D0855748

Penguin Books

Witchcraft and Sorcery

Max Marwick has held chairs in anthropology and/or sociology at Witwatersrand, Monash and Stirling universities and, before he retired to live in England, was Reader in Humanities at Griffith University, Brisbane, Australia.

Witchcraft and Sorcery

Selected Readings
Second Edition

Edited by Max Marwick

Penguin Books

PENGUIN BOOKS

Published by the Penguin Group
Penguin Books Ltd, 27 Wrights Lane, London W8 5TZ, England
Penguin Books USA Inc., 375 Hudson Street, New York, New York 10014, USA
Penguin Books Australia Ltd, Ringwood, Victoria, Australia
Penguin Books Canada Ltd, 10 Alcorn Avenue, Toronto, Ontario, Canada M4V 3B2
Penguin Books (NZ) Ltd, 182–190 Wairau Road, Auckland 10, New Zealand

Penguin Books Ltd, Registered Offices: Harmondsworth, Middlesex, England

First published in Penguin Books 1970
Second edition 1982
Reprinted in Pelican Books 1986
Reprinted in Penguin Books 1990
10 9 8 7 6 5 4 3 2 1

 # 25479620

Printed in England by Clays Ltd, St Ives plc
Filmset in Monophoto Times

*To the late Professor Sir Edward Evans-Pritchard
to whom all modern students of witchcraft and sorcery
are deeply indebted*

Contents

Part Three Theories of Witchcraft 231

Introduction

Each of us in modern society becomes aware of the sinister figures of witch and sorcerer through myth and fairy-tale, and they therefore belong to our world of fantasy. This makes it difficult for us to appreciate that there are societies actually existing in which these characters have a much clearer and threatening reality. Similarly it is hard to realize how recently it was that they were part of the reality of the societies from which ours is directly descended. It is only within the past three hundred years that our emancipation from widespread belief in witchcraft has been achieved. It is true that from time to time newspaper reports appear about the esoteric practices of present-day 'witches'. These accounts sustain the belief that witchcraft has never died out in modern society, that it has continued as an underground movement since the seventeenth century when it – or rather concerted opposition to it – emitted a final flare before smouldering through the intervening years, and that its flames have found new fuel in Britain since 1951 when, after more than two centuries, the old Witchcraft Act was repealed. But this point is debatable, and, whether or not one accepts the view that there has been an underlying continuity of belief from the seventeenth century to the present, it is clear that modern 'witchcraft' is very different from the conceptions Europeans had of it at the time of the religious conflicts at the close of the Middle Ages and, in turn, from the traditions of an earlier period. It differs, too, from the parallel notions of present-day non-literate, so-called 'primitive' peoples.

Our emancipation from belief in magic is still far from complete, as is shown by our credulous attention to the utterances of authorities such as doctors and scientists, even when they make pronouncements outside their narrow fields of competence, and by our continued observance of superstitions.

'Witchcraft' and 'sorcery' are terms referring to closely related systems of belief of wide distribution among human societies. Common to the two systems, which often exist side by side in the same society, is the cardinal belief that certain members of the community harm their fellows illicitly by supernatural means. In most English dictionaries 'witchcraft' and 'sorcery' are roughly synonymous. In anthropological usage they have acquired distinct meanings because an African tribe, the Azande,[1] are more precise in their categories of the supernatural than we are; and Sir Edward Evans-Pritchard, the anthropologist who studied them and who wrote what has become a classic in this field (1937), found the existence in English of those two words a useful means of translating the distinction that his informants perceived.

To appreciate the Zande distinction between 'witchcraft' and 'sorcery', adopted by most anthropologists, though now with more reservations than when the first edition of these Readings appeared, it is first necessary to define 'magic'. This is a morally neutral term in the sense that magic may be used with or without social approval. It refers to the activities or craft of the magician, a person who, suitably prepared, performs rituals aimed at controlling impersonal supernatural forces held responsible for the succession of events. In these rituals, the magician manipulates material objects and substances, often having characteristics or origins symbolically related to the objectives desired, while reciting an appropriate verbal formula. Although a non-literate (so-called 'primitive') society usually has its expert magicians, many forms of magic are available to its ordinary members, and the equivalents of do-it-yourself kits may be inherited, bought or borrowed.

According to the Zande distinction, the main difference between a sorcerer and a witch is that the former achieves his evil ends by magic, whereas the latter (often though not invariably conceived of as a woman) achieves hers by some mystical power inherent in her personality, a power that does not require the help of magic. There are other differences between them. As to motive, witches are considered to be slaves of aberration and addiction, and, thus conceived, are weird, sometimes tragic, figures. Sorcerers, on the other hand, are considered to be ordinary people driven by understandable, even if disapproved, urges, such as malice, envy or revenge, which are part of everyone's experience.

Propensity to witchcraft is usually considered to be hereditary or at least constitutional in the sense of having been implanted – in various ways – at an early age, whereas sorcery usually demands no special personal attributes and is believed to be practised by anyone who can

1. The Zande people have been referred to throughout as the Azande and not the A-Zande, the rendering used in Evans-Pritchard's earlier papers. The use of a plural prefix, A-, is a Bantuism unusual in a Nilotic language. Had we adopted in this instance the now common practice among students of Bantu languages and peoples of dropping prefixes from tribal names, the appropriate form would have been Zande, not only for the adjective and the singular, as Evans-Pritchard uses it, but also for the plural. However, as Evans-Pritchard's usage pre-dates the wide adoption among Bantuists of this usage, and as his plural form, Azande, has become one of the household words of anthropology, this has been retained – *Ed.*

acquire the necessary magical substances (especially in Africa) or the appropriate spells (especially in Oceania).

While most anthropologists see the advantage of following the Zande distinction between witchcraft and sorcery, there are some, particularly those writing on Oceania, who use the term 'sorcery' for all forms of destructive magic regardless of whether it is socially approved – as it may be in property-protection, for instance – or considered illicit. Similarly the term 'witch' does not invariably have a sinister or evil connotation. There are and were societies in which she was believed on occasion to cure ailments as well as attack people, their interests or their property.

In this connection Harwood, in a book from which excerpts are included in this edition of the Readings (see below, pp. 119–31), raises a more fundamental problem. He points out that, in two Tanzanian societies, the Nyakyusa (G. Wilson, 1936; M. Wilson, 1963) and the Safwa (Harwood, 1970), terms that might conceivably be translated as 'witchcraft' signify in fact a morally neutral power, believed to be used sometimes legitimately for protecting the community and effecting social control; and sometimes illicitly for harming other people. Furthermore, from a careful reworking of Evans-Pritchard's account, he concludes that the same applies among the Azande and that Evans-Pritchard's finding that the Zande word *mangu* denotes an exclusively anti-social power – and should therefore be translated as 'witchcraft' – comes from his particular interpretation of his material.

In view of the seminal influence that Evans-Pritchard's definitions have had, Harwood's examination of their validity – even for the Azande – has far-reaching implications. For instance, common to most of the papers in the first edition was the assumption that witches and sorcerers are by definition anti-social and immoral. Harwood challenges this assumption for the Azande study, and thus for others that have followed Evans-Pritchard's translation of what he perceived to be the Zande distinction; and he points out that it derives from Evans-Pritchard's having espoused the perspective of the witch-doctor rather than that of the ordinary villager.

One of the corollaries of the assumption that witches and sorcerers are by definition anti-social is that no one in his or her right mind – or in modern society not deluded by Margaret Murray's romantic theory (see below, pp. 146–52, 233–4 and 327–9) – would claim to be one of these evil dealers of misfortune and death by making a voluntary confession. Yet, in the time since the first edition appeared, evidence has increasingly come forward, especially from West Africa, that the confession of witchcraft is common if not institutionalized. Wyllie's paper (see below, pp.

132–9) is included as being representative of this growing body of data.

Because both witches and sorcerers incur social disapproval, generalizations about both are often made. This fact calls for a generic term that includes both. Hitherto 'witch', in addition to having the more specific meaning outlined above, has served as such a term and will be so used in this Introduction unless the context indicates the contrary. Middleton and Winter (1963, p. 3) have suggested 'wizard' and 'wizardry' as generic terms to include respectively witches and sorcerers on the one hand and their believed activities on the other. This usage does not seem to have caught on; for instance, in the works included in this volume, only the excerpts from Harwood's and Crawford's books follow it.

The antiquity of the belief in witches and sorcerers is indicated by its present wide distribution. While there are some human societies other than our own that lack this belief, they are exceptional, and those, the majority, that have it are found in all parts of the world – 'from Africa to the South Seas and from Asia to America', as Mayer (1954, p. 3) puts it in the lecture included in these Readings.

Whereas there must inevitably be some debate about the nature of beliefs that may be inferred from rock paintings, burials and other kinds of archaeological evidence, there is clear historical documentation in the chronicles and creative writing of classical antiquity for the existence of beliefs in witches and sorcerers. There is a close relationship, and frequently an identity, between beliefs held in these early periods of recorded history and those of later ages or those reported by modern anthropologists working among contemporary non-literate societies. In the historical societies from which ours is descended, the continuity in the conceptions of these mystical evil-doers from classical through medieval to early modern times is striking. Among human societies as a whole, it is less certain, though still highly probable, that beliefs among peoples now widely separated had a common origin in the prehistorical period. Thus Clements (1932, p. 240) has suggested that many primitive, widely distributed concepts of disease, including those relating to witchcraft, may be traced back to the dispersal of the Palaeolithic ancestors of modern humankind.

Until the close of the medieval period, European beliefs in witchcraft and sorcery seem to have had much in common with those prevailing among present-day non-literate peoples. Apart from a similarity in the content of the beliefs themselves, there also appears to be a resemblance in the relatively slight degree to which they occupied people's minds. They were a part of the pattern of life, but a relatively small part, activated in times of crisis and misfortune rather than being a source of continuous worry.

Most of the innumerable works on European witchcraft deal, not with the earlier periods when it showed a similarity to the 'witchcraft' familiar to modern anthropologists, but with the period when preoccupation with beliefs in it had reached the proportions of an epidemic. This development of an acute witch-scare on the basis of the long-standing, chronic system of beliefs was symptomatic of the rapid and fundamental changes the society of Europe was undergoing in its transition from the relatively undifferentiated feudalism of the Middle Ages to the varied, flexible and uncertain social organization that started with the Renaissance and the Reformation. During this period of institutional change, long-standing beliefs in witchcraft became entangled in the new religious and political issues of the day. Witches were identified with heretics, and this brought a new weapon to the armoury of the Church. A surviving pagan moral indignation against witches could now be pressed into service against those who failed to conform with official Christianity. As a result of this entanglement, European witchcraft acquired some of its distinctive features, of which the most important was the notion that witches had made compacts with the Devil. Whereas in other societies witches personify evil in general, in European history they did this in a very specific way by being the earthly representatives of the Prince of Evil.

Thus it is that European witchcraft, as most of the literature portrays it, is paralleled, not by the normal, chronic belief system of a non-literate society, but rather by the millenarian movements that, since the second half of the nineteenth century, have been reported from virtually every part of the world where native peoples have had to adjust themselves suddenly to the advent of Western ways of life. These millenarium movements, according to Worsley (1957, pp. 24–5), represent 'desperate searchings for more and more effective ways of understanding and modifying' a confused environment. Similarly the witch-scares of Europe and of Old and New England seem to have been part of the general reaction to a period of rapid and uncertain change.

The ethnography of witchcraft is understandably rich. Given Western society's emancipation from it, Western travellers, missionaries, administrators and even anthropologists have often selected this, the most bizarre and exotic aspect of native life, for a disproportionate share of attention. People's witch-beliefs are as often recorded for their sheer entertainment value as for their scientific interest. They seem to reward the romantic search by both writers and readers for fantasies that come true.

15

Nevertheless these systems of belief are of scientific interest and importance. Though from our point of view they represent the standardized delusions of the societies concerned, the comparative analysis of such delusions is, as Monica Wilson (1951, p. 313) has expressed it, 'not merely an antiquarian exercise but one of the keys to the understanding of society'. Indeed, they have been approached from the theoretical vantage points of a number of social sciences because of the light they throw on human behaviour in general, including that of ourselves among whom they no longer command credence. Even those accounts of witchcraft that are primarily descriptive are often based on an implicit set of theoretical assumptions that serve to make them intelligible when viewed from some other society such as our own. The theories of witchcraft that have been implicitly or explicitly put forward fall into three main categories, historical or ethnological, psychological, and sociological; and the last of these may be subdivided into those theories that emphasize normative aspects of social organization and those centring on tension and social change.

The first main category includes theories which, on the basis of history or conjectural history, account for the present distribution of witch-beliefs and for the developments within a particular society that have given rise to its characteristic pattern of beliefs. Here may be included theories such as Elsie Clews Parsons's relating to the diffusion of witch-beliefs in the American South-west; Ewen's on the importation to England of ideas emanating from the Continent (1933, pp. 44–50); and Margaret Murray's well-known but no longer well-supported hypothesis (1921) that the witches of Western Europe were the lingering adherents of a cult forming part of the pagan religion displaced by Christianity. Psychological theories accounting for witchcraft are found in the writings of Kluckhohn and of Krige (specifically on witchcraft and sorcery) and of Malinowski (1954, pp. 59–60, 63, 70–72) (on magic in general, of which sorcery is a specific form). These theories stem from Freud's doctrine of the displacement of affect and derivative neo-Freudian hypotheses about the projection of urges and conflicts into culturally standardized fantasies (Dollard, 1937, pp. 442–4).

During the eleven years that separate this edition from its predecessor, anthropologists have followed paths that increasingly diverge. One path, that of the empiricist, keeps closer to Durkheim's original sociological direction, treating social relations as primary and regarding rituals and belief systems as reflections or expressions of these. The other path, signposted 'rationalist' (Leach, 1976, pp. 4–5), 'cognitive' or 'semantic', instead of exploring the relation between behaviour and belief, seeks to analyse belief systems as logical structures in their own right. This divergence has left its mark on the study of witchcraft, as papers by Crick and Hammond-Tooke in Part Three illustrate. The concern with cognitive systems that are taken to be virtually autonomous is not as new as its protagonists seem to be claiming. It was implicit in papers published in the 1950s, such as those by Wilson and Nadel included in the first edition and retained in this one.

Of the two variants of the sociological theory of witchcraft, the one having to do with social norms is, because of its semantic emphasis, closely related to the psychological approach exemplified by Kluckhohn, Krige and Malinowski (see above) and the more recent cognitive approach just referred to. And this variant is more often encountered in the literature than the one that concerns the relation between social tensions and the incidence of accusations (see below). In most accounts following the normative approach the witch is depicted as the very antithesis of the social ideal, as the one who portrays the villain in the society's morality plays. So numerous and so revolting are the believed practices of witches that to accuse anyone of witchcraft is a condensed way of charging him with a long list of the foulest crimes. By graphically summing up all forms of deviance, such an accusation throws into sharper relief the positive moral precepts of the society to which the accused person belongs. The alleged witch's believed victim may also illustrate these precepts. It is a common practice for people in all societies to seek retrospectively for the causes of misfortune; and in those societies in which a belief in witchcraft exists, people who suffer misfortunes often examine their past social conduct, especially in so far as it affects people in the community who have been or who could be identified as witches. Thus, while witches are primarily negative models, they may also play positive moral roles in being the points of retrospective projection for feelings of guilt resulting from acts of foolishness and meanness that a believed victim may have committed.

The other variant of the sociological theory of witchcraft treats accusations of it as indices of social tension and as vehicles of social change. The relative frequency of accusations in various social relationships provides us with a set of social strain-gauges for detecting where the tensions and role-conflicts in a particular society lie. In keeping with the abandonment by anthropologists of a static functional model in favour of a more dynamic view of social trends and processes, this theory is undergoing modification, greater attention now being paid to the part accusations play in manipulating social situations and involving the community as a whole in issues hitherto confined to those persons directly enmeshed in the quarrel from which the accusation stems.

All these types of theories in differing degrees raise the study of witch-craft from the level of travellers' entertaining tales and 'straight' eth-nography to that of scientific analysis aimed at making generalizations about repetitive social situations and processes, and, within the range of statistical probability, at making predictions of their outcomes.

A recent development has been the merging by anthropologists and historians of their theoretical orientations to the study of witchcraft. This is exemplified in the work of Macfarlane (1970) and Thomas (1971). This trend has not been without its problems. Firstly, its wide comparative spectrum has raised the question whether, in giving similar attention to the large-scale epidemics of witch-hunting that swept early-modern Europe and the chronic, but cosmologically reconciled, belief-systems of non-literate peoples, it is attempting to compare the incomparable. This problem is basically one of definition, and some useful solutions to it are suggested in Part One, especially in the paper by Larner (see pp. 48 ff.).

Secondly, anthropological and historiographical approaches are them-selves subject to debate and development. Consequently, as often happens in interdisciplinary collaboration, a member of one discipline seeking theoretical aids in another may not, through coming late to it, be fully familiar with the theoretical minefield he is traversing; and, by espousing a particular theoretical position, may unwittingly subject him-self to the criticisms of those who are opposed to it. This problem is discussed in two of the papers in Part Three, by Kephart (pp. 326 ff.) and Crick (pp. 343 ff.).

In addition to these somewhat indirect contributions that the study of witchcraft can make to behavioural science, it has more direct appli-cations as well. Thus Evans-Pritchard's classic analysis of the part played by witch-beliefs in the total world-view of the Azande has not only clarified some of the problems relating to believed mental differences between 'primitive' and 'civilized' but it has even served as a model for the clearer understanding of the logic of scientific discovery (Polanyi, 1958, pp. 286–94). Similarly the analysis of past witch-scares provides prin-ciples for the better understanding of present mass movements. The parallel between the beliefs of seventeenth-century Western, or modern African, witch-finders and Joseph McCarthy's fevered dreams about red agents (Wilson, 1951) is indeed a close one, as Arthur Miller showed with subtle insight in *The Crucible* (1952).

References

CLEMENTS, F. E. (1932), 'Primitive concepts of disease', *University of California Publications in American Archaeology and Ethnology*, vol. 32, pp. 185–252.

DOLLARD, J. (1937), *Caste and Class in a Southern Town*, Yale U.P.

EVANS-PRITCHARD, E. E. (1937), *Witchcraft, Oracles and Magic among the Azande*, Clarendon Press.

EWEN, C. L. (1933), *Witchcraft and Demonianism*, Heath Cranton.

HARWOOD, A. (1970), *Witchcraft, Sorcery and Social Categories among the Safwa*, Oxford U.P. for International African Institute.

LEACH, E. (1976), *Culture and Communication*, Cambridge U.P.

MACFARLANE, A. [D. J.] (1970), *Witchcraft in Tudor and Stuart England*, Routledge & Kegan Paul.

MALINOWSKI, B. (1954), 'Magic, science and religion', in R. Redfield (ed.), *Magic, Science and Religion and Other Essays*, Doubleday. (Essay originally published in 1925.)

MAYER, P. (1954), *Witches*, Inaugural Lecture, Rhodes University, Grahamstown.

MIDDLETON, J., and WINTER, E. H. (eds) (1963), *Witchcraft and Sorcery in East Africa*, Routledge & Kegan Paul.

MILLER, A. (1952), *The Crucible*, Viking Press.

MURRAY, M. A. (1921), *The Witch-Cult in Western Europe*, Clarendon Press.

POLANYI, M. (1958), *Personal Knowledge*, University of Chicago Press.

THOMAS, K. (1971), *Religion and the Decline of Magic*, Weidenfeld & Nicolson.

WILSON, G. (1936), 'An African morality', *Africa*, vol. 9, pp. 75–99.

WILSON, M. [H.] (1951), 'Witch beliefs and social structure', *American Journal of Sociology*, vol. 56, pp. 307–13.

WILSON, M. [H.] (1963), *Good Company*, Beacon Press (paperback edition).

WORSLEY, P. M. (1957), 'Millenarian movements in Melanesia', *Human Problems in British Central Africa*, vol. 21, pp. 18–31.

Part One **Orientation**

The first six Readings in this volume provide materials towards defining and distinguishing the various aspects of the subject. We assume that Evans-Pritchard's classic study of the Azande (1937) will be consulted in the original by any serious student of witchcraft and sorcery; no excerpts from it have been included in this volume, though Gluckman's review-article on it will be found in Part Four. Thus, although Evans-Pritchard brought his influential working definitions conveniently together in his book on the Azande (1937, pp. 8–11), we go for them in this part to two of his earlier papers; and the second of these describes the important process of divination by oracle. Then follows Firth's concise discussion of terminology, which allows for differences in usage between Africanists and Oceanianists. Since modern anthropology necessarily gives arbitrary technical meanings to English words of long standing, the discussions of terminology by Thomas and Macfarlane serve as correctives to a complete surrender to professional jargon. Larner's paper supplements Thomas's in clearing the way for the comparative leaps that this volume makes from the witch-beliefs of historical societies to those of contemporary non-literate peoples. The basic definitions considered, we join Philip Mayer for a preliminary conducted tour.

Reference

EVANS-PRITCHARD, E. E. (1937), *Witchcraft, Oracles and Magic among the Azande*, Clarendon Press.

1. E. E. Evans-Pritchard

Sorcery and Native Opinion

Excerpt from E. E. Evans-Pritchard, 'Sorcery and native opinion', *Africa*, vol. 4, 1931, no. 1, pp. 23–8.

The problem before us is to analyse native ideas about magic and to find out what types of magic they regard with approbation, and what types they regard with disapprobation; whether their opinions in this respect are clearly defined and held by all members of the community and backed by legal sanctions; and what are the distinguishing attributes by which we can class any type of magic as good or bad. A complete analysis of this kind has never been made either in theoretical treatises on magic nor in field-work monographs on primitive peoples. Writers of books on magic generally regard all magic which produces or protects as white magic, and those types which destroy as black magic. As we shall see later, such a classification is based entirely on European ideas and does not correspond to modes of native thought. Though much has been written about magic, the native viewpoint has been little studied. The monumental works of Frazer (1911) contain nothing strictly germane to our problem, since 'homeopathic' and 'contagious' magic may be either black or white (in whatever sense we use these colour-symbols); and whilst it can hardly be said that 'black' magic is ever 'public' it would be equally incorrect to suppose that 'white' magic is necessarily so. Many shortcomings in Frazer's treatment of magic (1890) were revealed in the first competent analytical study of magic by Hubert and Mauss. They were anxious to show how magic is a social fact and is not merely composed of mistaken and illogical processes of individual psychology. In demonstrating how magic is not simply an individual psychological process but is a traditional complex of ideas, beliefs and rites which are handed down from one generation to another, they laid a broader basis of approach to the problems of magic than either Frazer or their other predecessors had done (Hubert and Mauss, 1902–3). Against criticism that it would therefore appear that the traditional social facts of magic were often at war with tradition and society itself, they replied by showing that not only was sorcery, as they understood the term, beyond all doubt part and parcel of transmitted culture, but also that it was often not illicit but rather a tool of government, a fact which had emerged as clearly from Frazer's work, and it was later to be demonstrated by Malinowski's first-hand observations in the Trobriands. The problem really resolved itself into a question of how 'crime' could be said to have a useful social function. There was little data to answer this question when Hubert and Mauss wrote their paper: especially was information lacking about the concepts of 'crime' and 'law' in primitive societies. Later writers on primitive jurisprudence have assumed that in all savage communities some acts of magic are disapproved of and punished by society (e.g. Sidney Hartland, 1924). This assumption has lately been challenged by Malinowski.

Malinowski has broken away from the formal treatment of the legality of magic and has given us a more dynamic account of the actual workings of 'black' magic in a Melanesian community. The views which he presents appear, however, to spring rather from a sociological analysis of the workings of black magic than from native commentary on the same. In this community sorcery acts as a legal force upholding the norms and rules of society. Its 'criminal' aspects, if we can so term them, are restricted to an abuse of proper legal machinery in much the same way as a chief may abuse the powers with which he is invested. 'Black' magic is used by a limited number of specialists, either for personal reasons or for a fee from a chief or rich commoner, to kill those whose success in love or gardening or trading has aroused the envy of their neighbours and those who show lack of respect to their chiefs and betters. They act as a conservative agency which gets rid of the *parvenus* of native society without grave scandals and disorder. Public opinion does not appear to react strongly on moral grounds either for or against black magic. This interpretation of sorcery strikes at the roots of our problem, since Malinowski (1926a) asserts that primitive peoples do not make any clear-cut moral distinctions between the legal and criminal uses of sorcery. 'These contributions,' he says, 'show clearly how difficult it is to draw a line between the quasi-legal and quasi-criminal applications of sorcery. The "criminal" aspect of law in savage communities is perhaps even vaguer than the "civil" one, the idea of "justice" in our sense hardly applicable, and the means of restoring a disturbed tribal equilibrium slow and cumbersome.'

Dr Schapera (1927) in an able review of Malinowski's book has pointed out that the chief criticism to be levelled against it is that the author has generalized from a restricted range of data in one community in formulating a theory applicable to all savage tribes. We hope to show in this paper from data collected in an African community that whilst the dividing line between the 'criminal' and the 'legal' is often indistinct, the natives clearly mark off some types of magic as 'criminal', and that they do so according to moral principles which are vital to the whole theory of magic in this community. The problem is really to know what the natives understand by such terms as 'crime' and 'justice' in their relation to magic.

The theoretical writer on magic has been severely handicapped by lack of reliable information about savage tribes, for in field-work accounts there is seldom to be found a competent analysis of native magic, and they generally lack in particular a clear understanding of the difference between black magic and witchcraft. If the reader will look at the better-known and easily accessible books on African tribes, such as those on the Bathonga, Baila, Akamba, Ashanti, Baganda, Shilluk, Bakongo, Lango and others, he will not find in them any detailed consideration of the legality of magic. It may be that such moral attitudes as we noted amongst the Azande are lacking amongst these other peoples, or it may be that this particular line of investigation was not followed by their observers.

Since, therefore, the particular problem which we are considering has not, to our knowledge, been thoroughly inquired into, it is inadvisable to attempt to make our treatment of it a comparative one. Consequently we shall restrict our observations to a people whom we know at first hand, the Azande of the Nile–Uelle Divide. Whether the moral distinctions made by this people about their magic are common to many societies can only be answered by future field-workers, for it is essentially a field-work question and one which can only be answered at the later stages of an investigation when the observer is already well acquainted with the natives amongst whom he is working.

In the opinion of the Azande what types of magic are reputable (white) and what types are disreputable (black)? The answer to this question is that just as a good man is one who acts in accordance with the established principles of social behaviour, whereas a bad man is one who flouts the accepted laws and customs of his country, so good magic acts in favour of, and black magic acts against, justice and order. This paper will explain the Zande point of view, and will illustrate the moral grading of their magic.

Terminology of Zande Magic

First of all we must clear the ground so that we may isolate the problem and focus it clearly. Much obstruction is caused by the loose use of terms such as 'witchcraft', 'black magic', 'white magic', 'sorcery', and so on. If the reader will turn to the books by theorists and field-workers which we have mentioned above he will find that such terms are used by one writer to refer to one feature of native culture, and are used by another writer to describe a totally different feature. They are often used indiscriminately by the same writer to refer to first one thing and then another in the same book. Without expressing any opinion as to whether the terminology used in this paper is generally applicable to other cultures we find it necessary both here and in our future writings on the Azande to use terms such as 'witch', 'magician', 'sorcerer', and symbols referring to the moral and legal attributes of magic, with strict reference to what are to the Azande distinct cultural concepts. We are taking several distinct Zande ideas and are using for them a distinguishing symbol in English. To the Zande *mangu* (witchcraft) and *ngwa* (medicine or magic) are quite different things. *Mangu* is an hereditary trait which can be discovered in the stomach of a witch (*ira mangu*, possessor of *mangu*). It is a physiological fact and its functioning needs no use of the concreta of magic, the material substance of medicine, the spell, and the rite.[1] *Ngwa* on the other hand is characterized by the special attributes of magic all over the world, the material element, the spell, the rite, the condition of the performer (taboo etc.) (Evans-Pritchard, 1929a; Hubert and Mauss, 1902–3, *passim*; Malinowski, 1926b). Within the complex of an act of magic particular emphasis is placed by the Azande and probably by all African peoples on the material element, generally botanical, to which we propose to restrict the term 'medicine', using the term 'magic' in a wider sense to refer to the whole complex of which medicine forms the nucleus, i.e. the spell (*sima-sima* in Zande), the rite, the condition of the performer, and the 'représentatives magiques' which comprise ideas and beliefs (embodied in myth or current tradition) associated with the performance. Another difference between *mangu* (witchcraft) and *ngwa* (magic) lies in the fact that it is highly improbable that an act of witchcraft ever takes place, whereas acts of magic may be witnessed daily in the life of the Azande.

We shall not discuss Zande witchcraft in this paper, as we have given a long account of it elsewhere,[2] but restrict ourselves to a consideration of magic and the people who perform magic, 'magicians' (*ira ngwa*, possessor of magic). All people who perform an act of magic are magicians,

1. Zande witchcraft, which is characterized by a special condition of the entrails, is a form of vampirism. Of the same genus are the *aira kele linde*, men whose upper teeth broke through before the lower ones, and whose influence is baneful. Other types of witchcraft, which employ no technique of magic, which we find in different African societies, are the 'evil eye', twins, monorchids, and so on (Evans-Pritchard, 1929b).

2. See next Reading – *Ed.*

whether they are professional departmental experts or merely amateur practitioners of sporadic rites. Amongst these magicians there are some who are criminals, whose magic is illicit, and it is to identify these men that we are devoting this essay. We shall use the word 'sorcerers' to symbolize these criminals and the word 'sorcery' to represent their criminal activities. Actually the Azande have no single lexicographic expression to denote sorcery and sorcerers, but they use the same terms for all acts of magic and magicians, *ngwa* and *ira ngwa*; but the context of utterance makes it clear whether they refer to magic in general or to its legal or criminal uses respectively. If they wish to specify they will either speak of magic as being good or bad (*wene* or *gbigbita*) or they will use a circumlocutory expression referring to the method or function of the magic by which the listener will know at once whether it is regarded with approval or not. We shall do the same, using the adjectives 'good' and 'bad' to denote the moral qualities of magic rather than the terms 'black' and 'white'.

For the guild or association of magicians who are found amongst the Azande in common with most African peoples we shall use the good old expression 'witch-doctors', since their main function amongst the Azande is to detect witches and to combat witchcraft. Thus in Zande society we have:

Witchcraft (*mangu*)
performed by witches (*ira mangu*)

Magic (*ngwa*)
performed by magicians (*ira ngwa*) a special association of whom are witchdoctors (*abinza* or *avule*). There are two types of *ngwa*: *wene ngwa*, good magic, and *gbigbita ngwa*, bad magic or sorcery, performed by sorcerers (*ira gbigbita ngwa*).

References

EVANS-PRITCHARD, E. E. (1929a), 'The morphology and function of magic', *American Anthropology*, vol. 31.

EVANS-PRITCHARD, E. E. (1929b), 'Witchcraft (*mangu*) amongst the Azande', *Sudan Notes and Records*, vol. 12.

FRAZER, J. G. (1890), *The Golden Bough*, 2 vols, Macmillan [and Co. (?)].

FRAZER, J. G. (1911–15), *The Golden Bough*, 3rd edn, 13 vols, Macmillian [and Co. (?)].

HARTLAND, E. S. (1924), *Primitive Law*, Methuen.

HUBERT, H., and MAUSS, M. (1902–3), 'Esquisse d'une théorie générale de la magie', *L'Année Sociologique*, vol. 7; reprinted in M. Mauss (1950), *Sociologie et Anthropologie*, Presses Universitaires de France.

MALINOWSKI, B. (1926a), *Crime and Custom in Savage Society*, Kegan Paul, Trench, Trubner.

MALINOWSKI, B. (1926b), 'Magic, science and religion', in J. Needham (ed.), *Science, Religion and Reality*, Macmillan; reprinted in R. Redfield (ed.), *Magic, Science and Religion and Other Essays*, The Free Press, 1948; Doubleday, 1954.

SCHAPERA, I. (1927), review of B. Malinowski's *Crime and Custom in Savage Society*, in *Man*, vol. 27, July.

2. E. E. Evans-Pritchard

Witchcraft amongst the Azande

Excerpts from E. E. Evans-Pritchard, 'Witchcraft (*mangu*) amongst the Azande', *Sudan Notes and Records*, vol. 12, 1929, pp. 163–249.

Witchcraft (*mangu*) and magic (*ngwa*) have quite different connotations in Zande culture and should be clearly distinguished in an ethnological account.[1] In certain respects witchcraft and sorcery are similar. Probably neither, certainly not *mangu*, has any real existence. Both have common functions, since they are used for pernicious private ends against the lives and property of law-abiding citizens. But their technique is quite different. Zande magic comprises the common characteristics of magic the world over, rite, spell, ideas, traditions, and moral opinion associated with its use, taboo and other conditions of the magician and the rite (Evans-Pritchard, 1929; Hubert and Mauss, 1902–3; Malinowski, 1926). All these are traditional facts transmitted from one generation to another. Witchcraft operates through different channels though in similar situations to sorcery.

Let us commence our analysis of Zande witchcraft from its concrete elements, for as the nuclear equipment of sorcery is a concrete, generally botanical, medicine, so the nuclear equipment of witchcraft is an abdominal condition (*mangu*). We have never actually seen a *mangu*, but it has often been described to us as an oval, blackish swelling or sack which sometimes contains various small objects. In size about the elbow-width of a man's bent fore-arm, it is situated somewhere in the upper abdomen near the bile tract. It cannot be observed from the outside during a man's lifetime, but in the past it used often to be extracted by a post-mortem operation, and was sometimes placed hanging from a tree bordering one of the main paths leading to a chief's court. We are ignorant about the real nature of this abdominal condition, but think that it is probably the gall-bladder or the stomach itself in certain digestive periods. [. . .]

Here we wish to state the main attributes of *mangu* in a preliminary manner before discussing the part the concept of witchcraft plays in native life and the complex and often contradictory notions associated

1. See previous Reading – *Ed.*

with it in Zande mentality. The first of these attributes is its physical character. It is a physical or physiological fact, a thing, which is situated, so far as we have been able to gather, in the abdomen just below where the breast-bones meet. The second important fact which we wish to bring out about *mangu* is that it is an hereditary anatomical endowment which is transmitted in unilinear descent from parents to children. There is sex dichotomy in the biological transmission of witchcraft. Thus whilst the sons of a male witch are all witches his daughters are not, and whilst all the daughters of a female witch are also witches her sons are not.[2] Witchcraft thus regarded as an inherited biological trait transmitted along the lines of sex does not run counter to Zande ideas of kinship and descent, but is complementary to their notions about procreation and their escatalogical beliefs. We will summarize these briefly in so far as they concern our subject.

The birth of a child results from a unison of spiritual properties in the womb of a woman with spiritual properties in the sperm of a man. The foetus is derived from the union of two principles, male and female. When the spirit (*mbisimo*) of the male is stronger than that of the female a boy child is born. When the woman's spirit (*mbisimo*) is stronger, a girl child will be born. Thus, whilst a child is thought to partake of the spirits of both parents, a girl is believed to partake more of the spirit of her mother, and a boy of his father, but in certain respects a child takes after one or other parent according to its sex, in the inheritance of sexual characteristics [and] of *mangu*. [...]

Some nocturnal birds and animals are very definitely associated with witchcraft and are thought to be the servants of human witches, and to be in league with them. Such are bats, which are universally feared for their evil attributes, and owls, which hoot forebodings of misfortune in the night. These nocturnal creatures are associated with witches because witchcraft is especially active at night, where it may sometimes be seen in motion.

For, like many primitive peoples, the Azande believe that witchcraft emits a bright light which can only be seen in the daylight by witch-doctors and by witches themselves, but which is occasionally visible at night to persons who are neither witches (all such being *amukundu*) nor

2. Lagae (1926, pp. 107–8), with his usual care, quotes a Zande text for the doctrine of unilateral inheritance of witchcraft: 'If a man with witchcraft in his stomach gives birth to a male child, he also is a witch because his father was one before him. It is the same with women. If a woman has witchcraft in her stomach and gives birth to a female child she also is a witch because her mother was one before her. Thus witchcraft does not worry a man who is born free from it by entering into his stomach.' (Our own free translation.)

witch-doctors.[3] The light of *mangu* is described as being similar to the little lights of firefly beetles, which move about like sparks kicked from a log-fire, only it is ever so much larger than they. The beetles themselves arouse no suspicion of witchcraft, but the Zande compares their phosphorescence to the emanation of *mangu*, adding that it is a poor comparison, since *mangu* has a so much greater and brighter light. [. . .]

We will naturally wonder what the light [is], whether it [is] the actual witch stalking his prey or whether it [is] some emanation which he [emits] to do the murder. On this point Zande theory is quite decided. The witch is asleep during the period of his activity on his bed in his hut, but he has despatched the spirit of his *mangu* (*mbisimo mangu*) to accomplish his ends. The spirit of *mangu* removes parts of the spirit of the victim's flesh (*mbisimo pasie ni: mbisimi*=spirit, *pasie*=flesh, *ni*=pron. suff.) and devours it. The whole act of vampirism is a spiritual one; the spirit of *mangu* removes and devours the spirit of the body. I have never been able to obtain a more precise explanation of witchcraft activities by enquiring into the meaning of *mbisimo mangu* and *mbisimo pasie*. The Zande knows that people are killed in such a way, but only a witch himself could give a circumstantial account of what exactly happens.

Witches usually combine in their destructive activities and subsequent ghoulish feasts. They assist each other in crime and they arrange their nefarious schemes in concert. They are believed to possess a special kind of ointment (*mbiro mangu*) with which they rub their bodies and little drums which they beat to summon others to congress, where their discussions are presided over by old and experienced members of the brotherhood. For witches have their hierarchy and status and leadership in the same way as all other Zande social groupings have.[4] Experience must first be obtained under tuition of elder witches before a man is able to kill his neighbours. Growth in experience goes hand in hand with physical growth of *mangu* itself.

A child born of a witch parent of its own sex has such a small *mangu* that it can do little injury to others. It is possible that his *mangu* will remain inoperative or largely so throughout life, but generally it grows both in size and in exercise of its powers. Hence, a child is never accused of murder, and even grown boys and girls are not suspected by adults of

3. Lagae's textual note reads: 'Those people who see witchcraft when it goes by night to injure someone say witchcraft is on its way shining bright like fire, it shines a little and again obfuscates itself' (1926, p. 108). (Our own free translation.)

4. Reference to other Readings, for instance Parsons (Reading 24, p. 235) will show how widespread this kind of belief is – *Ed.*

serious offences of witchcraft, though they may be a more serious menace to their child contemporaries. Generally speaking, the older a man grows the more potent becomes his *mangu* and the more violent and unscrupulous its use. The reason for this genetic concept of witchcraft will become apparent when we explain its situations in Zande social life and its place in their system of morals.

Sooner or later, a witch will probably fall a victim to vengeance or, even if he is clever enough to avoid retribution, he will be killed by another witch or by sorcery. Is the distinction between witches (*aboro mangu*) and non-witches (*amukundu*) operative beyond the grave? We have never been given a spontaneous statement to this effect, but in answer to direct and leading questions we have been told that at death witches become ... evil spirits ... known as *agilisa*. [...]

Mangu is ubiquitous. It plays its part in every activity of Zande life, in agricultural, fishing, and hunting pursuits; in domestic life of homesteads as well as in communal life of district and court; it is the essential theme of mental life, in which it forms the background of a vast panorama of magic; its influence is plainly stamped on law and morals, etiquette and religion; it is prominent in such different spheres as technology and language; [there is] no niche or corner of Zande culture into which it does not twist itself. If blight seizes the ground-nut crop it is *mangu*; if the bush is burnt vainly in pursuit of game it is *mangu*; if women laboriously ladle out water from a pool and are rewarded by but a few small fish it is *mangu*; if termites do not rise when they are due and a cold, useless, night is wasted in waiting for their flight it is *mangu*; if a wife shows herself sulky and unresponsive to her husband it is *mangu*; if a chief is cold and distant with his subject it is *mangu*; if a magical rite fails to achieve its purpose it is *mangu*; if, in fact, any failure or misfortune falls upon anyone at any time and in relation to any of the manifold activities of his life he believes that it is due to *mangu*. Those acquainted either at first hand or through reading with a normal day-to-day life of an agricultural African people will understand that there is no end to possible misfortunes arising in routine tasks and relaxations from miscalculation, incompetence, laziness, but mostly from causes over which the native has no control, since he possesses little scientific knowledge. All these are regarded as being due to *mangu* unless there is strong internal evidence and subsequent oracular confirmation that sorcery or one of those species of evil-bringing agents which we have described in the preceding section have been at work. But unless a man had previously had the misfortune of seeing *adandala*,[5] touching his wife's menstrual blood, seeing her anus, or similar experience, he would not attribute any casual misfortune to these causes.

It is strange at first to live amongst the Zande and to listen to their naïve explanation of misfortunes with the most obvious origin as products of witchcraft. A European cannot repress a smile at such crude and childish shelving of responsibility. A boy knocked his foot against a small stump of wood in the centre of a bush path, a daily occurrence in Africa, and suffered considerable pain and inconvenience in consequence. The sore, owing to its position on his toe, was continually receiving dirt and refused to heal. It was *mangu*. I pointed out that it was carelessness and advised him to look out where he was going in future, but he replied that it was quite true witchcraft had nothing to do with the stump of wood being in the path but that he had kept his eyes open, and if he had not been bewitched he would of course have seen the stump. As a conclusive argument for his view he remarked that all sores did not take days to heal, but generally close quickly, since that is the nature of sores and their usual behaviour; why, then, had not his wound closed unless there were *mangu* behind it? This I discovered before long was to be regarded as the general theory of ailments, and that there was little knowledge as to the real causes of disease. Thus, for example, when feeling unfit for several days I consulted native friends whether they thought that my consumption of bananas could have anything to do with my indisposition, but was at once informed that bananas do not cause sickness however many are eaten unless one is bewitched.[...]

Though a Zande will always place his misfortunes at the door of witchcraft, it must not be thought that he regards every enterprise as potentially successful so long as it is not interfered with by *mangu*. He is fully aware that people who traverse the bush will get cuts and scratches, and you will see how carefully he searches the ground in front of his bare feet whilst you, poor stranger, stumble along admiring the rich variety of the bush, but are, fortunately, provided with boots. His knowledge and absence of adequate protection make him careful. It is knowledge which each learns for himself from experience in childhood and uses throughout life. However, in spite of all precautions, cuts are sometimes unavoidable, since stumps of wood are often so close to the ground and so covered with dust or ashes that they are invisible to the most accustomed eye, or night conceals stumps and thorns from the late traveller; or a man must pursue game through sharp-edged grasses and tangled thorny undergrowth,

5. A species of wild cat associated with witchcraft, the sight of which is believed to be fatal (Evans-Pritchard, 1937, p. 51) – *Ed.*

where he can no longer keep to his beloved paths, and his attention to minor discomforts is distracted by excitement in the chase. Moreover, there are several different kinds of magic which protect him against minor injuries of this kind. I know of none which are specifically devoted to ward off bush cuts, but Zande magic is often wide-embracing and gives general protection to travellers and huntsmen away from home. If, in spite of practical caution and protective magic, he receives a nasty cut he will attribute it to the malice of his neighbours who have bewitched him. He will not, however, trouble very much about the matter unless the cut festers or refuses to close. He will then be certain that *mangu* is the cause and will begin to be resentful and possibly he will consult the oracles to find out who is causing such prolonged discomfort and inconvenience. [. . .]

If an illness continues in spite of the precautions taken, the relatives of the sick man will try and find out who is responsible. They will probably commence their enquiries through the *iwa*[6] oracle[7] and then check its verdict with the *benge*[8] oracle. One by one they place the names of people whom they suspect before *iwa*, and, when *iwa* has chosen one of them as the culprit, they ask it whether this is the only man responsible, or whether there are others acting in concert with him. If *iwa* says that this man is acting alone they put his name before *benge*. As we do not wish to enter here into the complicated technicalities of oracle-magic we will suppose that *iwa* chooses the name of one man and that *benge* supports the lesser oracle. The sick man and his relatives now have in their possession the name of the witch. This man was previously suspected, otherwise his name would not have been put before the oracles, and now they are certain that it is he who is bewitching their friend. As the feeling of the sick man and his relations is one of great indignation, and their first impulse is to assault the witch, it is highly important at this juncture that their actions should be well controlled by traditional procedure. There are two lines of action considered socially commendable. They may make a more or less public accusation of the witch face to face in a manner to be described shortly, or they may make a public declaration in his presence

6. '. . . rubbing-board oracle, which operates by means of a wooden instrument' (Evans-Pritchard, 1937, p. 11) – *Ed.*

7. The *iwa* is not so greatly relied upon as *benge* and *dakpa*, ['termites oracle' (Evans-Pritchard, 1937, p. 11) – *Ed.*], and a man accused of witchcraft on the strength of *iwa* alone may fairly say he is being wantonly insulted. Only in the case of serious illness is it proper (though many persons do it on other occasions) to act on the verdict of *iwa* alone since, in case of severe illness, it is necessary to save time.

8. '. . . poison, oracle, which operates through the administration of strychnine to fowls, and formerly to human beings also' (Evans-Pritchard, 1937, pp. 10–11) – *Ed.*

without mentioning any names, so that only they and the witch will know whom is being referred to. This latter method has an advantage where the witch is a person of social standing whom they do not wish to offend, or someone enjoying the respect and esteem of his fellow citizens, whom they do not wish to humiliate. This latter method is known as *kuba*. [. . .]

Those who have listened to this dramatic declaration know the voice which has spoken, who is ill, and all the circumstances of his sickness. As the witch listens he knows that his plot is discovered and that, being a marked man, if he continues to torture his victim his name will be revealed, and that, if he kills him, the death will be avenged. Self-preservation and self-respect will make him stop before it is too late. Moreover, he will be honoured by the deference which has been paid to him by concealment of his identity from the general public, so that he may yield to flattery where he will not yield to fear.

If this effort to get the witch to cease his activities is unsuccessful, the relatives of the sick man will resort to the procedure which is generally used alone without being preceded by a *kuba*, for a *kuba* is only used if they think that it is more convenient and if the *iwa* oracle sanctions its use. The normal procedure is to put the names of all suspects before *iwa* and let it select those guilty of causing sickness. Unless the man is dangerously ill, when they will at once make known *iwa*'s selection, they will place the names chosen by *iwa* before the more reliable oracle *benge*. A red strychnic powder is given to chicken, whilst the names of the suspects are mentioned one by one, and by either killing or sparing these chicken the oracle separates the innocent from among the guilty. Maybe several will be found guilty, maybe only one, but the procedure is the same for many as for one. They cut off a wing from the hen which died to the name of the witch and thrust it on to the end of a little pointed stick, spreading its wing out in the shape of a fan, and take it home with them. One of the relatives will then go with it to a neigh-bouring chief's deputy, since the chief is not always accessible, and does not wish to be troubled with every little affair of this kind, and they will tell him the name of the man denounced by *benge*. Or, instead of going to him, they may again consult *iwa* about several reliable men of good social position in order to choose one of them to notify the witch of *benge*'s verdict. If they go to the chief's deputy, the wiser course, he will promise to notify the witch. He calls one of his dependants and sends him with the fowl's wing to the homestead of the witch and tells him to present him with it, to note what happens and to bring back word accordingly. The messenger goes with the wing and lays it on the ground in front of the witch, saying that his master has sent him with it because of the illness of so-and-so. Generally a witch will protest his innocence of intention and his ignorance of the harm that he is doing to his neighbour. He calls for a gourdful of water, and when his wife brings it he takes a draught, swills it round in his mouth, and blows it out in a spray over the wing. He says aloud, so that the messenger can hear his words, that if he is a witch he is unaware of his possession of *mangu*, and that he is not causing injury to others with intent. He addresses the *mangu* in his stomach beseeching it to become inactive. If he makes this appeal from his heart and not in mere pretence with his lips, then the sick man will recover. The messenger returns to his master with news of what he has seen, and the deputy tells the relatives of the sick man that his duty has been performed satisfactorily. The relatives will wait anxiously for some days to find out what effect this ceremony will have. If the sick man shows signs of recovery they will praise *benge* for having revealed so quickly and surely the name of the witch and opened up a road to recovery. If sickness continues they will again consult the oracles to find out whether the witch was only pretending repentance or whether some new aggressor had arisen to trouble their ill friend, and in this case the same formal ceremony of presentation of hen's wings will again take place.

Though chiefs appear in the past to have sometimes taken more drastic steps to ensure their safety, the procedure described above has always been the normal everyday usage of every section of society. It is an usage which maintains generally an orderly outcome to a situation fraught with considerable emotional stress on both sides of the conferring of a hen's wing upon a man often leads, on the part of the *boro mangu*,[9] to concealed anger and permanent estrangement, whilst the relatives on their part feel themselves face to face with what amounts to murder of their friend and kin. The great authority of the *benge* oracle, the use of an intermediary to carry out the more offensive part of the performance, the social standing of a deputy backed up by the political power of a chief, the stereotyped mode of behaviour expected of a witch under the trying publicity which accompanies his humiliation, are factors which help to tide over this difficult impasse in human relations, whilst at the same time allowing expression of indignation along prescribed channels of conduct. For a man who were to accuse another man wantonly of witchcraft without being able to produce an oracular verdict to back up his statement would be merely laughed at for his

9. '*Boro* (*ira*) *mangu* witch: a person whose body contains, or is declared by oracles or diviners to contain, witchcraft-substance and who is supposed to practise witchcraft' (Evans-Pritchard, 1937, p. 9). Cf. previous Reading, which gives *ira mangu* for 'witch' – *Ed.*

pains if he were not beaten into the bargain. A man who went himself to deliver a hen's wing or who sent some unsuitable messenger without first consulting either the oracles or an old man of high social standing would run the risk of initiating a violent scene, and people would say that he got what an ignorant 'provincial' deserves. While, on the other hand, the man who showed temper on being presented with a hen's wing in the proper traditional manner would, as we shall show more fully in a later section, not only be considered a boor, but his behaviour would reveal blackness of heart and confirm the worst suspicions. The Zande can always tell you what is the correct behaviour in any situation, the ideal of conduct based on tradition; but people are always doing things the wrong way and troublesome consequences arise. Nevertheless, by a traditional sequence of activities from a preliminary consultation of the *iwa* oracle to a consultation of *benge*, from *benge* to *iwa* once more, from *iwa* to a dramatic declaration in the *kuba*, from the *kuba* to *iwa* again, from *iwa* to *benge*, from *benge* to a formal request to a chief's deputy and the sending of a messenger and the carrying out of a simple ceremony in the homestead of a witch, all is regulated by a well-known sequence of traditional moves and a series of behaviour-patterns which give firm social control over the unruly passions of men under severe emotional stress. [...]

References

EVANS-PRITCHARD, E. E. (1929), 'The morphology and function of magic', *American Anthropologist*, vol. 31.

EVANS-PRITCHARD, E. E. (1937), *Witchcraft, Oracles and Magic among the Azande*, Clarendon Press.

HUBERT, H., and MAUSS, M. (1902–3), 'Esquisse d'une théorie générale de la magie', *L'Année Sociologique*, vol. 7; reprinted in M. Mauss (1950), *Sociologie et Anthropologie*, Presses Universitaires de France.

LAGAE, C. R. (1926), 'Les Azande ou Niam–Niam', *Bibliothèque Congo*, vol. 18.

MALINOWSKI, B. (1926), 'Magic, science and religion', in J. Needham (ed.), *Science, Religion and Reality*, Macmillan; reprinted in R. Redfield (ed.), *Magic, Science and Religion and Other Essays*, The Free Press, 1948; Doubleday, 1954.

3. Raymond Firth

Reason and Unreason in Human Belief[1]

Excerpts from Raymond Firth, *Human Types: An Introduction to Social Anthropology*, Nelson, 1956, revised edition, chapter 6, pp. 155–6, 163–5.

Magic, as commonly accepted, comprises a rite and verbal formula projecting man's desires into the external world on a theory of human control, to some practical end, but as far as we can see based on false premises. A broad classification of magic in terms of these practical ends, whether the promotion of human welfare, the protection of existing interests, or the destruction of individual well-being through malice or the desire for vengeance, is given in the following table:

AIM AND SPHERE	SOCIAL ASPECT
A. *Productive.*	Performed either by private individuals for themselves, or by specialist magicians for others or the community as a whole. Socially approved. A stimulus to effort and a factor in organisation of economic activity.
Magic of hunting.	
Magic of fertility, planting, and harvest in agriculture	
Magic of rain-making.	
Magic of securing a catch in fishing.	
Canoe and sailing magic.	
Magic for trading profit.	
Magic of love.	
B. *Protective.*	Performed as above, and socially approved. A stimulus to effort and a force of social control.
Taboos to guard property.	
Magic to assist collection of debts.	
Magic to avert misfortune.	
Magic for the cure of sickness.	
Magic for safety in travelling.	
Counter-magic to C.	

1. The definitions given in these two excerpts from *Human Types* are of general applicability. For a useful discussion of how they fit the beliefs and practices of the Tikopia, see Raymond Firth (1954) – *Ed.*

Sorcery: performed as above, sometimes socially approved, sometimes disapproved. Often a force of social control.

C. *Destructive.*
Magic to bring storms.
Magic to destroy property.
Magic to produce sickness.
Magic to bring death.
[...]

Witchcraft: sometimes attempted, often doubtful if actually performed; and sometimes of imaginary occurrence. Classed as morally bad. Provides a native theory of failure, misfortune and death.

We may now turn to an analysis of destructive magic. Let us first compare the pattern of destructive magic in several primitive societies. Destructive magic among the Maori consists essentially in destroying some part of the victim's clothing or hair or nails or even his excreta with the recital of a powerful spell. Among the Zande of Central Africa *mangu* or witchcraft is a kind of emanation from an imaginary material substance in the bodies of some persons. It is thought to be capable of being diagnosed by oracles in the living, and is said to be discovered by autopsy on the dead. To the Zande ordinary magic and witchcraft are of quite a different order. In comparing the magic of these two societies we see that among the Maori there is no use of medicine, that destructive magic and productive magic are of the same generic kind, and that destructive magic is actually practised and relies for its success on the use of objects associated with the victim. But whereas the productive magic of the Zande is very similar to that of the Maori, Zande destructive magic has an additional category to the Maori type. Side by side with the sorcery which is actually performed and follows a special technique, is witchcraft, which does not require either formulae or exuviae of the victim, and is not actually capable of human performance. This duality in the sphere of destructive magic is commonly found in Africa as well as in Australia and parts of Melanesia. It does not, however, appear to exist in Polynesia.

Among the Daly River people of Australia two varieties of destructive magic are actually practised: the rite to bring on storms and damage one's enemies; and the burning or burying of personal exuviae to cause sickness and death. Also, there is a belief in and a great terror of *mamakpik*, the stealing of a living man's kidney fat with his resultant rapid decline and death. This presents the features of the Zande *mangu* in that it is never witnessed, and though a person may be accused of practising it he never admits to doing so, and its activity is diagnosed essentially by its supposed effects. But unlike the possessor of *mangu*, the practitioner of *mamakpik* has no supposed organic peculiarity of his body. In rare cases an attempt has actually been made to steal kidney fat in the prescribed fashion, but has naturally failed. In some parts of Melanesia there is a strong belief in a type of destructive magic, some of the cardinal features of which are physically impossible to carry out; yet there are people who actually profess to perform it. Such is the *vele* of Guadalcanal and the *vada* of south-eastern New Guinea, in which a magician is believed to daze his victim, extract vital organs, miraculously close the wound, and resuscitate him for a short time, though he cannot name his assailant and dies soon afterwards. The major difference of this from the Australian *mamakpik* is the existence of men who purport to practise this magic.

There is in all this destructive magic a set of common elements, though the emphasis upon each may vary from one community to another, and a fairly clear distinction can be drawn between one type, the practice of which is imaginary, and another type, where some ritual is actually performed. It is common to describe the first type as witchcraft and the second as sorcery, though these terms are not always uniformly so used. [. . .]

Reference

FIRTH, R. (1954), 'The sociology of "Magic" ', *Sociologus*, n.s., vol. 4, pp. 97–116, reprinted as chapter 9 of R. Firth, *Tikopia Ritual and Belief*, Allen & Unwin, 1967.

4. Keith Thomas

The Meaning of the Term 'Witchcraft'

Excerpt from Keith Thomas, *Religion and the Decline of Magic*, Weidenfeld & Nicolson and Charles Scribner's Sons, 1971, Penguin Books, 1973, pp. 463–5 (pp. 551–4 in the Penguin edition).

Modern social anthropologists have drawn a distinction between 'witchcraft' and 'sorcery' along the following lines. Witchcraft is an innate quality, an involuntary personal trait, deriving from a physiological peculiarity which can be discovered by autopsy. The witch exercises his malevolent power by occult means, and needs no words, rite, spell or potion. His is a purely psychic act. Sorcery, on the other hand, is the deliberate employment of maleficent magic; it involves the use of a spell or technical aid and it can be performed by anyone who knows the correct formula. Witchcraft, on this definition, is thus an impossible crime and not empirically observable, whereas sorcery really is practised in many primitive societies.[1]

This distinction arose out of the study of Azande witchcraft, but it has been applied to other contexts, even though its relevance to other African societies is nowadays much disputed.[2] Up to a point it can be made to fit English conditions, since there were at least some contemporary writers who perceived a difference between 'witchcraft', which was an occult power given by the Devil, requiring no tools or spells, and 'sorcery', which involved the use of images, poisons, etc. Thus, one writer declared in 1653 that sorcery was 'a thing or mischief which is distinct from witchcraft, as thus, witchcraft being performed by the devil's insinuation of himself with witches, ... sorcery being performed by mere sophistication and wicked abuse of nature in things of nature's own production, by sympathy and antipathy'. To exploit nature for a good purpose was legitimate; 'it is the evil of the end which is sorcery'. This comes very close to the modern anthropologist's description of sorcery as 'that division of

1. The original distinction was made by Evans-Pritchard, *Witchcraft, Oracles and Magic among the Azande*, pp. 21, 387, and had been amplified by M. G. Marwick in *African Systems of Thought*, with preface by M. Fortes & G. Dieterlen (1965), pp. 23–4.

2. See, e.g., *Witchcraft and Sorcery in East Africa*, ed. Middleton & Winter, pp. 2–3, 61, n.2; V. W. Turner, 'Witchcraft and sorcery: taxonomy versus dynamics', *Africa*, vol. 34, (1964), pp. 318–24; M. Douglas, 'Witch beliefs in Central Africa', *Africa*, vol. 37 (1967); J. R. Crawford, *Witchcraft and Sorcery in Rhodesia* (1967), p. 95.

destructive magic that is socially disapproved or deemed illegitimate'.[3] Francis Bacon anticipated it even more closely when he distinguished witchcraft from sorcery, by noting that a magical technique, like tying knots to prevent the consummation of a marriage, had 'less affinity with witchcraft, because not *peculiar persons only* (*such as witches are*), but anybody may do it'.[4]

The English witch, like her Azande counterpart, was also sometimes believed to have physical peculiarities, in addition to the witch's mark. In 1599, for example, a judge, Sir Richard Martin, said that he had heard that the hair of a witch could not be cut off.[5] Others asserted that a witch sitting in bright sunshine would leave no shadow[6] and that witches could shed no tears.[7] The author of a pamphlet account of a trial at Maidstone in 1652 reported that some bystanders wanted the witches burned, 'alleging that it was a received opinion amongst many that, the body of a witch being burnt, her blood is prevented thereby from becoming hereditary to her progeny in the same evil, which by hanging is not'.[8] The idea that witchcraft went in families and might be hereditary was often put forward.[9] But perhaps the closest approximation to the African conception of completely involuntary witchcraft was the belief in the existence of persons whose eyes had a special power of fascination, like the man who accidentally killed his own cattle by looking at them: one JP called such persons 'involuntary witches'.[10] These figures, however, were primarily creations of folklore and seldom made any appearance in the trials. One commentator declared that

the bodies of aged persons are impure, which, when they wax cankered in malice, they use their very breath and their sight, being apt for contagion, and by the Devil whetted for such purpose, to the vexation and destruction of others. For if they which are troubled with the disease of the eyes called *opthalmia* do infect others that look earnestly upon them, is it any marvel that these wicked creatures, having

3. W. Freeman, 'Artificiall Alligations and Suspentions shewing the Conjunction of Art and Nature' (1953) (Ashm. 1807). f. 82ᵛ. Cf. Marwick in *African Systems of Thought*, p. 22.

4. Bacon, *Works*, ii, p. 660 (my italics).

5. Ewen, ii, p. 190.

6. 'A Touchstone or Triall of Witches discoveringe them by Scripture', B.M., Royal MS 17 C XXIII, p. 13.

7. Scot, *Discoverie*, II. vi; Bernard, *Guide*, p. 239; Gaule, *Select Cases of Conscience touching Witches and Witchcrafts*, p. 76; Ewen, ii, p. 328; Cf. Lea, *Materials*, p. 568.

8. *A Prodigious and Tragicall History of the Arraignment, Tryall, Confession and Condemnation of Six Witches at Maidstone* (1652), p. 5.

9. Ewen, ii, index, *s.v.* 'heredity in witchcraft' (to which p. 264 should be added).

10. Ewen, ii, p. 356; above, p. 438.

both bodies and minds in a higher degree corrupted, should work both these and greater mischiefs[11]

But this idea also seems to have hardly ever been invoked in the courts.

In general, therefore, the anthropological distinction between witchcraft and sorcery is of limited utility when applied to England.[12] It can be said that the sorcerer used material objects, whereas the witch did not.[13] But the presence or absence of magical techniques does not seem to have been of great concern to those who took part in the trials. It was the fact of the witch's malignity which interested them. The evidence for this might come from her use of image-magic, animal familiars, curses or other magical techniques, but it could also be inferred from her social situation. She might wreak her malice by using techniques, which were observable, or by ill-wishing, which was not. But the two methods were interchangeable and there was no suggestion that they belonged to different species of offender.

The historian cannot even say, with the anthropologist, that sorcerers existed, whereas witches were imaginary. For some of those accused of being witches really had tried to harm others by mere ill-wishing, unaccompanied by magical techniques. In intention, at least, witchcraft was not an impossible crime. In execution, it was neither more nor less effective than most of the methods of the sorcerer. It is very probable that a higher proportion of those accused of attempting mental witchcraft were innocent than was the case with those charged with using observable magical techniques. But this is essentially unprovable. What is clear is that the person charged with witchcraft in sixteenth- and seventeenth-century England was never thought to have acted involuntarily. She was the victim of her evil thoughts, but not of any innate physical peculiarity.

Note: Readers wishing to follow up references in detail should consult the Notes on References and the Table of Abbreviations at the beginning of *Religion and the Decline of Magic* – Ed.

11. W. Fulbecke, *A Parallele or Conference of the Civil Law, the Canon Law, and the Common Law* (1618), f. 97.

12. *Pace* M. Gluckman, *Politics, Law and Ritual in Tribal Society* (Oxford, 1965), p. 266, n. 2.

13. Mair, *Witchcraft*, p. 23.

5. Alan Macfarlane

Definitions of Witchcraft

Excerpt from Alan Macfarlane, *Witchcraft in Tudor and Stuart England*, Routledge & Kegan Paul, 1970, Appendix 2.

Recent historians of English witchcraft have had considerable difficulty in their attempts to define the basic terminology.[1] Similarly, there is no unanimity among anthropologists. The classic distinction between 'witchcraft' and 'sorcery' in Africa was first outlined by Professor Evans-Pritchard (1937, p. 21) in the following words:

Azande believe that some people are witches and can injure them in virtue of an inherent quality. A witch performs no rite, utters no spell, and possesses no medicines. An act of witchcraft is a psychic act. They believe also that sorcerers may do them ill by performing magic rites with bad medicines.

The distinction here is between different types of means: the end is similar. Both witches and sorcerers injure people. Among the Azande a person *is* a witch. Witchcraft is an inherent quality, whereas sorcerers *act* in a certain way. Sorcerers are conscious of their activities, whereas witches, whose power is internal, may not be aware that they are witches until they are accused. While the witch is the vehicle for a power greater than herself, often the unwilling agent of vast evil forces, the sorcerer controls the power inherent in certain 'medicines' or other objects. Although both are driven by antisocial feelings, the witch is permanently malicious, having inherited her power or been taught it very early in life, while the sorcerer is only dangerous at specific times and acquires the power of evil later in life by a more self-conscious transmission.

Unfortunately, these analytic distinctions have not always worked when applied to societies other than the Azande. Thus, in Cewa society, there are 'sorcerers' who always use outward medicines or gestures and are conscious agents, but who, like 'witches', are permanently evil and learn their evil power early in life.[2] Even the Azande themselves do not

1. Briggs (1962, p. 3) discusses various definitions and suggests the effects of definitional differences among historians. Among other recent discussions, those of Ewen (1929, pp. 21–4) and Parrinder (1958, pp. 8–13) are the most helpful.

2. Marwick (1965, pp. 81–2) discusses the inapplicability of the 'witchcraft/sorcery' distinction in the Cewa setting. (Various renderings of this ethnic designation exist; Cewa has been adopted throughout – *Ed.*)

have 'witches' by all these criteria: people are not permanently motivated by witchcraft, but only on specific occasions.[3] There have been other criticisms of the whole distinction,[4] yet it has been found a useful tool in the analysis of witchcraft beliefs in Tudor and Stuart Essex. We may therefore ask to what extent people distinguished between various types of 'witchcraft' and how far there were generally accepted definitions.

Examination of historical definitions on the basis of the above distinctions immediately reveals that there was immense confusion and variation. There are a number of obvious reasons for this. Some authorities based their definitions on the works of Continental demonologists; others on the opinions of country folk. Opinions of witchcraft changed between 1560 and 1680. Attitudes differed between social and religious groups. An illustration of the way in which a number of opposing concepts were subsumed under the word 'witchcraft' occurs in the work of the Kentish squire, Reginald Scot (1584). 'Witchcraft', he said, was both good and bad in its effects, both inward and outward in its means, at least in the 'estimation of the vulgar people'. 'The effect and end' of witchcraft was 'sometimes evil, as when thereby man or beast, grasse, trees, or corne, &c., is hurt: sometimes good, as whereby sicke folkes are healed, theeves bewraied (*sic*), and true men come to their goods, &c.' Thus a person who cured an animal by magical means was, in common parlance, a 'witch'. Likewise, although outward rituals and medicines were used, inherent power of a personal kind was also needed. 'The matter and instruments, wherewith it is accomplished, are words, charmes, signes, images, characters, &c.' – external qualities. But their power depended on a certain personality. 'The which words although any other creature doo pronounce, in maner and forme as they doo, leaving out no circumstance requisite or usuall for that action: yet none is said to have the grace or gift to performe the matter, except she be a witch.' A person *was* a witch and also acted as a witch.

Other writers did not agree with Scot that the 'vulgar people' did not distinguish between types of witchcraft. In fact, it was just such a tendency to make a distinction between the 'good' and the 'bad' witch that angered John Gaule. As he wrote in the middle of the seventeenth century:

According to the vulgar conceit, distinction is usually made betwixt the White and the Blacke Witch: the Good and the Bad Witch. The Bad Witch, they are wont to

3. 'A Zande is interested in witchcraft only as an agent on definite occasions ... and not as a permanent condition of individuals' (Evans-Pritchard, 1937, p. 26).

4. One of the most forceful of the attacks on the widespread use of such a distinction was made by V. W. Turner (1964, pp. 319–24).

45

call him or her, that works Malefice or Mischiefs to the Bodies of Men or Beasts:
The good Witch they count him or her that helps to reveale, prevent or remove the
same (1646, p. 30).

The Witchcraft Statutes also distinguished between different ends. The
punishments for attempting to find lost goods, for instance, were different from those for trying to kill someone by witchcraft. Yet the Statutes,
by including both offences, blurred the differences. Thus a 'good witch' in
popular estimation might, theoretically, be executed just like a 'bad
witch'.

There seems to have been, in fact, a constant struggle between those
who wished to differentiate and those who wished to amalgamate. On the
one hand, there were those who wished to punish equally all who used
'magical' power, irrespective of their ends, and irrespective of the degree
of their control over such power. For them all 'superstition', especially
that emanating from Rome, was 'witchcraft' (cf. Perkins, 1608, pp.
150–52, 167). For them the words 'witch' and 'conjurer' were synonyms
(Ady, 1656, pp. 63–4). On the other hand, there were those who wished to
differentiate 'good' and 'bad' witches by their effects, and 'witches' and
'conjurers' by their degree of control over their power. The first of these
distinctions we have seen in the passage by John Gaule quoted above.
The second can be illustrated by the words of Sir Edward Coke (1644,
p. 44):

A Conjurer is he that by the holy and powerful names of God invokes and conjures
the Devill to consult with him, or to do some act. A Witch is a person, that hath a
conference with the Devill, to consult with him or to do some act.

The conjurer commands; the witch obeys.[5]

Two conclusions emerge from this short discussion of definitions of
terminology. The first is that, although anthropologists have provided
some useful analytic distinctions, these do not really help in a number of
societies. The second is that words like 'witchcraft' and 'sorcery' were
used in a number of different senses in seventeenth-century England. To
avoid confusion, therefore, words have been used as follows: Contrasting
means and ends, 'witchcraft' is predominantly the pursuit of harmful
ends by implicit/internal means. 'Sorcery' combines harmful ends with
explicit means. 'White witchcraft' pursues beneficial ends by explicit
means.

5. As Sir Walter Raleigh (1614, I, xi, 6, p. 209), echoing James I, put it.

Alan Macfarlane

References

ADY, T. (1656), *A Candle in the Dark: or, A Treatise Concerning the Nature of Witches and Witchcraft*.

BRIGGS, K. M. (1962), *Pale Hecate's Team*, Routledge & Kegan Paul.

COKE, Sir E. (1644), *Third Part of the Institutes of the Laws of England*.

EVANS-PRITCHARD, E. E. (1937), *Witchcraft, Oracles and Magic among the Azande*, Clarendon Press.

EWEN, C. L. (1929), *Witch Hunting and Witch Trials*, Kegan Paul, Trench, Trubner.

GAULE, J. (1646), *Select Cases of Conscience Touching Witches and Witchcraft*.

MARWICK, M. G. (1965), *Sorcery in its Social Setting*, Manchester U.P.

PARRINDER, G. (1958), *Witchcraft*, Penguin Books.

PERKINS, W. (1608), *A Discourse of the Damned Art of Witchcraft*, Cambridge.

RALEIGH, Sir W. (1614), *History of the World*.

SCOT, R. (1584), *The Discovery of Witchcraft*, p. 389 of the 1964 reprint, Preface by H. R. Williamson, Centaur Press.

TURNER, V. W. (1964), 'Witchcraft and sorcery: taxonomy versus dynamics', *Africa*, vol. 34, no. 4.

6. Christina Larner

Is All Witchcraft Really Witchcraft?

Christina Larner, 'Is all witchcraft really witchcraft?', *New Society*, vol. 30, 1974, pp. 81–3.

Whenever someone digs up a grave, or crucifies an acquaintance on Hampstead Heath, or carelessly leaves a skull lying around, those of us who have research interests in the field of pre-industrial witchcraft, whether as anthropologists, sociologists or historians, tend to get telephoned by the press, radio and television. I normally make stone-walling remarks, and these remarks run as follows: 'So-called witchcraft today in modern industrial cities is an entirely different phenomenon from the witchcraft of pre-industrial Europe or the witchcraft of primitive tribes. The difference lies in the social context: in pre-industrial witchcraft the community as a whole believed in the possibility and power of witchcraft, and the witch was therefore seen as a public menace; an enemy of the people. We have our enemies of the people today. They are, according to your collective demons: Jews, capitalists, communists, polluters, Catholics or Protestants; but they are not witches. Witches today are private persons doing their thing. They inhabit the world of fringe religion. They do not matter to anyone but themselves.'

Repetition of such an unencouraging formula, against a still apparently rising tide of interest, eventually creates doubt – rather than confirms certainty – in the mind of the speaker. It therefore seems worthwhile to examine in more detail to what extent it holds: and if it holds, why it makes no impression.

It seems reasonable to assume that the witchcraft that is ascribed to early modern Europe and to today's primitive societies should be allowed to set the standard as to what constitutes witchcraft. The problem here is that most witchcraft scholars in recent years, of whatever disciplinary persuasion, have been anxious – rightly – to establish a general theory of witchcraft. The practical effects of this concern have been most encouraging. Historians have drawn on anthropological theory to redirect their own research, and have produced a new kind of detailed survey of cases for limited areas: for example, the work of Alan Macfarlane on witchcraft in Tudor and Stuart England, E. W. Monter on sixteenth- and seventeenth-century Geneva, Eric Midelfort on witch-hunting in south west Germany, and Keith Thomas on religion and the decline of magic. Anthropologists have invoked the work of these historians in support of particular anthropological interpretations; and one thinks here especially of Mary Douglas, Max Marwick and Lucy Mair.

There is now fairly widespread agreement that pre-industrial European witchcraft has enough in common with contemporary primitive forms to be accounted the same phenomenon. But there is a danger that we will continue to push in the same direction, ensuring that new empirical studies will be tailored to one procrustean theoretical bed, or that general witchcraft theory will be so general as to say very little of value. One clear factor, which emerges from the empirical work so far done, is that the lowest common denominator is very low, and that divergences are very great. What we should now be doing, therefore, if we are to further comparative studies of witchcraft, is to break down the elements of witchcraft into their component parts. To this end I would suggest the following preliminary set of types:

Type A is *maleficium*. This is the simplest and most basic form of witchcraft. It can include both sorcery – physical manipulation of objects and/or incantation of words; and witchcraft – harming through the release of power activated by hatred.

Type B is *compact witchcraft*. Here the essence of witchcraft lies in a pact with Satan, the Christian devil. It does not matter whether the power realized through the pact is used for harming or healing. Compact witchcraft therefore blurs the secular distinction between black and white magic; between *maleficium* and *curing*.

Type C is *sabbath witchcraft*. It could be described as an extension of compact witchcraft, but in fact the addition of the sabbath, the idea that witches having made a pact with the devil combine with other witches to pay him homage, is commoner in Europe than the pact on its own. Witches' sabbaths or meetings also occur in non-Christian primitive cultures where pacts with one personalized devil are unknown.

These types can then be further subdivided. Type A has as its most simple form A^1, when the witch is accused of an act or acts of *maleficium*. A^2 represents the complications that occur when *maleficium* is fed into a legal system which has a pre-existing formula for interpreting the significance of *maleficium*. 'Curing' is represented by a^1. This is the other side of the *maleficium* coin, but one individual may be accused of practising both. And a^2 represents curing in a society which is likely to penalize it in the same way as it would *maleficium*. The types of sabbath witchcraft can also be sub-divided: C^1 are any witches' meetings. C^2 are meetings with the devil which may take any random form. C^3 is a deliberate inversion of Christian worship: the Satanic black mass.

The spread of types when applied to witch-believing societies then looks like this:

Primitive tribal	English (sixteenth and seventeenth centuries)	Scottish (seventeenth century)	Continental (fifteenth to seventeenth centuries)
A^1a^1	$A^1a^1a^2$	A^2a^2	A^2a^2
—	—	B	B
C^1	—	C^2 (rare)	C^2C^3

This indicates the pattern of the various ingredients of witchcraft exhibited by some of the witch-believing societies that have been studied. The question arises as to what extent these different elements are manifested in the witch cults of today's industrial cities. What of the despoilers of Highgate cemetery? What of our nude dancers in the Birmingham semi-detached?

There are two main types of contemporary witch cult: there are the groups who expressly embrace 'evil', whose centre point is Satan laced with sex; and there are the groups who regard themselves as the inheritors of a totally innocuous, pre-Christian fertility religion. Both these groups are backed by the products of the entertainment industry and the mass media, and are given some peripheral encouragement by panicky high churchmen.

The first type has had a long, if spasmodic, history. The eighteenth-century Hell Fire Club has its twentieth century successors in such people as Aleister Crowley. (The murdering Satanists of California are an extreme variety.) They tend to crop up when the rich and the bored get together. Money and leisure have usually been the background necessities for the trappings of a Black Mass, but the groups are totally eclectic in their ritual: they use any aspects of Black Mass folklore that take their fancy; and, as an activity, Satanism has undoubtedly been downwardly socially mobile in the second half of the twentieth century. The candlesticks do not have to be silver; and black candles can be had in any craft boutique.

The second type is quite distinct, and their groups tend to be connected with each other. Occasionally members write to me to explain that they are the true surviving witches. They have the characteristics of a sect, though there is little proselytizing. The basic belief is that they are a fertility religion which had to go underground during the period of Christian dominance. They meet to perform 'ancient rites', which consist essentially of forms of dance. None of these groups date from earlier than the 1920s, which was when the idea of witches as innocent exponents of an underground rival religion was first invented and popularized by Dr Margaret Murray. The key document for these groups is the article by Murray in the 14th (1929) edition of the *Encyclopaedia Britannica* which was replaced only in the 1968 reprinting by one by Clyde Kluckhohn and subsequently in the 15th (1974) edition by one by Max Marwick.

These two types of group could be seen as modern representatives of black and white magic; but there is no direct rivalry and little connection between them. They draw on different psychological types: while Satanism attracts the bored and the curious, the Murrayesque fertility cults are status-giving in a way that is analogous to that of orthodox religious sects. The actual numbers of people involved in either of these types of groups are unknown, and are likely to remain unknown, though sociologists are studying them. They are far outnumbered by consumers of the entertainment industry, who will apparently absorb any amount of films, plays, paperbacks on the theme of witchcraft, and magazines such as *Man, Myth and Magic* and *Witchcraft Today*.

The really striking factor about all this latter material – parasitic as it is on the few who actually participate – is that though much of it is wildly inaccurate, hysterical in its claims, overtly pornographic, and grotesquely spine-chilling, none of it ever admits to being the result either of a free-ranging imagination or of a straight journalistic investigation of the here-and-now. None of it ever emerges unadorned by the trappings of scholarship. The film-makers consult *bona fide* Jesuit exorcists. Paperbacks may have naked women on the front: they will have sixteenth-century woodcuts and Goya paintings within. Footnotes and bibliographies litter all copy. The standard witchcraft magazines all look as though a copy of *Penthouse* has been crossed with a Ph.D. thesis.

The explanation I would like to suggest for this remarkable dependence on scholarship and quasi-scholarship is that when the witch cults of contemporary western industrial societies are held against a model of witchcraft drawn from the classic witch-believing societies, they do not measure up. The only element which comes through strongly in the typology I have suggested is type C: the element of ritual. Type A, which is the one held in common by all witch-believing societies, is absent. Exponents would no doubt protest that they are constantly sticking pins into wax figures, and that they ritually curse three enemies a day before breakfast. But the truth is that nobody cares. *Maleficium,* unlike private ritual, cannot be committed in a social vacuum. To be effective, it must be generally believed to be effective. If ten covens were to write to me on the publication of this article to inform me that my name was being pronounced backwards while they danced widdershins around a casket containing a milk tooth from my younger son, a hair from the underbelly of my cat, and sealing wax from my desk, I would not be unduly dismayed: nor would I be in any way remarkable for not being dismayed. The social backing essential to the effective performance of *maleficium* simply is not there.

Nor do contemporary witchcraft practices fill any of the other social needs which they did (and do) fill in classic witch-believing cultures. The answer to the open question of whether or not these practices justify the name, 'witchcraft', does not affect this. It would be possible to do a different, more analytic, and rather more speculative categorization of witchcraft beliefs, in terms not of their external manifestations but of their relationship to internal social needs.

Featuring prominently in this would be witchcraft as decision-making; witchcraft accusations as a safety valve or as a gauge of social tension: witchcraft as explanation; and, by extension, witches as scapegoats. These are the principal social needs to which classic witch beliefs have been a response. And however strong the attraction of romantic atavism for individuals, it is inconceivable that in our highly diversified industrial society, where a variety of other responses to these needs have been developed, witchcraft can ever again play a significant part.

The reason, then, for the total dependence of all aspects of the contemporary culture of the occult on scholastic embellishment, is that the social need for which it currently caters is a secondary and not a basic need. It is the need for entertainment, diversion and titillation. Yet it cannot cater for that need without pretending to do much more. Identification with an era of general witch belief is therefore essential to the occult industry in all its forms. Hence the learned footnotes, the bibliographies, and the woodcuts.

Yet I do not think that scholars need to beat their breasts unduly when their works are press-ganged into this cause, nor even cast aside any silver pressed into their hands as ill-gotten. It may be, and probably is, true that much psychological damage is done to individuals in the pursuit of the occult. But the same could also be said of some adherents of standard sects and religions. What is quite clear is that the major and regular misfortunes that afflict mankind, and from which industrial societies are not immune (fire, flood, earthquake, disease, famine and war) will not, in the present social context, be ascribed to witchcraft.

References

DOUGLAS, M. (ed.) (1970), *Witchcraft Confessions and Accusations*, Tavistock.

MACFARLANE, A. (1970), *Witchcraft in Tudor and Stuart England*, Routledge & Kegan Paul.

MARWICK, M. (ed.) (1970), *Witchcraft and Sorcery*, Penguin.

MIDELFORT, E. (1972), *Witch-hunting in Southwestern Germany 1562–1684*, Stanford U.P.

MONTER, E. W. (1971), 'Witchcraft in Geneva, 1537–1662', *Journal of Modern History*, vol. 43, no. 2.

THOMAS, K. (1971), *Religion and the Decline of Magic*, Weidenfeld & Nicolson.

WILSON, B. (1972), *Religious Sects*, Weidenfeld & Nicolson.

7. Philip Mayer

Witches

Philip Mayer, *Witches*, Inaugural Lecture, Rhodes University, Grahamstown, South Africa, 1954.

Reality of Witchcraft in Human Experience

The idea of witchcraft, as you will know, is not confined to any one set of peoples, but is distributed through many different races, cultures, and environments. It occurs among primitive peoples from Africa to the South Seas and from Asia to America. Its record among civilized peoples is only a little shorter. Everyone knows that Joan of Arc was a convicted witch. However, it is not always recalled that witches were still being burnt in Europe down to the age of the French Revolution. The last occasion was in 1782 in Switzerland.

My object tonight is to discuss withcraft beliefs and witch persecutions as they appear from the standpoint of modern anthropology. Our science has learnt a great deal about witches since the pioneering days of Sir James Frazer and Edward Tylor. Besides collecting much more exact knowledge we have gained a far deeper insight into the social meaning of witchcraft.

It is pleasant to be able to say that some of the most notable advances in knowledge and understanding are owed to former holders of this Chair of Anthropology at Rhodes: to Professor and Mrs Krige who studied witchcraft in the Transvaal among the Lovedu[1] (1943), and to Professor Wilson who, with her husband, studied it in Tanganyika among the Nyakyusa (Hunter, 1936; Wilson, 1951a, 1951b, 1952). My third and last predecessor, Professor Radcliffe-Brown, has been prudent enough to work only among tribes where there are no witches. But to him is due the great general illumination of principles and methods without which modern Social Anthropology could not have progressed as it has. I feel that it is a special privilege and honour to have him here tonight.

In what I say tonight, I shall be drawing together some of the important points about witchcraft that have been made by various anthropol-

1. The *v* in this tribal name is a bilabial fricative (ß in I.P.A. script; ɞ in that of the International African Institute); in Krige's paper (Reading 27, pp. 263–75) it is represented by a *b* – *Ed.*

ogists studying particular tribes; and I shall also be outlining some general conclusions which have been suggested to me both by the literature and by my own field-work.

When one starts to think about witchcraft, commonsense suggests the first question how it is that ideas so absurd, fantastic and often horrible have been so widely distributed in place and time. At the same time, since witchcraft ideas are widespread without being universal, one wants to account for their absence too. Some of the most primitive peoples on earth, including Australian aboriginals and Bushmen here in South Africa, do not believe in witches.

One thing is clear: the witchcraft idea must be related to something real in human experience. Occurring at so many different times and places and cultural levels it cannot be lightly dismissed as a frill on the edge of human fantasy. Social Anthropology, then, is concerned with finding out what is the basic reality underlying witchcraft ideas. When I say reality I do not mean physical fact. Even the most optimistic field-worker does not expect to see anyone flying on those well-known broomsticks. The kind of reality we are searching for is social and psychological. The witchcraft belief, and the persecution of witches, are a response to social and psychological strains. The more exactly we can identify those strains, the better we can hope to understand the response.

I shall first have to say what witches are. This is not a simple matter. Until Evans-Pritchard's classic work on the Azande there was little serious effort to distinguish witchcraft from sorcery or to isolate it from black magic generally. But as we have to choose a working concept, I would suggest that the essence of the witchcraft idea is simply this: people believe that the blame for some of their sufferings rests upon a peculiar evil power, embodied in certain individuals in their midst, although no material connexion can be empirically demonstrated between those individuals and the ills they are supposed to have caused.

The witch then is held to be a person in whom dwells a distinctive evilness, whereby he harms his own fellows in mysteriously secret ways. To this central mystical idea each society adds its own embellishments.

One of the fascinations of these mystical embellishments is the recurrence of identical details in astonishingly different surroundings. Shakespeare writing in seventeenth-century England about medieval Scottish witches makes them recite a list of creatures that would be just as appropriate to witches in primitive Africa. Or again: the Pueblo Indians in Mexico say that witches go round at night carrying lights that alternately flare up and die down (Parsons, 1936, p. 131); exactly the same thing was said to me in Western Kenya by the Bantu tribe among whom I worked.

One could quote many of these minute parallels. It is not my task tonight to deal with them as such nor to interpret their symbolism. But perhaps it may help us to discern order in the symbolism if we list the major elements that seem to be common to witchcraft myths nearly everywhere:

First, the myth defines a category of persons who may be witches, and states how they can be recognized by particular signs. Witches are practically always adults, very often women, and apt to spring from witch families. They may bear physical stigmata – either external, like a red eye or a Devil's mark, or internal, like a snake in the belly or a special witchcraft substance. Personally they are often reserved, stingy and quarrelsome.

Secondly, the myth tells what sorts of misfortune can be caused by witches. Often these include natural calamities such as death, sickness, drought or plague. However, the context of the misfortune is usually more significant than its intrinsic nature. Witches typically send particular and unaccountable blows that seem somehow out of the common run.

Thirdly, the myth states that witches turn against their own neighbours and kinsmen; they do not harm strangers or people from far away.

Fourthly, they work from envy, malice or spite, against individuals, rather than in pursuit of material gain as such. Sometimes they are 'just greedy', or they may have no conscious motive at all.

Fifthly, witches always work in secret, and especially at night.

Sixthly, witches are not entirely human. Their evil power is something *sui generis*, quite unlike ordinary ways of dealing injury such as force or poison. It may work upon its victims immediately, that is to say without the use of any instrument at all. The witch only has to wish you harm, and the harm is as good as done. A witch then is a human being who incorporates a non-human power. When a myth refers to snakes or other objects in the belly of the witch, it seems to be reflecting this notion. Other myths reflect it by saying that witches are possessed by spirits or devils, or that at night they forsake human form and turn into were-creatures.

Seventhly, witches reverse all normal standards. They particularly delight in 'unnatural' practices such as incest or bestiality; they eat their own children, they dig up corpses. They go naked instead of clothed; they excrete in the middle of the dwelling. Even when they knock on your door they stand backwards; or when they ride on baboons, as the Pondo witches do, they face towards the tail. In Christian countries witches repeat prayers or the whole Mass in reverse order.

Lastly, witchcraft is always immoral. At best it is disapproved; at worst it inspires horror like other so-called unnatural practices. Witchcraft properly so-called cannot be justified.[2]

So much for the myth of witchcraft. But though Social Anthropology is concerned with myths and beliefs, it is even more directly concerned with actions, with what men actually do and not how they live. Malinowski made popular the saying that a myth provides charter for action. We have to study the witchcraft system as a whole, the actions as well as the myths, the entire complex of beliefs, attitudes and activities. And having done this we should try to relate it to other social systems, and to find out what part it plays in the working of society as a whole.

Whether anyone ever tries to be a witch and actually perform witchcraft is a question that has to be separately determined in each society we study. In some primitive tribes the answer seems to be yes. More often there is no positive evidence, but even so things sometimes happen in the field that shake one's scepticism. Like Evans-Pritchard (1937) among the Azande, I have seen among the Gusii at night suggestive lights moving near my camp, lights that died down and flared up again exactly as the witchcraft myth alleges. Gusii say that witches produce this effect by raising and lowering the lids of covered fire-pots which they carry with them.

However, Social Anthropology only claims to analyse behaviour that has been properly observed, and observed with some regularity. This condition, which does not as yet apply to witchcraft practices, does of course apply to the counter-action that people take against witches. Even if some individuals do try to be witches, the witchcraft power itself is surely imaginary, but the power of the idea regularly inspires people to defence or counter-attack. This therefore is the kind of action that field-workers have observed and analysed. We can analyse it irrespective of whether its referent is real or unreal, much as we could analyse a church service while leaving the existence of God an open question.

Let us start by distinguishing two broad categories of action against witches. These categories correspond to the two elements in the nature of the witch, who is non-human and yet human. In so far as the witchcraft power is non-human, one may try to nullify it by antidotes as mystical as itself. One may recite spells or wear amulets or put down medicines. This is a kind of duelling in the realm of fantasy, a duel between two equally imaginary forces. Judged by rational standards it cannot produce any

2. Exception may be taken to stating this as a general rule in the light of instances such as the Heiban and Tira, cited by Nadel (1947, pp. 157 and 202). Personally, I would prefer to define witchcraft as something essentially immoral. See also Wilson (1951a, p. 97, note 2), about her substitution of the term 'defender' for 'defender witches'.

concrete effects, as distinct from psychological ones. But because the wielder of witch-power is also a human being, one may also try to evade or control him as a human being. This is another kind of duelling, not mere fantasy but working social effects that are plain for all to see. For example, among the Gusii it is quite common for whole families to leave their homes through fear of witches; or the self-styled victims might seek reconciliation or pick quarrels, or start whispering campaigns, or complain to the elders. Or they might call in a 'smeller' which is the name they give to professional witch-detectives; in former days a witch who had been duly smelt out might be put to death, but nowadays the use of criminal sanctions against witches is not allowed by the Kenya Administration.

When we consider all the activity that is directed against supposed witches, the question must be asked when or why people start going to all this trouble: what events or situations give them the impulse to start fighting this imaginary menace. It is clear that the stimulus is a feeling of unease or anxiety; but this statement needs to be analysed further. After all, many events and many situations regularly create anxiety, but not all of them bring the witchcraft idea into operation. Death and sickness, for instance, always create anxiety, but the emotion can often be dealt with by the ordinary routine responses. The routine response to a death is a funeral, the routine response to a sickness is medical treatment. The idea of witchcraft is invoked on occasions when these routine responses alone do not give emotional satisfaction.

Events are creating a special anxiety when they are termed unnatural, or uncanny. They are seeming to run counter to the ordinary course of things. The anxiety fastens on to the question of what deeper causation can have underlain the observed event. Among ourselves, we know that some deaths arouse a special anxiety so that we feel impelled to investigate their deeper causation. It is not enough to bury the man who got drowned in the river. We may also insist on finding out why he got drowned – whether he jumped in, whether someone pushed him in, or whether it was just an accident.

The witchcraft idea is commonly invoked as a concept for explaining the deeper or indirect causation of events which seem unnatural. Evans-Pritchard has brilliantly analysed Azande witchcraft beliefs in this light. Of course, the sphere of the 'unnatural' is defined differently in every culture. The Azande explain very many deaths by witchcraft: they think it is unnatural to die unless one is very old. Other peoples explain things differently.

Within a given culture, we have also to reckon with the individual point of view. Subjective factors may largely influence the tendency to suspect witchcraft in particular cases. You may think that you have an unnatural illness; I may see nothing odd about it. And the observed facts can nearly always be given a different twist by a person with a different point of view. This was nicely illustrated for me by an old Gusii man.

Suppose there is a cattle plague [he said]. Nearly all of my cattle die, but my neighbour loses only a couple of beasts. I wonder whether he has bewitched me; it was strange that I should lose so many, and he only so few. Now that neighbour has seen that I am still able to lead out my plough with a pair of strong oxen, but the plague has killed just those two animals of his that he always used for ploughing. He says to himself how strange it is that I can still plough and not he. Perhaps *I* am the one who has bewitched *him*.

Even if only for reasons like these, the anthropologist would hardly expect to be able to predict by rule of thumb just what events will lead to the suspicion of witchcraft and what will not. But there is another limitation too. Witchcraft is usually not the *only* mystic agency that can be suspected of sending peculiar or unnatural misfortunes. Many a primitive universe is peopled with numbers of mystic agencies whose hand may be suspected behind any unusual event. Among the Gusii, for instance, strokes of bad luck may be interpreted as the work of witches, but they may also be attributed to sorcerers, or to the evil eye, or to ancestor spirits, or to broken taboos, or to perjured oaths, or to ritual uncleanliness or perhaps just to luck, 'the luck of God', as they say. A different kind of remedy or protection will be used according to which of these agencies is held responsible.

The Cosmological Setting of Witch-Beliefs

If we want to understand the functions of the witchcraft system as a response to human sufferings and anxieties, I think we have to consider how it fits into a people's entire cosmology, or view of the universe, or philosophy of life. I am especially thinking of what we ourselves call the problem of evil. For example, among those mystic agencies which I have just enumerated, the Gusii regard some as fundamentally just or good and others as fundamentally unjust or evil. Ancestor spirits belong to the first category: they are like angry fathers – always right; they do not trouble people except those who deserve to be troubled. When a Gusii thinks that his bad luck was sent by ancestor spirits, he is construing it as a moral sanction called down by some misconduct of his own. Witches belong to the second category; they are always wrong. When a Gusii thinks that his bad luck was sent by witches he is construing it as unprovoked aggression against himself. The former is a response in terms of guilt and atonement, the latter in terms of resentment and counter-attack.

Take by way of contrast the cosmology of the Andaman Islanders. They too have a cult of ancestral spirits, but unlike the Gusii they find it no blasphemy to accuse the spirits of doing wrong. As Radcliffe-Brown (1922) has shown us, when a death occurs among these people the anger is directed against the spirits and may find expression in violent railing against them. This contrast must obviously be relevant to the fact that the Andamanese do not believe in witches and the Gusii do.

Again, among the Tallensi, as Fortes (1949) has shown, the ancestor and earth cults can on the whole deal adequately with most social or psychological tensions. The idea of witchcraft, though it does exist, does not rank as equal to these in the cosmology: it appears mainly as a mixture of superstition and folklore.

The Gusii witchcraft belief helps to maintain their picture of the moral universe. By blaming witches they escape the need or temptation to blame spirits. The spirits can remain good because the witches are bad. (Incidentally, the Gusii have no answer to the question why these good and just spirits fail to protect virtuous men against evil witches. That problem is more directly tackled, among others, by the Venda in the Northern Transvaal, who say that before a witch can harm anyone the protective ancestor spirits must be caught off guard (Stayt, 1931, p. 275).

There are some cosmologies into which the concept of witchcraft does not fit at all, because they represent everything that happens as being fundamentally right, proper, or natural. Some religions, for instance, teach a Job-like submission to a divine will which brings about everything and is always just. With similar effect, Rationalism teaches that everything may be interpreted as the outcome of natural causes. In neither of these idea systems, if consistently held, is there any room for the witchcraft idea. Witches can only have place in a cosmology that admits to the possibility of things going wrong, that is, departing from the natural and the moral order. We ourselves, in spite of Christianity and Rationalism, appear to admit this possibility up to a point, as when we speak of 'uncanny' luck, meaning contrary to natural order, or of 'unfair' luck, meaning contrary to moral order.

I have been discussing how the witchcraft belief can serve to protect the picture of the moral universe, but as we know it can also protect many other ideas and beliefs. If you have cultivated your fields in the usual way, you may blame a witch for the failure of your crop, and so be saved from the thought that accepted farming techniques might be at fault. If your illness does not respond to treatment, you may blame a witch, and so be saved from doubting the worth of medical knowledge and practice. The witch system can save other belief systems from being deluged with the blame which might otherwise often deservedly fall upon them. It gives a channel into which the blame can be turned more conveniently. The power of the witch is conceived as something that can put a spoke into any wheel; this helps one to assume that, but for witchcraft, all the wheels would always be turning smoothly.

When we ourselves speak of natural disasters such as drought or epidemic, we sometimes call them 'Acts of God', meaning that no human being can be held responsible. Primitive peoples who attribute these disasters to witches are taking the opposite view; they are blaming human beings, and they may even be asserting that those human beings caused the disaster just by willing it. I think that this notion, bizarre to us at first sight, begins to look much more familiar if it is translated into slightly different wording: let us put it that the witch is debited with the moral responsibility. That is a thing distinct from the immediate physical agency. If so-and-so has been wishing for me to suffer, he seems to me morally guilty when I do suffer, no matter what the direct physical causation may be. It is but a short psychological step from attributing moral guilt in this sense to attributing clear responsibility; one is only invoking the common principle which Freud has called 'the omnipotence of thought'.

Witchcraft and Social Relationships

So far I have been discussing the witchcraft idea as a cosmological device, accounting for sufferings that people cannot or will not explain otherwise, and providing a pattern of action that the sufferer may follow when his misfortune makes him particularly uneasy. But the witchcraft idea has of course quite a different kind of social importance as well as this. It is a force in social relations; it is something that can break up a friendship or a marriage or a community; it is a banner under which people hate, denounce, and even kill one another. That is the aspect in which I now want to discuss it.

When we speak loosely of witches being tried or condemned we mean of course that individuals are being tried or condemned as witches. The witch does not exist in his own right; it is the judgement of society that creates him. Society creates the image of the witch, and pins this image down onto particular individuals. If we want to find out what individuals are chosen to fill this unenviable role, there are two ways to go about the inquiry. The first is to try to define a general category of witches. Natives define such a category when they say that all individuals with pythons in their bellies or with red rims round their eyes are witches. We might hope to substitute a more scientific formulation: we might, for instance, be able to show what personality types are most commonly associated with the role of witch in a given society.

The second way, which has been used to such excellent effect by the Kriges and the Wilsons, is to define witches in relation to those whom they bewitch. Instead of asking 'who are the witches?' *in vacuo*, one asks how witches stand related to their supposed victims or their actual accusers. A witchcraft case may end in the uprising of a whole community, but it begins as a duel between two antagonistic individuals, or even as a one-sided mistrust. Our question then is: In a given society, who is most likely to accuse whom?.

Thanks to the admirable field-work that has now been done in many parts of the world, we should be able to answer this question with some confidence. Two general rules seem to emerge from the literature. The first is that witches and their accusers are nearly always people close together, belonging to one neighbourhood community or even to one household. This principle is expressed in the witchcraft myth by the notion that witches cannot harm you from far away but only from close by. The second rule is that a witchcraft accusation nearly always grows out of some personal antipathy or hostile emotion. In the myth this is expressed by saying that witches attack where they feel dislike or envy.

In the typical case, then, the alleged witch is a neighbour and perhaps a kinsman of the accuser who has not been getting on well with him or her. I think that most of the apparent exceptions to this rule, if analysed, turn out not to relate to genuine witchcraft but to other phenomena such as sorcery or the evil eye. There are a few societies where the rule does not hold, but even these exceptions may be of the sort that prove the rule, as Kluckhohn has suggested in his studies of the Navaho (Kluckhohn, 1944; Kluckhohn and Leighton, 1946).

It is by now well established that witchcraft accusations may be significantly frequent in one or more specific relationships. For example, among many African peoples it is especially common for a woman to accuse her husband's other wife of being a witch. Among the Mesakin in the Southern Sudan, Nadel (1952, p. 24ff.) found that the accusation commonly occurred between a man and his maternal uncle. As Nadel has suggested, frequencies of this kind should be interpreted as pointers to weak spots in the social structure.

We must conclude that witches and their accusers are individuals who ought to like each other but in fact do not. The two elements in the situation – the demand for a positive sentiment and the inability to provide it – are equally essential to the picture. Painful tension arises because one individual cannot feel towards another as society expects him to feel. By the standards of society one ought to get on well with one's kinsman or neighbour, one's co-wife or maternal uncle. If in fact one cannot get on well with him or her, the situation may become tense. When such a tension becomes insupportable, the only ways to resolve it are reconciliation on the one hand or rupture on the other. Marwick (1952, p. 126) has shown that among the Ceŵa accusations of witchcraft serve the purpose of rupturing or blasting away relationships that have become insupportable.

When someone starts to argue that someone else is bewitching him, this notion may serve to bring to a head the tensions and strains of their relationship. It gives a pretext for quarrelling. There is no law under which you can denounce a person for being personally distasteful to you, but you can denounce him on grounds of witchcraft. The witch idea then is a device that enables people to dress up their animosities in an actionable guise – in the guise of an offence committed against themselves.

Although the condemnation of witches may seem arbitrary in a deeper sense, it is nevertheless carried out in due legal form. The witch's guilt is not taken on trust but is determined by some supposedly objective standard. We know of many magico-religious tests for guilt, such as ordeals, oracles, or diagnosis by magical specialists, and of judicial forms, hearings by a court or a body of elders. We know that even when a supposed witch is set upon by an angry mob and beaten or stoned to death, as used to happen in many African tribes, this is a judicial execution and not an uncontrolled lynching. The crowd is the public executioner in a non-centralized society: it is not the judge as well.

It has been observed, again by Marwick (1952, p. 129), that people accuse one another of witchcraft when they are prohibited from expressing their aggression in other ways such as physical brawling or going to law. From my experience among the Gusii, I would qualify this by adding that people who have both possibilities may still prefer to accuse each other of witchcraft, rather than to pick a legal quarrel, because the witchcraft case has a different objective. Legal cases among primitive people are usually meant to smooth out relationships by patching up quarrels over specific issues. However, among the Gusii and perhaps in most other societies the parties to a witchcraft case probably do not want to be reconciled. What they want is an excuse for rupture. In a witchcraft case the thing at stake is not a specific legal issue but the whole tone of the relationship.

It is an extremely important question what kinds of sanction are used against a witch: when will the suspect be only pursued as a private enemy by his self-styled victim, and when will he be hounded down as a public enemy by community or state? For this largely determines the degree of danger to life and liberty.

Let us consider how the matter is handled by the Gusii. Among the Gusii, for reasons I shall mention later, there was and still is a great reluctance to publicize witch cases. The first recourse is to private magic. If this does not give satisfaction, the easiest and best way to resolve the tension is to break off relationships altogether. For where there is no active relationship there can be no active danger, either of being bewitched or of being suspected. If a man suspects his wife, then he will divorce her; if he suspects his sweetheart he will stop courting her; if he suspects his neighbour he may leave the neighbourhood. By these and similar personal adjustments, rupture is achieved without calling in public sanctions or even trying to enlist public opinion; in fact, secrecy is usually a great object. But there remains an alternative way of achieving rupture, and this is by an open legal challenge, which constitutes a direct appeal to public opinion. If the challenge is successful, the witch is liable to be pursued with the whole weight of public sanctions, ending in his death or banishment; at best he has become a 'known witch', a person ready to be blamed and hounded down in any future private or public calamity. If the challenge is not successful, the challenge itself has at any rate dramatically registered the quarrel as open and bitter, since witchcraft is one of the most serious accusations a Gusii can make against another.

Modern administrations and governments in Africa have tried to lessen the social perils of the witchcraft belief by refusing to recognize witchcraft as a criminal offence. In that case it is not permitted to try people for witchcraft in the public courts nor to use criminal sanctions against supposed witches. Witchcraft cases are therefore kept down to the private level. They are duels between A and B, not public issues between A and the community.

This solution has undoubtedly removed the most dramatic dangers to life and liberty. But it brings other problems in its train. The public condemnation and execution of a witch, however repugnant it was, may be considered to have served a useful function from one point of view. It was cathartic; it purged the whole community of certain anxieties for the time-being. They had found the public enemy who made things go wrong for all of them; they had destroyed him; they could all breathe more freely.

But now that the anxieties cannot be purged by a few great public witch-hunts, they have to find outlet in countless little private hunts. Every sufferer has to find his own witch. It is less dangerous to be thought a witch, but there is much more likelihood of being thought one.

Since the accusation of witchcraft can be such a dangerous weapon, we have to enquire what safeguards there are against its being used too freely. We all feel that a society that gives excessive prominence to witchcraft must be a sick society, rather as a witch-ridden personality is a sick personality. This is confirmed by anthropological studies which in several cases have shown an increase of witchcraft phenomena in communities undergoing social breakdown. The native peoples of South Africa during the difficult phase of urbanization provide several cases in point.

In a normally stable society the witchcraft system is effectively controlled. It admittedly provides a vent for hatreds and anxieties that society cannot repress, but this remains after all a controlled outlet: the frequency or severity of convictions is somehow kept within bounds. It should be anthropologically valuable to compare the ways in which different societies achieve this control. Tonight, however, I shall only single out one aspect. In many societies, including the Gusii, the weapon of witchcraft accusation is given a double edge. There is good reason to think twice before you denounce your enemy as a witch, for the denunciation may very well recoil upon your own head.

The literature shows how common it is for witchcraft cases to be ambiguous in this sense. Prima facie the signs that point to a person's being a victim of witchcraft can equally well point to his being a witch himself. Let me give a few examples: I take them from the Gusii, but they would fit many other peoples too. If you have been out alone in the night you could well have been attacked by the witches whom you saw prowling in the dark. But to the person you met you looked just like a prowling witch yourself. If you have a peculiar illness, it may mean that you are being bewitched; but it may mean that someone whom you yourself have bewitched is using revenge magic against you. If you have become unusually prosperous, the witches will probably be attacking you, because they always go for people whose good fortune they envy. On the other hand, the kind of person who grows prosperous while all around him are poor is very likely to be a witch himself. If you marry into a witch family, or otherwise consort with known witches, who is more likely than you to become their next victim? On the other hand, why did you ever take up with such people if you were not yourself a witch? If you have left your home and gone to settle in a far-away place, you may say that you fled

65

from witches who threatened you at the old home. But other people may say that you fled as a witch fearing detection.

It may sound paradoxical to say that witches and their victims look much the same in the public eye, but it makes good sense if we remember that the matter really at stake is a sensation of distrust or hatred. There is not much essential difference between the statement 'I hate X', and the statement 'X hates me'. Even if the hatred is not actually mutual, the one who feels it will probably project it onto the other party. As Lienhardt (1951, p. 317) puts it, a man who easily hates is also one who easily believes himself to be hated.

At any rate, among the Gusii, as among many other peoples, it is almost as dangerous to accuse a witch, or to defend yourself against a witch, as it is to be a witch. The three kinds of activity merge into one another. The act of defending oneself involves a dangerous kind of black magic called *mosira*, so deadly that its use against anyone, except a witch, is considered anti-social. *Mosira*, like witchcraft itself, produces death or sickness. In view of this, the facts in a given case can always be interpreted in opposite ways. Each party can say that his own sufferings are due to his enemy's witchcraft and that his enemy's sufferings are due to his own *mosira*. A's interpretation of the evidence will thus exactly contradict B's. Besides, if a person uses *mosira* and has great success with it, people will suspect that he is probably a witch too. They will feel that if he can defeat other witches so triumphantly he must also have been well versed in their tricks himself.

To accuse a witch in public is dangerous, if only because the ordeal has to be taken by both parties; the ordeal can turn against the accuser and show that he himself was really the witch. But even if things do not get to this stage, it must be remembered that slandering a person by wantonly calling him a witch is in itself a very grave offence. The Gusii say that this kind of back-biting is just as bad as witchcraft itself; and in this they are quite logical, since both witchcraft and back-biting contain the same element of turning disloyal to one's own neighbour. Nowadays, though the government tribunals refuse to try witchcraft cases as such, they are often called upon to try cases of back-biting in this technical sense.

The Traitor within the Gates

I want to end by stating some general conclusions about the reality underlying the notion of witchcraft.

The figure of the witch, clearly enough, embodies those characteristics that society specially disapproves. The values of the witch directly negate the values of society. Typical witchcraft myths attribute to witches many kinds of vices including those that are considered unnatural or specially horrible. Lienhardt (1952, p. 317) has written of the Dinka witch as one who 'embodies those appetites and passions in every man which if un- governed would destroy any moral law'. That is well said; and it reminds us that the witchcraft myth has after all a certain educative or normative function. In the words of Kluckhohn (Kluckhohn and Leighton, 1946, p. 179) 'Witchcraft lore affirms solidarity by dramatically defining what is bad.'

The witch myth then recognizes an opposition of moral values; an opposition of good and bad, right and wrong, proper and improper, sinful and righteous. The witch is always on the wrong side of the moral line, he is a figure of sin incarnate. However, I think that another or a more particular kind of opposition is also vitally involved. I mean the opposition between 'us' and 'them', between in-group and out-group, between allies and foes. The witch is the figure of a person who has turned traitor to his own group. He has secretly taken the wrong side in the basic social opposition between 'us' and 'them'. This is what makes him a criminal and not only a sinner.

As we have seen, the witch is conceived as a person within one's own local community, and often even within one's own household. All human societies require a basic loyalty between members of the small cooperative and defensive group. The local community, the family, the household, all in one way or another make this demand of loyalty as a categorical imperative. Persons who stand in these intimate relations must on the whole work together, not against one another, if the group is to survive as a group. In one word they have to pursue common or joint interests. Injury to one should be felt as injury to all. But the witch is conceived as a person who withholds this elementary loyalty and secretly pursues opposed interests. He wants to spoil what his fellows most want to preserve: their life, health, strength, and fertility; their children and their livelihood. He wants to blast their crops and dry up the milk of their cattle. These fundamental interests of life, strength and subsistence are legitimately attacked by enemies in open warfare, but the witch is not fighting open war; he does not come from outside like a raider; he dwells within the group and destroys by stealth. The witch is the hidden enemy within the gate. He eats away like the maggot in the apple.

If we look upon the witch figure in this light as the arch traitor, the type of the fifth column, I think that several facts about witch beliefs are more readily understood; the main features all seem to fit readily into this pattern.

In the light of this principle we understand why the witch is regarded as not altogether human, why witchcraft is a so-called unnatural offence. The person who denies those basic loyalties to family and community outrages the sentiments, on which all social life must rest. The witch has denied the social nature of man; that is as much as to deny human nature itself. No wonder if the myth represents witches as eating their own children or consorting with hyenas and corpses. Anyone who can turn secret traitor to his nearest fellows is surely capable of all other unnatural sentiments too.

In this sense witchcraft is exactly parallel to incest. As Radcliffe-Brown (Radcliffe-Brown and Forde, 1950, pp. 70ff.) has pointed out, the great social danger of incest is that it threatens to overthrow the sentiments on which the family depends for its organized existence. It is entirely logical, on this showing, that witchcraft and incest both rank as unnatural offences, and that often both are attributed to the same individuals.

Further, we understand why witchcraft is always secret, and always associated with the night. The witch is essentially a hidden enemy but an apparent friend. If he did not appear to be one of ourselves he would not be betraying our trust. In the day he looks like anyone else; only at night does he reveal his secret inclinations. As the Lovedu say: 'You eat with him, yet it is he who eats you' (Krige and Krige, 1943, p 263).

Above all, we understand why witchcraft is treated as a criminal offence, even in those primitive societies where criminal sanctions otherwise hardly exist. By his treason the witch has forfeited his rights as a member of the in-group; he has outlawed himself; he has pursued the interests of an enemy; then let him be treated like an enemy, killed or put to flight.

We know that some peoples punish repeated petty theft within the community in the same manner as witchcraft – in fact they make these the only two offences punishable by death. The element of disloyalty provides the link between these two offences, which to the western mind seem so different. The petty thief who steals from his own neighbours is like the witch secretly attacking the interests of his own group.

I think that the same principle helps to some extent to explain how society chooses the individuals who fill the role of witches. The disloyal person will be sought among those who have failed to give public demonstrations of their loyalty. Accordingly the witch is the woman who fails to give tokens of goodwill to her neighbours: she is reserved, uncommunicative or stingy; a withholder of gifts, or of hospitality, yet greedy for the good things that other people have.

Possibly we might also use the concept of withheld loyalty to help to explain why witches are so often women. It would seem appropriate enough in those patrilineal societies where the new wife is brought in to join the household and community as a person from an outside group. There is a demand for the woman to merge interests and loyalties with those of her marital home, but she still keeps in her heart some private personal loyalties to her home of origin. She is thus the person who most readily fits into the image of an enemy within the gate.

What I have been saying relates to the witches of primitive society, but I think it applies equally well to certain phenomena of the civilized world. For we too are often found in situations where our basic values and basic loyalties seem threatened; and we too are apt to seek out the enemies within our gates.

In civilized societies other demands for over-riding loyalties have been added to those of the family and community. We are divided not only into groups but also into parties. We stand or fall by our ideologies, in a manner quite foreign to the primitive society with its general ideological uniformity. Civilization brings with it an opposition of sects; of orthodoxies and heresies; of rival religions and political 'isms'. Civilization still has its witches, but it is more apt to call them traitors to a cause, or an idea, or a way of life. It was consistent that for so many centuries in Christian Europe the witch was identified with the heretic or the devil worshipper, and persecuted as such by the Church. Given the idea of basic opposition between Christ and the devil, the witch would be conceived as one who had secretly left Christ and gone over to the devil. In our day we also have a feeling of fundamental cleavage, between the Communist and the Non-Communist world. When people in one of these camps start looking into corners and under beds to find hidden enemies who secretly sympathize with the other camp, we get what is very properly called a witch-hunt. The classic examples of witch-hunting in modern society are the purges of the Communist Party in Soviet Russia and other communist countries. The witch figure in the communist purge is a person who has turned traitor in this basic opposition, by harbouring secret bourgeois sympathies or secret leanings towards capitalism. He is identified and by 'confessing' at his trial he takes the blame for things he could not possibly have caused. He is purged, and the group has reaffirmed its solidarity.

It is equally proper to call McCarthyism a witch-hunt, as distinct from a simple political persecution. It is a witch-hunt because it too goes out and meets its selected victims much more than half way. It takes people who have not yet committed any crime, and tries by all means to fit them into the image of traitors to a cause, the American way of life.

Witch-hunting, then, goes together with a feeling that basic sentiments, values and interests are being endangered. A society in order to feel secure must feel that not only its material interests but also its way of life, its fundamental values, are safe. Witch-hunting may increase whenever either of these elements seems gravely threatened. Among primitive peoples, as we have seen, an increase in witch-hunting is apt to occur both when natural disasters threaten their material interests, and when culture contact threatens their way of life. If witch-hunting is a reaction to a society's feeling of insecurity, it seems unlikely to disappear from the civilized world at present, unless we can remove the radical feeling of insecurity which haunts our nations today.

References

EVANS-PRITCHARD, E. E. (1937), *Witchcraft, Oracles and Magic among the Azande*, Clarendon Press.

FORTES, M. (1949) *The Web of Kinship among the Tallensi*, Oxford U.P. for International African Institute.*

HUNTER, M. (1936), *Reaction to Conquest*, Oxford U.P. for International Institute of African Languages and Cultures*; 2nd edn, 1961.

KLUCKHOHN, C. (1944), *Navaho Witchcraft*, Papers of the Peabody Museum of American Archaeology and Ethnology, Harvard University, vol. 22, no. 2; Beacon Press, 1962.

KLUCKHOHN, C., and LEIGHTON, D. (1946), *The Navaho*, Harvard U.P.; rev. edn Doubleday, 1962.

KRIGE, E. J., and KRIGE, J. D. (1943), *The Realm of a Rain Queen*, Oxford U.P. for International Institute of African Languages and Cultures.

LIENHARDT, G. (1951), 'Some notions of witchcraft among the Dinka', *Africa*, vol. 21.

MARWICK, M. G. (1952), 'The social context of Cewa witch beliefs', *Africa*, vol. 22.

NADEL, S. F. (1947), *The Nuba*, Oxford U.P. for International African Institute.

NADEL, S. F. (1952), 'Witchcraft in four African societies', *American Anthropologist*, vol. 54.

PARSONS, E. C. (1936), *Mitla: Town of the Souls, and Other Zapoteco-Speaking Pueblos of Oaxaca, Mexico*, University of Chicago Press.

RADCLIFFE-BROWN, A. R., (1922), *The Andaman Islanders*, Cambridge U.P.; The Free Press, 1964.

RADCLIFFE-BROWN, A. R., and FORDE, D. (eds.) (1950), *African Systems of Kinship and Marriage*, Oxford U.P. for International African Institute; paperback, 1967.

STAYT, H. A. (1931), *The Bavenda*, Oxford U.P. for International Institute of African Languages and Cultures.

WILSON, M. Hunter (1951a), *Good Company: A Study of Nyakyusa Age-Villages*, Oxford U.P. for International African Institute.

WILSON, M. Hunter (1951b), 'Witch-beliefs and social structure', *American Journal of Sociology*, vol. 56, January.

WILSON, M. *et al.* (1952), *Keiskammahoek Rural Survey*, vol. 3, *Social Structures*, Shuter & Shooter, ch. 6.

* Until the mid 1940s the International African Institute used the longer title, International Institute of African Languages and Cultures – *Ed.*

Part Two

From the Ethnography of Witchcraft

As Kluckhohn has remarked (1962, p. 72), 'the essentially world-wide distribution of a number of beliefs about witches ... gives probability to Clements's intimation that a complex of certain witchcraft beliefs was part of a generalized Palaeolithic culture which, in some sense, forms the ultimate basis of all known cultures' (Clements, 1932, p. 240). Moving from the realm of archaeological and ethnological probability to that of documented historical virtual certainty, we find in respect of Europe an account of beliefs of this kind extending over at least two millennia. For the earlier periods, both in the south and in the north, the two readings from Caro Baroja provide the documentation; and those from Apuleius, the closer, more intimate, vicarious experience. A sideways glimpse at some pre-industrial societies, one in Melanesia and three in Africa, reminds us of the near-universality of beliefs in witches and sorcerers before we examine the final flare-up in Europe and in New England from the dying embers of belief, a critical period, now being repeated, three centuries out of phase, in the hitherto relatively isolated societies of East Central Africa.

References

KLUCKHOHN, C. (1962), *Navaho Witchcraft*, Beacon Press (first published as Papers of the Peabody Museum of American Archaeology and Ethnology, Harvard University, 1944).
CLEMENTS, F. E. (1932), 'Primitive concepts of disease', *University of California Publications in American Archaeology and Ethnology*, vol. 32, pp. 185–252.

8. Julio Caro Baroja

Magic and Religion in the Classical World

Excerpts from Julio Caro Baroja, *The World of the Witches*, translated by Nigel Glendinning, Weidenfeld & Nicolson, 1964, pp. 18–20, 24–8, 39–40.

Let us start by studying the situation as it was in classical times.[1] According to the leading authorities on magic in Greece and Rome, processes believed to be specifically magical are known to have been employed in both these societies to produce rain, prevent hail-storms, drive away clouds, calm the winds, make animals and plants prosper, increase wealth and fortune, cure sickness and so on. But magic was also used in Greece and Rome for more obviously perverted reasons: in country areas, for instance, it might be used to ruin an enemy's crops or make his cattle sicken; in the city, it was used to strike down an enemy when he was on the point of making a speech or taking an important part in some public celebration; or it was used to prevent a rival from winning a race or some other event in the public games. Death was quite frequently considered to be the result of witchery, and such beliefs were not confined to any one sector of society.[2] What we might call erotic magic is a whole world in itself.[3]

It is important to realize that any description or analysis of Graeco-Roman magic which fails to take into account the intention, whether good or bad, underlying specific acts, or the social stratum in which they take place, is bound to be invalid. Acts may be produced by similar processes, and yet be essentially and radically different in their ends.

1. For the following pages I have drawn on my essay 'Magia en Castilla durante los siglos XVI y XVII', in *Algunos mitos españoles y otros ensayos* (Madrid, 1944), pp. 185–213, particularly. But I have revised my views since writing this work.

2. A good deal of well-organized material can be found in the article on magic by H. Hubert, in the *Dictionnaire des antiquités grecques et romaines*, edited by Daremberg and Saglio (Paris, 1904), III, 2, pp. 1494–1521. Hopfner is less systematic in Pauly-Wissowa (ed.), *Real-Encyclopädie der Classischen Alterumswissenschaft*, N.B. (Stuttgart, 1930), XIV, cols. 301–93. L. F. Alfred Maury's book, *La Magie et l'Astrologie dans l'Antiquité et au Moyen Âge ou étude sur les superstitions païennes qui se sont perpétueés jusqu'à nos jours* (Paris, 1877), can still be read profitably in spite of its poor organization.

3. General histories of witchcraft contain a fair number of passages from works of the classical period. cf., for example, Soldan, *Geschichte der Hexenprozesse* (Stuttgart, 1880), I, pp. 35–51, for references to the Greeks; pp. 52–85, for the Romans.

Thus the practice of magic for beneficent purposes was considered legal and even necessary in Greece and Rome. It was commonly practised by a great variety of people: the priests of specific deities on the one hand, and professional people, such as doctors, on the other.[4] The state itself supported those whose business it was to augur the future or make prognostications for special occasions, and those who, in the public interest, discovered by divination what had happened or what was about to happen. A variety of techniques was used for this purpose, and these have been studied in detail in books on the religion and cults of the Greeks and Romans. It is not, therefore, necessary to go over the same ground here.[5]

Even the austerest Roman authors included magic formulae for obtaining useful and beneficial results in their work. Treatises on agriculture and medicine and the offices used by priests for certain cults and rites contain collections of spells and obscure writings probably of an invocational nature.[6]

Occasionally it is possible to detect a kind of scepticism even there. For the same technical treatises warn farmers and country-folk not to believe foreign diviners and sorcerers[7] nor women referred to as *sagae*.[8]

What of the magic and spells which were intended to cause harm? These were always held to be illegal. From the earliest times and even when there was some doubt about the spells' effectiveness, it was considered a serious criminal offence to make them. Plato made a distinction between those with a professional knowledge of maleficent practices and mere amateurs. Doctors were included among the professionals, but, speaking as a statesman rather than as a religious individual, Plato thought that professionals who tried to do evil should be condemned to death. Amateurs, on the other hand, ought to be let off more lightly.[9]

But that is not all. Although almost anyone might use spells in moments of violent stress, it was generally felt that they were more usually used by a particular type of person and in very specific circumstances. And Plato attacked those who believed they could summon up the dead and even bend the gods to do their will by spells as well as by prayers.[10] It is possible that the passage which contains this particular attack is a

4. A significant passage is that of Seneca, *Nat-Quaest*, IV, 6–7.
5. See Frazer, 'The magic art and the evolution of kings', *The Golden Bough*, I, chs. 3 and 4.
6. Cf., for example, Cato's *De agr. cul.*, 160; cf. also 5, 4, of the same work.
7. Cato, in his *De agr. cul.*, 5, 4, writes 'Haruspicem, augurem, hariolum, Chaldaeum nequem consuluisse velit'.
8. Columela, *De re rustica*, I, 8.
9. Plato, *Leg.*, XI, 932 e, 933 d.
10. ibid. X, 909 b.

specific reference to followers of the Orphic cult. But it should be remembered that there were a number of divinities in the ancient world known to be propitious to evil actions, however odd this may seem to us today, brought up as we are, whether believers or agnostics, in an era of Christianity.

In the Christian religion, God is the very image of Good, and the Devil of Evil. But the gods of the pagans – and some pagans were shocked by this – were subject to the same forces of evil and passions as men; even to the same fleeting and capricious desires. Maleficent magic has to be seen in relation to this kind of god. And this is not easy. The simplest thing to do is to examine the concrete forms which magic took, and see whether they were the result of belief in the power of spells and invocations, or belief in the power of supplications. But the whole relationship between magic and religion in antiquity appears complex, even if we follow the views put forward by classical authors themselves.

Take Lucan for example. He was a man who liked mystery and was keen on posing questions it was difficult to answer. In the course of discussing the objects, which were capable of *forcing the gods to do something* ('vim factura deis'),[11] owned by a sorcerer called Erichtho, and after enumerating the more extraordinary unnatural acts which it was possible to perform with the aid of Black Magic, Lucan asked himself how it was possible to force the gods in this way. Did the gods like obeying the spells of the sorcerer, he wondered? And did the power of these spells lie in some unknown form of piety, or were they the result of some mysterious ability to threaten?[12]

These are some of the fundamental problems of magic common to many different peoples. Lucan has expressed them very clearly. But he has not solved them. He merely presents us with three hypotheses which the student of magic and religion must constantly bear in mind.

When the magician invokes, curses or threatens the gods, he assumes that they have certain weaknesses he can exploit. This is either because the gods are capricious, or because the magician knows their secrets, which are withheld from other mortals, sometimes because of their shameful nature. Or there may be other explanations still stranger than these, such as, for instance, the existence of some strange *kinship* between the magician and the gods, or a certain affinity and sympathy with them, such as those to which Plotinus refers.

In order to understand the mentality of the magician it must first be realized that the gods of the Greeks and Romans were held to be largely

11. Lucan, *Bell. civ.*, VI, lines 440–41.
12. ibid., lines 492–6.

subject to the same physical and spiritual laws as men. The ideas of good and evil were related to physical feelings and experiences even in the case of the gods. In other words, nature and morality, divinity and humanity could not be put in the same watertight compartments as they are today, in the philosophical and religious systems of a world ruled by science and largely secular in character. [. . .]

Maleficent Magic

Evil has its own proper setting – the night. And gods who are propitious. It also has its own qualified ministers. For evil is ultimately achieved by combining a series of techniques which have been passed down from one generation to the next. It would be out of place to mention here all the Greek and Roman texts which prove that the night was looked upon as the proper time for committing evil deeds, because of its silence and the atmosphere of secrecy that surrounds it. However, some of the more important and significant passages are perhaps worth quoting.[13]

It is certainly a commonplace in classical poets for witches to appear at the most obviously secret hours. As Ovid has it:

> Nox, ait arcanis fidissima, quaeque diurnis
> aurea cum Luna succeditis ignibus, astra. . . .[14]

In these well-known lines the Latin poet is in fact describing Medea, one of the greatest witches of classical mythology, when she is on the point of committing a particularly evil action.

Horace's witch, Canidia, invoking the powers of night, is also well worth quoting for the realistic qualities of the passage:

'Night and Diana, ye faithful witness of all my enterprises, who command silence when we are celebrating our most secret mysteries, come to my assistance, and turn all your power and wrath against my enemies'.[15]

Here we find two of the deities who preside over magical acts mentioned in the same text. But the qualities of night are always less clearly

13. Virgil, *Aeneid*, II, line 255, '. . . tacita per amica silentia lunae'.
14. Ovid, *Metamorphoses*, VII, lines 192–3. 'O night,' she prayed, 'most faithful guardian of my secrets, and golden stars, who, with the moon, succeed the brightness of the day. . . .'
15. Horace, *Epodes*, 5, lines 49–54:

> 'O rebus meis
> non infideles arbitrae,
> Nox et Diana, quae silentium regis
> arcana cum fiunt sacra,
> nunc, nunc adeste, nunc in hostilis domos
> iram atque numen vertite.'

defined than those of the moon. The moon, perhaps because it changes shape, changes its name. In Horace it is Diana: since, whatever the origin of this Roman goddess, she was held to be the equivalent of the Greek Artemis. In Theocritus, we find a similar invocation addressed to Selene.[16] But there is another name which is also associated with the moon: that of Hecate, a goddess with more than one side to her nature. She was primarily looked upon as queen of the spirits of the dead, and was believed to be present both when the spirit entered the human body and when it left it, that is, at birth and at death. She lived in tombs, although she could also sit by the hearth, perhaps because that was at one time the place for family burials. And she also appeared at cross-roads on clear nights with a following of spirits and dogs who set up terrifying howls.[17]

At these cross-roads offerings were placed each month to propitiate the goddess. These consisted of the remains of purifying sacrifices. Initially Caria (in Asia Minor) seems to have been the centre of the Hecate-cult, but it also existed in Thessaly. This is particularly interesting because Thessaly was always well known for its witches. Hecate is, in fact, a deity around whom secret cults and ideas of terror could easily develop.[18] Her help was sought in cases of madness, since madness was believed to be caused by the souls of the departed.[19]

A whole group of ideas that might be termed 'cthonic' evolved around the deities Selene, Hecate and Diana. And even today the power of the moon in relation to the mind continues to find expression in such common terms as 'lunatic', referring to someone who is thought to be under the influence of the moon, and 'moonstruck' etc. But there is more to it than that.

In my view it is clear that a particular sexual significance was attached to these deities. They are either virgin goddesses or goddesses of erotic mysteries; not mother goddesses, for whom love meant principally fertility.

Now let us turn to their ministers. The existence of two sorceresses, the celebrated sisters Medea and Circe, who are even believed to be

16. Theocritus, *Idyl.*, II ('Pharmac.'), line 10 *et passim*.

17. cf. Heckenbach's article on 'Hekate' in Pauly-Wissowa (ed.), *Real Encyclopädie der Classischen Alterumswissenschaft*, N.B. (Stuttgart, 1912), VII, cols. 2769–82. Even more important is Erwin Rohde's invaluable book *Psyché: le culte de l'âme chez les grecs et leur croyance à l'immortalité*, ed. Auguste Reymond (Paris, 1928), pp. 328–35, 607–11.

18. Certain of Hecate's banquets can be compared to those of the witches. The Εχατιχὰ ψασματα have much in common with witches.

19. cf. Erwin Rohde, *Psyché*, op. cit., p. 325, note 1, for references to mental illnesses.

daughters of Hecate, traditionally dates back to heroic times.[20] Circe symbolizes seduction and is the archetype of the woman who, by being 'enchanting' or 'bewitching' as well as by her skill, makes all men bow to her will. (It is interesting to notice the sexual significance which we attach to these words, regardless of their original magical connotations.)[21]

Circe turns Ulysses's companions into pigs, but they still retain as animals the mental faculties they had as human beings – $νοῦς$.[22] In Homeric times, then, people believed the reverse of what St Augustine was to believe. For the latter, metamorphosis was the direct result of a mental derangement induced by the Devil, but with no physical reality. Circe ends up by falling in love with Ulysses, who turned out to be her equal in diplomacy.

Medea is perhaps less complex: she is the archetype of the tragic female and has been immortalized as such in drama. 'You have knowledge and wisdom' – she says to herself in the soliloquy in which she declares her intention of avenging herself on her unfaithful husband. 'Besides,' she adds, 'nature has made us women absolutely incapable of doing good and particularly skilful in doing evil'.[23] In the same soliloquy she admits her reverence for Hecate above all other gods and speaks of her as her helper.[24] In this short text, in fact, we have a woman, albeit a particular type of woman with a violently sensual and frustrated nature, who is bent on doing evil, in possession of recondite knowledge [$τέχνη$], and a vassal or dependent of a feminine goddess associated with terror and the night. This is the basis of a system: the 'logos' of maleficent magic or witchcraft. But Medea, like Circe, is the protagonist of events which took place in legendary times. So let us turn to texts which refer to a less obscure period.

Other texts speak of the $τέχνη$ or *scientia* of the more ordinary witches. Even Horace, in *Epode* 17, when writing a satire on a witch he frequently attacked elsewhere, begins by speaking of the science itself. After mentioning its patrons, Proserpina and Diana, he refers to the books of incantations, *libros carminum*, and to the chief instrument used in making spells of all sorts, the *turbo* or $ρόμβος$ (which had only to be

20. Diodorus Siculus, IV, 45.

21. She also controls animals; cf. *Odyssey*, X, 240. Circe has a pleasant singing voice (X, 220–21) and can make people forget (X, 236).

22. Homer, *Odyssey*, X, 240.

23. Euripides, *Medea*, more especially lines 401–9. There are frequent references to Medea as a sorceress in Latin poets; cf., for example, Horace, *Epodes*, lines 76–81.

24. Cf. Seneca's rhetorical invocation in his *Medea*, 1–55, and the more restrained speech in Euripides.

rotated in the reverse direction to undo what had already been done). He goes on to list the various arts that are the witch's pride, such as the ability to call down the moon from the sky with her chanting, to make waxen figures move, to invoke the spirits of the dead, to make love philtres[25] – all the skills, in fact, mentioned time and again by earlier and subsequent writers. [...]

Conclusion

There is documentary evidence of the existence over a period of *centuries* of the belief that certain women (not necessarily always old ones) could change themselves and others at will into animals in classical times; that they could fly through the air by night and enter the most secret and hidden places by leaving their bodies behind; that they could make spells and potions to further their own love affairs or to inspire hatred for others; that they could bring about storms, illness both in men and animals, and strike fear into their enemies or play terrifying jokes on them. To carry out their evil designs these women met together after dark. The moon, night, Hecate and Diana were the deities who presided over them, helping them to make philtres and potions. They called on these goddesses for aid in their poetic conjurations, or threatened and constrained them in their spells when they wanted to achieve particularly difficult results.

Apart from these powers, the women who were believed to attend such meetings were supposed to be experts in the manufacture of poisons and also in cosmetic arts; sometimes they were used as go-betweens in love affairs.

In fact, a whole series of nouns can be found in the classical Greek and Latin languages which refer to the various acts, operations and materials carried out and used by the witches. And these constitute a nucleus which has its place both in the history of witchcraft and in the history of humanism. Indeed, we can put forward the theory that when Fernando de Rojas, during the Renaissance, described in his *Celestina* the kind of woman we have been discussing and what has come to be called her 'laboratory', he could do so without being thought a pedant, in spite of the fact that he based himself on Horace, Ovid and other classical writers. His literary sources provided him with material about witchcraft that was still valid in his own time, as it had been in that of the Romans.

Another important point is the condemnation of magic for evil

25. Horace, *Epodes*, 17, lines 16–81.

purposes which we find in pagan laws. This was formally laid down from the very earliest Roman times,[26] and continued to be the case at the period when the Roman authorities had still not accepted Christianity officially. Tacitus has painted a brilliant picture of the terror felt in Rome when the spells which were believed to have caused Germanicus's illness (some of them described as *devotiones*) were discovered.[27]

Ammianus Marcellinus has also referred to prosecutions for crimes of magic in the reigns of Constantius, Valens and Valentinian I. His writings and others on the same subject were later the basis for some of Gibbon's most eloquent pages – pages which reflect only too clearly the disbelief in magic common in Gibbon's time. But when we come to these obscure figures of the Roman Empire's declining years we are already in a new world, with a new view of the beliefs we have been discussing.

26. Seneca, *Nat. Quaest.*, IV, 7: 'et apud nos in XII tabulis cavatur, nequis alienos fructus excantassit...'.

27. Tacitus, *Annals*, II, 69; III, 13; cf. Suetonius, *Caligula*, 3.

9. Apuleius

The Story of Thelyphron

Excerpt from Apuleius, *The Golden Ass*, translated by Robert Graves, Penguin Books, 1950, pp. 63–71.

'While I was still a University student at Miletus I came over to attend the Olympian Games. Afterwards, feeling a strong desire to visit northern Greece, I travelled through most of Thessaly. One unlucky day I arrived at Larissa, having run through nearly all the money I had brought with me, and while I was wandering up and down the streets, wondering how to refill my purse, I saw a tall old man standing on a stone block in the middle of the market place. He was making a public announcement at the top of his voice, offering a large reward to anyone who would stand guard over a corpse that night.

'I asked a bystander: "What is the meaning of this? Are the corpses of Larissa in the habit of running away?"

'"Hush, my lad," he answered. "I can see that you are very much of a stranger here, else you would realize that you are in Thessaly where witches are in the habit of gnawing bits of flesh off dead men's faces for use in their magical concoctions."

'"Oh, I see! And would you mind telling me what this guardianship of the dead involves?"

'"Not at all. It means watching attentively the whole night, one's eyes fixed on the corpse without a single sideways glance. You see, these abominable women have the power of changing their shape at pleasure: they turn into birds or dogs or mice, or even flies – disguises that would pass scrutiny even in a Court of Law, and by daylight too – and then charm the guardians asleep. I won't try to tell you all the extraordinarily ingenious tricks that they use when they want to indulge their beastly appetites; at any rate, the usual reward of from a hundred to a hundred and fifty drachmae for the night's job is hardly worth the risk. Oh – I was almost forgetting to tell you that if next morning the guardian fails to hand over the corpse to the undertakers in exactly the same condition as he found it, he is obliged by Law to have bits cut from his own face to supply whatever is missing."

'That did not frighten me. I boldly told the crier that he need not repeat the announcement. "I'm ready to undertake the job," I said. 'What fee do they offer?"

'"A thousand drachmae, because this is a job that calls for more than usual alertness against those terrible harpies: the deceased was the son of one of our first citizens."

'"All this nonsense leaves me unmoved," I said. "I am a man of iron, I never trouble to go to sleep, and I have sharper eyesight than Lynceus, the *Argo*'s look-out man. In fact, I may say that I am all eyes, like the giant Argos whom Jupiter once put in charge of the nymph Io."

'I had hardly finished recommending myself for the job before the old man hurried me along to a big house with its gates locked and barred. He took me through a small side door and along corridors until I reached a bedroom with closed shutters, where a woman in deep black sat wailing loudly in the half-light.

'The crier went up to her and said: "This man undertakes to guard your husband's body tonight; and he agrees to the fee."

'She pushed back the hair that shaded her beautiful grief-stricken face, and implored me to be vigilant at my post.

'"You need have no anxiety, Madam, if you make it worth my while afterwards."

'Nodding absently, she got up and led me into an adjoining room, where she showed me the corpse lying on a slab and wrapped in a pure white linen shroud. After another fit of weeping, she called in seven mourners as witnesses, also her secretary who had his writing materials with him. Then she said: "Gentlemen, I call you to witness that the nose is undamaged, so are both ears, the eyes are still in their sockets, the lips are whole, the chin the same." She touched each feature as she mentioned it, and the secretary wrote out the inventory, which the witnesses signed and sealed.

'I asked her as she was going away: "Will you be good enough, Madam, to see that I have everything I need for my vigil tonight?"

'"What sort of things?"

'"A good large lamp with enough oil in it to last until daybreak; pots of wine; warm water for tempering; a cup; and a plateful of cold meat and vegetables left over from your supper."

'She shook her head angrily: "What an absurd request! Cooked meat and vegetables indeed in this house of mourning, where no fire has been lighted for days! Do you imagine that you have come here for a jolly supper party? You are expected to mourn and weep like the rest of us." Then, turning to her maid: "Myrrhina, fill the lamp, bring it back at once, shut the door and leave the guardian to his task."

82

'All alone with the corpse, I fortified my eyes for their vigil by rubbing them hard and kept up my spirits by singing. Twilight shaded into night, and night grew deeper and deeper, blacker and blacker, until my usual bed-time had passed and it was close on midnight. I had been only a little uncomfortable at first, but now I was beginning to feel thoroughly frightened when all of a sudden a weasel squeezed in through a hole in the door, stopped close by and fixed her eyes intently on mine. The boldness of the creature was most disconcerting, but I managed to shout out: "Get away from here, you filthy little beast, or I'll break your neck. Run off and play hide and seek with your friends the mice. Do you hear me? I mean it."

'She turned tail and skipped out of the room, but as she did so, a sudden deep sleep stole over me and dragged me down with it into bottomless gulfs of dream. I fell on the floor and lay there so dead asleep that not even Delphic Apollo could have readily decided which of us two was the corpse; the body on the slab or the body on the floor. It was almost as though I had actually died and my corpse had been left without a guardian.

'At last the darkness began to fade and

The sentries of the Crested Watch 'gan shout

– crowing so loud that I eventually awoke, picked up the lamp and ran in terror to the slab. I pulled back the shroud and examined the corpse's face closely; to my huge relief I found it unmutilated. Almost at once the poor widow came running in, still weeping, with the seven witnesses behind her. She threw herself on the corpse and after kissing it again and again had the lamp brought close to make sure that all was well. Then she turned and called: "Philodespotus, come here!"

'Her steward appeared. "Philodespotus, pay this young man his fee at once. He has kept watch very well."

'As he counted me out the money she said: "Many thanks, young man, for your loyal services; they have earned you the freedom of this house."

'Delighted with my unexpected good luck, I gently tossed the bright gold coins up and down in my hand and answered: "I am much obliged to you, Madam. I shall be only too pleased to help you out again, whenever you may need my services."

'These words were scarcely out of my mouth when the whole household rushed at me with blows and curses, in an attempt to cancel their dreadful ominousness. One punched me in the face with his fists, another dug his elbows into my shoulder, someone else kicked me, my ribs were pummelled, my hair pulled, my clothes torn and before they finally threw me out of the house I felt like Adonis mauled by the wild boar, or Orpheus torn in pieces by the Thracian women.

'When I paused in the next street to collect my senses, and realized what I had said – it had certainly been a most tactless remark – I decided that I had got off lightly enough, all considered.

'By and by, after the customary "last summons", the agonized calling of his name by the relatives in case he might be only in a coma, the dead man was brought out of the house; and since he had been a man of such importance he was honoured with a public procession. As the cortège turned into the market place, an old man came running up, the tears streaming down his face. In a frenzy of grief he tore out tufts of his fine white hair, grabbed hold of the open coffin with both hands and screamed for vengeance.

'"Gentlemen of Hypata!" he cried, his voice choking with sobs, "I appeal to your honour, I appeal to your sense of justice and public duty! Stand by your fellow-citizen, this poor nephew of mine; see that his death is avenged in full on that evil woman, his widow. She, and she alone, is the murderess. To cover up a secret love-affair and to get possession of her husband's estate she killed him – she killed him with a slow poison." He continued to sob and scream, until the crowd was stirred to indignant sympathy, thinking that he probably had good ground for his accusations. Some shouted: "Burn her! Burn her!" and some: "Stone her to death!" and a gang of young hooligans was encouraged to lynch her.

'However, she denied her guilt with oaths and tears (though these carried little conviction), and devout appeals to all the gods and goddesses in Heaven to witness that she was utterly incapable of doing anything so wicked.

'"So be it then," said the old man, "I am willing to refer the case to divine arbitration. And here is Zatchlas the Egyptian, one of the leading necromancers of his country, who has undertaken, for a large fee, to recall my nephew's soul from the Underworld and persuade it to re-animate the corpse for a few brief moments."

'The person whom he introduced to the crowd was dressed in white linen, with palm-leaf sandals on his feet and a tonsured head. The old man kissed his hands and clasped his knees in a formal act of supplication. "Your reverence," he cried, "take pity on me. I implore you by the stars of Heaven, by the gods of the Underworld, by the five elements of nature, by the silence of night, by the dams that the swallows of Isis build about the Coptic island, by the flooding of the Nile, by the mysteries of Memphis, and by the sacred rattle of Pharos – I implore you by these holy things to grant my nephew's soul a brief return to the warmth of the sun, and so re-illumine his eyes that they may open and momentarily regain the sight that he has forfeited by his descent to the Land of the Dead. I do not argue with fate, I do not deny the grave what is her due; my plea is only for a brief leave of absence, during which the dead man may assist me in avenging his own murder – the only possible consolation I can have in my overwhelming grief."

'The necromancer, yielding to his entreaties, touched the corpse's mouth three times with a certain small herb and laid another on its breast. Then he turned to the east, with a silent prayer to the sacred disk of the rising sun. The whole market-place gasped expectantly at the sight of these solemn preparations, and stood prepared for a miracle. I pushed in among the crowd and climbed up on a stone just behind the coffin, from which I watched the whole scene with rising curiosity.

'Presently the breast of the corpse began to heave, blood began to pour again through its veins, breath returned to its nostrils. He sat up and spoke in a querulous voice: "Why do you call me back to the troubles of this transitory life, when I have already drunk of the stream of Lethe and floated on the marshy waters of the Styx? Leave me alone, I say, leave me alone! Let me sleep undisturbed."

'The necromancer raised his voice excitedly: "What? You refuse to address your fellow-citizens here and clear up the mystery of your death? Don't you realize that if you hold back a single detail, I am prepared to call up the dreadful Furies and have your weary limbs tortured on the rack?"

'At this the dead man roused himself again and groaned out to the crowd: "The bed in which I lay only yesterday is no longer empty; my rival sleeps on it. My newly married wife has bewitched and poisoned me."

'The widow showed remarkable courage in the circumstance. She denied everything with oaths, and began contradicting and arguing with her late husband as though there were no such thing as respect for the dead. The crowd took different sides. Some were for burying the wicked woman alive in the same grave as her victim: but others refused to admit the evidence of a senseless corpse – it was quite untrustworthy, they said.

'The corpse soon settled the dispute. With another hollow groan it said: "I will give you incontrovertible proof that what I say is true, by disclosing something that is known to nobody but myself." Then he pointed up at me and said: "While that learned young student was keeping careful watch over my corpse, the ghoulish witches who were hovering near, waiting for a chance to rob it, did their best to deceive him by changing shape, but he saw through all their tricks. Though the bedroom doors were carefully bolted, they had slipped in through a knot-hole disguised as weasels and mice. But they threw a fog of sleep over him, so that he fell insensible, and then they called me by name, over and over again, trying to make me obey their magical commands. My weakened joints and cold limbs, despite convulsive struggles, could not respond immediately, but this student who had been cast into a trance that was a sort of death, happened to have the same name as I. So when they called: 'Thelyphron, Thelyphron, come!' he answered mechanically. Rising up like a senseless ghost he offered his face for the mutilation that they intended for mine; and they nibbled off first his nose and then his ears. But to divert attention from what they had done, they cleverly fitted him with a wax nose exactly like his own, and a pair of wax ears. The poor fellow remains under the illusion that he has been well rewarded for his vigilance, not meanly compensated for a frightful injury."

'Terrified by this story, I clapped my hand to my face to see if there were any truth in it, and my nose fell off; then I touched my ears, and they fell off too. A hundred fingers pointed at me from the crowd and a great roar of laughter went up. I burst into a cold sweat, leaped down from the stone, and slipped away between their legs like a frightened dog. Mutilated and ridiculous, I have never since cared to return to Miletus; and now I disguise the loss of my ears by growing my hair long and glue this canvas nose on my face for decency's sake.'

10. Apuleius

The Transformation of Lucius

Excerpt from Apuleius, *The Golden Ass*, translated by Robert Graves, Penguin Books, 1950, pp. 88–93.

We spent the next few nights in the same delightful way, and then one morning Fotis ran into my room, trembling with excitement, and told me that her mistress, having made no headway by ordinary means in her affair with the Boeotian, intended that night to become a bird and fly in at his bedroom window, and that I must make careful preparations if I wished to watch the performance.

At twilight, she led me on tip-toe, very, very quietly, up the tower stairs to the door of the cock-loft, where she signed to me to peep through a chink. I obeyed, and watched Pamphilë first undress completely and then open a small cabinet containing several little boxes, one of which she opened. It contained an ointment which she worked about with her fingers and then smeared all over her body from the soles of her feet to the crown of her head. After this she muttered a long charm to her lamp, and shook herself; and, as I watched, her limbs became gradually fledged with feathers, her arms changed into sturdy wings, her nose grew crooked and horny, her nails turned into talons, and soon there was no longer any doubt about it: Pamphilë had become an owl. She gave a querulous hoot and made a few little hopping flights until she was sure enough of her wings to glide off, away over the roof-tops.

Not having been put under any spell myself, I was utterly astonished and stood frozen to the spot. I rubbed my eyes to make sure that I was really Lucius, and that this was no waking dream. Was I perhaps going mad? I recovered my senses after a time, took hold of Fotis's hand and laid it across my eyes. 'Dearest love,' I said, 'I beg you, by these sweet breasts of yours, to grant me a tremendous favour – one which I can never hope to repay – in proof of your perfect love for me. If you do this I promise to be your slave for ever more. Honey, will you try to get hold of a little of that ointment for me? I want to be able to fly. I want to hover around you like a winged Cupid in attendance on his Goddess.'

'H'm,' she said, 'so that is your game, is it, my darling? You want to play me a foxy trick: handing me an axe and persuading me to chop off my own feet? That's all very well, but it hasn't been so easy for me all this time to keep you safe from the she-wolves of Thessaly. You would have been easy meat if I hadn't protected you with my love. Now if you become a bird, how shall I be able to keep track of you? And when will I ever see you again?'

I protested: 'All the gods in Heaven forbid that I'm such a scoundrel as you make out. Listen: If I became an eagle and soared across the wide sky as Jupiter's personal courier, his thunderbolt proudly grasped in my claws, do you really suppose that even such winged glory as that would keep me from flying back every night to my love-nest in your arms? By that enchanting knot of hair on your head in which my soul lies helplessly entangled, I swear that I'm incapable by nature of loving any other woman in the whole world but my dearest Fotis. And anyhow, when I come to think of it, if that ointment really does turn me into a bird, I'll have to steer clear of the town; owls are such unlucky birds that when one blunders into a house by mistake, everyone does his best to catch it and nail it with outspread wings to the doorpost. Another thing, if I played truant from you and made love to the ladies in my owl disguise, what sort of a jolly welcome do you think they would give me? But that reminds me: once I'm an owl, what is the spell or antidote for turning me back into myself?'

'You need not worry about that,' she said. 'My mistress has taught me all the magical formulas. Not, of course, because she has a kindly feeling for me, but because when she arrives home from one of her adventures I have to prepare the necessary antidote for her to use. It really is extraordinary with what insignificant herbs one can produce a total transformation: tonight, for instance, she will need only a little anise and laurel leaves steeped in spring-water. She will drink some of the water, wash herself with the rest, and be a woman again at once. You can do the same after your flight.'

I made her reassure me on this point several times before she went, twitching with fear, up the tower stairs and brought me out one of the boxes from the casket. Hugging and kissing it I muttered a little prayer for a successful flight. Then I quickly pulled off my clothes, greedily stuck my fingers into the box and took out a large lump of ointment which I rubbed all over my body.

I stood flapping my arms, first the left and then the right, as I had seen Pamphilë do, but no little feathers appeared on them and they showed no sign of turning into wings. All that happened was that the hair on them grew coarser and coarser and the skin toughened into hide. Next, my fingers bunched together into a hard lump so that my hands became hooves, the same change came over my feet and I felt a long tail sprouting from the base of my spine. Then my face swelled, my mouth widened, my nostrils dilated, my lips hung flabbily down, and my ears shot up long and hairy. The only consoling part of this miserable transformation was the enormous increase in the size of a certain organ of mine; because I was by this time finding it increasingly difficult to meet all Fotis's demands upon it. At last, hopelessly surveying myself all over, I was obliged to face the mortifying fact that I had been transformed not into a bird, but into a plain jackass.

I wanted to curse Fotis for her stupid mistake, but found that I could no longer speak or even gesticulate; so I silently expostulated with her by sagging my lower lip and gazing sideways at her with my large, watery eyes.

When Fotis saw what had happened she beat her own face with both hands in a frenzy of self-condemnation. 'Oh, this is enough to kill me!' she wailed. 'In my flurry and fear I must have mistaken the box; two of them look exactly alike. Still, my poor creature, things are not nearly so bad as they seem, because in this case the antidote is one of the easiest to get hold of; all that you need do is to chew roses, which will at once turn you back into my Lucius. If only I had made my usual rose-garlands this evening! Then you would have been spared the inconvenience of being an ass for even a single night. At the first signs of dawn I promise faithfully to go out and fetch what you need.' Over and over again she cursed her own stupidity and carelessness, but though I was no longer Lucius, and to all appearances a complete ass, a mere beast of burden, I still retained my mental faculties. I had a long and furious debate with myself as to whether or not I ought to bite and kick Fotis to death. She was a witch, wasn't she? And a very evil one, too. But in the end I decided that it would not only be dangerous but stupid to kill the one person who could help me to regain my own shape. Drooping my head and shaking my ears resignedly, I swallowed my rage for the time being and submitted to my cruel fate. I trotted off to the stable, where I would at least have the company of my white thoroughbred who had carried me so well while I was a man.

He was there with another ass, the property of my host – my former host – Milo, and really I did expect that, if dumb beasts have any natural feelings of loyalty, my horse would know me and take pity on my plight, welcoming me to his stable with as much courtesy as if I were a foreign ambassador on a visit to the Imperial Court at Rome. But – O Hospitable Jupiter and all the Gods of Faith and Trust! – my splendid horse and Milo's horrible ass put their heads together at once, suspecting that I had designs on their food, and formed an alliance against me. The moment I approached their manger they laid their ears back, wheeled round, and started kicking me in the face. My own horse! What gratitude! Here was I, driven right away from the very barley which only a few hours before I had measured out for him with my own hands.

As I stood in my lonely corner, banished from the society of my four-footed colleagues and deciding on a bitter revenge on them next morning as soon as I had eaten my roses and become Lucius again, I noticed a little shrine of the Mare-headed Mother, the Goddess Epona, standing in a niche of the post that supported the main beam of the stable. It was wreathed with freshly gathered roses, the very antidote that I needed. I balanced hopefully on my hindlegs, pushed my forelegs as far up the post as they would go, stretched my neck to its fullest extent and shot out my lips. But by a piece of really bad luck, before I could eat any of the roses, my slave who was acting as groom happened to catch me at work. He sprang up angrily from the heap of straw on which he was lying and shouted: 'I've had quite enough trouble from this damned cuddy. First he tries to rob his stablemates and now he plays the same trick on the blessed gods! If I don't flog the sacrilegious brute until he's too lame to stir a hoof ...' He groped about until he found a bundle of faggots, picked out a thick knobbly one, the biggest of the lot, and began unmercifully whacking my flanks.

A sudden loud pounding and banging on the outer gate. Distant cries of 'Thieves! Thieves!' The groom dropped his faggot and ran off in terror. The next moment, the courtyard gate burst open and armed bandits rushed in. A few neighbours hurried to Milo's assistance but the bandits beat them off easily. Their swords gleamed like the rays of the rising sun in the bright light of the torches that they carried. They had axes with them, too, which they used to break open the heavily barred door of the strong room in the central part of the house. It was stuffed with Milo's valuables, all of which they hauled out and hastily divided into a number of separate packages. However, there were more packages to carry than robbers to carry them, so they had to use their wits. They came into our stable, led the three of us out, loaded us with as many of the heavier packages as they could pile on our backs, and drove us out of the now ransacked house, threatening us with sticks. Then they hurried forward into trackless hill-country, beating us hard all the way.

11. Julio Caro Baroja

Witchcraft amongst the German and Slavonic Peoples

Excerpts from Julio Caro Baroja, *The World of the Witches*, translated by Nigel Glendinning, Weidenfeld & Nicolson, 1964, pp. 47–57.

The type of witch known in classical antiquity is not very different from the one with which we are familiar today. She continued to exist in Europe a long time after the fall of the Roman Empire and even down to our own times. The same, as we shall see, is true of the witch amongst European peoples who were not part of the classical world.

In the first place, let us consider those peoples of Germanic origin whose magical interests and activities are well documented. If we accept the evidence about them, it would appear that, among the Germanic tribes too, each individual social class had its own particular brand of magic; even the gods used magic in certain circumstances. The practice of magic in these tribes also corresponded to their logical and social order (the 'logos' and the 'ethos'), however surprising this may seem. This is also true, of course, of other communities which have recently been studied in detail; maleficent magic flourishes during certain states of tension.

In the highest levels of Germanic society the kings practised magic publicly, and their success was more or less generally admitted.

Among the Swedes, Erick 'of the windy hat' had remarkable powers as king and magician.[1] In other cases, the trials and misfortunes of the community were attributed to the fact that the reigning monarch lacked the necessary magical power to deal with the adverse circumstances. But coming down in the social scale we also discover that in ancient Scandinavia every magical activity was thought to be the property of a particular family. Thus, 'all' the sooth-sayers, 'all' the witches and 'all' the magicians could be traced back to three specific forebears, just as the giants could.[2]

The division of human activities according to families presupposes the handing down of knowledge from the period of myths. Witchcraft or

1. John Magnus, *Gothorumque sueonumque historia, ex probatis antiquorum monumentis collecta* ... (Basle, 1558), XVII, ch. 12, p. 640.
2. Mlle R. du Puget, *Les Eddas traduites de l'ancien idiome scandinave* (Paris, n.d.), p. 21 (p. 5 of Gylf's voyage) and p. 249 (p. 32 of Hyndla's poem).

maleficent magic has its own special terminology, and is completely defined by the word *seid*.[3]

There are passages in Icelandic Sagas in which whole families are accredited with the power of witchcraft: father, mother and children.[4] However, as in the classical world, women, or particular types of women, were believed to have more special powers.

The passage in Tacitus's *Germania* which relates how the men of that country believed women to be sacred and always attached great importance to their opinions, warnings and advice,[5] has been the object of numerous conflicting interpretations – like other parts of that work.

But if the cases of Velleda[6] or Ganna,[7] both heroines of German history, can be adduced in support of this view, there is also good reason to believe that fear as well as respect and veneration was sometimes felt for women; fear of the spells of which they were held to be capable.

Both early Germanic literature and historical works, written in Latin about the Germanic peoples at a later date, make frequent references to the ambivalent position of women in that society.

There are, for example, numerous passages in the *Edda* which allude to the skill of women in magic and the dangers run by those who allow themselves to be dominated by women:

Flee from the dangers of sleeping in the arms of a witch; let her not hold you close to her. She will make you disregard the assemblies of the people and the words of the prince; you will refuse to eat and shun the company of other men, and you will feel sad when you go to your bed.

Such were the supernatural warnings given to Lodfafner.[8] These and other passages seem to support the case for the existence of a 'Circean complex' which has completely controlled men's actions at various periods.

The picture of the *old witch* is also extremely common in the *Edda*. Such a one, for example, was Angerbode, mother of the wolves who will ultimately eat the sun and the moon:

> East of Midgard, in the iron forest,
> Sat the old witch.
> She fed the fearful race
> of Fenrer ...[9].

3. H. Ch. Lea, *Histoire de l'Inquisition au Moyen Age*, III, pp. 486–90.

4. Fernand Mossé, *La Laxdoela Saga: Légende historique islandaise traduite du vieux norrois avec une introduction et des notes* (Paris, 1914), pp. 99, 103, 104, 105–7, 111–12.

5. Tacitus, *Germ.*, 8.

6. Tacitus, *Hist.*, IV, 61–6; VI, 22–4. Dio Casius, LXVII, 5.

7. Velleda's successor.

8. *Les Eddas*, op. cit., p. 138 (pp. 4–5 of Lodfafner's song).

9. ibid., p. 27.

At the same time, witchcraft, or magic for evil ends, is the constant subject of criticism as one of the most anti-social activities possible.

But it must be emphasized that in the pagan German world the gods were not only aiders and abetters of witchcraft but sorcerers themselves. Loke or Loki, the evil one, was able to say to Odin, the Father of the gods: 'They say you have practised magic in Samsoe, that you have made spells like any *Vala*: you have wandered through the country disguised as a witch. What, I say, could be viler in a man than this'.[10] The same Loki could shout at Freya: 'Be silent! You are a poisoner and you work magic. Thanks to your spells the powers that were propitious to your brother have turned against him'.[11]

There can be no doubt, therefore, that magic has its place in the life of gods as well as men. The question that Lucan asked himself about the gods on Olympus might well have been put by a German about those in Valhalla. A *vis magica* exists which fascinates or coerces 'them' just as it controls the strong and the meek in the world.

Several legends which have survived in more modern versions than those which have so far been quoted prove that the Germanic peoples were dominated by fear of witches in their everyday life.

They frequently attributed the misfortunes of their kings to witches. One of the best known of these legends is the one about the death of the Danish king Frotho III. The usual source for this tale in books on magic is the German historian, A. Krantz.

The king, who is said to have lived at the same time as Christ, seems to have used magic in much the same way as other more or less legendary figures. He had a witch at his court who was famed for her magic. Her son had great faith in her powers and plotted with her on one occasion to rob the king's treasury, since the king was advanced in years. When they had carried out the robbery, they went to an isolated house they owned far from the court. The king, following the hints of a number of people, connected their flight with the robbery and decided to go in person to look for them. When the witch saw him coming she used her magical powers to change her son into a bull who went out to meet him. The king sat down to look at the animal. But the witch gave him little time for contemplation. The bull charged him violently and killed him.[12]

This is roughly the story as Krantz has it, although it should be borne

10. ibid., p. 188 (p. 24 of Aeger's feast). Cf. also p. 115 (p. 34 of Wola the Wise's prediction).

11. ibid., p. 190 (p. 32 of Aeger's feast). A further accusation is on p. 195 (p. 56 of Aeger's feast).

12. A. Krantz, *Regnorum Aquilonarium, Daniae, Sueciae, Noruagiae Chronica* (Frankfurt, 1583), fols. 20 v–21 i (Book I, ch. 32).

in mind that there are other slightly different versions.[13] For present purposes, however, this will serve. The important thing in this instance is the general outline of the legend. It is also worth while pointing out that the person chiefly responsible for popularizing the story believed that old witches were perfectly capable of achieving the same or even more astounding results in his own times (i.e. in the fifteenth and sixteenth centuries).[14]

The Germanic world was dominated by belief in witchcraft from its northern extremities to the shores of the Mediterranean where the Visigoths and Lombards lived; from the steppes of eastern Europe to the Atlantic islands. Even at the height of their power, men lived in constant fear of witches.

This fear and hatred led the Germans to accuse their enemies of practising witchcraft or of being descended from evil witches. An example of this is the traditional story about the origin of the Huns. This was first written down by a historian of the Goths called Jornandes, or Jordanes, in the sixth century, and it was later reproduced and modified by many other historians. According to the legend, King Filimer, after conducting a survey into the customs of his people at a very early period, discovered that a number of sorceresses lived among them. These he banished to the remote and deserted regions of Scythia so that they should have no ill-effect on others. However, as a result of the contact between these women and certain foul spirits who wandered about the same deserts, the Huns were born.[15] Those were the sorceresses called *alrunae* or *haliurunnae* which also appear in other texts. To call someone a 'son of a witch' is a very ancient insult.

It is an equally hallowed custom to attribute black powers to one's nearest communal enemy. So far as the specific case of the Huns is concerned, it is highly probable that witchcraft was common among them (just as it later was among the Magyars and Hungarians). But their bad reputation may have been partly due to the intense fear they inspired in others; in other words, it may have been due to the feeling of comparative impotence that others felt in their presence.

More or less mythical stories about the power of specific witches are also to be found in the old Slav chronicles.

13. See, for example, Pierre le Loyer, *Discours, et histoires des spectres, visions et apparitions des esprits* (Paris, 1605), Book II, ch. 7, p. 142.

14. A. Krantz, op. cit., fol. 16 v (Book I, ch. 23).

15. Jordanes, *De rebus gothicis*, 24. Many years afterwards, John Magnus maintained that witches had intercourse with men and not with spirits (*Gothorumque sueonumque historia*, VI, 24, pp. 258–9). The number of witches varies considerably from one edition to the next.

There is, for instance, a legendary episode in the earliest history of Bohemia which is worth recording. A certain chief named Krok died at the end of the seventh century, in 690, and left three daughters. The first, Kazi or Brelum, had a considerable knowledge of medicinal plants which she put to practical use. The second, called Tecka or Tekta, was a soothsayer and diviner; whenever there was a robbery in the country she revealed the person who was responsible and, if anything was lost, she could tell where it was. The third, Libuscha, Libussa or Lobussa, was a sybil, skilled in witchcraft and vastly better at it than any other man or woman of her times. Thanks to her magic, she was able to make the Bohemians elect Przemislaw as their leader, and then marry him. She predicted the rise of Prague and died after a long and glorious life. However, when she died, women had become so accustomed to directing affairs that they refused to submit to the rule of men again. A young maid named Wlasca, a born leader, called the women together and addressed them in approximately these words:

Our lady Libussa governed this kingdom while she was alive. Why should not I now govern with your help? I know all her secrets; the skill in spells and the art of augury which were her sister Tecka's are mine; I also know as much medicine as Brelum did; for I was not in her service for nothing. If you will join with me and help me I believe we may get complete control over the men.

Her ideas met with the approval of the women she had gathered together. So she gave them a potion to drink to make them loathe their husbands, brothers, lovers and the whole male sex immediately. Fortified by this, they slew nearly all the men and laid seige to Przemislaw in the castle of Diewin. The women are supposed to have ruled for seven years, and a series of rather comical laws are said to have been passed by them. However, in the end Przemislaw returned to the throne, for he too was something of a magician. Later authors retold this story and added their own particular interpretations.[16]

The Middle Ages was a great period for preserving traditions as well as for making them, and the magical processes described in the texts are monotonously repeated. Ones which are already to be found in the Vedic poems reappear in the darkest years of the Middle Ages and continue to recur even today.

The story of King Duff of Scotland, for instance, supposed to have taken place at some time between A.D. 967 and 972, follows a typically

16. 'Chronicon Bohemiae', Book II, ch. 3–10, in *Reliquiae manuscriptorum omnis aevi diplomatum ac monumentorum ineditorum* (Halle, 1737), XI, pp. 131–45, cf. P. J. Schafarik, *Slawische Alterthümer*, II (Leipzig, 1844), p. 421.

well-worn pattern. According to the chronicles, an illness which he caught was attributed to witchcraft. Investigations were made and some witches were eventually found cooking a waxen image of the king over a slow fire. This explained the nature of the king's illness, since he was in a continual sweat. Once the women had been condemned the king was restored to health.[17]

The Nature of Civil and Religious Laws

The laws of the barbarians, written in Latin and devised for the northern peoples who ruled for centuries over former provinces of the Roman Empire, abound in provisions against sorcerers and those who followed their advice.

In Book 6, subtitle 2, of the Spanish *Fuero Juzgo*, for example, one finds four laws of the Chindasvint period which condemn all the possible varieties of magic. The first of these applies to servants and simple folk who consult *ariolos, aruspices* and *vaticinatores* – diviners, fortune-tellers and enchanters – about the health or death of the king. The second refers to those who give poisonous herbs to others. The third is about sorcerers and rain-makers who ruin the wine and the crops by their spells; those who disturb men's minds by invoking the Devil; and those who make nocturnal sacrifices to the Devil. The fourth condemns those who use verbal or written spells to harm the bodies, minds and property of others.[18]

These Spanish laws and others, both civil and ecclesiastical, of the same period, condemn magic in general without any specific reference to the sex of the person in question. But similar laws in old Gaul, and other countries which were also under the rule of christianized barbarians, make frequent references to the sex of the sorcerers and also make other allusions which are worth examination. Perhaps certain types of witches were more common in Gaul than in Spain under the Visigoths.

A passage in Pomponius Mela which has often been discussed seems to imply that there were women who practised magic for beneficent purposes among the ancient Gauls. Nine of them were attached to a temple, and lived under a rule of perpetual chastity.[19] Whatever the truth of this may be, it does not seem to affect the general point about the place of women in witchcraft.

17. H. Boethius, *Scotorum Historiae a prima gentis origine* (Paris, 1574), Book XI, fols. 220 v–221 v. Pierre le Loyer, *Discours*, op. cit., Book IV, ch. 15, pp. 369–70.

18. *Fuero juzgo en latin y castellano, cotejado con los más antiguos y preciosos códices por la Real Academia Española* (Madrid, 1815), pp. 81–2 and 104–6 (Latin with Spanish translation).

19. Pomponius Mela, III, 7.

We know from other sources – not wholly reliable ones however – that witches abounded in Gaul in the later period of the Roman Empire. They were occasionally consulted by people of high rank, and were equated with druids (as 'druidesses' are called in texts which relate to the third century A.D.).[20] These witches continued to multiply and thrive in later periods, and they were a source of worry to more than one family of high social standing at the court of the Merovingian kings. This is revealed in the works of the best-known historians of the period, who also point out that more than one woman paid dearly for her reputation as a witch.

In 578 Queen Fredegond lost a son. Suspicious individuals suggested that his death had been caused by magic and spells. A courtier accused Mummolus, one of the prefects (who was also disliked by the Queen), of instigating the crime. But those who actually committed it were said to be certain women of Paris. The latter confessed under torture to the murder of the Queen's son, and admitted killing many other people too.[21] It is not hard to imagine the fate of the prefect and the ladies in question.

This was not the only episode in the violent life of Queen Fredegond in which witches had an important role. Earlier, she accused her step-child Clovis of killing two of her sons with the aid or complicity of an old witch and her daughter. These three she also managed to kill.[22] Yet this did not stop her from making spells and consulting witches herself when she felt like it.[23]

Fredegond was no exception in the land over which she reigned. The repression of magic, which she herself practised and which she accused others of practising, was one of the major concerns of the civil and religious authorities at the time and at later periods.

Sometimes, however, there are noticeable variations in the ways in which repressive measures are carried out: a divergence of opinion between legal and ecclesiastical authorities.

It is a long time since a Frenchman called Garinet collected together the most famous laws passed by the Frankish kings and their successors against the practice of magic. This was ranked as one of the manifestations of paganism which had to be eradicated (as it was in the last laws made under the Roman Empire). More recently these laws have been studied in a more scholarly way. But Garinet's book is still useful.[24]

20. *Scriptores Historiae Augustae: Alex-Sev.* (biography ascribed to Lampridius); *Numerianus* (biography ascribed to Flavius Vopiscus).

21. Gregory of Tours, *Hist. franc.*, VI, 35.

22. ibid., V, 40.

23. ibid., VII, 44.

24. Jules Garinet, *Histoire de la magie en France, depuis le commencement de la Monarchie jusqu'à nos jours* (Paris, 1818), pp. 6–7, 39–40, etc., and appendices.

Superficially there is little difference between these laws and those passed by the Christian Roman Emperors and by the Visigothic and Ostrogothic rulers in their respective kingdoms. Nor do these laws differ from others known to have been passed during the same dark ages in England, Germany and Hungary. The laws are apparently so similar that books on them are inevitably boring to read. But they are worth studying, even if not in great detail: for, suddenly, amongst the mass of virtually identical items, we find one that is quite different and extremely significant. As early as A.D. 743, Childeric III published an edict condemning pagan and magical practices as if they were much the same thing. Amongst the former are included sacrifices to the dead, and other sacrifices which were still being made at that time not to the old gods, but to Holy Martyrs and confessors in places close to the churches themselves. Among magical practices listed, we find ligatures, fortune-telling, augury, incantations and phylacteries.[25]

Charlemagne, following in the footsteps of Childeric and other Merovingian kings, published several edicts urging his subjects to forsake their superstitious beliefs. When mere exhortation proved useless, he resorted to edicts which laid down sentences appropriate to these crimes. These edicts specifically condemned all kinds of witchcraft, such as the making of wax figures, summoning devils and using love philtres, disturbing the atmosphere and raising storms, putting curses on people and causing the fruits of the earth to wither away, drying up the milk of some people's domestic animals to give it to others, practising astrology and making talismans. The law laid down that, in future, those who practised the arts of the Devil would be dishonoured and treated like murderers, poisoners and thieves; those who consulted them and made use of them would be given a similar sentence, and in some cases that meant death.[26]

In A.D. 873, Charles the Bald issued a decree in Quierzy-sur-Oise, declaring that he desired to fulfil his kingly duties laid down by the saints in the proper manner. He had learnt that sorcerers and witches had appeared in various parts of his kingdom, bringing illness and even death to a number of people. And his intention was to drive out the godless, and those who made philtres and poisons: 'We therefore expressly recommend the lords of the realm to seek out and apprehend with the greatest possible diligence those who are guilty of these crimes in their respective

---

25. Baluze, *Capitularia regum francorum*, I (Paris, 1677), cols. 150–52, ch. 4 of the Capitular, comprising an 'Indiculus superstitionum et paganiarum'.

26. Baluze, op. cit., I, cols. 220 (ch. 18, dated 789), 518 (ch. 40, uncertain date), 707 (ch. 21 of Book I of Ansegisus' collection), 837 (ch. 69 of Book V of the same collection), 929 (ch. 26 of Book VI), 962 (ch. 215 of Book VI), 999 (ch. 397 of Book VI), 1104 (ch. 369–70 of Book VII).

countries. If they are convicted, whether they are men or women, they must perish, for justice and the law demand it. If they are under suspicion or accused without being convicted, and if the testimony against them is not sufficient to prove their guilt, they shall be submitted to the will of God. This shall decide whether they are to be pardoned or condemned. But the associates and accomplices of those who are really guilty, both men and women, shall be put to death, so that all knowledge of such a heinous crime may vanish from our dominions'.[27]

These three texts of three different periods may suffice to show how hard civil law was on those who were accused of crimes of witchcraft in the eighth and ninth centuries. Probably, these laws were often enforced in an arbitrary way, and people must frequently have been accused of such crimes in much the same violent and fanatical manner as Queen Fredegond accused her step-son. The danger of arraigning people who might be totally innocent had yet to be recognized.

This explains why the Church, which absolutely condemned paganism, let alone magic, from a theological point of view, promulgated a series of dispositions which would, on occasion, soften the harsh effects of civil law. This moderation may partially have been due to propagandistic motives, aimed to attract the great mass of people who remained unconverted to Christianity in the country areas and small towns. But perhaps the more moderate dispositions of the Church also reflect the ideas of St Augustine.

J. B. Thiers in his *Traité des superstitions* collected together a large number of references to Canon laws of Church Councils, and to other decrees which severely condemned the practice of magic, dating from the sixth, seventh and eighth centuries and later periods also.[28] Some of these emphasize the dangerous spiritual effects of magic, but others insist that sorcerers themselves are often victims of the illusions and deceits of the Devil, and deny that it is necessary to believe categorically in their powers.

Even after the promulgation of the decrees of Charlemagne which have already been mentioned, the prelates who were summoned to the Council of Tours in 813 still felt the need for priests to warn the faithful that spells could not help sick or dying persons or animals; they were nothing but illusions and tricks of the Devil.[29] In other instances the same

27. Baluze, op. cit., II, cols. 230–31 (§VII).

28. J. B. Thiers, *Traité des superstitions qui regardent les sacremens*, I (Paris, 1741), pp. 178, 198, and *passim*.

29. Title 3 of Canon 42. cf. Joseph Hansen, *Zauberwahn, Inquisition und Hexenprozess im Mittelalter und die Entstehung der grossen Hexenverfolgung* (München-Leipzig, 1900), pp. 66–7.

99

ecclesiastical authorities disputed the validity of facts which civil law accepted, or qualified the conclusions that were drawn from them.

A good example of this is that of Agobard, Archbishop of Lyons (779–840), who, in spite of the general views held at the time, severely criticized those who believed that certain human beings were capable of bringing on rain and hail-storms. He also censured those who held Duke Grimald responsible for sending sorcerers to throw harmful magic powders into fields, forests and streams, when the oxen belonging to the smallholders in the diocese were stricken by an epidemic.[30]

The prelates who attended the sixth Council of Paris in 829 were in closer agreement with the civil laws and edicts. The eleventh canon of the Council expressed the following opinion:

There are other very dangerous evils which are certainly legacies of paganism, such as magic, astrology, incantations and spells, poisoning, divination, enchantment, and the interpretation of dreams. These evils ought to be severely punished, as the laws of God ordain. But there is no doubt, as many learned men have witnessed, that there are some people capable of so perverting the minds of others with the Devil's illusions, (by giving them philtres, drugged food and phylacteries), that they become confused and insensible to the ills they are made to suffer. It is also said that these people can disturb the air with their spells, send hail-storms, predict the future, take produce and milk from one person to give to another, and do a thousand similar things. If any such be found, be they men or women, they should be severely punished, particularly since, in their malice and temerity, they fear not the Devil nor do they renounce him publicly.[31]

There is undoubtedly a conflict between these views and Agobard's: one which is to be found time and again in later periods. It even occurs in certain civil laws, some of which put forward opinions which are flatly contradicted by other laws in the same code.

There is, for example, an act dated 789 amongst the laws of the Frankish kings; it refers to Saxony and condemns belief in *strigae* and their ability to eat men, expressing the view that they ought to be burnt for it. The same act prescribes capital punishment for all who believe such things.[32] There is clearly a connection between this and another law to be found in the *Leges Langobardicae,* dating probably from the reign of

30. Agobard's work, 'Liber contra insulsam vulgi opinionem de grandinem', can be found in Migne's *Patrology,* CIV, cols. 147 ff. Nearly all writers on the subject quote it. See, for example, Hansen, op. cit., p. 73.

31. Cf. J. B. Thiers, op. cit., note 28.

32. Baluze, op. cit., I, cols. 251–2: 'VI. Si quis a diabolo deceptus crediderit, secundum morem paganorum, virum aliquem aut feminam strigam esse et homines comedere, et propter hoc ipsam incenderit, vel carnem ejus ad comedendum dederit, vel ipsam comederit, capitis sententia punietur.'

King Rotharius. Yet although it is conceived in much the same spirit, this law holds that, from a Christian point of view, *strigae* or *mascae cannot* be capable of the acts they are believed to perform.[33]

On the other hand, the popes who were concerned with the conversion of central European and, above all, Northern peoples, gave very categorical instructions on the subject to kings and prelates of the Church. Pope Gregory II, for example, ordered Bishop Martinian and the priest called George who went with him to Bavaria, to forbid spells and enchantments, which were relics of paganism, although he makes no reference to the punishment of those involved.

On once occasion Pope Gregory VII wrote to the King of Denmark asking him to avoid, as far as possible, persecuting innocent women who were thought to have caused storms or epidemics. Earlier, Pope Leo VII had sent an instruction dated 936 to Archbishop Gerhard of Lorch, intended for the authorities of southern Germany, which again took a lenient view of those accused of witchcraft. Answering a specific enquiry he maintained that 'although, by the old law, such people were condemned to death, ecclesiastical law spared their lives so that they could repent'.

This rather ambiguous situation is typical of a period of transition like the Middle Ages. On the one hand, we have the passionate beliefs of the masses just converted to Christianity or still pagan, and on the other, the doubt and pragmatism of the ecclesiastical authorities in the face of popular beliefs and civil law.

---

33. Joseph Hansen, 'Zauberwahn, Inquisition und Hexenprozess im Mittelalter und die Entstehung der grossen Hexenverfolgung' (München–Leipzig, 1900), pp. 76–7, also refers to the laws promulgated by Stephen of Hungary (A.D. 997–1038). General histories like Soldan's, or the more recent one by Baissac, contain plenty of material on this period.

12. R. F. Fortune

Sorcerers of Dobu

Excerpt from R. F. Fortune, *Sorcerors of Dobu: The Social Anthropology of the Dobu Islanders of the Western Pacific*, Routledge, 1932, pp. 150–54.

Witchcraft and Sorcery

Death is caused by witchcraft, sorcery, poisoning, suicide, or by actual assault. There is no concept of accident. Falling from coconut palms or other trees is due to witchcraft; similarly of other accidents.

When the Tewera* men were in the Amphletts on an overseas voyage they went for the night to a small sandbank near by to obtain sea-birds' eggs. The canoe was not well beached. It floated off in the night, the supports of the outrigger boom smashed, and outrigger boom and canoe sank separately. Fortunately both were washed up on a sand-bar within swimming distance. Every man blamed the flying witches. 'They charm so that we sleep like the dead and do not ground our canoe. They lay no hand on the canoe. They say "you go to sea" and the canoe goes.' Some of the men blamed their own women of Tewara, declaring that their habits were vile. Some blamed the women of Gumasila, who were jealous, presumably, of their taking sea-birds' eggs from an island near Gumasila.

Witchcraft is the woman's prerogative, sorcery the man's. A witch does all of her work in spirit form while her body sleeps, but only at the bidding of the fully conscious and fully awake woman and as the result of her spells, it is said. Not only is all that we term accident as opposed to sickness ascribed exclusively to witchcraft, but a particular way of causing illness and death is the monopoly of women. This method is that of spirit abstraction from the victim.

The man, as sorcerer, has the monopoly of causing sickness and death by using spells on the personal leavings of the victim. When the diviner of the person responsible for an illness beards a witch he says: 'Restore X's spirit to him'; when he beards a man he says: 'Produce X's personal leavings that you have in your house.' Such personal leavings may be remains of food, excreta, footprints in sand, body dirt, or a bush creeper

*The island on which Fortune carried out most of his research. He describes it as 'an outlying small island, with a population of forty-four in 1928, twenty-two in 1959'. It lies about twenty-three miles north-north-east of Dobu – *Ed.*

with a malevolent charm first breathed into it which the sorcerer watched his victim brush against and which he subsequently took to his house to treat further.

Moving among the men mainly I soon became aware of a convention. Death is always referred to the *werebana*.* That village is weeds and grass, that island is uninhabited now – the flying witches. Yet these same men in reality feared sorcery as much as witchcraft, all had their killing powers, and little by little I heard of what they had done with them. By convention only, death is referred to the women's activities. Underneath the convention was the knowledge that men themselves had a great hand in it – only this is not referred to by men, except in great confidence that usually betrays itself first in a panic and is pressed home from the panic by the field-worker. The sorcery of other places is referred to freely – the sorcerers there, the danger of poison in the food offered one.

The women do not seem to have enough solidarity to turn the tables and to blame all death upon the *barau,* the male practitioner, as they might. Instead, they voice the general convention – the flying witches are responsible. The diviner takes no notice of this convention of speech. He is as likely to divine a sorcerer as a witch in any concrete case of illness.

The women, however, have a counter convention established. No woman will admit to a man that she knows a witchcraft spell. The men have the benefit of a general alibi. But a man will admit to his wife that he knows death-dealing spells, whereas she will not reciprocate. The women have the benefit of an individual alibi. The diviner, and all persons discarding courtesy of speech, take no more account of the women's alibi than of the men's. Courtesy of speech in direct conversation matters greatly in Dobu. If A tells B that B's greatest friend is vile, B replies: 'Yes, he is vile.' B may take secret measures to revenge himself on A, but in conversation there is never any controversy in such a matter.

The Dobuan men are quite certain that the women of the Trobriands do not practise witchcraft spells, as they are equally certain that their own women do so practise. Accordingly the men of Dobu feel safer in the Trobriands among a strange people of a strange speech than they do in their own homes – in direct and striking contrast to their greater fear in the Amphletts and in parts of Fergusson Island than in their own homes, and in contrast also to their greater fear in other Dobuan districts than in their own home districts. I saw this most clearly for myself; there was no doubt about their attitudes – considerable fear at home, sharpened greatly in all strange places, but blunted in the Trobriands. Whether this great certainty of feeling is founded on a solid fact that women in Dobu do

* Flying witches –*Ed.*

practise witchcraft spells, or merely on acceptance of the Trobriand freedom from Dobuan-like fears, I should be loath to say. I have worked with the men intimately and I know that the diviner's discarding of the convention clearing the male sex is correct. I know the men complain about the lying they believe there is in the women's convention. But only a woman working with women could tell what the facts are – whether they are really innocent or whether they are putting up a convention counter to the men's. Personally I suspect the latter. The women certainly own *tabus*. A few men say themselves that they penetrated beneath the women's convention and actually got witchcraft spells from women by threatening them with violence. Such men are few, and may be telling the truth or not. The probability is that women do own spells, however. The witch charged as a witch by the diviner summoned to a sick person does not deny witchcraft any more often than a sorcerer in a similar position denies sorcery. Such denials are few in all, for a reason that we shall discuss later. It would be unreasonable that women should suffer so without benefit when spells may be so easily made from the natural expression of hate. Innovation in spells occurs despite native belief to the contrary. In the *kula* magic we shall meet Tauwau, the culture hero who created galvanized iron roofs, nailed houses, bully beef in tins, and European diseases. Side by side with Tauwau in the magic are lines that are as old as any. Sometimes *kaiana,* fire vented forth from the pubes of flying witches, is seen at night. Then the village gathers together around its fires, which are kept burning all night, and none retires to the house to sleep. The entire village became more than usually dormant in the afternoon on such occasions. On other occasions a woman would wake from a nightmare convinced that the flying witches were chasing her spirit and were just outside baulked by her spirit's good luck in getting home before them. Then the night would be hideous with a ghastly yelling or alternate high and low shrieking, expressing such fear in its very sound as to be contagious enough to myself who knew its origin. Next day sometimes the woman and her husband were outwardly serene and I had to get the whole story from someone else. But sometimes the woman or her husband would be shaken and ill and drawn in appearance all day, confined to the mat – in which case I dosed the patient with salts or quinine according to taste.

Because of danger from witch or sorcerer it is not advisable to go alone. Frequently in broad daylight I was warned not to do it. 'You go alone' in surprise and in dissuasion. In strange places they looked after me well. Once in Raputat of Sanaroa I went with three natives, fresh from the canoe under the hot sun, to bathe in a cool spring ten minutes away from the shore. Two bathed and went away on an errand. One remained. I was resting in my bathing V's and not going back. My native hung about chewing a stem of grass and gazing at the distance. This lasted a long while. Finally I said: 'It's all right, Kisian, I know the track now.' 'No, I shall wait for you. New Guinea vile – witchcraft, sorcery is here.' That is typical. Even at home it is rare for anyone to be alone except on adultery or stealing bent; and often adultery and stealing are cooperative ventures, two men going together. Many means of death exist by day. Only in the night, however, bats are abroad. If a bat approaches a house, crying aloud, panic rises. They pale quite visibly, talk stops abruptly; and on several occasions it happened when natives were in my house by night, they said '*werebana*' in an undertone, sat saying nothing for five or ten minutes, and then as soon as was decent got up and slunk away. The night is a little more feared than the day because it is the time for sleep when the spirits of the sleepers go abroad in the pursuit of the black art. Most of the black art of the daytime is done in the flesh. But fear of the night work is only slightly greater than fear of the day work.

The situation created by witchcraft beliefs in marriage we have already treated. The members of village X may refer freely to their fear of certain women of village Y, until inter-marriage takes place. Then comment is forced underground, as it is a great insult to 'call witchcraft' within a husband's range of gaining report of comment upon his close relatives in law or upon his wife. All men have a nervousness of their wives' complicity, and a fear of mothers-in-law. Only the most reckless will say privily of another man: 'It would appear that last night he slept with his wife – but did he sleep with his wife? Or was she far away? With an empty skin at his side he slept.'

I may add as well as witches who are mortal women (*werebana*) there are also sea witches (*gelaboi*) who have no present human embodiment.

Methods of Divination

Divining is usually done by water-gazing or crystal-gazing. In the former case water is put into a wooden bowl and hibiscus flowers thrown on the water. The divine charms: 'the water is water no longer'. He cuts the water-in-changed-nature open. At the bottom of the cut he sees the spirit of the witch who has abstracted the spirit of his patient and who now has it concealed, or the spirit of the sorcerer who has the *sumwana*, body leavings of the patient, and now has them concealed. Volcanic crystals may be used instead of water.

Spirit abstraction by a *gelaboi* may be indicated by the patient making delirious or semi-delirious statements about canoes at sea, canoes used by these spiritual *gelaboi*. Great attention is paid to the patient's ravings if there are any.

If the patient runs about in delirium then again his *sumwana* has been taken by a sorcerer. The sorcerer in such case has bound up the *sumwana,* winding it about in some receptacle with bush creeper. This winding is compared to the way in which the tree opossum, *Cuscus*, winds its tail around branches and darts about apparently aimlessly. The sorcerer's winding of *sumwana* has made the patient run about like the opossum.

The diviner may bend forward the middle finger of the patiebt, grasping it tightly at the first joint. If the tip of the finger does not flush then spirit abstraction by a witch has occurred. If it does flush then the patient's *sumwana* has been taken by a sorcerer.

Again the diviner may tell by the body odour of the patient the sex of the person responsible. None could define how this was done.

These measures of noting the symptoms of delirium, or of trying the finger bending or the smelling tests, precede the water or crystal gazing which finally determines the exact identity of the person responsible for the illness. The attention paid to delirium narrows down the circle of people within which the diviner's judgement may operate, but the other two tests leave him free by their nebulousness. Flushing or no flushing in the finger bent is rarely so obvious as to rule out subjective appraisal of the results, a subjective factor that is even more obvious in the smelling test.

Unless the agent revealed is a *gelaboi,* a *yatala* or, as it is also called, a *bwokumatana,* follows. The diviner summons the village, a member of which he has 'seen' in his water-gazing. The person divined is charged with the deed by the diviner. Then follows a promise of cessation of enmity and of active black magic by the witch or the sorcerer charged, provided her or his just complaint against the patient is remedied by the patient immediately. The patient pays the black magician and the diviner, and recovers – unless unremedied grudges undivined as yet still exist elsewhere.

After a death the kin of the dead divine whose grudge killed their kinsman by watching the corpse as the mourners file by one by one as is the custom. When the guilty person passes the corpse it is believed to twitch in one place or another. So strong is this belief that twitches are probably often fancied. In any case common fact is often relied on rather than the pure magic of divination. If one man has sought out another's company too much and for no reason that appears customary, and the latter dies, suspicion falls on his unexplained companion. False friendship is suspected. I heard from three different sources: 'If we wish to kill a man we approach him, we eat, drink, sleep, work, and rest with him, it may be for several moons, and we wait our time; we *kawagosiana*, call him friend.' It will be recalled that the black art is believed to be ineffective at a distance as it is conducted by men. Men have to work in the flesh. Even witches are believed to confine their work to within the locality to which they belong.

It is realized by the Dobuan that relationship considerations debar certain persons who might be responsible for the death from mourning, so that divination by the corpse is not perfect. As well as consideration of unreasonable companionship there is consideration of possible grudges left unhealed. Then again the possibility of poison in food eaten is canvassed. I have heard these considerations being turned over in the heat that followed the sudden death of a father and child together without marks of violence. Every meal for several days back was considered in detail. So also of companions of the pair, and old hostilities. It was all done in my presence in about ten minutes, provoked by the sudden reception of the news by two men related to the dead.

Divination in Dobu is practised by everyone without magic, and by a special class with more authority and with magic.

13. Isaac Schapera

Sorcery and Witchcraft in Bechuanaland*

Excerpt from Isaac Schapera, 'Sorcery and witchcraft in Bechuanaland', *African Affairs*, vol. 51, 1952, pp. 41–52.

I

In 1825 the heir to the chieftainship of the BaTlhaping, a young man named Phetlhu (son of Mothibi), died suddenly of a disease that Robert Moffat, who was present at the time, described as 'Hottentot sickness' (i.e., anthrax). His parents, however, maintained that he had been bewitched by the relatives of a girl to whom he had been formerly betrothed, but whom he had jilted for someone else. A raiding party was therefore sent to seize and kill those people, but they were forewarned and managed to escape by fleeing to a neighbouring tribe.

In 1889, a correspondent to the vernacular journal *Mahoko a Becwana* (published at Kuruman mission station) asserted that Sechele, chief of the BaKwena, had recently caused five men to be killed for witchcraft, on the accusation of a single servant maid. Sechele (who, it may be remembered, had been baptized by Livingstone in 1849) replied shortly afterwards. He admitted having killed the men, but said that there was overwhelming proof of their guilt, and that he had released many others against whom the evidence was less convincing.

Among the BaNgwaketse, during the chieftainship of Seepapitso (1910–16), records were kept of 464 cases tried at the chief's court. Of these, no fewer than twenty-six (i.e., about one in eighteen) were directly concerned with charges of witchcraft, and in another seven accusations of witchcraft figured incidentally.

In 1927 the Kwena chief Sebele II (great-grandson of Sechele) accused his paternal uncle Kebohula of having tried to bewitch him by burying a 'doctored' hoe in the royal council-place (*kgotla*). The matter was discussed for three days at a large tribal gathering, which decided that Kebohula was guilty and should be banished from the tribal Reserve. At this stage the Administration intervened, induced Sebele to withhold the order of banishment, and passed a Proclamation (no. 17 of 1927) which made it a penal offence, both for people to accuse others of practising witchcraft, and also for people to attempt, by the use of magic, to inflict harm upon others.

* Now the Republic of Botswana – *Ed.*

The Native Tribunals Proclamation of 1934 removed from the jurisdiction of tribal courts all statutory offences. This included cases of witchcraft. The Proclamation also provided that all cases tried before the established Native Tribunals should be recorded. An inspection that I made of 850 case records, from five different tribes for the period 1935–40, showed that despite the Proclamation thirty-one of the cases had actually been concerned with witchcraft.

In 1937 the divorced wife of the Ngwato chief Tshekedi was, under the Proclamation of 1927, tried in the Court of the District Commissioner at Serowe for attempted witchcraft against her husband. She herself maintained that the 'medicines' she had used were intended to restore his love, but the court found her and the two magicians whom she had employed guilty of the offence as charged, and sentenced them all to imprisonment. Shortly afterwards, at the request of Tshekedi, they were banished from the tribal Reserve. It was alleged at the time that she had also caused the death of Tshekedi's mother by the use of poison, but the Crown apparently did not think that there was sufficient evidence for this to justify prosecution.

II

As shown by the instances just given, the belief in sorcery was noted among the Tswana at least 130 years ago; and, although all the tribes in the Protectorate have been considerably influenced during the past eighty years by contact with Western civilization, to such an extent that the official religion of them all at the present time is Christianity, that belief still persists very strongly. It has even been given official recognition by the Administration. The (revised) Native Courts Proclamation of 1943 repeated the stipulation that tribal courts had no jurisdiction over statutory offences; but it also provided that their warrants might be specially endorsed to allow them to deal with cases of witchcraft. Since the Proclamation was passed, the right to deal with such cases has been granted to the chief's courts of three tribes (BaNgwato, BaNgwaketse, and BaKgatla).

It will, of course, be remembered that during the sixteenth and seventeenth centuries belief in witchcraft also flourished in Western Europe, when many thousands of people were tortured and brutally put to death as witches. However, no matter what our predecessors may have thought, we at least maintain nowadays that these beliefs were largely superstition, with no real justification in fact. Must the beliefs of the Tswana be similarly dismissed as empty superstition, indicative merely of intellectual backwardness, or is there in fact, as suggested by the recent action of the

Administration, some valid reason for their existence? To put it very simply: do people amongst the Tswana really practise sorcery, or are the accusations so often made devoid of any factual substance? The answer, if I may anticipate much of what I am going to say, is that sorcery is, in fact, practised amongst the Tswana; there are indeed people who try to inflict harm upon others by means of the various techniques locally classed together as *boloi* ('sorcery and witchcraft', or 'black magic').

In many parts of Africa, two kinds of 'black magic' are commonly distinguished. In the one, people deliberately try, with the aid of magic, to injure some specific enemy or enemies. In the other, the persons termed 'witches' are said to suffer from some hereditary pathological condition; they seek to harm others, not of their conscious volition, but because it is inherent in their nature; and in some forms of the belief it is held that they themselves are ignorant of their dreadful powers, all their activities being carried out at night by their spirits or souls while their bodies repose in sleep. Following Evans-Pritchard, it has become customary in anthropological literature to refer to the first class as 'sorcerers', and to the second as 'witches'.

The Tswana do not believe that there is any hereditary condition by virtue of which people unwittingly become witches. They maintain that all who practise *boloi* are fully aware of what they are doing, i.e. always act 'of malice aforethought'; their motive is invariably one of envy, vengeance, or greed, and any person, male or female, may become one of them. In other words, the Tswana do not believe in 'witches', but only in 'sorcerers'.

Nevertheless, in many respects some of the Tswana beliefs about sorcerers are strongly reminiscent of what is said elsewhere about witches. They distinguish between *baloi ba bosigo,* 'night witches', and *baloi ba motshegare*, 'day sorcerers'. Of the former, many weird and wonderful beliefs are held. It is said that people of this class consist mainly of elderly women, who are not content to employ magic solely in order to injure some particular enemy, but who make a habit of bewitching. By day they go about their routine everyday activities just like other people, but at night they gather in small groups and visit one homestead after another, carrying on their nefarious practices. They wear nothing on such occasions, or very little, and their bodies are smeared with white ashes or the blood of dead people. Admission into the group is apparently open to anyone, but, before being admitted, a woman must give evidence of her zeal by causing the death of some very close relative, preferably her own firstborn child. Once initiated, she is given an ointment with which to smear her body when she goes to bed at night; this will cause her to wake instantaneously when her colleagues come to call her. Alternatively, in some tribes, it is said that a special 'medicine' is injected into her thumb, whose itching will then awake her when necessary.

Among the activities attributed to these 'night witches' is the exhumation of newly-buried corpses. This, it is said, is generally done by means of a special magic that causes the grave to open of itself and the corpse to float to the surface. The witches then take from it such parts as they wish to use with their other medicines. It is believed also that they have special medicines that will enable them to throw the inhabitants of a homestead into a deep sleep, so that they may enter at will and do what they wish. Locked doors are no barrier against their magic; and, once inside, they cut the body of their victim and insert small stones, fragments of flesh, etc., which will cause him to fall ill and ultimately die, unless he is 'doctored' in time.

Associated with these night witches are various kinds of animal familiars. Foremost among them is the owl, which acts as their spy and whose hooting warns them that someone is approaching. This bird is greatly feared by the people, who regard it as ill-omened, and if it comes near their home they try to kill it and then throw it far away. It is said also that, when the witches wish to go to a distant place, they ride on hyenas; they keep one leg on the ground, and put the other on the animal's back, and in this way are able to progress at great speed! The BaKgatla say that some witches make their own hyenas, moulding the body from porridge, which is then vitalized by means of special medicines; but the belief in robots of this kind does not appear to exist elsewhere.

It should be said at once that beliefs of the kind just mentioned, although very widely held, are not really taken seriously by most of the people. Few claim to have actually seen 'night witches' at work, and very many are openly sceptical of the practices and powers attributed to them; some even say that such persons are mere figments of the imagination.

On the other hand, there is virtually unanimous belief in the existence and activities of the *baloi ba motshegare,* 'day sorcerers'. Unlike their nocturnal counterparts, these sorcerers do not belong to bands, nor do they practise the black art habitually. They use magic solely in order to inflict harm upon some specific enemy; and the only reservations about them are in regard to some of the methods they are said to employ. All these methods involve the use of herbs or other material substances, collectively known as *ditlhare* ('medicines'), which as a rule must be obtained from professional magicians or 'doctors' (*dingaka*). Magicians themselves may be hired to inflict harm upon a person's enemies, and may do so too against their own hated rivals. In such cases they also are said to practise *boloi,* although normally their activities are regarded with great respect as being beneficial to the community.

The following are some of the more commonly described methods of bewitching. The sorcerer may sprinkle 'doctored' blood over the court-yard of his enemy, the blood being as a rule that of the latter's totem animal, or of some member of his family. Should the victim then step upon the blood, his feet become affected, and he will either die or lose the use of his limbs. Alternatively, the sorcerer may conceal a bundle of rags containing 'doctored' roots in the eaves of his victim's hut, or he may bury them in the ground at the entrance to the homestead. The mere presence of these substances about the place will bring illness or death to one of the inhabitants. Again, the sorcerer may take some dust from his victim's footprint and work upon it with medicines; or he may blow some prepared powder in the victim's direction, at the same time calling upon his name; or he may send an animal, such as a lion or leopard or snake or ox, to inflict direct bodily injury upon him. This last method, known as *go neelela,* 'to give over', is said to be very commonly used.

There is one other method, allegedly used mainly by professional magicians in disputes with their colleagues, which deserves to be mentioned. It consists in working with lightning as a destructive agent. By using the appropriate medicines, the sorcerer can direct the lightning so that it strikes his victim or the latter's hut or cattle; some magicians are even said to have the power of making themselves fly through the air and then descend upon their victim in the guise of lightning.

From our point of view, obviously none of the methods just described can really achieve the purpose for which it is intended. Were they the only ones employed by sorcerers – and, it must be noted here, at least some of them are practised in all seriousness – we would be fully justified in regarding the whole of the Tswana belief in sorcery as nothing more than fantasy or hallucination. In all fairness, however, it must be added at once that nowadays many of the Tswana themselves do not consider such methods worthy of credence. Tshekedi, for instance, has on several occa-sions openly stated in court, when trying cases of sorcery, that some of the practices alleged against the accused were merely 'fairy tales' (*mainane*), incapable of causing physical injury.

But there is one other method, which the Tswana almost invariably mention first when asked how people bewitch, and which they regard as by far the most efficacious and dangerous. This method, known as *go jesa,* 'to feed' or 'to give to eat', consists in putting some poisonous substance into beer or porridge or other food, which is then given to the person whom one intends to bewitch. Here, also, there is sometimes an element of fantasy. Some people, for instance, say that when the victim swallows the food, the poisonous substance changes into a miniature lion or crocodile or some similar animal, which gnaws away persistently at his entrails until he dies in excruciating pain. But the majority maintain that the substance put into the food is actually poisonous (in our sense of the term). There are several well-known herbs said to be used for the purpose, including a few whose action is very slow, so that death does not take place suddenly enough to arouse immediate suspicion of foul play. It is clear also, from the records of several cases tried in the courts, that sometimes poisons are used with which we are more familiar; for instance, caustic soda (readily purchased at the trading stores) is fairly often mentioned in this connection.

III

It is often said by Europeans claiming to know something about tribal life that the African lives in perpetual dread of sorcery. It is true that he regards sorcery as an ever-present danger. But he is no more obsessed by fear of it than is the average inhabitant of a large city in Western Europe obsessed by fear of being involved in a traffic accident. Both are dangers that must be faced almost daily; but just as we can avoid a collision by exercising caution, so do the Tswana believe that it is possible to protect oneself against sorcery.

It is an almost universal practice amongst them that whenever a new homestead, hut, or cattle kraal, is being built, it is fortified by means of 'doctored' pegs or other objects, which are either buried in the ground or applied in some other way. The aim of the rite is to counteract any medicines that a sorcerer may bring into the place. It is believed that, as soon as he enters, his medicines will lose their power and be rendered ineffective. Some magicians claim that if the site has been properly doctored the sorcerer's medicines will turn against himself, so that the harm he intends will in fact fall upon him. It may be noted, incidentally, that one form of 'fortifying' a homestead is to bury at the entrance a long stick smeared with medicine. Then, so it is believed, if a sorcerer or any other evil-doer steps over the entrance, the stick will become a snake that bites him fatally.

However, the principal form of protection used by most people is to have their own bodies magically 'strengthened' by a doctor. In its most widespread form the doctoring consists in making small cuts on every joint of the person's body, and into each cut is smeared a little of the magical ointment specially prepared by the doctor to combat sorcery.

113

Henceforth, not only is the client regarded as immune from the attacks of sorcerers, but if any of them try to bewitch him the attempt will rebound disastrously upon them. This ceremony of 'strengthening' the body is usually performed simultaneously on all members of a family, especially when they are building a new homestead and the doctor comes to fortify it. In such cases the father is treated first, then the mother, and then all the children in descending order of age.

Apart from this special doctoring, many people, before going to a feast or to some other place where they fear that they may be given poisoned food, take special precautions. They swallow a certain medicine with which they have been supplied by their doctor. Then, so it is believed, if they are in fact given poisoned food the medicine will cause them to vomit it out and so escape the threatened consequences. At such feasts, too, the head of the household generally gets a magician to smear protective medicines on the base of every pot in which food is to be cooked. I myself have on several occasions seen such protective magic being employed at such essentially Christian feasts as those held when a person is being baptized or married in church.

IV

In the old days, when a person had died, fallen ill, or been afflicted with some other misfortune, a doctor was invariably called to divine the cause. Occasionally the misfortune might be attributed directly to the action of God (*Modimo*), in which case nothing could be done. Far more commonly, it might be attributed to *kgaba*, i.e., punishment inflicted by the ancestral spirits because some senior member of the kinship group had been insulted or otherwise injured by a junior relative. In such cases, a sick person would usually recover after the performance of a special cleansing ceremony by the person held to have been the source of the *kgaba*. It was also fairly common, however, for the doctor to attribute the misfortune to sorcery. In such cases he would never directly mention any person by name as responsible, but would state his sex, totem, skin complexion, and the direction from which he usually came when bewitching. If the people could from the description identify the sorcerer, they would normally hold an inquiry and try to obtain further evidence of his guilt. Then, if satisfied that he was in fact the culprit, they would report him to the chief, who alone had the right to prosecute and to punish sorcerers.

The trial of a sorcerer was generally conducted along the same lines as any other case that came before the chief. If it was clear from the evidence

114

that the accused was guilty, the chief would order him to 'undo' the patient (*go mo dirolola*), i.e., to remove the effects of his sorcery so that the patient should recover. If he refused, he would be tortured until he consented. This seems to have been the only contingency in which torture was normally employed. If the patient then recovered, the sorcerer would be let off with a severe reprimand, although sometimes he might also be removed from his home and settled somewhere else. But if the patient died, or if he was already dead when the case first came to court, the sorcerer would be killed. In several tribal capitals, there are steep precipices still pointed out today as the places where, in the old days, sorcerers and others condemned to death were executed, their bodies, after they had been clubbed or speared, being tumbled over the cliff and left to lie at the base as food for the vultures and hyenas.

Since the introduction of European rule, the chiefs no longer have the right to impose the death penalty; nor, except in the three tribes previously named, have they even the right to try any person accused of sorcery. Nevertheless, such trials are still held from time to time. It must be said at once that tribal courts are generally cautious about the type of evidence that they will accept before convicting persons accused of sorcery. For instance, judging from the records that I have consulted, they do not regard the bare findings of a divination as sufficient. They must be satisfied, beyond doubt, that the accused has in fact been discovered using one or other of the methods already described. In particular, they pay special attention to his possession of medicines. It is fairly common, for instance, for a court to order his huts to be searched, and if any medicines are found he is asked to state where he got them and what their uses are. There are always magicians present at the hearing who will be able to check the statements that he may make in this connection. If he is able to show that his medicines are innocuous, i.e., intended for treating sickness, or for any other lawful purpose, or if none at all are found in his possession, the case against him is seldom regarded as serious.

It should also be noted here that a malicious and unfounded accusation of sorcery is itself an offence in tribal law, the accused in such cases being entitled to receive damages for 'the spoiling of his name'. Many accusations of sorcery seem to be based upon little more than the statements made by magicians when divining. Not only is such evidence, if unsupported, not accepted in the courts; but time and again chiefs have warned their people against relying too much upon the words of the magicians, and some of the latter have even been punished for falsifying the verdicts of their divining-bones.

The sentences imposed upon convicted sorcerers vary according to circumstances. Perhaps the most common nowadays is to remove the culprit from his home to some other part of the tribal territory. The reason for this will be mentioned below. Occasionally, however, if medicines are found in his possession, and he cannot satisfactorily account for them, he may be told to swallow them, the argument being that if they are not poisonous no harm will befall him, whereas if they are he deserves the fate that he will suffer. At least one instance was described to me in which the accused had died very shortly after swallowing his own medicines; but this, I hasten to add, took place in the days before the Witchcraft Proclamation of 1927 had been passed.

If the accused, although guilty, has employed methods other than the use, or attempted use, of poison, he is sometimes fined or thrashed. Or, as in the old days, he may simply be ordered to 'undo' his victim, the implication being that drastic action will be taken against him should the latter die. Sometimes, again, the court will permit the victim to have his own doctor treat him, or, if the victim is dead, his relatives will be authorized to have his grave doctored; should any misfortune then overtake the culprit, it is attributed to the 'vengeance magic' used against him. One chief, in describing to me his use of this particular type of sentence, said that he did not really believe such 'vengeance magic' could work, but at least its use gave satisfaction to the people claiming to have been harmed.

V

From the records of cases heard in court, and from other evidence, it is abundantly clear that sorcery is, in fact, employed amongst the Tswana. It is not a mere figment of the imagination, nor are people always accused without any foundation at all. Sorcery is a recognized method of trying to inflict harm upon one's enemies, and persons accused of the crime have at times freely admitted that they resorted to it; and although some of the techniques employed are by our standards either stupid or ridiculous, they are nevertheless employed in all seriousness, and sometimes, as when poison is used, they can be really deadly.

One very important aspect still remains to be noted. In the vast majority of instances for which I have adequate data (ninety cases in a sample of 105), the sorcerer and his victims were usually very closely related. The most common types of relationship were those of husband and wife, parent and child, brother and brother; less commonly, but also fairly frequent, the parties involved were parent-in-law and child's spouse, master and servant, or doctor and client. It is extremely rare for people to be accused of bewitching either strangers or persons living away from their own part of the tribal territory.

These facts throw a revealing light upon the nature of Tswana sorcery. It is employed predominantly in situations of domestic conflict. The immediate causes are innumerable; there may be disputes about marital fidelity, about ownership of property or succession to office, about favour shown to one member of the family at the expense of another, etc. In our own society such disputes, if they cannot be settled amicably or adjusted by process of law, generally result in the separation of the persons concerned. But in tribal law people are not free to change their residence when and as they wish; they are expected to remain living among their kinsmen, and only in exceptional circumstances will the tribal authorities permit a man to move away from his own group. Consequently, the people on terms of hostility may find themselves forced to continue living in close daily contact, and unable to avoid one another; and it is in situations of this sort that they sometimes fall back upon the traditional weapon of sorcery. It is for this reason, too, that a convicted sorcerer is generally removed from his home. Obviously, if the Tswana thought that one could harm people through sorcery at a distance, this particular remedy would be useless. But the Tswana do not have that belief; and the reason given by chiefs for ordering the removal of a sorcerer is that unless such a step is taken in time he may ultimately try more drastic methods, for instance by way of poison or the use of physical violence.

If it is asked why the Tswana continue to believe in sorcery, although so many of its techniques are (to us, at least) obviously futile, several answers can readily be given. The first, as we have seen, is that not all the techniques are in fact futile; on the contrary, the use of poison must be regarded as decidedly effective. Secondly, since sorcery is not necessarily held to achieve its purpose immediately, the chances of a victim's meeting with misfortune at some time or other are fairly considerable, no matter what technique is employed; and time and again, when one has attempted to argue on this point with the Tswana, their reply is to quote instances where people have in fact been injured by sorcery. Their evidence often rests upon little more than divination by the magicians; and it is only fair to add that at least some people accuse the magicians of deliberately fostering the belief in sorcery so as to have more employment for themselves. And it must be remembered in this connection that there are magicians in virtually every village in Bechuanaland. Their influence is continuous and always present, and there is still very little to counteract them. Finally, it must be emphasized that belief in sorcery is still part of the cultural tradition of the Tswana. From childhood onwards, every person grows up in an environment where it not only flourishes, but is still taken for granted as a recognized method of dealing with one's enemies; and on the whole it is much easier for the average tribesman to fall into line with his fellows than to break away completely from his native beliefs.

Nevertheless, even if we characterize much of it as folk-lore or sheer fantasy, Tswana sorcery has a solid core of fact, viz., the employment of poison as a means of injuring an enemy who is at the same time a close relative or neighbour from whom one is normally unable to move away. There is nothing superstitious or fantastic about this element of the concept, nor can we dismiss it as lightly as most of the other elements. As I have already indicated, the Tswana themselves are tending more and more to be sceptical about such features as many of the beliefs relating to 'night witches', and several chiefs are nowadays stressing the absurdity of such techniques as doctoring a person's footprint; but even the most enlightened continue to believe that people can bewitch others by poisoning their food, and this belief, I submit, is well founded. People are often punished for the same offence in our own society; and the fact that the Tswana call it 'sorcery' does not justify our maintaining that it therefore cannot exist at all among them.

14. Alan Harwood

Witchcraft, Sorcery and Social Categories*

Excerpts from Alan Harwood, *Witchcraft, Sorcery and Social Categories among the Safwa*, Oxford University Press for International African Institute, 1970.

Introduction

In a recent volume on witchcraft and sorcery in East Africa (Middleton and Winter, 1963), the editors raise a number of questions about beliefs in wizardry[1] which, they claim, 'have not as yet been raised in any systematic form, let alone answered' (p. 8). One of these questions concerns the reasons why some societies maintain beliefs in both witchcraft and sorcery.

Witchcraft, as defined by Middleton and Winter (p. 3),[2] is 'a mystical and innate power, which can be used by its possessor to harm other people'. Sorcery, on the other hand, is 'evil magic against others'. In further developing this second concept, the editors note that: 'In Africa the most common belief is that sorcerers use "medicines" to harm those against whom they bear ill will' (p. 3). For the purposes of this study, we shall follow Middleton and Winter in their interpretation of these terms and define 'witchcraft' as a belief which attributes misfortune to innate psychic powers and 'sorcery' as a belief attributing misfortune to maleficent physical substances.[3]

Middleton and Winter reason that since either of these beliefs by itself can logically function as an explanation of misfortune and an aid to action in the face of uncertainty, 'one set of beliefs, either those regarding sorcery or those concerning witchcraft, is redundant' (p. 8). They continue,

*I am grateful to the author for the care and trouble he took to write bridge passages linking the excerpts from his book. These are contained in square brackets. He has thus made this highly condensed version of his argument much clearer than I could have rendered it following my usual policy of keeping editorial insertions to a minimum and using them only when it is unlikely that I am making unjustified inferences from authors' statements – *Ed.*

1. We are here adopting Middleton and Winter's use of 'wizardry' as a cover term for both witchcraft and sorcery.

2. These definitions derive from Evans-Pritchard's pioneering study of the Azande (1937).

3. Douglas's recent (1967, pp. 72–3) comments concur with these criteria for defining the distinction between witchcraft and sorcery.

If, however, these two types of ideas were fully substitutable for one another, while we might expect to find them co-existing in an occasional society, we would not expect to find them together in one society after another as is the case in Africa. The only reasonable inference is that they must fit into social systems in different ways (p. 8).

In this study we attempt to make a start in answering Middleton and Winter's important question as to the reasons why beliefs in both witchcraft and sorcery frequently exist simultaneously in the same society by showing how both these beliefs 'fit into' the social system of one African society of which we have first-hand experience: the Mwanabantu tribe[4] of the Safwa dialect group of south-western Tanzania.

In the course of eighteen months' field-work among these people, we observed the importance of both witchcraft and sorcery beliefs as explanations of disease and death and undertook a study of the place of these beliefs in the social life of the Mwanabantu. By describing the different, yet complementary, roles that each of these sets of beliefs plays in processes of social control within the tribe, we show that these beliefs not only 'fit into' the social system in different ways, to use Middleton and Winter's phraseology, but are indeed integral to a scheme of classification which is central to the whole social structure of the tribe. [. . .]

Social Structure

[Social relations in Mwanabantu tribe are characterized, on the one hand, by interactions among certain individuals and groups that are carried out in an idiom of patrilineal descent and an ethic of sharing and unity, and, on the other hand, by interactions that are based on exchange and an ethic of reciprocity.

The first kind of social relations, which (following Barth, 1966, pp. 23–4) we shall call relations of incorporation,] are conceived in terms of the mystical protection and assistance of named patrilineal forebears. This mystical unity, which is demonstrated in ancestor rites, constitutes the minimal expression of incorporation in Mwanabantu society [and applies not only to patrilineally related kinsmen, but also to co-residents of communities and to tribal areas, which consist of several communities

4. The term 'tribe' is defined in the Safwa context as all those communities whose headmen recognize common patrilineal descent. This usage is taken from Evans-Pritchard (1940), who uses it to describe much the same kind of social unit among the Nuer, although he defines the unit in terms of political rights and obligations rather than lineage (p. 5). He notes, however, that Nuer 'habitually' express tribal obligations in a kinship idiom' (p. 143). We have chosen to define the unit as Safwa speakers do, in lineage terms.

socially and politically linked through the patrilineal ties of their respective headmen.] Various economic rights and obligations may also be entailed in this mystical tie, but these economic aspects of the incorporative relationship become gradually attenuated with increasing generational removal from the common ancestor. [As a result, most incorporative groups in Mwanabantu society are solely convening groups, which assemble to express their unity with respect to the ancestors.]

[In contrast to incorporative relations, other social relations in Mwanabantu society are ones in which strict reciprocity is supposed to be maintained, and mutual prestations are the rule. Typically these relations are between non-kinsmen and affines.]

Deviance, Disease and Death

Deviance in Mwanabantu society consists in pursuing one's personal ends to the point of disrupting an incorporative social relationship or weakening a transactional one. [Both these forms of deviance are believed to cause a condition in individuals known as *empongo*. Signifying the weakening or withdrawal of life force (*inzyongoni*),[5] *empongo* may be glossed as both 'disease' and 'death' in English. When a person falls ill, it is incumbent on close kinsmen to consult diviners to discover the deviance which has caused the *empongo*.] In this way, *empongo* serves as an indicator of disrupted social relations.

[To understand better the consequences of this linkage between disease and death (*empongo*) on the one hand, and deviance on the other, we must investigate ideas about the causes of *empongo* in greater detail. For, as we shall see, the classification of the causes of *empongo* parallels the classification of social relationships.

Itonga as a Cause of *Empongo*

[. . .] The term *itonga* [may be] simply defined as 'the power to understand and perform "hidden things".' When asked outright 'What is *itonga*?' (*Itonga lyɛnu*? or *Itonga lili wili*?), trusted informants invariably answered that it is doing things to others without being seen [. . .] – the power to act, unperceived by others.

This defining characteristic of the term leads to its use in two ways.

---

5. The concept of the *inzyongoni*, as found among Safwa-speakers, and the concept of 'life force', ascribed by Tempels (1959) to all 'Bantus', are obviously similar in many respects. Since I did not read Tempels until after I returned from the field, however, I had no way of checking on specific similarities and differences in belief.

First, it may be used in a general sense to describe any situation in which the underlying interpersonal causes are not apparent. It is merely a way of expressing confusion over the precise causality of an event. The range of possible causes entertained by Safwa and by Westerners are of course different, as our present discussion of the causes of disease will indicate; but whenever the cause is unknown, people may speak of *itonga*. The second use of the term derives both from the notion of invisible power and from the idea that in many cases diminutions of [life force] are humanly caused. [...] The logic of these two assumptions leads to the postulation that there are certain humans, the *abitonga* (singular, *omwitonga*), who possess the power to act invisibly and employ this power in interpersonal relations. In short, the term in the first sense refers to an attribute of a situation, while in the second sense it refers to an attribute of a person. These two senses fuse in situations when a diviner has ruled out all other possible causes and indicates that a person with *itonga* is responsible for bringing about a disease or a death.

The power of *itonga* may be inherited patrilineally by both males and females, but not all children need inherit. There is no physical manifestation of this power observable either externally or internally, although post-mortem evidence of the *empongo* called '*endasa*' indicates that the victim was engaged in a mutual battle of *itonga* and thus a possessor of the power himself. The activities which are inspired by *itonga* are carried out at night by the [life force] of the possessor of this power.

There are two kinds of *itonga*, good (*linza*) and bad (*libibi*). Good *itonga* is used for the benefit of a social unit, while bad *itonga* is used against it.

Good *itonga* may be used both to divine and to protect people without this power from the attacks of those who use it in a malicious manner. Thus within every community there is said to be a league of elders who by means of *itonga* not only protect residents from attacks from without but also punish their co-residents for uncooperative behaviour ... Bad *itonga*, on the other hand, is used to introduce foreign substances (*amalila*) into another person's body or into his gardens to diminish their effectiveness. It is also said to enable possessors to 'consume' (*alye*) members of their own lineage.

One kind of *itonga* may be converted to the other so that a person, who has previously used his powers for the benefit of the community, may suddenly employ them to its detriment. Good *itonga* may be converted to bad *itonga* privately by the will of the possessor, but bad *itonga* may be changed to good only by drinking a 'medicine' prepared by a person with stronger powers or by public avowal of a change of heart. It is said that a person whose *itonga* has been converted from bad to good would die should he revert to his old, malevolent ways.

Thus *itonga* itself is a neutral power which can be used in either a moral or immoral fashion. As one informant described people with *itonga,* 'They are like keys, which can both open and close doors'. Employed in either a moral or immoral manner, however, *itonga* is always a matter of conscious intent and the user considered morally responsible. [...]

'Medicine' (*Onizi*) as a Cause of *Empongo*

Onzizi is a general term for substances which alter a vexing situation. It is usually made from plants, although the term may be extended to include oil for a bicycle, insecticide, or spirit for lighting pressure stoves. Its use was also recorded with reference to taxes as 'the medicine of the government (*onzizi gwas εrikali*)' in a speech by the Chief to explain the workings of the central government. These examples are obviously all applications of the term to new situations but are nevertheless revealing of its root meaning. [...] Safwa [...] recognize a functional classification in which medicines are conceived as performing the following tasks (*imbombo*): (1) enhancing already existing interpersonal relations or individual states; (2) repairing (*-lengany-*) a spoiled relation or state; or (3) degrading or spoiling (*-nandy-*) a pre-existing favourable condition or situation. [...]

The use of medicines [of the third category, those aimed at] spoiling a social relationship or another individual's vital state of being, is called *ogulugulu*. The two most frequently discussed practices which fall under the rubric *ogulugulu* are *akulε* ('poisoning') and *atεdyε* ('trapping'). *Akulε* is to swallow a lethal medicine placed in food or beer. (Whether all such medicines are poisonous by empirical standards is questionable but in any case irrelevant to the Safwa classification.) *Atεdyε*, which is the same word used to refer to trapping wild animals, involves spreading a medicine, specifically concocted to kill a particular person, across a path which the intended victim uses. To prepare a trapping medicine, the hair, nail parings, faeces, or earth from a footprint of the victim must be used.

While both 'poisoning' and 'trapping' are directed against people, a third malicious medicine, *ihobε*, is designed primarily to kill livestock. Only after decimating a family's herds is it then believed to attack the herd-owners with a gradually debilitating condition in which the victims are said to eat but never feel full. *Ihobε* medicine is inserted in the bone or horn of a cow or bull, and the whole is buried in the house or cattle byre of the victim.

Ogulugulu is said to be used by those who do not have *itonga* to attack others, although in practice the two powers are employed against entirely different categories of victims. Thus a man generally conceded to possess *itonga* may nevertheless be accused of causing a particular instance of death or disease by means of medicines rather than his mystical power.

Ogulugulu, however, is a double-edged sword. On the one hand, it is considered to be quite a dangerous mode of attack for the user. Because its success depends upon the strength of both the life forces and other medicines involved in the situation, it may conceivably rebound upon its owner at any time. On the other hand, because of the many forces involved, it is relatively easy for a person accused of *ogulugulu* to disclaim responsibility for its results. In cases of *ogulugulu* the responsibility tends to become diffused among several people rather than focused on one (as is the case of attacks by people with bad *itonga*).

The Relationship between *Itonga* and 'Medicines'

Although the effects of malicious medicines are always detected by a diviner and thus a person with *itonga*, the use of medicines itself is not considered to be *itonga*. As one informant put it, 'Medicines are not like *itonga*. We can see medicines.' Medicines thus constitute a 'visible' cause of disease and death in Safwa terms. No matter how mystical or improbable *ogulugulu* may seem to the Western observer as a cause of disease or death, it is a natural and comprehensible one to the Safwa.

Although medicines and *itonga* are conceived as being different by the Safwa, there is nevertheless a relationship between them. Just as medicines enhance the life state of individuals who are ill or spouseless, they may also enhance one's power of *itonga*. Thus an informant described one compound head in the community as having much *itonga* (*itonga ligɔsi* because he had many medicines made from the faeces, urine and footprints of others. When I asked him if it was the medicines which gave the man *itonga*, he replied no, that the man had been born with *itonga* and that the medicines had only strengthened it. This interpretation was later confirmed by other informants. [. . .]

Itonga and Witchcraft, 'Medicines' and Sorcery

Given this summary of Safwa concepts about two causes of disease and death, one is faced with the problem of fitting them into the larger context of African belief. We wish to concentrate here on the Safwa notions of *itonga* and medicine. [. . .] In many respects the *abitonga* clearly resemble the witches of other African societies. Their powers are innate and can harm people, and witchcraft is used to account for misfortunes. Since the Safwa concept of *itonga* thus fulfills these minimal requirements of the definition of witchcraft proposed by Middleton and Winter and recapitulated above in the Introduction, we shall henceforth consider it as a member of this analytic class. We shall nevertheless continue to use the term *itonga* in the Safwa context and only employ 'witchcraft' in discussion of comparative, analytic problems.

In one important respect, however, *itonga* and witchcraft seem quite different. For, apart from the one example of the Nyakyusa (G. Wilson, 1936, pp. 86–9; M. Wilson, 1963, pp. 96–102), anthropologists have tended to portray African witches as by definition antisocial – an attribute which, as we have seen, is not characteristic of the *abitonga*. Our purpose in this section is to show that, appearances to the contrary, the Safwa are not alone with their neighbours the Nyakyusa in believing that the mystical power of 'witches' is morally neutral, and that perhaps the ethnocentric preconceptions of ethnographers are responsible for the dim light in which African 'witches' have traditionally been painted.

In speaking of witchcraft in Africa, one begins almost by necessity with Azande belief. On the matter of the moral implications of Zande witchcraft, Evans-Pritchard is quite clear: 'The Zande phrase "It is witchcraft" may often be translated simply as "It is bad" ... A man must first hate his enemy and will then bewitch him' (1937, p. 107). Elsewhere Evans-Pritchard says,

To Azande themselves the difference between a sorcerer and a witch is that the former uses the techniques of magic and derives his power from medicines, while the latter acts without rites and spells and uses hereditary psycho-psychical powers to attain his ends. *Both alike are enemies of men*, and Azande class them together. (1937, p. 387; emphasis mine.)

Thus according to the ethnographer, it would seem that Zande witches are by definition antisocial.

If we examine Zande belief more closely, however (Evans-Pritchard, 1937, pp. 187, 219), [it] does not appear to differ significantly from that of the Safwa. [According to Zande laymen,] *mangu*, like *itonga*, seems to be a neutral power which can be used to effect both moral and immoral ends. On the one hand it may be used to detect and control malevolent people with mystical power; on the other hand it may be used antisocially to sicken or kill one's enemies (Evans-Pritchard, 1937, p. 187).

Only if we dismiss [this] generally accepted Zande view and espouse the witch-doctors' perspective, does there appear to be a difference between Zande and Safwa ideology. For if the *mangu* of witchdoctors is truly 'another thing' from the *mangu* of witches, as the doctors claim (p. 225), then [the latter] power may indeed have only immoral effects, as Evans-Pritchard avers. Yet if we accept this viewpoint, we are confronted by serious problems in connection with his entire analysis. On the one hand Evans-Pritchard claims that *mangu* is an inherited substance and uses this attribute to differentiate *mangu* from another key Zande concept *ngua*, which is not inherited and achieves its effects through medicines. However, the witch-doctors claim that their *mangu* is not inherited but comes from medicines, an assertion which clearly controverts the basic distinction drawn between *mangu* and *ngua*. Surely something is amiss here. Either Evans-Pritchard's understanding of the basic distinction between *mangu* and *ngua* is erroneous, or the witch-doctors' claim that their *mangu* comes from medicines is specious and demands further investigation. It would seem that Evans-Pritchard accepted the witch-doctors' claim without probing its implications, because he already had a predilection for viewing *mangu* as entirely anti-social and could not accept the generally reported fact that the same *mangu* that 'bewitches' also detects. In short the Zande data would suggest that *mangu* is a morally neutral power, although this fact is somewhat obscured by the ethnographer's interpretation.

Let us turn now from this classic of African witchcraft and sorcery to the work which provides the point of departure for this book – Middleton and Winter's *Witchcraft and Sorcery in East Africa*. In this work, too, the authors seem to prejudge witches adversely. At one point the editors (p. 8) refer to witches as 'personifications of evil, as innately wicked people who work harm against others', and many of the individual contributors to the volume similarly portray witches as anti-social and immoral – even in some cases when their own data suggest another interpretation. [. . .]

This brief and by no means exhaustive survey clearly shows that the Safwa and Nyakyusa are not alone among African peoples in having a concept of a mystical power which can be used for both socially beneficial and maleficent ends. It also apprises one of the dangers of terming this power 'witchcraft' with the load of negative connotations which this term bears in Western tradition. We suggest that viewing a person with mystical power who harms others as necessarily evil is a predilection born of our own Western witchcraft traditions where the category 'witch' necessarily has the attribute 'anti-social' attached to it. Among the Safwa, however, this attribute does not cling to the category *omwitonga*. For the Safwa the question of whether or not a given individual is an *omwitonga* is quite separate from the question of whether he acts anti-socially (*-nandy-*, *-tul-*) or not. [. . .]

Although ethnographers of African peoples have been negligent in describing the use of personal mystical powers for moral purposes, they have long noted the use of medicinal substances for both beneficial and maleficent ends. Again dating from Evans-Pritchard's seminal work, the terminology for the various uses of medicine has become standardized in African ethnographic literature. 'Magic' has been adopted to refer to the use of medicines in general, regardless of purpose; while the term 'sorcery' has been reserved for their use for immoral ends. No standard term has been adopted specifically for the use of medicines to effect moral aims, and Evans-Pritchard himself simply speaks of 'good magic' or 'good medicines'.

Yet neither 'magic' nor 'sorcery' quite conveys the spirit of Safwa belief, since both terms smack of supernaturalism. For the Safwa, medicines do not act in a mysterious way – their action is visible and comprehensible. In fact this is one of the main distinctions between medicines and *itonga*, as we have noted above. The point here is not whether the Safwa 'really' know how medicines work but that they *think* they know. This fact should certainly influence our ethnographic approach to the subject.

This criticism may sound like a mere quibble over labels; and it would be, if labels did not have a profound effect on our thinking about these matters. For by lumping both witchcraft and magic together through the common feature of supernaturalism, ethnocentrically defined, we tend to look for a common logic behind both activities, when this may not be the case. It is manifestly not so for the Safwa, as we shall show.

To avoid the supernatural implications of the traditional terminology, when operating strictly within the Safwa context, we shall speak of the use of medicines and qualify this, as necessary, to indicate either malicious or philanthropic intent. When we move [later] to the analytic level [...], however, we shall perforce adopt the traditional terminology. The reader should nevertheless bear the distinctive quality of Safwa medicines in mind.

Studying Conceptual Categories in their Natural Context

The data for this analysis consist primarily of cases of disease or death which occurred during the ethnographer's stay in Mwanabantu tribe. Cases which antedated this visit were usually collected only if they were conceived as historically related to contemporary events by the actors involved. This procedure was followed to ensure that the data were collected in the natural context which made them meaningful to the

127

participants. Several initial attempts to elicit case material from the past under abnormal conditions – by asking questions in a conversational setting without provocation that was locally meaningful – produced bare facts about accusations or divinations but nothing about the tensions or disputes underlying them.

In the process of collecting these data, the writer attempted to get at least two informants to discuss each case and noted differences in interpretation when these occurred. Although a number of ethnographers of African peoples have noted that a single instance of disease or death may evoke from different members of the community a number of different interpretations as to its cause (Douglas, 1963, pp. 129–30; Evans-Pritchard, 1937, p. 129), none to our knowledge has examined these variant interpretations systematically. This fact is particularly startling because the basic assumption among most writers on the subject of witchcraft is that this presumed cause of death and illness reflects social tensions. Since tensions are usually diffuse, it would seem highly important to collect the variant interpretations of individual instances of disease or death which presumably stimulate expression of these pre-existing tensions. As we shall see in the following analysis of case histories, the data on variant interpretations contribute much to our understanding of the uses to which diagnoses about the causation of disease or death are put.

The matter of collecting variant interpretations raises another point which has often been neglected by many writers on witchcraft and sorcery – namely, the immediate social context of accusations. [...]

For example, Marwick's elaborate statistical analyses (1952, 1963, 1965) distinguish between cases in which the sorcerer's accuser is known and those in which the 'sorcerer [is] designated by diffuse gossip' (Marwick, 1965, p. 106). Yet in cases of the first category we are never informed of how and where an accusation has been made. Most of the older literature on witchcraft and sorcery (e.g. Krige, 1947; Wilson, 1951, 1963; Nadel, 1952) also suffers from this deficiency, although the best recent examples of the so-called 'extended case study' method (e.g. Turner, 1957; Middleton, 1960) contain these relevant details, the full importance of which we shall observe in the following analysis. [...]

Conclusions

Our analysis has shown that disputes in the social field become symbolized by cases of *empongo* and that the cause assigned to the *empongo* depends on the social relationship between the principal parties to the dispute signified. [. . .] There is a clear contrast between the social relationships symbolized by medicines and those symbolized by manifestations of *itonga*. Medicine symbolizes disputes between non-kinsmen of different communities, people between whom no relationship of descent can be established. *Itonga*, on the other hand, symbolizes disputes between actors in those social relationships which can be conceptualized in terms of descent. Thus disputes between patrilineal kinsmen, between residents of the same community (which [. . .] is structured and conceived by Safwa as a compound with the headman as father and compound head) and between residents of communities whose headmen are linked by a patrilineal tie all find expression in terms of *itonga* – that mysterious, unseen, inherent power. [. . .]

What is the effect of diagnosing a case of *empongo* in one way as opposed to another? That is, once a decision has been reached concerning the cause underlying a case of *empongo*, how does this decision influence the behaviour of the people involved? Diagnosing a case of *empongo* in terms of medicines initiates a different chain of behaviour, a different set of social processes and dynamics from that which follows a diagnosis in terms of . . . *itonga*. A diagnosis of medicine typically leads to the covert accumulation of additional medicines. On the other hand, a diagnosis of *itonga* initiates social processes that result in either reconciliation or severance of the incorporative relationship between the disputants. The aetiological categories of *itonga* and medicine thus guide the ways in which disputes are handled because they implicitly associate disputes with particular categories of social relations. The process of labelling makes the relationships between the disputants a salient aspect of the case, and the norms and values of these relationships can then be utilized to regulate the outcome.

In sum, beliefs about *itonga* and medicines would seem to 'fit into' the Mwanabantu social system (to use Middleton and Winter's phrase) as part of a more inclusive classificatory scheme which regulates social relations . . . [These terms, in short,] provide the idiom for expressing the 'negative' aspect (Simmel, 1964, pp. 15–16) of the fundamental social relationships of incorporation and transaction in Mwanabantu society . . .

We are not necessarily suggesting that this particular correlation, found in Mwanabantu society, is universally true, however. In answer to Middleton and Winter's question, we cite Mwanabantu data as illustrative of a general proposition that witchcraft and sorcery beliefs may be utilized in a single society to express conflict involving any two contrasted social categories. In Mwanabantu tribe these happen to be incorporative as opposed to transactional relations; they might be used instead, for example, between males as opposed to females or between age sets as opposed to within age sets. This conclusion must be tested cross-culturally. At the present time, however, comparative work is hampered by two major flaws in the literature.

First, the terms 'witchcraft' and 'sorcery' have for the most part been employed in a thoroughly chaotic manner. (See Turner [1964] for examples of their inconsistent use even within the single symposium edited by Middleton and Winter.) This situation would appear to be due largely to the fact that investigators have often imposed these analytic categories on the data before examining them first to see what distinctions the people under consideration make themselves. Thus Marwick (1965, pp. 81–3), for example, distinguishes witchcraft from sorcery by five criteria *which derive from Zande folk belief.* He then goes on to apply the term 'sorcery' to all beliefs about 'mystical evil-doers' among the Cewa, although some of his own data show that these beliefs share attributes which he claims characterize witchcraft. [Earlier in this analysis] we have cited other examples of this practice. This terminological morass is a formidable obstruction to comparative work. For one must first uncover the ethnographic reality behind each investigator's terminology, and, in so doing, one often brings unresolvable inconsistencies to light.

These inconsistencies are unresolvable largely because of the paucity of recorded case material, which is the second feature of the literature that presently hampers comparative research on this subject. The generalizations which characterize most ethnographic accounts of witchcraft and sorcery do not provide much data for reanalysis. Only in recent ethnographies employing the extended case study method (e.g. Turner, 1957; Middleton, 1960) do we find adequate data for further analysis.

In short, the literature itself reflects certain weaknesses in ethnographic method or reporting which presently obstruct comparative work on the problem of the relationship between witchcraft and sorcery, on the one hand, and social categories, on the other. Nevertheless, the effort required to unravel the existing data from various societies (a project beyond the scope of the present inquiry) would undoubtedly be well repaid. In the meantime, collection in the field of detailed case histories should contribute towards a greater understanding of this interesting relationship.

References

BARTH, F. (1966), *Models of Social Organization*. Royal Anthropological Institute Occasional Paper, no. 23. Glasgow U.P.

DOUGLAS, M. (1963), 'Techniques of sorcery control in Central Africa', in *Witchcraft and Sorcery in East Africa,* John Middleton and E. H. Winter (eds), Routledge & Kegan Paul.

DOUGLAS, M. (1967), 'Witch beliefs in Central Africa', *Africa*, vol. 37, no. 1, pp. 72–80.

EVANS-PRITCHARD, E. E. (1937), *Withcraft, Oracles and Magic among the Azande*, Clarendon Press.

EVANS-PRITCHARD, E. E. (1940), *The Neur,* Clarendon Press.

KRIGE, J. D. (1947), 'The social function of witchcraft', *Theoria*, vol. 1, no. 8, p. 21.

MARWICK, M. G. (1952), 'The social context of Ceŵa witch beliefs', *Africa*, vol. 22, no. 1, pp. 120–35, vol. 22, no. 2, pp. 215–33.

MARWICK, M. G. (1963), 'The sociology of sorcery in a central African tribe', *African Studies*, vol. 22, no. 1, pp. 1–21.

MARWICK, M. G. (1965), *Sorcery in its Social Setting: a Study of the Northern Rhodesian Ceŵa,* Manchester U.P.

MIDDLETON, J. (1960), *Lugbara Religion: Ritual and Authority among an East African People*, Oxford U.P. for the International African Institute.

MIDDLETON, J, and WINTER, E. H. (eds) (1963), *Witchcraft and Sorcery in East Africa,* Routledge & Kegan Paul.

NADEL, S. F. (1952), 'Witchcraft in four African societies: an essay in comparison', *American Anthropologist*, vol. 54, pp. 18–29.

SIMMEL, G. (1964), *Conflict and the Web of Group Affiliations*. Translated from the German by Kurt H. Wolff and Reinhard Bendix, Free Press of Glencoe (paperback edition).

TEMPELS, P. (1959), *Bantu Philosophy*. Translated by C. King, Paris, Présence Africaine.

TURNER, V. W. (1957), *Schism and Continuity in an African Society: a Study of Ndembu Village Life*. Manchester U.P. for the Rhodes-Livingstone Institute.

TURNER, V. W. (1964), 'Witchcraft and sorcery: taxonomy versus dynamics', *Africa*, vol. 34, no. 4, pp. 14–25.

WILSON, G. (1936), 'An African morality', *Africa*, vol. 9, no. 1, pp. 75–99.

WILSON, M. (1951), 'Witch beliefs and social structure', *American Journal of Sociology*, vol. 56, pp. 307–13.

WILSON, M. (1963), *Good Company: a Study of Nyakyusa Age Villages*, Beacon Press (paperback edition).

15. R. W. Wyllie

Introspective Witchcraft among the Effutu

R. W. Wyllie, 'Introspective witchcraft among the Effutu of southern Ghana', *Man*, n.s., vol. 8, no. 1, 1973, pp. 74–9.

Anthropologists have usually approached witchcraft from the point of view of t : accuser, always assuming that the accusation is false. This has made it hard for us to interpret witchcraft confessions. Threats to practise witchcraft against an enemy, these we can interpret as empty boasting. But the idea that a person may sincerely believe himself a witch and go to a diviner to be cured of his state is difficult to understand within the terms of our analysis (Douglas, 1970: p. xxxiv).

At the heart of modern social anthropological theory relating to witch-craft is a form of structural–functional analysis which focuses upon witchcraft accusations and treats these as indices of social tension and vehicles of social change (Marwick, 1970, p. 17). In studies conducted by the leading exponents of this approach (Marwick, 1965; Middleton, 1960; Mitchell, 1956; Turner, 1954) the relations between the principal actors in witchcraft situations are traced and explicated to show the underlying social strains and tensions. Thus we have learned that, in situations where roles are ambiguous or ill-defined, witchcraft accusations may serve as a means of dismantling relations and rejecting obligations which have become redundant; that they may facilitate periodic changes in the social system, as in cases of village or lineage fission; and that they tend to flow down the status hierarchy, or are at least directed against social equals, only rarely being levelled against social superiors.

Despite a certain difference of opinion on matters of research tech-nique, these investigators have continued to regard the *accusation*, rather than the *confession*, as the most significant expression of witch beliefs. This emphasis is understandable in the work of anthropologists who have operated primarily in societies of central and east Africa, where witch-craft 'cases' invariably appear to be initiated by an accuser, who is either the imagined 'victim', or someone acting on his behalf. In parts of west Africa, however, we have reports of witchcraft in which specific ac-cusations against others are rarely made and where the self-accusing witch initiates witchcraft enquiries. This confession-oriented, or intro-spective, form of witchcraft has been described in Ghanaian studies, by

Debrunner (1961), Field (1960) and Ward (1956), while Ruel (1970, pp. 333–50) has shown that it exists among the Banyang of West Cameroon and suggests that it is found also among neighbouring Cross River peoples such as the Ejagham, Efik, and Ibibio. Further indications of the presence of introspective witchcraft in West Africa are offered in studies of the new 'spiritual' or 'prophet-healing' sects, whose leaders perform witch-cleansing functions for persons – mainly women – who confess to involuntary witchcraft activity (Baëta, 1962; Parrinder, 1953; Peel, 1958; Turner, 1967).

To date no serious attempt has been made to interpret introspective witchcraft within the terms of the prevailing structural–functional paradigm. Indeed, the existence of this form of witchcraft appears to have been largely ignored by anthropologists reared on a rich diet of witchcraft accusations, who tend to use terms like 'witchcraft' and 'witch beliefs' in a general sense when they really seem to mean only those beliefs expressed in witchcraft accusations.[1] This assumption that there can be no witchcraft without accusations is, perhaps, most clearly expressed by Lewis (1971, p. 118),

Let us first be clear, however, that although in witchcraft (or sorcery) it is always the bewitched subject who thrusts himself forward to catch our attention and sympathy as the innocent 'victim' of evil machinations, the real victim in any objective sense is the accused 'witch'.

Such a proposition is clearly inappropriate for much West African witchcraft, where it is the self-accusing 'witch', rather than the 'bewitched subject', who engages our attention as prime mover and central actor in witchcraft situations.

Among the Effutu of southern Ghana there is a widespread belief in witchcraft (ogyapa, 'the fire within'), but specific accusations against supposed witches are seldom made.[2] A person who feels himself bewitched may seek protection from his unknown assailant by consulting a traditional priest (okomfo) who will, after consulting the deity whose medium he is, supply anti-witchcraft medicine. Most priests limit their activities to providing a kind of blanket protection for their clients, but there are some whose deities are supposed to be able to do more than

1. General suspicions, however, may be voiced. For example, an okomfo, when asked what he thought about the leaders of the new prophet-healing sects, ventured the opinion that 'they must be witches – no one can heal people the way they say they do, without herbs or medicines, unless they are witches.'

2. Marwick, for example (1972), includes some comments on 'the crucially important question of how witch beliefs decline with increasing social differentiation', but these deal only with the decline of witchcraft accusations.

deter witches. Their anti-witchcraft medicine is so strong that the witch who comes in contact with it becomes ill and can only find relief by coming to the priest to confess. Among the best known of the modern witch-finding deities is *Tigare*, whose cult emerged in the northern part of the Ivory Coast during the second quarter of the present century and reached the Effutu around 1948 (Christensen, 1954). Today there are two branches of this cult operating in Winneba, the chief Effutu town (pop. 25,376 in 1960), although their importance has diminished in recent years. At present 'bewitched' persons and self-accusing 'witches' are more likely to be found attending the prophet-healing sects, of which there are some fifteen in the town. Here the fearful seek the protection of the 'Holy Spirit', while those who believe themselves witches may undergo treatment and exorcism.

Most Effutu believe that witchcraft powers are inherited from parents – the father as well as the mother – and that the witch is active at night, when her spirit (*sunsum*) leaves her body as she sleeps. Witches, it is felt, usually have little or no control over their actions and wish to be rid of their powers. It is this notion of involuntary witchcraft which makes self-accusation and confession a less shameful experience than might otherwise be the case. Treatment of self-accusing witches, whether at the hands of traditional priests, *Tigare* priests, or local prophets, is normally a prolonged affair. A confession may be heard in the course of several visits to shrine or sect and particularly difficult cases may require the 'witch' to spend a period in residence at the shrine or sect. During this time she will be visited frequently by relatives and friends who bring her special items of food prescribed by the priest or prophet. The cost of the treatment is usually borne by the husband of the 'witch', assisted by other kinsfolk. Neither priest nor prophet can, however, guarantee a complete and effective cure in such cases. The former claim to be able to cut the spiritual 'web' or 'wire' upon which a witch moves, but concede that this may be repaired by the witch in the course of time. Prophets see witchcraft as evidence of Satan's power to infect those whose thoughts and hearts are impure; through exorcism the power can be banished, but may return if the person concerned does not keep his spiritual defences in good order.

Most of those who engage in self-accusation and confess to witchcraft are women and it is generally believed (and this is supported by their confessions) that their witchcraft, like that of child-witches, is always destructive and anti-social. Their confessions typically involve assertions that they have caused the death or illness of children (usually their own, but sometimes those of their brothers or sisters) by spiritually devouring the life-force or soul (*nkra*) of the victim. While claims to have killed or harmed siblings are also made, it is only rarely that husbands, co-wives, parents or grandparents are mentioned as targets for malevolent witchcraft by women.[3] Self-accusing child-witches, on the other hand, tend to include almost all close relatives, together with school-mates and friends, in their long and exhaustive list of 'victims'. In contrast to the destructive witchcraft of women and children, that of the few men witches is thought to be constructive and socially beneficial. Most men witches say that they act as 'witch-lawyers', defending those selected as victims by members of the coven, or witch association, in their nightly gatherings. It is usual also for diviners and herbalists to admit to having *ogyapa* and using it constructively.

As in Akan and Banyang witchcraft, Effutu witches say that they assume the forms of animals or reptiles as they go about their business. Moving across their spiritual 'web' or 'wire' in search of prey, they may also appear as bright lights flashing in the sky and, occasionally, may render themselves quite invisible. Few witches claim to have only one *ogyapa* dwelling within themselves, the majority identifying by name several of these entities, e.g. 'spit-fire', 'it will destroy the home', and 'it has no consideration for his mother's son'. Ruel (1970, p. 335) is correct in pointing out the similarities between Akan and Banyang witch beliefs in these respects and my own observations lend support to his view that introspective, or confession-oriented, witchcraft requires a more sophisticated and complex system of witch beliefs than does accusation-oriented witchcraft:

If the witch is the 'other' person, one can be content with a simple representation of his moral character and actions; but such a simple stereotype is no longer appropriate to any self-conscious inquiry about one's own implications in potentially evil actions.

Unlike witchcraft accusations in central and east African societies, the self-accusations of Effutu witches appear to have little to do with the termination of redundant social relations and obligations, or with facilitating periodic, cyclical changes in the social system. We see too that the targets of Effutu witches are mainly children and belong to a quite different social category from that of the typical 'imagined victim' in

---

3. Of thirty-seven confessions of involuntary witchcraft recorded during visits to prophet-healing sects in 1967–8, all but two were made by women. The exceptions were two adolescent boys. Of the sixty-nine 'victims' claimed by the women: 42 were children of the 'witch', 9 were children of her siblings, 5 were children of her co-wives, 8 were siblings of the 'witch', 2 were mothers of the 'witch', 2 were the 'witch's' mother's brothers, 1 was a non-relative.

central and east African witchcraft. The confessions of women, contrary to what we might have expected, tend to flow down the status hierarchy towards children; they rarely flow up the hierarchy towards husband, uncle, aunt, parent and grandparent, or across a status group towards sibling, co-wife, or some other competitor. Does this mean that the introspective witchcraft of the Effutu is not amenable to structural–functional analysis and must await an ethno-psychiatric interpretation, such as that offered by Field (1960) for Akan witchcraft? To this question I would reply in the negative, while conceding that such an interpretation might well prove interesting and valid in its own right.

A useful starting-point in a structural–functional analysis of Effutu witchcraft may be found in the work of Lewis (1970, pp. 293–309; 1971). Here a promising lead is provided by his concept of 'peripheral possession', by which he means the possession of deprived and socially subordinate persons by spirits which are not charged with upholding public morality (1970, p. 294). Lewis argues (1971, p. 32) that the actions of those so possessed represent an indirect strategy of 'mystical attack' whereby persons who are politically impotent seek to manipulate, and exact support from, those in dominant positions:

In its primary social function, peripheral possession thus emerges as an oblique aggressive strategy. The possessed person is ill through no fault of his own. The illness requires treatment which his (or her) master has to provide. In his state of possession the patient is a highly privileged person: he is allowed many liberties with those whom in other circumstances he is required to treat with respect. Moreover, however costly and inconvenient for those to whom his normal status renders him subservient, his cure is often incomplete. Lapses are likely to occur whenever difficulties develop with his superiors. Clearly, in this context, possession works to help the interests of the weak and downtrodden who have otherwise few effective means to press their claims for attention and respect.

The parallels between peripheral possession, as outlined in the passage above, and self-accusation on the part of Effutu witches, are obvious and striking. In both cases little or no blame can be attached to the person concerned, whose behaviour is caused by forces which were unsolicited and beyond his control. Self-accusation of witchcraft, like peripheral possession, typically involves persons in socially subordinate positions who, while they are being cured of the affliction, receive material and moral support from their husbands and relatives. In introspective witchcraft the underlying social strains and tensions are revealed both in the confessions and in the treatment accorded the 'witch' during her rehabilitation. By voicing hostile and destructive sentiments towards children (especially her own), the self-accused woman casts herself in the stereotyped role of 'wicked mother', while the involuntary nature of her misdeeds places her beyond serious criticism. In this personal 'ritual of rebellion' she emphasizes the motherly ideal by making a dramatic statement of its opposite, thereby reminding others (who may be inclined to take it for granted) of the value and importance of her domestic roles. Her cure involves personal recognition, consideration and attention from her husband and relatives who, through their supportive actions, demonstrate their appreciation of her worth and their desire that she should return to her place as a valued member of the household. Here we see that those who 'foot the bill' in terms of moral and material support are the kinds of people who, in central or east Africa witchcraft situations, might well be playing the role of accuser or imagined victim. But while witchcraft accusations often serve to dismantle tension-fraught relationships, self-accusations and confessions represent a less drastic form of attack. Introspective witchcraft, among the Effutu at least, may be seen as a relatively mild form of protest and an appeal for recognition and respect by people in subordinate social positions. This protest and appeal stops short of a demand for independence and is similar in its function to peripheral possession, which:

... expresses insubordination, but usually not to the point where it is desired to immediately rupture the relationship concerned or to subvert it completely. Rather it ventilates aggression and frustration largely within an uneasy acceptance of the established order of things (Lewis, 1971, pp. 120–21).

It is difficult to extend this analysis to other societies in which introspective witchcraft is found because comparative data are generally lacking. Ruel's account of Banyang witchcraft (1970) gives no indication of the kinds of social categories from which self-accusing 'witches' are drawn, nor of any clear pattern in their confessions regarding the identities of typical 'victims'. Ward's short study (1956) together with the various discussions of modern prophet-healing sects do point to the preponderance of women among self-accusers, but provide little information on the confessions themselves, or on the relations between the principal characters in witchcraft situations. Only in Field's book (1960) is found the kind of information necessary for any useful comparison and this strongly suggests that my interpretation of Effutu witchcraft fits the Ashanti case also.[4]

4. Field describes in some detail a number of specific case histories of persons who had engaged in self-accusation and confession. The overwhelming majority of these were women and their confessions showed that children were by far the most popular targets or 'victims'. Only two of the twenty-four women whose cases are discussed claimed that they had used witchcraft against their husbands.

Finally, I end with a suggestion that more attention may have to be paid to introspective witchcraft in future discussions of the impact of urbanization upon witch beliefs. It has been cogently argued by Marwick (1970, pp. 379–81), Mitchell (1965, pp. 201–2) and Swartz (1969, pp. 27–31)* that witchcraft accusations decline in African urban areas, primarily because social relations become more fragmented and increasingly involve 'strangers', between whom hostility can be expressed openly (and even by means of social separation) rather than mystically, as in witchcraft accusations. No doubt this is true, but it would be unwise to assume that all expressions of witch belief decline in the urban situation. We have shown that tension and hostility may be expressed in the idiom of witchcraft without resort to specific accusations against others. In towns like Winneba there are still persons whose subordinate positions and lack of power and status make any open expression of hostility or resentment on their part a somewhat risky business. For married women and children, social separation from their husbands and families is not an easy step to take, even in the more impersonal urban system. Here, self-accusation and confession of witchcraft may be one of the least dangerous and more certain ways of giving vent to frustration and resentment and of pressing one's claim for consideration and respect.[5] I am not in possession of the data needed to determine whether or not the incidence of self-accusation and confession of witchcraft in Winneba has declined in recent years. My impression is that these manifestations of witch beliefs have not declined since 1950, the heyday of the *Tigare* cult in Winneba, and have probably increased. The Effutu themselves are convinced that there are more 'witches' about today than ever before.

References

BAETA, C. G. (1962), *Prophetism in Ghana*, S.C.M. Press.

CHRISTENSEN, J. B. (1954), 'The Tigare cult of West Africa', *Pap. Mich. Acad. Sci. Arts Lett.*, vol. 39, pp. 389–98.

DEBRUNNER, H. (1961), *Witchcraft in Ghana*, Accra, Presbyterian Book Depot.

DOUGLAS, MARY (ed.) (1970), *Witchcraft Confessions and Accusations* (Ass. Social Anthrop. Monogr., vol. 9), Tavistock.

FERNANDEZ, J. W. (1967), *Divinations, Confessions, Testimonies: Zulu Confrontations with the Social Structure*, University of Natal, Institute for Social Research.

FIELD, M. J. (1960), *Search for Security*, Faber and Faber.

*The papers of both Mitchell and Swartz are included in Part Four of these Readings – Ed.

5. Fernandez (1967) has put forward the interesting theory of a swing away from divination towards confession in South African urban areas. This he views as an attempt to restore, by the voluntary release of personal secrets, some form of communal life in the midst of associational relationships between 'strangers'.

LEWIS, I. M. (1970), 'A structural approach to witchcraft and spirit possession', in *Witchcraft Confessions and Accusations*, M. Douglas (ed.) (Ass. Social Anthrop. Monogr., vol. 9), Tavistock.

LEWIS, I. M. (1971), *Ecstatic Religion: an Anthropological Study of Spirit Possession and Shamanism*, Penguin.

MARWICK, M. G. (1965), *Sorcery in its Social Setting: a Study of the Northern Rhodesian Ceŵa*, Manchester U.P.

MARWICK, M. G. (ed.) (1970), *Witchcraft and Sorcery*, Penguin.

MARWICK, M. G. (1972), 'Anthropologists' declining productivity in the sociology of witchcraft', *Am. Anthrop.*, vol. 74, pp. 378–85.

MIDDLETON, J. (1960), *Lugbara Religion*, Oxford U.P.

MITCHELL, J. C. (1956), *The Yao Village*, Manchester U.P.

MITCHELL, J. C. (1965), 'The meaning in misfortune for urban Africans', in *African Systems of Thought*, M. Fortes and G. Dieterlen (eds), Oxford U.P. for International African Institute.

PARRINDER, G. (1953), *Religion in a West African City*, Oxford U.P.

PEEL, J. D. Y. (1958), *Aladura: a Religious Movement among the Yoruba*, Oxford U.P.

RUEL, M. (1970), 'Were animals and the introverted witch', in *Witchcraft Confessions and Accusations*, M. Douglas (ed.) (Ass. Social Anthrop. Monogr., vol. 9), Tavistock.

SWARTZ, M. J. (1969), 'Interpersonal tensions, modern conditions, and changes in the frequency of witchcraft/sorcery accusations', *Afr. urban Notes*, vol. 4, pp. 25–33.

TURNER, H. W. (1967), *African Independent Church*, Clarendon Press.

TURNER, V. W. (1954), *Schism and Continuity in an African Society*, Manchester U.P.

WARD, B. (1956), 'Some observations on religious cults in Ashanti', *Africa*, vol. 26, pp. 47–60.

16. Norman Cohn

The Non-Existent Society of Witches

Excerpts from Norman Cohn, *Europe's Inner Demons*, Chatto–Heinemann for Sussex University Press, 1975, chapter 6 and pp. 251–5.

I

Hundreds of books and articles have been written about the great European witch-hunt of the fifteenth, sixteenth and seventeenth centuries, and during the last few years the subject has received more attention from historians than ever before. But that does not mean that nothing remains to be said. On the contrary, the more is written, the more glaring the disagreements. Were there people who regarded themselves as witches? If so, what did they do, or believe themselves to do? Were they organized, did they hold meetings? What are we to make of covens and sabbats? Again, when and where did the great witch-hunt begin? Who launched it, who perpetuated it, and for what motives? And just how 'great' was it – did the numbers of those executed run into thousands, or into tens of thousands, or into hundreds of thousands? On most of these questions there is still no consensus amongst historians – and even where consensus exists, it is not necessarily correct. [...]

We may start with the stereotype of the witch as it existed at the times when, and the places where, witch-hunting was at its most intense. The profile of that stereotype at least is established beyond all dispute. We possess not only the records of innumerable witch-trials, but also memoirs and manuals by half a dozen witch-hunting magistrates; and the figure of the witch that emerges could not be clearer or more detailed.

A witch was a human being – usually a woman but sometimes a man or even a child – who was bound to the Devil by a pact or contract, as his servant and assistant.

When the Devil first appeared to a future witch he was clad in flesh and blood; sometimes his shape was that of an animal but usually it was that of a man, fully and even smartly dressed. Almost always he appeared at a moment of acute distress – of bereavement, or of utter loneliness, or of total destitution. A typical pattern was that an elderly widow, rejected by her neighbours and with nobody to turn to, would be approached by a man who would alternatively console her, promise her money, scare her, extract a promise of obedience from her, in the end mate with her. The money seldom materialized, the copulation was downright painful, but the promise of obedience remained binding. Formally and irrevocably the new witch had to renounce God, Christ, the Christian religion, and pledge herself instead to the service of Satan; whereupon the Devil set his marks on her – often with the nails or claws of his left hand, and on the left side of the body.

If becoming a witch rarely brought either wealth or erotic pleasure, it had other rewards to offer. A witch was able to perform *maleficium*, i.e. to harm her neighbours by occult means. The pact meant that the Devil would demand this from his servant, but it also meant that he would supply her with supernatural power for the purpose. With the Devil's aid a witch could ruin the life of anyone she chose. She could bring sudden illness, or mental disorder, or maiming accidents, or death, on man, woman or child. She could bedevil a marriage by producing sterility or miscarriages in the woman, or impotence in the man. She could make cattle sicken or die, or cause hail-storms or unseasonable rain to ruin the crops. This was her reward; for a witch's will, like her master's, was wholly malignant, wholly set on destruction.

Witches were believed to specialize in the killing of babies and small children. More than mere malice was at work here – witches needed the corpses for all sorts of reasons. They were cannibals, with an insatiable craving for very young flesh; according to some writers of the time, to kill, cook and eat a baby which had not yet been baptized was a witch's greatest pleasure. But the flesh of infants was also full of supernatural power. As an element in magical concoctions it could be used to kill other human beings, or else to enable a captured witch to keep silent under torture. It could also be blended in a salve which, applied to a witch's body, enabled her to fly.

At regular intervals witches were required to betake themselves to the sacrilegious and orgiastic gatherings known first as 'synagogues', later as 'sabbats'. There were ordinary sabbats, which were usually held on Fridays and were small affairs, involving only the witches of a given neighbourhood; and there were œcumenical sabbats, held with great ceremony three or four times a year, and attended by witches from all quarters. A sabbat was always a nocturnal happening, ending either at midnight or, at the very latest, at cockcrow. As for the locality, it might be a churchyard, a crossroads, the foot of a gallows; though the larger sabbats were commonly held at the summit of some famous mountain in a faraway region.

To attend the sabbat, and in particular to attend the œcumenical sabbat, witches had to cover great distances in very little time. They did so by flying. Having anointed themselves with the magic salve they would fly straight out of their bedrooms, borne aloft on demonic rams, goats, pigs, oxen, black horses; or else on sticks, shovels, spits, broomsticks. And meanwhile the husband or wife would sleep on peacefully, quite unaware of these strange happenings; sometimes a stick laid in the bed would take not only the place but also the appearance of the absent spouse. Thanks to this arrangement, some witches were able to deceive their mates for years on end.

The very numerous accounts of the sabbat differ from one another only in minor details, so it is easy to construct a representative picture. The sabbat was presided over by the Devil, who now took on the shape not of a mere man but of a monstrous being, half man and half goat: a hideous black man with enormous horns, a goat's beard and goat's legs, sometimes also with bird's claws instead of hands and feet. He sat on a high ebony throne; light streamed from his horns, flames spouted from his huge eyes. The expression of his face was one of immense gloom, his voice was harsh and terrible to hear.

The term 'sabbat', like the term 'synagogue', was of course taken from the Jewish religion, which was traditionally regarded as the quintessence of anti-Christianity, indeed as a form of Devil-worship. For the sabbat was above all an assertion of the Devil's mastery over his servants, the witches. First the witches knelt down and prayed to the Devil, calling him Lord and God, and repeating their renunciation of the Christian faith; after which each in turn kissed him, often on his left foot, his genitals or his anus. Next delinquent witches reported for punishment, which usually consisted of whippings. In Roman Catholic countries witches would confess their sins – for instance, attending church – and the Devil would impose whippings as a penance; but everywhere witches who had missed a sabbat, or who had performed insufficient *maleficia*, were soundly whipped. Then came the parody of divine service. Dressed in black vestments, with mitre and surplice, the Devil would preach a sermon, warning his followers against reverting to Christianity and promising them a far more blissful paradise than the Christian heaven. Seated again on his black chair, with the king and queen of the witches on either side of him, he would receive the offerings of the faithful – cakes and flour, poultry and corn, sometimes money.

The proceedings ended in a climax of profanity. Once more the witches adored the Devil and kissed his anus, while he acknowledged their attentions in a peculiarly noxious manner. A parody of the Eucharist was given, in both kinds – but what was received was an object like the sole of a shoe, black, bitter and hard to chew, and a jug full of nauseous black liquid. After this a meal would be served; and often this too would consist of revolting substances – fish and meat tasting like rotten wood, wine tasting like manure drainings, the flesh of babies. Finally, an orgiastic dance, to the sound of trumpets, drums and fifes. The witches would form a circle, facing outwards, and dance around a witch standing bent over, her head touching the ground, with a candle stuck in her anus to serve as illumination. The dance would become a frantic and erotic orgy, in which all things, including sodomy and incest, were permitted. At the height of the orgy the Devil would copulate with every man, woman and child present. Finally he would bring the sabbat to a close by sending the participants off to their homes, with instructions to perform every conceivable *maleficium* against their Christian neighbours.

That is how witches were imagined when and where witch-hunting was at its height. It will be observed that they were thought of as a collectivity: though they perform *maleficium* individually, they are a society, assembling at regular intervals, bound together by communal rites, subject to a rigid, centralized discipline. In every respect they represent a collective inversion of Christianity – and an inversion of a kind that could only be achieved by former Christians. That is why non-Christians, such as Jews and Gypsies, though they might be accused of *maleficium*, were never accused of being witches in the full sense of the term. Witchcraft was regarded as apostasy – and apostasy in its most extreme, most systematic, most highly organized form. Witches were regarded as above all a sect of Devil-worshippers.

II

How did this strange stereotype come into being? Ever since historical research into these matters began, in the second quarter of the nineteenth century, [...] some scholars have argued that a sect of witches really existed, and that the authorities who pursued and tried witches were in effect breaking the local organizations of that sect. [...]

When it was first propounded, [this theory] represented a radical innovation. In the eighteenth and early nineteenth centuries practically no educated person believed that there had ever been a sect of witches; it is only since around 1830 that this has gradually ceased to be taken for granted. Not, of course, that those scholars who have maintained that there really was a sect of witches have claimed that the sect did all those things it was originally believed to do. They have not argued that witches flew through the air to the sabbat, or that the Devil presided over it in

143

corporeal form. But they have argued, and very forcibly, that witches were organized in groups under recognized leaders; that they adhered to a religious cult that was not only non-Christian but anti-Christian; and that they assembled, under cover of night, at remote spots, to perform the rituals of that cult. On this view, what we find in the witch-trials and the writings of witch-hunters represents a distorted perception of groups that really existed, of meetings that physically took place. Propounded by academics at leading universities in Europe and North America, often in works published by university presses, this interpretation has been taken on trust by multitudes of educated people. It still is: when conversation turns to the great witch-hunt, it is assumed more often than not that the hunt must have been directed against a real secret society.

The founding of this school of thought has sometimes been ascribed to the Italian cleric Girolamo Tartarotti-Serbati, who published *Del Congresso Notturno delle Lamie* in 1749, or else to the great German folklorist Jacob Grimm, on account of certain passages in his *Deutsche Mythologie*, first published in 1835; but in both cases wrongly. Tartarotti and Grimm merely drew attention to the fact that folk beliefs dating from pre-Christian times had contributed something to the stereotype. Neither even hinted that the great witch-hunt was directed against an anti-Christian sect. The first modern scholar to advance that view seems to have been Karl Ernst Jarcke. In 1828, when Jarcke was a young professor of criminal law at the University of Berlin, he edited the records of a seventeenth-century German witch-trial for a legal journal, and appended some brief comments of his own. He argued that witchcraft was above all a nature religion that had once been the religion of the pagan Germans. After the establishment of Christianity this religion survived, with its traditional ceremonies and sacraments, as a living tradition amongst the common people; but it took on a new significance. The Church condemned it as Devil-worship, and in the end this view of the matter was adopted even by those who, in secret, still practised it. At the core of the old pagan religion were secret arts for influencing the course of nature – arts which, in the view both of the adherents of that religion and of the Christian clergy, depended on the Devil for their efficacy. As the Christian religion became the religion of the common people, the practice of those arts came to be regarded, and experienced, as a conscious, voluntary service of the evil principle; to be initiated into them was to choose the Devil's service. That explains why, in the later form of witch-belief, anyone adept in those arts was expected to employ them for the purpose of harming others, i.e. was expected to perform *maleficia*.[1] [. . .]

1. K. E. Jarcke, 'Ein Hexenprozess', in *Annalen der deutschen und ausländischen Criminal-Rechts-Pflege*, vol. I, Berlin, 1828 (esp. p. 450).

Jules Michelet, in *La Sorcière* (1862), [. . .] portrays witchcraft as a justified, if hopeless, protest by medieval serfs against the social order that was crushing them. Michelet imagines serfs coming together secretly, at night, to perform ancient pagan dances, with which they blended satirical farces directed against lord and priest. This, he thinks, happened already in the twelfth and thirteenth centuries; in the fourteenth, when both the Church and the nobility were largely discredited, the sabbat turned into a ritualized defiance of the existing social order, epitomized by the Christian God. Michelet calls it 'the black mass'; and at its centre he puts not the Devil, nor a man impersonating the Devil, but a woman – a female serf in her thirties 'with a face like Medea, a beauty born of sufferings, a deep, tragic, feverish gaze, with a torrent of black, untamable hair falling as chance takes it, like waves of serpents. Perhaps, on top, a crown of vervain, like ivy from tombs, like violets of death'.[2]

This romantic figure is the priestess of the cult; indeed, Michelet credits her with inventing, organizing and staging the entire sabbat. [. . .] She sets up a giant wooden figure, hairy, horned, with a great penis. It represents Satan, imagined as 'the great serf in revolt'. [. . .] At the sabbat [she] ritually mates with Satan: before the assembled multitude, she seats herself on his lap and, in a simulated copulation, receives his spirit. Later, after the banquet and the dance, she turns herself into an altar. A man disguised as a demon makes offerings on her prostrate body: corn is offered to Satan to ensure a good harvest, a cake is cooked on her back and distributed as Eucharist. Finally the priestess shouts defiance at the Christian God; while a horde of 'demons' rush out and jump over fires, to cure the assembled peasants of their fear of hell-fire.

Now, none of this figures in any contemporary account of the witches' sabbat. Not one mentions a priestess, or so much as hints that a single woman dominates the ritual. As for the 'black mass' celebrated on a woman's back – that notion was born in an entirely different historical context: the 'affair of the poisons', which took place in Paris around 1680.[3] Nor was the sabbat, even at its first appearance, imagined as a festival of serfs – already in 1460, at Arras, rich and powerful burghers were accused of attending it, along with humbler folk. To give his account even a shadow of plausibility, Michelet has to pretend that all extant accounts of the sabbat date from the period of its decadence, the true, original sabbat being something quite different. The argument is not likely to commend itself to historians. [. . .]

La Sorcière, [. . .] despite the special pleading, the suppression of texts and the fatuities of exegesis on which the interpretation depends, was not

2. J. Michelet, *La Sorcière*, chap. xi (p. 128 in the edition by P. Viallaneix, Paris, 1966).
3. Cf. G. Mongrédien, *Madame de Montespan et l'affaire des poisons*, Paris, 1953.

without influence. For in *La Sorcière* Michelet deployed all those visionary and poetic gifts that make him so compelling a historian. Though he
protested that the book was free from emotional romancing, was indeed
the most unquestionably true of all his works, the opposite is the case. *La
Sorcière* was written when Michelet was sixty-four, and it was written
fast: the two chapters on the sabbat took a day each, almost the whole
book was finished in two months.[4] Driven by a passionate urge to
rehabilitate two oppressed classes – women, and the medieval peasantry –
the aging romantic radical had neither time nor desire for detailed research. The result was an imaginative creation of such power that it has
continued to be reprinted, and read, and taken seriously, for generation
after generation. [. . .]

But *La Sorcière* also contains hints of a different interpretation. In
passing, Michelet suggests that the sabbat was really the celebration of a
fertility cult, aimed at securing abundance of crops. At the hands of later
scholars this notion was to undergo some startling elaborations.

In his notes to *The Waste Land*, T. S. Eliot lists, as one of the works to
which he was most indebted, *The Golden Bough* by Sir James Frazer – 'a
work of anthropology ... which has influenced our generation pro-
foundly'. Unlike some of Eliot's other notes, this one was perfectly
serious: first published in 1890, reissued with enlargements in twelve
volumes between 1907 and 1915, *The Golden Bough* had indeed launched
a cult of fertility cults. At least in the English-speaking world it became
fashionable to interpret all kinds of rituals as derivatives of a magic
originally performed to encourage the breeding of animals and the
growth of plants, and to see in the most diverse gods and heroes so many
disguises for the spirit of vegetation. It was to be expected that this kind
of interpretation would be applied also to the history of European witchcraft; and so it was, in *The Witch-Cult in Western Europe*, by Margaret
Murray. The year was 1921, and the influence of *The Golden Bough* was at
its height. (*The Waste Land*, with Eliot's comment, appeared the following year.)[5]

The impact of *The Witch-Cult in Western Europe* has been extraordinary. For some forty years (1929–68) the article on 'Witchcraft' in successive editions of the *Encyclopaedia Britannica* was by Margaret Murray
and simply summarized the book's argument, as though it were a matter
of established fact. By 1962 a scholar was moved to comment with
dismay: 'The Murrayites seem to hold ... an almost undisputed sway at

4. P. Viallaneix, preface to *La Sorcière*, pp. 17–18.

5. Margaret Murray first expounded her views a few years earlier, in two articles in *Folk-
Lore*, vols. XXVIII (1917) and XXXI (1920).

the higher intellectual levels. There is, amongst educated people, a very widespread impression that Professor Margaret Murray has discovered the true answer to the problem of the history of European witchcraft and has proved her theory'.[6] Since that was written the Murrayite cause has received formidable reinforcements. The Oxford University Press, the original publishers of the *Witch-Cult*, re-issued it in 1962 as a paperback, which has been frequently reprinted since and is still selling well. In a foreword to this new edition the eminent medievalist Sir Steven Runciman praises the thoroughness of the author's scholarship and makes it plain that he fully accepts her basic theory. Some leading historians of seventeenth-century England have shown themselves equally trusting. Even amongst scholars specializing in the history of witchcraft the book has exercised and – as we shall see – continues to exercise considerable influence. It has also inspired a whole library of new works, which have disseminated the doctrine amongst more or less serious readers. It is significant that in Britain even that respectable series, Pelican Books, having published an anti-Murrayite work on witchcraft by Professor Geoffrey Parrinder in 1958, replaced it in 1965 by the Murrayite work of the late Pennethorne Hughes. More dramatically, the *Witch-Cult* and its progeny have stimulated the extraordinary proliferation of 'witches' covens' in Western Europe and the United States during the past decade, culminating in the foundation of the Witches International Craft Association, with headquarters in New York. In 1970 the association, under the leadership of Dr Leo Martello and his 'high priestess' Witch Hazel, held 'the world's first public Witch-In for Halloween' in Central Park. Even Margaret Murray, one imagines, would have been surprised by the development of the Witches' Liberation Movement, with its plans for a Witches' Day Parade, a Witches News Service, a Witches' Lecture Bureau and a Witches' Anti-Defamation League.[7]

The argument presented in the *Witch-Cult* and elaborated in its successor *The God of the Witches* (1933) can be summarized as follows:

Down to the seventeenth century a religion which was far older than Christianity persisted throughout Western Europe, with followers in every social stratum from kings to peasants. It centred on the worship of a two-faced, horned god, known to the Romans as Dianus or Janus. This 'Dianic cult' was a religion of the type so abundantly described in *The Golden Bough*. The horned god represented the cycle of the crops and the seasons, and was thought of as periodically dying and returning to life. In society he was represented by selected human beings. At national level

6. E. Rose, *A Razor for a Goat*, Toronto, 1962, pp. 14–15.
7. Cf. Florence Hershman, *Witchcraft U.S.A.*, New York, 1971, pp. 149–56.

these included such celebrated personages as William Rufus, Thomas à Becket, Joan of Arc and Gilles de Rais, whose dramatic deaths were really ritual sacrifices carried out to ensure the resurrection of the god and the renewal of the earth. At village level the god was represented by the horned personage who presided over the witches' assemblies. Hostile observers, such as inquisitors, naturally took this personage to be, or at least to represent, the Devil; so that to them witchcraft seemed a form of Satan-worship. In reality, the witches were simply worshipping the pre-Christian deity Dianus; and if they appeared to kiss their master's behind, that was because he wore a mask which, like the god himself, had two faces.

The preservation of the Dianic cult was largely the work of an aboriginal race, which had been driven into hiding by successive waves of invaders. These refugees were of small stature – which was the reality behind stories of 'the little people', or fairies. Shy and elusive, they nevertheless had sufficient contact with the ordinary population to transmit the essentials of their religion. The witches were their disciples and intellectual heirs.

The organization of the Dianic cult was based on the local coven, which always consisted of thirteen members – twelve ordinary members, male and female, and one officer. The members of a coven were obliged to attend the weekly meetings, which Dr Murray calls 'esbats', as well as the larger assemblies, or sabbats proper. Discipline was strict: failure to attend a meeting, or to carry out the instructions given there, was punished with such a beating that sometimes the culprit died. The resulting structure was remarkably tough: throughout the Middle Ages the Dianic cult was the dominant religion, Christianity little more than a veneer. It was only with the coming of the Reformation that Christianity achieved enough hold over the population to launch an open attack on its rival – the result being the great witch-hunt.

Margaret Murray was not by profession a historian but an Egyptologist, archaeologist and folklorist. Her knowledge of European history, even of English history, was superficial and her grasp of historical method was non-existent. In the special field of witchcraft studies, she seems never to have read any of the modern histories of the persecution; and even if she had, she would not have assimilated them. By the time she turned her attention to these matters she was nearly sixty, and her ideas were firmly set in an exaggerated and distorted version of the Frazerian mould. For the rest of her days (and she lived to 100) she clung to those ideas with a tenacity which no criticism, however well informed or well argued, could ever shake.

There has been no lack of such criticism. George Lincoln Burr, Cecil L'Estrange Ewen, Professor Rossell Hope Robbins, Mr Elliot Rose, Professor Hugh Trevor-Roper, Mr Keith Thomas are amongst those who, from the 1920s to the 1970s, have either weighed the theory and found it wanting, or else have dismissed it as unworthy of consideration. But other scholars have taken a different view and have maintained that beneath its manifest exaggerations, the theory contains a core of truth. The reason is given by Arno Runeberg in his book *Witches, Demons and Fertility Magic* (1947). He points out that some of the accounts of witches' assemblies quoted by Murray have no fantastic features but are perfectly plausible. The witches go to and from the sabbat not by flying but on foot or on horseback: the 'Devil' has nothing supernatural about him but sits at the head of the table like an ordinary man; the meal is quite unremarkable; the participants even specify who supplied the food and drink. Runeberg concludes: 'That such drinking-bouts should be only hallucinations ... is indeed curious. Neither is it probable that the persecutors by leading questions would have caused people to tell such stories'.[8] According to this view these commonplace happenings, themselves perhaps neither very frequent nor very widespread, represent the reality around which fantasies clustered, gradually building up the whole phantasmagoria of the witches' sabbat as we find it in other and better known accounts. It would be a powerful argument if the accounts quoted by Murray were really as sober as they appear to be – but are they? The only way to find out is to examine her sources in their original contexts – a tiresome task, but one which is long overdue.

The relevant passages in the *Witch-Cult* carry references to some fifteen primary sources, mostly English or Scottish pamphlets describing notorious trials. Now, of all these sources only one is free from manifestly fantastic and impossible features – and even in that one the Devil, though 'a bonny young lad with a blue bonnet', has the conventional requirements of a cold body and cold semen, and gladly mates with a witch aged eighty.[9] To appreciate the true import of the other sources one has only to compare [...] what Murray quotes with what she passes over in silence. [...]

The Somerset trials of 1664 are regarded by Murray as particularly illuminating. She quotes from the evidence of Elizabeth Styles:*

*In this and the following quotations I have modernized the spelling and replaced a few obsolete words by their modern equivalents. N.C.

8. A. Runeberg, *Witches, Demons and Fertility Magic*, Helsingfors, 1947, pp. 230–1.

9. R. Burns Begg, 'Notice of Trials for Witchcraft at Crook of Devon, Kinross-shire in 1662', in *Proceedings of the Society of Antiquaries of Scotland*, vol. XXII, Edinburgh, 1888, pp. 212 *et seq.*, 223.

At their meeting they have usually wine and good beer, cakes, meat or the like. They eat and drink really when they meet in their bodies, dance also and have music. The man in black sits at the higher end, and Anne Bishop usually next to him. He uses some words before meat, and none after, his voice is audible, and very low.[10]

She does not quote the sentence immediately preceding: 'At every meeting the Spirit vanishes away, he appoints the next meeting place and time, and at his departure there is a foul smell.' Nor is there any mention of certain other details supplied by the same witness. For Elizabeth Styles said that, while the Devil sometimes appeared to her as a man, he usually did so in the form of a dog, a cat or a fly; as a fly, he was apt to suck at the back of her head. He also provided his followers with oil with which to anoint their foreheads and wrists – which enabled them to be carried in a moment to and from the meetings. On the other hand, Elizabeth added that sometimes the meetings were attended by the witches' spirits only, their bodies remaining at home.[11]

A Scot herself, Murray draws heavily on the records of Scottish trials for her material. A typical source, covering both the feast at the sabbat and the return from it, is the confession of Helen Guthrie, one of the alleged witches tried at Forfar in 1661. The *Witch-Cult* gives the following excerpts:

They went to Mary Rynd's house and sat down together at the table, the devil being present at the head of it; and some of them went to John Benny's house, he being a brewer, and brought ale from hence ... and others of them went to Alexander Hieche's and brought aqua vitae from thence, and thus made themselves merry; and the devil made much of them all, but especially of Mary Rynd, and he kissed them all except the said Helen herself, whose hand only he kissed; and she and Jonet Stout sat opposite one to another at the table.[12]

Herself, Isobell Shyrie and Elspet Alexander, did meet together at a house near to Barrie, a little before sunset, after they had stayed in the said house about the space of an hour drinking three pints of ale together, they went forth to the sands, and there three other women met them, and the Devil was there present with them all ... and they parted so late that night that she could get no lodging, but was forced to lie at a dike side all night.[13]

All very normal – until one looks at the original source and discovers what those sets of dots represent. With the lacunae filled in the passages read as follows:

10. M. Murray, *The Witch-cult in Western Europe*, Oxford, 1962, p. 140.

11. J. Glanvill, *Sadducismus Triumphatus*, London, 1689, pp. 353–4.

12. Murray, op. cit., p. 141.

13. Ibid., p. 98.

... and brought ale from hence, and they (went) through at a little hole like bees, and took the substance of the ale ...

... and the Devil was there present with them all, in the shape of a great horse; and they decided on the sinking of a ship, lying not far off from Barrie, and presently the said company appointed herself to take hold of the cable tow, and to hold it fast until they did return, and she herself did presently take hold of the cable tow, and the rest with the Devil went into the sea upon the said cable, as she thought, and about the space of an hour thereafter, they returned all in the same likeness as before, except that the Devil was in the shape of a man upon his return, and the rest were sorely fatigued ...[14]

After this it comes as no surprise to learn that another member of the group was accustomed to turn herself into a horse, shod with horseshoes, and in that guise transport her fellow witches, and even the Devil himself, to and from the sabbat – with the result that the following day she was confined to bed with sore hands. Nor is it unexpected that the Forfar witches should sometimes have had less ordinary meals than those described above. In the event they confessed to digging up the corpse of a baby, making a pie of its flesh, and eating it; the purpose being to prevent themselves from ever confessing to their witchcraft. [. . .]

Similar use is made of Isobel Gowdie's confession (or rather confessions, for under increasing pressure she made four) at Auldearn, in Nairn, in 1662:

We would go to several houses in the night time. We were at Candlemas last in Grangehill, where we got meat and drink enough. The Devil sat at the head of the table, and all the Coven about. That night he desired Alexander Elder in Earlseat to say the grace before meat, which he did; and is this: 'We eat this meat in the Devil's name' (etc.) And then we began to eat. And when we had ended eating, we looked steadfastly to the Devil, and bowing ourselves to him, we said to the Devil, We thank thee, our Lord, for this. – We killed an ox, in Burgie, about the dawning of the day, and we brought the ox with us home to Aulderne, and feasted on it.[15]

The simple dash between the two stories conceals much, including the following items:

All the coven did fly like cats, jackdaws, hares and rooks, etc., but Barbara Ronald, in Brightmanney, and I always rode on a horse, which we would make of a straw or a bean-stalk. Bessie Wilson was always in the likeness of a rook ... (The Devil) would be like a heifer, a bull, a deer, a roe, or a dog, etc., and have dealings with us; and he would hold up his tail while we kissed his arse.[16]

14. (G. R. Kinloch, ed.), *Reliquiae Antiquae Scoticae, illustrative of civil and ecclesiastical affairs*, Edinburgh, 1848, pp. 121–3.

15. Murray, op. cit., pp. 141–2.

16. R. Pitcairn, *Criminal Trials ...*, Edinburgh, 1833, vol. III, Appendix, p. 604; cf. pp. 609–11.

Isobel Gowdie had much more to say. When she and her associates went to the sabbat they would place in the bed, beside their husbands, a broom or a three-legged stool, which promptly took on the appearance of a woman. At the sabbat they made a plough of a ram's horn and yoked frogs to it, using grass for the traces. As the plough went round the fields, driven by the Devil with the help of the male officer of the coven, the women followed it, praying to the Devil that the soil might yield only thistles and briars. [...]

Murray is of course aware of these fantastic features – but she nevertheless contrives, by the way she arranges her quotations, to give the impression that a number of perfectly sober, realistic accounts of the sabbat exist. They do not; and [...] the stories of witches' sabbats adduced by Murray [contain such an abundance of manifestly impossible features that they cannot be taken seriously as evidence of anything that physically happened.] As soon as the methods of historical criticism are applied to her argument that women really met to worship a fertility god, under the supervision of the god's human representatives, it is seen to be just as fanciful as the argument which Michelet had propounded, with far greater poetic power, some sixty years earlier. [...]

There is a further reason why the notion of a secret society of witches cannot be satisfactorily explained by postulating the real existence of such a society. [...] Present-day anthropologists have found very similar notions firmly embedded in the world-views of 'primitive' societies in various parts of the world. Bands of destructive witches who kill human beings, especially children; who travel at night by supernatural means; and who foregather in remote spots to devour their victims – these crop up again and again in anthropological literature. But anthropologists are agreed that these bands exist in imagination only; nobody has ever come across a real society of witches. And that indeed is the nub: from Jarcke ... onwards, the tradition we have been considering has suffered from the same defect, of grossly underestimating the capacities of human imagination. There existed, [in fact,] two completely different notions of what witches were.

For the peasantry, until its outlook was transformed by new doctrines percolating from above, witches were above all people who harmed their neighbours by occult means; and they were almost always women. When the authors of the *Malleus Maleficarum* produced quasi-theological reasons to explain why witches were generally female, they were simply trying to rationalize something which peasants already took for granted.[17]

17. *Malleus Maleficarum*, part I, question vi.

Why was it taken for granted? The answer has sometimes been sought in the circumstances of village life in the early modern period. It has been argued that, as the traditional sense of communal responsibility declined, elderly women who were unable to provide for themselves came to be felt as a burden which the village was no longer willing to shoulder;[18] or else that spinsters and widows increased so greatly in number that they came to be felt as an alien element in a society where the patriarchal family still constituted the norm.[19] Such factors may well have provided an additional impetus for witch-hunting in the sixteenth and seventeenth centuries, but they certainly do not fully account for the notion that the witch is, typically, a woman. At least in Europe, the image of the witch as a woman, and especially as an elderly woman, is age-old, indeed archetypal.

For centuries before the great witch-hunt the popular imagination, in many parts of Europe, had been familiar with women who could bring down misfortune by a glance or a curse. It was popular imagination that saw the witch as an old woman who was the enemy of new life, who killed the young crops, caused impotence in men and sterility in women, blasted the crops. And it was also popular imagination that granted the witch a chthonic quality. The *Malleus* again reflects a popular, not a theological, belief when it recommends that a witch who is to be taken into custody should first be lifted clear of the earth, to deprive her of her power.[20]

The other notion of the witch came not from the peasantry but from bishops and inquisitors and – to an ever-increasing degree – from secular magistrates and lawyers. Admittedly, rural magistrates were often themselves of peasant origin; but they were literate, which meant that a view of witchcraft which was enshrined above all in written texts was current amongst them, and in this view a witch was above all a member of a secret, conspiratorial body organized and headed by Satan. Such a witch could just as well be a man as a woman, and just as well young as old; and if, in the end, most of those condemned and executed as witches were still elderly women, that was the result of popular expectations and demands. [...] The earliest witch-trials were quite free from such one-sidedness; and still at the height of the great witch-hunt, in the sixteenth and seventeenth centuries, many men, young women and even children were executed.

18. A. Macfarlane, *Witchcraft in Tudor and Stuart England*, London, 1970, pp. 161, 205–6; K. V. Thomas, *Religion and the Decline of Magic*, London, 1971, pp. 560–7.

19. H. C. E. Midelfort, *Witch-Hunting in Southwestern Germany*, Stanford University Press, 1972, pp. 184–5.

20. *Malleus Maleficarum*, part III, question viii.

The complaint against these people was not primarily or necessarily that they harmed their neighbours by occult means but that they attended the sabbat. Collective worship of the Devil in corporeal, usually animal form; sexual orgies which were not only totally promiscuous but involved mating with demons; communal feasting on the flesh of babies – these constituted the essence of witchcraft as it was imagined and formulated by educated specialists during the fifteenth, sixteenth and seventeenth centuries. Practices which in earlier centuries had been vaguely ascribed to certain heretical groups, notably the Waldensians, now constituted an independent offence, which in time came to be called the *crimen magiae*. Admittedly, *maleficium* was not excluded – at the end of the sabbat the Devil commonly required his followers to report on the harm they had recently brought about, and instructed them on the harm they were expected to do during the coming weeks or months. Nevertheless, in this version of witchcraft, *maleficium* was of secondary importance. Here a witch was not simply a malicious, dangerous person but an embodiment of evil: above all, an embodiment of apostasy.

Left to themselves, peasants would never have created mass witch-hunts – these occurred only where and when the authorities had become convinced of the reality of the sabbat and of nocturnal flights to the sabbat. And this conviction depended on, and in turn was sustained by, the inquisitorial type of procedure, including the use of torture. When suspected witches could be compelled, by torture, to name those whom they had seen at the sabbat, all things became possible: the mayor and town councillors and their wives were just as likely to be accused as were peasant women.

The great witch-hunt itself lies outside the scope of this book, but a few brief comments are called for. It reached its height only in the late sixteenth century, and it was practically over by 1680 – with the trials at Salem, Massachusetts, in 1692 as a belated epilogue. It was an exclusively western phenomenon – eastern Europe, the world of Orthodox Christianity, was untouched by it. Within western Europe, no distinction can be drawn between Roman Catholic and Protestant countries – both were equally involved. On the other hand, not all areas of western Europe were equally involved. Spain, Italy, Poland, the Low Countries, Sweden experienced mass witch-hunts, but only in limited areas and for limited periods. England saw little of mass witch-hunts, though some hundreds of women were executed (by hanging, not burning) for doing harm by occult means. In Scotland, France, the German states, the Swiss Confederation, mass witch-hunts were carried out with great intensity and ferocity. Yet even there, the centres of activity constantly shifted: an area which had never burned a single witch would suddenly begin to burn witches by the dozen; another, which had been burning witches for years, would suddenly stop; in some areas little or no witch-hunting took place. Everything depended on the attitude of the authorities – the prince, or the town council, or the magistrates. The authorities in turn could be influenced to take up witch-hunting by the writings of such codifiers as Bodin or Del Rio, or by the example of neighbouring states. They could also be influenced to abandon it by writings of such men as Weyer or Spee, or by some particular paradox arising from the trials – not least the risk that they themselves would be accused of attending the sabbat.

Many attempts have been made to estimate the total number of individuals burned as witches in Europe during the fifteenth, sixteenth and seventeenth centuries, but it is a fruitless enterprise: the records are too defective. Some of the best-known estimates, which put the figure at some hundreds of thousands, are fantastic exaggerations. On the other hand those who would argue, from the statistics for English witch-trials, that there never was a great European witch-hunt at all are also in error. For certain areas of the European mainland reasonably complete records do exist, and some of these have been studied in detail. They show beyond all possible doubt that the great witch-hunt is no myth. [...]

Dr H. D. Erik Midelfort has made a detailed study of south-west Germany.[21] He calculates that in a period of little more than a century, from 1561 to 1670, at least 3,229 persons were executed in that area.[22] The figures for particular places are even more startling. In the little town of Wiesensteig, sixty-three women were burned in a single year, 1562.[23] In the small, secluded territory of Obermarchtal, with a population of some 700 poor peasants, in the three years 1586–8 forty-three women and eleven men were burned, i.e. nearly 7 per cent of the population.[24] Such massive killings occurred only when supposed witches were forced by torture to denounce others whom they had seen at the sabbat. Midelfort gives an example: 'When Ursula Bayer denounced eight other persons, we know that four of them were executed with her on 16 June 1586, and two later; only two escaped trial and torture'.[25] In June 1631 the small town of Oppenau, in Württemberg, with a population of 650, was drawn into the witch-hunt that had been proceeding in the neighbouring territories for a couple of years. In less than nine months fifty persons had been

21. Midelfort, op. cit.
22. Ibid., p. 32.
23. Ibid., p. 89.
24. Ibid., pp. 96–8.
25. Ibid., p. 97.

executed in eight mass burnings, and 170 further denunciations were awaiting consideration by the court – at which point the judges began to have doubts about the correctness of their proceedings.[26] It would be easy, but pointless, to multiply the examples; those given are enough to show how untypical the English case was. The decisive factors are not in doubt: really massive witch-hunts occurred only where the concept of witchcraft included the sabbat and where judicial procedure included torture – and in England, save in rare instances, neither circumstances applied.

The great witch-hunt is only now beginning to be studied on a European scale, but already this much is certain: it was not, in the main, a cynical operation. Financial greed and conscious sadism, though by no means lacking in all cases, did not supply the main driving force: that was supplied by religious zeal. Even torture appeared, to most of those who employed it, not only legitimate but divinely required. The witch was regarded as being not only allied to the Devil but in the grip of a demon, and the purpose of torture was to break that grip. Each trial was a battle between the forces of God and the forces of the Devil – and the battle was fought, *inter alia*, for the witch's own soul: a witch who confessed and perished in the flames had at least a chance of purging his or her guilt and achieving salvation. On the other hand, it was held that God would give an innocent person strength to withstand any amount of torture. And it is true that the few – about one in ten, at the height of the witch-hunt – who could hold out were usually set free.[27] [...]

The great witch-hunt can in fact be taken as a supreme example of a massive killing of innocent people by a bureaucracy acting in accordance with beliefs which, unknown or rejected in earlier centuries, had come to be taken for granted, as self-evident truths. It illustrates vividly both the power of the human imagination to build up a stereotype and its reluctance to question the validity of a stereotype once it is generally accepted.

Much work remains to be done before the dynamics of the great witch-hunt can be fully understood. Meanwhile it is at least possible to suggest one fruitful line of enquiry. When operating separately the two different notions about witches inspired two very different kinds of witch-trial; but they could also be combined, and this is what commonly happened at the

26. Ibid., p. 137.

27. The point is well documented in E. Delcambre, 'Les procès de sorcellerie en Lorraine. Psychologie des juges', in *Tijdschrift voor rechtsgeschiedenis*, vol. XXI, Groningen, Brussels, The Hague, 1953, pp. 389–420; see also the same author's 'La psychologie des inculpés lorrains de sorcellerie', in *Review historique de droit français et étranger*, series 4, vol. XXXII, Paris, 1954, pp. 383–404, 508–26.

height of the great witch-hunt. A certain collusion, no doubt unconscious, occurred between the peasantry on the one hand and the authorities – and notably the magistrates – on the other. An old woman is arrested for witchcraft. At once, neighbours come forward to accuse her of harming their children or their cattle – whereupon the magistrates compel her to admit not only to those acts of *maleficium* but also to having entered into a pact with a demon, having copulated with him for years and having formally renounced Christianity. They also compel her to speak of the sabbat and to name those whom she saw there.[28] Behind the accusations from below and the interrogations from above lie divergent preoccupations and aims. Just how they interlocked deserves detailed examination. It might well provide the key to what still remains one of the most mysterious episodes in European history.

28. For a particularly clear example, studied in detail, see P. Villette, 'La sorcellerie à Douai', in *Mélanges de Science religieuse*, vol. 18, Lille, 1961, pp. 124–73.

17. Keith Thomas

The Decline of Witchcraft Prosecutions

Keith Thomas, *Religion and the Decline of Magic*, Weidenfeld & Nicolson and Charles Scribner's Sons, 1971, Penguin Books, 1973, chapter 18.

They say miracles are past; and we have our philosophical persons to make modern and familiar, things supernatural and causeless.

W. Shakespeare, *All's Well that Ends Well.* II, iii

The later seventeenth century saw the decline of witch-prosecution in England and the spread of scepticism about the very possibility of the offence. Long before the repeal of the Witchcraft Act in 1736 it had become increasingly difficult to mount and sustain a successful prosecution in the courts. The explanation for this lies in the changed attitude of the educated classes who provided the judges, lawyers, Grand Jurymen and Petty Jurymen, whose collective resistance effectively brought the trials to an end.

But how is this change of attitude to be accounted for? Here we encounter the most baffling aspect of this difficult subject. For the revolution in opinion about witchcraft was almost as silent as the decay in the intellectual prestige of astrology. The topic inspired a continuous flow of controversial writing, it is true. But the arguments employed on either side hardly changed at all. What has to be explained is why it should have taken over a hundred years for the case urged by the sceptics to become generally acceptable.

The sceptical argument was not necessarily linked to any new assumptions about the natural world. On the contrary much of the debate was deliberately conducted within a framework of Protestant fundamentalism. The leading sceptical writers – Reginald Scot, Samuel Harsnet, Sir Robert Filmer, Thomas Ady, John Wagstaffe, John Webster, Francis Hutchinson – all urged that the 'continental' conception of witchcraft as devil-worship was unacceptable because it had no Biblical justification. This type of witchcraft was not to be found in the Scriptures, and, as Webster emphasized, 'What the Scriptures have not revealed of the power of the kingdom of Satan is to be rejected and not to be believed'.[1] Of

1. J. Webster, *The Displaying of Supposed Witchcraft* (1677), p. 47.

158

course, there was Exodus, xxii, 18, which declared that a witch should not be suffered to live. This was the text which led John Wesley to assert that 'giving up witchcraft is, in effect, giving up the Bible'. But the sceptics urged that these Old Testament witches had not been devil-worshippers; they were merely wizards and diviners; and the harm they did their enemies was by the use of poisons and similar natural means. Most of them were frauds, who deserved punishment for their impostures, but were incapable of making a corporal pact with Satan. The modern myth of devil-worship, with its night-flying and its sabbaths, was a gross invention of 'friarly authors', an amalgam of Papal fabrication with ancient pagan superstition.[2] In elaborating this theme the sceptics were essentially continuing the traditional Protestant onslaught upon the relics of paganism to be found in the teachings and practice of the Roman Church.

But in arguing that the popular image of Satan lacked scriptural foundation, the sceptics could also draw powerful reinforcement from a new current in contemporary philosophy. Materialists, like Thomas Hobbes and the followers of Descartes, rejected the whole concept of incorporeal substances as a contradiction in terms. By doing so they effectively jettisoned demons from the natural world. Hobbes did not deny that there could be spirits whose bodies were too fine to be perceived by human beings. But he emphatically asserted that they could never be capable of possessing men's bodies or assuming human form. Most demons, he declared, were 'but idols or phantasms of the brain'. Locke did not say that there were no spirits, but he thought it impossible to arrive at any certain knowledge of them.[3] For the opponents of witch-craft prosecution it was a cardinal tenet that the Devil had no temporal power; he could not assume bodily form and his assaults were purely spiritual.[4] Since Satan was a relatively inconspicuous figure in the Old Testament, a plausible case for this view could be made on purely Biblical

2. Scot, *Discoverie*, esp. V.ix; VI.i, ii, v; VII.i; S. Harsnet, *A Declaration of Egregious Popish Impostures* (1603), pp. 132–8; J. Gaule, *Select Cases of Conscience touching Witches and Witchcrafts* (1646), p. 57; (Sir R. Filmer), *An Advertisement to the Jury-Men of England touching Witches* (1653); Ady; J. W(agstaffe), *The Question of Witchcraft Debated* (1669); Webster, op. cit., esp. pp. 57–8; B. B(ekker), *The World Turned Upside Down* (Eng. trans., 1700); F. Hutchinson, *An Historical Essay concerning Witchcraft* (1718: 2nd edn, 1720), chap. xii; *A Discourse on Witchcraft occasioned by a Bill now Depending in Parliament* (1736); J. Juxon, *A Sermon upon Witchcraft* (1736), cf. *Journal of John Wesley*, ed. N. Curnock (1909), v, p. 265.

3. T. Hobbes, *Leviathan* (1651), chaps. 34, 44 and 45; J. Locke, *An Essay Concerning Human Understanding* (1690), ii. 23, 31; iv.3.27.

4. Scot, *Discoverie*, I II.iv, vi, xix; VIII.iv; *A Discourse upon Divels and Spirits*; Webster, *The Displaying of Supposed Witchcraft*, pp. 73, 95.

grounds. Several of the religious sects of the Interregnum were to encourage this mode of thinking. Lodowick Muggleton stressed that devils had no bodily existence but were merely evil thoughts in men's minds.[5] The Ranters also interpreted the Devil symbolically; he represented suppressed desires and was not literally a person or creature.[6]

By the end of the seventeenth century this interpretation was becoming more acceptable in orthodox circles. Sir Isaac Newton thought that evil spirits were mere desires of the mind. Devils may have had physical powers before the coming of Christianity, declared Bishop Stillingfleet, but men who accepted the Gospel were no longer capable of receiving any hurt from them in their persons, children or goods.[7] The metaphorical interpretation of the demonic possessions in the New Testament was also gaining ground. 'To have a devil', explained a writer in 1676, 'was a kind of phrase or form of speech'.[8] These trends were emphasized by the decline of Hell – the tendency of many seventeenth-century intellectuals to question the existence of Hell as a localized place of physical torment, and to re-interpret it symbolically as a state of mind, an inner hell.[9] As late as the nineteenth century it was still possible for an ecclesiastical court to rule that a man who denied the personality of the Devil was to be deemed a 'notorious evil liver'. But this opinion was reversed by the Judicial Committee of the Privy Council; and according to the twentieth-century *Encyclopaedia Britannica*, 'it may be confidently affirmed that belief in Satan is not now generally regarded as an essential article of the Christian faith'.[10] But the mere banishment of the Devil to his infernal kingdom had in itself been enough to refute the possibility that witches might make compacts with him, save in their minds; even if an old woman wanted to give herself to the Devil, there could be no prospect of her gaining any influx of supernatural power as a result.

Those influenced by these theological currents of thought thus came to think it increasingly improbable that God could ever have allowed

5. L. Muggleton, *A True Interpretation of the Witch of Endor* (1669), p. 4; idem, *The Acts of the Witnesses* (1699), p. 12; idem, *A Looking-Glass* (1756 edn), p. 47.

6. *H.M.C., Leybourne-Popham*, p. 57; J. Bauthumley, *The Light and Dark Sides of God* (1650), pp. 28–31. The heterodox Catholic, Thomas White, also took a highly naturalistic view of fantasies about the Devil; *The Middle State of Souls* (1659), p. 190.

7. F. E. Manuel, *Portrait of Isaac Newton* (Cambridge, Mass., 1968), p. 369; *Letters Illustrative of the Reign of William III*, ed. G. P. R. James (1841), ii, pp. 302–3.

8. *The Doctrine of Devils* (1676), p. 36, cf. above, p. 585.

9. See D. P. Walker, *The Decline of Hell* (1964); and C. A. Patrides, 'Renaissance and modern views on Hell', *Harvard Theol. Rev.*, lvii (1964); above, pp. 202–3.

10. T. A. Spalding, *Elizabethan Demonology* (1880), p. 83; *Encyclopaedia Britannica* (11th edn, Cambridge, 1911), *s.v.* 'Devil'.

witches to exercise any supernatural power, or have intended that they should be persecuted for supposedly doing so. The standard sceptical position was well defined by Reginald Scot in his *Discoverie of Witchcraft* (1584), and did not change much thereafter. All witches, said Scot, came in one of four categories. First there were the innocent, falsely accused out of malice or ignorance. Next came the deluded: malevolent, half-crazed persons, who had convinced themselves that they were in league with the Devil and made absurd confessions to that effect, but who were actually incapable of harming anyone. Thirdly, there were the genuinely maleficent witches, who injured their neighbours secretly, not by supernatural means, however, but by the use of poison. Finally, there were the cozeners and impostors, the wizards and charmers who gulled country folk by falsely pretending to heal disease, tell fortunes or find lost goods. These last two categories were the witches who the Bible had said should not be allowed to live. To this extent, therefore, Scot admitted the existence of 'witches'. But he was certain that none of them could have made a corporal pact with the Devil or succeeded in harming her neighbours by supernatural means. He was all for the prosecution of the cunning men and wise women. But he was implacably opposed to putting old women to death for being guilty of an impossibility.[11]

At the time Scot's work was said to have made 'a great impression in the magistracy and also in the clergy'. It was not reprinted in England until 1651, but it nevertheless had a considerable influence. Elizabethan sceptics, like Samuel Harsnet and the physician John Harvey, drew heavily upon it in their published writings, and there is evidence to suggest that its arguments were familiar among the educated laity. The Kentish sceptic, Henry Oxinden, for example, rehearsed them fluently in a private letter of 1641.[12] Even the supporters of the belief accepted much of what Scot had to say on the subject of counterfeits. But most members of the educated classes remained slow to accept the full implications of his

11. Professor Trevor-Roper, by contrast, argues that Scot and his followers did not shake the foundations of the belief in witchcraft, but merely questioned its practical interpretation: 'the basis of the myth was beyond their reach'; *The European Witch-Craze of the 16th and 17th Centuries* (Harmondsworth, 1969), pp. 75, 88–9, 94, 101. This, however, is to misrepresent Scot's refusal to deny that 'witches' existed. Scot admitted the reality of impostors, poisoners, scolds and deluded persons, but he made no concessions to the notion that they had any supernatural power ('My question is not (as many fondly suppose) whether there be witches or nay; but whether they can do such miraculous works as are imputed unto them'; *Discoverie*, sig. Aviij^v).

12. Ady. sig. A3; *The Oxinden Letters, 1607–42*, ed. D. Gardiner (1933), pp. 220–23. On Scot's supporters, see Kocher, *Science and Religion*, chap. 6; Notestein, *Witchcraft*, p. 77, p. 9; The *Discoverie* was reprinted in 1651, 1654 and 1665.

thesis. 'Many deny witches at all, or, if there be any, they can do no harm,' wrote Robert Burton in 1621, 'but on the contrary are most lawyers, divines, physicians, philosophers.' Scot's position remained that of a self-conscious minority. Many contemporaries regarded it as tantamount to atheism to deny the reality of spirits or the possibility of supernatural intervention in daily affairs.[13] It was certainly a more rigid position than that actually adopted by the judges and jurymen who brought the witch-trials to an end. So far as can be told, they were not motivated by any coherent ideology of this kind. Their attitude was more modest. What influenced them was not a denial of the possibility of witchcraft as such, but a heightened sense of the logical difficulty of proving it to be at work in any particular case.

This was a difficulty of which everyone had long been aware. Not even the most zealous witch-hunter had ever said that *all* misfortunes were the work of witches. On the contrary the leading authorities always stressed that allegations of witchcraft were not to be made before other possible explanations of the apparent *maleficium* had been considered: it might be an act of God; it might be the direct work of the Devil without the intervention of a witch; it might be the result of imposture; or it might have purely natural causes. All these possibilities were to be carefully investigated before a witchcraft accusation was levied.[14] But this advice posed two perplexing questions. How was one to distinguish witchcraft from all the other possible causes? And how was one to know for certain the identity of the witch?

In order to distinguish *maleficium* from natural illness the demonologists listed various criteria. These usually boiled down to saying that the disease should have supernatural symptoms incapable of natural explanation; as, for example, when a possessed person displayed superhuman strength or spoke fluently in foreign languages with which he was unacquainted; or when the application of conventional remedies to the patient produced unconventional results.[15] It is obvious that these 'tests' depended entirely upon a consensus of learned physicians as to what was or was not natural. If this consensus broke down, then there was no way of proceeding. Since in any case a minority of intellectuals held that witches could inflict their victims with the symptoms of some ordinary

13. Burton, *Anatomy*, i, pp. 202–3. cf. M. Casaubon, *Of Credulity and Incredulity in Things Divine* (1670), p. 171.

14. Cf. Bernard, *Guide*, and Gaule, *Select Cases of Conscience, passim*.

15. J. Cotta, *The Infallible True and Assured Witch* (1624), esp. chap. 10; Bernard, *Guide*, pp. 26–8, 49–52.

natural disease,[16] the difficulty of recognizing witchcraft when one saw it became even greater.

Contemporaries with open minds on the subject of witchcraft thus became increasingly aware of the logical difficulties involved in making an accusation. Those who saw this problem ranged from the London preacher in 1603 who pointed out that diabolical possession could never be confidently identified, 'because there cannot be assigned any proper token or sign to know that any is essentially possessed; which sign must be apparent in all such as are so possessed and not in any others',[17] to the former Secretary for Scotland who wrote in 1697 that he had no doubt that witches could exist, but that 'the Parlements of France and other judicatories who are persuaded of the being of witches never try them now, because of the experience they have had that it is impossible to distinguish possession from nature in disorder; and they choose rather to let the guilty escape than to punish the innocent'.[18]

Even if the fact of witchcraft could be established, there still remained the problem of identifying the witch. At a popular level this was, as we have seen, no problem. Evidence of *maleficium,* accompanied by express or tacit hostility, was enough to convince the neighbours. In Elizabethan times it also seems to have been enough to secure a conviction in the courts. As William Perkins lamented, 'Experience shows that ignorant people ... will make strong proofs of such presumptions, whereupon sometimes jurors do give their verdict against parties innocent'.[19] In the early seventeenth century, however, after the passing of the 1604 statute, with its emphasis on the diabolical compact, the commentators set aside the 'presumptions' which had been 'ordinarily used', in favour of stricter standards of proof, based primarily upon evidence of compact. What they now wanted was sworn evidence that the witch kept a familiar or bore the devil's mark on her person; most decisive of all, they hoped for her free confession that she had entered into a pact with Satan.[20] This new emphasis upon evidence of compact can be seen in seventeenth-century legal proceedings, especially during and after the period of the Hopkins campaign. Yet none of these new 'proofs' was infallible. The

16. Sir Thomas Browne declared at the trial of two witches at Bury St Edmunds in 1664 that the Devil could make natural illnesses worse (Ewen, ii, pp. 350–51). cf. Cooper, *Mystery*, pp. 265–8.

17. *Diary of John Manningham*, ed. J. Bruce (Camden Soc., 1868), p. 128.

18. *H.M.C.*, 14th rep., appx, pt. iii, p. 132.

19. Perkins, *Discourse*, p. 210.

20. Perkins, *Discourse*, pp. 199–219; Ewen, i, p. 61; Cotta, *The Infallible True and Assured Witch, passim*; Cooper, *Mystery*, pp. 276–9; Bernard, *Guide*, ii, chaps. 17–18; Gaule, *Select Cases of Conscience*, pp. 80–83.

'familiar' might be a harmless domestic pet and the 'mark' a natural excrescence.[21] The 'confession' itself could be plausibly discredited by sceptics as the product of fantasy or 'melancholy'. How could one distinguish a true confession from a false one?[22] The more the demonologists insisted on the need for certain proof, the greater the logical difficulties they ran into. The paradox was that their severer view of witchcraft as devil-worship led ultimately to a rise in the acquittal-rate for, without torture of the kind used on the Continent, confessions to such a crime were often unobtainable.

On the Continent the mechanism of prosecution was at times so infallible that, when a contemporary asked some experienced German judges how an innocent person, once arrested for witchcraft, could escape conviction, they were at a loss for an answer.[23] In England the situation was never as bad as this, for even Hopkins, with his modified form of torture, did not achieve a hundred per cent conviction-rate. Unfortunately the evidence is inadequate for us to know how it was that most acquittals during the period were obtained and what reasoning led a Grand Jury to reject any particular indictment or persuaded a Petty Jury to refuse to convict. But Richard Bernard in 1627 listed a number of the objections which a Grand Jury might raise: perhaps the victim was a counterfeit; perhaps he was suffering from a natural disease, which a better doctor might be able to identify; or perhaps it was a supernatural disease which the Devil had inflicted directly without the intermediate agency of a witch.[24]

Such evidence as there is suggests that acquittals were usually made along these and similar lines. Demonstrations of the victims' imposture are particularly well recorded in the pamphlet literature of the time. But other cases suggest that juries would acquit when they thought the witch's malice had not been proved; when the witnesses against her were disreputable; when the testimony offered seemed unduly far-fetched; or when the accused had a record of regular church-going and godly living. Neither a 'confession' nor a whole army of hostile witnesses was necessarily enough to secure a conviction if judge or jury felt unhappy about the case.[25]

21. For attempts to distinguish between the appearance of 'natural' and 'unnatural' marks see, e.g. Gaule, *Select Cases of Conscience*, pp. 104–6; M. Hopkins, *The Discovery of Witches*, ed. M. Summers (1928), pp. 52–3.

22. Hopkins, however, claimed to be able to do so (op. cit., pp. 57–9).

23. Lea, *Materials*, p. 707.

24. R. B(ernard), *The Isle of Man* (1627), *Epistle to the Reader*.

25. For examples of such factors at work, see Ewen, i, pp. 59–60; Ewen, ii, pp. 116–18, 149, 190, 229, 236–7, 243, 251, 364–5, 378, 381, 390.

What is certain is that the mounting rate of acquittals was the work of tribunals which did not deny the possibility of witchcraft as such, but were perplexed by the impossibility of getting certain proof of it in any particular case. This was partly a tactic adopted by thoroughly sceptical judges, like L. C. J. North, who advised his colleagues to display 'a very prudent and moderate carriage' in face of popular fury against witches, endeavouring 'to convince, rather by detecting of the fraud, than by denying authoritatively such power to be given to old women'. This was the attitude of Archbishop Abbot, when dealing with the alleged bewitching of the important Earl of Essex in the reign of James I. He would not deny that there was such a thing as witchcraft, but how was he to distinguish it by its external symptoms from any other physical malady?[26] This was a real difficulty and not necessarily a mere device employed by the pusillanimous who did not believe in witchcraft, but were afraid to say so. But it was a difficulty which had been implicit in the conduct of witch-trials from the beginning. Why did it take so long for men to grow sensitive to it? This is an impossible question to answer categorically. All that one can do is to sketch some of the circumstances by which the change seems to have been precipitated.

In the first place it must be recognized that the hypothesis of witchcraft, like any other explanatory mechanism, was bound to crack under its own weight, if too frequently invoked. The accusation was easy to make and hard to disprove. It was therefore particularly likely to be animated by malice or imposture. But one had only to be an eye-witness of a patently unjust accusation to be converted to a belief in the need for exercising greater caution in future. The leading sceptical writers seem, almost without exception, to have been provoked into publication by personal acquaintance with incidents of this kind; from Reginald Scot, who had witnessed a number of fraudulent accusations in nearby Kentish villages, to Francis Hutchinson, the future Bishop of Down, whose *Historical Essay Concerning Witchcraft* (1718) was precipitated by the condemnation and subsequent reprieve in 1712 of the Hertfordshire woman, Jane Wenham, whom he visited after her release and of whose piety he was convinced.[27] In France it was the series of scandalous cases of hysterical

26. R. North, *The Lives of the ... North*, ed. A. Jessopp (1890), i, pp. 166–7; Notestein, *Witchcraft*, p. 234.

27. Scot, *Discoverie*, I.ii; VII.i–ii; XII.xvi; Hutchinson, *An Historical Essay concerning Witchcraft*, p. 165 cf. the cases of Harsnet, provoked by the activities of Darrell and the recusants; Jorden, by the conviction of Elizabeth Jackson (above, pp. 610, 651); Arthur Wilson by the executions at Chelmsford in 1645 (F. Peck, *Desiderata Curiosa* [new edn, 1779], ii, p. 476); Filmer, by executions in Kent in 1652 (*An Advertisement to the Jurymen*, sig. A 2); Ady, by a female impostor at Braintree, and the memory of Matthew Hopkins (pp. 79, 101–2);

imposture which led the *parlementaires* to discontinue witchcraft pros-ecution.[28] In England the stimulus seems to have been much the same.

Apart from the influence of individual miscarriages of justice, it is possible to discern the growth of two essentially novel attitudes. The first is the assumption of an orderly, regular universe, unlikely to be upset by the capricious intervention of God or Devil. This view of the world was consolidated by the new mechanical philosophy, but the way to its ac-ceptance had long been prepared by the emphasis of theologians upon the orderly way in which God conducted his affairs, working through natural causes accessible to human investigation. In the presence of such reason-ableness, talk of miraculous happenings came to appear increasingly implausible. It was this conviction, rather than any new psychological insight, which accounts for the scepticism displayed towards the con-fessions of old women who said that they had seen the Devil, or flown through the air, or killed men by their secret curses. The confessions on which the demonologists laid such weight were unacceptable *a priori*, because as John Webster said, 'it is ... simply impossible for either the Devil or witches to change or alter the course that God hath set in nature'.[29] Accusations of diabolical witchcraft were thus rejected not because they had been closely scrutinized and found defective in some particular respect, but because they implied a conception of nature which now appeared inherently absurd.

The increasing prevalence of this attitude was to vitiate the last-ditch attempts of some later seventeenth-century intellectuals to place the an-cient belief in witchcraft upon a genuinely scientific foundation, by sifting through the many inherited tales of the supernatural in order to arrive at those which were authenticated beyond any doubt. This was the motive underlying the psychical researches of Meric Casaubon, Henry More, George Sinclair, Joseph Glanvill and Richard Baxter: even Robert Boyle thought that 'one circumstantial narrative fully verified' was all that was necessary to confound the sceptics.[30] But the task proved impossible. For no one can be persuaded to change his mind by evidence which he regards as implausible. 'Without many witnesses', thought the Deist Charles

Webster, by the impostures of Edmund Robinson (*The Displaying of Supposed Witchcraft*, p. 277); the author of *The Doctrine of Devils*, by a case in his parish (pp. 60, 197). Even Bernard's revisionism was prompted by a trial at Taunton Assizes in 1626 (*Guide*, sig. A3; *The Isle of Man*, sigs. A8ᵛ–9), just as John Gaule wrote in response to the activities of Hopkins. Thomas Cooper also had direct experience of witchcraft accusations (*Mystery*, sig. A3, p. 14).

28. R. Mandrou, *Magistrats et sorciers en France au XVIIᵉ siècle* (Paris, 1968).

29. Webster, *The Displaying of Supposed Witchcraft*, p. 68.

30. *The Works of the Honourable Robert Boyle* (1744), v. p. 244. For the others see Robbins, *Encyclopedia*, pp. 44–5, 223–4, 350–51, 470; Notestein, *Witchcraft*, chaps. xii and xiv.

Blount, 'the testimony of one person alone ought to be suspected in things miraculous'. Many anecdotes were assembled and published, but none was strong enough to pass the test which the sceptics were now in practice applying, and which David Hume was later to elevate into a philosophical principle: namely, that no testimony could establish a miracle unless it were of such a kind that its falsehood would be more astonishing than the fact it was meant to establish.[31]

The second assumption underlying the sceptical attitude was the optimistic conviction that it would one day be possible to uncover the natural causes of those events which still remained mysterious. Already it was possible to suggest natural explanations for such phenomena as the insensible witch's 'mark', or the incomprehensible 'confessions'. 'Melancholy' underlay the witches' delusions; the 'incubus' was not a visitation, but a disease; and natural illnesses could account for supposed cases of diabolical possession. Much remained perplexing, but, as John Wagstaffe pointed out,[32] the study of mental illness had barely begun, and there was no telling what future discoveries might be made. The progress made by seventeenth-century scientists was dramatic enough to make most contemporaries aware of the elasticity of natural knowledge, and to imbue some of them with immense confidence in the potentiality of future human achievement. This was a theme which some of the sceptics were to reiterate;[33] and it made it possible for them to discard the explanatory role of witchcraft without leaving too unbearable a void behind.

In the short run, moreover, the sceptical attitude was greatly assisted by the vogue, particularly in the late sixteenth and early seventeenth centuries, of the neo-platonic conception of the universe as pulsating with many undiscovered occult influences. Many writers were sceptical about witchcraft, precisely because they were so credulous in other matters. They accepted the possibility of sympathetic healing and action at a distance; they believed that stones might have hidden properties, that a corpse might bleed at the approach of its murderer, and that some men could 'fascinate' others by the emanations from their eyes. Scot's scepticism was made possible by his commitment to this tradition, and it was no coincidence that John Webster was sceptical about witchcraft, but

31. C. Blount, *Anima Mundi* (1679), p. 51 (in *The Miscellaneous Works of Charles Blount, Esq.* [1695]); D. Hume, *Essays, Moral, Political, and Literary,* ed. T. H. Green and T. H. Grose (1875), ii, pp. 88–108.

32. Wagstaffe, *The Question of Witchcraft Debated,* p. 67.

33. e.g., Scot, *Discoverie,* sig. Biij; Filmer (quoted below, p. 790); Webster, *The Displaying of Supposed Witchcraft,* p. 17 and chap. 13.

believed in the weapon-salve, astral spirits, satyrs, pygmies, mermaids and sea-monsters. It was because these men accepted so wide a range of supposed natural phenomena that they were able to dispense with witchcraft as an explanation of mysterious happenings. It was much easier for them to advance a 'natural' explanation for the witches' *maleficium* than it was for those who had been educated in the tradition of scholastic Aristotelianism.[34] The sceptics thus explained away apparent mysteries by proffering hypotheses about natural events which we should regard as entirely spurious. In the same way, rationalist physicians like Edward Jorden could reinterpret diabolical possession as hysteria produced by the 'rising of the mother', a natural explanation but a mistaken one.[35]

Renaissance neo-platonism and its affiliated schools of thought thus provided the vital intellectual scaffolding necessary to prop up the hypothesis that there was a natural cause for every event. When in the later seventeenth century this scaffolding collapsed under the onslaught of the mechanical philosophy it did not need to be replaced. The absurdity of witchcraft could henceforth be justified by reference to the achievements of the Royal Society and the new philosophy.[36] It is true that some of the early converts to the mechanical philosophy had difficulty in making up their minds on the subject of witchcraft, but in the long run theirs was to prove a comprehensive explanation for natural phenomena, and one which needed no external assistance. By an appropriate coincidence, one of the three M.P.s who initiated the repeal of the Witchcraft Act in 1736 was John Conduitt, who married Sir Isaac Newton's niece and was one of his leading admirers and memorialists.

There was, therefore, a continuing stream of scepticism throughout the whole period of witchcraft prosecution in England. Scot's great work was probably no more than an elaborate application of a type of rationalist criticism already in vogue. As early as 1578 a Norwich physician, Dr

34. See, e.g. Scot, *Discoverie*, XII and XVI.viii–ix; J. H(arvey), *A Discoursive Probleme concerning Prophesies* (1588), p. 79; S. Boulton, *Medicina Magica* (1656), pp. 166–67; Webster, *The Displaying of Supposed Witchcraft*, pp. 290–311; above, p. 520. So far as the belief in spirits was concerned, however, neo-platonic influence worked in the other direction by upholding faith in all sorts of occult influences, cf. Wagstaffe, *The Question of Witchcraft Debated*, pp. 75–7. There are brief but valuable remarks on this subject in Kocher, *Science and Religion*, pp. 67–70, and Trevor-Roper, *The European Witch-Craze*, pp. 59–60.

35. Above, p. 584.

36. Cf. Richard Bentley; 'What then has lessen'd in England your stories of sorceries? Not the growing sect [of free-thinkers], but the growth of Philosophy and Medicine. No thanks to atheists, but to the Royal Society and College of Physicians; to the Boyles and Newtons, the Sydenhams and Ratcliffs.' ('Phileleutherus Lipsiensis', *Remarks upon a late Discourse of Free-Thinking* (2nd edn, 1713), p. 33). cf. Webster, *The Displaying of Supposed Witchcraft*, p. 268, and Hutchinson, *An Historical Essay concerning Witchcraft*, pp. 169–70.

Browne, was accused of 'spreading a misliking of the laws by saying there are no witches'.[37] Scot himself was deeply read in the literature of witch-craft and drew in particular upon the medical findings of the Cleves physician Johan Weyer, whose *De Praestigiis Daemonum* (1563) had urged that many supposed witches were innocent melancholics and that even the guilty ones were mere tools of Satan, incapable of doing harm by their own activities. Scot took this position further by denying even Satan any physical power.

Outside intellectual circles, the movement of opinion is difficult to chart. There is much to support the view that 'doubt was only silenced, not convinced'.[38] The evidence for this does not lie in the isolated utter-ances of sceptics, like the Elizabethan lawyer, Serjeant Harris, who de-clared in court in 1593 that the idea that one could do harm by melting wax images was 'a vain and fond conceit'.[39] Rather it is to be found in the many areas of contemporary society where the subject of witchcraft seems to have been seldom or never mentioned: in the world of business-men and financiers; in the practice of many contemporary doctors; and in most aspects of politics and administration.

In the later seventeenth century the growing volume of scepticism is unmistakable. In 1668 Joseph Glanvill admitted that 'most of the looser gentry and the small pretenders to philosophy and wit are generally deriders of the belief in witches'.[40] In the following year appeared John Wagstaffe's *Question of Witchcraft Debated*, a sweepingly sceptical per-formance, which was controversial among Cambridge dons, but widely esteemed elsewhere.[41] 'We live in an age and a place,' wrote Robert Boyle to Glanvill in 1677, 'wherein all stories of witchcrafts, or other magical feats are by many, even of the wise, suspected; and by too many that would pass for wits derided and exploded.' There were so many would-be exploders of immaterial substances about, thought Henry Hallywell in 1681, that to talk of devils and possession was to invite mockery and contempt. When, around 1694, the Marquis of Halifax compiled his list of 'fundamentals', he had to set against the proposition 'that there were witches', the significant qualification – 'much shaken of late'.[42]

37. *C.S.P.D., Addenda, 1566–79*, p. 551.

38. *George Lincoln Burr, Selections from his Writings*, ed. L. O. Gibbons (Ithaca, N.Y., 1943) p. 372.

39. P. B. G. Binnall, 'Fortescue *versus* Hext', *Folk-Lore*, liii (1942), pp. 160–61.

40. J. Glanvill, *Saducismus Triumphatus* (1681), Preface (dated 1668), sig. F3.

41. North, *The Lives of the ... North*, ed. Jessopp, ii, p. 287; Casaubon, *Of Credulity and Incredulity in Things Divine*, p. 177.

42. *The Works of the Honourable Robert Boyle*, v, p. 244; H. Hallywell, Melampronoea (1681), p. 3; *The Complete Works of George Savile, First Marquess of Halifax*, ed. W. Raleigh (Oxford, 1912), p. 210.

Of course, the belief still retained some vitality in clerical circles; when Francis Hutchinson came to write his book on the subject in 1718 he could cite nearly thirty works published in defence of the notion since 1660. Yet even potential believers were aware of the difficulty of obtaining satisfactory proof in any particular case,[43] while many of the educated laity had come to regard the very notion of witchcraft as an absurdity. Even before the Act was repealed in 1736, the fact that a man feared witches could be cited in the courts as evidence of his insanity. When the Scottish judge Lord Grange opposed the repeal in 1736, Walpole is said to have commented that from that moment he knew he had no more to fear from him politically.[44] By the middle of the century, Conyers Middleton could remark that 'the belief in witches is now utterly extinct'.[45]

At a popular level, of course, this was far from the truth. There had been occasional traces of scepticism, even in the sixteenth century. As early as 1555, one John Tuckie of Banwell, Somerset, said that in his opinion no man or woman could do anything by witchcraft,[46] and he must have had his successors. But few village Scots or mute, inglorious Harsnets have left any trace on the records. If there was a decline in the belief in witchcraft among seventeenth-century cottagers and husbandmen it has yet to be demonstrated. The dwindling number of prosecutions is not evidence that allegations were no longer levied. It only shows that they were no longer seriously entertained by the courts.

But although popular feeling against witches survived the repeal of the Act in 1736, it is possible that the volume of accusations had begun to dwindle. If so, the reasons for this may have been as much social as intellectual. For by the later seventeenth century the conflict between charity and individualism, which had generated so many of the witch accusations in the past, was well on the way to being resolved. The development of the national Poor Law converted the support of the indigent into a legal obligation. In the process, it ceased to be regarded as a moral duty.[47] '[when] the poor man ... makes known his distress to the parish officers,' William Cobbett was to write, 'they bestow upon him,

43. Hutchinson, *An Historical Essay concerning Witchcraft*, sigs. a1v–a2v, cf. R. T. Petersson, *Sir Kenelm Digby* (1956), p. 171; Notestein, *Witchcraft*, p. 341; Bentley, *Remarks upon a Late Discourse*, p. 33.

44. N. Walker, *Crime and Insanity in England*, i (Edinburgh, 1968), pp. 55, 58; *D.N.B.*, 'Erskine, James, Lord Grange'.

45. Quoted in L. Stephen, *History of English Thought in the Eighteenth Century* (3rd edn, 1902), i, p. 268.

46. D. R. Wells, D7 (16 May 1555). He was, however, facing a charge of sorcery at the time.

47. Cf. R. Bernard, *The Ready Way to Good Works* (1635), p. 439.

not alms, but his legal dues.'[48] The Poor Law had, of course, been established in Tudor times. But its implications were not at first fully appreciated, for it was invoked only intermittently and as a last resort. Private charity remained an important source of maintenance and the authorities often turned a blind eye to begging at the door.[49] From the early seventeenth century onwards, however, the Poor Law became less of an emergency expedient, more of a regular system of relief. During the century the amount of money raised annually in this way increased more than tenfold. With such organized means of support, the indigent were no longer so dependent upon the voluntary help of their neighbours. 'I am certain,' wrote a late-seventeenth-century commentator, 'that now, care being taken by overseers publicly chosen in every parish, a great many that have compassionate hearts do not much in that kind as they would do otherwise; for what is more natural than to think such care needless ... Many people not only think it needless but foolish to do that which is parish business.'[50] Private charity continued, but its nature was altering. The merchants and gentry who established the large philanthropic foundations did not give away food at the door; neither did old women come to ask them for it.

In such circumstances the tensions and guilt which had produced the old allegations of witchcraft gradually withered away. A man who turned away his neighbour empty-handed could do so with a clearer conscience, for he could tell himself that other ways now existed of dealing with the problem. He need no longer feel the torments of remorse which would once have culminated in an accusation of witchcraft. Witch accusations had reflected a conflict between the communal norms of mutual aid and the individualistic ethic of self-help. But by the end of the seventeenth century, this conflict was on its way to being resolved by the disappearance of the old norms. When this happened the stimulus to witchcraft accusation was to dwindle.

Significantly, witch-beliefs lasted longest in the village communities,

48. Quoted in M. D. George, *England in Transition* (1935), p. 137.

49. The Act of 39 Eliz. c. 3 (1597–8) allowed begging within the parish when authorized by the authorities, cf. *Poor Relief in Elizabethan Ipswich*, ed. J. Webb (Suffolk Rec. Soc., 1966), pp. 18–19. The intermittent nature of the Poor Law is demonstrated by W. K. Jordan, *Philanthropy in England, 1480–1660* (1959), chap. 5.

50. D. North, 'Some Notes concerning the Laws for the Poor' (B.M., Add. MS 32, 512), f. 31. The annual yield of the poor rate was estimated in 1614 at £30,000–40,000. By 1685 it was put at £665,362 (Jordan, op. cit., p. 141 n; *The Political and Commercial Works of ... Charles D'Avenant* (1771), i, p. 41). The depressing effect of poor relief upon private charity is discussed by C. Wilson, 'The Other Face of Mercantilism', *T.R.H.S.*, 5th ser., ix (1959), pp. 93–4.

where the causes of misfortune could still be seen in personal terms. In country villages the conventions of neighbourliness and mutual help survived into the nineteenth century. Women still came to the door to beg and to borrow, and the man who turned them away empty-handed did so with mixed feeling. It was no accident that Ruth Osborne, who was lynched for witchcraft by a Hertfordshire mob in 1751, had been previously refused buttermilk by the farmer whose subsequent mysterious illness provoked the accusation against her. The majority of other informal witch accusations recorded in the eighteenth, nineteenth and even twentieth centuries conform to the same old special pattern of charity evaded, followed by misfortune incurred.[51]

After 1736 when the possibility of formal prosecution was no longer open, villagers turned to informal violence, counter-magic and the occasional lynching. This procedure was both illegal and a poor substitute for the old witch-trials. For it was not the mere allegation of witchcraft which had had the cathartic effect, but its acceptance and proof;[52] and after 1736 proof had become difficult and means of redress prohibited. In these circumstances witch-beliefs inevitably declined.

The history of witchcraft *prosecutions* in England thus reflects the intellectual assumptions of the educated classes who controlled the machinery of the law courts. The decline in formal prosecution was a consequence of their increasing scepticism about the possibility of the offence, or at least about the possibility of proving it. The history of witchcraft *accusations* on the other hand can only be explained in terms of the immediate social environment of the witch and her accuser. Their highly informal nature makes it impossible to measure fluctuations in its volume with any precision. There seems no way of telling, for example, how far the drop in indictments before the courts in the early eighteenth century was caused by the known hostility of judges and juries to such accusations, how far it reflected a dwindling demand for prosecution on the part of the villagers themselves.

These considerations make it rash to draw too many conclusions from the actual trends in formal prosecution. But it may be stated categorically that no convincing correlation can be established between the chronology

51. Robbins, *Encyclopedia*, pp. 368–9 (for Osborne). For others, see e.g., *Folk-Lore Journ.,* v. (*1887*). p. 158; *Shropshire Folk-Lore,* ed. C. S. Burne (1883–6), pp. 147, 151, 154; *County Folk-Lore*, i, (Folk-Lore Soc., 1895), ii, pp. 168–9; *County Folk-Lore*, v (Folk-Lore Soc., 1908), pp. 73, 78; E. J. Begg, 'Cases of Witchcraft in Dorsetshire', *Folk-Lore*, lii (1941), pp. 70–72; R. L. Tongue, *Somerset Folk-Lore*, ed. K. M. Briggs (Folk-Lore Soc., 1965), pp. 69–70; E. J. Rudsdale, 'Witchcraft in Essex', *Essex Rev.,* lv (1946), pp. 187–9; E. W. Martin, *The Shearers and the Shorn* (1965), pp. 72–3.

52. Cf. J. R. Crawford, *Witchcraft and Sorcery in Rhodesia* (1967), pp. 281–2.

of witch-persecution and such general events as the incidence of plague, famine, unemployment or price fluctuations. Neither, in the light of what has been seen about the personal nature of the misfortunes attributed to witches, is there any reason why we should expect such a correlation to exist. It is also wrong to think of 'scares' and 'panics' sweeping the country. Such an impression might be derived from the intermittent survival of pamphlet accounts of the more sensational trials. But the judicial records show that witchcraft prosecution was a regular phenomenon through most of the period. There seems to have been a drop in the number of prosecutions in the twenty years before the Civil War, though this may be partly an optical illusion created by the uneven survival of records.[53] There certainly was an upsurge in the time of Matthew Hopkins, whose activities show to what extent it was possible to stimulate prosecution from above. But even his campaign would have been impossible without the underlying tensions of village society. The animosities which led to the indictment of his victims were much the same as those which underlay the other trials of the century. Witchcraft accusation was endemic in English society, but it was essentially a local phenomenon, and it will be better understood when more is known about the history and structure of the English village.

(Note: Readers wishing to follow up references in detail should consult the Notes on References and the Table of Abbreviations at the beginning of *Religion and the Decline of Magic*. References preceded by 'above' or 'below' are to the Penguin edition of this book – *Ed.*)

53. At least eight executions are known to have taken place in the 1630s (Ewen, ii, pp. 394, 409–10, 416, 439; Kent R.O., SA/AC 7, f. 198).

18. H. C. Erik Midelfort

The Social Position of the Witch in Southwestern Germany

Excerpt from H. C. Erik Midelfort, *Witch-Hunting in Southwestern Germany 1562-1684,* Stanford University Press, 1972, pp. 179-90.

The assembled information regarding the ratio of men to women in fifteen separate hunts is summarized in Table 1. In two early hunts (Wiesensteig and Rottenburg), we find overwhelming proportions of women (98-100 per cent). These trials were also in two regions that proved most persistent in witch-hunting. Wiesensteig repeated the spasm of 1562-3 a mere twenty years later, whereas Rottenburg continued to execute people at a high rate over a thirty-year period. It is as if the stereotyped identification of witches and old women suffered so little shock that the crisis of credibility or confidence that we found elsewhere could not operate in these places.* One could speculate that those hunts that produced high proportions of men among the executed (20-40 per cent) would tend to have trials that ended abruptly, and would tend to resist backsliding into panic again. More work must be done to test the hypothesis that severe shock to stereotypes of witchcraft tended to inhibit future panic. It would be a good chance to test and develop dissonance theory from a novel point of view.[1] Certainly it is significant that the proportion of women dropped from 87 per cent in the first six large hunts to 76 per cent during and after the crisis of confidence of 1627-31. In summary, it is fair to say that, as a hunt developed, the number of men suspected usually rose, and that from the 1620s on men were generally more prevalent. One stereotype had broken down, a stereotype by which society had been able to hunt its hidden enemies without inviting social chaos.

Another stereotype disintegrated: that of age. If witches were predominantly old before 1600, more and more trials after 1600 came to feature children as central actors.[2] Children were not only bewitched like those at

---

*The crisis of confidence in mass denunciations which brought mass witch-hunting to an end is the subject of Chapter 6 of Dr Midelfort's book – *Ed.*

1. For a not very novel use of dissonance theory, cf. Rosenthal and Siegel, 'Magic and Witchcraft'.

2. Cf. Tramer, 'Kinder im Hexenglauben'.

Table 1
Males and Females Executed in Large Witch-hunts of the German Southwest

| Place and year | Sex of persons executed | | |
	Female	Male	Percent women
Wiesensteig:			
1562–63	63[a]		100%
1583	25[a]		100
Rottenburg, 1578–1609[b]	147	3	98
Rottweil, 1561–1600	36	6	86
Obermarchtal, 1586–96:			
1586	15	8	65
1587	24	1	96
1588	4	2	67
1589	1	0	100
1590	1	0	100
1592	1	0	100
1593	3	1	75
1596	1	0	100
Total	50	12	81
Ellwangen, 1611–18:			
1611	91	7	93
1612	73	23	76
1613	10	4	71
1614	16	11	59
1615	20	13	61
1616	8	5	62
1618	2	0	100
Total	220	63	78
Schwäbisch Gmünd, 1613–17:			
Burning no. 1	6	0	100
Burning no. 2	5	2	71
Burning no. 3	6	0	100
Burning no. 4	9	1	90
Burning no. 5	2	0	100
Burning no. 6	1	1	50
Burning no. 7	5	0	100
Burning no. 8	3	0	100
Burning no. 9	2	0	100
Total	39	4	91

Table 1 (*continued*)

	Sex of persons executed		
Place and year	*Female*	*Male*	*Percent women*
Ortenau, 1627–30:			
1627	4	0	100
1628	33	1	97
1629	20	2	91
1630	10	4	71
Total	67	7	91
Oberkirch, 1631–2:			
Cappel, 1631	16	4	80
Ulm, 1631	7	2	78
Renchen, 1632	15	8	65
Sasbach, 1632?	41	23	64
Oppenau, 1631–2	40	10	80
Total	119	47	72
Wertheim, 1616–44:			
1616–17	Sex unknown		
1629	9	1	90
1630–32	2	0	100
1633	Sex unknown		
1634	16	0	100[a]
1641	2	0	100
1642	4	0	100
1644	2	1	67
Total	35	2	95
Baden-Baden, 1627–31:			
Steinbach, 1628	24	9	73
Bühl, 1628–29	47	23	67
Baden, 1627–31	Sex unknown		
Total	71	32	69
Offenburg, 1627–9:			
1627	6	1	86
1628	22	0	100
1629	21	11	66
Total	49	12	80
Mergentheim, 1628–31:			
1 Jan.–4 May 1629	34	2	95
17 May–31 Dec. 1629	44	15	75
1630	8	5	62
1631	0	1	0
Total	102	24	81

Table 1 (*continued*)

	Sex of persons executed		
Place and year	Female	Male	Percent women
Esslingen, 1662–5	15	22	41
Reutlingen, 1665–6	11	3	79
Calw, 1683–4	1	1	50
Total, six witch-hunts before 1627	580	88	87
Total, nine witch-hunts after 1627	470	150	76
Grand Total	1,050	238	82

^aSex unknown, but the implication is that all were women. By implication we can often surmise that only women were involved when words like 'sagae' or 'veneficae' were used.

^bThe implication is that all were women until 1602, and that from 1602 to 1609, fourteen were female and three male.

Table 2
Würzburg Witchcraft Trials, 1627–9

Execution groups (in time sequence)	Total executed			Children			Adults			Percent adults in total
	F	M	%F	F	M	%F	F	M	%F	
1–5	22	4	85%	0	0	0%	22	4	85%	100%
6–10	16	12	57	2	0	100	14	12	54	93
11–15	10	4	71	2	1	67	8	3	73	79
16–20	15	13	54	6	11	35	9	2	82	39
21–25	7	27	21	1	13	7	6	14	30	59
26–29	9	21	30	2	3	40	7	18	28	83
Subtotal	79	81	49%	13	28	32%	66	53	55%	74%
Total	160			41			119			

Salem, Massachusetts; they were witches themselves. The iron Bishop of Würzburg, Philipp Adolf von Ehrenberg, even executed his own young nephew.[3] From 1627 on, every large witch-hunt began with children.

This suggestion concerning sex and age in the dynamic of witch-hunting agrees well with what we know regarding the persons executed in the Würzburg trials. In a well-known list from 1629, 160 persons were

3. Karl Vierordt characteristically saw even this incident as a persecution of Protestantism. *Geschichte*, II: 127–28.

named, in twenty-nine burnings.[4] When we group these execution days, the patterns of sex and age become clear (see Table 2).

Clearly the proportion of females dropped rapidly, from 85 per cent to a low of 21 per cent before recovering slightly in the last group of four executions. The same pattern prevails for girls and boys, with a drop from 100 per cent to 7 per cent, and with a recovery to 40 per cent in the last four burnings. Among adults only, the drop was more rapid, but recovery set in earlier, to be followed in executions 21–29 by another drop in the percentage of women burned. When we look at the proportions of adults and children, we notice an identical pattern, starting with all adults, declining to only 39 per cent adults in burnings 16–20, with a subsequent recovery to levels still well below the first ten burnings. Overall, the break-up of stereotypes is clear. In fact, the first eight persons executed were exclusively adult women. Slowly age and sex came to matter less, leaving society with no protective stereotypes, no sure way of telling who might be, and who could not be, a witch.

Despite these significant increases in men and children, witch panics almost always singled out adult women for special attention. This is not the place to review all of the suggested reasons for this emphasis, but a few salient points deserve mention.[5] First, women were viewed as particularly prone to diabolical contracts, not only because they were thought weak of mind but also and especially because they were lusty. Unlike the Victorian woman from whose standard women have only recently and imperfectly escaped, women in the sixteenth and seventeenth centuries were supposedly aggressive and lustful.[6] Sexual intercourse was an explicit delight for women. Other women were pictured whose primary desire was the satisfaction of sensuality. Only a background of this sort made the stories of seduction by the devil, repeated endlessly in confessions, at all psychologically plausible. The judges could understand, apparently, that a woman would feel drawn to a man and succumb to him on first meeting because such behaviour accorded well with ideas of female nature. Just as common are the confessions that intercourse with the devil turned out to be far less enjoyable than with their own husbands, owing to the devil's 'hard and cold nature'. Regardless of the origin of such confessions, whether spontaneous or suggested, these details pro-

4. Soldan-Heppe, *Geschichte der Hexenprozesse*, II: 17–20

5. For general treatments see Hansen, 'Die Zuspitzung des Hexenwahns auf das weibliche Geschlecht', *Quellen*, pp. 416–44; Paulus, *Hexenwahn,* pp. 195–247; Caro Baroja, *The World of the Witches*, pp. 18–40, 47–48, 101–4; Harper, 'Fear and the Status of Women'.

6. R. Schmidt, *Die Frau*, pp. 40, 122–28, 134; Janssen, *Geschichte*, VI: 430–37.

vided a convincing rationale for witch-hunters trying to explain why women fell prey to the devil in such large numbers.[7]

Beyond psychological plausibility, women seemed also to provoke somehow an intense misogyny at times. In some instances this hatred reflected traditionally tense family relationships. In the case of Barbara Rüfin of Ellwangen* we noticed a mother-in-law problem that had got totally out of hand. Such relationships, in which hate could not easily be admitted, might occasionally have disintegrated into wild name-calling of the sort that led to examinations and trials.[8] But surely a bad relation with one's mother-in-law or other kinsman could not have soured whole groups of men against women. And the literary tradition of Eve, Circe, Hecate, and Jezebel cannot explain much more than literary convention. We touch at last a sensitive nerve in the passing observation that during plagues men sometimes suffered and died at a rate six to ten times that of women, perhaps because women stayed at home more than men.[9] Even if the ratio in Germany never reached these heights, it is easy to imagine that occasional disproportions of this sort might have led examiners to look especially diligently for the *women* responsible for plague.[10] More work on plague needs to be done before we can make this more than a rather unlikely suggestion, but at least here one would have a real cause of resentment.[11] It is not enough to assert that a particular social group has been chosen as a scapegoat. One must also examine the reasons why that group *attracted* to itself the scapegoating mechanism.[12]

A much more attractive explanation of the attack on women in witch-hunts could also be constructed on what we know of the changing role of women in the early modern period. Scholars have often remarked that the sixteenth century was one of the most bitterly misogynistic periods ever

*A case described on pp. 101–103 of Dr Midelfort's book – *Ed.*

7. These details may be found in virtually any of the confessions throughout the German Southwest. Cf. esp. Mergentheim and Ellwangen, whose trials produced hundreds of them.

8. Middleton and Winter, *Witchcraft and Sorcery*, pp. 18–19.

9. Wilson, *The Plague*, p. 3, n. 3.

10. Carl Bücher thought that he saw this phenomenon in fourteenth- and fifteenth-century Frankfurt, since the number of widows on tax lists rose after plague years. This was faulty reasoning, since when women died, there was no change in a man's tax status, whereas a husband's death brought the widow into the tax lists; Bücher, *Frauenfrage*, pp. 6, 58.

11. It would seem unlikely that this kind of disproportion in favour of women in plague could have been at all common without provoking comment. What we know of later plagues certainly fails to show any violent disproportion. Women usually suffered on an equal basis with men in early modern Germany too. Cf. Woehlkens, *Pest und Ruhr*, p. 91. Cf. also the recent dispute between Russell, 'Effects of Pestilence', and Thrupp, 'Plague Effects'.

12. Berkowitz and Green, 'Stimulus Qualities'.

known.[13] Some have attempted to tie this new flood of anti-feminine attitudes to the Renaissance or to the Reformation,[14] an attack that has naturally provoked vigorous rebuttal.[15] No scholars have until now been successful in tying such ideas to more than literary tradition. The attempts at a psychology of misogyny have also shown pronounced weakness in explaining why the sixteenth century brought anything new.[16] Recently, however, it has become clear that the sixteenth century brought one of the most profound demographic changes that Europe ever experienced. John Hajnal has demonstrated that the 'European marriage pattern' dates roughly from the fifteenth or sixteenth century, a pattern characterized by late marriage and large proportions of both men and women who never married at all.[17] For the first time in all Western history, it seems, men's ages at first marriage rose to twenty-five or even thirty, whereas women's ages at marriage rose to twenty-three and up to twenty-seven. The proportion remaining single probably rose from about 5 to 15 per cent or even 20 per cent. In specific instances we now know that these numbers were even higher.[18] In nineteenth-century Carinthia, to take an extreme case, 45 per cent of all women never married.[19] In sixteenth-century Württemberg we can see 'hints ... of a non-European marriage pattern in the earlier centuries'.[20] In southwestern Germany, therefore, like the rest of Western Europe, the sixteenth century seems to have brought a profound shift in family patterns. The causes of such a change are as yet poorly understood.[21]

The massive implications are only now being explored.[22] In addition to obvious ramifications in the field of economic history, this shift towards later marriage would lay a social basis for trends towards crystalization of the nuclear family as well as emphasis on marriage by choice (and not

13. Kelso, *Doctrine for the Lady*, pp. 6, 10–13.

14. Janssen, *Geschichte*, VI: 430–37.

15. Kawerau, 'Lob und Schimpf des Ehestandes'; Siegel, 'Milton'.

16. Cf. Rogers, *Troublesome Helpmate*, pp. 100–134; Powell, *English Domestic Relations*, pp. 147–78.

17. Hajnal, 'European Marriage Patterns in Perspective'. Many scholars have endorsed these views: Wrigley, 'Family Limitation', p. 87; Spengler, 'Demographic Factors'; Van de Walle, 'Marriage', p. 489; Demeny, 'Early Fertility Decline', pp. 514–16.

18. Cf. Litchfield, 'Demographic Characteristics', p. 197. Between 1450 and 1649 men married between 29 and 35 years of age, and 30–55 per cent of all daughters were still single at age 50.

19. Demeny, p. 514.

20. Hajnal, p. 116.

21. Noonan, 'Intellectual and Demographic History', pp. 480–81.

22. Spengler, 'Demographic Factors'; Hajnal, p. 132.

by arrangement) found among Lutherans and Puritans alike.[23] Just as important no doubt was the social impact of a large proportion of people who never married at all. In a society accustomed to placing 95 per cent of all women in marriage, the identity problems and role conflict of perhaps 20 per cent of all women might now prove enormous. Here for the first time in European history was a large group of women who remained spinsters. Their numbers were of course augmented by widows, who often formed 10–20 per cent of the tax-paying population. We know from other studies that such sexual disbalance away from marriage provoked social problems and affected social attitudes.[24] We know that theoretically, legally, and perhaps emotionally the patriarchal family was considered the basis of society.[25] In the light of these concepts, the growing number of unmarried women would have appeared as a seditious element in society, especially after the death of their fathers removed them from patriarchal control altogether. Nunneries even in Catholic countries seem to have been in decline in the sixteenth century. Until society learned to adjust to the new family patterns, one could argue that unmarried women would have been especially susceptible to attack.

This conclusion would support the commonplace observation that widows and spinsters were most commonly accused of witchcraft, far out of proportion to their numbers in society. Certainly it was against them that many hunts were initially directed; later when that stereotype dissolved, large numbers of married women and young unmarried girls were suspected, accused, and convicted of witchcraft. Much more demographic work needs to be done to turn these conjectures into demonstrations. But the model of changing social roles holds out more hope of solving the knotty problem of sixteenth-century misogyny than a dozen studies of classical or biblical origins.

Two attributes of women did obviously increase the likelihood that they would be suspected of witchcraft. One was melancholy, a depressed state characterized occasionally by obscure or threatening statements and odd behaviour. Many women in their confessions emphasized the fact that they were seduced into witchcraft at a time when they were sad, dejected, or even desperate – often because of ill treatment by husbands.

23. Ariès, *Centuries of Childhood*, pp. 69–75, 403–4; Morgan, *Puritan Family*, chaps. 2 and 3; Luther, 'Das Elltern die Kinder zur Ehe nicht zwingen'.

24. Moller, 'Sex Composition'.

25. The structure of Althusius's thought regarding politics revolves constantly around the family. Morgan's conclusions (pp. 78–89) would seem to apply far beyond the restricted New England horizon.

Johann Weyer found melancholy so frequently among old women accused of witchcraft that he made it central to his picture of the poor deluded witch.[26]

The other dangerous attribute, as already suggested, was isolation. Women belonged under the protection and legal power of their father until they married.[27] When they married, their husbands took over this power intact. Maids and servants too were part of the household in which they lived and were subject to the discipline of the family.[28] The structure of society was so completely geared to the family that persons without families were automatically peculiar, unprotected, and suspect. Widows in particular were defenceless until they remarried.[29] So were spinsters. For this reason, husbands urged their wives to remarry if death should separate them. Thomas Schreiber, the unfortunate innkeeper in Mergentheim*, wrote to his wife shortly before his execution, lamenting that 'I can no longer be your father', but urging her to remarry 'on account of the children, for widows and orphans are despised and pushed down in this vile world'.[30] In some cases the courts even seemed to recognize that the problem of dangerous women was related to their unattached, uncontrolled existence. In 1571 the court at Horb, a few miles up the Neckar from Rottenburg, released Agatha, the widow of Hanns Bader of Bildechingen, on the condition that she swear 'to live quietly and chastely, and not to leave the jurisdiction of Bildechingen any more, and to stay day and night in the household of her son-in-law'.[31] Putting her under masculine rule would help solve the problem. We are now in a better position to reflect on the impact a larger proportion of unmarried women might have on such a society.

---

*The case of Thomas Schreiber is described on pp. 150–53 of Dr Midelfort's book – *Ed.*

26. E. William Monter has asserted that Bodin was correct in rejecting Weyer's claim that witches were melancholy, befuddled old women. Bodin had argued that such women *could* not be melancholiacs. Such a statement merely proves Bodin's ignorance of the state of the literature in the sixteenth century and his total reliance on the classics. Galen was not accepted uncritically in the sixteenth century as Monter implies, 'Inflation and Witchcraft', p. 382. Cf. Babb, *Elizabethan Malady*, p. 191 (for a *lady* suffering from melancholy), p. 28 (for 'uterine' melancholy). Melancholy was itself often pictured as a woman; cf. Klibansky, Panofsky, and Saxl, *Saturn and Melancholy*, pp. 220 *et seq.*, and the plates. For Bodin and melancholy, cf. Brann, 'Renaissance Passion of Melancholy', pp. 361–67, with the proof of how thoroughly out of tune Bodin was with contemporary thinkers on the subject.

27. Eberle, 'Probleme', p. 91–92.

28. Morgan, pp. 62–77, 84–87.

29. R. Schmidt, *Die Frau*, p. 125.

30. Württemberg, Staatsarchiv Ludwigsburg, Repertorium B262. Mergentheim Gerichtsakten, Bü. 103 (undated letter to his wife).

31. Giefel, 'Zur Geschichte der Hexenprozesse'.

The family context in which witch-trials took place often complicated the trials. In a large panic in a small town, it is clear that the judges or jurymen might quickly come to situations in which their own relatives, even wives, were suspected. The chance for political accusation was large and inviting, but it is very difficult without diaries or personal letters to prove this sort of motivation in any specific case. Factionalism, however, may have played a larger role than most historians have assumed. Julio Caro Baroja, the anthropologist, has drawn the suggestive parallel between medieval feuding and witch-hunting, but he had little evidence to support it.[32]

It has been commonplace since Michelet to remark the high incidence of trials in which mother and daughter(s) were executed. In Mergentheim nearly one-half of the persons arrested for witchcraft were related to at least one other suspect. In the case of the Weit family, eight members were tried and executed between November 1628 and June 1630. In a story included by Martin Crusius in his chronicle, certain features of factional tension between town and village emerge with startling clarity. Although he did not label it an example of witchcraft, the details are so exceptionally similar that we can be fairly sure that it was. In 1588 it seems that the wine steward at a tavern in Habsburg Bernau[33] failed to keep accurate records. Wine was missing and unaccounted for. The innkeeper stayed in his wine cellar overnight and watched as seventeen old women 'poured wine for themselves and drank joyously with one another according to their established custom'. When the innkeeper brought charges against them, they admitted that they had done this and 'other such evil deeds for the past seventeen years; therefore, they were burned to death. But some of them had relatives in a village of that region, and they came to Bernau around 1 January 1589, and set it afire at five places; 129 buildings burned down including the town hall and all its contents, and twenty-three persons besides.'[34] Here at least was a perfectly clear case of family factionalism and the dire effects it could have in witch panics. It was perhaps a fear that family complications would develop that led the magistrates to pause so long in the case of Thomas Schreiber. We may recall that his friends and relatives from several surrounding towns petitioned for his release. Certainly the courts had to be circumspect before taking action. Only after receiving advice from the

32. Caro Baroja, *The World of the Witches*, pp. 89–91. He says that inquisitors thought of witches as an organized band, hardly a novel observation.
33. Bernau is about five miles northwest of St Blasien.
34. Crusius, *Schwäbische Chronik*, II: 378.

learned of Würzburg did they feel confident enough to torture, condemn, and execute Schreiber.

Turning from the family nexus in which early modern society both thought and acted, we may treat briefly a few of the persistent questions regarding the status and character of those executed for witchcraft. It is sometimes asserted that witchcraft was a *Modeverbrechen,* a fashionable crime under which many old-fashioned, genuine crimes were subsumed. There can be no doubt that in the many small, isolated witchcraft trials that went on throughout the sixteenth and seventeenth centuries, many crimes like fornication, abortion, infanticide, and poisoning were connected to witchcraft.[35] It is another matter, however, to assert that those caught up in severe witch panics were real criminals. One would then be faced with explaining a sudden crime wave of enormous proportions. The persons caught up in such years of terror ranged from the ugliest hag to the Bürgermeister himself. Often accusations at first were aimed at the stereotyped examples of old, secluded, peculiar women. It is false to assume that this stereotype originated only in the modern age, as many scholars assert. The age of witch-hunts thought first in terms of old women, just as we do. But the mechanism of the hunt has shown us in many cases what happened. Denunciations spread rapidly from tortured suspects until a hundred or more persons were implicated. Those who accumulated the most denunciations were of two groups: (1) the people of notoriously bad reputation (especially midwives), and (2) the better known men and women of a town, like magistrates, teachers, innkeepers, wealthy merchants, and their wives. Our analysis of confiscations* confirmed the early interest of the courts both in the very poor and in men of wealth. One cannot simply speak glibly of who 'the witch' was, what his or her character reveals. We must learn to deal with sixteenth-century stereotypes and become sensitive to the crisis that developed when stereotypes broke down, especially in the seventeenth century.

Historians have also noted occasionally that wealthy persons sometimes received better treatment and less severe torture than their poorer neighbours. Judging by modern standards, they have assumed that bribery eased the lot of the wealthy. Of course it was true that wealthy persons could afford to buy better food than prison fare and to keep warmer in their cells. But by imperial law, persons of high estate were actually entitled to better treatment and less degrading punishments. The

*In the first part (pp. 164–78) of Chapter 7, from which this excerpt also comes – *Ed.*

35. This appears very clearly in the consultations of the Tübingen legal faculty throughout the seventeenth century: Tübingen Universität, Universitätsarchiv. 84/1–70. Libri Sententiarum ... facultatis jur. Vols. 1–60.

Carolina,* for example, referred often to 'estate' (*Stand*) and gave alternatives in punishment in nineteen articles.[36] Later interpreters used Roman law to argue that social class was always a relevant factor in determining punishment.[37] We noticed in our account of the witch-hunt at Rottenburg† that Agatha von Sontheim escaped the full extent of the ordinary law and was released in return for money and a change in religion.

It may well be generally true that the nobility received light treatment, since we know of only two other instances in the German Southwest in which persons of the nobility were even accused of witchcraft between 1500 and 1700. In one case, the knight Hans Ritter von Gnöztheim was executed in 1591 for practicing 'unchristliche Zauberei'.[38] In the other case, Sabina von Schellenberg (*née* von Freiberg) was accused of witchcraft in 1635. The court at Bräunlingen arrested her, but finally let her go without seriously questioning her.[39] In a few other incidents, nobles appeared as plaintiffs, as in 1590 when Leo von Freiberg tried and executed a man for witchcraft after aspersions had been cast on Freiberg's wife.[40] Again in 1621 a certain Jacob der Schwabe zu Bamlach was executed at Kleinkems for having used magic to kill Junker Dietrich von Andlaw.[41] An exactly similar case in 1737 in which a person was executed for bewitching Count Neipperg concludes our series.[42] It is evident from so short a list that the nobility did not in this period play anything like the major role it had in the witch-trials of the Middle Ages. In that earlier period nobles were often suspected of using magic for political and personal ends.[43] The crucial element of this shift would seem to lie in the group of people who feared the action of witchcraft. As long as kings, princes, and the high nobility feared the effects of evil magic, we can expect that they would have concentrated on rivals and schemers within their own ranks.[44] But in an age when the populace at large lived

Constitutio Criminalis Carolina, 1532, the basic criminal code of the Holy Roman Empire (see pp. 22–27 of Dr Midelfort's book) – *Ed.*

†Described on pp. 91 f. of the book – *Ed.*

36. Gwinner, *Der Einfluss des Standes*, pp. 43–46, 87–89, 117, 125.

37. For Rome, cf. Garnsey, 'Legal Privilege'.

38. Walcher, 'Ein Hexenprozess', p. 345.

39. Balzer, 'Die Bräunlinger Hexenprozesse', p. 24; cf. the weak study by Heinrich Schreiber, *Die Hexenprozesse*, pp. 25–32.

40. Meyer, *Heimatbuch*, p. 76.

41. Albert Ludwig, *Die evangelischen Pfarrer*, p. 73.

42. Willburger, 'Hexenverfolgung in Württemberg', p. 144.

43. Caro Baroja, *World of the Witches*, p. 83.

44. A late example is the famous Voisin affair in France, 1676–87; see Mandrou, *Magistrats et sorciers*, pp. 468–72.

in fear of witchcraft, the prince or lord was too remote to seem a likely suspect. At most the town magistrates or the administrators of the lord would fall prey to the suspicions of the populace. That, in fact, did happen.[45] Doctors, lawyers, and university professors, in addition to the nobility, seemed to enjoy considerable immunity from witchcraft accusations. Often they too legally avoided the grossest tortures.[46] Even university students who came under suspicion were generally punished by expulsion only.[47]

Aside from these generally privileged groups, it seems clear that Jews and Gypsies were almost never accused of witchcraft. We know of no instance in the German Southwest in which they were victims of witch-trials. The standard explanation for this phenomenon has been that witchcraft was a heresy, and therefore one had to be a Christian to become a witch.[48] That made good theological sense, and Christian Thomasius emphasized the point while attacking the witch-hunt. 'No one,' he said, 'calls Jews or Gypsies witches (*Hexenmeister*) or says that they have a pact with the devil,' despite their common reputation for magic.[49] Yet the most severe judges of witchcraft scoffed at this distinction. Jean Bodin, for example, argued learnedly in 1580 that even pre-Christian Rome and Greece had had witches. They were persons who renounced their own religion and gave themselves to the devil.[50] In struggling to make the classical world relevant to Renaissance Europe, Bodin was continually forced to generalize, and to define matters in such a way that uniquely Christian doctrines became culturally relative. Bodin, therefore, opened the door to witchcraft to even Jews and Gypsies. Similarly in 1667 Johann Jacob Faber asserted that Gypsies actually *were* witches.[51] In 1581 a woman from Cappel near Rottweil even described the devil as a Gypsy.[52] No doubt there were ways of getting around a strict reading of theology if there had been any desire to persecute Jews and Gypsies as witches. After all, the *Carolina* had said nothing of heresy; it

45. Franck, 'Der Hexenprozess'; Balzer, p. 7; Strukat, 'Hexenprozesse'.

46. Gwinner, *Der Einfluss des Standes*, pp. 203–4.

47. E.g. in Freiburg i. Br. in 1613; Janssen, *Geschichte*, VIII: 681, n. 2. In 1588 two Tübingen students received light punishment for their version of Faust in verse; cf. Boeckh, *Geschichte*, p. 421; Engel, *Bibliotheca*, no. 212, pp. 67–71. The unique copy of this version is in Copenhagen.

48. 'Only a Christian could be a witch'; Robbins, *Encyclopedia*, p. 550.

49. Philipp, *Zeitalter der Aufklärung*, pp. 291–92.

50. Ordinary pagans were idolators whose religion at least 'restrains men somehow by the barriers of the law of nature', Bodin, *De la démonomanie*, fols. 69r–79r.

51. Faber, *Specimen Zeli*, p. 12.

52. Ruckgaber, 'Die Hexenprozesse', pp. 184 *et seq.*

spoke only of harmful or harmless magic. It seems necessary to conclude that these two groups were simply not appropriate scapegoats in the sixteenth and seventeenth centuries.[53] Perhaps after the great pogroms of the fifteenth and early sixteenth centuries, the Jews found a social position, in villages and small towns, that was less threatening to their neighbours. Gypsies on the other hand were migrant. They never stayed long enough in one place to become part of the local social structure, and perhaps for that reason were suspected only of thefts and other secular crimes. Gypsies were continually forced and herded from one place to another without becoming part of a witch hunt.[54] Perhaps too their well-known elusiveness made apprehension impossible.

References

Primary printed sources

BODIN, JEAN. *De la démonomanie des sorciers*. Paris, 1580.

CRUSIUS, MARTIN. *Schwäbische Chronik, worinnen zu finden ist, was sich von Erschaffung der Welt an biss auf das Jahr 1596 in Schwaben … zugetragen … Aus dem Lateinischen erstmals übersetzt, und mit einer Continuation vom Jahr 1596 biss 1733 … versehen*. Ed. and trans. Johann Jacob Moser. 2 vols. Frankfurt, 1733.

FABER, JOHANN JAKOB. *Specimen Zeli justi Theologici contra Maleficos et Sagas. Das ist Muster und Prob eines recht Theologischen Eifers wider die Zauberer und Hexen*. Foreword by Tobias Wagner. Stuttgart, 1667.

LUTHER, MARTIN. 'Das Elltern die Kinder zur Ehe nicht zwingen noch hyndern, und die Kinder on der elltern willen sich nicht verloben sollen' (1524), in *D. Martin Luthers Werke* (Weimar, 1883–), 15, pp. 163–69.

Secondary sources

ARIÈS, P. (1962), *Centuries of Childhood*, New York.

BABB, L. (1951), *The Elizabethan Malady. A Study of Melancholia in English Literature from 1580 to 1640*, East Lansing, Mich.

BALZER, E. (1910), 'Die Bräunlinger Hexenprozesse', *Alemannia*, 3rd series, vol. 2, pp. 1–42.

BERKOWITZ, L., and GREEN, J. A. (1962), 'The stimulus qualities of the scapegoat', *Journal of Abnormal and Social Psychology*, vol. 64, pp. 293–301.

BOECKH, J. G., et al. (1961), *Geschichte der deutschen Literatur von 1480 bis 1600*, Berlin.

BRANN, N. L. (1965), 'The Renaissance passion of melancholy: the paradox of its cultivation and resistance', unpublished Ph.D. dissertation, Stanford University.

BÜCHER, C. (1882), *Die Frauenfrage im Mittelalter*, Tübingen.

CARO BAROJA, J. (1964), *The World of the Witches*, Chicago.

53. Trevor-Roper oversimplifies when he suggests that Jews and witches were interchangeable victims of pressures for social conformity. He fails to analyze the specific cases in which it was either Jews or witches who were persecuted; *Crisis*, p. 112.

54. As in Rottweil; Stadtarchiv, Repertorium, Vols. 12–13, 1570–89. In 1580 Rottweil was much taken up with the problems of Gypsies.

DEMENY, P. (1968), 'Early fertility decline in Austria-Hungary: a lesson in demographic transition', *Daedalus*, vol. 97, pp. 502–22.

EBERLE, E. (1964), *Probleme zur Rechtstellung der Frau nach den kursächsischen Konstitution von 1572*, Dr. jur. dissertation, Heidelberg University, 1964; published Stuttgart.

ENGEL, K. (1885), *Bibliotheca Faustiana, Zusammenstellung der Faustschrigen vom 16. Jahrhundert bis Mitte 1884*, 2nd edn, Oldenbourg.

FRANCK, W. (1870–72), 'Der Hexenprozess gegen dem Fürstenbergischen Registrator, Obervogteiverweser und Notar Mathias Tinctorius und Consorten zu Hüfingen. Ein Sittenbild aus den 3oer Jahren [1630's]', *Zeitschrift der Gesellschaft für Beförderung der Geschichts-Altertums- und Volkskunde von Freiburg, dem Breisgau und den angrenzenden Landschaften*, vol. 2, pp. 1–42.

GARNSEY, P. (1968), 'Legal privilege in the Roman Empire', *Past & Present*, no. 41, pp. 3–24.

GIEFEL, J. (1902), 'Zur Geschichte der Hexenprozesse in Horb und Umgebung', *Reutlinger Geschichtsblätter*, vol. 13, pp. 90–92.

GWINNER, H. (1934) *Der Einfluss des Standes im gemeinen Strafrecht*, Dr. jur. dissertation, Breslau-Neukirch University. Published as No. 345 of the Strafrechtliche Abhandlungen.

HAJNAL, J. (1965), 'European marriage patterns in perspective', in *Population in History* (D. V. Glass and D. E. C. Eversley eds), Chicago, pp. 101–43.

HANSEN, J. (1901), *Quellen und Untersuchungen zur Geschichte des Hexenwahns und der Hexenverfolgungen im Mittelalter*, Bonn.

HARPER, E. B. (1969), 'Fear and the status of women', *Southwestern Journal of Anthropology*, vol. 25, pp. 81–95.

JANSSEN, J. (1924), *Geschichte des deutschen Volkes seit dem Augsgang des Mittelalters*, 8 vols., 15th edn Freiburg i. Br.

KAWERAU, W. (1892), 'Lob und Schimpf des Ehestandes in der Litteratur des 16. Jahrhunderts', *Preussische Jahrbücher*, vol. 69, pp. 760–81.

KELSO, R. (1956), *Doctrine for the Lady in the Renaissance*, Urbana, Ill.

KLIBANSKY, R., PANOFSKY, E., and SAXL, F. (1964), *Saturn and Melancholy: Studies in the History of Natural Philosophy, Religion and Art*, London.

LITCHFIELD, R. B. (1969), 'Demographic characteristics of Florentine patrician families, sixteenth to nineteenth centuries', *Journal of Economic History*, vol 29, pp. 191–205.

LUDWIG, A. (1934), *Die evangelischen Pfarrer des badischen Oberlandes im 16. und 17. Jahrhundert*, Lahr. No. 9 of the Veröffentlichungen des Vereins für Kirchengeschichte in der evangelischen Landeskirche Badens.

MANDROU, R. (1968), *Magistrats et sorciers en France au XVIIe siècle*, Paris.

MEYER, K. (1928?), *Heimatbuch für Kirchheim unter Teck und Umgebung*, 4th edn, Kirchheim.

MIDDLETON, J., and WINTER, E. H. (eds) (1963), *Witchcraft and Sorcery in East Africa*, London.

MOLLER, H. (1945), 'Sex composition and correlated culture patterns of colonial America', *William and Mary Quarterly*, 3rd series, vol. 2, pp. 113–53.

MONTER, E. W. (1969), 'Inflation and witchcraft: the case of Jean Bodin', in *Action and Conviction in Early Modern Europe: Essays in Honor of E. H. Harbison* (T. K. Rabb and J. Seigel eds), Princeton, N.J., pp. 371–89.

MORGAN, E. (1944), *The Puritan Family*, Boston.

NOONAN, J. T. (1968), 'Intellectual and demographic history', *Daedalus*, vol. 97, pp. 463–85.

PAULUS, N. (1910), *Hexenwahn und Hexenprozess vornehmlich im 16. Jahrhundert*, Freiburg.

PHILIPP, W. (ed.) (1963), *Das Zeitalter der Aufklärung*. Vol. 7 of *Klassiker des Protestantismus*, Bremen.

POWELL, C. I. (1917), *English Domestic Relations 1487–1653*, New York.

ROBBINS, R. H. (1959), *The Encyclopedia of Witchcraft and Demonology*, New York.

ROGERS, K. M. (1966), *The Troublesome Helpmate: A History of Misogyny in Literature*, Seattle.

ROSENTHAL, T., and SIEGEL, B. J. (1959), 'Magic and witchcraft: interpretation from dissonance theory', *Southwestern Journal of Anthropology*, vol. 15, pp. 143–67.

RUCKGABER, H. (1838), 'Die Hexenprozesse in Rottweil a. N.', *Württembergische Jahrbücher*, pp. 174–96.

RUSSELL, J. C. (1965–6), 'Effects of pestilence and plague, 1315–1385', *Comparative Studies in Society and History*, vol. 8, pp. 464–73.

SCHMIDT, R. (1917), *Die Frau in der deutschen Literatur des 16. Jahrhunderts*, Strassburg.

SCHREIBER, H. (1836), *Die Hexenprozesse zu Freiburg im Breisgau, Offenburg in der Ortenau, und Bräunlingen aus dem Schwarzwalde*, Freiburg i. Br.

SIEGEL, P. N. (1950), 'Milton and the Humanist attitude toward women', *Journal of the History of Ideas*, vol. 11, pp. 42–53.

SOLDAN-HEPPE (1912), *Geschichte der Hexenprozesse*. Ed. Max Bauer. 2 vols, Munich.

SPENGLER, J. (1968), 'Demographic factors and early modern ecomonic development', *Daedalus*, vol. 97, pp. 433–46.

STRUKAT, A. (1927), 'Hexenprozesse in den fürstenbergischen Gemeinden', *Aus dem Schwarzwald*, vol. 35, p. 139.

THRUPP, S. (1965–6), 'Plague effects in medieval Europe', *Comparative Studies in Society and History*, vol. 8, pp. 474–83.

TRAMER, M. (1945), 'Kinder im Hexenglaube und Hexenprozess des Mittelalters', *Zeitschrift für Kinderpsychiatrie*, vol. 11, pp. 140–9, 180–7.

TREVOR-ROPER, H. R. (1968), 'The European witch-craze of the sixteenth and seventeenth centuries', in *The Crisis of the Seventeenth Century: Religion, the Reformation and Social Change*, New York, pp. 90–192.

VAN DE WALLE, E. (1968), 'Marriage and marital fertility', *Daedalus*, vol. 97, pp. 486–501.

VIERORDT, K. F. (1847–56), *Geschichte der evangelischern Kirche in dem Grossherzogthum Baden. Nach grossentheils handschriftlichen Quellen bearbeitet*, 2 vols, Karlsruhe.

WALCHER, K. (1892), 'Ein Hexenprozess im Jahr 1591', *Württembergische Vierteljahrshefte für Landesgeschichte*, n.s. vol. 1, pp. 345–53.

WEYER, J[ohann], *De Praestigiis Daemonum*, Basel, 1577.

WILLBURGER, A. (1929–30), 'Hexenverfolgung in Württemberg', *Robbenburger Monatschrift für praktische Theologie*, vol. 13, pp. 135–45, 167–73.

WILSON, F. P. (1963), *The Plague in Shakespeare's London*, London.

WOEHLKENS, E. (1954), *Pest und Ruhr im 16. und 17. Jahrhundert*, Hanover, n.s. 26; Schriften des niedersächsischen Heimatbundes.

WRIGLEY, E. A. (1966), 'Family limitation in preindustrial England', *Economic History Review*, vol. 19, 82–109.

19. Joyce Bednarski

The Salem Witch-Scare Viewed Sociologically

Abridged version of Joyce Bednarski, *The Salem Witch-Scare Viewed Sociologically*, 1968, original MS.

The Salem witch-scare has become a classic part of American history, if for no other reason than because it is unique on the American continent. Historians have been enthralled with its brutality and hysteria since its occurrence almost three hundred years ago. Immediately following the incident, several books were published, the most notable being: Cotton Mather's *Wonders of the Invisible World* and Robert Calef's *More Wonders of the Invisible World*, (see Burr, 1914) the latter author making the former one appear to be a somewhat foolish and superstitious man blinded toward the facts (Starkey, 1961, p. 246). The clash of opinions about the witch-scare was the first in a long line of disagreement which was to follow. Even the men who witnessed the trials could not agree on their meaning and relevance. This, one might suggest, is not unusual; people involved in an event are often led by their emotional attachment to the situation to interpret it according to their bias.

However, this uncertainty about Salem did not end with the generation who lived through it. Interestingly enough, it has continued to our own day, and the fanatical goings-on of that year are still surrounded by an aura of mystery and superstition which even the scientific age of the twentieth century has not successfully dispelled. In the nineteenth century, more literature was written on Salem in an attempt to explain the seemingly inconsistent outbreak of passion in the severe Puritan Community. Charles W. Upham's *Salem Witchcraft* (1867) is an extensive study of, not only the witch trials, but also the way of life which existed in the Bay Colony, and provides sketches of the personalities involved in the trials. For all his work, however, Upham seems to come up with few answers. Indeed, in his more than 500 pages, he does little more than relate the history of those few years; admittedly he sets forth some causal hypotheses, but all of these he concludes are not valid after investigation of the facts. Many other documents could be cited: there is Brooks Adams's *The Emancipation of Massachusetts* (1887), one section of which deals with witchcraft, Winfield S. Nevin's *Witchcraft in Salem*

190

Village in 1692 (1892), somewhat a repetition of Upham, but not chronologically organized and therefore confusing to the student who is not already familiar with the story. This list is hardly exhaustive, but it serves to illustrate my point that the Salem witch-hunt has been a subject of continuous interest ever since it occurred and continues to the present day to haunt the minds of American historians of this early era with its seeming incongruity and ill defined effects on our culture.

The aim of this paper is to re-examine the major events of the trials and analyse them sociologically. My account is based on Marion Starkey's *The Devil in Massachusetts* (1961) as well as extensive reading in the earlier accounts of Cotton Mather, Robert Calef and others, tempered with some general background reading on the life and times, the *mores* and customs, of these early Puritans (see, Miller (1952), Taylor (1908), Winthrop (1853)). In the absence of any sociological evaluation of the events of 1692, much of my paper will be speculative.

A brief account of what took place in Salem Village (now the Boston suburb of Danvers) towards the close of the seventeenth century is a necessary preliminary to sociological analysis and should provide a deeper understanding of the social and emotional climate which nurtured the witch-scare.

The Salem witch-scare began quietly and gradually in the home of the Reverend Samuel Parris, minister in the local church. Several of the young girls of the village had taken a liking to listening to Parris's colored domestic servant, Tituba, tell stories of the supernatural which she had learned in Barbados. They were enthralled by the excitement of her tales of witches, curses and spells, and began to spend more and more time at her feet listening to these accounts. She, too, was probably encouraged by their admiration and attention to rack her memory for the most fantastic and hair-raising of her repertoire. At what point this harmless pastime turned into the tragic action which was to sweep the community, no one knows. At any rate, some of the children were so taken by these stories that they began to feel supernatural powers working upon them.

By the end of the winter, several of the children began to suffer from a strange malady. They would, for no apparent reason, fall into convulsions, scream inhumanly, and engage in other extraordinary behavior. As their malady became public knowledge, more and more of the village children succumbed to it. While some adults were sceptical about their antics, most were horrified and puzzled by the onslaught and could do little but stand in helpless awe of the situation.

And so Dr Griggs, the town physician, was called in. He tried all his remedies; he reread all of his medical books, but to no avail. Finally he admitted that the affliction of these children was outside the realm of medicine; his considered opinion was that they were bewitched. Given the stage of medical knowledge at that time, this was not an unreasonable assumption.

The problem was passed on to the spiritual mentors of the community. Parris took the situation in hand and called together ministers from the neighboring area to decide what should be done. After witnessing the girls' contortions, the clergy agreed that Satan had come to Salem; and the only recourse was immediate action; the children would have to identify the witches who were harassing them. All this talk of witchcraft, coupled with Tituba's hair-raising tales, certainly helped to convince the girls that they were bewitched. In addition, the continuous pleading from the clergy that they reveal the identity of their tormentors must have induced them to accuse their first three 'witches'.

The character and background of those they named are significant. The first was Tituba, an obvious choice because of her vast knowledge of the 'art' and her cultural alienation from the community. The second, Sarah Good, was the town hag; a pipe-smoking tramp who wandered over the countryside begging from everyone and cursing those who refused her. Hated and disdained by all the upright Salemites, she was a prime target. The third, Sarah Osbourne, was of high social status, but her reputation was tainted by the scandal that she had lived with a man nearly a year before marrying him. To the Puritan mind, this was among the worst of sins. Besides, she had not attended church in fourteen months, and that was judged as a further sign of her degeneracy and involvement with the forces of evil.

If the coaxing of the girls can be said to have elicited the first accusations, it was the hearings at which the three accused women were examined that produced the snowballing effect which was to follow in which no one, no matter how virtuous, could feel secure from the barrage of name-calling. The children were in attendance at the hearings, where they made their presence known by crying out and rolling on the floor in agony. Everyone assumed that the women on trial were responsible for their suffering. Furthermore, when Tituba was put on the stand, she did not deny the accusations as had Sarah Good and Sarah Osbourne, but rather gave her audience an exuberant confession. She warned the onlookers that, besides herself and her two fellow accused, Satan had many more conspirators in the village.

The hearing then, which was supposed to bring a quick end to the scare, had exactly the opposite effect. The people began to look around

192

for the additional witches to whom Tituba had made reference; the girls' status was elevated — no longer were they merely afflicted children, but oracles or diviners who could help to weed out the evil elements in the community. All the attention they received must have encouraged them to continue their antics so that they would not fall from favor. Indeed, once one had become one of the 'diviners', there was virtually no way out. This fact is exemplified by the case of Mary Warren who tried to renounce her accusations when her master, John Proctor, was cried out upon. Not only would no one listen to her, but several of the girls intimated that Mary had finally succumbed to the power of the Devil and was trying to undermine the forces of good working against him. So, within a short time, Mary 'repented' and returned to the fold.

After the initial hearings, accusations fell like raindrops. Most of the village would have been happy if the scandal had ended with the indict-ment of the first three 'witches', but anyone with insight might have guessed that this was not to happen. Barely a week had passed when another accusation was made, this time not of a ne'er-do-well, but of an upstanding and pious member of the community – Martha Cory. Hers was followed by those of Dorcas Good, the five-year-old daughter of Sarah Good, and of Rebecca Nurse and her two sisters, Mary Esty and Sarah Cloyce, three of the most saintly and respected members of the Church. And so it went – John Proctor, Giles Cory, Abigail Hobbes, Bridget Bishop, Sarah Wild, Susannah Martin, Dorcas Hoar and the Reverend George Burroughs – most of whom had previously been con-sidered fine, God-fearing members of the community. The county jail was bursting at its seams, and the list of upcoming trials grew to an unpre-cedented length.

The hysteria had run wild. By spring, it no longer confined itself to Salem, but spread to Andover and other surrounding towns. At this point, the colonial officials intervened. They decided to set up a Court of Oyer and Terminer to try the cases of the suspected witches. Even this move was not sufficient to stem the growing tide of mass mania. The judges who were appointed were as easily convinced of the girls' sincerity and the accused's dishonesty as the Salem magistrates had been before them. Those who confessed were spared (but kept in prison), while those who refused to admit that they were agents of the Devil were hanged.

William Phips, the new governor of the Colony, admitted that he had no solution to the problem, and busied himself with the Indian wars which had been causing some trouble on the northern frontier. Mean-while, the girls continued to cry out against an extraordinary number of people. At one point, even Lady Phips was named. When Samuel

Willard, president of Harvard College and pastor of the First Church of Boston, was accused, the magistrates flatly told the girls that they were mistaken. This act marked the beginning of the end. As more and more persons of irreproachable character were cried out upon, more and more of the judges and men in authority questioned the justice of the whole procedure. The validity of spectral evidence had always been a bone of contention, and now seemed even more in doubt in view of the worsening situation. It was brought to the attention of the authorities that in the Bible the Devil had appeared in the form of Samuel, a highly regarded saint. This raised the question of whether Satan might indeed be able to impersonate an innocent person. If this were so, the spectres haunting the girls could very well be 'freelance' apparitions; and thus the prosecution would have no case at all.

In the face of growing doubts, Governor Phips dismissed the Court of Oyer and Terminer in October, and released several persons from prison. However, more than one hundred and fifty remained in custody, and an additional two hundred had been accused. In December, Phips instituted the Superior Court of Judicature to try those cases still on the calendar. The magistrates agreed to admit spectral evidence only in marginal cases. Of fifty-two persons tried, only three were found guilty – an amazing reversal, considering that, up to that time, there had not been a single acquittal. Phips responded by signing reprieves for the three accused as well as for five others who had been condemned previously. Finally the governor issued a general pardon for those still under suspicion, and discharged all who remained in jail. This marked the end of the Salem witch-hunt. It was over less than a year after it began, but in the course of that time nineteen persons had been hanged, two had died in prison, and Giles Cory, who had adopted the course of standing mute at his trial, had been crushed under a pile of rocks (a persuasive procedure used by the magistrates to induce confession) – a grand total of twenty-two lives sacrificed to the hysterical screechings of a pack of adolescent girls.

This is the story. Many things have been left out. Only a detailed reading of the annals of 1692 can communicate the full horror of what went on. But from this sketchy account the trend is clear; it is the story of a society gone mad – a society blind to rationality and reason, driven by fear and distrust. The question remains as to the reasons for this outburst and the effects it had on the development of events after its conclusion.

An answer to this question must be qualified by the recognition that human interaction is subject to many influences, and single causes of events can seldom be determined. Another qualification needs to be made. George Kittredge has said: 'It is easy to be wise after the fact –

especially when the fact is two hundred years old' (1929, p. 373). This he sets forth as an admonition to those who would judge seventeenth-century actions by twentieth-century standards. Many ascribe the tenets of the New Englanders in the matter of witchcraft to their Puritan theology. This, he feels, is a serious error. He argues that: 'Our forefathers believed in witchcraft, not because they were Puritans, not because they were Colonials, not because they were New Englanders, but because they were men of their own time and not of ours' (1929, p. 357). He then goes on to substantiate his statement with copious evidence of a universal belief in witchcraft in the seventeenth century. This point is not ill taken. There is always the chance that the analyst will try to superimpose his cultural values and judgements on a situation in which they do not pertain and will subsequently come up with conclusions which are equally unbased. Our ideas and values have changed considerably since 1692, and therefore I am perhaps unjustified when I speak of Salem as a society gone mad – blind to all rationality and reason – for indeed this kind of rationality and reason did not come into its own until about the time of the French Revolution, almost a century after the Salem incident. However, if kept within the context of what Salem appears to be to our contemporaries, I think it is a valid statement: such hysteria is madness in any age. So long as the reason for its existence, i.e. the belief in witches, is not viewed as foolish and insane, there seems to be no injustice done.

What were the conditions which caused the Salem witch-scare? Broadly speaking, most writers will agree that scares and crazes arise during a time of struggle, upheaval and change. In an era of uncertainty men will act and react in extraordinary ways. Sometimes they will make amazing strides and on other occasions they will revert to anti-social behavior. It is a simple sociological hypothesis that when conventional avenues of conduct in a society are blocked or cut off, men will be forced to establish new ones. In this process, several structures may be tried before an acceptable one is found, and in the interim anomie may prevail.

The Bay Colony was experiencing a metamorphosis of this sort in both her political and religious-moral realms at the end of the seventeenth century. Because of the overemphasis on the Puritan ethic as the driving force behind the colonists, the political dilemma is not commonly understood. At best, the political situation in 1690 could be described as uncertain. The problems had begun more than 30 years earlier during the Quaker persecutions. King Charles's decrees had brought about only minor changes in the political outlines of the Colony; however, they had made the people uneasy about their future. The King's dispatching of four commissioners to the Commonwealth of Massachusetts to see that his orders were being carried out made the colonists even more apprehensive. In 1676, Charles II began to review property claims; in 1679, he ordered Massachusetts to allow the establishment of an Anglican Church (hitherto outlawed by the colonists). One event led to another and in 1686 James revoked the Charter and sent a Royal Governor named Andros (both an Anglican and a disdainer of colonial self-assertion) to govern the Colony. In 1689, Bostonians revolted and imprisoned Andros. Luckily for them, William of Orange had succeeded in overthrowing James, in the Glorious Revolution, and they were not reprimanded by William for their revolt against James's lackey (Erikson, 1966, p. 138).

Meanwhile, Increase Mather had gone to England in 1688 to negotiate for the reinstitution of the Charter (Kittredge, 1929, p. 371). He returned home in 1692 with a new charter instead, some of the provisions of which would make the colonists very unhappy. Indeed they had already gotten wind of the bad news, for two of Mather's fellow delegates had refused to accept the new charter and had sailed home early to warn the populace and denounce Mather. The change which incensed them stated that the electorate was no longer to be limited to members of the Covenant, but broadened to include propertied members of every Christian sect except Catholics. This provision was a considerable blow to the Puritan political theocracy: previously, law had ensured that the elect, i.e., members of the Covenant, would remain in power, regardless of their numbers. With the new ruling, there was a strong possibility that the damned would rule (those outside the Covenant heavily outnumbered those within it). Furthermore, William insisted that he name the governors of the Commonwealth, a bitter pill for the colonists to swallow, since they had been electing their own governors since the founding of the Colony more than fifty years before (Starkey, 1961, p. 131).

From this, it is apparent that the political structure of the Commonwealth had collapsed. Not only had the machinery broken down, but the theocratic philosophy which upheld it had been abandoned as well. The whole system was ready for the scrap-heap – and there were no alternatives to replace it. This fact is most significant. That the Colony was left without a measuring stick of its actions, a standard for evaluating its past and directing its future, is the very fact which generated a climate receptive to an outburst like the witchcraft mania of 1692.

The crisis in the political sphere was paralleled by one in the religious-moral realm. This was inevitable in a theocratic society such as that of the Puritans. The 'Puritan ethic' was undergoing a metamorphosis, too. But its upheaval was not the action of an outside force, as was the political change; its destruction came from within. The Puritan movement, when founded in England, had been international in scope. After fifty years in the New World, the Colonial Puritans had lost most of their meaningful contacts with the outside world, and no longer looked forward to a worldwide communion of the elect (Erikson, 1966, p. 156). The sense of mission which had sustained the sect in its infancy was gone.

Furthermore, the Puritan God was omnipotent. Believers had learned to accept tragedy and failure as God's will. However, by the 1690s, they saw all around them nothing but progress (Erikson, 1966, p. 156). Man had worked, and what he had produced was good. Where effort was put forth, progress had been made. There was no evidence of a God Who, by the wave of His mysterious hand, brought tragedy or plenty. And so the people began to move from a reliance on fate to a confidence in man's ability. This idea was not congruent with the original Puritan belief in predestination and was thus another rent in the fabric of the Puritan ethic.

Still another factor which undermined the stability of the society and laid it open for the witchcraft episode was the deterioration of the strong sense of community within the Colony. When the settlers landed in America, they were a body united against the evil world. Their very existence was threatened by the wilderness, full of dangerous wild beasts and hostile Indians. Only as a unit could they hope to stand up to these adversaries which they believed to be a manifestation of Satan. Now these adversaries had been overcome. The Indians and the wild beasts had retreated with the frontier – and Massachusetts was no longer the frontier (Erikson, 1966, p. 158). Even their righteous opposition to those who did not profess the 'True Faith' was taken away from them when the decree of 1679 ordered religious toleration (at least for Anglicans) in the Bay Colony (Erikson, 1966, p. 138). It is a simple sociological fact that a strong sense of community cannot exist without a purpose and there seemed to be no purpose for unity among the Puritans by 1690. And so the people grew away from their neighbors. Feelings of distrust and suspicion built up within the community because there was no effective avenue for channeling them toward an outside enemy.

The foregoing reasons, I feel, are causes of the Salem incident which stem from the breaking down of the system. The men of the Bay had lost their purpose and, in so doing, had lost their way. In the process of redirecting themselves, there ensued a brief period of anomie, the primary manifestation of which was the witch-scare.

On the other hand, I feel that there are factors within the workings of Puritanism which also contributed to the witch-scare. Admittedly, they may be secondary, but I still feel they are worth mentioning. In many

197

ways, the Puritan ethic is not unlike Lockean philosophy, both subjectively and structurally. Both are highly idealistic, and yet both are racked by confusion and latent contradictions. The subjective parallel carries through on the political level, where both attempt to reconcile authority and freedom. In the Puritan treatise, man is told on the one hand that he should cling to authority, dogma and revelation while on the other hand he is permitted to appeal to nature, reason and logic. The juxtaposition of these two propositions is paradoxical, because they are polemically removed from each other and have never been successfully reconciled. These inconsistencies exist within the spiritual realm of Puritan theology as well – in the fruitless attempts meaningfully to reconcile piety with intellect and spirit with reason (Miller, 1939, p. 430). These inconsistencies loom large in the trial procedures, which serve as a classic illustration of how these opposing qualities cannot exist together. It is apparent that all reason and logic had given way to dogma and revelation at the height of the hysteria and that no reason existed until the validity of dogma and revelation was dispelled.

The Puritan spirit is often looked upon as being tragic; a point with which Perry Miller strongly disagrees. Conversely, he feels that there is no sense of tragedy in Puritanism, that there is no provision in the philosophy for failure, and, therefore, no capability for its perception (1939, p. 38). Furthermore, Puritanism is unique in its absolutism and its refusal to make allowance for weakness (1939, p. 57). Coupling these two factors, one can see how the Puritan ethic encouraged a belief in witchcraft, i.e. if human failure is impossible, then any human flaw must be the work of the Devil.

There is also the possibility that the Salem witch-scare served as nothing more than a valve by which the community let off steam. They adopted the desperate piety and sense of impending doom from late medieval religion, but rejected the festivities and color which softened the harshness of that theology. Consequently, they were left without an emotional outlet. As the pressure built up, the society looked for a release, and it pounced on the first opportunity – the witch trials. That this is a major causal factor seems doubtful, but it may have had a secondary effect.

Another aspect of Puritanism is its lack of intermediaries between God and man. The pre-Calvin God was a personal God, easily accessible through saints and symbols. Reformation God, however, became elevated and aloof – outside of man's reach and understanding. Denied of this relationship, man looked for signs of God elsewhere – and the only place for him to turn was the world. If man could discern the faces of good and evil in material form, he felt more secure in his faith. From this it might be hypothesized that the aloofness of the Puritan God drove man to seek the struggle between good and evil within men in the persons of the bewitched and the witch. A further corollary to this point is that, once man no longer could find the faces of evil (the Devil) working from outside the community, he would be forced to look inward and accuse his fellows.

In summary, then, I would contend that the causes of the Salem witch-scare were both external and internal. In one respect the system was too weak to withstand the test of unity; in another it was too rigid to make allowances for the needs of its adherents not specifically provided for by the system. In the 1690s, then, Puritanism was like a rusty bridge girder: it was too brittle to stand up under the weight of controversy and not flexible enough to bend and make allowances for the changing tide of the times. In a word, it was antiquated.

What, then, were the ramifications of the Salem witch trials? Their most apparent effect was that they hastened the end of the Puritan era, and ushered in the age of reason. However, there is a more subtle proposition which I wish to set forth: that the Salem witch trials in some way affected and influenced the growth of New England as a major intellectual community. This hypothesis rests on Turner's analysis of the social drama which he sums up as follows:

Implicit in the notion of reintegration is the concept of social equilibrium. This concept involves the view that a social system is made up of interrelated units, of persons and groups, whose interests are somehow maintained in balance; and further, that when disturbance occurs, readjustments are made which have the effect of restoring the balance. But it is necessary to remember that after disturbance has occurred and readjustments have been made, there may have taken place profound modifications in the internal relations of the group. The new equilibrium is seldom a replica of the old. The interests of certain persons and groups may have gained at the expense of those of others. Certain relations between persons and groups may have increased in intensity while others may have diminished. Others again may have been completely ruptured while new relationships have come into being. A social system is in dynamic movement through space and time, in some way analogous to an organic system in that it exhibits growth and decay, in fact, the process of metabolism (1957, p. 161).

In essence, he is saying that a disturbance such as a witch hunt can act as a dynamic of social change. It can rearrange social units on the preference ladder by the very nature of its phases: breach, crisis, operation of redressive mechanisms, and either reintegration of the social groups or social recognition of irreparable schisms (1957, p. 161). A simple analogy could be made between a pyramid of children's blocks and a social system. The weak spot in both is the breach. The crisis occurs when the blocks fall down and when the basic values of the society are evaluated (indirectly by the witch-hunt). The last phase entails the rebuilding of the pyramid on the one hand and the reshaping of the society on the other. Neither is likely to have all the same parts in the same places. To continue the analogy, some blocks will be higher on the pyramid than before, others lower.

This is what I contend happened in Salem in 1692. Although the intellectual heritage was a definite part of the Puritan ethic, it ranked pretty low on the pyramid. Above it were authoritarianism, pietism, revelation, dogma, and moralism, to mention only the major ones. The crisis (the trials) proved that the most elevated values left something to be desired, and therefore when the system was rebuilt, another arrangement was tried. This rearrangement of values was taking place in the beginning of the eighteenth century when the scientific method and the concept of reason were coming into their own. These were the new and exciting ideas of the time. New England had some basis for accepting them in her intellectual heritage and high opinion of education left over from the Puritan era; and so she adopted them, and they grew and gained respect throughout the world. Consequently, by her early acceptance of these tenets, combined with their existence in an environment favorable for growth, they have developed to such a degree as to make New England an outstanding intellectual community.

References

ADAMS, B. (1887), *The Emancipation of Massachusetts*, Houghton Mifflin.
BURR, G. L. (ed.) (1914), *Narratives of the Witchcraft Cases 1648–1706*, Scribners.
ERIKSON, K. T. (1966), *Wayward Puritans*, Wiley.
KITTREDGE, G. L. (1929), *Witchcraft in Old and New England*, Harvard U.P.
MILLER, A. (1952), *The Crucible*, Viking Press.
MILLER, P. (1939), *The New England Mind*, Macmillan & Co.
NEVINS, W. S. (1892), *Witchcraft in Salem Village in 1692*, North Shore Publishing Co.
STARKEY, M. L. (1961), *The Devil in Massachusetts*, Knopf, 1950 (references are to the 1961 edn by Dolphin Books).
TAYLOR, J. M. (1908), *The Witchcraft Delusion in Colonial Connecticut*, Grafton Press.
TURNER, V. W. (1957), *Schism and Continuity in an African Society*, Manchester U.P.
UPHAM, C. W. (1867), *Salem Witchcraft*, 2 vols., Frederick Unger.
WINTHROP, J. (1853), *The History of New England*, vol. 2, Little, Brown.

20. Audrey Richards

A Modern Movement of Witch-Finders

Audrey Richards, 'A modern movement of witch-finders', *Africa*, vol. 8, 1935, no. 4, pp. 448–61.

All over present-day Africa witch-finders seem to appear, as it were from nowhere, flourish for a time, and then disappear. Either it is some individual of unusual personality in his community who announces a magic remedy for human sufferings, and so obtains a following, or else it is a more or less organized band of wonder-workers which crosses the border from some neighbouring territory with all the kudos attached to the foreign and the strange. Among these latter the celebrated *Bamucapi*, who recently swept from Nyasaland into Northern Rhodesia and later reached Southern Rhodesia and the Congo, are an interesting example. The actual origin of this movement is difficult to discover, but I watched it at its height in the Bemba country of N.E. Rhodesia in the summer of 1934, and I want in this article to describe very shortly the methods of these witch-finders, and to try to account for their success.[1]

The *Bamucapi* themselves were for the most part young and dressed in European clothing. They went about the country in ones and twos, usually paying local assistants to help them. Their leader, they said, was one Kamwende of Mlanje in Nyasaland, but he was spoken of as a person of mythical attributes rather than as an organizer in actual control. The procedure of the witch-finders was impressive. Arrived at a village, they summoned the headman, who was bidden to gather his people together and to kill and cook a chicken for the ritual meal of which all were to partake. Once assembled the men and women were lined up in separate files and passed one by one behind the back of the witch-finder, who caught their reflections in a small round mirror by a turn of his wrist. By his image in the glass it was claimed that a sorcerer could be immediately detected, and thus discovered, he was immediately called upon to yield up his horns (*nsengo*), a term which included all harmful magic charms. Wonderful stories were told of the perspicacity of the witch-finders.

1. During this time Professor Malinowski, then on a tour of inspection of his pupils' fields of study, visited my area, worked himself on this problem, and generously allowed me to add his notes to my own.

Horns wilfully concealed were apparently always unmasked. 'Look under the roof of his granary', the *Bamucapi* would cry in case of a denial by the sorcerer, and there the hidden danger would be immediately brought to light. 'We know they made no mistakes', was the significant comment of natives, 'because the men and women they spotted as sorcerers were people we had been afraid of all along!'

But with the detection of the sorcerer a cure was provided. Each man and woman drank a sip of the famous *mucapi* medicine – a fine red powder which gave a soapy solution when shaken with water in a bottle – the name of the witch-finders being said to come from the Cinyanja word *kucapa,* to rub or wash clothes. For this medicine the claim of the *Bamucapi* was staggering. It was nothing less than the complete removal of witchcraft from the territory. A man who had drunk the *mucapi* medicine, and then returned to his evil practices, was liable to instant death – a grisly death in which he was to swell to enormous proportions, his limbs crinkled with dropsy, and his body too heavy to be carried to the grave. Nor could a cunning sorcerer escape by refusing to pass in front of the magic mirror. He would merely be caught at a kind of second coming of the founder of the movement, who was to return beating a mysterious drum outside each village at night. At its sound all witches and wizards as yet undetected would be compelled to follow to the graveyard where their crimes would be finally unmasked. Some told also of the coming of a mythical woman with one breast in front and one behind. The good she would suckle in front, while the wicked would find themselves following willynilly behind. Such stories were told and retold in the villages with the myth of the original Kamwende, who, it was said, had received his revelation in the grave from which he had been resurrected after two days, with one eye, one arm, and one leg powerless, but with the secret of the *mucapi* medicine and the power to resist poisons of all kinds.

As a secondary object the *Bamucapi* sold protective charms, pinches of powder sewn up in small cloth bags. For 3d. charms could be bought against wild beasts and snakes, for 6d. powder to protect the gardens from animal pests, for 6d. a charm for luck and success and for 5s., it was rumoured, a charm for winning the favour of the local Government official. 'But you can see for yourself', my informant added, 'that very few natives have had as much money to spend as that!'

The success of the movement was from the first overwhelming. It completely captured the people's imagination, and created its myths as it spread. From hut to hut of an evening men shouted the latest exploits of the witch-finders – the number of horns found in such and such a village, or the people miraculously saved from snakes or lions. The Government, which at first allowed the movement to proceed unchecked, was universally praised. 'This is the best thing the Bwanas have ever done for us,' many natives told me. 'Now at last they are allowing us to free our country from witchcraft.' Adverse criticism of missions which refused to allow their Christians to drink the medicine was frequent. The suspicion, and often the accusations of witchcraft commonly made against unpopular Christian teachers, seemed at last to be publicly substantiated. 'If they have nothing to fear', the natives said, 'why are they afraid to put themselves to the test?' At the cross-roads outside each village was a pile of horns and other magic objects – horns which many missionaries had tried unsuccessfully for years to remove and forbid.

The cause of the success of this movement is therefore of considerable interest, the more so since it is in many ways typical of many such organizations of witch-finders which have sprung up in other parts of Africa. We have to ask ourselves first, then, why the methods of the *Bamucapi* appealed to the natives so strongly? To what fears did they seem to provide such an immediate and universal panacea? These are questions that cannot be answered by a study of the ritual and myths of the *Bamucapi* as an end in themselves. To assess the strength of the movement in any particular area we have to consider it against a background of tribal structure and belief.

In the Bemba country, for instance, it may be said that novelty was enough to account for the success of any native movement, religious or secular. The Babemba are known to be unusually credulous and unstable in temperament, the first to adopt and discard anything new. Nyasaland, the reputed home of the movement, has also a high reputation among Rhodesian natives as the land of high wages and educational facilities, and most of the clerks employed in the country are still of Nyasaland origin. Further, the Babemba are among those African peoples with whom every form of Europeanism is a positive cult. The *Bamucapi* appealed because they presented a dogma that satisfied native belief, while their ritual contained many superficial features of the white civilization. The witch-finders came as well-dressed young men, not as wrinkled old native doctors (*ŋanga*) in greasy bark-cloth. They worked in the open and lined up the natives after the manner of an official taking a census. They sold their medicine in stoppered chemist's bottles rather than in dirty old horns pulled from a skin bag. Their teaching, too, was an interesting blend of the old and the new. Their power, they said, came from Lesa, the High God on whom the *ŋanga* calls when preparing his medicine, the term being used by the missionary also to describe the Christian God. But curiously enough the efficacy of the medicine depended on the keeping of a number of taboos which are deeply embedded in native belief, such as, for instance, the taboo on a man having intercourse with a woman in the bush. Some natives said that Marya also helped the *Bamucapi*, but added quickly not the Marya of the Catholic missions, but another one; for there is no doubt the movement was antimission as a whole. Phrases reminiscent of Christian teaching were also used. The witch-finders addressed the villagers with a preliminary sermon, a technique quite foreign to the native *ŋanga*, and stressed such ideas as the washing of sins. Kamwende, it will be remembered, descended into the grave and rose again, and was expected to reappear at a second coming. It is interesting, too, that the *Bamucapi* followed the distinctions made by the Roman Catholic missions in the classification of native medicines. Those that contained medicine (*muti*) only were permitted, but those that contained what the Babemba call a *ciſimba*, an activating principle, such as an eagle's claw or the bone of a squirrel, were to be forbidden.

But over and above the attraction of novelty there were deeper causes behind the success of the *Bamucapi*. The witch-finders claimed, as I stated, to remove the dangerous weapons of the sorcerer. We have to ask ourselves, then, whether the fear of witchcraft is one which dominates native belief. Is black magic, in the sense of a definite ritual actually performed by a man in the belief that it will harm his enemy, very constantly performed among the Babemba?

An analysis of the horns collected by the *Bamucapi* throws an interesting light on this question. I took possession in one instance of the complete heap of horns and magic charms, 139 in all, which had been found in a village of some seventy huts. These lay in a tumbled heap at the cross-roads outside the village, surrounded by knots of people, mostly young men and women, murmuring under their breath at the horrors from which they had been saved. These onlookers seemed to assume to a man that the horns were dangerous objects without exception. Excited comment identified this and that small object as coming from a dead man's grave, as almost certainly part of the bone of a sorcerer's victim, or as soaked in the blood of a dead child.

The actual analysis of these horns was therefore interesting. The collection included forty-five duiker horns, admitted by most to be used as containers for charms or medicines (*muti*) usually of a harmless type such as hunting magic. Sixteen were the horns of big buck such as roan antelope, the usual containers for medicine good and bad, and even for snuff or any other substance which needs to be carried in a stoppered vessel. It would be difficult, informants admitted, to tell a container of black magic from a simple box of snuff. Of the rest of the charms, seventeen were small gourds (*misafi*) used as containers for snuff or oil with a wooden stopper fixed in the narrow end. In such tiny gourds, magic of good luck or popularity is often carried (*muti ua cisense*). Thirty-six more charms were the small cloth bags (*mikoba*) in which medicines of various sorts are sewn to be worn round the owner's neck, the *Bamucapi* themselves supplying their medicine in this form. Such medicines would be nearly always protective to the owner and not destructive to somebody else. To cut a long story short then, out of a collection of 135 horns which had drawn cries of horror and execration from the passers-by, 125 were mere containers, possibly filled with nothing more than the ordinary household remedies which the English mother keeps against coughs and digestive ailments.

Of the remainder of the horns, some were admittedly doubtful or definitely suspicious. Five were wristlets made of the skin of the water lizard or the tree iguana, which are considered ill-omened animals. Nine were bush-buck horns, and this buck (*cisongo*) has a very bad reputation among the Babemba. The animal is believed to be a *cibanda* or evil spirit, and is tabooed to chiefs, to pregnant women and others. By such a horn a sorcerer would be able to lay the spirit of his victim, sending it flying through the air by night 'glowing like a white man's torch' (*lulebanga torchi*) to the grave of the recently buried man, where it would be found sticking upright on the mound in the morning full of grave-earth and hence the injured spirit of the dead.

Some of the other objects the natives condemned in spite of all evidence of common sense, so much had they made up their minds already as to the horrors they expected to find. The parietal bone of a monkey recently shot in a garden raid was sworn to be that of a baby. The skull of a vulture with its characteristic beak was identified as an owl by natives who are good naturalists, since sorcerers are known to prowl at night with owl-like birds (*ntitimufi*) to steal grain from the granaries of others. A polished bit of wood was dubbed the wrist-bone of a lion by one of the best-known hunters in the district. Lastly, the two horns which raised the greatest outcry were *fimango*, or horns specially prepared by the *ŋanga* of a chief in old days to lay the spirits of sorcerers burnt after death by the *mwafi* poison ordeal; that is to say, horns which are specially made to protect people against witchcraft. These objects, filled with medicines to attract evil spirits, the ends netted in and covered with red dye and black beads for the same purpose, acted, as it were, as lightning conductors, kept outside a chief's village to attract the evil spirits to the ground. *Fimango* were also used in the most important form of divination known as '*kutinta*' practised by the *ŋanga* of the chief. The main protection of the native against witchcraft in the old days was therefore cheerfully discarded on the heap at the bidding of a couple of quacks! In fact the *Bamucapi* depended a good deal for their effects on the ignorance of the young of the use of Bemba magic. Their own ignorance on the subject, and their lack of knowledge of the language, was of no account, since they defended the throwing away of a charm admittedly harmless by declaring it contained a *cifimba* unseen to the ordinary man.

Our examination of a typical heap of horns has therefore shown us that only eleven out of 135 horns were admitted by everyone to be undeniably bad destructive magic, that is to say, prepared for the injury of others. For the rest, two were actually protective magic intended to save the whole community against witchcraft, while the majority were containers of medicine, some curative and some mere charms for success, dangerous only in so far as success could be considered to be obtained at the expense of others. It would appear thus to be part of the skill of the *Bamucapi* to create the sense of danger from which they professed to save the people so miraculously. That is to say they drew out the maximum number of charms from a village by convincing each owner that detection was inevitable, either now or in a mythical future, and that even harmless charms were better out of the way. Besides, never was immunity against the charge of witchcraft secured with such ease – a penny a time and 'they give you change'! Old people who had at one time or another been accused of witchcraft, walked miles in search of the *Bamucapi* in order to drink the medicine, and so be publicly passed as free from suspicion. The pile of horns at the cross-roads naturally grew and its very height proved to the rest of the world the dangers from which it had been saved.

Are we then to believe that the sorcerer proper does not exist among the Babemba; or does he exist only, as Evans-Pritchard suggests may be the case among the Azande, not in fact, but in native opinion? (Evans-Pritchard, 1931). We know that primitive peoples are alike in their almost universal belief that death and disaster are due to supernatural agencies. They differ, on the other hand, greatly as to the proportion of human ills which they attribute to hostile fellow beings with supernatural powers and that which they believe to be inflicted by supernatural beings, angry spirits and the like, themselves.

Some communities, that is to say, are more witch-ridden than others. The Trobriand Islander, Malinowski tells us, considers 'every death, without exception, as an act of sorcery' (Malinowski, 1929, p. 127). Similarly, a neighbouring Melanesian people, the Dobu Islanders, believe 'that all good luck is due to one's ritual being stronger than the ritual of others, which is aimed at results contrary to one's own aims' (Fortune, 1932, p. 101). Of the Babemba this is emphatically not so. They believe good and bad fortune to be due to a variety of causes of which witchcraft is only one.

The place of the sorcerer in the community also varies tremendously. In some cases he practises his art, as Malinowksi says, 'almost openly' (Malinowski, 1922, p. 75), the magic of healing and the magic of destruction being vested in one practitioner, who acts in the interests of the man who employs him. In such a community 'there can be no doubt that acts of sorcery are really carried out by those who believe themselves to possess black powers'. In other areas, the possession of powers of black magic is inherited in certain families and openly recognized. In other tribes, among them the Babemba, no witch-doctor will ever admit that he possesses any magic of destruction, although he may grudgingly allow that he can sometimes protect those who are attacked by the spell of a sorcerer. In this particular the natives believe that they differ from neighbouring tribes, for I heard of a man who had made a journey to the country of the Batabwa to the North-West, where he said black magic could be openly bought and sold.

This, then, is the question we shall have to ask ourselves in trying to assess the strength of the *Bamucapi*. In accounting for failing luck and disaster, what sum of human ills is debited to the sorcerers' account? It is obvious that the problem is one of practical importance to the administrator. If a native announces that his child has been killed by the evil magic of a fellow human being, he is probably punished with a legal penalty, but if the same native volunteers his bereavement to be due to the anger of his dead great-grandfather, to him an equally credible statement, he will merely be received with a tolerant smile.

Now a characteristic of Bemba belief is the number of different causes to which human ills may be attributed, and of these witchcraft is at first sight not the most important. A man may suffer harm (a) because of the anger of his ancestral spirits (*mipafi*) to whom he owes certain duties of respect, and who are ultimately responsible for punishing any infringement of tribal law. The spirit of a commoner will punish members of his own particular family, though admittedly not mortally, while the *mupafi* of a chief may inflict disaster on the whole land, either in the form of general bad luck, or some dramatic disaster such as a locust plague: (b) through the vengeance of a haunting spirit (*ciwa*), the avenging ghost of an ancestor who died neglected, injured, or wrongfully accused by his relatives: (c) through the neglect of some important ritual, such, for instance, as that protecting the purity of the household fire; or the breaking of some moral rule such as adultery committed in special circumstances: (d) through punishment sent by a chief's *mupaſi* as the result of a human curse (*kulapiyſia*) when the individual concerned cannot find out who has injured or stolen from him, and calls for divine aid. In all these cases there is one common feature. Punishment is only inflicted by the supernatural power when it is deserved. The religious dogma follows strictly the tribal morality and gives it its sanction. It stresses particularly that basic sentiment of Bemba society – the attitude of a man to authority in general and in particular to his chief. *Mipaſi* are injured if not given proper respect, while the whole land suffers if the chief defaults. So also in the case of the avenging *ciwa*, it is the failure to honour and stand by your relations which is punished, the typical case always given being that of the old mother who dies of starvation and neglect. Here again the *ciwa* may not even return and haunt the living without the permission of Lesa, the High-God, and only a spirit suffering under a legitimate grievance is allowed to avenge. The curse by the name of a dead chief will only light on the real offender.

To sum up, according to Bemba dogma most misfortune is believed to be due to wrong-doing, and in particular transgression of the rules of respect to authority. The cause of the disaster can be ascertained by divination, itself a mechanism socially approved and carried out by a reputable character, the *ŋanga*. The remedy can be procured by the purchase of medicine, by the performance of a laborious rite, and perhaps, most important of all, by the public admission of guilt.

In this apparently logical and orderly system there is, according to theory, only one incalculable element – the sorcerer (*muloſi*) who kills without rhyme or reason, for the sake of doing harm. The *baloſi* are enemies of society and running counter to its laws. They actually start their careers of crime by committing some outrageous act, such as father-daughter incest, or the murder of a baby of their own clan. They have various mythical attributes. They can make themselves invisible; kill at a distance; send magic birds to steal food from their enemies; and of course perform secret rites and possess and sell evil medicines. Now it is obvious that such sorcerers are actually non-existent, though their mythical attributes are readily credited to unpopular people of dour or difficult temperaments, bad mixers in the American sense, bad sharers, or persons who seem to be winning unusual success at others' expense. I would not be bold enough to say that no rites of evil magic are performed in Bemba country, or that there do not exist here and there individuals who believe themselves to possess such powers. But it is the reflection of the *buloſi* belief in the widespread use of protective magic which is, I believe, the important practical issue. In an atmosphere of suspicion and hatred, natives will believe themselves forced to buy charms from the reputable *ŋanga* of the neighbourhood, or very commonly from a witchdoctor of another tribe, to protect themselves (*kuʃilika mubili*), such charms being naturally viewed with alarm by others. In such an atmosphere of mistrust, too, ordinary magic of success, hunting, and agricultural charms, or those for luck in personal relations, such as formed the bulk of the horns on our heap, assume a sinister aspect. Beauty magic bought by a young unmarried girl is not a dangerous possession, but the same charm purchased by one of two jealous co-wives would be considered a hostile act. All magic of luck and self-protection becomes dangerous, that is to say, just in so far as the success it brings is believed to hurt another. Protective magic, like protective armaments, increases the sense of insecurity it was bought to end. Herein lies the danger, especially as contact with white civilization has, in many cases, actually increased the use of such charms and counter-charms.

A little consideration will in fact show us, what is not at first sight evident, that a change in the native belief in sorcery inevitably follows changes in social structure. The strength of the fear of witchcraft in any community obviously depends on the nature of its tribal institutions.

It is clear that the strength of the belief in the power of sorcery in any community depends on the nature of its tribal institutions and, in particular, the type of authority exercised, and its legal machinery. Its incidence will vary with its system of social grouping, local or kinship, and the absence or presence of emotional tension between these groups. To explain by a contrast between two widely different cultures, the Trobriand Islander is afraid his chief may bewitch him, and hence magic acts in this community as a conservative force backing up his authority. Witchcraft has its appointed place in the whole political system. The Mubemba, living under a far more autocratic and powerful chief, says simply, 'Why should a chief bewitch a commoner since he can so easily beat him or mutilate him?' Evans-Pritchard, in fact, suggests that we shall find an interesting correlation between the morphology of magic and the type of political system in a primitive society (Evans-Pritchard, 1929).

The presence or absence of legal machinery for settling grievances obviously also affects the incidence of magic throughout the society. The Melanesian often has no way of venting his grievance against his fellows except by the practice of the magic of hate. The Mubemba, in common with most other Bantu peoples, can obtain redress in a legal court. He brings a case where the former would besiege the sorcerer for more and more spells.

Again there are patterns of culture in which two social groups are legally bound together in a network of obligations mutually burdensome, and providing perpetual cause for emotional tension. Two individuals may be placed by society in a position of constant rivalry from the start. In such an atmosphere suspicion and charges of witchcraft flourish. I will instance only from the same two Melanesian societies, the relation in Trobriand matrilineal society between a man's heir, his maternal nephew, and his son; or in Dobu the hostility between the .groups united in marriage (*susu*) between which the fear of witchcraft is an absolutely dominating dread. Among the Babemba differences in the marriage and kinship system do not provide groupings with interests so sharply contrasted, although the co-wives in a society where the women have never really accepted polygamy as an institution, or the rival heirs to great chieftainships, are always suspected of bewitching each other. But I believe conflicting elements in the society have lately increased.

This is, in fact, the crux of the whole matter. Missionaries all over Africa are teaching a religion which casts out fear, but economic and social changes have so shattered tribal institutions and moral codes that the result of white contact is in many cases an actual increase in the dread of witchcraft, and therefore in the whole incidence of magic throughout the group.

In Bemba society the position of the chief has materially altered. One of his functions was formerly the administration of the poison ordeal (*mwafi*) to those accused of sorcery, and this gave an ultimate sense of security to the community at large. Now he no longer performs this duty, and his subjects know, moreover, that they cannot charge a witch in a legal court, black or white. 'No one will help us now', said an informant about the *Bamucapi* movement, 'unless we help ourselves.' It must be remembered, too, that divination, itself an essential part of the native system of fixing guilt, can no longer be publicly practised. It exists, but is discredited, and in this transition stage its loss has certainly robbed the native of some of his old moral certainties.

Further, with alterations in the sanctions for the power of the chief – his wealth, military supremacy, and the belief in his supernatural powers – that attitude to authority, on which, as we saw, tribal morality so largely depended, has been rudely shaken, and with it the whole system of beliefs in supernatural punishment for wrong-doing. Some natives are abandoning tribal rules because they find them burdensome; and some are living in conditions where it is impossible to carry them out – perhaps working at a mine too far to be able to care for their kinsmen or to carry out certain religious rites. Other natives again, many of them Christians, are caught between clashing moralities. In either case the majority are suffering, I believe, from a perpetual sense of guilt, expressing itself in a constant anxiety for some kind of supernatural defence. Nowhere did I feel this more strongly than in the most civilized part of Northern Rhodesia, the copper belt. Here a Bemba woman no longer feels it necessary to keep the wearisome taboos for the protection of her household fire, but just for that reason she feels herself bound to pay as much as she can for protective charms to save the life of her child – 'just in case'. The influence of wage-earning is here again all-powerful. Money seems to the urban native his only asset in this insecure world. By it he can in effect exchange a belief in a system of ancestral spirits who demand respect, the performance of exacting ceremonial, and the keeping of tribal morality, for safety bought on a hard cash basis open to all who have money, whatever their position in the society. What wonder, then, that he rushes to the seller of charms? And wherever protective magic is freely bought and sold there is an atmosphere of mutual suspicion between individuals. The fear of witchcraft increases, and witch-finders flourish.

Again, social grouping has been altered by white contact, with, as a transition stage, new causes of hostility between the individual components. In villages near European settlements, natives from other areas have intruded on original kinship units because they want to live near their work. 'We don't feel safe in this village. There are so many strangers here', an old woman said to me in a village near Kasama. In the mines it is the tribal admixture which is, I believe, at the basis of the natives' positive obsession by the fear of witchcraft. Each tribe credits the other with absolutely diabolical powers. Paralysed by the fear of the unknown, what can they do but buy more charms? Moreover, wage-earning in a large industrial undertaking provides opportunity for advance through individual initiative, and hence jealousy is rife. I know few successful clerks raised above the heads of their fellows who have not been accused at one time or another of sorcery. 'How else did he gain the bwana's favour?' is the natural question. And it is in the ranks of such men that, paradoxically enough, the most money is spent in the purchase of protective charms. I know of one ex-Government clerk in the Kasama area who had spent a Government bonus of £15 on the purchase of protective magic from a neighbouring tribe. Jealousy of the man who has adapted himself more quickly than his fellows to Europeanism is, I believe, inevitable in this transition stage.

Here, then, we must leave our study of the *Bamucapi* movement. We have seen that part of the success of these charlatans was due to their clever blend of the old and the new, and I believe that such a combination will be almost invariably found in modern witch-finder movements. Added to this we must reckon the cleverness of a technique that drew from a village its harmless as well as its dangerous horns, and by the multiplicity of charms thus produced increased the sense of the risk the whole community had run. An analysis of the horns collected led us to doubt the existence of sorcerers proper in the community, a doubt confirmed by a study of Bemba belief as to the supernatural causes of death and disaster. But native belief in witchcraft, and the widespread use of protective magic and counter-charms of all kinds, was confirmed. This latter I believe to have been actually increased by contact with the white civilization, and the resultant economic and social changes in Northern Rhodesia. Hence follows the success of modern movements of witchfinders, movements which are, I believe, inevitable as a product of violent changes in tribal organization and belief.

References

EVANS-PRITCHARD, E. E. (1929), 'The morphology and function of magic', *American Anthropologist*, vol. 31.
EVANS-PRITCHARD, E. E. (1931), 'Sorcery and native opinion', *Africa*, vol. 4, no. 1.
FORTUNE, R. F. (1932), *Sorcerers of Dobu*, Routledge.
MALINOWSKI, B. (1922), *Argonauts of the Western Pacific*, Routledge.
MALINOWSKI, B. (1929), *Sexual Life of Savages*, Routledge.

21. Max Marwick

The Bwanali–Mpulumutsi Anti-Witchcraft Movement[1]

From M. G. Marwick, 'Another modern anti-witchcraft movement in East Central Africa', *Africa*, vol. 20, 1950, pp. 100–112. Abridged by the author.

The movement to be described is the one initiated by Bwanali in Southern Nyasaland, and extended by his disciple, Mpulumutsi, alias Bonjisi, whose headquarters were near Furancungo in the district of Tete, Portuguese East Africa. Wherever possible I have quoted my own fairly literal translations of statements made in Nyanja to me or to my assistants by informants who belong to 'tribal' designations such as Ceŵa, Ntumba, Nyanja etc. who in the past were collectively known as the Malawi; a small minority, however, are Nyanja-speaking Ngoni – descendants of the Zulu–Swazi invaders who enslaved many of the Malawi peoples from about a century ago until, fifty years later, their power was broken by the Europeans.

The Nyanja witchcraft system is characterized by beliefs that witches are necrophagous, and that they attack only their matrilineal relatives. Their motives are said to be 'hunger for meat' (*nkhuli*) and/or the hatred of a kinsman, because, people say, there is no way of resolving hatred between matrikin other than the use of witchcraft. Nyanja make no clear distinction between witchcraft and sorcery. And they believe witches have familiars such as hyenas and owls.

The general opinion among Nyanja informants is that witchcraft is on the increase; and they certainly believe that it operates especially in the new situations arising from modern social changes, e.g. in quarrels between mother's brothers and sister's sons over the ownership of cattle bought with wages earned by the latter at the labour centres. The alleged increase in the incidence of witchcraft is attributed, however, to the fact that the *mwabvi* poison ordeal, which in the old days was regularly applied as a measure of public hygiene, has been suppressed by the Europeans.

In my notes the first reference to Bwanali occurs in a text written in

1. The field-work on which this paper is based was generously financed by the Colonial Social Science Research Council.

June 1947. Within a month or two of this time Bwanali's fame and that of his disciple, Bonjisi, alias Mpulumutsi, had quickly spread over Nyasaland and the adjoining parts of Northern Rhodesia and Portuguese East Africa. In December 1947 I was able to have a short interview with Bwanali.

When I visited him, he was living in a village on the Chikwawa side of the boundary between Neno and Chikwawa Districts, Southern Nyasaland. I found him seated on a new reed mat outside a hut. He was simply dressed in new blue shirt and shorts, and he had a white cotton robe over his shoulder, though he left this behind when he showed me over the barrack-like shelters that had been built for his patients. These shelters were occupied by people who, he told me, were not yet well enough to go home. Next to him on his mat, Bwanali had a copy of the Nyanja Bible.

He told me that for many years he had been a hunter in Portuguese East Africa, but that he had given this up some time back in order to become a 'doctor' (herbalist). His present work started in July 1946. Contrary to rumour, he asserted, he did not die and wake up again or have any revelations that God wanted him to do this work: he simply found that the number of his successful cures suddenly increased. From this he felt that God was helping him.

Referring to his general procedure, Bwanali said that if a person comes to him, he makes incisions in his skin on various parts of his body and rubs medicine into them. If a person wants medicine to take home, he gives it to him, but taking medicine home is not a condition of being treated. If people want to dig the medicinal roots for themselves, he tells them all they want to know – how to identify the trees, dig the roots, prepare and administer the medicine. Those with intelligence, he added, go back and become 'doctors' among their own people. He does not receive any payment for his work.

When I asked him to explain the relationship between Bonjisi (Mpulumutsi) and himself, Bwanali said that after Bonjisi had been killed by the witchcraft of his relatives, his corpse was brought to him (Bwanali) and he revived him. Bonjisi stayed on to learn all about the medicines, and then went back to his own area to do work similar to his (Bwanali's).

Asked whether people really confess their witchcraft to him, he said that they do. He emphasized that they do this before being given the medicine. He exhorts them to give up their evil practices. He points out to them that God did not create them bad, and that they should conduct themselves in a manner worthy of their creation. If they return to their tricks, he warns them, they will not continue to live. A return to witchcraft will make them feel ill, and this will be the sign that they are not behaving themselves as they should.

While I do not exclude the possibility that Bwanali was keeping information from me (our interview was rather a hurried one), the general impression I got of him was that he is very genuinely concerned with the growing incidence of man's wickedness (in the form of witchcraft) and that he considers it his divine calling to help man throw it off. His system of morality seems consistent with both Nyanja and Christian patterns. Though his belief in witchcraft and his encouragement in others of this belief would probably be condemned by certain missionaries, no one can say that he is not a deeply religious man. From the mental hygiene viewpoint he probably does more good than harm. His function is comparable with that of a father-confessor or a psychiatrist in our own society. Though, according to Western standards, he may be misguided, his sincerity seems striking.

For various reasons I was unable to pay a visit to Mpulumutsi and the nearest approach I have to a factual account of him is the following statement made to me by a man who had just returned from a visit to him.

We were ten days travelling before we arrived at his 'compound' which is at a place called Matenje in Portuguese territory. Mpulumutsi got his knowledge and technique from Ce Bwana Ali[2] who does similar work at a place near Blantyre. It was after he had died and risen again that he went to Bwanali. We arrived on the morning of the eleventh day, and at two o'clock that afternoon he called us and made us stand in a long queue – men and women together. He then started to make incisions in our skins and rub medicine into them, He did this on our insteps, throats, chests and backs. He rubbed some medicine on our heads, gave us some to drink and some to take home with us. As he gave us the medicine, he told us to throw away all the medicines we had in our houses, especially those for killing people. Medicines not used for killing people, he said, should be thrown away, too, but fresh supplies of them might be dug without any danger – expecially if they were mixed with some of the medicine he now gave us. That which he now handed to us we should use for this purpose, as well as for treating our relatives at home.

The person who gave these instructions was the one who died and woke up after his corpse had been two days in his house. After he had woken up he came with a book. It was a Christian book – the Nyanja Bible. This man was formerly a cook in Johannesburg. He is an Ngoni of Gomani's group, still quite young – about my age [between thirty and forty]. His name is Joni [John], but he admits to the name of Mpulumutsi. When we got there, he asked us, 'Why have you come here?' We replied, 'We heard that Mpulumutsi was here.' 'O.K.',[3] he said, 'you've found me today. But if you've come with two hearts, you won't get home again. You must

2. *Ce* is the Yao equivalent of 'Mr'; *Bwana* is the Nyanja for 'master'.
3. The most adequate translation of the much-used Nyanja expression, *cabwino*.

come with one heart only.' 'We want people of good heart', he continued, 'we don't want people who kill one another. This season the people will not get their hoeing done easily because they'll be too busy carting one another back and forth [i.e. burying one another]. This is because many people will forget my warning and die as a result of returning to their practice of killing their fellow men by witchcraft or of eating human flesh [i.e. of people killed by other witches].'

After we had been treated and given medicine to take away with us, we retired. Some people woke up with headaches, and went and complained of them to Mpulumutsi. He said to them, 'You've been eating your fellow men.' One confessed: 'Yes, I've eaten two of my children.' Another said, 'I've eaten my mother-in-law and her husband.' A third admitted to having brought a human head with him and to having used flesh from it as a 'relish' to eat with his maize porridge on the very journey to Mpulumutsi! He had thrown it away just before arriving. Mpulumutsi warned these people that they should give up their evil practices. After that he gave them medicine to drink.

Those who, having been treated with Mpulumutsi's medicines, don't confess their witchcraft, or resume it after having confessed, are sure to die. Many die on the way home to their villages. [Q.] No, I didn't see any dead people, but on the way there I saw a number of trees from which bark had been stripped in order to make coffins for those who had died by the way.

People don't have to pay anything; they simply receive treatment and medicine. Some bring castor oil and give it to Mpulumutsi for mixing with the medicine. Others don't bring anything. Why should they? Why should Mpulumutsi have a return for his work, seeing that God told him to do it?

A person on his return from being treated by Mpulumutsi should not touch his medicines but should get an untreated person to throw them away for him. They should be thrown away in water.

Mpulumutsi said nothing about beating a drum, but other people we met told us that he would beat a drum and all the witches would be forced by its sound to go to him and be caught.

The treatment given by Bwanali and Mpulumutsi is believed to have two functions, a protective one and a destructive one. There is a suggestion that the attraction of the first function causes witches to undergo the treatment and expose themselves to the dangers inherent in the second one. The belief in the destructive function of the medicine implies that it has a selective effect similar to that of the poison ordeal: it spares the innocent and kills the witches.

The reader will have noticed a number of similarities between the Bwanali–Mpulumutsi and Mcape* movements. Both started in Nyasa. land and spread into adjoining territories. Both aimed at the complete removal of witchcraft from the country by the systematic destruction or reform of witches and by the protection of their potential victims. And

*See previous Reading – *Ed*.

the same beliefs have occurred in association with both: for instance, that the originator of the movement had died and been resurrected; that the medicine would lead to death in those who resumed their witchcraft; that on the 'second coming' or at some significant future date a drum would be beaten which would inexorably attract witches to their death; that Maria (Marya) would assist in the destruction of the witches; and that certain rules and taboos should be observed by persons who had been treated with the medicine.

The differences between the two movements are usually to be found in those activities to which European control might have been applied in the case of the Mcape movement. There were three ways in which the Mcape vendors threw themselves open to European control. Firstly, they made their patients drink medicines said to have divining properties. This was bound to evoke opposition since it so clearly resembled the *mwabvi* poison ordeal, which had been suppressed. Secondly, not necessarily by administering medicines, but by using mirrors and other devices, they made direct accusations of witchcraft. This again was bound to conflict with the requirements of European Administrations whose concern to keep the peace had made them declare accusations of witchcraft illegal. Finally, they sold medicines and charms, a step that rendered them liable to prosecution for fraudulent dealing.

The most important differences between the Bwanali-Mpulumutsi and Mcape movements are in these three spheres. Firstly, the evidence suggests that, although it is not unknown for Bwanali and Mpulumutsi to administer medicines orally, they generally do this only after a confession has been made. Normally they apply the medicines to incisions made in the skin, a course of action that has no resemblance to the traditional poison ordeal. Secondly, judging from reports, they do not make a practice of openly accusing people of witchcraft; listening to confessions of witchcraft can hardly be an offence. Thirdly, the available evidence suggests that they do not receive any payment for their work. The movement of 1947 as compared with that of the 1930s is basically more like a religious movement than a commercial 'racket'. Its emphasis on divine inspiration, the sharing of sins by confession, and back-to-God moral rearmament classes it with a religious revival rather than with the patent medicine trade.

22. R. G. Willis

The Kamcape Movement

Excerpts from R. G. Willis, 'Kamcape: an anti-sorcery movement in south-west Tanzania', *Africa*, vol. 38, 1968, pp. 1–15.

While doing field-work among the Fipa of south-west Tanzania between December 1962 and June 1964 I collected evidence about an anti-sorcery cult or movement called Kamcape which was then active in the area.[1] The present article describes this evidence and seeks to assess its sociological significance. [...] The Fipa are a Bantu group inhabiting the high plateau at the south end of Lake Tanganyika [...]. They are primarily agriculturalists, with millet, maize and beans as the major crops. They also keep livestock: mainly cattle, goats and sheep. Many of the Fipa [...] inhabiting the Rukwa valley and Lake Tanganyika shore are fishermen. [...]

The Idiom of Mystical Belief

Traditionally, Fipa explained unfortunate or unusual events by reference to one of three kinds of mystical or invisible agency. There were the non-human divinities (*imyaao* or *amaleesa*) who were identified with some particular natural object and often reincarnated in pythons; there were the ancestral spirits (*imisimu*); and there was sorcery (*uloosi*). Which agency was responsible in any particular case was decided by divination. Against attack by sorcery, Fipa had two methods of defence: as individuals, they had recourse to magician-doctors for protective or countervailing medicine; and as communities, they periodically subjected those of their number who were suspected of being sorcerers to the ordeal of drinking a vegetable poison, *umwaafl*.[2] Those who vomited the poison were proved innocent; those who did not were considered guilty and either died or were put to death. As a precautionary measure,

1. The research was paid for by a generous grant from the Emslie Horniman Anthropological Scholarship Fund.
2. Village headmen obtained the poison on behalf of their villages from their district governor, who had custody of it. The poison ordeal was also employed to settle other disputed criminal cases, such as theft and murder.

poison was often administered to entire village populations, except children.

Seventy years of Christian missionary activity, and other Westernizing influences, have substantially eroded Fipa belief in the traditional divinities and, though to a lesser extent, in the ancestral spirits. On the other hand, belief in sorcery is general, even among many educated people. Fipa see the sorcerer (*unndoosi*; pl., *aloosi*) as a hereditary specialist analogous, in his own sinister way, to the magician-doctor (*siŋaanga*; pl. *asiŋaanga*). Like the magician-doctor, the sorcerer operates with a wide assortment of symbolic material ingredients which are divided into two categories: primary ingredients, *ifiti fikola*; and secondary ingredients, *ifisiimba* or *ifingila*, whose purpose is to augment and intensify the power of the primary ingredients. The primary ingredients are collected *ad hoc* by the magician-doctor (and supposedly by the sorcerer also). Secondary ingredients are kept by both classes of expert in a special bag, called *intaangala*. Sometimes Fipa implicitly recognize the similarity between sorcerers and magician-doctors by referring to the latter as 'doctors of life' (*asiŋaanga ya uumi*). The word for the lore and practice of magician-doctors, *ugaanga,* may also serve as a euphemism for sorcery.

A common image of a sorcerer is an old man who goes around his village naked at night, seeking to enter huts and removed head and pubic hair from their magically stupefied occupants, later using the hair to make noxious medicine. A more complex image consists of an old man and his wife, also naked, who carries her husband suspended upside-down from her shoulders, while she clasps his lower legs to her breasts.

Sorcerers are said to have many ways of injuring their victims at a distance. Sometimes they send a certain fly, whose bite is said to be fatal, or a mole, or a pigeon, or a kind of meteor called *ilyaŋoombe*. The most dreaded weapon of all is a preparation called *ulupekeso*, which is said to wipe out entire extended families.

Sorcerers are said to have means of turning their victims into zombies (*amasea*), which are then forced to work in their masters' gardens at night, sleeping on top of his hut by day. Certain experts in sorcery are said to have the power to metamorphose themselves (*ukusaangooka*) into the form of a ferocious animal, such as a lion or leopard, in which shape they attack and kill their human prey.

An Anti-Sorcery Movement in Action

The existence in Ufipa of an anti-sorcery cult first came to the notice of the authorities there near the end of 1963, when a man called Yasita

Mtontela was severely beaten and injured by fellow villagers of Kapenta, a small settlement in the south-east corner of Ufipa. Four men and a woman were subsequently accused and convicted in the magistrate's court at Sumbawanga, central Ufipa, of assaulting Mtontela.

In their defence the accused said the assault on Mtontela followed a visit to Kapenta by adherents of a movement called Kamcape, whose object was to abolish sorcery. The visitors, who numbered about twenty, were led by the accused woman, Luse Pesambila, whose home was near Mpui, about thirty miles away. Her followers were all strangers to Kapenta.

The exponents of Kamcape required all the villagers to drink of a special potion and to have 'medicine' rubbed into incisions made in the centre of their foreheads and between the thumb and forefinger of their right hands. They were told that this treatment guaranteed immunity from sorcery. Several old men who were accused by the villagers of practising sorcery were similarly treated, and it was explained that if they reverted to sorcery afterwards the 'medicine' would kill them.

According to the five accused persons, Mtontela, who was believed to have killed a fellow villager by sorcery, refused to drink the Kamcape potion or submit to being cut. His hut was then searched and several animal horns were found concealed in the roof.

What happened next was described to me in an interview in prison with two of the convicted men:

The horns taken from Mtontela's hut were filled with a special medicine, made of zebra meat and oil, prepared by Luse Pesambila [the woman leader of the Kamcape party]. They were placed on a two-legged stool set upright in the ground in the middle of the *baraza* [a large open hut used for public and official business]. Three local headmen were among the crowd assembled there. Luse Pesambila then laid beads on the horns, which soon began to emit red smoke, of the kind sorcerers send to injure and kill their victims.

Confronted with this evidence of his guilt, Mtontela thereupon confessed his crime, describing how he had secretly taken samples of the dead man's excrement, spittle and urine and mixed them with medicine in order to kill him.

It was after this that we beat Mtontela.

The prisoners' statement added that the potion and medicine brought by the Kamcape cult members had originated in Nyasaland (Malawi), with a man called Icikanga, and had been brought from Unyamwanga (a tribal area to the south-east of Ufipa) by a certain Paulo Mombo.

In the following year, 1964, the Kamcape movement spread through southern Ufipa, giving rise to considerable and increasing concern among the officers of the local administration (as I learned from the then Area Commissioner, Mr Philip Mbogo).

There was a common pattern underlying Kamcape operations. The first move was for several cult members (referred to as 'scouts' by my informants) to visit a village and have secret conversations with the headman. The latter, it seems, could usually be persuaded that a Kamcape 'cleansing' operation in his village was desirable. A suitable fee was then agreed on. The visitors would spend the night in the headman's hut and disappear early the next morning.

Several days, or weeks, later, a party (which was always said to be 'large') of Kamcape cult members and supporters would arrive in the selected village and begin operations.

In March 1964 I visited several villages just after Kamcape had been there. In Kapele, a hamlet of about fifty inhabitants, seven old men had been accused of sorcery and 'branded' with deep razor or knife cuts in the centre of the forehead.

At this hamlet I saw a basket about two feet high and eighteen inches in diameter, which was full of animal horns, cowtails, pieces of wood, and animal bones. All these objects were said to have been removed from surrounding huts during the Kamcape operation. Near by was an earthen pot containing a pint-size tin and an orange-coloured fluid said to have been made by boiling the bark of a tree called *nacifuumbi*.

On the seven alleged 'sorcerers' in this hamlet, Mikaeli, told me he had been accused by Kamcape of killing five people and causing cattle to become lame. A young woman there admitted she had held the head of this old man, who was her mother's father, while he was 'branded'. Mikaeli vehemently denied his guilt to me, and publicly, and expressed his intention of going to Sumbawanga to complain to the police. A score or so people standing around, however, were apparently convinced of Mikaeli's guilt. The most vocal of these was a youth called Danieli who said he came from the village of Chianda, about five miles away. Mikaeli, he said, had made lethal medicine from the footprints of his victims. Asked how he knew this, he said he had been told by several people, whom he refused to name.

Danieli said that the object of Kamcape was to 'cleanse' the country and the villages. He claimed to possess official authorization to combat sorcery in the form of a certificate (*cheti*).

At another and larger settlement about three miles from the hamlet of Kapele, and on the same day, I saw a girl called Natalia whom I judged to be about sixteen years old and who was said to have taken a leading part in the Kamcape operation in Kapele. She admitted administering 'medicine' and making cuts on the foreheads and hands of alleged sorcerers, including Mikaeli.

Natalia said she had learned the technique of Kamcape from an elder sister who lived in the village of Mchima, about sixteen miles south-east of Kapele. The sister had in turn been instructed by a magician-doctor called Pita Ote, also of Mchima village, who was a disciple of Icikanga, the founder of the Kamcape movement.

How 'Icikanga' came to originate the Kamcape anti-sorcery movement is described in the following story:

Two brothers were at the seaside. They had collected a lot of money and one day the elder brother said he would go home, taking the money with him in a bag. The younger brother said he would follow him later. So the elder brother went home and a few days after arriving there he died, through sorcery. The other villagers buried him, together with the bag he had brought home.

Some time later the younger brother arrived and was told of his elder brother's death. Then he asked, 'What of the bag he brought with him?' and was told it had been buried with his brother. He then said he would dig up the corpse and recover the bag of money, and after considerable trouble obtained permission to disinter, the police coming along to watch. When he had been digging for a while there was a strange noise and the 'corpse' sat up, with the bag under its arm, and said: 'I have come back to rid the world of sorcery.'

Icikanga then arose and went and branded the man who had ensorcelled him, and that was the beginning of Kamcape.

The movement continued to spread northwards and westwards from its point of origin in south-eastern Ufipa throughout 1964. In November, according to my informants, Kamcape was active near and around the large village and port of Kirando, in the north-western corner of Ufipa. It was noticeable that the movement made no attempt to operate in the populous (and relatively well-policed) villages clustered around the administrative centre of Sumbawanga, but confined its activities to the more remote settlements. By the beginning of 1965 there were no more reports of such disturbances in any part of Ufipa.[3]

Earlier Movements

The anti-sorcery cult that flourished in Ufipa in 1964 was not the first movement of this kind to occur in the area or in this general region of central Africa. In 1933–4 a movement called *Mcape* (or *Mcapi*) swept from Nyasaland into Northern Rhodesia and later reached Southern Rhodesia, Mozambique and the Congo. The initiates of this movement or cult are said to have derived their authority and knowledge from a

3. According to an informant in contact with the administrative and judicial authorities at this time.

certain Kamwende of Mlanje in Nyasaland, who was resurrected after two days in the grave.[4]

In 1943–4 an anti-sorcery movement called Kamcape was active in some parts of Ufipa, particularly the Rukwa valley (eastern Ufipa).[5] In 1947 an anti-witchcraft movement called Bwanali-Mpulumutsi arose in Nyasaland and spread into Northern Rhodesia.[6] In 1954 a movement, or movements variously called Kamcape, *Wacilole*, or *WaCauuta*,[7] flourished in Ufipa. The *Wacilole* (literally, 'People of the Mirror') employed a hand mirror with which they claimed to detect sorcerers, by studying the reflections in it of villagers lined up for the purpose.[8] The *WaCauuta* ('People of Cauuta') apparently recruited only women; members painted their faces white (this colour symbolizes spiritual power among the Fipa) and danced themselves into a state of dissociation, when they were supposed to be able to discover sorcerers.

Comparisons

The Kamcape anti-sorcery movement of 1963–4 in Ufipa bears certain obvious resemblances to earlier movements directed against mystical evil-doers in this part of Africa. The similarity between the name 'Kamcape' and the 'Mcape' (or 'Mcapi') movement of 1933–4 in Northern Rhodesia is at once apparent. According to Richards, 'Mcape' was derived from a Nyanja verb *ku-capa*, to rub or wash clothes. 'Kamcape' appears to be the same word prefixed by the common Bantu particle *ka*.[9] Like the Mcape and Bwanali–Mpulumutsi movements, the Kamcape movement of 1963–4 looked to an origin in Nyasaland (Malawi); and the return from the grave of Icikanga, Kamcape's supposed founder, recalls the 'resurrection' of Kamwende, originator of the 1933–4 movement.

The methods employed by Kamcape to combat, or neutralize, the

---

4. Richards (1935). According to an unpublished paper by Professor T. O. Ranger, who has drawn upon archival material in Dar es Salaam, this movement was active in south-west and southern Tanganyika, and particularly so in Ufipa.

5. I owe this information to missionary sources in Ufipa.

6. Marwick (1950). This movement, which was also associated with a resurrection myth, did not spread to Ufipa, as far as I know.

7. According to missionary and other informants. The 1954 Kamcape movement in Ufipa is also referred to in Marwick (1965, p. 94).

8. A similar method of divination was employed by the Mcape movement of 1933–4 (Richards, 1935).

9. In Fipa the particle *ka* is used to express a consequential action or end-result. 'Kamcape' might also be connected with a Swahili word *chapa*, a print or brand, in view of the Kamcape practice of 'branding' alleged sorcerers.

power of alleged sorcerers again resemble the procedure of Mcape[10] – and also of many Congolese anti-sorcery, or anti-witchcraft, cults.[11] The most recent Kamcape movement in Ufipa also resembled the Mcape cult of 1933–4 (and the Congolese cults too, apparently) in its insistence that villagers surrender (or submit to confiscation of) all objects of magico-medical significance.[12] Richards makes the point that most of the 'witch-craft objects' thus revealed were probably innocuous in both fact and purpose – though in the emotionally charged atmosphere of a witch-hunt the Bemba villagers found it hard to realize this (Richards, 1935). The same sort of thing seems to have happened during the Kamcape operations in Ufipa.

As well as administering an anti-sorcery potion, the Kamcape cultists of 1963–4 in Ufipa rubbed anti-sorcery 'medicine' into incisions made in the skin.[13] It may be that this combination of two traditional methods of introducing substances into the body represented some recognition of the apparent failure of earlier movements (including the Kamcape movements of 1943–4 and 1954 in Ufipa) and a consequent need to 'do better' this time.

Another feature of the most recent Kamcape movement in Ufipa was the conspicuous 'branding' of alleged sorcerers, who were compelled to submit to having large double crosses incised on their foreheads.

This combination of different techniques and practices appears to distinguish Kamcape from the recorded methods of other such movements in this part of Africa[14] and affords a clue to the complexity and variety of social factors involved.

Problems and Theories

In analysing a people's ideas and behaviour in the context of mystical evil-doing it seems important to distinguish between *beliefs* about witches

10. Every villager had to drink a sip of Mcape medicine, 'a fine red powder which gave a soapy solution when shaken with water in a bottle' (Richards, 1935).

11. Referred to by Douglas (1963). The earliest of these cults was active about 1910, and Douglas suggests there may have been previous ones.

12. Douglas (1963, p. 158); Richards (1935). Similar demands were apparently made, with success, by some of the first European missionaries to arrive in Ufipa.

13. The Bwanali–Mpulumutsi movement of 1947 in Northern Rhodesia also used this latter technique.

14. The Mcape movement of 1933–4 relied on the administration of a potion and the Bwanali–Mpulumutsi movement of 1947 on a 'medicine' rubbed into incisions in the skin. Neither movement seems to have treated alleged witches or sorcerers differently from those presumed innocent.

and sorcerers – who and what they are, the conventional image or images of such figures[15] – and specific *accusations* of witchcraft or sorcery; the significance of the latter can only be assessed empirically, by observing the behaviour of a group over time. It may then be discovered that a pattern of accusations emerges which is more or less at variance with the accepted indigenous theory of witchcraft or sorcery.[16]

Like Zande witchcraft, day-to-day sorcery accusations among the Fipa are a function, firstly, of misfortune, and secondly, of personal relations (cf. Evans-Pritchard, 1937, p. 106). These inter-personal accusations are initiated by such events as sickness or death, or loss of crops or livestock, and occur between coevals in situations of sexual or status rivalry. Inter-generational accusations are rarely, if ever, heard. Moreover, the accusations that are made are essentially private and not of communal concern. Usually the alleged sorcerer does not know that he has been accused.

The accusations made during a Kamcape operation are of quite a different nature. The accusations are not a response to any particular personal misfortune (though personal sufferings, bereavements and losses may be retrospectively invoked by the accusers to substantiate their allegations). The accusations are public and the whole community participates in making them; and most of the accusers are of a different and junior generation to the accused.

It may be assumed, then, that the accusations made during a Kamcape operation relate primarily to general and social, rather than inter-personal, conflicts within a village community. What are these conflicts, and how can the activities of Kamcape be thought of or felt by the Fipa as resolving or alleviating them?

It was seen earlier that in every Fipa village there is, or tends to be, a polarization of political opinion and sentiment into 'traditionalist' and 'progressive' parties. The 'traditionalists' draw their inspiration and ideology from their own village, its past and present, and their champion is the headman – the office-holder who represents the village to, and against, the outside world. The 'progressives' are involved intellectually and emotionally in a wider universe of interests and ideology, in the area and national organization and propaganda of TANU, Tanzania's governing party.

15. In Monica Wilson's arresting phrase, 'the standardized nightmares of a group' (Wilson, 1951).

16. Thus although the official doctrine of the Ceŵa of eastern Zambia is that sorcerers are women, in nearly three-fifths of 101 cases reported, accusations were made against men (Marwick, 1965, p. 103).

Economic conflict in Fipa villages is generated by a shortage of accessible land. Although Ufipa as a whole is quite sparsely populated, the stability of Fipa villages in space and time results in the exhaustion of nearby land, so that many villagers often have to go several miles to find suitable plots. Fipa cope with this problem by building hut-shelters of timber and turves in which they camp during specially busy times of year, such as tilling and harvesting. The more convenient plots adjacent to the village tend to be in the hands of a few elder men.

Both political and economic conflict in Fipa villages is thus to some extent also a conflict of generations: the 'traditionalists' are usually the elder (and largely illiterate) men who are also economically privileged; the 'progressives' tend to be younger and relatively better educated, but to have a smaller economic stake in the community.

Religious differences are another, if latent, source of conflict in many villages. The Christians tend to associate paganism with every kind of evil, including, and especially, sorcery; while the pagans tend to see the Christians as a divisive element opposed to the traditional ethos of village comradeship and unity.

Here then, in the different spheres of politics, economics and religion, are three of the commonest causes of intra-village conflict among the Fipa – and no doubt many other causes, potential and actual, could be discovered and enumerated. Although there is a tendency, noted earlier, for conflicts to follow generational lines, there is certainly much overlapping and even cross-cutting of age-groups and their respective political, economic and religious affiliations and interests.

Social and ecological factors combine to generate conflicts within village communities. Probably this has always been so, though in the more homogeneous society of pre-colonial Ufipa the causes of conflict may have been fewer and less complex. Even so, traditional Fipa society had several institutionalized means of coping with the problem.

If the headman of a village felt that sorcery had become a serious threat to the peace of his community, he could apply to his district governor (*umweene nkaandawa*) for *umwaafi* poison; this was then administered to suspects at a public ceremony. Often every adult member of a village had to participate (see above, p. 218 f.).

Douglas has drawn attention to the formal and functional similarity between the mass administration of the poison ordeal to detect and eradicate mystical evil-doers (an institution found in many parts of Africa, and particularly common in central Africa and the Congo) with the techniques of modern movements directed against witches and sorcerers. An implication of Douglas's argument is that anti-witchcraft and

226

anti-sorcery movements have emerged to fill the gap in society's defences against mystical enemies left by the suppression of the poison ordeal by colonial governments. This is almost certainly part of the truth. In Ufipa the gap has been further widened by the suppression of the indigenous religion, in which village headmen played the role of priests at communal sacrifices. Another socially integrative institution of traditional Fipa religion, also suppressed, was that of public confession: a man who was conscious of having wronged his neighbours filled a winnowing tray with sand and shouted his confession, shaking the sand to the winds as he did so.

Modern Fipa village society has to make do without any of these integrative devices, in a situation in which external ideological influences, many of them destructive of traditional values, are stronger than ever. In such a situation it would seem that tensions and conflicts are likely to increase, in the absence of traditional palliative mechanisms, until they threaten the complete disruption of village society. To this problem there are two possible solutions: revolution, a radical change in the system of social relations; or millenarianism, a general attempt, in the form of a 'revivalist' movement, to reassert and re-establish the traditional ethos of communal solidarity.

What happens when Kamcape take over a village in a 'cleansing' operation has certain resemblances to a miniature revolution. The abrupt assumption of authority by young men and young women – those categories with least status in traditional and normal Fipa society – together with the degradation of members of the most prestigious class, the male elders, would seem to suggest that the old order has been overturned. But this reversal of social roles and values exists only for the hour or two that the Kamcape operation lasts. Afterwards the community returns to normal: the alleged 'sorcerers' become respected elders again and the youths and girls revert to their former subordinate status.

Kamcape shares with the Bwanali-Mpulumutsi movement, with Mcape, and with the Congolese movements described by Douglas, the millenarian intention of 'turning over a new leaf', of 'wiping the slate clean'. Moreover the whole tenor of a Kamcape operation, the explicit and implicit meaning of the entire performance, makes good sense in terms of indigenous social theory. As Fipa see it, the class or category of male elders, the *akombe* or *ayiikolo*, possess, by virtue of their privileged status, joint and collective responsibility for the whole village community, for its physical and spiritual integrity and harmony. If there is tension and conflict then, blame has to be levelled at this class or category of elders; or if not at the whole lot of them, then at a sub-group within that class or category who can be held to have betrayed their fellows and thus to be the enemies of the whole community. To identify this anti-social sub-group and ritually and magically render its members harmless is the purpose of the 'branding' by Kamcape of those accused of sorcery, coupled with the administration to them of anti-sorcery 'medicine'.

A Kamcape operation is thus a kind of ritual drama in which the whole community participates, in which a number of elder men play the scapegoat role of 'sorcerer', and in which the most active participants, appropriately, are those members of the community with least status, and therefore least responsibility for, and identification with, the old state of affairs. The purpose of this ritual drama is to effect a radical change in the moral climate of the community by abolishing what is felt to be the root cause of all social tensions and conflicts – the practice of sorcery.

Kamcape is then partly a magico-medical operation analogous to the traditional mass ordeal by poison; but it is also more than this, as is indicated by the Kamcape practice (superfluous if the object were merely the 'practical' one of eradicating sorcery) of publicly and conspicuously 'branding' those accused of being sorcerers. This act of 'branding' is the climax of the ritual drama of Kamcape, the purpose of which is moral and symbolic. In the acting-out of this drama the 'sorcerers' symbolize, visibly and concretely, the evil, destructive, disintegrative forces menacing village society. That the identification and 'branding' of the 'sorcerers' is a dramatic and symbolic act is further confirmed by the fact that those 'branded' are not banished or ostracized after the Kamcape operation is over but reassume their former place in village life.

The overt purpose of the Kamcape movement, its manifest function, is to eradicate sorcery. Its latent function is to effect a resolution at the psychic level of a generalized sense of internal conflict and to recreate the moral climate of village communities in accordance with the traditional ethos of unity and harmony. But the internal conflicts which give rise to this generalized sense of social unease are endemic in village communities. Therefore Kamcape can provide only a temporary, and not a permanent, solution of the problem. Eventually the social situation will be ripe for another 'millenarian' movement, perhaps employing new and more elaborate techniques, to appear on the scene. This cycle appears to have recurred several times in Ufipa, with anti-sorcery movements flourishing at roughly ten-yearly intervals in 1933–4, 1943–4, 1954 and 1964.

The quasi-revolutionary overtones of the Kamcape movement have already been remarked – the active leading part played in its operations by youths and girls, the temporary degradation of a segment of the dominant, prestigeful class of male elders. What are the prospects of such movements becoming genuinely revolutionary in aim and practice, of actually changing the pattern of social relations instead of playing at it?

Kamcape as it appeared in Ufipa could not have instituted a permanent change in social relations because it had no permanent organization of its own and no directing head: it had no existence as a political entity. Yet just as the ritual drama enacted by Kamcape in numerous villages contained in germ the idea of society remade, so the notion of a hierarchical political organization was also latently present in the ideology of Kamcape's followers. They looked to a founder in Malawi called Icikanga from whom the esoteric knowledge of Kamcape is said to have been obtained and handed down through a chain of disciples and followers to the local leaders in various parts of Ufipa. Whoever 'Icikanga' is, it seems unlikely that he knew what was being done in his name in south-west Tanganyika in 1963–4. What happened, I think, was that the exponents of the Kamcape movement in Ufipa found it convenient to invest their activities with a mystical authority by associating them with this renowned seer and eradicator of witchcraft and sorcery who is said to have experienced a Christ-like resurrection.

The idea of a hierarchical political organization under a mystical-religious head was certainly abroad in Ufipa at the time of the Kamcape movement of 1963–4, even though the movement itself, passing across the country in a wave of seemingly spontaneously generated action, had no such formal shape. Kamcape might be described as a proto-church with an incipiently revolutionary and totalitarian doctrine of millenarian revivalism, a more developed form of which could be seen in the Lumpa organization of Alice Lenshina in neighbouring Zambia.[17] When such movements achieve political organization they are likely, at any rate in the beginning, to turn their energies away from an internal struggle against witchcraft or sorcery and into resistance to, or even insurrection against, the established state power.[18]

The political potentialities of such seemingly non-rational movements as Kamcape have been noted by Simone Clemhout:

Nativistic movements represent a cultural innovation in that they try ... to modify the institutionalized means to revitalize traditional values. These movements take

17. The struggle against witchcraft was a central preoccupation of the cult and church founded by Alice Lenshina, who was said to have died and then returned to earth after a visionary experience. Those wishing to join her church had first to surrender their magical objects and confess their wrong doings. (See Rotberg, 1961; Fernandez, 1964.)

18. Rotberg (1961) notes that at a later stage such organized movements may lose much of their insurrectionary ardour and achieve a *modus vivendi* with the state power, as happened with the Kibanguist movement in the Congo.

mostly a religious form because they are innovations at the cathetic or symbolic level. These movements, as far as they involve political elements, are a very great help to rationalizing political leadership (Clemhout, 1966).

References

CLEMHOUT, S. (1966), 'The psycho-sociological nature of nativistic movements and the emergence of cultural growth', *Anthropos*, vol. 61, nos. 1–2.

DOUGLAS, M. (1963), 'Techniques of sorcery control in Central Africa', in J. Middleton and E. H. Winter (eds.), *Witchcraft and Sorcery in East Africa*, Routledge & Kegan Paul.

EVANS-PRITCHARD, E. E. (1937), *Witchcraft, Oracles and Magic among the Azande*, Clarendon Press.

FERNANDEZ, J. W. (1964), 'The Lumpa uprising: why?', *Africa Report*, November.

MARWICK, M. G. (1950), 'Another modern anti-witchcraft movement in East Central Africa', *Africa*, vol. 20, no.2.

MARWICK, M. G. (1952), 'The social context of Cewa witch-beliefs', *Africa*, vol. 22, nos. 3–4.

MARWICK, M. G. (1965), *Sorcery in its Social Setting*, Manchester U.P.

RICHARDS, A. I. (1935), 'A modern movement of witch-finders', *Africa*, vol. 8, no. 4.

ROTBERG, R. (1961), 'The Lenshina movement of Northern Rhodesia', *Rhodes-Livingstone Journal*, vol. 29.

WILSON, M. Hunter (1951), 'Witch-beliefs and social structure', *American Journal of Sociology*, vol. 56.

Part Three Theories of Witchcraft

With the exception of a few self-conscious, artificial cults, witches and sorcerers belong to our fantasy-world. This may account for the considerable effort that has gone into explaining their believed existence in those societies where they were, or still are, experienced as real threats to life, health and property. This urge for reasonable comprehension is probably the mainspring of Margaret Murray's theory, here succinctly and fairly presented by Macfarlane before he tests it against the empirical evidence he won from the records of sixteenth and seventeenth-century Essex.[1] Elsie Clews Parsons's account of Pueblo witchcraft seems to be prompted less by the desire to give comprehensibility to exotic beliefs than by the sheer momentum of American anthropological diffusionism. With more comparative material at our disposal than she had, we can now be critical of some of her conclusions, especially her tendency to attribute to European influence many features since found to be nearly universal. A similar but more sober diffusionist approach is to be detected in some of Ewen's writings, not represented here but referred to in the Introduction (see p. 16). Psychological explanations of witchcraft, stemming from Freud's doctrine of the displacement of affect and mediated by Malinowski's general theory of magic (which draws some of its examples from Melanesian sorcery), are here represented most clearly by Kluckhohn. Krige's paper merits inclusion for its ethnographic richness alone, and could have gone into Part Two; but its penultimate paragraph contains a trenchant exposition of what we class as a psychological theory. Sociological theories, as we are reminded by the Readings from Wilson and Nadel, relate beliefs and attendant behaviour to the mesh of social relationships and to the moral values that keep it in workable shape. But, as no society is static, its shape is fluid, and these beliefs provide media for social dramas, which, in Turner's phrase, are either indices or vehicles of change (1957, p. 162). Accusations of witch-

1. The origins of this theory and the historiographical inadequacy of Murray's work are discussed in the excerpts from Norman Cohn's book in Part Two – see pp. 140–57 – *Ed.*

craft and sorcery usually uphold the *status quo*, but may sometimes punctuate the abandonment of the old order to make room for the new; and their incidence in categories of social relations provides pointers to recurrent problems and structural instabilities. Crawford emphasizes the part accusations play in social change, and insists that, far from being mere indices of change, they are crucial influences in the quality of the interaction that follows change. His remarks thus provide a corrective to functionalist exaggeration of the benefits of a system of witch-beliefs (to be detected, for instance, in the excerpts from Kluckhohn's book).

Many of the accounts of the European witch-scare imply that it was sustained, not by ordinary village folk, but by those whom Thomas designates as 'the educated classes who controlled the machinery of the law courts' (1971, p. 583). Harris (not represented in the Readings) has perhaps been the most explicit exponent of the view that the European witch-craze was one of the means by which the ruling classes of the day maintained their hegemony. He asserts that the craze 'was largely created and sustained by the governing classes as a means of suppressing Christian messianism' (1974, p. 225); that it led the poor to believe 'that they were being victimized by witches and devils instead of princes and popes' (ibid., p. 237); and that it thus demobilized the poor and the dispossessed, drawing them 'further and further away from confronting the ecclesiastical and secular establishment with demands for the redistribution of wealth and the leveling of rank' (ibid., pp. 239–40). In her paper in this Part, Kephart deals incidentally with Harris's political interpretation of the witch-craze.

As we mentioned in the general Introduction, the increasing interest of anthropologists in structuralist analysis has implications for the study of witchcraft. The chapter from Crick's book presents a programme in which the author goes so far as to suggest that the concept of 'witchcraft' should be 'analytically dissolved into a larger frame of reference' (see below, p. 346). Hammond-Tooke's paper, though belonging to the same genre, is both less radical and more empirical than Crick's contribution, and serves to illustrate how rationalist, cognitive or semantic anthropology might approach the subject.

References

HARRIS, M. (1974), *Cows, Pigs, Wars, and Witches*, Random House.

THOMAS, K. (1971), *Religion and the Decline of Magic*, Weidenfeld & Nicolson, and Penguin Books (1973).

TURNER, V. W. (1957), *Schism and Continuity in an African Society*, Manchester U.P.

23. Alan Macfarlane

Murray's Theory: Exposition and Comment

Excerpt from A. D. J. Macfarlane, *Witchcraft Prosecutions in Essex, 1560–1680: A Sociological Analysis*, D.Phil. thesis, University of Oxford, 1967, pp. 16–18.

The most radical attempt to provide a new explanation of witchcraft prosecutions was made by Miss Margaret Murray (1921).[1] Her work was based on the two assumptions that witchcraft beliefs cannot be profitably examined in isolation from other systems of ideas and that they cannot be dismissed as mere nonsense. These convictions were shared by G. L. Kittredge whose wide learning illuminated the subject (1929, pp. 372–3). Having decided that quite reasonable people really did fear witches and that others, without torture, freely confessed to this crime, Margaret Murray took what in many ways was a logical step and argued that there really must have been witches. They were, however, not the evil creatures described by their persecutors, but a highly organized pagan cult. She applied a number of Sir James Frazer's theories to English witchcraft, for instance the importance of rituals for increasing fertility in primitive religion, and thereby constructed a detailed picture of this 'witch-cult'. Witches, she claimed, met regularly at their 'Sabbats', they formed 'covens' of thirteen, each of which had a leader dressed in animal guise. They feasted, danced, and sang. This she termed 'ritual' witchcraft. Then the Christian inquisitors, in their attempt to stamp out paganism, turned this cult of pre-Christian gaiety into a deadly onslaught on the values of society. The leaders of the covens were transformed in their hands into the Devil, the innocent meetings were described as orgies. The 'witches' were believed to have made a secret or open compact with the Devil whereby they exchanged their soul for transitory power and pleasure.

Miss Murray's work was immediately criticized and has continued to be attacked (Burr, 1922, pp. 780–83; Ewen, 1938, n.p.; Robbins, 1959, pp. 116–17; Rose, 1962). The major criticism is that by extracting and quoting out of context from the whole of European folklore she created a totally false picture. She mistook what people believed to be happening for what actually did happen. Though she showed that people thought

1. As Professor Trevor-Roper recently pointed out, however, many of Murray's theories were anticipated by Jakob Grimm (Trevor-Roper, 1967, p. 15).

there was a witch-cult, she failed to demonstrate that there actually was one. Her thesis will not be examined directly in the following pages. There are very few descriptions of the phenomena which she discusses in Essex witchcraft; for instance, the Sabbat, coven and diabolic compact are absent, except in the exceptional trials of 1645.* Nor does more detailed examination of those accused of witchcraft in Essex lend any support to the argument that there really was an underground pagan cult. Probably there were those who came to believe themselves to be witches, but there is no evidence that they formed a self-conscious organization. This is a negative conclusion and impossible to document. All that can be said is that the Essex evidence does not support her conclusions and, indeed, makes her picture of the witch-cult seem far too sophisticated and articulate for the society with which we are concerned. Yet her assumptions about the necessity to treat accusations as something more than intolerant superstition are subscribed to.

* In another chapter of his thesis the author attributes the exceptional nature of these trials to the influence of the witchfinders, Hopkins and Stearne, and to tensions following the Civil War. Of over twelve hundred cases he reviews, only one is a clear instance of 'ritual witchcraft' though it could hardly be regarded as confirming Murray's theory – Ed.

References

BURR, G. L. (1922), 'A review of M. A. Murray's *Witch-Cult in Western Europe*', *American Historical Review*, vol. 27, no. 4.

EWEN, C. L. (1938), *Some Witchcraft Criticisms: A Plea for the Blue Pencil*, n.p.

KITTREDGE, G. L. (1929), *Witchcraft in Old and New England*, Harvard U.P.

MURRAY, M. A. (1921), *The Witch-Cult in Western Europe*, Clarendon Press.

ROBBINS, R. H. (1959), *Encyclopedia of Witchcraft and Demonology*, Crown.

ROSE, E. E. (1962), *A Razor for a Goat: Witchcraft and Diabolism*, University of Toronto Press.

TREVOR-ROPER, H. R. (1967), 'Witches and witchcraft', *Encounter*, vol. 28, nos. 5 and 6.

24. Elsie Clews Parsons

Witchcraft among the Pueblos: Indian or Spanish?

Abridged from Elsie Clews Parsons, 'Witchcraft among the Pueblos: Indian or Spanish?', *Man*, vol. 27, 1927, pp. 106–12, 125–8.

Beliefs and Practices

In the Zuñi origin myth (Parsons, 1923, pp. 37–138) a witch pair, male and female, come up from the under worlds after the other people and bring with them two gifts – death to keep the world from being crowded, and corn. The tradition implies that in Zuñi opinion witchcraft is magical power which is not necessarily differentiated into good or evil. 'The best men of the pueblo may be witches', I have been told in Laguna, and there, as in Zuñi and in other pueblos, charges of witchcraft have been brought against high officials. The Pueblo curing societies work against witchcraft, but there are said to be society practices in black magic as well as in white, particularly among the clown societies. In short, although black magic is plainly distinguished from white magic and the witch is he or she who is habitually engaged in the practice of black magic, witchcraft may be practised by any person or by any group.

There is individualistic practice of witchcraft, but witchcraft also runs in families, and in several towns there is believed to be a society of witches which is organized like any other society, with the same officials. Members, it is said at Laguna, have to obey the orders of their officers, orders to go out and make people sick. To be initiated the candidate must sacrifice some one, i.e. bewitch some one to death. In the instances cited to me at Zuñi the sacrificed one has always been a member of the household of the candidate.

In the initiation, the candidate has to go under an arch or bow (Laguna). With him goes the member of the society whose type of animal transformation the candidate chooses for his own, i.e. if he wants to be a witch cat he goes under the bow with a witch cat – a variant of the familiar Pueblo pattern of society sponsor or ceremonial father. In Pueblo folk-tales going under a bow or through a ring or hoop to produce a metamorphosis is a common incident. A still more common means of metamorphosis is by putting on the skin of the creature one is to be

changed into. The creatures most commonly mentioned for witch transformation are cats, dogs, burros, bears, owls.

Insects are controlled by witches as their agents. They can send
caterpillars or grasshoppers to destroy crops, and they send insects
into the body of a victim similarly to destroy it.[1] Witches may also
'send in' a piece of flesh from a corpse or a shred of funeral cloth
or a splinter of bone; any sharp or pointed thing is serviceable,
thorn, cactus point, glass, etc. Sending things into the body is the
commonest form of witch attack, but, at Zuñi at least, witches may also
attack through the ghosts (*ahoppa*) of members of the family they are
persecuting.

Epidemic is always imputed to witchcraft; but not every individual
ailment. The ailment from which recovery is rapid is much less likely to be
attributed to a witch than that which is lingering, on and off.

Besides causing sickness, individual and epidemic, and insect plague,
witches can control the weather, keeping the rain off[2] or causing wind.

Bewitching is very commonly the result of a grievance, since a witch
who feels injured will retaliate. Now as you never know who is a witch,
you are always careful not to give offence – unless you are yourself a
witch. A reckless attitude towards others, 'not caring what you say',
seems to be one indication of witchhood. I cannot help but connect the
very striking social timidities of the Pueblos with their witchcraft theories.
Father Dumarest had the same impression. 'Why are the Pueblo Indians
so pacific?' he writes. 'Why do they not try even to defend themselves in
quarrels? Because from their youth their elders have taught them that
nobody can know the hearts of men. There are witches everywhere'
(1919, p. 162).

Envy is a very common motive in witchcraft.

The most abusive and the most dreadful charge you can bring against
anyone is that of being a witch. In some towns such charges are quite
commonly bandied about; although how much colour an accused has to
lend it by his behaviour in general it is difficult to determine. Besides
reckless speech, dishonesty in regard to property, or, still more, the
possession of wealth from sources unknown[3] and roaming about at night
or looking into windows seem to be characters or habits open to suspicion. Lurking at night about the house where a person is sick is par-

1. For such use of a centipede see Parsons (1917, part 2, p. 270, no. 2).

2. Feathers of the owl and the crow are associated with witchcraft because, I was told at
Zuñi, these birds keep away other birds and hence keep away the rain.

3. For example, a certain member of the council at Taos is reputed a witch since without
working he wears good clothes and, an extra touch, 'he looks under his eyes'.

ticularly questionable and the house of an invalid will be watched in order to catch the operating witch.

Persons may labour under the suspicion of witchcraft for years without decisive action being taken against them. They are said to be more or less shunned.

Decisive action is taken against witches in case of a public misfortune like an epidemic or a grasshopper plague or a drought. Then some person, either long under suspicion or but freshly suspected, is likely to be tried. Formerly at Zuñi the suspect was hung by his arms tied behind his back to a projecting beam of the Catholic Church until he confessed. Nowadays, he is 'talked to' by the bow-priests. This nagging is felt to be very trying [and he may be advised to] tell them something to get rid of them.

In individual cases of bewitchment the curing societies are called upon. The particular doctor is invited by a relative of the invalid to make the cure.

The use of arrow points on altars and attached to fetishes is a charm against witchcraft.

The animal paws which figure on altars are also charms against witches or agents in fighting them. In this turning of the wild animals against the witches who can themselves become wild animals, may be seen the conceptual closeness between witches and medicine-men, of which we have already spoken. The connexion appears again in the sucking cure of the medicine-man, he sucking out of the invalid's body what the witch has sent into it.

Ashes are also a charm or prophylactic against witchcraft.

It is believed in Zuñi and Taos, probably elsewhere, that witches can use hair cuttings in their black magic, so hair cuttings are burned or thrown into the river.

[In a Tewa folk-tale Coyote marries Yellow Corn Girl and teaches her how to transform herself into an animal by jumping through a ring. He then helps her to kill her mother and brother by witchcraft.] 'After this there were witches. There were never witches before the girl married Coyote. That is the reason why people are witches now. They have been taught by Coyote.'

Indian or Spanish?

In Pueblo folk tales, as in Plains Indian tales, Coyote is frequently the arch trickster, so holding him responsible for the introduction of witchcraft is characteristically Indian; but what of other features in this tale as

237

well as in the foregoing account in general: causing sickness by image or by injection, killing relatives, the witch assembly, transforming into animal form by putting on an animal skin, or jumping through a ring or under a bow, – are these European or Indian features? Belief in animal metamorphosis is certainly both European and Indian; transformation by ring seems more European, by skin, more Indian (although this can be found as a medieval belief). The witch assembly is, of course, a European idea, but is so thoroughly worked into the Pueblo idea of ceremonial organization that it would be rash to hold that it was not a pre-Spanish idea. Killing relatives is European, although killing by taking out the 'heart' (soul) is Indian. Causing sickness is both European and Indian, but causing it by sending something into the body is Indian;[4] whereas the use of an image to represent the invalid seems European.

Is the use of ashes as a witch prophylactic Spanish or native, or both? Marking a cross on the head with ashes on Ash Wednesday is a prevalent Catholic rite, one that seems to be the origin of rubbing ashes on a baby at Laguna and at Zuñi. But is it also the origin of the practice at Laguna of a medicine-man rubbing his legs that he may not tire in his witch contest, or of the use of ashes in the exorcising rite of waving around the head, familiar at Zuñi and among the Hopi? Probably not.

Again, what is European and what is native in the belief that persons in high office are open to the charge of witchcraft? In early days the Spaniards were continually abusing the medicine-men as witches, the very kind of abuse and suspicion the Indians are quick to indulge in today. And yet even before the advent of the Spaniards, medicine [-men] may have been suspected of black magic.

In contrast with these dubieties certain miscellaneous witch beliefs and practices may be mentioned as plainly European: the belief in Taos and Laguna that witches travel as balls of fire, and the related belief that a light which is seen to vanish betokens a death in the family (Laguna, Zuñi); to catch a witch, the practice of turning one's clothes inside out, trousers, coat, etc. (Zuñi); the belief that the footfall of a witch animal is inaudible (Laguna and Santa Clara). The belief that the witch animal which is wounded is subsequently found as a wounded person I would also classify as European, together with the belief about hair cuttings and the practice in the Eastern towns of burning anti-witch root. The burning of the witch with green wood in the Tewan folk-tale appears to point back to the witch executions which actually took place in New Mexico under Spanish administration.

4. See R. H. Lowie (1924, pp. 176–80), for the distribution among Indians of the theories of sickness from intrusion and from soul-kidnapping.

In conclusion, I venture this general reconstruction. In pre-Spanish days the ceremonial groups were considered capable of black as well as of white magic, they could cause the same inflictions they could cure and, in particular, their members could send harmful substances into the human body. Their members got their medicines through the prey animals, and, by wearing portions of the animal, were endowed with the powers of the animals, by putting on the whole skin of the animal might even transform into it. All these beliefs (except that of sending things into the body, which belief is unfamiliar to the Mexican neighbours of the Pueblos) were enriched by Spanish witchcraft theory, which also spread, if it did not introduce, the idea that anybody might practise witchcraft. In this connexion it is significant that among the Hopi there is much less reference to witchcraft in the daily life or of its practice on the part of any evilly disposed person than there is at Zuñi or in the east. Here, I infer, as in other particulars, the Hopi are a touch-stone of Spanish influence. In other words, where Spanish influence has prevailed, witchcraft has been secularized and witch notions have tended to permeate the daily life.

References

DUMAREST, NOËL (1919), 'Notes on Cochiti, New Mexico', *Memoirs of the American Anthropological Association*, vol. 6.

LOWIE, R. H. (1924), *Primitive Religion*, Boni & Liveright.

PARSONS, E. G. (1917), 'Notes on Zuñi', *Memoirs of the American Anthropological Association*, vol. 4, no. 4.

PARSONS, E. C. (1923), 'The origin myth of Zuñi', *Journal of American Folk-Lore*, vol. 36, pp. 137–38.

25. Bronislaw Malinowski

Sorcery as Mimetic Representation

Excerpts from Bronislaw Malinowski, *Magic, Science and Religion and Other Essays*, edited by Robert Redfield, Doubleday, 1954, pp. 70–84; Free Press, 1948. The essay from which these excerpts are taken was first published in 1925.

Let us have a look at a typical act of magic, and choose one which is well-known and generally regarded as a standard performance – an act of black magic. Among the several types which we meet in savagery, witch-craft by the act of pointing the magical dart is, perhaps, the most wide-spread of all. A pointed bone or stick, an arrow or the spine of some animal, is ritually, in a mimic fashion, thrust, thrown, or pointed in the direction of the man to be killed by sorcery. We have innumerable recipes in the oriental and ancient books of magic, in ethnographic descriptions and tales of travelers, of how such a rite is performed. But the emotional setting, the gestures and expressions of the sorcerer during the perfor-mance, have been but seldom described. Yet these are of the greatest importance. If a spectator were suddenly transported to some part of Melanesia and could observe the sorcerer at work, not perhaps knowing exactly what he was looking at, he might think that he had either to do with a lunatic or else he would guess that here was a man acting under the sway of uncontrolled anger. For the sorcerer has, as an essential part of the ritual performance, not merely to point the bone dart at his victim, but with an intense expression of fury and hatred he has to thrust it in the air, turn and twist it as if to bore it in the wound, then pull it back with a sudden jerk. Thus not only is the act of violence, or stabbing, reproduced, but the passion of violence has to be enacted.

We see thus that the dramatic expression of emotion is the essence of this act, for what is it that is reproduced in it? Not its end, for the magician would in that case have to imitate the death of the victim, but the emotional state of the performer, a state which closely corresponds to the situation in which we find it and which has to be gone through mimetically.

I could adduce a number of similar rites from my own experience, and many more, of course, from other records. Thus, when in other types of black magic the sorcerer ritually injures or mutilates or destroys a figure or object symbolizing the victim, this rite is, above all, a clear expression of hatred and anger. Or when in love magic the performer has really or symbolically to grasp, stroke, fondle the beloved person or some object representing her, he reproduces the behavior of a heartsick lover who has lost his common sense and is overwhelmed by passion. In war magic, anger, the fury of attack, the emotions of combative passion are frequently expressed in a more or less direct manner. In the magic of terror, in the exorcism directed against powers of darkness and evil, the magician behaves as if himself overcome by the emotion of fear, or at least violently struggling against it. Shouts, brandishing of weapons, the use of lighted torches, form often the substance of this rite. Or else in an act, recorded by myself, to ward off the evil powers of darkness, a man has ritually to tremble, to utter a spell slowly as if paralysed by fear. And this fear gets hold also of the approaching sorcerer and wards him off.

All such acts, usually rationalized and explained by some principle of magic, are *prima facie* expressions of emotion. The substances and paraphernalia used in them have often the same significance. Daggers, sharp-pointed lacerating objects, evil-smelling or poisonous substances, used in black magic; scents, flowers, inebriating stimulants, in love magic; valuables, in economic magic – all these are associated primarily through emotions and not through ideas with the end of the respective magic.

Besides such rites, however, in which a dominant element serves to express an emotion, there are others in which the act does forecast its result, or, to use Sir James Frazer's expression, the rite imitates its end. Thus, in the black magic of the Melanesians recorded by myself, a characteristic ritual way of winding-up the spell is for the sorcerer to weaken the voice, utter a death rattle, and fall down in imitation of the rigor of death. It is, however, not necessary to adduce any other examples, for this aspect of magic and the allied one of contagious magic has been brilliantly described and exhaustively documented by Frazer. Sir James has also shown that there exists a special lore of magical substances based on affinities, relations, on ideas of similarity and contagion, developed with a magical pseudo-science. [...]

Magic is not born of an abstract conception of universal power, subsequently applied to concrete cases. It has undoubtedly arisen independently in a number of actual situations. Each type of magic, born of its own situation and of the emotional tension thereof, is due to the spontaneous flow of ideas and the spontaneous reaction of man. It is the uniformity of the mental process in each case which has led to certain universal features of magic and to the general conceptions which we find at the basis of man's magical thought and behavior. It will be necessary to give now an

241

analysis of the situations of magic and the experiences which they provoke. [. . .]

Now we must analyse this belief from the point of view of the sociological observer. Let us realize once more the type of situation in which we find magic. Man, engaged in a series of practical activities, comes to a gap; the hunter is disappointed by his quarry, the sailor misses propitious winds, the canoe builder has to deal with some material of which he is never certain that it will stand the strain, or the healthy person suddenly feels his strength failing. What does man do naturally under such conditions, setting aside all magic, belief and ritual? Forsaken by his knowledge, baffled by his past experience and by his technical skill, he realizes his impotence. Yet his desire grips him only the more strongly; his anxiety, his fears and hopes, induce a tension in his organism which drives him to some sort of activity. Whether he be savage or civilized, whether in possession of magic or entirely ignorant of its existence, passive inaction, the only thing dictated by reason, is the last thing in which he can acquiesce. His nervous system and his whole organism drive him to some substitute activity. Obsessed by the idea of the desired end, he sees it and feels it. His organism reproduces the acts suggested by the anticipations of hope, dictated by the emotion of passion so strongly felt.

The man under the sway of impotent fury or dominated by thwarted hate spontaneously clenches his fist and carries out imaginary thrusts at his enemy, muttering imprecations, casting words of hatred and anger against him. The lover aching for his unattainable or irresponsive beauty sees her in his visions, addresses her, and entreats and commands her favors, feeling himself accepted, pressing her to his bosom in his dreams. The anxious fisherman or hunter sees in his imagination the quarry enmeshed in the nets, the animal attained by the spear; he utters their names, describes in words his visions of the magnificent catch, he even breaks out into gestures of mimic representation of what he desires. The man lost at night in the woods or the jungle, beset by superstitious fear, sees around him the haunting demons, addresses them, tries to ward off, to frighten them, or shrinks from them in fear, like an animal which attempts to save itself by feigning death.

These reactions to overwhelming emotion or obsessive desire are natural responses of man to such a situation, based on a universal psycho-physiological mechanism. They engender what could be called extended expressions of emotion in act and in word, the threatening gestures of impotent anger and its maledictions, the spontaneous enactment of the desired end in a practical impasse, the passionate fondling gestures of the lover, and so on. All these spontaneous acts and spontaneous works make man forecast the images of the wished-for results, or express his passion in uncontrollable gestures, or break out into words which give vent to desire and anticipate its end.

And what is the purely intellectual process, the conviction formed during such a free outburst of emotion in words and deeds? First there surges a clear image of the desired end, of the hated person, of the feared danger or ghost. And each image is blended with its specific passion, which drives us to assume an active attitude towards that image. When passion reaches the breaking point at which man loses control over himself, the words which he utters, his blind behavior, allow the pent-up physiological tension to flow over. But over all this outburst presides the image of the end. It supplies the motive-force of the reaction, it apparently organizes and directs words and acts towards a definite purpose. The substitute action in which the passion finds its vent, and which is due to impotence, has subjectively all the value of a real action, to which emotion would, if not impeded, naturally have led.

As the tension spends itself in these words and gestures the obsessing visions fade away, the desired end seems nearer satisfaction, we regain our balance, once more at harmony with life. And we remain with a conviction that the words of malediction and the gestures of fury have traveled towards the hated person and hit their target; that the imploration of love, the visionary embraces, cannot have remained unanswered, that the visionary attainment of success in our pursuit cannot have been without a beneficial influence on the pending issue. In the case of fear, as the emotion which has led us to frenzied behavior gradually subsides, we feel that it is the behavior that has driven away the terrors. In brief, a strong emotional experience, which spends itself in a purely subjective flow of images, words, and acts of behavior, leaves a very deep conviction of its reality, as if of some practical and positive achievement, as if of something done by a power revealed to man. This power, born of mental and physiological obsession, seems to get hold of us from outside, and to primitive man, or to the credulous and untutored mind of all ages, the spontaneous spell, the spontaneous rite, and the spontaneous belief in their efficiency, must appear as a direct revelation from some external and no doubt impersonal sources.

When we compare this spontaneous ritual and verbiage of overflowing passion or desire with traditionally fixed magical ritual and with the principles embodied in magical spells and substances, the striking resemblance of the two products shows that they are not independent of each other. Magical ritual, most of the principles of magic, most of its spells and substances, have been revealed to man in those passionate experiences which assail him in the impasses of his instinctive life and of his practical pursuits, in those gaps and breaches left in the ever-imperfect wall of culture which he erects between himself and the besetting tempt-ations and dangers of his destiny. In this I think we have to recognize not only one of the sources but the very fountainhead of magical belief.

To most types of magical ritual, therefore, there corresponds a sponta-neous ritual of emotional expression or of a forecast of the desired end. To most features of magical spell, to the commands, invocations, meta-phors, there corresponds a natural flow of words, in malediction, in entreaty, in exorcism, and in the descriptions of unfulfilled wishes. To every belief in magical efficiency there can be laid in parallel one of those illusions of subjective experience, transient in the mind of the civilized rationalist, though even there never quite absent, but powerful and con-vincing to the simple man in every culture, and, above all, to the primitive savage mind.

Thus the foundations of magical belief and practice are not taken from the air, but are due to a number of experiences actually lived through, in which man receives the revelation of his power to attain the desired end. We must now ask: What is the relation between the promises contained in such experience and their fulfilment in real life? Plausible though the fallacious claims of magic might be to primitive man, how is it that they have remained so long unexposed?

The answer to this is that, first, it is a well-known fact that in human memory the testimony of a positive case always overshadows the negative one. One gain easily outweighs several losses. Thus the instances which affirm magic always loom far more conspicuously than those which deny it. But there are other facts which endorse by a real or apparent testimony the claims of magic. We have seen that magical ritual must have originated from a revelation in a real experience. But the man who from such an experience conceived, formulated and gave to his tribesmen the nucleus of a new magical performance – acting, be it remembered, in perfect good faith – must have been a man of genius. The men who inherited and wielded his magic after him, no doubt always building it out and developing it, while believing that they were simply following up the tradition, must have been always men of great intelligence, energy, and power of enterprise. They would be the men successful in all emergencies. It is an empirical fact that in all savage societies magic and outstanding personality go hand in hand. Thus magic also coincides with personal success, skill, courage and mental power. No wonder that it is considered a source of success.

This personal renown of the magician and its importance in enhancing the belief about the efficiency of magic are the cause of an interesting phenomenon: what may be called the *current mythology* of magic. Round every big magician there arises a halo made up of stories about his wonderful cures or kills, his catches, his victories, his conquests in love. In every savage society such stories form the backbone of belief in magic, for, supported as they are by the emotional experiences which everyone has had himself, the running chronicle of magical miracles establishes its claims beyond any doubt or cavil. Every eminent practitioner, besides his traditional claim, besides the filiation with his predecessors, makes his personal warrant of wonder-working.

Thus myth is not a dead product of past ages, merely surviving as an idle narrative. It is a living force, constantly producing new phenomena, constantly surrounding magic by new testimonies. Magic moves in the glory of past tradition, but it also creates its atmosphere of ever-nascent myth. As there is the body of legends already fixed, standardized and constituting the folklore of the tribe, so there is always a stream of narratives in kind to those of the mythological time. Magic is the bridge between the golden age of primeval craft and the wonder-working power of today. Hence the formulas are full of mythical allusions, which, when uttered, unchain the powers of the past and cast them into the present.

With this we see also the role and meaning of mythology in a new light. Myth is not a savage speculation about origins of things born out of philosophic interest. Neither is it the result of the contemplation of nature – a sort of symbolical representation of its laws. It is the historical statement of one of those events which once for all vouch for the truth of a certain form of magic. Sometimes it is the actual record of a magical revelation coming directly from the first man to whom magic was revealed in some dramatic occurrence. More often it bears on its surface that it is merely a statement of how magic came into the possession of a clan or a community or a tribe. In all cases it is a warrant of its truth, a pedigree of its filiation, a charter of its claims to validity. And as we have seen, myth is the natural result of human faith, because every power must give signs of its efficiency, must act and be known to act, if people are to believe in its virtue. Every belief engenders its mythology, for there is no faith without miracles, and the main myth recounts simply the primeval miracle of the magic.

26. Clyde Kluckhohn

Navaho Witchcraft

Excerpts from Clyde Kluckhohn, *Navaho Witchcraft*, Beacon Press, 1962, pp. 67–121 (first published as Papers of the Peabody Museum of Archaeology and Ethnography, Harvard University, 1944).

[The next section] will [...] be given over to structural analysis. The hypothesis will be developed that the euphoric effects of the witchcraft pattern assemblage are considerable, perhaps even outweighing the dysphoric effects at the present moment. It is hoped that this may influence anthropologists more frequently to examine without prejudice the contributions of any pattern assemblage to the total social system and to resist the tendency to label 'witchcraft' or 'sorcery' as 'evil' – in accord with the connotations which such words as 'witchcraft' and 'sorcery' have in our language, conformant to our system of sentiments. It is hoped that this exercise in structural analysis may contribute to the general understanding of some aspects of Navaho social structure which have perhaps been insufficiently appreciated. At the same time, the emphasis upon structure will by no means preclude other kinds of interpretation.[1] Thus witchcraft as an expression in fantasy for the culturally disallowed, but unconsciously wanted, will be considered because such wish fulfilments are of obvious utility to individuals in the preservation of their equilibrium. [...]

A structural analysis (an investigation of 'functional dependences') is a study in the interrelation of parts. All of the parts must be described before their interrelationships can be understood. A description of many aspects of Navaho social structure will, therefore, be a necessary back-

1. These interpretations were partially developed in the course of participation in the seminar on Culture and Personality conducted by A. Kardiner and R. Linton in Columbia University, 1939–40. For the opportunity of sharing in this seminar I am grateful to the Carnegie Corporation. While I benefited markedly from association with Dr Kardiner, it is only fair to him to state that few of his psychoanalytic interpretations of Navaho witchcraft material are here incorporated, and that he has not commented upon many of the hypotheses in this section because they have been formulated subsequent to the time of my contact with him. Membership in Dr Sandor Rado's seminar on psychoanalytic theory at the New York Psychoanalytic Institute during the same period should also be mentioned as an important influence underlying the type of analysis attempted.

But for direct revisions of this section I am most indebted to a painstaking criticism (both factual and theoretical) by David Aberle.

ground to comprehension of the workings of witchcraft. This becomes clear immediately when we ask the question which is actually most central to our conceptual scheme: why have witchcraft patterns (whatever their historical source!) survived through the periods to which our material relates? If we look at a few features of the Navaho socialization process and at some conditions of Navaho life which the child early experiences, we at once gain a partial (though by no means complete) enlightenment.

Early Life as Background for the Survival of Belief in Witchcraft

Let us observe, first of all, how socialization implements the persistence of witchcraft beliefs. The child, even before he is fully responsive to verbalizations, begins to get a picture of experience as potentially menacing. He sees his parents, and other elders, confess their impotence to deal with various matters by technological or other rational means in that they resort to exoteric prayers, songs and 'magical' observances and to esoteric rites. When he has been linguistically socialized, he hears the hushed gossip of witchcraft and learns that there are certain fellow tribesmen whom his family suspect and fear. One special experience of early childhood which may be of considerable importance occurs during toilet training. When the toddler goes with mother or with older sister to defecate or urinate, a certain uneasiness which they manifest (in most cases) about the concealment of the waste matter can hardly fail to become communicated to the child. The mother, who has been seen not only as a prime source of gratification but also as an almost omnipotent person, is now revealed as herself afraid, at the mercy of threatening forces. The contrast must be uncommonly great between the picture of the world which the child had during what the psychoanalysts call the period of 'oral mastery' and the picture of the world which he gets from the words and acts of his elders during the period when he is being obliged to give up the 'instinctual gratifications' of unrestricted urination and defecation.

Other early experiences of the child help to create a soil fertile for the implanting of belief in such a phenomenon as witchcraft. What with a diet which no longer has even the advantages of being a trial and error adaptation over many generations to the peculiar conditions of Navaho life, with no skills for combatting the disease introduced by Europeans, with drafty hogans and wet clothing and other inadequate protections, it is hardly surprising that Navaho children are frequently ill. The threats to health which were characteristic of the aboriginal culture are still largely present, but additional threats arising out of unwise adoption of our

247

dietary habits, and from other European borrowings, have been added. In short, it is inevitable that the Navaho child experiences discomfort and pain – without quick or satisfactory means of alleviation. The child likewise sees others ill and suffering. Hunger, too, is an early experience. Not many Navaho have attained adulthood without knowing starvation for short periods and hunger rations for long periods. Since the child soon discovers that even his mother cannot control these things and since the doings and sayings of his elders make it plain that all of these privations occur even when people work very hard and very skilfully, it is small wonder that experience has a capricious and malevolent component for most Navahos.

Thus we see, in a very general way, how a belief in witches fits with what the young Navaho very soon comes to expect of living. But as yet we have learned little as to why these particular forms of belief in *witchcraft* should be perpetuated. The learning of urine and faeces concealment may act as a conditioning mechanism specific to witchcraft belief. Otherwise, however, the only thing which seems demanded by the conditions listed is fear of *some* sort of malevolent forces. To get beyond the demonstration of a social matrix favourable to the survival of beliefs of the generic type of witchcraft, we must examine systematically the contributions which the witchcraft pattern assemblage makes to the maintenance of personal and social equilibrium. [...]

What are the 'functions', the sociological *raison d'être*, of belief in (and perhaps practice of) witchcraft by the Navaho? It will be convenient to consider this question first from the standpoint of the adjustive responses which such beliefs and practices make possible for the individual. We shall then see how they constitute, up to a point, adaptive responses for the society. Since a society is made up of individual organisms, the two categories inevitably merge, but an emphasis upon the two angles of perspective will show the 'functions' in sharper focus.

Manifest 'Functions' of Witchcraft for the Individual Navaho

The manifest 'functions' are limited in number. So far as practice is concerned, witchcraft is obviously a means of attaining wealth, gaining women, disposing of enemies and 'being mean'. In short, witchcraft is a potential avenue to supernatural power. Power seems to be an important central theme in Navaho culture of which gaining wealth, disposing of enemies, and even, to some extent, obtaining possession of women are merely particular examples.

An inadequate memory, lack of the fees for teachers (the teacher of witchcraft needs to be paid only by the sacrifice of a sibling!), or other factors prevent some Navahos from attaining supernatural power through the socially approved route of becoming a singer. For such persons learning witchcraft is a manifest antidote to deprivation. Indeed, the presence of the witchcraft patterns must be a constant 'temptation' to Navahos who lust for power but have not attained it by other means. The practice of witchcraft similarly supplies an outlet to those Navaho in whom aggressive impulses are peculiarly strong. Old Navahos often comment that the men who used to organize war parties were of a special personality type: 'they were the ones that always like to stir up trouble.' One may speculate that personalities who found leading a war party an especially congenial occupation would find becoming a witch the most congenial substitute in the contemporary Navaho world.

But since most of the data evidence belief in witchcraft rather than practice of witchcraft, our major attention must be given to seeing how witchcraft 'functions' in the lives of Navahos who are not witches. At the manifest level, it may be pointed out, first of all, that witchcraft stories have the obvious value of the dramatic – the exciting story. They partially fulfil the 'functions' which books and magazines, plays and moving pictures carry out in our culture. In the second place, it must be realized that witchcraft ideology gives a partial answer to the problems which disturb the Navaho as well as other peoples – stubborn illness without apparent etiology, death without visible cause. One of man's peculiarities is that he requires 'reasons' for the occurrence of events.[2] One of the manifest 'functions' of belief in witchcraft is that such belief supplies answers to questions which would otherwise be perplexing – and because perplexing,

2. Lee (1940, pp. 356–7) has argued that 'An analysis of Trobriand behaviour and language shows that the Trobriander, by custom, focuses his interest on the thing or act in itself, not on its relationships . . . he deduces no causal connexion from a sequence. . . . The Trobriander has no linguistic mechanism for expressing a relationship between events or acts. Culturally, causation and teleology are either ignored or non-existent.' She is, however, careful to say, 'By this I mean, not that the individual Trobriander cannot understand causality, but that in his culture, the sequence of events does not automatically fall into the mould of causal or telic relationship.'

Whether or not all peoples employ a category which may be roughly equated with our 'causation' or even our 'mutual interdependence', all human beings whom I have known or read about seem to go to considerable trouble to find and to express 'reasons' for what they say and do. The giving of justifications which are 'rational' with reference to the logics of that culture seems to be one of the most universal of adjustive responses. This does not mean, of course, that 'the function' of such behaviour is usually that of 'satisfying intellectual curiosity', although this motivation must not be too dogmatically and cavalierly excluded in every case (cf. Kluckhohn, 1942, p. 56, fn. 46).

So far as the Navaho are concerned, the statement hardly needs qualification. For the Navaho language is marked by elaboration and refinement of causative categories.

disturbing. More specifically, the availability of witchcraft as an explanation helps to maintain the Navaho's conviction in the efficacy of the curing ceremonials. If a chant which has been performed without a hitch by a singer of great reputation fails, nevertheless, to cure, the Navaho need not wonder: 'Are the chants really any good? Or are we perhaps, after all, hopelessly at the mercy of the forces that cause illness?' A culturally acceptable alternative explanation is at hand: 'The disease was caused by witchcraft, *that's why* the chant didn't work.' This line of reasoning also gives an obvious out for the singer who has failed. Unless he feels the situation to be of a kind that voicing such a suspicion will be a boomerang against himself, he may say, 'Well, my friends, I have done my best and my chant is very powerful. But your unfortunate kinsman has clearly been witched. As you know, only Evil Way chants will do any good against those who have been witched. And the best medicine is not a chant but a prayer ceremonial. That is why I have failed. I am sure that the man who did divination should have found out that a witch was behind this illness.'

But would the convenience of witchcraft as an explanation be, of itself, sufficient to ensure the survival of such beliefs at the expense of more rational modes of explanation? It must be remembered that acculturated Navahos characteristically continue to fear witches after they have lost all trust in Navaho medicine. Even in a more complex culture like our own which prides itself upon its rationality, belief in 'black magic' is by no means totally extinct. After all, until comparatively recent times, the Christian Church taught – not that witchcraft was untrue but that it was an evil religion. Our culture hardly needs witchcraft as explanation. The tenacity of such beliefs must have additional supports. To understand fully why witchcraft belief has such survival value among the Navaho, we must look at the latent 'functions' of belief in witchcraft for the individual.

Latent 'Functions' of Witchcraft for the Individual Navaho

The most obvious of these is that the individual can capitalize on the credence of his fellows in these patterns to gain the center of the stage for himself. It is difficult to know how often Navahos complain of the symptoms of witchcraft as a device for getting attention. But close analysis of some cases where the personal context is well known indicates that this mechanism is sometimes employed. A high proportion of those who have suddenly 'fainted' or gone into a semi-trance state at 'squaw dances' or other large gatherings are women or men who are somewhat neglected or occupy low status. The rich and powerful (who are usually, of course, somewhat aggressive types) tend to announce or to have it discovered by a diagnostician in the privacy of their homes that they are victims of witchcraft. But, out of seventeen cases where I have the relevant facts, eleven of those who collapsed at large gatherings were women and thirteen of those were persons known to receive a minimum of prestige responses in the normal run of things. These facts fit well with similar phenomena which have been reported from other cultures. It is a commonplace that European and New England witch trials were frequently started by publicity seekers, often children. It is probable that in the South frustrated women make up a considerable proportion of the accusations which get Negroes lynched. Linton points out that among the Tanala of Madagascar 'most of those subject to *tromba* [a neurotic seizure indicated by an extreme desire to dance] are persons of minor importance' (Kardiner, 1939, p. 270). Mead's material on the differential participation in certain trance states in Bali suggests somewhat similar interpretations (1939).

A second latent 'function' of the corpus of witchcraft lore for individuals is that of providing a socially recognized channel for the expression (in varying degrees of obliquity) of the culturally disallowed. Certain aberrant impulses (such as those toward incest and necrophilia) may achieve some release in phantasy. Of course, a man can have a day dream involving intercourse with a dead women without recourse to a witchcraft setting. But he is then likely to have his pleasure dampened by worry over the abnormality of his phantasy. In the Navaho phrase 'he will wonder if he is losing his mind'. He will probably feel under the necessity of having Blessing Way sung over him at once. Whereas, if the phantasy takes the form of repeating (or manufacturing) a witchcraft tale involving this incident or visualizations while listening to another telling such a story, the psychological mechanisms of identification or projection permit the outlet in phantasy without conflict.

Quantitatively more significant as adjustive responses are the ways in which witchcraft beliefs and practices allow the expression of direct and displaced antagonisms. The Leightons found that into their category of 'difficulties with other Navahos' fell 26 per cent of the 859 'threats' which were mentioned in their interview material. They note that intra-tribal friction ranks second only to the disease-accident and injury-religious beliefs as a source of the worries which Navahos reported to them (Leighton and Leighton, 1942, p. 206). My own material abundantly confirms this indication of the importance of the problem of aggression in Navaho society at the present time. Witchcraft is, of course, only one of many possible ways of handling this problem and is indeed only one of a number of ways utilized by the Navaho. Fights occur; aggression is expressed against dead relatives as ghosts; there are other cultural devices for meeting the hostility problem which will be discussed in due course. But if myths and rituals provide the principal means of *sublimating* the Navaho individual's anti-social tendencies, witchcraft provides one of the principally socially understood means of *expressing* them. [...]

The two most important latent 'functions' of Navaho witchcraft for the individual relate to the crucial Navaho problems of aggression and anxiety. These latent 'functions' seem to be less related to individual status than to certain general pressures which affect (to varying degrees) all Navahos. Let us briefly review the picture. The intra-societal tensions which are present in every society (Dollard, 1938) are aggravated in the case of the Navaho by their uncushioned dependence upon a capricious physical environment, by emotional inbreeding, by insecurity consequent upon the pressure of our culture and society, by restrictions upon various methods of discharge of aggressive impulses. Non-aggressive ways of handling hostile feelings are inadequate. Most direct forms of intra-group aggression constitute too great a challenge to social solidarity and to subsistence survival. Under these circumstances the beliefs and practices related to witchcraft constitute eminently adjustive cultural solutions for Navaho individuals.

Displacement of aggression

There are few socially legitimated hostilities among the Navaho. The witch is the person whom the ideal patterns of the culture say it is not only proper but necessary to hate. Instead of saying all the bitter things one has felt against one's stingy and repressive father-in-law (which would threaten one's own economic security as well as bring down upon one's head unpleasant social disapproval), one can obtain some relief by venting one's spleen against a totally unrelated witch in the community. This displaced aggression does not expose one to punishment so long as one is discreet in the choice of the intimates to whom one talks. And if one rages against a witch who isn't even in the locality but lives over the mountain a safe hundred miles away one is perfectly assured against reprisals.

The fact that a high proportion of witchcraft gossip refers to *distant* witches makes Navaho witchcraft much more adaptive than most patterns which center witch activity within the group. At Zuni where everyone knows everyone else the effect appears to be much more destructive. But in a Navaho story the witch can be specified as a Navaho – with a gain to the imaginative reality of the tale – and yet never have been seen by narrator and hearers, or perhaps seen only rarely when he visited the community to conduct a ceremonial. In such cases the social visibility is sufficient for credence but the social distance great enough to make the origin of feuds unlikely. Since Navaho witches (with the partial exception of the de Chelly and Cañoncito populations) are a distributive rather than a segmental minority, persistive sadism of the type directed against Jews in Germany does not appear. [...]

Direct aggression

Witchcraft, however, not only provides 'scapegoats' against whom hostile impulses may be displaced. Under some circumstances, witchcraft provides a means for attack upon the actual targets of my hostile feelings. If I am a singer and smarting under professional jealousy of another singer I can whisper accusations of witchcraft against my rival (cf. Newcomb and Reichard, 1937, p. 16; Reichard, 1939, pp. 7, 8). Or I can mitigate the burning of my envy of a rich neighbor by suggesting that perhaps the way his riches were obtained would not bear too careful scrutiny. If my wife runs off with another man, I can often say to my relatives 'Oh, he got her by Frenzy Witchcraft.' This both permits intensified and socially justified indignation on my part and also reduces my shame: it is not that the seducer is a better man than I – *he* used magical powers.

Nor does witchcraft belief merely channelize antagonisms between one individual and another. The feuds between different extended family groups (which perhaps often actually rest primarily upon a realistic conflict over land or water resources) are frequently given a formulation in witchcraft terms (cf. Kluckhohn, 1962, p. 208). For instance, one group had complained to the Indian agent of the drinking and fighting of some of their neighbors; these retaliated by threatening to kill an old man of the accusing group as a witch.

Witchcraft belief also permits a limited amount of direct verbal expression of aggression against relatives. Guarded gossip about a tyrannical maternal uncle is a useful safety valve! On several occasions I have had a Navaho in a communicative mood say to me, 'Yes, my maternal uncle is a big singer all right. But some people say he is a witch too.' Such gossip about close blood relatives is relatively rare, but cases of direct accusation against affinal relatives are not infrequent (cf. Kluckhohn, 1962, Part I, section 10, para. 10). My material confirms Morgan's suggestion that such accusations are notably more frequent among patrilocal consumption groups.

This is doubtless partly because such patrilocal residence creates new strains in social relationships within a social organization which is still dominantly matrilineal and matrilocal. [...]

In summary, witchcraft is one Navaho means of handling the hostility problem. The existence of this belief in Navaho culture permits the socially tolerated expression of direct and displaced aggression. It channels the expression of aggression. It possibly forces the expression of aggression. But my thesis is not that given the amount and kind of aggression which exists in Navaho society witchcraft belief *must* exist. My thesis is only that given these conditions some forms of release must exist. When other forms are inadequate, and when the witchcraft patterns were historically available, witchcraft belief is a highly adjustive way of releasing not only generalized tension but also those tensions specific to Navaho social structure. [...]

It is almost inevitable that Navaho life today should be anxiety ridden. But nothing is more intolerable to human beings than being persistently disturbed without being able to say why or without being able to phrase the matter in such a way that some relief or control is potentially available. It is worth noting that man not only craves reasons and explanations, but in most cases these reasons involve some form of personification, some human-like agency either natural or supernatural. It seems that only a small minority among highly sophisticated peoples can fairly face impersonal forces and the phenomena of chance. Doubtless the explanation for this attitude is that during the years of dawning consciousness practically everything that happens is mediated by human agents – the parents or their substitutes.

Witchcraft belief allows the verbalization of anxiety in a framework that is understandable and which implies the possibility of doing something. Witches (who are living individuals) are potentially controllable by the society; the caprices of the environment are not. Likewise, it is important for the adjustment of the individual that witchcraft is a focus of anxiety which the culture recognizes as valid. The symptoms of anxiety which the members of different societies manifest under conditions of stress are characteristically different. For a Navaho, witchcraft is something in terms of which he can acceptably justify his anxiety to his fellows. It is a peculiarly adjustive response in that he can justify his anxiety without taking any blame himself. For in the case of those illnesses which are normally treated by Holy Way chants the ultimate etiology from the Navaho point of view rests in the infraction of some cultural prohibition. To some degree, it is the individual's own fault that he is sick. However, the Navaho consider the witch victim as guiltless. Thus, between various possibilities for the objectification of anxiety, witchcraft is one of those which is most wholly advantageous. But the cultural validity is the issue which concerns us immediately here. [...]

To sum up: witchcraft is a major Navaho instrument for dealing with aggression and anxiety. It permits some anxiety and some malicious destructiveness to be expressed directly with a minimum of punishment to the aggressor. Still more anxiety and aggression is displaced through the witchcraft pattern assemblage into channels where they are relatively harmless or where, at least, there are available patterns for adjusting the individuals to the new problems created. Individual adjustment merges with group adaptation.

Witchcraft as an Adaptive Structure for the Local Group and for Navaho Society

That most Navahos believe in witchcraft is, up to a point, a danger not merely to the solidarity but to the very existence of the society. The informant's remark, 'If the white people hadn't stopped us, we'd have killed each other all off' has more than a grain of truth in it. Paradoxically, however, belief in witchcraft, so long as other forces hold the disruptive tendencies in check, is an adaptive structure of a high order. The principal manifest 'function' is that witchcraft lore affirms solidarity by dramatically defining what is bad: namely, all secret and malevolent activities against the health, property and lives of fellow tribesmen. This sanction is reinforced by attributing to witches all the stigmata of evil: incest, nakedness and other kinds of forbidden knowledge and act.

But credence in witchcraft likewise has many specific latent 'functions' which make for the preservation of the group's and the society's equilibrium. It tends, along with other social mechanisms, to prevent undue accumulation of wealth and tempers too rapid a rise in social mobility. A rich man knows that if he is stingy with his relatives or fails to dispense generous hospitality to all and sundry he is likely to be spoken of as a witch. Individuals know also that if they accumulate wealth too rapidly the whisper will arise that they got their start by robbing the dead of their jewelry. In a society like the Navaho which is competitive and capitalistic, on the one hand, and still familistic on the other, any ideology which has the effect of slowing down economic mobility is decidedly adaptive. One of the most basic strains in Navaho society arises out of the incompatibility between the demands of familism and the emulation of European patterns in the accumulating of capital. The rich tend to have considerable prestige, but they are also much hated. The reasons for this are many-sided. Among others, there is the association between polygyny and wealth. 'I might lose my wife because rich people can have more than one wife.' One is tempted to speculate on the associations between Frenzy Witchcraft, polygyny and wealth, but in the absence of fuller information about the history of the various sub-patterns of polygyny and of any historical knowledge of Frenzy Witchcraft, such speculations would be empty. To return to the point at issue, the best hope for the preservation of the coherence of Navaho culture and the integrity of the Navaho way of life seems to rest in there being a gradual transition between the familistic type of social organization and a type more nearly resembling our own. A man cannot get rich very fast if he does his full duty by his extended family. Any pattern, such as witchcraft, which tends to discourage the rapid accumulation of wealth makes, therefore, for the survival of the society.

Similarly, the threat of an accusation of witchcraft acts as a brake upon the power and influence of ceremonial practitioners. They are effectively warned that their capacity of influencing the course of events by supernatural techniques must be used only to accomplish socially desirable ends. The fact that witches are depicted as using whistles, pollen, turquoise, sandpainting, songs (cf. Kluckhohn, 1962, pp. 54, 77, 81, 97) and that there are many other highly specific parallels between witchcraft and chant practice (e.g., sorcerers bearing [burying?] materials under a tree struck by lightning[3] indicates that witchcraft is thought of as *bad* ceremonialism (Kluckhohn, 1962, fn. 1, Appendix 9). The whole association of practitioners and ceremonial practices with witchcraft reflects the central ambivalence of feeling which the Navaho have for this sector of the culture. Singers are valued – but distrusted. Witchcraft gossip and potential trials and executions guarantee the lay Navaho that practitioners will think twice before they abuse their powers. How this works in the concrete is well illustrated by an incident which occurred at Red Rock in 1937. A man went to his maternal uncle and asked him to sing over his wife. The uncle was not satisfied with the number of sheep offered and evaded performing the chant. The wife died. The nephew first accused his uncle as a witch but was unable to muster family or community support for disciplining. He thereupon killed the uncle himself. Such events must surely reinforce the disposition of singers to be liberal to their kin and prompt in acceding to requests for ceremonial help.

3. Cf. 'disposal' in chants.

Clyde Kluckhohn

Witchcraft as a Technique of Social Control

Accusation of witchcraft is, indeed, a threat which Navaho social organization uses to keep all 'agitators', all individuals who threaten to disrupt the smooth functioning of the community, in check. When Manuelito in 1884 brought about the execution of more than forty 'witches' (Van Valkenburgh, 1938, p. 47), there is good evidence that this was a very astute way of silencing leaders throughout the Navaho country who were beginning to advocate another armed resistance to the whites. Manuelito was convinced that the only hope for his tribe lay in peace. He knew that if he caused the troublemakers to be arrested and turned over to the United States government his own prestige would suffer and possibly be destroyed. But they could be tried and killed as witches with full social approval. I may here be attributing undue prescience to Manuelito, but the interpretation has the support both of Navaho informants and qualified white observers. Perhaps, all of this is rationalization after the fact; I merely report what Navahos and whites who either knew Manuelito personally or knew some member of his immediate family have told me. Certainly, however, the use of this device for social control is in most cases less consciously carried out. The introduction of the Ghost dance cult among the Navaho was blocked by spreading the word that proponents of the new religion were witches (cf. Kluckhohn, 1962, p. 232). Any powerful instigator of trouble in a local Navaho group simply tends to be talked about as a probable witch, and this tendency operates to reduce intra-group friction. Realization that someone who 'acts mean' is likely to be accused as a witch acts as a deterrent of hostile acts. The corollary is that an offended person may avenge himself by witchcraft.

There are other respects in which witchcraft belief is an effective sanction for the enforcement of social co-operation.[4] The aged, whether they have a claim as relatives or not, must be fed or they will witch against one. The disposition to aid siblings who are ill is reinforced by the realization that the death of siblings may give rise to suspicion that a survivor is learning witchcraft. The effectiveness of leaders is sometimes increased by the fear that they are witches and that if they are disobeyed they will use witchcraft against those who fail to follow them. While this sometimes doubtless has the consequence of perpetuating bad leadership, it has its good side too in that the anarchistic tendencies of Navaho society make it

4. For an excellent discussion of witchcraft as a device for social control see Gayton (1930, pp. 409–11).

peculiarly vulnerable when facing a society organized like our own. The survival of Navaho groups is favored by any sanctions which assist a united front behind leaders of some permanence. The singer's care and best efforts for his patients are reinforced by his knowing what the consequences of his losing too many patients will be: suspicion of witchcraft, perhaps open accusation, possibly trial and execution. Even the fear of going about at night has social value. One of the principal sources of friction among Navahos is sexual jealousy. Fear of witches at night acts to some slight extent as a deterrent of extra-marital sex relations because night-time would otherwise provide favorable conditions for a secret rendezvous. [...]

Discussion and Summary

After presenting patterned cultural theory and practice relating to one sector of Navaho culture which may be referred to in English by the one word 'witchcraft',[5] an attempt at 'explanation' has been made. That is, I have tried to show that certain available data bear a determinate relationship to other data and to generalized propositions. In particular, we have seen that the data did not bear a haphazard relationship to the physical environment, economic problems, health conditions, the concrete situation of the individual and to such other sectors of culture as the forms of habit training and general social organization.

The study of Navaho witchcraft does not stop, then, with the bringing to light of bits of curious and sometimes terrible belief. Systematic analysis of observed behaviors and of the latent and manifest content of interview material suggests clues as to the stresses and strains of Navaho social organization and the dynamics of social process generally. The outstanding conclusions specific to the Navaho may now be briefly reviewed.

Burke has remarked, 'Human beings build their cultures, nervously loquacious, upon the edge of an abyss.' This is even more true of the Navaho than of many human societies. Witchcraft supplies a partial

5. It is true that I have not found any single Navaho word which lumps together Witchery, Sorcery, Wizardry and Frenzy Witchcraft. So far as 'conceptual category' is concerned, the category 'witchcraft' is probably the observer's and not a native category. I do think that evidence has been presented that the Navaho do treat the separate varieties as a 'feeling category'. In any case from the standpoint of the observer attempting a structural analysis, there can be no doubt that all of these patterns are crystallized around a common focus: private manipulation of the supernatural for socially disapproved ends. Moreover, there are more explicit elements common to each. For example, the use of the personal name enters in all four techniques. As one informant remarked, 'They used to say you can't witch a person until you know his name.'

answer to some of the deeper uncertainties supplementing the answers provided by myths and rituals. If myths and rituals are the principal integrative and instrumental patterns for meeting the need-persistive (cf. Rosenzweig, 1941) reactions to frustration, witchcraft patterns are instruments of no mean importance in adjusting to the ego-defensive (Rosenzweig, 1941) reactions in deprivation. Those substitute responses which do not constitute aggressive acts in the social sense cannot, for the Navaho, discharge the cumulative tensions. In a society where the relative strength of anticipations of punishment for overt aggression is high, witchcraft allows imaginary aggression. Witchcraft channels the displacement of aggression, facilitating emotional adjustment with a minimum of disturbance of social relationships. Even direct aggression through witchcraft helps to maintain societal inhibitions consonant with the old native culture. Likewise, the witch is a convenient anxiety object. Anxieties may be disguised in ways which promote individual adjustment and social solidarity. The threat of accusation of witchcraft is a check upon the strong and powerful. The belief that the destitute, the aged – and even animals – may, if treated too unkindly, turn with witchcraft upon those who neglect or oppress them is, up to a point, a protection for these unfortunates. Many sorts of cultural values are reinforced by the corpus of witchcraft lore. It is probably no accident that the bogeymen who are used to socialize children have so many characteristics in common with the were-animals dreaded by adults (cf. Kluckhohn, 1962, part 1, section 3, fn. 8).

The extent to which Navahos avail themselves of these cultural instruments is related to place in the social structure, temporary social situation and probably to constitutional factors. All of these are determinants of the level of tolerance of frustration. 'If the tolerance is poor, then some aggressor must be fabricated. A thwarted individual would then displace the aggression onto a system or onto any group representing a constellation of ideas that evoked hostility, no matter how mild, in the previous experience of the individual' (Levy, 1941, p. 356). With the Navaho – as with, I suspect, all peoples – beliefs and practices related to witchcraft are, to some extent, infantile, regressive instrumental patterns differentially invoked by those persons who are more 'on the spot' or more under the stress of misfortune than others, or by those who for constitutional or whatever factors are less able to 'take it' than others.

Similarly, those who are suspected or accused of witchcraft do not constitute a random sample of the Navaho population generally. A large majority consist of two groups of people: the rich,[6] and old and powerful

6. Cf. Horney (1937, pp. 171–5). Power, prestige and possessions serve not only as a reassurance against anxiety but also as a means of releasing hostility.

259

singers. Gossip against the rich almost always takes the form of the rationalization that they got their start by stealing jewelry and other valuables from the dead.[7] But actually the prevalence of this rationalization acts as a kind of economic leveler. The rich feel pressure to be lavish in hospitality, generous in gifts to needy relatives and neighbors and prodigal in the ceremonies they sponsor. Otherwise, they know the voice of envy will speak out in whispers of witchcraft which would make their life in society strained and unpleasant. Similarly, the existent mechanism regulates the power and influence of the singer. Feeling toward singers always tends to be somewhat ambivalent. On the one hand, they have great prestige, are much in demand and may obtain large fees. On the other hand, they are feared, and the border of active distrust is always close. A singer must not lose too many patients. He must also be more generous and hospitable than the model Navaho. It is also well documented that at various crucial times in the history of the Navaho clever leaders have used the accusation of witchcraft as an effective means of social control. During the post-Fort Sumner period, the chiefs in power took care of advocates of renewed resistance to the whites by spreading the word that these persons were witches. Many were killed. There seems evidence that a correlation exists between the amount of fear and talk about witches and general state of tension prevailing among the Navaho.

7. The constant association of witchcraft with the dead is a problem which can be regarded at present as only partially understood. The explanation is doubtless historical, in part. That is, the generalized complex of witchcraft idea patterns which has been transmitted to the Navaho contains this as one element – for the witch-ghoul notion has a very wide distribution. But the Navaho have intensified and reified the association. The linking of almost all types of witchcraft activity with the dead or with objects connected with the dead is approximately to be explained as part of the pattern which attributes all the Navaho 'worst things' to witches. Likewise, the association is to be understood on the ground of the partial equivalence of witches and ghosts (ghost = witch from the company of the dead). In this connexion, Opler's (1936) hypotheses of ambivalence may, in my opinion, profitably be invoked.

The peculiarly morbid Navaho fear of the dead, however, is a topic which deserves an essay of its own. Among other things, this almost pathological (as it seems to the observer from our culture) fear may perhaps be related to the configuration of individualism and its sub-configuration of modesty. These are manifested in many other witchcraft data. Note that modesty and privacy are to some extent preserved even in a witchcraft context (Kluckhohn, 1962, p. 54, where the boy is allowed to be apart while he urinates and thus escapes).

I suggest that such dread of the dead is likely to be at a maximum in a culture which glorifies the individual. The later Middle Ages where the salvation of the individual was the great goal and where St Thomas Aquinas expressed the dominant attitude as 'persona est, quod est perfectissimum in natura' is a good parallel. Here also the macabre, the gruesome, the dismal aspects of death seem to have been deliberately exploited (cf. Huizinga, 1927, esp., chap. 11, 'The Vision of Death'). One may contrast cultures where societies are extended by generations as in India and China.

Thus, during the last difficult years of controversy over the stock reduction programme, there has been appreciably more witchcraft excitement than for some time past. The resentment over stock reduction must itself be seen in the context of the general disequilibrium of the Navaho economy. The 'depression' of the 'thirties had much more direct and sharply felt effects upon the Navaho than did earlier down shifts in American business cycles – because, prior to 1929, Navaho economy was much less fully integrated with American economy, generally. Since Navahos suffered as a result of the fall in the price of sheep and wool, the loss of market for their craft products, unemployment at wage work, this factor alone helps us understand increased antagonism against the rich during the last decade.

But witchcraft is not something which need be viewed with naïve abhorrence. It has been seen to have its manifest and its latent 'functions' both for the individual and for social groups. At the same time, witchcraft has its *cost*[8] for the individual and for the group. Given the conditions of Navaho life and the Navaho socialization process, given the guarantee in the background that the Indian Service will prevent wholesale slaughter of 'witches', Navaho witchcraft does constitute an adjustive and an adaptive structure. Its *cost* is projected aggression and some social disruption. Probably, as a natural consequence of the insistence that witchcraft *does* have important adaptive and adjustive effects, the *cost* has been too little stressed. In many cases witchcraft belief undoubtedly does more to promote fear and timidity than to relieve aggressive tendencies. The fears consequent upon witchcraft tend to restrict the life activities of some persons, to curtail their social participation. Perhaps the witchcraft pattern assemblage tends to be mainly adjustive for individuals who tend to be aggressive, mainly disruptive for those who tend to be non-aggressive. Such a view would fit well with the suggestions which have been made of the relationship between witchcraft patterns and war patterns (Kluckhohn, 1962, part 2, section 3, paras. 3 and 4).

Another aspect of the *cost* of witchcraft belief to which attention should be drawn is that probably this is a basis for unwillingness to undertake or to continue the burdens of leadership. For example, a young Navaho who has made a splendid record during the past two years as a judge has told his friends that he was resigning because he felt that his father's serious illness was traceable to witchcraft activities occasioned by resentment at some of the judge's decisions. Likewise, to counterbalance the tendency to economic leveling, there is to be reckoned the power and

8. I am indebted to David Aberle for suggesting to me this concept of 'cost' to balance that of 'function'.

instrument for domination which accrues to the rich in so far as they are dreaded as witches. A statement in *Son of Old Man Hat* is a classic in this connexion:

Bunch of Whiskers wasn't a headman, but everybody knew him and feared him. He was the richest Navaho on the reservation. They used to say, 'He's a witch. That's why he has lots of sheep, horses and cattle, and beads of all kinds, and all kinds of skins.' He had everything, and by that everyone knew him and was afraid of him (Dyk, 1938, p. 357).

References

DOLLARD, J. (1938), 'Hostility and fear in social life', *Social Forces*, vol. 17.

DYK, W. (1938), *Son of Old Man Hat: A Navaho Autobiography*, New York.

GAYTON, A. H. (1930), 'Yokuts-Mono chiefs and shamans', *University of California Publications in American Archaeology and Ethnology*, vol. 24.

HORNEY, K. (1937), *The Neurotic Personality of Our Time*, New York.

HUIZINGA, J. (1927), *The Waning of the Middle Ages*, Arnold; Penguin Books, 1955.

KARDINER, A. (1939), *The Individual and His Society: The Psychodynamics of Primitive Social Organization*, New York.

KLUCKHOHN, C. (1942), 'Myths and rituals: a general theory', *Harvard Theological Review*, vol. 35, no. 1.

KLUCKHOHN, C. (1962), *Navaho Witchcraft*, Beacon Press.

LEE, D. (1940), 'A primitive system of values', *Philosophy of Science*, vol. 7, no. 3.

LEIGHTON, A. H. and LEIGHTON, D. C. (1942), 'Some types of uneasiness and fear in a Navaho Indian community', *American Anthropologist*, n.s., vol. 44.

LEVY, D. M. (1941), 'The hostile act', *Psychological Review*, vol. 48, no. 4.

MEAD, M. (1939), 'Researches in Bali', *Transactions of the New York Academy of Sciences*, series 2, vol. 2, no. 1.

NEWCOMB, F. J., and REICHARD, G. A. (1937), *Sandpaintings of the Navaho Shooting Chant*, New York.

OPLER, M. E. (1936), 'An interpretation of ambivalence of two American Indian tribes', *Journal of Social Psychology*, vol. 7.

REICHARD, G. A. (1939), *Navajo Medicine Man: Sandpaintings and Legends of Miguelito*, New York.

ROSENZWEIG, SAUL, (1941), 'Need-persistive and ego-defensive reactions to frustration as demonstrated by an experiment on repression', *Psychological Review*, vol. 48, no. 4.

VAN VALKENBURGH, R. F. (1928), *A Short History of the Navaho People*, Window Rock.

27. J. D. Krige

The Social Function of Witchcraft

J. D. Krige, 'The social function of witchcraft', *Theoria*, vol. 1, 1947, pp. 8–21.

Introduction

My objective is to show that witchcraft is something more than meaning-less superstition. I can do so most effectively by restricting myself to a single Bantu tribe, the Lobedu of the far N.E. Transvaal. For in this way I shall be able to analyse some of its relations to the ideas and values of the society and perhaps also to achieve my aim of making some sense of an institution which, owing to its associations among ourselves, seems to be utterly devoid of sense.

Among the Lobedu, just as of course among other Bantu people, witches and sorcerers, so far from playing the role of unreason, make a rational contribution to the fulfilment of men's needs and purposes. This is almost immediately evident when we remember that witchcraft and sorcery are explanations of evil in the universe. They enable men to account for their failures and frustrations. Moreover, since the evil operates only through the medium of human beings, it can also be brought under human control. The parts assigned to these characters, the witches and sorcerers, presuppose a just world, ordered and coherent, in which the evil is not merely outlawed but can be overcome by man-made techniques. In the result men feel secure and the moral order is upheld.

I cannot undertake the task of demonstrating the validity of the under-lying conceptions and presuppositions, because the whole setting is en-tirely different from anything with which we are familiar. I have to limit myself to a small segment of the circle circumscribing the magical back-ground against which witchcraft assumes meaning. But I shall have failed in my purpose if I fashion the witch to a shape that cannot be articulated with ordinary human needs such as we ourselves have.

Let us at the outset see how the Lobedu phrase the roles of those arch-enemies of society, the witches and sorcerers. They picture witchcraft as criminality incarnate, an intrinsically evil influence in the universe which can manifest itself only through a human being; it is independent of all the other supernaturals, but it is not a capricious power; and it is thought

263

to be set into motion only by malice, hatred and similar motives and generally only against some specific individual.

The phraseology used indicates that the Lobedu make a major distinction between witchcraft proper, which is the wickedness, sometimes without overt rhyme or reason, of the night-witch, and sorcery, which is the destructive technique of the day-witch; witchcraft implies personal relationships with the supernatural, sorcery means manipulation of magic which is not supernatural by Lobedu conceptions. An elaborate moral grading of magic indicates, however, that many other distinctions are drawn. At the one extreme good magic or medicine – the two conceptions are identical – safeguards the moral order and is approved; for it is the application in the public interest of the properties of matter, as when the queen, transformer of the clouds, makes rain or the doctors heal disease. At the other extreme, evil magic or sorcery is bad and frowned upon. Between these extremes there are several grades of magic (or rather uses of magic since magical power in itself is generally neutral) some within the law but ethically disapproved and some about which opinions differ. Often enough the victim places an interpretation upon his misfortunes which differs from that of his fellows: he may try to incriminate a sorcerer, but they will tell you that he is merely blaming others to escape a sense of his own inadequacy or incompetence. Perhaps I shall be able to turn later to some of these complications in the moral scheme. At the moment my point is that it is essential to understand that sorcery which falls into the category of magic is entirely different from witchcraft proper. Sorcery is neither wonderful nor above ordinary matter-of-fact physical laws; but witchcraft involves supercausation, is mysterious and transcends the operation of natural cause and effect.

The night-witch is accordingly a sinister character. He belongs to an unholy fraternity, whose members meet at night to deliberate upon their deeds of darkness. For these deeds are always mysterious in the sense that no one knows how they are done, and they are physically impossible by natural means. The idea is that he disposes of the powers of darkness rather than that he does his evil work by night. The night-witch uses no medium of destruction such as poison; he himself has inborn powers to ride through the air, prowling over villages like night bombers over our cities, but invisible, infiltrating unobserved into the defences and insinuating himself through the smallest crevices. He uses no spells or incantations; nor indeed does he employ medicines or send his soul on these miraculous excursions. But he has familiars who have various functions: he may send them out as vampires or leave them at his home in his own image as an alibi. No one, however, knows precisely what his methods are except that they are all supernatural.

It is his mystical presence which paralyses you when you wake in a sweat after a terrifying nightmare. He maliciously excises parts of your body in order to insert sand or millet, which accounts for the excruciating pains familiar to anyone who has experienced foreign matter impinging upon exposed tissues. When unaccountably your bones ache or you feel tired as on the morning after the night before, you know that it is a night-witch who has set you to hoe all night in his garden. Nowadays, in the more sophisticated culture-contact situation, you ascribe lassitude for which no ostensible reason exists to such new devices of night-witches as causing you in your sleep to cycle aimlessly up hill and down dale.

Night-witches, like the succubi of medieval times, are almost invariably women, not men, but the rationalization incriminating the gentler sex is rather different. According to popular opinion as reflected, e.g., in Dr Wier's disquisition in 1563 on the credulity and fragility of the female sex, medieval women were considered to be peculiarly susceptible to evil influences owing to their mental and moral infirmities. The Lobedu have a much higher estimate of women's nature and role, for women are the supreme rulers, the high priests, the great go-betweens in quarrels, the final adjudicators in questions of inheritance and succession and, as may be suspected in a society that does not rely on force or coercion, the guarantors of the effectiveness of all the major sanctions. Nevertheless, the Lobedu seem to have succumbed to the masculine illusion that what is feminine is often inexplicable, instinct with inscrutability. With such credentials Lobedu women both become psychological substitutes on whom people tend to project their failures and frustrations and are believed to be endowed with inscrutable powers such as the night-witch disposes of.

The province of the night-witch is not limited to destruction by disease and death. Among other things, barrenness, marked differences in the productivity of adjoining fields, the wind that breaks the growing crops, are attributed to witchcraft of this brand. And rather more sinister is the power to enslave souls and to send familiars and vampires upon nefarious errands. The addition of the familiar to the scheme permits of its further elaboration; but I have to content myself by saying that the relationship between witch and familiar is not invoked as an explanation of frigidity in women as is the case among some Xhosa tribes. Lobedu familiars are often obnoxious animals such as polecats and hyenas, though the most fearful of them all is the *khidudwane*, a human being killed in such a way that when he is buried only his shadow is interred, the real personality being imprisoned in a large earthen pot by day and dispatched by its mistress upon sinister missions by night. Quite unlike the *khipago*, a conception borrowed, as the name indicates, from the European spook, which is comparatively harmless and can easily be laid by appeasing his complaint or pouring medicine on his grave, this fearful familiar of the witch causes one to faint, waste away and die, and nothing will avail except discovery of and a direct attack upon the witch.

There is a great deal more to the witch than this, for the analysis of wickedness is taken far back and is closely articulated with conscious as well as subconscious, hidden, human motivations. The night-witch, e.g., is born not made; but, since criminality is by Lobedu conceptions a product of both nature and nurture, the potentialities with which the witch is born unfold apace as she imbibes the evil secretions in her mother's milk. Moreover she must learn how to put her power into practice. This learning process begins on the second or third day after birth when mother-witch flings infant-witchling up against the wall to which it will cling like a bat and so learn its first lesson in flying.

The sorcerer by Lobedu conceptions is an entirely different character. He is usually a man whose machinations involve the use of medicines and incantations, ordinary natural techniques 'of the day' as they phrase it, not the inscrutable and supernatural devices 'of the night'. Sorcery operates by natural laws. It is not the nature of its power that is evil, but only its perverted application. Its essence is the criminal use of the potency of medicines, which can be and usually are in the service of legitimate ends. The sorcerer's techniques are simply those of lawful medical practice; but they are lawful means put to unlawful ends. Spells are not essential, since the destructive potency is usually inherent in the poisons used, not in the sorcerer himself. For the sorcerer is not evil incarnate: he belongs to no criminal gang, does not inherit either his knowledge or his sinful propensities, and has no power to tame and teach familiars. The Lobedu have in mind a normal human being, a man even of good character and generous instincts, who owing to some temporary aberration succumbs to the temptation of injuring an enemy by using some poison – an extract of the ordinary properties of material things, which he may acquire from another. Unlike the night-witch who might send a hyena to take up its abode in your body and eat your food, the sorcerer's method is to cause you to eat some indissoluble toxic substance which clings to your oesophagus and from there poisons your whole system. There is no known antidote to the internal hyena, except of course the long-range attack upon the unknown witch; but the foreign substance introduced by the sorcerer can be removed by means of an emetic.

A favourite technique of the sorcerer is to challenge enemies by pitting the potency of his poisons against the drugs they use to protect themselves. This conception of medicines warring against one another, like our toxins and anti-toxins, is the reason why everyone must be inoculated with anti-sorcery serum, just as we guard ourselves in anticipation by vaccination. It is also obvious that such techniques as placing poisoned thorns in your path, or pointing a medicated forefinger, are used by sorcerers not night-witches. It suffices to ground an imputation of sorcery when a man menaces you with the words *u do bona* (you will see) and evil subsequently befalls you.

The Moral Grading of Magic

Since sorcery is simply lawful means put to unlawful ends, the same techniques may be moral and approved in one context but immoral and outlawed in another. And a study of these different contexts casts considerable light upon a number of underlying conceptions. Take, e.g., the technique of challenging or in Lobedu phraseology 'trying' others with medicines. The medicines are called *malego* and the technique *hu lega*, and *hu lega* is sorcery and illegal except when employed by doctors against one another. It is legal in this context not merely because the trial of strength has social value and the quacks are discredited, but also for a much subtler reason. Lobedu society is fundamentally cooperative and frowns upon all forms of rivalry. Even when the good things of life, the prizes, or the means for achieving desired ends such as land, are, objectively considered, limited, the scarcity is rephrased in such a manner that rivalries are avoided. It is as if everything for which people might compete is made to fall into the category of free commodities, or rather, since psychological principles are involved, objective facts are reinterpreted in a way that shifts the problem to a subjective setting in which the scarcity no longer appears as a significant factor. The population, e.g., presses hard upon the natural resources but the periodical threat of starvation, even the scarcity of relishes, is attributed not to the limited resources, but to some shortcoming in men such as indolence; and the virtue of rephrasing the difficulty in this way is that rivalries for the scarce things are obviated while the merit of, say, industry is stressed. This is naturally only part of the explanation, for the functioning of the culture relies on co-operativeness: aggressiveness and the measurement of one's achievement against that of another are never rewarded, the social structure places barriers between potential competitors and, among a multitude of other cultural arrangements tending in the same direction, the whole educational system – the absence of any comparison of the attainments of children, the insistence upon sharing (even the head of a locust, as the Lobedu say), the team work and mutuality that are given a high cultural rating, the disapproval of any form of personal display – all this inculcates values that are incompatible with competitiveness.

Now when one doctor tries another with *malego*, the intention to injure does not constitute sorcery. I have said that the Lobedu themselves rationalize what appears to be an inconsistency by saying that this licence, that is allowed doctors, is a guarantee of the effectiveness of their medicines, since if they cannot immunize themselves against the poisons of others, they are little use as guardians of the public health. But partly also *legal*ing is the projection of rivalries into the magical world since it is disallowed in ordinary life. There cannot be competition for clients or their custom, for any rivalry on the economic level is simply inconceivable. Nevertheless, the implications of scarcity of clients are inescapable. The attention is, however, diverted from the objective situation of a limited clientele to the warring of medicines in the magical world, and this vicarious outlet for, instead of complete repression of, competition is condoned not merely because it is to the public benefit but also because it is compartmentalized, as completely segregated from the conception of rivalry as heroic deeds in war involving the killing of the enemy are among us segregated from foul murder in peace.

Many other uses of the power which we call magic are moral and hence medicinal, or immoral and hence sorcery according as the motive is approved or not. Some of them, curiously enough in a co-operative society, are concessions to the impulse of revenge; some are methods of frustrating an enemy by making his objective invisible; and there are today also techniques to secure the favour of others, like love-magic or medicine to attract trade customers, but these are introductions from other tribes, incompatible with the Lobedu pattern, and hence always reprehensible. The power is in itself neutral; it is the objective which makes it moral or immoral. That, of course, is not the whole story; the handling of human motivations is much subtler; but I must content myself with this over-simplification, which at all events is a sufficient approximation to Lobedu conceptions to enable us to take our analysis a little further.

One type of vengeance magic is *madabi* which is the use of powers – really certain properties of matter – to transmute the thing to which it is applied, e.g., *madabi* will enable you to turn pieces of the skin of an animal into the animal itself. A deserted husband may legitimately so manipulate *madabi* as to frighten his erring wife into running back to him, for instance, by causing monkeys to appear whenever his unfaithful spouse cooks or draws water for her new found lover. Among us mice rather than monkeys might occasion misgivings in a conscience-stricken wife. But the use of *madabi* for purely personal ends is sorcery and hence criminal, as when a man takes revenge upon a girl, whom he has seduced and who subsequently jilts him, by changing her sex whenever the child is about to be born, and thereby endangering her life. In the first instance *madabi* functions as a moral sanction and its psychological effect reflects the effective internalization of a sense of guilt which nothing will remove except repentance and restitution; in the second, it conceptualizes a sense of frustration seeking an outlet in unlawful revenge. Like other vengeance or rather justice magic, *madabi* continues to act unless and until the person who dispenses it reverses its power. To apply *madabi* is *hu dabeka*; to arrest or reverse its action is *hu dabekulla*; and this reversal has been very neatly linked up with conceptions of fair play and the ultimate triumph of justice. Let me illustrate from the technique called *mutsikela*, the most dreaded form of vengeance magic which, even when lawfully used, is considered to be so drastic that preliminary public warning of its being put into operation is necessary.

Mutsikela, or working on the grave of a victim killed by sorcery or witchcraft, is lawful if directed against the criminal murderer, even though its effects are so deadly that it destroys not merely the criminal but also his relatives; for either they are accomplices or the homicidal propensity is inherent in them and has been nurtured in the same home. While medicine to reanimate the spirit of the deceased victim is being poured down a hole in the grave, the most diabolical spell known to the Lobedu – it is *ex tempore* but follows a familiar pattern – is uttered sending the spirit on its mission of stern justice. Spirit and medicine are instructed to search for and strike down the homicidal witch, the phraseology I heard on one occasion being, 'to cause them to follow you to the grave; and we say not one of them but the whole brood of culprits'. There are, however, dangers in using this method of restituting a wrong. It is perfectly legal in untainted hands, though its morality is doubted. It must be preceded by the public warning, *hu ebela*, which consists in a warning shouted out from some vantage point, within earshot of the suspected witch, that, unless he desists and makes amends, retaliatory action will be taken. One must remember that in the Lobedu pattern of justice, the repressive sanctions, such as penalties, fines, punishments, indeed any measure involving physical coercion, are practically unknown; all wrongs fall under the restitutive sanction and the procedure given the highest cultural rating is *hu khumelwa*, mutual reconciliation. The criminal, even if he has murdered your son, is wherever possible converted into a kinsman: he gives his daughter and so becomes a son-in-law who has many obligations to you and in return receives beer, the bond *par excellence* of brotherhood, from you.

Mutsikela, like all justice magic, searches for the evildoer and passes judgement upon him; but if the culprit has made suitable restitution and you neglect to recall the forces you have set into operation, or if the witch who has caused the death himself *tsikela*'s for you in an attempt to disarm suspicion against him, the omniscient medicine will seek the culprit in vain and returning will strike down the guilty sender. And so the engineer of evil is hoist with his own petard; the criminal use of this kind of magic not merely constitutes sorcery of the worst brand but also rebounds upon the criminal. It is, however, more than suspected that the cleverest sorcerers and witches have methods of confusing these medicines, though in the last resort the greatest magicians, the specialists whose function it is to protect the society against witchcraft and sorcery, are superior and the operation of their medicines cannot be circumvented.

Anti-Witchcraft Defences

As *mutsikela* indicates, the Lobedu have effective anti-witchcraft defences. Of course a victim may always consult the divinatory dice, those specially prepared bones that take the place of our stethoscopes and X-rays in diagnosis. No one believes, as we naïvely imagine, that bones are in themselves endowed with perspicacity; but properties and powers can be imparted to them by subjecting them to certain treatments. I am not concerned to explain how such a conception can be justified, except to say that at the level of observation, technology, and scientific verification of these people it is impossible to demonstrate its invalidity. Now, if the bones have identified the witch, it is open to the victim to accuse him and risk the legal proceedings that follow. But resort to law is not altogether satisfactory: it tends to harden animosities in this case whereas appeasement is the accepted function of law; the court is liable to dismiss the accusation as based on idle gossip, or to procrastinate in the hope that the parties will forget their grievances in letting off steam again and again as the case drags on: and there is the danger that the attempt to invoke legal sanctions against a witch will spur him to greater activity against you. It depends entirely upon a man's estimate of the total situation whether he will rely mainly on legal justice or other means to deal with harm caused by the witch or sorcerer; but in any case anticipatory protective measures are always taken. The type of defence is determined by the kind of attack that is feared. A few examples will suffice to indicate the general principles of anti-witchcraft defences.

Protection against the parachutists that ride through the air, the night-flying witches, not unnaturally takes the form of camouflaging the village or other objective of the enemy. Hence the *diphaba*, medicine encircling the village or placed at strategic points, such as the gates. This medicine masks the village, making it appear like an expanse of water so that the witch is deluded and concludes that he has come to the wrong place. Logically enough, the camouflaging effect is obtained by using the properties of products of the ocean, such as whale-oil and sea sand. Medicated pegs around the village block the passage of poisoned shafts hurled by sorcerers. So-called witch-doctors of various kinds, for some establish contact with the forces involved through the diagnostic bones, some through their own innnate powers and some others through the medium of ancestral spirits, are the detectors and predictors. They divine the nature and direction of the attack, smell out the quislings and send back with interest the death and destruction. Vengeance-magic with its preliminary warning to the enemy is nothing else than the legitimate reprisal.

The usual defences are unavailing against the witch within the village, since he probably knows the disposition and nature of the precautions taken. There are, therefore, methods of dealing with fifth-columnists. Traitors within the gate may be expelled but a much more favoured solution than physical coercion, which is always regarded as objectionable, is to *fera* the witch. *Fera*ing consists in surreptitiously introducing into his system, through his food or beer, a drug which calms the irritation impelling him to bewitch. It stops that itching of the fingers which constrains him to commit crimes and causes him to forget his frustrations and to seek compensation in day-dreaming or loquacity instead of in action. He may become gossipy and guileless. An examination of the ingredients of the medicine used throws a good deal of light upon the conceptions that they are handling in this case, but the thought-pattern can hardly be explained here and I must content myself by saying that the objective is to convert the compulsion to do evil into conduct that is aimless and harmless.

The Incidence and Function of Witchcraft

I have so far confined myself to description and have mentioned a few of the Lobedu rationalizations. But it is necessary to pursue the analysis very much further in order to understand the real role of witchcraft and sorcery and to show to what needs in human nature the institution is a response. I need hardly reiterate that witches and sorcerers are considered to be the embodiment of malignant forces ever on the alert to enter into unholy matrimony with the criminal impulses of the human heart. Witchcraft particularly is the essence of evil, vicious and inscrutable, that whirls through the universe and seeks asylum in sinful souls in which the germs of wickedness lie ready to be quickened into life. Sorcery is not transmitted in the germ-plasm: a child can never be guilty of sorcery, but the kind of precocity in him which enables him to circumvent an adult or the accepted code is a sure sign of incipient witchcraft. Both vices are, however, identified with the malice and jealousies that motivate anti-social conduct. Both of them occur only where you find stresses and strains in life, where, in other words, there are tensions, actual or potential, between people. Hence it is relatives and neighbours, but never strangers, who use witchcraft or sorcery against one another.

Merely to say that we have here the projection of conflicts that in a non-aggressive social environment are driven underground because they are not permitted to find expression in open dissension, is not enough. Some kinds of tension are rather differently canalized; they are given other avenues of vicarious expression. There are, e.g., relatives such as the father's sister towards whom, according to the behaviour patterns of the Lobedu, onerous obligations and an extreme delicacy of conduct are enjoined; they are easily aggrieved and readily nurse grievances; and they may have concealed complaints, repressed and subconscious wants. A father's sister's subconscious grievance is actually conceptualized as *mahava*, which may cause illness in the family of her brother's home. And when he calls her, as he may, to remove the cause, she often uses the phraseology (in the conciliation rite she performs): 'if I have been aggrieved and am harbouring ill-will in my heart, I am quite unaware of it. . . .' The interesting point is not merely this conception of hidden frustrations, but also that *mahava* is in quite a different category from witchcraft or sorcery. The position is that the father's sister's displeasure or frustrations cannot be projected as witchcraft or sorcery; and the technique of handling tensions of this kind is entirely different.

It is, however, not merely the incidence of witchcraft and sorcery as between persons, i.e., the types of personal tensions involved, that raises numerous interesting problems; there is a different problem in attempting to explain why these evils are invoked for only a limited range of situations. Why, e.g., can you never ascribe the cracking of your pot in the process of burning to these destructive forces, while you do so when the crops in your garden, also the fruits of your labour, unaccountably fail? Why, when you are caught out telling lies, cannot you incriminate a witch maliciously intent upon discrediting you? After all the Lobedu have a technique, *hu nielela*, which can quite legitimately be used to cause a thief who has escaped detection to repeat his thieving so that he may be caught red-handed. A criminal may be made the victim of an obsessive compulsion to relapse into crime so that he will once more be tried for an offence for which he has, say, been let off with a light sentence in our European courts; for as the Lobedu see things, our justice causes criminals to multiply and witches to become more aggressive and the clemency we exercise to reform the offender presents itself as a challenge to which they respond by magically constraining him to crime. *Hu nielela* is never antisocial and hence can never fall in the category of sorcery; and while it will take me too far afield into Lobedu cultural arrangements, orientations of values and conceptual categories to demonstrate the good sense and coherence of these apparent incongruities, I can say, generally, that when the total situation considered against the background of the knowledge and control of nature available demands an explanation in terms of lack of skill, incompetence or other inadequacy, a man is not permitted to attribute his misfortune or failure to sorcery or witchcraft. Moreover the fundamental presupposition, that the social order is dominated by moral forces, must not be invalidated by the interpretation of causes that a man invokes to account for his shortcomings.

Leaving on one side these difficult questions, let us for a moment revert to the incidence as between persons of witchcraft and sorcery. A statistical analysis reveals that some relatives never bewitch one another, even though their relationship is subject to the severest conflicts. A brother can, for instance, never impute witchcraft or sorcery to his cattle-linked sister, that is, the sister through whose marriage he obtains the cattle for his own marriage. She is the builder of his home and can intervene in it; indeed, he can never divorce the wife obtained with his sister's cattle unless she consents; and in the last resort she may give refuge to that wife if he drives her away and so can prevent the annulment of the marriage and cause the wife to bear children by anyone she likes: the children will still be his and she may still require one of the daughters to marry her son (or if she has none, a supposititious one) so as to become her daughter-in-law who will care for her in her old age. The situation is obviously one that is pregnant with potential stresses and strains. Yet, as I have seen, the ill-conceived idea of a brother to impute witchcraft or sorcery to this sister is ridiculed as a mental aberration or treated as a psychopathic compensatory adjustment. The Lobedu rationalization is usually that brother and sister know one another's medicines and hence cannot harm one another in this way, but underlying this rationalization is the realization that to admit the possibility of witchcraft between these two relatives would endanger the whole social structure, the delicately-balanced edifice built upon the *lobola* exchanges.

On the other hand the most prolific source of witchcraft and sorcery is the conflict of co-wives. They become entangled (if I may use the metaphor of the eternal triangles of our monogamy) in the polygons of jealousy that arise in polygamy. The specific cause of the frustration that is projected may be neglect or favouritism of the husband, status of one wife relative to the other co-wives, indeed any kind of differential treatment or attempt by the husband to benefit the house of one wife at the expense of another. Sexual jealousies do not, however, take a prominent place, since the structure of the family is such that the husband-wife relationship is primarily the link holding together two larger groups, the intermarrying lineages whose interlocking rights and duties constitute the basis of social solidarity as well as of the political organization. A very considerable portion of the total cultural energy goes to devices for ensuring the smooth running of these crucial institutions; and the solutions for difficulties that are ranked highest are always compromise, give and take, conciliation. Dissension and open conflict between co-wives is severely frowned upon, while agreement even in the humblest home receives royal recognition, which means a great deal since the queen is divine and only rarely accessible to ordinary mortals. The consequence is that co-wives can express their resentments only indirectly in some substitute activity. This is, of course, good soil for the growth of grievances for which witchcraft and sorcery provide a very natural vicarious outlet – hence the high incidence among co-wives of vicarious fights in the world of fantasy.

It would serve no good purpose to analyse the various conflict situations in which imputations of witchcraft and sorcery arise. They are quite unintelligible in our setting since the different ways in which men account for their failures and frustrations are always relative to the functioning and values of their society. But a few facets of these situations can be dealt with fairly generally. The first is the psychological function of witchcraft and sorcery. They enable men to believe that their failures are due not to any fault of their own, but to the machinations of others; and it is very necessary, in a world in which the technology is inadequate for the satisfaction of the complex culturally created needs, that men should be able to compensate for their inadequacy and continue to feel that they are masters of their own fate. Moreover, witchcraft and sorcery provide avenues of vicarious achievement to those who, because of their aggressive temperaments or disharmonious conditioning, find it impossible or extremely irksome to conform to the pattern of co-operativeness and reciprocity.

Another point worth mentioning is that witchcraft and sorcery do not operate automatically, as a number of other forces do; they must always be set into motion by a specific individual; and consequently there must be some theory incriminating such an individual. Part of the theory is that there are people with innate perverse impulses, and since the values and institutional arrangements of the society reflect an ultimate and universal sanity, they are abnormal and can have intimate relations with the supernormal. Their techniques therefore override ordinary physical laws. But it is impossible to impute witchcraft or sorcery to certain individuals, since they cannot have the necessary evil motivations, or a logical inconsistency would be involved: the society has found it useful to convert the misfortune suffered into a social sanction. There is, in other words, a good deal more in witchcraft and sorcery than meets the eye, and they can be shown to be intelligent responses to man's fundamental needs in the context of the society in which they are found.

28. Monica Hunter Wilson

Witch-Beliefs and Social Structure

Monica Hunter Wilson, 'Witch-beliefs and social structure', *American Journal of Sociology*, vol. 56, 1951, pp. 307–13. The first draft of this paper was delivered as a lecture to the Chicago Anthropological Society in April 1950.

Many anthropologists are concerned just now with the relation between values and social structure. My subject is a facet of that problem. I shall try to show that witch beliefs are one expression of the values of a society and that these vary with the social structure. My analysis is based on the comparison of two African peoples among whom I have done field work, the Nyakyusa of Tanganyika (G. Wilson, 1936a, 1936b, 1938; M. Wilson, 1937, 1950, 1951) and the Pondo of South Africa (cf. Hunter, 1936).

These peoples are similar in many respects: they are both cattle people and cultivators, traditionally having had a subsistence economy but now drawn into the world economy, the Pondo as migrant laborers in the gold mines of South Africa, the Nyakyusa as migrant laborers on the mines and sisal plantations of Tanganyika and as peasant producers of coffee and rice. Both peoples were, and still are, organized under chiefs and have well-developed legal institutions; both peoples are patrilineal, and marriage is legalized by the transfer of cattle from the groom's group to that of the bride; both speak a Bantu language, with all that that implies in similarity of concepts and categories of thought; and both have the type of religion so general in Bantu Africa, viz., an elaborate ancestor cult, a belief in the power of medicines (that is, in mystical power residing in certain material substances), and a belief in witchcraft.

I am using 'witchcraft' in the sense in which Professor Evans-Pritchard uses it for the belief in a mystical power innate in certain individuals and exercised by them to harm others, and I distinguish it from sorcery, which is the illegal use of medicines to harm others. In doing so, I follow precisely the Nyakyusa verbal usage, for they distinguish between *ubulosi*, an innate power used to work evil, and *ubutege*, the illegal use of destructive medicines. The distinction is an important one; for sorcery, as I have defined it, is practiced, that is, people use medicines (which are sometimes poisons) with the object of harming others, while few anthropologists would admit the reality of witchcraft – the exercise of an innate

276

power to harm others directly. But, though both Nyakyusa and Pondo have a lively fear of witchcraft, there are marked variations in the forms of their beliefs and in the incidence of accusations, and it is these differences which I wish to discuss.

The Nyakyusa believe that witches exist as pythons in the bellies of certain individuals. They are something tangible, discoverable at an autopsy, and inherited. The incentive to witchcraft is said to be the desire for good food. Witches lust for meat and milk – the prized foods of the group – and it is this which drives them to commit witchcraft. They delight in eating human flesh and gnaw men inside, causing death to their victims. The witches also steal milk, sucking the udders of cows, so that the cows dry up and later abort. All this happens in dreams. Nightmares of being throttled, of being chased, of fighting, and of flying through the air are taken as evidence of an attack by witches; and, if a man wakes up suddenly at night in fear and sweating, he knows that 'they' – the witches – have come to throttle him. The witches are thought to fly by night on their pythons or 'on the wind'; they attack either singly or in covens; and they feast on human flesh.

Though the first incentive to witchcraft is said to be the lust for food, witches select as their victims those against whom they have a grudge; they act illegally and immorally but not without cause. They attack those with whom they have quarreled, so that the good man who keeps on friendly terms with his neighbors has little to fear from the witches. Children are warned not to be quarrelsome or boastful or brusque in their manners, lest they arouse the anger of witches. People also fear to be conspicuously successful, lest, exciting envy, they bring upon themselves the attack of a witch. One can show off a bit, but not too much. Thus a man may safely hoe a garden bigger than that of his neighbors, but it must not be too conspicuously bigger, and he must not boast of its size; a woman may carry home a heavier load of faggots than her fellow, but it must not be too conspicuously heavier; and so on. To be a Don Juan, carrying on many intrigues, or the favorite wife of one's husband is also dangerous, provoking jealousy. Above all, witches are thought to attack those who are stingy with food, and a direct connection is made between feeding potential witches on beef and protecting one's self against attack. Well-fed pythons stay quiet.

The kind of person accused of being a witch is very like the person thought to be attacked. He (or she) is proud and boastful, morose, or aloof and unsympathetic to neighbors in trouble. The 'strong, silent man' depicted as a hero by Hollywood would very likely be labeled a witch in African society. The unusually successful man, the go-getter, is also liable to be accused of practising witchcraft or sorcery, for it is argued that his success can only have come through some mystical power and *at the expense of his fellows*.

The Nyakyusa believe that witchcraft is extremely dangerous but that the danger is limited in two ways: first, witchcraft rarely operates beyond the village – a private person can be attacked only from within his own village – and, second, the good man is defended by his neighbors. It is thought that in every village there are 'defenders' (*abamanga*) who see the witches in dreams and fight them and drive them off. The leader of 'the defenders' is the headman of the village.

But not only do 'the defenders' protect the innocent, they also punish the guilty. They bring upon a wrongdoer a chilling breath which paralyses him or causes him to sicken with a fever or some debilitating disease. The supposed victim of such an attack will complain angrily of 'witchcraft' (*ubulosi*), but other people will speak of his sin and the just retribution that has fallen upon him through 'the breath of men' or 'the curse'. The source of this power of defense and punishment is almost identical with that of witchcraft: it comes from pythons in men's bellies, though, curiously, defenders have only one python, whereas witches have several, and the defender's python is not visible at an autopsy like that of a witch. The sins which are believed to bring down the anger of the defenders are many, but the commonest are failure to provide feasts on certain specified occasions, disrespectful behavior towards parents or by a woman towards her husband or parents-in-law, incest, and a breach of conventions regarding the limitation of pregnancies. Ill health in man and beast and field was directly linked to sin by our informants; Job, who suffered misfortune, though he was righteous, is foreign to Nyakyusa thought. Hence a study of cases of misfortune provided concrete data on values; it shows very clearly what was judged good and what evil.

The categories of people suspected by the Nyakyusa of practicing witchcraft are, first and foremost, village neighbors – more than a third of the cases of witchcraft we collected were of this type – second, fellow-workers in a mining camp, and, third, wives. Only very rarely is an accusation of practicing witchcraft lodged against a kinsman.[1]

The Pondo ideas about witchcraft are rather different. First, they think that a witch always works by means of a familiar – a fabulous hairy being with exaggerated sexual characteristics called *Tikoloshe*, or a baboon, a wild cat, a snake or a lightning bird. The familiar is of opposite sex to that of the witch and is often spoken of as taking the form of a

1. This account is based on the general statements of our Nyakyusa friends and an analysis of ninety-one cases of misfortune, all of which were attributed to mystical causes.

beautiful girl or a handsome man, very light in color, and the witch and familiar have sexual relations. Usually the familiar is acquired by inheritance (Hunter, 1936). The basis of these beliefs is against dreams, sex dreams being frequently interpreted in terms of witchcraft. The Pondo do not distinguish so sharply between witchcraft and sorcery as the Nyakyusa do; nevertheless, they speak of two types of power used illegally, viz., familiars and medicines. Familiars are regarded as altogether and utterly evil, and there is no idea of their being used in defense or to punish a wrongdoer. A homestead is defended against witches by its ancestors and by medicines placed round about it, not by some of its members who see and fight the witches in dreams. And the range of witchcraft is not limited in the way in which it is among the Nyakyusa; nowadays it is even said to be sent by post.

I know much less about the kind of behavior thought to excite the attacks of witches or to lead to an accusation against one among the Pondo than among the Nyakyusa, for I was less interested in this problem when I was in Pondoland than I became later on and also I was less intimate with the Pondo than with the Nyakyusa. I do know, however, that envy, roused by conspicuous success, is a cause very commonly cited. I am inclined to think that misfortune is less closely linked with morality among the Pondo than among the Nyakyusa, that is, that they conceive of the witches acting without cause in a way in which the Nyakyusa do not; but I have not the evidence to substantiate this. Further investigation will be necessary to prove or to disprove such a hypothesis. But, even though witchcraft and morality may not be so closely linked by the Pondo as by the Nyakyusa, a study of Pondo witch beliefs throws a good deal of light on Pondo morality.

The typical accusations of witchcraft in Pondoland are between mother and daughter-in-law who live in the same homestead and between fellow-employees in the mines or elsewhere. Accusations against neighbors, people of other homesteads, occur but are less frequent. I have no figures to support this impression of the incidence of accusations among the Pondo, but it is largely confirmed by the analysis of accusations now being made by a young anthropologist, Miss Selma Kaplan, in another Xhosa-speaking area, the Keiskamma Valley, which is culturally very similar to Pondoland.

Now the differences between the Nyakyusa and Pondo ideas about witchcraft are not absolute; there is some overlapping between them. There are some hints among the Nyakyusa of sex associations with witchcraft, though they have no theory of familiars with whom the owner has sex relations and do not interpret sex dreams in terms of witchcraft,

and there is some suggestion among the Pondo of witches seeking food –
the baboon familiar is said sometimes to milk cows. There is also some
overlapping in the type of behavior thought to anger the witches in the
two societies and in the relationships within which accusations occur. But
the difference in emphasis is very great. I went straight to the Nyakyusa
after working with the Pondo, and I was puzzled by the contrast. What
was the reason for it? Why should the Nyakyusa always talk about the
witches lusting for food and the Pondo talk about witch lovers? Why do
the Nyakyusa have this theory of a power akin to witchcraft used in
defense and to punish evildoers, and not the Pondo?

With the reports of the dreams of men in half-starved prisoner-of-war
camps in mind, I began, first, to reflect on the differences in Nyakyusa
and Pondo diet, but I found no answer there. The Nyakyusa have long
been among the best-fed people in Africa (Lugard, 1893, vol. 1, p. 131;
Thomson, 1881, vol. 1, pp. 268–74), while the Pondo are nowadays very
badly fed. The Nyakyusa eat only a limited amount of meat but have a
good deal of milk and ample supplies of bananas and plantains, maize,
beans, finger-millet, groundnuts, sweet potatoes, pumpkins and greens:
and many of them get fish and rice. The Pondo, on the other hand, have
no more meat than the Nyakyusa and almost certainly less milk, while
their supplies of fruit, grains, pulses, greens and fish are much more
limited in quantity and variety. It is true that a century ago the Pondo
probably had much more meat and milk than they have today: but, if
meat hunger really produces the idea that witches kill to get flesh, then it
would have appeared among the Pondo long before this. There is no
tradition of cannibalism among either people, though it may conceivably
have been resorted to by both in periods of extreme privation. Neither
people have ever had the reputation among their neighbors of being
cannibals, as the Azande had.

What, then, are the other conspicuous differences between Nyakyusa
and Pondo societies? The Nyakyusa are peculiar in that they live not in
kinship villages, like most African peoples, but in age-villages. A group of
boys build a village when they are still quite young – about ten or eleven
years old – and they remain together through life, bringing their wives to
this village when they marry. Tremendous emphasis is laid on enjoying
the company of age-mates, on eating and drinking with them, and avoiding quarrels with them. Until he marries, a boy is fed by his mother,
though he sleeps in the boys' village and spends his spare time there, but
he does not come home alone for meals. Instead, a group of boys visits
the mother of each member in turn, and this habit of eating in a group is
ideally maintained all through life. A man cannot eat with women, and he

cannot eat with his sons; to do so would imply a familiarity wholly immoral in Nyakyusa eyes; but he should eat with neighbors who are age-mates of his own standing. Generosity with food and hospitality to neighbors is the first virtue and the basis of prestige in the society. The village is the landholding group and joins in common defense under the leadership of the village headman in the 'war by day and war by night' (*ubwite pa musi nobwite pa kelo*), 'war by night' meaning the war against witches. Traditionally, also, the members of a village have certain re-sponsibilities for torts committed by one of their fellows.

In spite of living and fighting with his age-set, however, a Nyakyusa man has very close ties with his kinsmen. He is bound to them by a supposed mystical interdependence and the performance of rituals di-rected to common ancestors, on which health and fertility are thought to depend, and by interest in the cattle owned by members of his agnatic lineage. I have not space now to go into the very complicated system by which cattle are acquired and distributed; it must suffice to say that they circulate within agnatic lineages and between lineages; a man acquires cattle primarily through kinship connections, and his kinsmen have cer-tain claims on the cattle he holds. Fellow-villagers have no claims on his cattle other than food; they do not inherit from him or get cattle from him with which to marry, but they do expect to receive a share of his milk and to feast on beef upon certain recognized occasions, when he should kill cattle for a ritual. There are no clans or large exogamous groups. Descen-dants of a common grandparent cannot marry, and those with a common great-grandparent should not marry; but, since kinsmen are scattered, the limitation on choice within one neighborhood is small.

Nyakyusa country has been under European control since 1893 and, as we saw earlier, some of the men are in European employment, but relations between Nyakyusa and European are still fairly tenuous; the atmosphere is that of a frontier, and the caste system has not solidified as it has in South Africa. Racial segregation is not taken as an ultimate value by any group.

The Pondo social structure is quite different. Among them the local group, the homestead (*umzi*), is a kinship group, comprising an agnatic lineage, together with wives and unmarried daughters. The men of a homestead form a close-knit group, commonly eating in company and formerly being jointly responsible for each other's torts and fighting as a unit in the army of the district. A number of lineages make up a clan, which, though not strictly a territorial group, has a territorial headquar-ters, a substantial proportion of the men in any one area being of the same clan, that of the chief of the area. Tremendous emphasis is laid on clan exogamy and not marrying into the clan of one's mother or of either grandmother. Clans are large; they may have three thousand or four thousand members; and, since they tend to concentrate in different areas, a great many girls in one neighborhood are classed as sisters by a young man of the neighborhood. The emotional content of this taboo on clan incest is tremendous; it survives even among urbanized people, and it is one of the main cultural differences separating the Xhosa- and Zulu-speaking people from the Sotho, with whom they mingle in Johannesburg and other centers of employment.

Second, the Pondo are members of a color-caste society, in which one of the ultimate values is the exclusion of sex relations between members of different castes. They are in much closer contact with whites than the Nyakyusa are, and the emphasis on endogamy within each color group is much greater in South Africa than in Tanganyika. Sex relations between white and black, whether marital or extra-marital, are now a criminal offense in South Africa.

Now my hypothesis is that the differences between the Nyakyusa and Pondo ideas of witchcraft are directly connected with these differences in their social structure. The Nyakyusa emphasize the virtue of feeding village neighbors and regard the lust for meat and milk as the main incentive to witchcraft *because* they live not with kinsmen but with neighbors, and yet cattle, the main form of wealth, are controlled by kinship groups. Jealousy of a neighbor's wealth is common enough, but it is peculiarly keen among the Nyakyusa because non-relatives live close together in villages and the poor cannot help being aware when the rich feast on good food. Our Nyakyusa friends spoke of the witches *smelling* meat roasting or *smelling* milk, and that, I think, is very significant. A share in feasts is the only benefit a non-relative can expect to have from the wealth in cattle of a fellow-villager.

The Pondo setup is quite different. Among them, only kinsmen live together, and kinsmen can expect to benefit from the herd of their wealthy relatives either through inheritance or by assistance with marriage cattle, so every man has a personal interest in the increase of cattle belonging to the kinsmen with whom he lives. Pondo also crave meat feasts, but they speak of the pressure to kill cattle as coming from the ancestors, not from neighbors. When a sacrifice is made on behalf of a kinsman who is ill the Pondo say: *Balambile, bafuna ukudla ngaye*, meaning 'they are hungry, they want to eat with him', and 'they' refers to the ancestors, not to witches or neighbors. Neighbors play no necessary part in the ritual at all, and even if they do not come to share in the feast the patient will recover, whereas, if a Nyakyusa has been ill and sacrifices, the neighbors *must* eat of the meat of the sacrifice and bless him.

And what of the Pondo emphasis on sex in witchcraft? Are they a much more inhibited people than the Nyakyusa? At first sight it appears that they are not. There is, in fact, much greater freedom of premarital relations between the sexes among the Pondo than among the Nyakyusa, for the marriage age of girls is much higher and the marriage age of men rather lower. In Pondoland there is a large group of nubile girls who dance and flirt and cuddle with the young men, whereas among the Nyakyusa there is no such group. Among the latter most girls are betrothed well before puberty, and, once a girl is betrothed, any sex contact with her (outside the puberty ceremonies) is treated as adultery. But the Pondo prohibit sex relations with a much wider group of persons than do the Nyakyusa. I relate the emphasis on sex in witchcraft among the Pondo to the system of clan exogamy, which excludes large categories of individuals living in the same neighborhood from marrying or flirting with one another, and the idea that the familiar is a light-colored person to the caste system which almost excludes sex relations between persons of different colors. In short, I suggest that the familiar is a symbol of forbidden sex attraction and that such attraction is common in a society in which large categories of people who live in close contact with one another are forbidden to marry.

The belief in 'the breath of men', that is, in a power akin to witchcraft used in defense and to punish wrongdoers is also, I suggest, related to the age-village organization. It is matched in a kinship village by the belief that the ancestors are a shield against misfortune to the group and that senior living relatives have a mystical power over their descendants and juniors. The concept of 'the breath of men' gives a Nyakyusa village headman a power over the members of his village comparable to that of a headman in a Pondoland village. The fact that the power of the one is thought to derive from a python in his belly and the power of the other from his ancestors does not materially affect his relationship with members of his village.

The difference in the incidence of accusations of witchcraft in Nyakyusa and Pondo societies is also related to the differences in the social structure of the two groups. A Pondo bride joins the homestead of her husband and lives, often for many years, under the control of her mother-in-law. Friction between them is very common. Moreover, she is long regarded as a stranger and so is suspect because she is a member of another clan. The Nyakyusa wife, on the other hand, lives in a different village from her mother-in-law and does not necessarily see much of her.

Nor is she an outsider in a closely knit kin group as the Pondo woman is. In Nyakyusa society friction is most likely between neighbors who live close together, and it is between them that accusations of witchcraft are most frequent. Both societies are polygynous, and, in both, accusations are fairly frequent between co-wives. Individuals from both societies work for Europeans, and accusations are very common between fellow-workers.

There are indications that, as these two societies are drawn into closer relationship with the outside world, there is a change in the forms of belief, as well as in the incidence of accusations. Among the Nyakyusa, for example, the more sophisticated fear sorcery while denying belief in witchcraft. Sorcery is felt by them to be compatible with Western science in a way in which witchcraft is not, for *ubetege*, the word I have translated as 'sorcery', is usually interpreted as 'poisoning' by those Nyakyusa who know some English. It is quite true that it includes poisoning, but it also includes burying a medicine under an enemy's doorstep or in the thatch of his hut, and no consistent distinction is made by the Nyakyusa between these different types of *ubutege*.

But, though the forms of belief change, belief in witchcraft or sorcery of one kind or another continues, and this, I think, is the crux of our problem. What are the social conditions which produce a general belief in witchcraft and sorcery? Granted that accusations of practicing witchcraft or sorcery are an expression of conflict and that they are likely to be many when conflict is acute, as in a Johannesburg slum or a mining camp in Tanganyika, we still have to explain why such accusations are not common in London slums or Tyneside collieries. For example, what were the social conditions in seventeenth-century England that produced beliefs so very similar to contemporary beliefs in Pondoland – the parallels to the Pondo belief in familiars are very close indeed in seventeenth-century England – and what were the effective causes of the decline of these beliefs? I long to read an adequate analysis of this problem by some social historian aware of anthropological theory. The decline in belief in witchcraft and sorcery is not purely a matter of extending scientific knowledge – our answer must cover the astute Pondo teacher, who said to me: 'It may be quite true that typhus is carried by lice, but who sent the infected louse? Why did it bite one man and not another?'

I have suggested elsewhere (Wilson and Wilson, 1945) that witch beliefs are general in small-scale societies with inadequate control of their environment and dominated by personal relationships, societies in which people think in personal terms and seek personal causes for their misfortunes. This hypothesis may or may not prove to be part of the answer;

but, even if it is true, it does not take us far enough. Innumerable other questions crop up. For example, is the close connection which the Nyakyusa make between witchcraft and morality, between misfortune and sin, characteristic of all very small societies or of all relatively stable societies, or is it related to other, quite different factors? Supposing that I am right in thinking that the Pondo tie misfortune less closely to morality than the Nyakyusa do, what is the reason for this difference?

And when the belief in witchcraft in the sense in which I have defined it disappears, what takes its place? Are the witches but the primitive form of the scapegoat who is always with us? Are men with pythons in their bellies and those who ride baboons by night indeed a true parallel to the red agents of McCarthy's fevered dreams?

Understanding of these problems will, I think, proceed from a close analysis of the relation between witch-beliefs and other aspects of society, such as I have tried to paint on a very small canvas in this paper. I see witch-beliefs as the standardized nightmare of a group, and I believe that the comparative analysis of such nightmares is not merely an antiquarian exercise but one of the keys to the understanding of society.

References

HUNTER, M. (1936), *Reaction to Conquest*, Oxford U.P. for International Institute of African Languages and Cultures.

LUGARD, F. D. (1893), *The Rise of our East African Empire*, Blackwood.

THOMSON, J. (1881), *To the Central African Lakes and Back*, Sampson Lowe, Marston, Searle & Rivington.

WILSON, G. (1936a), 'An African morality', *Africa*, vol. 9.

WILSON, G. (1936b), 'An introduction to Nyakyusa society', *Bantu Studies*, vol. 10.

WILSON, G. (1938), *The Land Rights of Individuals among the Nyakyusa*, Rhodes-Livingstone Papers.

WILSON, G., and WILSON, M. H. (1945), *The Analysis of Social Change*, Cambridge U.P.

WILSON, M. Hunter (1937), 'An African Christian morality', *Africa*, vol. 10.

WILSON, M. Hunter (1950), 'Nyakyusa kinship', in A. R. Radcliffe-Brown and D. Forde (eds), *African Systems of Kinship and Marriage*, Oxford U.P. for International African Institute.

WILSON, M. Hunter (1951), *Good Company: A Study of Nyakyusa Age-Villages*, Oxford U.P. for International African Institute.

29. S. F. Nadel

Witchcraft in Four African Societies

S. F. Nadel, 'Witchcraft in four African societies: an essay in comparison', *American Anthropologist*, vol. 54, 1952, pp. 18–29.

In this paper[1] it is proposed to present a small-scale model of a comparative analysis, more precisely, of an analysis of 'concomitant variations' (to borrow Durkheim's term), such as any enquiry concerned with the explanation of social facts must employ. The facts in question are particular variants of the belief in witchcraft. Indirectly, the study will also refer to a much discussed hypothesis, the assumption that infantile experiences represent a paramount determinant of culture.

The comparison concerns two pairs of societies – the Nupe and Gwari in Northern Nigeria, and the Korongo and Mesakin tribes in the Nuba Mountains of the Central Sudan. Each pair shows wide cultural similarities combined with a few marked divergencies, one of these being the diversity in witchcraft beliefs. This discussion will proceed on two assumptions:

1. That any one relevant cultural divergence entails further, concomitant, divergences in the respective cultures.

2. That witchcraft beliefs are causally related to frustrations, anxieties or other mental stresses precisely as psychopathological symptoms are related to mental disturbances of this nature.

Witchcraft in Nupe and Gwari

The two societies are neighbors in an identical environment and also maintain frequent contacts. They speak closely related languages and have an identical kinship system, based on patrilineal succession, patrilocal residence, and localized extended families. Political organization and the regulation of male adolescence are closely similar in both tribes; so is their economy, though marketing and trade are on a much larger scale in Nupe. The religion of Nupe and Gwari is again closely similar

1. In slightly abridged form and under the title 'A comparative study of witchcraft', the paper was presented at the Berkeley meeting of the A.A.A. For a fuller account of some of the ethnographical material see Nadel (1942, esp. ch. 9; 1935; 1947).

(ignoring here the more recent spread of Islam), and the conceptions of life and death, of a body possessed of a double soul ('shadow-' and 'life-soul'), or of the reincarnation of ancestral souls, are identical even as regards nomenclature.

Both groups, too, firmly believe in witchcraft; several grave incidents showing the strength of the beliefs occurred even during the period of field work among the two tribes. Both conceive of witchcraft as un-equivocally evil, as destroying life, mainly through mysterious wasting diseases, and as implying the power of witches to 'eat' the 'life-soul' of their victims. Witches are active at night and cannot be seen or discovered by ordinary means. Everything connected with witchcraft takes place in a fantasy realm which is, almost *ex hypothesi*, intangible and beyond em-pirical verification. This is shown most clearly in the tenet that it is only the 'shadow-souls' of witches which roam about and attack victims, while their bodies remain asleep at home, thus deceiving any ordinary attempts at proving, or disproving, these mystic activities.

The two beliefs, however, differ radically in the ascription of sex to the witch. In Nupe witches are always women (called *gáci*, from *egá*, 'witch-craft'). They are thought to be organized in a society closely modelled on similar human associations and headed by the woman who is also, in real life, the titled official head of the women traders. It may be noted that this is the only instance of the fantasy world of witchcraft projecting into and becoming tangible in concrete, everyday life. The woman said to preside over the association of witches occupies an exceptional position also in another sense; for she is the only 'good' female witch, sometimes a 'reformed' witch, and hence a person willing and able to control the sinister activities of her companions.

The men fit into this pattern in an ambiguous way. Certain individuals are said to possess a power similar to witchcraft, which enables them to see and deal with witches. This power is known by a different name (*eshe*) and is essentially good; so that the men possessed of it can control and combat the women witches. At the same time the female witches need the co-operation of the men, for only when the female and male powers are joined does female witchcraft become fully effective, that is, deadly. Here again, the men are said to use their power not to assist, but to restrain the female witches, by withholding the required aid. The ambiguity referred to, then, lies in this: men are necessary for the fullest effect of witchcraft; but as a class, they also stand aloof and are not themselves evil; rather do they attempt to block evil witchcraft. Even so, the fatal effects of female witchcraft are admitted to occur; in which case one argues that a few evil individuals among the men (whom no one can name) have betrayed their

287

own sex and become the helpers of a woman witch. The general picture is that of a sharp sex-antagonism, which assigns the evil intentions to the female, and to the male a benevolent and ideally decisive – if somewhat Utopian – role.

Characteristically, the men are never blamed or accused of witchcraft, and the main collective weapon against witchcraft lies in the activities of a male secret society which, by threats and torture, 'cleanses' villages of witchcraft. The same idea that the men alone have the secret power of defeating female witchcraft is expressed in the legends on the origins of witchcraft and anti-witchcraft. The case studies collected add a further twist to this sex-antagonism; for in the majority of cases the alleged witch is a woman, usually an older and domineering female, who would attack a younger man who somehow fell under her dominance; which situation is again pictured in the legends. The men, therefore, though on the Utopian or fantasy plane the masters of female witchcraft, are, on the plane of 'real' incidents and fears, its main victims.

One case history and one legend may be quoted. The former concerns a young man from a village on the river Niger who one night suddenly disappeared. A body which the police had good reason to believe was his was later fished out of the river; but the people refused to accept this 'natural' explanation, maintaining that the young man had been spirited away by a witch. Suspicion at once fell on an elderly wealthy woman whose house the young man had frequently been visiting; he had, in fact, been something like a protégé of that woman or, in Nupe parlance, her *egi kata* – 'son of the house' – which term is applied to any individual who seeks the patronage of some influential older person and becomes dependent upon his patron's advice and material help.

The legend tells of a young king 'in ancient times', whose mother was an overbearing old woman, constantly interfering with her son's plans and actions. At last the son decided to rid himself of her influence. He consulted a (male) diviner, who told him the secret of a certain cloth mask, which would drop on his mother and remove her from the earth. Thus, it is said, originated the Nupe anti-witchcraft cult *ndakó gboyá*, which is today vested in the male secret society mentioned before and employs the cloth masks as its main paraphernalia.

As regards the Gwari beliefs, a brief outline will suffice. They involve no sex-antagonism or sex-polarity. Witches and their victims are indiscriminately male and female. Witchcraft is discovered by ordinary divination, practiced by both men and women, and anti-witchcraft measures consist in the main in an annual 'cleansing' ritual which embraces the whole community, again irrespective of sex.

So much for the general picture of the two cultures and their divergent conceptions of witchcraft. Turning now to the search for 'concomitant' divergences, and taking our lead from psychoanalysis, we might start with infantile experiences and the techniques of child-rearing. Here we meet with one relevant difference only, concerning children of two and over. Until a newborn child has reached the age of two or three the parents in both tribes refrain from cohabitation. Afterwards, when cohabitation is resumed, the Nupe wife visits the husband's hut, the children staying in her sleeping quarters, while in Gwari the husband visits the wife, so that cohabitation takes place in the presence of the young children. The people have no doubt that the children do in fact witness the sexual act. Assuming, with Freudian psychology, that this fact entails deeply unsettling psychological effects, it should foster the oedipus trauma and definite tensions between child (perhaps more specifically son) and father.[2] Assuming further that these tensions, normally repressed or blocked in overt behavior, might find an outlet in the fantasy of witchcraft beliefs, we should expect these to reveal some bias towards sex-antagonism and towards identifying the evil witches either with males (the hated father image) or perhaps, by a more devious transference, with females (the mother avenging herself on all males). In fact, neither assumption is borne out by the evidence, the sex-antagonism occurring in the tribe where the traumatic experience is absent.

Certain other cultural divergences, however, concerning adult life, seem to be congruent with the diversity in witchcraft beliefs. They resolve upon marriage, which, generally speaking, is without serious complications and relatively tension-free in Gwari, but full of stress and mutual hostility in Nupe. Two facts may be mentioned.

1. The economic position of the Nupe wives, many of whom are successful intinerant traders, is generally much better than that of their peasant husbands. Thus husbands are often heavily in debt to their wives, and the latter assume many of the financial responsibilities which should rightly belong to the men as fathers and family heads, such as finding bride-price for sons, paying for the children's education, bearing the expenses of family feasts and the like. This reversal of the institutionalized roles is openly resented by the men, who are, however, helpless and unable to redress the situation.

2. As has been said, many married women become itinerant traders. According to the tenets of Nupe morality, this occupation should be

2. Gwari informants in fact claimed that a marked hostility between father and son was a common feature of their family life. The writer's material on the Gwari, however, is not sufficiently full to permit any more definite statement.

reserved for childless women, in whose case one also excuses the moral laxity which, in that society, goes together with this livelihood. But in fact mothers too become itinerant traders, leaving their children once they are four or five years old; more importantly, women also refuse to have children, practising abortion and using alleged contraceptives, in order to be free to choose this occupation. Again, the men are helpless; they can only brand this voluntary sterility as the gravest possible form of immorality.

In practice, then, the men must submit to the domineering and independent leanings of the women; they resent their own helplessness, and definitely blame the 'immorality' of the women-folk. The wish to see the situation reversed is expressed in nostalgic talk about 'the good old days' when all this was unheard of (and which are disproved by all genealogies and concrete records of the past). Equally, it can be argued, the hostility between men and women *plus* this wish-fulfilment are projected into the witchcraft beliefs with their ambivalent expression of sex-antagonism, in which men are the 'real' victims but the 'Utopian' masters of the evil women. A final item of evidence, mentioned before, lies in the identification of the head of the witches with the official head of the women traders. It relates the 'projection' in a direct and overt manner to the conscious hostility and the concrete situations evoking it. The psychological 'symptom', we might say, and the anxieties and stresses which are its cause are connected by a clear thread of meaning.

Witchcraft in Korongo and Mesakin

These two tribes are once more neighbors in the same environment; though speaking different languages they know one another and are often bilingual. They share the same economy, political organization, and religious beliefs and practices. Both reckon descent in the mother's line and have the same kinship system and domestic arrangements; more particularly, in both groups children of six or seven are free to leave their father's house, where they were born, for that of their mother's brother to grow up under his tutelage. A detailed census showed that in each tribe this change of residence and affiliation occurred in about half of all cases. In all other respects, too, child-rearing is identical in the two societies.

So is the regulation of male adolescence, with one exception to be discussed later. It may be pointed out here that male adolescence and, indeed, the whole life-cycle of the men, revolve upon a highly formalized division into age classes, each of which is characterized by the right to engage in particular sporting contests, which are exhibitions of virility as well. These sports are light wrestling, wrestling of a more strenuous kind, and fighting with spears. In the first, lowest, age class, before puberty, no sports are practised. The severe variety of wrestling marks the peak of physical vigor, attained towards the end of adolescence; while spear-fighting, which implies more skill than bodily strength, is considered appropriate to an age of already declining physical vigor. After the spear-fighting stage, the tests or exhibitions of virility cease altogether, the men having become 'too old'. At the same time the men give up sleeping in the cattle camps out in the bush, which more arduous mode of life is once more regarded as appropriate for youths only. This decline in physical vigor at the end of adolescence is attributed to the cumulative effects of sexual activity, especially to the sex life involved in marriage and pro-creation. In both groups, finally, the first part of the sporting contests after puberty is celebrated with much ceremony and is made the occasion for an important gift on the part of the boy's mother's brother. This consists of an animal taken from the mother's brother's herd, the same herd which the sister's son is in due course bound to inherit. The gift therefore represents something like an 'anticipated inheritance', and is in fact known by the term 'inheritance', a point which is of crucial importance for the understanding of the witchcraft beliefs.

To turn now to the contrast between the two groups. The Korongo have no witchcraft beliefs at all; the Mesakin are literally obsessed by fears of witchcraft (known as *torogo*) and witchcraft accusations, entailing violent quarrels, assaults, and blood revenge, are frequent. Witchcraft itself is a mysterious, malignant and often deadly power, emanating directly from evil wishes, though it is subject to two significant restrictions. Mesakin witchcraft is believed to operate only between maternal kin, especially between a mother's brother and sister's son, the older relative assailing the younger. Mesakin witchcraft further operates only if there is a reason, some legitimate cause for resentment or anger; and the latter is almost invariably a quarrel over the 'anticipated inheritance' mentioned before. As has been said, both tribes acknowledge this particular duty of the mother's brother. But in Korongo it is never refused. The gift can be postponed, but is also sometimes made twice, and rarely raises any serious difficulty. In Mesakin the exact opposite is true. The gift is always refused to begin with and has often to be taken by force, a procedure which is fully sanctioned by public opinion. The gift cannot be postponed, nor is it ever repeated. Quarrels over it between the youth and his mother's brother are the rule; and if by any chance the former falls ill, dies, or suffers some other misfortune, the older man is invariably suspected of having employed witchcraft.

Practices of child-rearing, being identical in the two tribes, offer no clue either to the sharply divergent attitude towards the anticipated inheritance or to the witchcraft beliefs which, in one of the two groups, come into play in this connection. The clue seems to lie, rather, in certain cultural differences shaping the adult attitudes towards life and, more especially, towards the fate of growing old.

To begin with, the two tribes deal differently with pre-marital sex relations. Both groups, as will be remembered, firmly believe that regular sexual intercourse is physically weakening for the male, yet also glorify physical vigor and manliness. In both groups, for example, a 'born' coward or weakling is called by the name normally given to the male homosexuals (who invariably turn transvestite), is treated with the same contempt, and is often forced to join their ranks. In both groups, too, the men hate growing old, which means, above all, withdrawing from the 'manly' pursuits and admitting their physical debility; thus the 'old men' will always try to join the sports for which they are supposed to be no longer fit, even at the risk of being ridiculed, or sneak out for a night in the cattle camps to join the company of the younger men. Yet while among the Korongo pre-marital and highly promiscuous sex relations are fully accepted and openly engaged in, among the Mesakin they are carefully concealed; indeed, the Mesakin insisted that formerly pre-marital chastity was rigidly observed. In other words, the Korongo accept the 'dissipation' of strength through sexual intercourse as something one can do nothing about; the Mesakin at least believe that it should be restricted and postponed, and face the failure of the ideal with all the symptoms of a feeling of guilt.[3]

Furthermore, the two tribes schematize their age classes differently, thus establishing a different correspondence between 'social age', as indicated in the age class, and physical age.[4] The Korongo have six age classes, as against three among the Mesakin, so that in the former tribe the various phases of individual life are much more faithfully represented; also, the rights and responsibilities changing with age are more evenly spaced. Above all, the pursuits typical of youth, tribal sports and life in the cattle camps, are discarded gradually, allowance being made for transitional stages. Thus the severe wrestling, indicative of the peak of physical vigor, is assigned to the third age class, of as yet unmarried youths, but lasts into the next grade, when marriage, at the age of

3. There is an interesting trace of this also among the Korongo; for here the fiancée of a young man will refuse to have pre-marital relations with him (and with him only), thus avoiding responsibility for the dissipation of strength of her beloved (Nadel, 1947, p. 289).

4. See Table 1 (p. 294 f.).

twenty–twenty-two, and regular sexual relations are expected to show their weakening effect. At this stage spear-fighting is the appropriate sport, again lasting into the next higher grade. This, the fifth grade, starts with parenthood and the assumption of the responsibilities of a family head; but the final farewell to sports and life in the cattle camps does not take place until a few years afterwards, at the age of twenty-eight–thirty. The Korongo also specifically name their sixth and last grade the age class of 'old men', the criterion now being the visible physical decline of the really old. In short, the Korongo accept a gradual process of growing old, the social 'old age' being only one of many steps and congruent with physical age.

The Mesakin, on the other hand, distinguish explicitly only between boys before puberty, youths (unmarried and married) before parenthood, and 'men', without further separation of the really old. Wrestling, spear-fighting, and life in the cattle camps all cease together, at the end of the second grade, that is, at the age of twenty-two–twenty-four. The Mesakin, therefore, introduce the indices of social 'old age' early in life, and expect men to renounce the cherished privileges of youth abruptly and on purely conventional grounds, which take little account of physical age.

Let us now return to the demand for the anticipated inheritance which figures so prominently in Mesakin witchcraft beliefs. In both tribes the mother's brother must see in this insistent demand a reminder that he has definitely grown old; not only has he by then probably begotten children (which fact would merely announce his declining youth), but he has now a ward sufficiently old to claim his 'inheritance', that is, a gift explicitly anticipating the donor's impending death. Now, among the Korongo the older man is prepared for the gradual decline of age and accepts its onset, which coincides with sex life, with good grace or at least without struggle; furthermore, since among the Korongo the anticipated inheritance can be postponed, the mother's brother may by then be an older or old man also in the physical sense. Among the Mesakin, who know no such gradual transition to old age and idealize pre-marital chastity (which would postpone its onset), the 'reminder' must find the donor mentally unprepared; and since the gift cannot be postponed it will often be demanded of men still physically young. Hence the violent resentment on the part of the mother's brother when the demand is made and his invariable first refusal.

The resentment and refusal merely express the older man's envy of youth and virility, the loss of which is brought home to him by the very request for the anticipated inheritance. Clearly, every man in the tribe has

Table 1
Korongo and Mesakin Age Classifications and Activities

Approx. age	Korongo			Mesakin		
	Age class	Activities	General circumstances	Age class	Activities	General circumstances
Up to 12–13	1. belad	None	Pre-puberty	1. nate	None	Pre-puberty
13–16	2. dere	Light wrestling	Post-puberty; first sex-relations	2. kaduma	Light wrestling; severe wrestling; spear-fighting; live in cattle camps	Post-puberty; pre-marital sex relations; later marriage
17–20	3. adere	Severe wrestling; live in cattle camps	Unmarried; pre-marital sex relations			
21–25	4. adumok	Severe wrestling; later spear-fighting; live in cattle camps part of the time	Married			

Approx. age	Korongo			Mesakin		
	Age class	Activities	General circumstances	Age class	Activities	General circumstances
26–50	5. asnda-gan	Spear-fighting; visits to cattle camps; both end after 3–4 years	Fathers, family heads	3. mede	None	Fathers, family heads; including physically old men
50–	6. tgif	None	Physically old men			

gone through this phase or knows about it in the case of others; everybody also knows that the mother's brother's refusal is bound to be abortive in the end, that he can be forced to yield the gift, and that tribal morality is against him. It is suggested that the belief in the mother's brother's power to use witchcraft against his would-be heirs arises from this knowledge. The hostility which, one knows, the older man feels but should not feel, and which he has no means of realizing finally and successfully, is accepted as operating in the sphere of secret as well as anti-social aims, that is, in the sphere of witchcraft. Differently expressed, every man projects his own frustrations of this nature into the allegations that others are guilty of witchcraft. In punishing them, the accuser vicariously wipes out his own guilt, unadmitted or admitted.

The picture just drawn is to some extent over-simplified. For the Mesakin believe that witchcraft may also be practiced by a sister's son against his mother's brother or by full brothers against one another. Here, too, there must be a legitimate motive, which lies again in a grievance over inheritance; but this may be ordinary as well as 'anticipated' inheritance. Nor need the alleged witch attack only the kinsman by whom he feels he has been injured; he may equally attack a close relative (patrilineal or matrilineal) of that kinsman or any one of the latter's matrilineal kin, thus venting his anger almost at random. These facts, however, seem significant: the belief in the powers of witchcraft of a sister's son over his mother's brother is pure 'theory', for which the people themselves can cite no concrete cases; in all the remaining instances, too, including that of brothers bewitching one another, it is invariably the older man who is accused; and finally, even where witchcraft is believed to strike at random, both victim and assailant are always males.[5] If then, the accusations of witchcraft are not invariably directed against a mother's brother resentful of his kinship obligations, they are always directed against a person likely to feel the resentment and anxieties that go with mature age; and though the motives imputed to the witch are less single-minded than the previous discussion would suggest, and the occasions thought to provoke them less conspicuously 'reminders' of the loss of virility, the witchcraft accusations remain a projection of the hostility of the old towards the young and of the frustrations springing from such envy of youth. This is perhaps borne out most strikingly by the following, admittedly atypical, instance. In one of the witchcraft cases recorded the alleged witch was a transvestite homosexual who had no livestock pro-

5. Only in one case, said to have occurred 'a long time ago', a woman was accused of having bewitched her brother's young son. But the people considered this a most unusual case, which they themselves were at a loss to explain. Nor were they certain of the circumstances.

perty, so that the question of inheritance did not arise; he was said to have bewitched his sister's young boy for no reason other than 'envy of a true male'.

Conclusions

Before attempting to summarize our findings, some general remarks may be interjected. The correlations suggested in the preceding discussion, between witchcraft beliefs and particular features of the cultures in which they appear (or fail to appear), are not the only ones that can be discovered, even in the few societies here considered. These other correlations have been neglected mainly because they seem to be of lesser relevance; more precisely, they appear to belong only to the background of facilitating or impeding conditions, and not to the core of basic causes and determinants. Two examples may be given.

The Korongo, who have no witchcraft, possess a full and explicit mythology concerned with explaining all the things in the world – the creation of man and animals, the origin of death and disease, the invention of fire, and so forth. The witchcraft-ridden Mesakin, on the other hand, have nothing of the kind. Now it may be argued that an explicit explanatory mythology presents a picture of the universe less obscure and puzzling than does a religion backed by no such intellectual efforts; their absence, therefore, may be taken to foster anxieties and a sense of insecurity, and hence, indirectly, to predispose people towards also accepting the mysterious and malevolent powers of witches. Yet it seems clear that this factor can only have contributory significance since too many instances could be quoted of cultures combining an explicit mythology with belief in witchcraft.

The second example refers to the dualistic nature of the Nupe witchcraft beliefs, which occur in a culture and idea system generally characterized by a marked bias for dichotomous conceptions. Among the Gwari, where the witchcraft beliefs ignore the polarity of the sexes, the idea system is similarly devoid of any dualistic trend. Witchcraft beliefs, then, and that wider orientation hang together logically. Here we are once more dealing merely with predispositions of a general kind – with ways of thinking about the universe and of ordering its phenomena. Nor, in fact, does this last correlation exhibit any causal nexus, however indirect or contributory, but only a general 'fit', a logical consistency, linking witchcraft beliefs with a general mode of thought.

Even so, an exhaustive analysis must obviously include these and further, additional factors also. More generally speaking, in any inquiry like ours, based upon 'concomitant variations', we must be prepared to reckon with several concomitants and multiple forms of interdependence, rather than with simple one-to-one correlations. That only studies of this far-reaching order can do justice to the complexity of social situations need hardly be defended. As regards the present inquiry, this ideal degree of completeness was beyond its scope. Perhaps, too, such completeness will often remain an ideal, unattainable in the present stage of our science.[6]

To turn to the conclusions proper:

1. The witchcraft beliefs here examined are causally as well as conspicuously related to specific anxieties and stresses arising in social life. The word 'conspicuously' is relevant because the witchcraft beliefs also indicate the precise nature of the social causes of which they are the symptoms – marriage-relations in Nupe, and the relationship between mother's brother and sister's son in Mesakin.

2. The anxieties and stresses need not arise from infantile experiences alone; rather, the present evidence tends to show that adult experiences, too, may be responsible for their emergence, and hence for the emergence also of the particular cultural features indicative of the anxieties and stresses.

3. The witchcraft beliefs of the Nupe and Mesakin seem to represent two basic potentialities or types. In Nupe, the witch is identified with the person openly and successfully setting aside the social values and thus denying the state of society desired and thought 'good'; attacks against witches are thus attacks upon the successful enemies of the ideal society. In Mesakin, the witch is identified with the person who cannot live up to the social values yet cannot openly rebel against them; the attacks upon witches are attacks upon the victims of the ideal society. In the first case one punishes the human agents responsible for the frustrations suffered by the believers in the ideal; in the second, one punishes and tries to obliterate the very fact that submission to the social ideal can give rise to frustration. In both types, then, the imputation of witchcraft serves to uphold the desired, if Utopian, state of society by identifying the witch with the transgressor – whether in successful action or in unadmitted, suppressed desire. Gwari witchcraft, so far as the somewhat incomplete data go, seems to stand halfway between these extremes. We may note in passing that if the Mesakin belief in witchcraft wielded by aggrieved brother's and sister's sons were more than 'theory', this would illustrate a third type of witchcraft in which the witch is identified with the victim of

6. The methodological issues touched upon above have been treated more fully in Nadel (1951, pp. 234, 258 ff.).

the 'transgressor' and the act of witchcraft with punitive action – though of a disproportionate and unlawful kind.

4. It is sometimes said that witchcraft beliefs 'canalize' hostility or 'deflect' hostile impulses into socially relatively harmless channels, that is, help society to function. Our evidence does not quite bear out this assumption. The witchcraft fears and accusations only accentuate concrete hostilities and in fact give them free rein. The concrete hostilities *are* 'canalized', in the sense that they are directed against a few scapegoats rather than against more numerous victims. But every witchcraft accusation or punishment of witches adds to the stresses of the society, through causing a serious disturbance of social life, entailing blood revenge, and the like. The accusations of witchcraft *do* deflect tensions and aggressive impulses; these are deflected, as it were, from the maladjusted institutions which cause them – marriage and the economic system in Nupe, kinship relations and the regulation of adolescence in Mesakin – so that these institutions can continue to operate. But they remain maladjusted and their continued operation only creates further tensions. Each persecution of witches no doubt relieves the tensions and stresses in a cathartic manner; but the relief is itself creative of new difficulties; equally, it is short-lived, for witchcraft cases go on happening all the time.

In brief, the witchcraft beliefs enable a society to go on functioning in a given manner, fraught with conflicts and contradictions which the society is helpless to resolve; the witchcraft beliefs thus absolve the society from a task apparently too difficult for it, namely, some radical readjustment. But from the observer's point of view it is doubtful if this is more than a poor and ineffectual palliative or can be called a solution 'less harmful' than open hostility or even the break-up of the existing institutions and relationships.

References

NADEL, S. F. (1935), 'Nupe witchcraft and anti-witchcraft', *Africa*, vol. 8.

NADEL, S. F. (1942), *A Black Byzantium*, Oxford U.P. for International Institute of African Languages and Cultures.

NADEL, S. F. (1947), *The Nuba*, Oxford U.P. for International African Institute.

NADEL, S. F. (1951) *The Foundations of Social Anthropology*, Free Press of Glencoe.

30. Max Marwick

Witchcraft as a Social Strain-Gauge

Excerpts from M. G. Marwick, 'Witchcraft as a social strain-gauge', *Australian Journal of Science*, vol. 26, 1964, pp. 263–8. Presidential Address, Section F, Australian and New Zealand Association for the Advancement of Science, Canberra Congress, January 1964.

I have decided to examine some aspects of the sociology of witchcraft and sorcery that appear to me to be in need of clearing up and pruning if we are to make further progress in this field. I am encouraged to attempt this task because I now find myself better situated geographically for the exploration of a problem that has interested me for some time, and among colleagues better fitted to advise me on it. The problem to which I am referring is the fact that, in Oceania, one of the well-founded propositions of the sociology of sorcery and witchcraft does not seem to apply.

Elsewhere, especially in Africa, it has been repeatedly recorded (for instance Evans-Pritchard, 1937, pp. 105–6; Krige and Krige, 1943, p. 263; Hunter, 1936, p. 307; Schapera, 1952, p. 49) that both believed attacks and accusations of witchcraft and sorcery occur only between persons already linked by close social bonds; but in Oceania it is more often reported (for instance, Elkin, 1937, *passim*; Hogbin, 1935, *passim*; Lawrence, 1952, p. 342, and 1955, p. 12; Meggitt, 1962, pp. 249, 325) that the sorcerer, who seems to be commoner here than the witch, is believed to direct his destructive magic *outside* his own group; and Oceanian accusations of sorcery, in the rare instances where they are recorded, seem to be consistent with this belief. A corollary to the generalization supported by the African material is that the relationship between alleged witch or sorcerer and believed victim is not only close but also strained; and this fact gives us a means of detecting the tension-points of a social structure by the frequency with which attacks of witchcraft and sorcery are believed to occur between persons standing in various relationships. Thus among the South-Eastern Bantu-speaking peoples of Africa accusations of witchcraft are reported to be directed against the women who have been brought in as wives into the patriarchal, virilocal settlement; and this is taken as a pointer to the peculiar difficulty of adjusting affinal relationships in a society dominated by the twin principles of patrilineal descent and polygyny associated with the house property complex (Hunter, 1936, p. 307; Gluckman, 1956, p. 98; Middleton and Winter, 1963, pp. 10, 11). The fact that, in different societies, different types of persons accuse each other of witchcraft and sorcery provides us with what I am here calling a social strain-gauge. Thus Wilson has discovered a different incidence of accusations of witchcraft among the South African Mpondo, who typically accuse their daughters-in-law, and the East African Nyakyusa, who typically accuse their unrelated village neighbours. She has attributed the difference to the differing social conditions resulting from the fact that the Mpondo live in small hamlets with their paternal kinsmen and the latter's wives; and the Nyakyusa, in villages with unrelated age-mates (Wilson, 1951b, *passim*).

My main objective in this paper will be to examine the problems that arise if we try to apply this social strain-gauge, developed largely in Africa, to detecting the characteristic tensions of Oceanian societies, and from this exercise, as well as from retrospective glances at some of the inadequacies of my own fieldwork in Africa, to formulate some hints for future investigators in this field. [...]

I have already mentioned one of the differences that seem to exist between Oceania and the rest of the world, but particularly Africa, in reports on the social directions believed to be taken by witchcraft and sorcery. In Africa these belief systems seem to reflect tensions within a community, whereas in Oceania they more commonly express tensions between communities. The question arises whether this difference is a real one or one resulting, in part at least, from different definitions of terms and different conventions of field-work. As my knowledge of Oceanian ethnography is still very limited, I shall inevitably ask questions rather than answer them. In any event a consideration of this difference will serve as a starting point for an examination of how field-work methods might be developed to meet the need for wider comparability of data and consequently more soundly established generalizations.

To ensure that field material is comparable between societies and regions, anthropologists have to be in agreement on what they propose to observe, and they have to be explicit about the steps they take in making and recording their observations. I would add that, in presenting the final results of the analysis of their material, they should ingenuously take the reader into their confidence rather than employ literary forms that obscure the nature of the sources of their information.

To be in agreement about what we are to observe we must first agree on definitions. In investigating the difference I have mentioned between the reported actions, real or believed, of Oceanian sorcerers and witches and those of other regions, I have encountered a difference in definition. With a few notable exceptions,[1] Oceanianists usually equate the term 'sorcery' with destructive magic in general and do not apply it exclusively, as Africanists do, to destructive magic applied anti-socially or illegitimately. The precedents for the different usage of terms by anthropologists in these two regions go back 30 or 40 years. In Oceania, Melanesia in particular, Malinowski (1926, pp. 93, 94) and Fortune (1932, pp. 167, 176) used the term 'sorcery' to mean destructive magic in all its possible applications, socially approved or not, and this wider definition has been followed by other writers dealing with this wider region, for example, Firth (1956, p. 156), Hogbin (1934, pp. 221, 223), R. M. Berndt (1962, pp. 208, 211) and Meggitt (1962, p. 325), although some of the more recent writers, such as Berndt and Meggitt, explicitly recognize two categories of sorcery, on the one hand legal or retaliatory and on the other illegitimate or socially condemned. In contrast to this, anthropologists working in Africa have found it profitable to follow the usage established by Evans-Pritchard (1931, p. 26; 1937, p. 21) when, with apparently no necessary intention of standardizing terminology for the whole continent, or for the whole anthropological profession, he used terms such as 'witchcraft', 'sorcery' and 'magic' as the English equivalents of clearly distinguished native concepts. Important for our present purposes is the fact that, faithfully translating Zande terms, he differentiated between witches and sorcerers on the score of personality types, motivation and method, and threw them together on the score of social or moral status. He reported that, whereas the Azande believe witches to have aberrant personalities permanently addicted to evil-doing and harming others by mystical means, they look upon sorcerers as ordinary folk driven by possibly passing fits of anger or envy and employing destructive magic to attain their anti-social ends. He summed up their important social or moral similarity in the statement, 'Both alike are enemies of men' (Evans-Pritchard, 1937, p. 387). In other words, the activities of both are deemed anti-social or illegitimate.

Thus it has come about that, where Oceanianists refer to 'legal sorcery' or 'retaliatory sorcery', Africanists refer to 'destructive magic put to legitimate use', as in the protection of property or the prevention of adultery, or to 'vengeance magic', and they reserve the term 'sorcery' for the illegitimate applications of destructive magic.

Even with questions of definition settled, different results can be ob-

1. For instance, Spencer and Gillen (1899, pp. 532–3) distinguish between the roles of medicine-man and sorcerer even if they recognize that these roles are sometimes combined in the same person; and Burridge (1960, pp. 59–71) uses the term 'sorcerer' exclusively for the person among the Tangu of New Guinea whose evil machinations are blamed for misfortunes.

tained from different methods of field-work. Even in the same society there are, as we all know, differences between what informants tell us and what, when we are fortunate enough to have the opportunity, we see actually happening. More than that, there are different degrees of generality and specificity in informants' statements in those fields of enquiry, such as opinion and belief, in which we are obliged to rely heavily on them because the object of investigation eludes direct observation. The existence of these different and divergent sources and levels of information in the same society is, of course, recognized in the injunction by the writers of *Notes and Queries on Anthropology* (Committee of the R.A.I., 1951, p. 36) that the direct observation of events and the interrogation of informants are complementary and interdependent methods. The fact that varied and conflicting information can be wrung from the same society by different approaches was brought home to me when I was among the Cewa of east-central Africa. It was brought home to me in a number of ways, of which I shall mention two that are relevant to my present theme. I found that the informants whom I consulted casually and non-systematically were in close agreement on two points relating to the mystical evil-doers of their society, *nfiti*, a term I translate as 'sorcerers' rather than 'witches'. They affirmed (a) that virtually all deaths resulted from sorcery; and (b) that most sorcerers were women. When I put this informal consensus of opinion to quasi-statistical investigation by having one of my African assistants interview ten men and nine women individually, the picture was not greatly altered. The averages of the estimates of this small sample of informants showed no significant sex differences, and were to the effect that (a) 93 per cent of 20 hypothetical deaths would have been the result of sorcery, and (b) the sex ratio of 20 hypothetical sorcerers would have been 27 per cent male to 73 per cent female.

I later compared these estimates with the proportions obtained from another source. During the course of my field-work I collected nearly 200 explanations given for actual cases of misfortunes, mostly deaths. The main features of these cases were tabulated and the totals gave very different answers to these two questions.

1. Only 55 per cent of the misfortunes were attributed to sorcery.

2. Within these, 58 per cent of the alleged sorcerers were male and 42 per cent female.

Informants may thus make very different statements about the same phenomenon when they are speaking generally and when they are referring to a series of specific instances.

Another source of variation is to be found in the different levels of reality of aspects of the phenomenon being investigated, this being a point of some importance in the sociology of witchcraft and sorcery. In this field, the primary data of the field-worker are behaviour episodes such as accusations, protective measures and (conceivably but rarely) malevolent rites. From these he can infer a secondary order of data, viz., the beliefs themselves, whose existence helps to explain the behaviour. He can confirm his conclusions about the nature of these beliefs by noting what informants may say about them when asked, or in some other way moved, to introspect and describe them. When we record the relationship between an alleged witch or sorcerer on the one hand and his believed victim on the other, we are clearly in the secondary realm of informants' beliefs, and the degree of reality we attribute to what we are recording will depend on the extent to which we may or may not share such beliefs. Assuming that we are entirely sceptical of the existence of witchcraft and that we have reservations about the frequency with which sorcery is actually practised, we are, when we consider the witch or sorcerer *vis-à-vis* his believed victim, dealing more or less with an imaginary relationship. As Berndt (1962, p. 224) remarks, this does not mean that we should disregard it because it is imaginary: 'If people believe these things occur, that is sufficient reason to consider them. We are not, as anthropologists, concerned primarily with the empirical "reality" of the situation, with whether or not it actually takes place; local belief in it gives that degree of reality which is required for our purposes.' By this he presumably means that we are justified in studying beliefs because they have real social concomitants.

I agree with this approach to the extent that a record of people's beliefs about the relationship between alleged witches or sorcerers and their victims provides us with an interesting summary of their insights into their own social system. By noting the frequency with which persons in various categories of social relationship come together as witch and victim or as sorcerer and victim, we are reading the society's home-made strain-gauges, which in my experience are more reliable in their assessment of tension-points than are the general statements of informants. What I would like to emphasize, however, is that there is no need to be satisfied with the study of the realm of belief alone. There are many real manifestations of these imaginary beliefs, such as accusations and protective measures, and therefore more objective strain-gauges for exploring social tensions can be employed. Some of us in Africa (Wilson, 1951a, pp. 198–205; Marwick, 1952, 1963, 1965; Mitchell, 1956, pp. 156 ff.; Turner, 1957, *passim*) mainly at Mitchell's instigation, have come to concentrate our attention on that important and hitherto somewhat neglected character in a witchcraft or sorcery drama, the accuser. Whereas the relationship between alleged sorcerer or witch and believed victim is usually an imaginary one, that between accuser and alleged sorcerer or witch is one with a greater degree of reality, belonging to the primary order of data I have referred to. Though the person designated as a witch or sorcerer may in fact be entirely innocent of any of the actions or characteristics implied in such a charge, the relationship between him and the accuser is nevertheless real. It is real enough for the field-worker to observe it on occasion, and, if the accusation takes place in his absence, to feel reasonably certain of establishing the existence of the relationship from informants' statements. It is true that this external, more objective strain-gauge gives recordings of tensions that are often similar to those indicated by the way in which persons of various relationships are brought together in the roles of witch and victim or sorcerer and victim, by, that is what I have called the home-made strain-gauges; but some interesting differences may appear. For instance, my Cewa case material shows a statistically significant difference in the relative age of alleged sorcerers, their believed victims and their accusers. Sorcerers are older than their believed victims and accusers are younger than those whom they accuse, this relative age distribution reflecting in part the fact that an accusation of sorcery is often involved in a younger man's bid for leadership of one of the segments into which a Cewa matrilineage usually divides.

Once again the application of these more objective measures, such as an examination of the kinds of social relationship between accuser and accused or even accused and believed victim, may give a picture of social tensions very different from that derived from informants' general statements. There is a saying among the Cewa, ŋombe ndi cipali cikutha ŵanthu, 'Cattle and polygyny finish people', meaning that quarrels over the ownership and inheritance of cattle (which are relatively recent additions to Cewa culture) and over polygyny are frequent, and often culminate in believed attacks of sorcery. When the first part of this statement is put to the more precise test of the strain-gauges I have mentioned, it is confirmed, though in rather small measure; for cattle are the objects of competition in about 15 per cent of the 80-odd cases in my sample of believed attacks by sorcery said to have been preceded by quarrels. The second part of the statement is not confirmed by the case material; for cases involving polygyny account for only 1 per cent of the total relationships between sorcerer and victim and for only 2 per cent of those between accuser and sorcerer.

This experience of having obtained different results from different research procedures in the same society has made me very interested in the precise source of an investigator's information and correspondingly sceptical of arguments he may put forward to account for the tensions he believes he has found to be characteristic of the social system concerned. If he claims that witchcraft is believed to operate between half-brothers in a patrilineal society and proceeds to explain this in terms of a house property complex, we are entitled, before we examine his argument, to ask whether the data it seeks to explain are derived from informants' statements, introspective or otherwise, or from records of a series of believed attacks by witches.

My experience of finding that different methods of enquiry yielded different answers to the same questions seems to have been shared by the late Professor Kluckhohn. In *Navaho Witchcraft* (1944, p. 55) he reported a tendency for distant and totally unrelated witches to be blamed for people's misfortunes. However, in a commentary he was kind enough to send me on one of my papers, he stated that his more recent data had not confirmed his earlier conclusions in this respect, and that gossip about local witches was commoner than his first impressions had led him to believe. I get the impression that his earlier finding may have been based on informants' general statements; and his later one, on the examination of specific instances. It may be that both answers are right: that people put the blame for misfortunes in general on to distant witches and for a specific misfortune on to someone within the community who is a natural choice because he is eccentric in some way or because the believed victim offended him.

Middleton and Winter (1963, pp. 10–11), suggest that, if witchcraft is invoked for explaining one type, e.g. generalized misfortune, sorcery will be invoked for the other type. I believe that this might fit Kluckhohn's material and I find a hint of it in my own. I feel, however, that the argument of Middleton and Winter depends too heavily on taking Evans-Pritchard's distinction to its logical conclusion, and is not sufficiently concerned with the comparability of the terminological usage of those whose works they review.

If within a single society, such as that of the Ceŵa or the Navaho, different estimates of the incidence of social tensions accrue from different ways of collecting data, how much more likely are there to be differences and inconsistencies between different ethnographic regions where terms are differently defined and where different conventions of field-work methods may have developed. I say 'may have developed' because it is not always possible to judge from an anthropologist's writings what methods he in fact used. Too much attention to euphony of prose in general, and too much concern with the dilemma between repetition and elegant variation in particular, sometimes drive anthropological writers into possibly graceful but certainly obscure statements that hide from their readers the sources of their data and the bases of their conclusions. Thus when Kuper (1947, p. 175) writes in reference to the Swazi that 'witchcraft and sorcery ... are usually selective and take toll of people between whom bonds already exist', we are entitled to ask her a few questions about how she came to this conclusion. It might be a rather hair-splitting revocation of the licence we would readily grant someone of her literary grace to ask whether her statement implies that she herself believes in Swazi witchcraft and sorcery. It would not, however, be an unfair question to ask whether this dramatic sentence rests on informants' general statements about witchcraft and sorcery, whether it summarizes their beliefs about a series of specific cases or whether it represents the pattern of accusations revealed by case material.

Similarly when Berndt (1962, p. 217), in discussing the position of a person who practises sorcery against a member of his own political unit, writes '... in spite of examples to the contrary the assumption is that sorcery is, and should be, directed outside the district', one wishes he were more explicit about whose assumption he is referring to and about the extent of the disagreement between this assumption and the examples to the contrary. And though the following passage from Fortune (1932, p. 127) is a reminder that the role of the anthropologist is empathetic exploration, in the sense of feeling himself in the position of a member of the society he is studying and then reporting on his feelings, one could wish for an indication of a more objective basis for so important a conclusion:

The whole life of the people is strongly coloured by a thorough absence of trust in neighbours and the practice of treachery beneath a show of friendliness. Every person goes in fear of the secret war, and on frequent occasion the fear breaks through the surface.

Any comparative sociology built on the comparison of incomparables is doomed to failure. We cannot judge whether our comparisons are safe unless field workers are more explicit on how they collected their data and how they came to their conclusions.

In my cursory search through Oceanian ethnography for references to witchcraft and sorcery, I have found that most anthropologists in this region have not made a practice of systematically collecting specific instances of either believed attacks of sorcery or witchcraft or of observed or observable accusations of these. For instance, in an otherwise admirable analysis of the position of the sorcerer among the Tangu, Burridge

(1960, pp. 59–71) offers only hypothetical cases and, apart from saying (on p. 64) that 'first suspects are those most strange or distant', omits any information on how the believed sorcerer was related to his accuser and to his believed victim. Of the authors whose works I have examined, Berndt (1962, pp. 214–28) offers the most detailed illustrative cases; but only seven of these have to do with sorcery, and he does not indicate to which of the three periods mentioned in his Introduction (pp. 8–9) each case belongs.

A common failing in the case reports I have encountered in the Oceanian literature is an omission to specify the social relationships between the main characters concerned. This may be partly the result of the fact that most cases of sorcery reported are ones in which it is believed to have taken its traditional social direction, i.e. between members of different groups rather than of the same group; and in this type of case, if the ethnographer gives the group affiliations of the main characters, he is providing most of what is material to their social relationships. This applies to six of Berndt's seven cases. However, in the seventh case, which involves people in the same village (Berndt, 1962, p. 223), no details of social relationships are mentioned except that the sorcery was used by men to punish two women who had trespassed on an exclusively male preserve.

Sometimes Oceanian authors' incidental references to specific cases of sorcery do not necessarily confirm more general statements about the direction that attacks are believed usually to take. Thus Meggitt (1962, p. 325), who explicitly states that, among the Walbiri, it is usually someone outside the local community who is suspected of sorcery (though it can be a relative), happens to give two instances, one real and one hypothetical, of the believed operation of sorcery, and neither happens to fit the general pattern. The first (p. 176) involves an accusation between two women in the same community, the potential co-wives of an intended polygynist; and the second (p. 246) describes how a punitive party in pursuit of a wrong-doer from their own community who is seeking refuge in the territory of another community might confine itself to performing sorcery against him from a distance.

On the other hand there are a number of instances where the incidental illustration does confirm the general Oceanian belief that sorcery operates between communities rather than within the same community. Spencer and Gillen (1899, p. 533) report:

News was brought into the camp that a very celebrated old man had died far away out to the west. His death was due simply to senile decay, but along with the news of his decease word was brought that he had been killed by a charmed stick pointed at him by a man of a distant group, the locality of which was stated with certainty.

Reay (1959, pp. 136 ff.) makes some references to the witch's being suspected of cooperating with an enemy group. The Kuma witch is therefore in the interesting position of resembling the African witch or sorcerer by being the enemy within the community; and yet he conforms to the general Oceanian trend for beliefs in witchcraft or sorcery to provide a medium of inter-community strife. Two of the cases that occurred when Hogbin (1935) was on Wogeo, and the majority of other cases reported to him there, were ones in which a person from another district was held to have been responsible for the death of the victim. The Garia sorcery-feud reported by Lawrence (1952, p. 343) is consistent with his general finding (1955, pp. 11, 14) that sorcery is usually suspected outside one's 'security circle' of close kinsmen and in this respect it resembles the blood feud. Oliver (1955, pp. 241, 242), on the other hand, cites a case in illustration of his statement that 'suspicion is not limited to persons living *outside* the village'.

From this inadequate array of case material that I have picked up in my hasty and superficial examination of Oceanian literature, it would appear that the general statement that Oceanian sorcerers are usually believed to be outside the communities of their victims and presumably of their accusers, though at present sometimes supported by undisclosed if not dubious evidence, is likely to be sustained by more systematically collected case material. It may well be that social strain-gauges which in Africa have usually detected tensions within a community may serve in this region as measures of relationships between different social groups. As Berndt (1962, p. 209) puts it (although his definition of sorcery is wider than mine), 'Sorcery, like warfare, can throw into relief all those conflicts which are an accompaniment of inter-district relations'.

There certainly seems to be a close intertwining in this region of the mystical aggression of sorcery and the real aggression of war. Berndt (1962, p. 223) uses the presence or absence of associated physical aggression as the criterion for distinguishing his two major categories of sorcery in the Eastern Highlands of New Guinea; and the Australian Aboriginal techniques of sorcery are often described as though they were actual physical attacks on the victim (e.g. Spencer and Gillen, 1899, p. 536; Warner, 1937, pp. 194–206). In the Australian literature the sorcerer is sometimes referred to as the 'murderer' (Elkin, 1937, *passim*), and his dispatch by the emu-padded allies of the victim is an important part of sorcery-lore. It may be that the association between physical aggression and sorcery has had a part in the emergence of the wider definition of sorcery adopted by Oceanianists; for whether the destructive magic used is illegitimate or not depends upon the viewpoint of one or other of the groups concerned.

But all this is speculation. So far as I am aware, no book comparable with Evans-Pritchard's study of Azande witchcraft nor even Kluckhohn's of Navaho witchcraft has yet been written on the sorcery and witchcraft of an Oceanian people. Despite its title, Fortune's book on Dobu is largely confined to description of sorcerers' techniques and contains remarkably little that could be used for the detailed sociological analysis of sorcery. It is to be hoped that when such an analysis is made of the sorcery and witchcraft of an Oceanian people, the material used will include specific cases as well as informants' general estimates of the ways of sorcerers and witches, and that the style will not prevent the reader from judging which line of evidence is being led.

One of the problems relating to the use as strain-gauges of statistics derived from cases of accusation arises from the fact that the incidence of accusations of sorcery or witchcraft in various relationship categories is of complex determination. A high absolute frequency of accusations in a particular category, say that between matrilateral parallel cousins in a matrilineal society, is an index, not only of the degree of tension characteristic of the relationship, but also of the sheer frequency of interaction in it. Thus, to argue that a high frequency of accusations in a given relationship-category indicates a high degree of social tension in it is as naïve as contending that divorce is a more serious problem in the United Kingdom than among South African whites because the absolute number of divorces in any one year is greater in the former than in the latter population. Just as divorces can be compared only when considered as rates, i.e. in relation to the universe in which they occur, such as the total population or the total married population, so must accusations of sorcery and witchcraft somehow be related to the universe of social interactions in which they occur. In short, a person may accuse a cousin more frequently than a brother simply because he has far more cousins than brothers with whom he interacts; and the higher frequency for cousins does not necessarily indicate a tenser relationship with them than with brothers unless the differing sizes of the two universes of interaction can somehow be controlled. I cannot offer a solution to this problem which I have set out more fully elsewhere (Marwick, 1961, 1963, 1965), but I commend it to statistically minded social scientists.

What lessons are to be learned from the comparison I have attempted and from my experience and that of some of my colleagues in Africa? I suggest that the person who carries out field-work in preparation for the book on the sociology of Oceanian sorcery or witchcraft for which we are waiting might bear the following points in mind. Firstly, terms such as sorcery or witchcraft must be clearly defined and the differentiation between destructive magic socially approved and that socially condemned should be maintained; for the difference between them is for obvious reasons material to sociological analysis. Secondly, the well-established principle of comparing the ideal with the real applies in this field of inquiry as much as in any other, and should not be forgotten simply because it is obvious. The general statements that informants make about sorcerers and witches must be compared with specific ones they make in reference to particular cases and with what the ethnographer may observe of their and other people's actions. Thirdly, beliefs in sorcery and witchcraft invariably have a social setting in the sense that they mediate, though they sometimes complicate, the living together of people in the on-going process we call a society. They do this by providing a means of expressing tense social relationships. Sometimes they relieve the tension. Sometimes they end the relationship when it has become redundant and insupportable and yet, because of emotional investment in it, indissoluble by the quiet process of closing a contract. They also mediate social living by dramatizing moral values both in the retrospective reconstructions of disturbed relationships between the believed victim and his alleged attacker and in the negative example of the witch or the sorcerer who, by the African definition at least, is someone beyond the pale, the personification of evil, and a bogey man with which to frighten naughty children.

These considerations mean that, fourthly, the field-worker, in collecting his material, has to pay particular attention to the three central characters, the accuser, the alleged sorcerer or witch and the believed victim, and to the social relationships, the rivalries and the alliances between them.

Finally, the ethnographer should again apply a well-established canon of field-work to his particular topic, i.e. when he cannot observe the relationships believed to be involved in a particular instance of misfortune, and even when he can, and wishes to supplement his observations, he should not rely on only one informant for each case, but should record the interpretations of different persons differently placed in relation to the central characters.

I feel that, if the strain-gauge I have described is used according to these prescriptions, it may, through making field material from different societies more profitably comparable, advance our knowledge of the sociology of tension and conflict and once again demonstrate that the role of anthropology is the pursuit of exotic customs not merely for their own sake but for what they can contribute to the understanding of human behaviour in general.

References

BERNDT, R. M. (1962), *Excess and Restraint*, University of Chicago Press.

BURRIDGE, K. (1960), *Mambu*, Methuen.

COMMITTEE OF THE ROYAL ANTHROPOLOGICAL INSTITUTE (1951), *Notes and Queries on Anthropology*, R.A.I., 6th edn.

ELKIN, A. P. (1937), 'Beliefs and practices connected with death in north-eastern and western South Australia', *Oceania*, vol. 7.

EVANS-PRITCHARD, E. E. (1931), 'Sorcery and native opinion', *Africa*, vol. 4, no. 1.

EVANS-PRITCHARD, E. E. (1937), *Witchcraft, Oracles and Magic among the Azande*, Clarendon Press.

FIRTH, R. (1956), *Hyman Types*, Nelson, rev. edn.

FORTUNE, R. F. (1932), *Sorcerers of Dobu*, Routledge.

GLUCKMAN, M. (1956), *Custom and Conflict in Africa*, Blackwell.

HOGBIN, H. I. (1934), *Law and Order in Polynesia*, Christophers.

HOGBIN, H. I. (1935), 'Sorcery and administration', *Oceania*, vol. 6.

HUNTER (now WILSON), M. (1936), *Reaction to Conquest*, Oxford U.P. for International Institute of African Languages and Cultures.

KLUCKHOHN, C. (1944), *Navaho Witchcraft*, Papers of the Peabody Museum of American Archaeology and Ethnology, Harvard University, vol. 22; Beacon Press, 1962.

KRIGE, E. J. and KRIGE, J. D. (1943), *The Realm of a Rain Queen*, Oxford U.P. for International Institute of African Languages and Cultures.

KUPER, H. (1947), *An African Aristocracy*, Oxford U.P. for International African Institute.

LAWRENCE, P. (1952), 'Sorcery among the Garia', *South Pacific*, vol. 6.

LAWRENCE, P. (1955), *Land Tenure among the Garia*, Australian National University, Social Science Monographs, no. 4.

MALINOWSKI, B. (1926), *Crime and Custom in Savage Society*, Kegan Paul, Trench, Trubner.

MARWICK, M. G. (1952), 'The social context of Cewa witch-beliefs', *Africa*, vol. 22.

MARWICK, M. G. (1961), 'Some problems in the sociology of sorcery and witchcraft', Paper contributed to Third International African Seminar, Salisbury, Rhodesia, December (subsequently published as ch. 9 of M. Fortes and G. Dieterlen (eds), *African Systems of Thought*, Oxford U.P. for International African Institute, 1965).

MARWICK, M. G. (1963), 'The sociology of sorcery in a central African tribe', *African Studies*, vol. 22.

MARWICK, M. G. (1965), *Sorcery in its Social Setting*, Manchester U.P.

MEGGITT, M. J. (1962), *Desert People*, Angus & Robertson.

MIDDLETON, J., and WINTER, E. H. (eds) (1963), *Witchcraft and Sorcery in East Africa*, Routledge & Kegan Paul.

MITCHELL, J. C. (1956), *The Yao Village*, Manchester U.P. for Rhodes-Livingstone Institute.

OLIVER, D. L. (1955), *A Solomon Island Society*, Harvard U.P.

REAY, M. (1959), *The Kuma*, Melbourne U.P. for the Australian National University.

SCHAPERA, I. (1952), 'Sorcery and witchcraft in Bechuanaland', *African Affairs*, vol. 51, no. 41.

SPENCER, B., and GILLEN, F. J. (1899), *The Native Tribes of Central Australia*, Macmillan.

TURNER, V. W. (1957), *Schism and Continuity in an African Society*, Manchester U.P. for Rhodes-Livingstone Institute.

WARNER, W. L. (1937), *A Black Civilization*, Harper.

WILSON (née HUNTER), M. (1951a), *Good Company*, Oxford U.P. for International African Institute.

WILSON (née HUNTER), M. (1951b), 'Witch-beliefs and social structure', *American Journal of Sociology*, vol. 56, p. 307.

31. J. R. Crawford

The Consequences of Allegation

Excerpts from J. R. Crawford, *Witchcraft and Sorcery in Rhodesia*, Oxford University Press for International African Institute, 1967, pp. 160–61, 278–90.

Introduction

There are a number of aspects of wizardry allegations. [...] One problem is the extent to which fear of an allegation of wizardry assists to ensure conformity with the social norms of the community. Another, and perhaps greater problem, is whether allegations of wizardry are mere manifestations of social tensions or whether they are something more than this. Some social anthropologists write of wizardry allegations as if they were of little more significance than signposts to social friction – almost like a rash in the case of measles. On this aspect of the matter I shall let the case material speak for itself. Over and over again it is difficult not to come to the conclusion that the sequence of events related could not have come about had the accusation which was made not been made in the idiom of wizardry. Then there is the question as to whether persons deliberately or unconsciously make use of the wizardry allegation in the manipulation of the structure of society to their own advantage. Are wizardry allegations, in other words, 'merely a stereotyped response to misfortune' or are they 'an instrumental technique'? (See Beattie in Middleton and Winter, 1963, p. 31.) Do wizardry allegations resolve social tensions or intensify them? There are no doubt many other questions also. To some it is possible to suggest an answer, but more often the material at my disposal is insufficient or ambiguous. It may, perhaps, be wrong to assume that there is any very clear-cut answer. It is probable, for example, that among the Shona an allegation of wizardry is often no more than a stereotyped response to misfortune. It would, I think, be quite wrong to deduce from this that it can never be used as an instrumental technique. In certain circumstances, for example in the case of rivalry for political office, accusations of wizardry are clearly used as an instrumental technique.

In the following pages I shall give an account of a number of wizardry allegations, mostly taken from cases which have come before the courts. The accounts will give an illustration of the nature of the material used by me, the manner in which accusations may take place and, I hope, something of the atmosphere surrounding an accusation. It is very easy to discuss wizardry accusations in the clinical atmosphere of a sociological study, but it is as well to keep in mind the emotions of hate and terror, the feelings of doubt and of certainty, the moments of rationality and irrationality which accompany an allegation and of the brutality which may eventuate. [...]

The Normative Aspects of Wizardry Belief

A number of cases have been referred to where a breach of the social norms has been followed by an accusation of wizardry. In some cases it would seem that the breach has something to do with the accusation, in other cases after the allegation has been made the fact that the person accused has acted in an improper manner is seen as evidence confirming the truth of the accusation. On the face of it, if accusations follow breaches of the social norms, the fear of an accusation might be expected to operate as a sanction against the breach of these norms. Obviously it is important to establish whether, in fact, the fear of an accusation is a sanction against anti-social behaviour. Many anthropologists assume that it must be such a sanction. While, however, it is usually easy enough to decide why people depart from the social norms of the community in which they live, it is less easy to establish the reasons why people conform to those norms, although it is easy enough to appreciate that a group of persons can hardly live together as a group unless they do conform to certain standards of conduct. A large part is notoriously played by informal sanctions such as public opinion, reciprocity and so forth. Of course formal sanctions are, on occasion, necessary. In our own society the thief no doubt ordinarily appreciates the anti-social effect of his conduct but the financial rewards of his crime are such as to render this sort of conduct attractive notwithstanding this. It is, for this reason, necessary to impose an institutionalized sanction in the form of criminal punishment. A formal sanction such as this is no less a sanction because the chances of punishment for any particular offence are small as they are, in our own society, in the case of certain driving offences. It is, therefore, not fatal to the theory that wizardry accusations serve as a social sanction, that an accusation by no means necessarily, or even usually, follows certain sorts of anti-social conduct. What does, however, create a measure of doubt is that the types of anti-social conduct in respect of which the allegations of wizardry is supposed to serve as a social sanction are, among the Shona, the types of conduct which Shona society has not

315

singled out as being actionable wrongs. It is this very class of conduct which rural communities throughout the world control effectively whether or not they believe in wizardry. When I have discussed political or other matters with a Shona it is usually clear that public opinion or, as he would express it 'what the people say or think' is a matter which plays a considerable part, and often a conscious part, in the formation of his own views and attitudes. It is abundantly clear that, whether or not the fear of a wizardry allegation is, among the Shona, a sanction against social conduct, it is possible to explain the high degree of social conformity which exists among the Shona without invoking wizardry beliefs. Sorcery however is a sanction which can be of importance, particularly in the enforcement of a contract or in quasi-contractual relationships. If an employee, for example, finds a replacement while away on holiday, fear of sorcery may ensure that he regains his post on return.

Manipulating Public Opinion

While there may be a measure of doubt as to whether wizardry beliefs are an effective social sanction there can be no doubt that such beliefs can be used as a means of manipulating public opinion in much the same manner as allegations of heresy in medieval Europe or Communism in modern America and Southern Africa were, and are, used. Malice can be expressed as an allegation of wizardry and will find credence if the person against whom hostility is expressed is unpopular, particularly if he has also acted in an unusual manner. It is thus easy to marshal public opinion against the social non-conformist. The person manipulating public opinion in this manner need not do so consciously. If one person dislikes another he is likely to attribute to him evil ways. After all, everyone knows himself to be a reasonable person and he is hardly likely to dislike someone unless he merits this dislike! If the person has evil ways, one tends to define these in terms of one's social stereotype of an evil person, for most of us do our thinking in stereotypes. If one is a Shona, the stereotype is that of a wizard. When the suspect's behaviour is examined, it is found that he has acted suspiciously in disregarding social norms, and who of us always does everything he should do? This confirms one's views and, that being so, it is one's plain duty to tell one's friends of the danger in their midst. Whether or not one's friends will believe what they are told will depend in part on whether other people want to believe the accusation and whether reasonable grounds for suspicion exist. It is obviously easier to turn public opinion against an unpopular than a popular person. If the accusation is believed the accuser has successfully marshalled public opinion against the object of his dislike which is what he, consciously or unconsciously, set out to do. A person is most likely to dislike persons who are sexually, economically or politically in competition with him and the accusation of wizardry affords a technique for marshalling public opinion against the rival in what is, essentially, a private quarrel. It is suggested that beliefs in wizardry are more important as a means of social manipulation than as a sanction against anti-social conduct. An allegation of wizardry by a diviner is, however, not necessarily such an attempt at social manipulation but – in common with other accusations of wizardry – I see it as an attempt to associate the community as a whole with an event. There can be no doubt that the effect of an allegation of wizardry by a diviner is to make the divination the concern of the community as a whole. If this is the effect, it is probable that this is also the end desired. In the case of a professional diviner, the motive for the allegation may, no doubt, be primarily to enhance his prestige. An allegation of wizardry is, therefore, an appeal to the moral feelings of the community in an attempt to involve the community emotionally in a certain state of affairs. The reasons for making the appeal depend on the person making it and the events of the moment.

Cathartic Effect?

It is frequently suggested that wizardry allegations have a 'cathartic effect' in resolving the social tensions of a community. A moment's thought will convince one that this cannot be entirely true. A mere accusation of wizardry can do nothing except worsen social relationships. Immediately, of course, it will worsen relationships between the accuser and the accused. If some believe the accusation and some do not, then the community is likely to be divided into opposing groups, normally, no doubt, into groups reflecting a pre-existing segmentation or potential segmentation in the community. It is only 'proof' of an accusation – and, what is more, 'proof' of a nature which will convince everyone in the community or in a section of it – which can serve to resolve social tensions whether by the finding of a scapegoat, by the crystallization of the various interest groups or the exculpation of the suspect from all guilt. It is, therefore, vitally important to distinguish between the accusation of wizardry and the 'proof' of wizardry. Here, there can be no doubt that, in the past, the most convincing 'proof' of wizardry was, in the case of the Shona, the poison ordeal. Shona attitudes were very similar to those of a number of other African peoples. Douglas (in Middleton and Winter, 1963, p. 123) has a suggestion of some interest about the poison ordeal amongst groups in Central Africa north of the Zambesi and, in particular, about the Lele of the Kasai. She states that, in the past, the poison ordeal was the only sure way of indicating a sorcerer. If suspicion fell upon a young man he could move away from his village but the position was not the same with an old man who found it less easy to move and whose village became a closed community. If his quarrel built up cumulatively he could easily 'acquire the reputation of a fully committed sorcerer, responsible for every death in the village'. An ordinary oracle could not clear the name of such a person but the poison oracle could. In the absence of such an oracle he faced social extinction and, probably, social exile. In addition, if his name was not cleared his clansmen were faced with the payment of blood compensation. The ordeal provided a solution to the problem. If the person concerned survived the ordeal he could demand compensation, and make a new start. If he did not survive and died, his kin and supporters had no option but to pay compensation and, when this was done, there could again be a new start. With the prohibition of the ordeal by the Colonial Administration there remained no way of resolving social tensions by recourse to the ordeal and no one could be certain who was, and who was not, a sorcerer. The situation became intolerable. A way out of the problem was found in the various anti-sorcery cults which spread through Lele country at various intervals from 1910 onwards. By initiation into the cult, of which the *Kabenga-Benga* is the most recent, a person was cleansed of sorcery. Should a person, once initiated, practise sorcery again it was believed he would die. The cults, therefore, enabled a person to be cleansed of suspicion and to re-integrate himself into the community and also removed the tensions and suspicions which were making community life increasingly intolerable. Inevitably these cults collapse in the end as the theory that only sorcerers who have been initiated die becomes inadequate to account for the deaths of, for example, small children. Each cult becomes, in turn, discredited.

Divinatory Role of Pentecostal Churches

Among the Shona, diviners have never been supposed to be infallible, although they may have considerable reputations. The only way a person could finally clear himself of suspicion of wizardry was by means of the poison ordeal. I have already shown how women, in areas where the ordeal still survived may, of their own volition, seek the ordeal as a means of freeing themselves from an intolerable situation. Now that the ordeal is prohibited, recourse to it is, in most parts of the country, impossible. The

Shona solution to the problem has not been, however, the development of cults on the lines of the *Kabenga-Benga* cult or of those described by Marwick (1950, p. 2) or Richards (1935, pp. 448–61) although the *muchapi* movement, when it first spread to Rhodesia before the last war, was probably very similar. *Muchapi* is still known and persons still administer it; but the movement has long ago spent its force. Instead, the role of the anti-sorcery movements among the Lele is, among the Shona, largely taken by the Pentecostal Churches. I have previously described the manner in which these churches cleanse initiates of wizardry and divine wizardry. Some churches have even developed new forms of the ordeal; here the manner in which the churches have tried to make good the vacuum occasioned by the prohibition of the poison ordeal is particularly evident. If one accepts, as a believer must, that a Pentecostal prophet is speaking with the voice of God, his pronouncements are clearly infallible, unlike those of a doctor diviner. A prophet accepts no money for his services – at any rate directly – and that he has no obvious reason to tell lies is an added reason for credence. The prophet in his bright robes, with a mitre on his head and a crozier in his hand, is a much more impressive figure than the ordinary Shona diviner and his psychological impact on his congregation correspondingly greater. The Pentecostal Churches do not, of course, afford an entirely satisfactory alternative to the poison ordeal because many of them are comparatively small and not everyone belongs to them. Even if the church is large, the congregations are often widely scattered and their followers are seldom dominant in any particular community. Because of this, and because they cannot convince everyone of their power, the churches are probably less effective than the *Kabenga-Benga* cult or the poison ordeal in resolving social tensions. On the other hand, if a person becomes disillusioned with the church he can always transfer his allegiance to another. One does not, therefore, in Mashonaland get the widespread cycles of belief and disbelief which occur among the Lele, although there is undoubtedly a pattern of growth and decay among the individual Pentecostal Churches. From the point of view of the person suspected of wizardry the joining of a Pentecostal Church may not free him of suspicion as far as non-believers are concerned; but at least he is joining a group with whom normal social relationships can be established.

It should be stressed that the Pentecostal Churches are more than an anti-wizardry cult, for they manifestly have other social roles as well. Of these, perhaps the most important is their role in helping the Shona to adapt to the modern world and to provide an acceptable *tertium quid* between the beliefs of the past, and the beliefs of the various Europeansponsored Christian Missions with their discipline, prohibition of polygamy and their European background. The Pentecostal Churches have often an advantage over the Mission Churches, merely because they are African.

The Shona have developed a reasonably coherent cosmology and wizardry beliefs are in accord with their general religious beliefs. The religious beliefs do not, however, appear to be essential for the existence or survival of wizardry beliefs. If the religious framework of Shona wizardry beliefs were an essential part of those beliefs one would expect wizardry beliefs in societies with religious beliefs differing from those of the Shona to take a very different form. This is not the case. Again, if the religious aspect of Shona wizardry beliefs were an essential part of these beliefs they would be abandoned on the acceptance of Christianity. This is not so – the various spirits which the Shona believe are associated with wizardry are simply transformed into Biblical devils. It is because wizardry, although explained in terms of Shona religious beliefs, is not dependent for survival upon those beliefs that it shows such remarkable resilience to social change. As long as children and young people continue to die it is unlikely that belief in wizardry will be abandoned. The main importance of Shona religious ideas today (as far as we are concerned with them in this book), at least in the case of persons who no longer find these beliefs adequate for their needs, is that – being essentially belief in various forms of spirit possession – they prepare a person seeking fresh religious experience for the reception of beliefs of Pentecostal type. Traditional Shona beliefs also ensure that, where a church of essentially non-Pentecostal type is joined, it will tend, if controlled to any extent by the Shona, to conform increasingly to the Pentecostal pattern. The life of most of the Shona is today rather drab and in the circumstances, and even without the background of traditional beliefs, the colour and excitement of ceremonies of Pentecostal character would undoubtedly prove attractive.

Witchcraft and the Moral Community

An element which Shona witchcraft beliefs share with the beliefs of many other societies is the ascribing to a witch of perverted conduct or conduct which is an inversion of that approved of by society. An example of perverted conduct is the Shona witch's predilection for human meat; a food strongly disliked by ordinary men. It has been suggested by Winter (Middleton and Winter, 1963, p. 292) when discussing a similar situation among the Ambo that one of the reasons why it is believed that a witch can only harm persons within the village or neighbourhood is to be found in the fact that a witch's conduct is believed to be an inversion of socially acceptable conduct. The local community is a moral community where persons must conduct themselves in their relations with one another in an acceptable way and in accordance with the concepts of society in regard to good neighbourliness. It is, therefore, unnatural for a person living in the community to seek to harm it. On the other hand, communities living outside the neighbourhood are, among the Ambo, essentially hostile and, therefore, there is nothing unnatural about an attempt to harm a member of these groups. No question of inverted conduct and no question of witchcraft arises.

However probable this theory may seem among the Ambo it gives rise to difficulties if one attempts to apply it to the Shona. In the past the moral community of the Shona embraced at least the tribe and it is probably wider now. One was expected to conduct oneself in a proper way with other tribesmen even if they were not members of the village. In fact, members of the same tribe usually regarded one another as kinsmen even if blood relationship could not be established. Witchcraft allegations, however, as among the Ambo, are confined to the village or neighbourhood. While I am not suggesting that Winter's theory is wrong, for society is complex and there is often no single cause for any observed pattern of conduct, I think that, at least among the Shona, the reason for the confining of witchcraft allegations to a comparatively small territorial area is best explained – not in terms of any 'moral' community – but in the fact commented upon by many social anthropologists that accusations are most likely in situations of intimate personal contact where the status of the persons concerned is more or less equal. In rural areas one only normally comes into intimate personal contact of this nature with persons living in the same locality. Wizardry allegations also occur in factories and rural schools which cannot be regarded as 'moral communities' save in a rather extended sense of the term. The concept of the 'moral community' does not, in any event, explain why accusations are made against certain members of the community and not against others. It is surely best to apply Occam's razor and find the explanation for both the pattern of accusations within the community and the limitation of accusations to a village or neighbourhood in inter-personal contact and rivalry rather than to find a different reason for each. Even if Winter's theory is unsatisfactory the concept of the moral community is not without relevance as far as the study of Shona wizardry allegations is concerned. There is, among the Shona, nothing improper in the use of sorcery or magic to destroy a member of a hostile group. The person who uses such means against an enemy is not a wizard, as would be the case if he turned his supernatural weapons against one of his own community. Indeed, the ability to fortify one's own group magically against the machinations of an enemy group is obviously a socially desirable ability. In the past, no army would have set out to attack another group without being adequately fortified by means of magic.

Shona wizardry beliefs throw light upon what the Shona conceive the 'moral community' to be; but I am a little doubtful if the concept of the 'moral community' has any great effect as far as the pattern of wizardry allegations is concerned.

There is no need to say much here about the distinction the Shona make – but do not well express – between witchcraft and sorcery. I believe, however, that I have shown that this distinction is vital for the understanding of the nature of witchcraft allegations. The importance of the distinction arises from the fact that witchcraft allegations are made against women and sorcery allegations, which are less serious, are made against men. In a patrilineal society with virilocal marriage this inevitably means that witchcraft allegations are, in the main, made against the wives and mothers of lineage members and that sorcery allegations are made against lineage members. In other words, the solidarity of the lineage is maintained at the expense of non-lineage members. It is essential for my argument in this respect to show that witchcraft allegations against women are socially of greater consequence and are more serious from the point of view of the person accused of witchcraft than is the case where a sorcery allegation is made against a man. The figures given previously show, with very little doubt, that allegations resulting in serious consequences to the person accused are more often made against a woman than a man. This, of course, does not establish my case as one might, for example, argue that this does not mean that allegations made against a woman are, in themselves, more serious than those made against a man; all that is shown is that women are in a position of inferiority in Shona society and are thus less capable of coping with the situation which arises. There may be something in this argument; but in the few court records where a witchcraft allegation, as opposed to a sorcery allegation, was made against a man, the consequences to that man appear to have been as serious as is frequently the case in allegations made against women. In any event, even if an able-bodied Shona man can avoid the consequences of a believed allegation of witchcraft or sorcery by moving elsewhere, an old man, unless he is a chief or headman, is hardly in a better position to cope with his environment than a woman. In the result, therefore, the evidence in my opinion supports the view that the consequences of an allegation against a woman are more serious than against a man because the allegation against a woman is a more serious allegation, rather than the view that the differing consequences are merely the direct consequence of a difference in social status.

Accusations and Social Tension

I have referred on a number of occasions to allegations of wizardry which I have stated have arisen from or been generated by social conflicts of various sorts. The question now arises as to whether this is an altogether accurate statement of the origin of the accusation of wizardry and also whether it is entirely correct to regard an accusation of wizardry as an expression of social conflict. Where co-wives are competing for the favours of their husband and accuse one another of wizardry, it is very difficult not to regard the accusation as being a reflection of social conflict – although it may be other things as well. In such circumstances it would appear to be not incorrect to state that the allegation arises from the conflict. Where, however, the diviner is consulted about the death of a child and divines the cause of the death to be wizardry, naming a particular person to be a wizard, it is clear that the allegation does not arise directly from any social conflict. The diviner may, of course, be acquainted with, or may discover, the social conflicts in the community from which his consultants come and may make use of this knowledge when indicating a wizard; but it is clearly not correct to regard the accusation as arising from any particular social conflict. In both the case of the accusation by a co-wife and the accusation by a diviner the accusation will reflect social conflict in the community; but in the first case there is a direct causal link between the conflict and the accusation. In the second there is not. The diviner need not have divined the presence of wizardry at all and, if wizardry were divined, need not have named the person he did name as a wizard. A social conflict may have guided, but it did not determine, the diviner's choice. Although the two types of accusation have a different origin they both, as I suggested previously, are in essence an appeal to the community with the intention of involving the community as a whole emotionally in some particular occurrence.

Too much emphasis on the allegation of wizardry as being the reflection of social tension leads one into the error of supposing that an allegation is a mere symptom of social malaise and is not, in itself, a dynamic force in the community. There are, indeed, many social anthropologists who would appear to overlook the dynamic importance of wizardry allegations. An allegation of wizardry may originally reflect a state of enmity between two persons but, once made, a chain of events may be set in motion which can lead rapidly to the most unforeseen and often tragic consequences. There is no reason to suppose that any other form of expression of hostility would ordinarily result in the tragedies occasioned by an allegation of wizardry, nor is it easy to think, in the context of Shona society, of any other type of accusation which can so readily embitter social relations and increase social tension. One can no more regard wizardry allegations as a mere expression of social conflict than the all too common beer drink stabbings among the Shona. The accusation, as in the case of the stabbing, reflects social conflict; but the deed itself may entirely alter the nature of the conflict and, in any event, adds to it an entirely new dimension.

If the allegation of wizardry is primarily a device for involving the community as a whole in some particular happening then the reason why some sorts of social conflict result in a wizardry allegation is – at least in part – explained. One would really only expect allegations to occur in situations where the marshalling of public opinion against an offender serves a useful purpose. If, for example, one's daughter is seduced, a Shona man's primary interest is in obtaining recompense. The marshalling of public opinion against the offender, particularly if he is a member of another community (for public opinion is most effective within the community) does not serve any very real purpose, as the only reasonable way to recover damages, if the seducer will not willingly pay them, is action in the chief's court. What is primarily required is not emotion, but a good case. Of course, if legal proceedings become frustrated, as we have seen, an appeal to public opinion made in the idiom of wizardry is not unlikely. I would also suggest one reason why a commoner would not normally make an allegation of wizardry against a chief, and that is that the marshalling of public opinion against a chief would not only serve no useful purpose, but would be distinctly dangerous.

If any reason is to be sought for the limitation of wizardry allegations to a village or neighbourhood other than that allegations result from intense inter-personal relationships, it lies in the nature of the wizardry allegation as a device for controlling public opinion. If a person is a stranger from outside one's community the marshalling of public opinion in one's own community against the man serves little purpose and, indeed, is probably unnecessary. The views of the members of one's own community about the conduct of the stranger will probably coincide with one's own.

The use of the allegation of wizardry as a device for directing public opinion against a person is particularly obvious in a struggle for political power within a community in which each contestant tries to involve as many persons as possible in the dispute and get them on his side. The weapon is, of course, a two-edged weapon and is as useful in securing the retention of power in the face of a challenge as in securing the advantage of a person seeking to challenge established power. The use by the Ndebele kings of wizardry allegations to remove those who were politically dangerous is notorious. It would seem that this device was not entirely unknown in the Shona chieftaincies also.

References

MARWICK, M. G. (1950), 'Another modern anti-witchcraft movement in East Central Africa', *Africa*, vol. 20, no. 2.

MIDDLETON, J., and WINTER, E. H. (eds) (1963), *Witchcraft and Sorcery in East Africa*, Routledge & Kegan Paul.

RICHARDS, A. I. (1935), 'A modern movement of witch-finders', *Africa*, vol. 8, no. 4.

32. M. J. Kephart

Rationalists vs. Romantics among Scholars of Witchcraft[1]

M. J. Kephart, *Rationalists vs. Romantics: the Influence of 20th-Century Anthropology on the Scholarship of the Satanic-Witch Craze*, 1980, original MS.

Rationalists vs. Romantics

The satanic-witch craze, which lasted in Europe from around 1300 to around 1700, has turned from a social problem to a special problem in historical studies. Some reviews of the literature exist, and all imply that serious scholarship devoted to this topic has been divided into two schools, the rationalist and the romantic (Caro Baroja, 1961, pp. 79–82; Midelfort, 1968; Monter, 1972; Cohn, 1975: Chapters VI and VII; and Kephart, n.d.: Chapters II and III). Rationalists deny that any satanic-witches existed. Romantics affirm that there were 'witches' of some sort around during the satanic-witch-hunting period, or at least something was going on that might be interpreted by satanic-witch hunters and modern scholars as 'witchcraft'. The implications of this division are considerable. Rationalists focus on the hunting. They spend their time looking for connections between hunting and larger social issues of the period. Romantics focus on satanic-witchcraft. They spend their time searching for evidence for the existence of some sort of belief or behavior in the peasantry that can count as 'witchcraft'. These two schools were established by the nineteenth century. In this paper the effect of professional anthropology on the development of the scholarship devoted to the satanic-witch craze is examined. By the turn of the twentieth century rationalist scholarship was well developed in America and Europe, but, early in the new century, romantic scholarship gained ground and held it. It is my view that academic anthropology contributed largely, at the intellectual level, to this victory.

This paper is written from the rationalist standpoint. My precursors are the rationalists of the nineteenth and twentieth centuries, notable among whom are H. C. Lea, A. D. White, Joseph Hansen, Canon Dollinger, G. L. Burr and R. H. Robbins, whose *Encyclopedia of Witch-*

1. This essay has had the benefit of the editing of Mr Paul Shankman, Department of Anthropology, University of Colorado, Boulder. Dr Max Marwick, the editor of this book, has also taken trouble to improve it. My thanks to both, and, as usual, neither is responsible for any errors I may have made.

craft and Demonology (1959) is a culmination of the rationalist materials of the nineteenth and twentieth centuries. My particular sort of rationalism is a type of anthropology called cultural materialism. On this view, satanic-witch hunting is seen as part of a larger conflict between classes for political and economic power in Europe. This particular sort of treatment appears in a book called *Cows, Pigs, Wars and Witches* (1974) by the anthropologist Marvin Harris. The book is written to shed light, using cultural materialism, on seemingly mysterious cultural puzzles, among which happens to be the satanic-witch craze. Harris's theory is both a refutation of the romantic position and an important elaboration of the rationalist position. Before Harris, however, academic anthropology had not done much to help rationalist history.

Anthropologically Influenced Romanticism: Margaret Murray

In 1921 the British Egyptologist Margaret Murray brought out a book called *The Witch-cult in Western Europe*. Murray was, after that, considered an anthropologist by many historians of the satanic-witch craze. She was so considered because she had read Sir James Frazer's notion of early religions as fertility religions. This gave her the idea that 'witchcraft' in western Europe was a widespread, secret fertility religion existing just below the surface of orthodox Christianity. Murray took the content of tortured confessions very seriously* and concluded that real *covens* or cults of satanic-witches had existed, just as the satanic-witch hunters had claimed, but that far from worshipping satan with their hearts and bodies, they worshipped a pagan survival, a fertility deity. This view of a widespread secret folk religion with *covens* and *sabbats* may be farfetched, but it has been influential since its publication in both general history and specialist circles. For example, few general readers have ever heard of Wallace Notestein's rationalist book on the English satanic-witch craze (1911), whereas Murray's much less scholarly books are famous.

In 1970, in his book *Witchcraft in Tudor and Stuart England*, the historian Alan Macfarlane reviewed the anthropological literature on sorcery, or what I will call ethnographic-witchcraft, in preliterate cultures. His text and bibliography excellently cover the more modern writings, but, as we have seen, he was not the first British historian to turn to anthropology for inspiration. As Eliot Rose put it, in his book *A Razor for a Goat*, Margaret Murray seemed to 'unlock in the name of anthropology the door at which history might have hammered forever in vain'

* Even if, as Cohn demonstrates (above, pp. 149–57), she used records of them selectively to support her theory – *Ed.*

327

(1962, p. 15). Rose can see that 'Neither the anthropology nor the history involved is actually of the kind now regarded as "modern" by those who practice the arts in question . . .' (ibid.), but, however out of date Murray's views might be, as anthropology or history, they have continued down to the present to exert great influence, despite learned attacks on them. Russell, for example, in his book *Witchcraft in the Middle Ages*, says that he sees the lasting significance of Murray's work to lie in her claim that there were indigenous folkloric magical antecedents to satanic-witchcraft that rationalists largely ignore (1972, p. 37).

Though rationalist scholarship continued to develop during the period of Murray's influence, romanticism of some sort has been the dominant respectable tradition, ably and subtly defended by such scholars as Trevor-Roper, Monter, Thomas, and a group of French historiographers from whose works Monter includes excerpts in his fine reader (1969). Some romantic scholars are more overtly influenced by Murray than others. Rose spends some portion of his book attacking the pagan nature of the cult system Murray insists on, but in the end he offers yet another theory for the rise of some sort of cult-style goings-on, this one involving the Goliards. Other historians no less able in their defense of Murray's notions are Huxley (1952), Caro Baroja (1961), Hansen (1969) and Russell (1972). Russell considers that Carlo Ginzburg's work has confirmed the Murray theory in important part, namely that there were grass-roots fertility cults in Italy at just the interesting period (1972, pp. 41–2). This is not the place for another systematic critique of Murrayism, but only for mention of its features and followers in order to show the influence of twentieth-century anthropology on the scholarship of the satanic-witch craze.

The important thing about Murray's influence was that it not only swamped the hopeful beginnings of nineteenth-century rationalist discourse, it also distorted the almost equally hopeful beginnings of radical-style nineteenth-century romanticism made by Jules Michelet. While Michelet may have been wrong about the existence of real 'witches' in Europe, he was right to emphasize that the lowest classes were politically discontented at this period. For Michelet, peasants got together to meet needs not met by conventional social and religious services just then. For Murray, there is no need of political motivation for meetings. The peasants just got together for pagan fertility ceremonials, like the happy natives Frazer wrote about, dancing, feasting, engaging in spiritually and perhaps sexually satisfying nocturnal activities. Russell's conclusion to his book is nothing but updated Michelet, but with the political emphasis considerably dimmed.

A recent example of romanticism attempting to re-politicize itself and acknowledging its direct debt to Michelet, is a feminist book called *Witches, Midwives and Nurses* (1973) by Barbara Ehrenreich and Deirdre English. The book is not especially professional history but it does show how long it has taken for Michelet's political notions to regain currency in the romantic establishment after the great influence of Murrayism. After Murray, modern romanticism is cleansed of its political theory and real or spurious anthropology is made to take its place.

Subjectivism: Taking the Informant's Point of View

Taking the informant's point of view and trying to get inside the heads of informants has long been a stated goal of twentieth-century anthropology, so it is little wonder that historical treatments of the satanic-witch craze that took note of anthropological writings on magic and sorcery should be influenced by the prevailing fashion of the anthropology borrowed from. In anthropology this methodological stance is sometimes called subjectivism.

Russell exemplifies the force of this point of view when he proposes a way of getting out of the bind of having evidence of bad quality. Before presenting his solution, he shows that he knows just how bad the quality is:

No one interpretation is demanded by the sources, which are sparse, opaque, and difficult to penetrate. Almost all the documents we have relating to medieval heretics and witches were written by their adversaries – as treatises, descriptions in chronicles, or confessions forced on the heretics themselves. The Inquisitors in particular habitually used set formularies of questions and answers that determined in advance much of what they would 'discover'. These formularies were in Latin and could be 'translated' for the accused in such a way that he would understand whatever the Inquisitor chose. Having received the answer he wished, he had only to record it as a response to the Latin query, which might have a wholly different meaning from what the prisoner understood. If such devices failed, there was always torture, which was extensively, viciously, and persistently used and could break all but the most heroic spirits (1972, p. 42).

Earlier in this chapter, Russell had criticized Lecky because Lecky allegedly 'argued in Humean fashion that although the evidence for the reality of witchcraft is immense, it is unacceptable because it is rationally impossible' (1972, p. 32). The 'immense' body of evidence that Russell refers to is shot through with the very drawbacks he mentions himself, but since he is committed to the romantic position, he ends up being influenced by the suspect data. He apparently feels he can obviate the difficulties of the data by espousing a strictly subjectivistic approach. Russell sums this up when he says:

Some of the shortcomings of the sources are partly overcome by accepting, as we shall in this book, that what people thought happened is as interesting as what 'objectively did happen', and much more certain (1972, p. 43).

This view places a heavy burden on the informant's good-faith testimony, a burden which Russell's own description of how the informants gathered their evidence hardly seems to merit. Yet people's opinions in demonological writings and the forced confessions of suspects are made to bear the weight of Russell's analysis, and in this he is well within the subjectivistic tradition in anthropology and history.

Functionalism in Anthropology and History

Anthropological functionalism in this context is the doctrine that beliefs in magic and sorcery serve a useful function in the preliterate cultures that hold them. Functionalism was borrowed heavily by historians in their attempts to understand the satanic-witch craze. Because Macfarlane has done a thorough job of reviewing the modern anthropological literature I will not duplicate his work here but only expand it a bit, backwards, by reviewing the work of Bronislaw Malinowski, whom Macfarlane does not discuss.

A few years after Murray's book came out, another admirer of Frazer wrote about magic. Unlike Murray, Malinowski was well trained in anthropology. Malinowski's great contribution in 'Magic, Science, and Religion' (1925) has been that he salvaged both 'primitive' natural science and primitive magic from the category of the irrational, and showed how they were related to each other and to religion. Malinowski's refinement and elaboration of Frazer's insight that magic is 'pseudo-science' (1925, p. 87), using his own field-work for examples along the way, is an accomplishment for anthropology and for the history and philosophy of science. Malinowski wrote that, where human work and human natural science, however rudimentary from our point of view, fail, then magic and religion begin. Magic, rather than proving the primitive to be inherently irrational, reveals that he is rational to a degree modern people fail to appreciate. Malinowski says, for example:

Early man seeks above all to control the course of nature for practical ends, and he does it directly by rite and spell, compelling wind and weather, animals and crops to obey his will ... Magic, based on man's confidence that he can dominate nature directly, if only he knows *the laws which govern it* magically, is in this akin to science (1925, p. 19; italics added).

Toward the end of the essay Malinowski concludes that the cultural function of magic is to make human beings more secure.

Thus magic supplies primitive man with a number of ready-made ritual acts and beliefs, with a definite mental and practical technique which serves to bridge over the dangerous gaps in every important pursuit or critical situation. It enables man to carry out with *confidence* his important tasks, to maintain his *poise* and his mental integrity in fits of anger, in the throes of hate, of unrequited love, of despair and anxiety. The function of magic is to ritualize man's *optimism*, to enhance his faith in the victory of *hope* over fear. Magic expresses the greater value for man of *confidence* over doubt, of *steadfastness* over vacillation, of *optimism* over pessimism (1925, p. 90; italics added).

This gift of poise, this sense of control, is the legitimate function of magic meant in the most general sense in primitive cultures, but it is a function which cannot be found anywhere in either satanic-witchcraft or satanic-witch hunting. Even considering that evil or black magic is the sort meant, the European materials describing satanic-witchcraft do not reveal any of the features that functionalists usually regard as compensatory adaptations, such as, relatively easy counter-magic, 'witch doctors', curative or protective magic, ritual, sacrifice, etc., to help the distressed 'victim'. Ethnographic-witchcraft certainly can be very terrible in preliterate societies, but its virulence pales in comparison with the alleged dangers to mind and body of satanic-witchcraft in Europe, against which no spiritual protection sufficed, authorities insisted (Lea, 1888, p. 506). Thomas (1971) emphasizes this alleged virulence in his treatment of the English satanic-witch craze. Official Church doctrine after the Reformation was that the 'victims' of harm done by 'witchcraft' could only be helped by the imprisonment and death of the 'witch'. The state intervened in what had usually been a private matter, in English villages, *maleficium*.

Malinowski's functionalism has been elaborated by American and British anthropologists trained to be interested in magic and sorcery in preliterate cultures. Evans-Pritchard's explanatory model, which influenced Macfarlane's study of the 'witch-hunt' in England, allows, not only for explanations for misfortune but also for 'people to take action in the face of uncertainty and misfortune' (Middleton and Winter, 1963, p. 8), the gift of confidence. The tension people feel when misfortune occurs can thus be reduced by beliefs in sorcery or ethnographic-witchcraft. The notion that certain social structures will focus tension between certain categories of persons has been the social-structuralist complement to functionalist writings on sorcery.

331

Even putting aside satanic-witchcraft, and only discussing satanic-witch hunting, anthropological functionalism hasn't been much help. Macfarlane and Thomas try to see the 'witch-craze' in England in the context of anthropological functionalism. Neither has been successful in showing what the function of satanic-witch hunting was for English villagers, that is, over and above what the villagers had previously got out of the occasional prosecution or lynching of suspected practitioners of ordinary *maleficium* before 1563. Anthropologically influenced functionalism attempts to reduce the whole satanic-witch craze to peasant accusations of *maleficium* at the village level. Larner, for example, helps to achieve this reduction by defining English prosecutions at this period as being without the elements of compact or sabbath (1974, p. 82). In her typology and table based on the typology,* she claims that England during the sixteenth and seventeenth centuries was without her Type B, 'compact witchcraft', or her Type C, 'sabbath witchcraft'. But it happens that these elements were present in England during the 'witch-craze' period.

Functionalists are quite right to point out that, before the Elizabethan period, no compact or sabbath was believed in by the peasant villagers; but the whole point of the satanic-witch craze, in Britain as in Europe, was the heavy involvement of the nobility and the gentry, educated persons in university, Church, government and the judicial system. The satanic-witch ideology, including the notion that all magic was done by an implicit or explicit pact with Satan, had been invented and elaborated in the highest circles in Europe and when the ideology got to Britain, in the usual way, it was taken up by the highest in the land, from the reading gentry, up to and including the monarch. Whether or not the Marian exiles had a critical role in importing Continental notions, it was certainly educated people who did it, not peasants. Educated people formed opinions, imported and wrote books on satanism (Macfarlane, 1970, pp. 79–91; Robbins, 1959, pp. 167–9, 174; and Notestein, 1911, 227–53). Of the Elizabethan law of 1563, Robbins notes: 'Witchcraft was not merely the vulgar prejudice of uneducated people. This bill was framed by some of the ablest and most learned men in England . . .' (1959, p. 279). Notestein mentions that Henry More, for example, in the next century, believed that he had absolute proof of the 'nocturnal conventicle of witches' in his book, *Antidote to Atheisme* (1911, p. 239). As the upper classes spread beliefs in satanism, the peasantry came to hear of it. Finally, the highest personage in the land took active notice (1911, pp. 93–119). James Stuart, while still James VI of Scotland, developed an

*See above, p. 50 – *Ed.*

interest in satanism. He wrote a book on the topic called *Demonology*, first published in Edinburgh in 1597. Before writing his book James had involved himself in a famous 'witch' trial in North Berwick, 1590–2. Judicial torture was not permitted for this crime in England, but North Berwick is in Scotland and the peasant suspects were questioned under torture and a lot of 'evidence' of satanism was gathered. James played the role of the Continental demonologist (Robbins, 1959, p. 359). He was convinced that the trial proved the existence of Continental-style compact and sabbath in Britain. Upon becoming king of both Scotland and England, James I (as he was then styled) had *Demonology* reprinted in London, and personally supervised the passing of the new, harsher 'Witchcraft Statute' in 1604. This new law was critical for English prosecutions, and for my argument, because it 'changed the emphasis from *maleficium* to the pact with the Devil, in line with Continental thinking, and certainly heightened the attack against witches' (ibid., p. 277). Now peasant women could be executed for nothing more than 'entertaining evil spirits' or compact. Most often the charge was still for harm allegedly done, for *maleficium*, but any convictions for compact alone show that Larner's typology is inadequate. For example, 'at Chelmsford in 1645 seven women were hanged for the sole charge of entertaining spirits' (ibid., p. 280).

And the conventicles or sabbaths were also in existence in at least some English minds at this period, for in 1673, a female 'witch-finder' in New Castle, charged her neighbors with participating in 'witch gatherings or conventicles held at various times and places' (Notestein, 1911, p. 281). Earlier in the century, in the case of the 'Lancashire Witches' of 1633–4, a 'witch meeting or conventicle was confessed to' (ibid., p. 273). Though judicial torture was not usual in England, duress could be used.

It is odd that Larner's article is decorated with a print of Matthew Hopkins, when her point is that no satanism was believed in or prosecuted for in England (1974, p. 82). Hopkins had absorbed plenty of Continental notions about the nature of satanic-witchcraft and how to prosecute it. These included belief in *sabbats* and the use of methods verging on torture to obtain confessions. Hopkins believed that conventicles were being held in his own home town: 'the witches, he tells us, were accustomed to hold their assemblies near his house' (Notestein, 1911, p. 166). He found or implanted beliefs in satanism wherever he went and there were many trials during his 'witch-finding' career, which reached its height during 1645–6. The point is, the upper classes knew of satanism during the Tudor and Stuart period and it was this sort of 'witchcraft' that they were concerning themselves about, passing laws against, and prosecuting for, while the peasantry was still mainly concerned about ordinary *maleficium*. Village accusations of *maleficium* did not take place in a cultural vacuum but were directly influenced by the new interest the ruling classes were taking in Continental-style satanism. Ordinary interest in *maleficium* may well have had the usual anthropological function, but what was the possible function to the peasants of satanism, torture or duress, and mass trials during the Tudor and Stuart period? No one, however well versed in anthropology, has offered a convincing function, to the peasants, for this phenomenon.

Macfarlane's attempt to find the function to English villagers for satanic-witch-hunting may not have been totally successful, but Erik Midelfort's similar attempt for German villagers and townsfolk has been, according to Midelfort, totally unsuccessful. In my review of the literature (Kephart, n.d.), Midelfort is classified as a sort of romantic with strong, if episodic, rationalist tendencies. His approach to anthropology, however, is thoroughly rationalist by 1972. In his book Midelfort cautiously praises Macfarlane for 'a new and more cautious functionalism, a sympathetic but critical use of anthropology' (1972, p. 4), but Midelfort's own use of anthropology will be somewhat different, for though he claims a 'modest familiarity with social theory and the anthropological study of witchcraft' (ibid., p. 2), he sees that uncritical application of anthropological functionalism will 'ultimately yield confusion' (ibid., p. 3). Further, he does not want to compare seventeenth-century European villages with life in today's preliterate cultures. Though earlier Midelfort had faulted Robbins who '... necessarily denies whatever help the social sciences can offer to historians' (1968, p. 383), by 1972 Midelfort himself has taken a more critical view of what sort of help anthropology might have to offer when he says he wants to 'stop comparing the details of one society with those of another' (1972, p. 4) and 'thus the present study will not bristle with arcane allusions to the Navajo, Azande, or Ceŵa' (1972, p. 5).

Early on in this book Midelfort distinguishes between small-scale and large-scale trials (1972, p. 4). Small-scale trials, even during the hunting period, were similar to the occasional trial or lynching of a suspected practitioner of *maleficium* that had gone on from earliest Christian times. Large-scale trials were characteristic of the satanic-witch-craze period alone. Late in the book Midelfort says, of functionalism:

Turning briefly to the larger social question of function, we can concede that the small trials may indeed have served a function, delineating the social thresholds of eccentricity tolerable to society, and registering fear of a socially indigestible group, unmarried women ... In this restricted sense the small witch trial may have even been therapeutic, or functional. In its larger form however, these panics were clearly dysfunctional. They produced fear rather than dissipating it; they increased social tensions rather than relieving or purging them (1972, pp. 195–6).

Midelfort may have rejected anthropological functionalism, but it is plain that Macfarlane, Thomas, Monter, and others have not. The borrowing of anthropological functionalism has led historians to focus on the micro-situation in Europe, seeking the alleged function to local residents for local large-scale hunting, and to turn away from the macro-situation in Europe. The borrowing of anthropological functionalism has had the effect of yielding confusion in historical thinking on the satanic-witch craze.

The Ethnographic Analogy: Universal Sorcery as Reported by Anthropologists Becomes Confused with European Satanic-Witch Hunting

Russell (1972, p. 33) has criticized nineteenth-century rationalist historians for being anthropologically uninformed, just as the early Midelfort (1968, p. 383) criticized R. H. Robbins for refusing to use anthropology. But H. C. Lea knew quite well that sorcery and magic are universal, and, near the turn of the century, White wrote in his chapter 'From Magic to Chemistry and Physics' a passage that seems to show he understands nineteenth-century anthropology well enough:

In all the earliest developments of human thought, we find a strong tendency to ascribe mysterious powers over Nature to men and women especially gifted or skilled. Survivals of this view are found to this day among savages and barbarians left behind in the evolution of civilization, and especially in this case, among the tribes of Australia, Africa, and the Pacific coast of America. Even in the most enlightened nations still appear popular beliefs, observances, or sayings, drawn from this earlier phase of thought.

Between the prehistoric savage developing this theory, and thereafter endeavouring to deal with the powers of Nature by magic, and the modern man who has outgrown it, appears a long line of nations struggling upward through it (1896, p. 373).

Russell wants to take advantage of the ethnographic analogy and have real ethnographic-witchcraft prove the existence of real satanic-witchcraft, so he cannot admit the extent to which rationalists appreciate what anthropology has to offer. It is not that rationalists do not know about ethnographic-witchcraft, but that they do not wish to confuse it with European satanic-witch hunting. See, for example, Robbins (1959, pp. 1, 3) for this distinction. And, of course, Lea made the distinction between satanic-witch hunting and 'ordinary sorcery' in Europe

(1888: Chapters VI and VII). Conflating different sorts of 'witchcraft' enables romantics to support their premises with data from another field when their own data are suspect. Recently some anthropologists themselves have contributed to blurring the distinction among the several sorts of 'witchcraft'.

Lucy Mair, in her book *Witchcraft* (1969), is, on the whole, romantic in approach. Not only does she attack, throughout the book, rationalist history; she pretty constantly blurs the distinction among three sorts of 'witchcraft'. She blurs the distinction between *maleficium* in Europe and satanic-witch hunting in Europe, and she blurs the distinction between satanic-witch hunting and ethnographic-witchcraft. Early in the book, she takes certain (rationalist) historians to task for not being anthropologically informed:

The books on witchcraft in western Europe, in England, and in colonial America have nearly all been written by people who did not look for parallels to contemporary witch beliefs outside Europe, if they knew that these existed. Most of the [rationalist] writers have been interested rather in asking why persons in high authority persecuted witches than in asking what ordinary people did about them (1969, p. 32).

Late in the book she says:

The questions that have been asked by [rationalist] writers about Europe concern the reason why people should have believed in the compact with the Devil, and why those accused should have been tortured to make them confess to it. They do not ask why misfortunes were supposed to be caused by witches ... They are more interested in the activities of lawyers and churchmen seeking to root out heresy than in what ordinary people did when they thought they were bewitched. Hence the major works are studies of witch-finding rather than of witchcraft. They ask the legitimate question why this should be pursued more actively at one time than another, but they are concerned rather with the direction of witch-finding from above than with popular demand for the services of witch-finders (1969, p. 222).

But recently, as Mair points out, this state of affairs has been altered for the better, in the work of a scholar 'who combines the anthropologist's with the historian's approach' (ibid., p. 186). This is, of course, Macfarlane. After spending some portion of her book attacking rationalist notions, it is no surprise that Mair is glad to find that Macfarlane's Essex study disproves the notion that the satanic-witch hunts 'were nothing but a monstrously dramatic form of religious persecution' (1969, p. 187). Mair admires Macfarlane's study because 'this is the only attempt that has so far been made to treat the belief in witchcraft at any period of European history as the kind of social reality with which we are familiar in Africa' (loc. cit.). This is obvious blurring of the distinction between satanic-witchcraft and ethnographic-witchcraft. Mair continues:

Macfarlane's study is the first to show how much more closely the complex of behaviour surrounding the idea of witchcraft in seventeenth-century England resembles that in Africa than would be supposed if one looked only at the spectacular trials in which heretics are accused of witchcraft in the sense of diabolism. The Essex witches were not accused simply of *being* witches; before they could be indicted, they had to be charged with some specific damage to a neighbour's person or property, and this was still so even after the advent of Matthew Hopkins (1969, p. 198 f.).

This blurring causes Mair some unnecessary confusion, as when she says that in her view the anthropologist 'would not be likely to agree that the suspicions and accusations of witchcraft between neighbours became any more prevalent because church and state were taking a new interest in it' (1969, p. 196). An anthropologist is almost certain to notice such a social change as this, but Mair will not because she does not wish to distinguish, as Lea did, between satanic-witchcraft, meant as a punishable crime involving pacts with the Devil, and 'ordinary sorcery within Europe' (see above, p. 335 f.). As mentioned in the discussion of functionalism, on my view, the Essex trials all came after the 'Witchcraft Statutes' of the Tudor period and the later harsher one of 1604, precisely because peasants were influenced by the 'new interest' their betters were taking in 'witchcraft'. After 1604, we find reports of even the *sabbat*, which nobody can claim was an indigenous local village complex of beliefs. It is clear that, like Macfarlane and Thomas, Mair wants to find real 'witchcraft' of some sort beneath the trials. She says:

In the light of contemporary evidence from Africa and elsewhere, an anthropologist would not suppose that fifteenth-century Europeans needed any prompting to ascribe their misfortunes to the ill-will of their neighbours (ibid., p. 197).

This, however, does not explain the absence of trials for 'witchcraft' meant as *maleficium* in England before the fourteenth century (when satanic-witch hunting began on the Continent), their extreme rarity between 1300 and 1563, or take into account Evans-Pritchard's reservation about Macfarlane's work (preface, 1970, p. xvi) that 'it is not clear, however, since some of these misfortunes must have been very frequent events, why they so seldom led to legal action' even during the craze period. Even though Mair refutes certain of Murray's claims (1969, pp. 226–31), her own work is anthropologically informed romanticism.

A year after Mair's book came out, Douglas edited a volume of essays called *Witchcraft Accusations and Confessions* (1970). Douglas is the most social-structuralist of recent cultural anthropologists who take up this question. Yet the force of the ethnographic analogy has had its effect upon her. In her introductory chapter, she notes that Mayer disallows the comparison of European satanic-witchcraft with ethnographic-witchcraft. Mayer apparently views ethnographic witchcraft as a 'fully domesticated species, not to be compared with the wild, European sort' (1954 in ibid., p. xix). This seems the very distinction necessary for an understanding of the European situation, but then Douglas blurs this vital distinction when she goes on (1970, pp. xxiv ff.) to cite Lienhardt's research in the Dinka culture where belief itself creates the reality of the 'night witch' as if Dinka 'witch' beliefs were exactly comparable to European satanic-witch beliefs from the hunting period.

Douglas proposes a demographic-social-structural model for interpreting cultures in a general way in terms of beliefs in evil magic. She finds that in high density cultures, bad feelings among close associates in ill-defined situations can lead to a lot of accusations of sorcery. Evans-Pritchard's landmark treatment still applies to the relatively densely populated cultures he dealt with in Africa like the Azande and Nuer, but not to all preliterate and 'prescientific' cultures. In sparsely populated cultures, Douglas notices, people

... can do without explanations of misfortune. They can live in tolerance and amity and without metaphysical curiosity. The precondition is that they should be free to move away from each other whenever strains appear. The price of such a benign cosmology is a low level of organization (1970, p. xxxiii).

Douglas has hit upon a good idea, that population density is important, but as the population density of medieval Europe has always been high by preliterate standards, it is not clear how this alone could have brought forth satanic-witch hunting on so grand a scale just when it did. Population density is, indeed, important but it is what Douglas does not examine that is in my view equally important, namely that in the European case the dense population was stratified into mostly hereditary and often mutually competitive social classes. Douglas seems to be going in the right direction but she has not produced a general theory.

Norman Cohn and Marvin Harris

This was how things stood in anthropology up to 1974 when Harris applied cultural materialism to the satanic-witch craze in *Cows, Pigs, Wars and Witches*. In his treatment he used as a main reference a book by Cohn called *The Pursuit of the Millennium* (1961), in which Cohn described a little known phenomenon of medieval life, the military-messianic uprisings. These involved the peasantry at about the same time as the real, then later, alleged, heresies involved the Church. In Harris's opinion the satanic-witch craze was invented and imposed by the ruling classes in Church and government to disperse and fragment 'all the latent energies of protest' (1974, p. 239). The Church propagandists promoted fear of satanic-witchcraft because this fear 'gave everyone's anger and frustration a purely local focus ...' (ibid.) and 'in doing so, it drew the poor further and further away from confronting the ecclesiastical and secular establishment with demands for the redistribution of wealth and the leveling of rank' (1974, pp. 239–40). Since old women had been thought of as 'witches' from classical times, in Europe, they provided the perfect, low-cost scapegoat and red herring. Harris says:

The practical significance of the witch mania therefore was that it shifted responsibility for the crisis of the late medieval society from both Church and state to imaginary demons in human form. Preoccupied with the fantastic activities of these demons, the distraught, alienated, pauperized masses blamed the rampant Devil instead of the corrupt clergy and the rapacious nobility (1974, pp. 237–38).

In 1975 Cohn brought out his own book on the satanic-witch craze, *Europe's Inner Demons*. Cohn's approach is to treat the satanic-witch craze as if it had legitimate *intellectual* underpinnings in peoples' real beliefs and behaviors. While Cohn does attack traditional romantic theory in his chapter 'The Non-Existent Society of Witches', he also begins an attack on rationalist theory in the next chapter, which lasts through the rest of the book.

After refuting traditional romanticism in Chapter Six, Cohn begins his running attack on rationalist theory in Chapter Seven, by revealing some forgeries certain rationalist writers have used, which seem to give satanic-witch hunting an earlier date than it deserves (1975, pp. 126–46). This is certainly a service to satanic-witch hunting scholarship, but nothing he reveals destroys the main rationalist argument: namely, that the satanic-witch ideology was fabricated in the service of satanic-witch hunting, and that the hunting was an outgrowth of the previous attack on real or alleged heresies in Europe. After dispensing with rationalist theory to his own satisfaction, Cohn goes on to propose that real ritual magic in Europe gave the Church and legal authorities the idea that illicit metaphysical power was being resorted to. Cohn's history of ritual magic is good, and of particular interest to the science historian, but as an explanation for the rise of satanic-witch hunting, it will not do, because it presumes a form of romanticism; that is, it presumes that there had to be *something real* going on in order for Church and secular authorities to say and do the things they said and did. Furthermore, Cohn's attack on rationalist theory is internally inconsistent, as his own excellent history demonstrates. He says, in the first paragraph of Chapter Seven, 'Three Forgeries and Another Wrong Track':

Most historians who were not persuaded that a sect of witches really existed have accepted that the stereotype came into being during, and as a result of, the Inquisition's campaign against Catharism in southern France and northern Italy (1975, p. 126).

The Cathars were famous heretics in this period. The general rationalist argument is that heretic-hunting gave rise to satanic-witch hunting, but this hunt never took place as Cohn shows in this chapter. Cohn puts this forward as a definitive attack on rationalist theory; yet in the opening pages of Chapter Twelve, 'The Making of the Great Witch Hunt', in an attempt to discredit the notion that the *Malleus Maleficium* was critical to the satanic-witch picture, Cohn says, of the critical transitional trials, 'these trials were a by-product of the persecution of the Waldensians ...' (1975, p. 225), of heretics. And though the Inquisition did not have the all-pervasive role nineteenth-century rationalists assigned it, Cohn himself shows how the Inquisition in Milan, by 1390, was trying the followers or presumed followers of Diana and eliciting the details of sexual intercourse with a devil, and executing the female defendants (1975, pp. 217–18). During the critical period of the late thirteenth and fourteenth centuries, the Inquisition did not have to figure in trials for sorcery–heresy–witchcraft, but it did sometimes, and, of course, its procedure was used. It little matters if an inquisitor, a bishop, or a secular judge is ordering questioning under torture; the result is the same, confessions of whatever the interrogator wants to hear. It is trivial to argue that nineteenth-century rationalists were wrong about certain trials, or that they were wrong to attribute more to the Inquisition than it deserves, for inquisitorial procedure applied to real or alleged heretics did in fact give rise to the critical transitional trials which Cohn describes in Chapter Twelve. Cohn says, in the trials of alleged Waldensians from the 1420–30s, where 'the inquisitorial procedure was employed, though not necessarily by the Inquisition . . .' (1975, p. 225); the 'earliest formulation of the witches' sabbat ...' (ibid., p. 226) came into being. And 'on the French side of the Alps the trials were mostly initiated by the Inquisition . . .' (loc. cit.). Finally, 'the whole population of those remote areas came to be suspect – and suspect not simply of heresy but of the new-style witchcraft' (1975, p. 227). Cohn has indeed traced down the critical trials.

Even if nineteenth-century rationalists got certain facts wrong, their general theory is as yet unrefuted. On the content level the crimes attributed to heretics and satanic-witches were strikingly alike. But even if the content of the heresy picture and of the satanic-witch picture were different, the methods for finding and dealing with the two sorts of defendants were similar. Total suspension of ordinary rules of evidence, of ordinary civil rights of the defendants, the use of unremitting torture to obtain confessions of impossible acts, and execution by burning characterize both (real and alleged) heretic hunting and satanic-witch hunting. No *real* beliefs or behaviours need be scrupulously searched for, as Cohn does in this book, when we already know that it was perfectly easy to fabricate accusations of sorcery, heresy and sundry disgusting behaviors against any group or person whom authorities wanted to get rid of for any reason. Cohn shows how this can be done in his chapter on the destruction of the Templars (1975, p. 75–98), but he does not, for some reason, wish to turn the light of this analysis on satanic-witch hunting itself. Nothing I have said here should be interpreted as a rejection of Cohn's insight that ritual magic was around during this period, but as all sorts of magical thinking were extant in medieval Europe, this alone will not account for specific persecutions.

It has been my contention in this paper that one of the main intellectual reasons why historians will not approach satanic-witch hunting in a totally rationalist way is that they have before them the ethnographic analogy and half a century of history which confounds ethnographic-witchcraft and satanic-witch hunting. And among anthropologists only Marvin Harris has taken a strictly rationalist line on satanic-witch hunting. It is this that has allowed him to see the import of *The Pursuit of the Millennium*. In my view, only Cohn's romantic bias has prevented him from realizing the potential of his own materials. At the intellectual level, Cohn, like Macfarlane, Thomas and other good scholars, has been led astray by the sort of history that has previously influenced by use and misuse of anthropology. Before Harris, professional anthropology in this century had not only failed to provide a general theory for the rise of satanic-witch hunting, it blunted the rationalist sword unsheathed in the nineteenth century.

References

BURR, G. L. (1890), 'The literature of witchcraft', *Papers of the American Historical Association*, vol. 4, pp. 237–66.

CARO BAROJA, J. (1965), *The World of the Witches*, University of Chicago Press.

COHN, N. (1961), *The Pursuit of the Millennium*, Harper Torchbooks.

COHN, N. (1975), *Europe's Inner Demons*, Basic Books, New York.

Theories of Witchcraft

DOLLINGER, J. J. I. (1869), *The Pope and the Council*, Rivingtons.

DOUGLAS, M. (ed.) (1970), *Witchcraft Accusations and Confessions*, Tavistock.

EHRENREICH, B. and ENGLISH, D. (1974), *Witches, Midwives and Nurses: A History of Women Healers*, Compendium.

EVANS-PRITCHARD, E. E. (1937), *Witchcraft, Oracles and Magic Among the Azande*, Clarendon Press.

HANSEN, C. (1969), *Witchcraft at Salem*, George Braziller Inc.

HANSEN, J. (1900), *Zauberwahn, Inquisition und Hexenprozess im Mittelalter* (see E. W. Monter (1969), pp. 3–10; 31–6).

HARRIS, M. (1974), *Cows, Pigs, Wars and Witches*, Random House.

HUXLEY, A. L. (1952), *The Devils of Loudon*, Harper.

KEPHART, M. J. n.d., 'Cultural materialism and the problem of European satanic-witch hunting'. Unpublished MS.

KLUCKHOHN, C. (1962), *Navajo Witchcraft*, Beacon Press.

LARNER, C. (1974). 'Is all witchcraft really witchcraft?', *New Society*, vol. 30, no. 627.

LEA, H. C. (1888), *A History of the Inquisition of the Middle Ages*, vol. III, Harper & Brothers.

LEA, H. C. (1939), *Materials Toward a History of Witchcraft*, A. C. Howland (ed.), University of Pennsylvania Press.

MACFARLANE, A. (1970), *Witchcraft in Tudor and Stuart England*, Routledge & Kegan Paul.

MAIR, L. P. (1969), *Witchcraft*, McGraw-Hill.

MALINOWSKI, B. (1954), 'Magic, science and religion' in *Magic, Science and Religion and Other Essays*, Doubleday Anchor Books.

MIDDLETON, J. and WINTER, E. H. (eds) (1963), *Witchcraft and Sorcery in East Africa*, Praeger.

MIDELFORT, H. C. E. (1968), 'Recent witch-hunting research', *Papers of the Bibliographic Society of America*, vol. 62.

MIDELFORT, H. C. E. (1972), *Witch-hunting in Southwestern Germany*, Stanford University Press.

MONTER, E. W. (ed.) (1969), *European Witchcraft*, John Wiley.

MONTER, E. W. (1972), 'The historiography of European witchcraft', *Journal of Interdisciplinary History*, vol. 7, no. 4.

MURRAY, M. A. (1921), *The Witch-Cult in Western Europe*, Oxford U.P.

NOTESTEIN, W. (1965), *History of Witchcraft in England, 1558–1718*, Russell & Russell (first published by the American Historical Association in 1911).

ROBBINS, R. H. (1959), *The Encyclopedia of Witchcraft and Demonology*, Crown Publishers.

ROSE, E. (1962), *A Razor for a Goat*, Toronto U.P.

RUSSELL, J. B. (1972), *Witchcraft in the Middle Ages*, Cornell U.P.

THOMAS, K. V. (1971), *Religion and the Decline of Magic*, Scribner.

TREVOR-ROPER, H. R. (1967), 'The European witch-craze of the sixteenth and seventeenth centuries', in *Religion, the Reformation and Social Change*, ch. 3, Harper & Row.

WHITE, A. D. (1896), *History of the Warfare of Science with Theology in Christendom*, D. Appleton.

33. Malcolm Crick

Recasting Witchcraft

Malcolm Crick, *Explorations in Language and Meaning*, Malaby Press, 1976, chapter 6.

We have so far made but a few very general remarks on the differences
between structural-functionalism and semantic anthropology. Of course,
because the consensus in British anthropology has long been destroyed,
many of the developments of the last decade have already shown us in
concrete terms how two very different general outlooks concerning the
nature of the discipline may manifest themselves. One spectacular instance has been in kinship studies. Descent theorists, traditionally em-
phasizing institutions and social functions, have signally failed to see that
alliance theory is concerned with rules and categories and not with
behaviour. This chapter takes 'witchcraft' as a subject where the same
general cleavage has similarly already appeared. By showing below how
deliberately following a new type of interest can considerably reshape this
topic, the gulf between the newer and older styles of anthropology will
be made that much clearer. Only detailed ethnographic analysis can
establish the value of the proposals made below, and in this chapter
little more than an outline framework for a new style of approach
is given. Even so, the analysis (which makes considerable use of insights
from linguistic philosophy) provides a useful and specific demonstration of that broad link which exists between semantic anthropology
and language.

The topic of witchcraft is highly suitable for these purposes for several
reasons. Firstly, the deficiencies of the functionalist writings are here very
clear. Also, it has already constituted a bridge with other disciplines:
philosophers have used Evans-Pritchard's Zande study to debate general
issues concerning the nature of anthropological inquiry (Winch, 1964;
MacIntyre, 1964); and historians have recently made extensive researches into the subject. Whilst we may feel flattered that other scholars find
our work invaluable (Thomas, 1971, 436n), this interest places us under a
particularly heavy obligation to look carefully at our achievements in this
field. When this is done, it is apparent that anthropology has far less to
offer these other disciplines than some obviously think.

343

Two Styles in the Study of Witchcraft

Evans-Pritchard's 1937 study of Zande witchcraft is an undeniable land-mark in the history of anthropology, but the last two generations have not greatly advanced our understanding of the problems he wrote about. His book concerned the sociology of knowledge and perception (Douglas, 1970b, p. xiv), and it would be an understatement to comment that subsequent work has not done justice to its theoretical pregnancy. Like some of the other early 'paradigmatic' writings it has been emas-culated by being converted into a functionalist framework where it was interpreted as being about 'social control' and the like (Ardener, 1971b, p. lxxvi) – exactly the sort of approach from which Evans-Pritchard con-tinually distanced himself. The emphasis in most subsequent works in the field has been on the social locus of accusations, theories of 'social strain', and hypotheses concerning the dissolution of redundant relationships. The 'micro-sociological' conception of anthropology has almost completely submerged his most important ideas. From Evans-Pritchard's construction of the logic of the Zande conceptual structure which lay behind the perception and labelling of certain kinds of events, anthro-pology virtually went a full circle until it seemed to be suggested by some functionalists that witchcraft could be explained by misfortune.

Unfortunately, those historians who have lately studied witchcraft have failed to see the gulf between these two approaches. Macfarlane (1970), for instance, juxtaposes quotations from Marwick and Evans-Pritchard, seemingly oblivious of the fact that they represent two very different conceptions of a discipline. Thomas describes his work as 'mainly sociological' (1970, p. 47), and it is no surprise therefore that it is open to many of the criticisms which can be made of the sociological tradition in anthropology (Keynes, 1972). These scholars cannot be blamed here since the semantic style of tackling witchcraft has not been much in evidence for them to use. Of the many recent books on the subject – many ironically dedicated to Evans-Pritchard – almost all have been representatives of the old approach.

Mair's general survey (1969), for instance, does not go beyond the functionalist perspective. And one can see here plainly, in the very ar-rangement of the material, how the fact that her main interests are in the politico-jural field necessarily affects the treatment of witchcraft. Marwick, the figure in the field most associated with the 'social strain' hypothesis, still sees studies of witchcraft and sorcery as contributions to behavioural science. His is an attempt at 'making generalizations about repetitive social situations and processes, and, within the range of statistical probability, at making predictions of the outcomes' (1970, p. 17, 1965, p. 173). His remarks on the inadequacy of the sociological analyses by those like Lewis are completely justified. But when he suggests that the difficulty here 'springs from the failure of anthropologists to quantify and objectify their methods rather than that they are stuck with too rigid or too simple a model' (1972, p. 382), he evidently sees progress as consisting in the elaboration of a framework rather than requiring any substantial theoretical rethinking. A recent set of essays by Manchester anthropologists (Gluckman, 1972) similarly represents that easy resort to sociological generalizations which has been responsible for the virtual stagnation of whole areas of the discipline over the last generation.

Lastly, the A.S.A. monograph on witchcraft (M. Douglas, 1970b), by its very title stresses aspects like confessions and accusations, and thus reveals the divergence of interest between most of the contributors and Evans-Pritchard. Certainly the 'boundarism' of Douglas's introduction is a step forward, and cannot be located in the old style, but Beidelman's severe comments on the continuing propensity for taxonomic and functional thinking makes a rather dissonant epilogue in a volume which contains very few new insights. Lewis, for example, gives an old-fashioned comparative functional study of the social correlates of witchcraft and spirit possession, which rests upon the most simplistic of assumptions concerning the link between belief and social structure (1970). In a similar fashion, Esther Goody offers the sociological hypothesis that it is the ease of terminating marriage which lies behind the fact that Gonja believe that it is only the witchcraft of women that is evil and should be punished, without even a minimal attempt to construct the symbolic syntax which relates the categories of male and female in Gonja society (1970). As Ardener makes very clear in his analysis of Bakweri witchcraft notions, it is pointless to try to account for such facts without first constituting the conceptual 'templates' (1970, pp. 156, 159, n. 15), that is without trying to specify the ideological structures which generate such events.

In trying to reframe the topic of witchcraft, considerable emphasis will be placed on underlying classificatory structures in order to stress one aspect of the reorientation which a semantic approach involves. Of course Mair is quite correct to say that to advance our understanding there is no need to scrap everything which has been done on this topic in the last thirty years (1972b, p. 140), but no one would suggest this. On the other hand, there is a definite need for a 'rethinking of the approach itself, rather than simply more studies' (Beidelman, 1970, p. 356). Douglas has long criticized the narrow conception of the scope of witchcraft studies, and has suggested that advance to a broader frame of reference would require an atmosphere of debate and tension (1967, p. 80). We have seen some elements of cleavage appearing, but this atmosphere has not been in evidence in the recent literature to the extent one would wish. It is to be hoped that the recasting offered here will make the opposition between the older and the newer styles of anthropology in this field more striking.

An Analytical Dissolution: Society as a Moral Space

One of the reasons for the shortcomings of anthropological discussions of witchcraft is the idea that it is a phenomenon which should be treated as a topic at all. So, following Levi-Strauss's demolition of totemism and Needham's of kinship, my suggestion is that our understanding will advance when 'witchcraft' is analytically dissolved into a larger frame of reference. Some still argue that our first task is to define witchcraft, and then by comparison to see what the phenomenon really is (Standefer, 1970). But it is vital to locate the nature and dimensions of the field by which 'witchcraft' is constituted. Such a location can then define the phenomenon away. Studies of witchcraft – let alone comparative studies – would then appear a semantic nonsense, and the mark of our better comprehension would be a decreasingly frequent employment of the term.

In this connection it is important to see that witchcraft may have become a separate topic for anthropology because of its appearance in the history of our own society. This occurrence, by supplying us with a ready-made term, would be sufficient to destroy those cautions we observe in the translation of culture in connection with other problems. The gulf between the intellectual structures of seventeenth-century England and Zande society, for instance, is vast. Moreover, Evans-Pritchard himself emphasized that our historical witchcraft was not like anything we so label in primitive cultures (1937, p. 64) – a fact which historians should not underestimate the importance of when they use anthropological data in arriving at their interpretations.[1] English witchcraft existed in a culture which possessed such categories as 'natural philosophy' and a theological system upon which witch beliefs were partly parasitic. Great violence must be done to the conceptual structures of another culture in speaking of witchcraft if it lacks those environing categories which defined it in our own. Where the conceptual field is so different we could not reasonably

1. The idea employed below of a conceptual field may be of value for their work, since this perspective allows a structural approach to be followed in the diachronic dimension. Historians thus might be able to plot the changing dimensions and articulation of the historical field of which witchcraft was a part over a time span in a certain culture.

expect to find the same phenomenon, and so the one term should not be used twice. This just becomes an easy way by which a whole host of labels can be illicitly employed in describing other cultures.

This point, though it may strike a social scientist as of rather little import, is crucial in semantic anthropology and affects all the topics with which it deals. As Dumont has rightly insisted, it is only by a painstaking investigation of details that the route to the universal is kept open (1961, pp. 37–8). We simply cannot confuse categories like 'caste' and 'hierarchy' with the general sociological notions of stratification and inequality. This 'smug sociocentricity' merely sacrifices the goal of understanding to the convenience of an immediate discourse (1972, p. 261). Such social science does not even recognize the extent to which it is itself the product of a particular type of social system, and therefore uses almost unthinkingly the categories of thought which come most easily to it.

In the case of witchcraft just such a conceptual laziness has been at work. We require far more to observe the discriminations existing in the culture under study, instead of employing those which our own supplies. While doing this, advance can also be made by endeavouring to formulate a common framework which can absorb the details of particular cultural schemas. The common language used here to recast witchcraft seeks to sink beneath cultural terms which are not safely used in anthropology to an analytical level of sufficient depth that satisfactory commensurability between cultures can be attained. Indeed, the proposed framework may be a cultural universal.

Against those who associate convention with variability and nature with universality, one can argue that there are certain characteristics which are not optional for a culture because the idea of their absence is made unintelligible by basic features of the concept of the social life of human beings (Winch, 1960, p. 233). Because a society is a conceptual and normative system, students of human social life must deal with the 'actions' of 'persons' in an articulated 'moral space'. The total moral space of a culture will have many dimensions, each constituted by a system of collective representations. For dissolving witchcraft, only two primary structurings will be discussed: firstly, a system of concepts of human action and its evaluation; secondly, a system of person categories. Naturally, to understand any particular patterns of social action it would be necessary to relate these planes to the other classificatory structures.

Action and Evaluation Concepts

Cultural classifications of human action and its evaluation have been little studied by anthropologists. Of course, data have been obtained incidentally; but, for want of the relevant interests, it has rarely been a subject for inquiry in its own right. Anthropologists thus have attempted to explain 'sacrifice' or 'ritual', for instance, without investigating systematically the concepts of action of the culture in question, and without grasping therefore the kind of principles on which the distinctions of such a system were based. Partly this may have been due to a scientist presumption that human beings themselves have very little if any insight or worth to say about their own activities. Yet it is evident that there is a very rich and discriminating system of concepts concerning human action embedded in ordinary English, and there is no reason to suppose that a pre-literature culture would be less well endowed. Indeed, folk systems there could well be more elaborate and insightful.

Despite efforts of philosophers and anthropologists to investigate fundamental categories of the human mind, we cannot afford to be confident that the candidates that have already been proposed are sufficiently well grounded empirically. Hence it must be admitted that while the articulated 'moral space' is offered as a cultural universal, the term 'moral' is clearly one of our own culture's action and evaluation concepts. Consequently it cannot be entirely free of the translational difficulties which beset other cultural concepts. The best we can do is to acquire as broad a perspective as possible, and this is why it is so unfortunate that philosophical discussions of morals have normally been conducted on such a narrow cultural and historical basis (Collingwood, 1944, pp. 43, 46; MacIntyre, 1971, pp. 1–4). We have often been given general theories of ethics, yet it is surely important to observe that our moral 'ought', for instance, first appeared in the eighteenth century (MacIntyre, 1971, p. 165). Such a notion was absent in Greece, so it is only by a mistranslation that we can say that Kant and the Greek philosophers were arguing about the same subject. Moral concepts are so much a part of – indeed in large part constitutive of – different forms of social life that it is unrealistic to think in terms of a timeless discourse. What we need is less an abstract theory than a social history of moral notions – both a historical perspective on the basic items of our human vocabulary (such as 'person' itself) and the comparative data from students of other cultures. Only this kind of research can give us a better knowledge of what are social universals. Without such a perspective our interpretation is bound to be less refined.

Here perhaps is a role for the sociology of knowledge, for clearly there can be no history of ideas in a vacuum. The Cartesian *cogito ergo sum*, which has so little import for us now, can presumably be set against a general cultural configuration which made it of such concern to Descartes (Wilden, 1972, pp. 212 ff.). No doubt a certain type of social experience lies behind what may be our contemporary equivalent of his dictum – 'I speak, therefore I am a social being'. Mary Douglas has recently put forward the general argument that there is a concordance between social and symbolic experience: the image of the human body mirrors the perception of the body social (1970a). Such a thesis would naturally imply that very different ideas of duty, self, action, and so on, will be found under different social conditions. Durkheim made obligatoriness and desirability universals of morality, but he still suggested that their relative importance could vary considerably (1906, p. 46). It seems feasible, for instance, that there are cultural conditions where Kant's imperatival view of ethics would be barely intelligible since it contains that notion of universalizability by which 'ought' is severed from particular social ties. If Kant's view was partly a response to a growing individualism, obviously it will not suit a culture where the stress falls upon social role instead of the individual who acts a role. Certainly, if we are to understand institutional facts about responsibility and punishment we shall need to uncover the conceptual systems relating to ethics and the nature of the 'person' which they embody.[2]

There is a place for vital research on these subjects, and anthropologists could contribute usefully by giving a comparative perspective on basic concepts in the field of human action. What the outcome of such work will be we cannot tell. Perhaps it is unrealistic to expect complete relativity in the field of morals; but Mauss (1938) has shown how those seemingly basic concepts which we feel ought to be *a priori* and timeless in fact are the result of a complicated history in our own civilization. And Lienhardt, discussing the Dinka concept of self-knowledge, has pointed out how the whole area of 'mind' and 'experience' can be construed differently from the way it is in our culture (1961, pp. 149–50). That there are pre-literate societies with extensive 'psychological' vocabularies is well known. What is not certain are the divergences we may find in the fundamental presuppositions of such domains. A comparative study of human action cannot be just a survey of different evaluations, since the basic concepts may be too discrepant. We already have ethnographic evidence of striking differences in moral consciousness and perception (Read, 1955, p. 226). In some cultures, for instance, there is purportedly

2. The French sociological tradition of analysing systems of 'collective representations' has provided valuable comparative material on different cultural concepts of the person (see *La Notion de Personne en Afrique Noire*, Editions du Centre National de la Recherche Scientifique. Paris 1973).

not that clear differentiation between a 'person' and his situation or status that we find in our own (ibid, p. 196).

Such interests as these will require semantic anthropology to separate itself from that uncritical adherence to a Western philosophy of mind which has so impaired much of our work (Needham, 1972, p. 188). We need a broadly based empirical study of different cultural concepts of the human person and his powers. Some studies are already available (Geertz, 1966), but research on this topic must be an intensive analysis of cultural categories. Writings under labels like 'culture and personality' studies, or 'psychological anthropology', by virtue of being culture-bound could not be adequate.

A System of Person Categories

The second primary articulation of the moral space we have proposed as a framework for dissolving witchcraft consists of a set of person categories.[3] It is a classificatory system through which is distributed a range of cultural predicates ascribing attributes and powers to different types of human being. Of course we have much data on this subject, but because it was not a leading interest of the functionalist field-workers, the topic was not approached systematically, and so our information remains inadequate even for those cultures best known to anthropologists. For instance, in order to define a 'witch' we should need fully mapped out the different symbolic definitions of those sorts of person categories normally translated as 'sorcerer', 'diviner', 'prophet', 'priest' and so on.[4] So often we have been told that a witch is believed to possess such and such 'supernatural' powers, without being informed as to what the culture in question regards as the natural powers of other categories of human being.

We may regard the 'person field' as structured like a chess board. It forms one plane of the many which make up the total moral space, and therefore cuts through other classifying systems in the culture. With this image we have a framework which makes it clear why witchcraft cannot be approached as if it were a separate topic. The identity 'witch' is only

3. A debt to the work of Strawson must be acknowledged here (1958, 1964), although my interest is not in the philosophical 'primitiveness' of the notion of a person. Also, by virtue of its slender linguistic base, there must be a worry that Strawson's studies of the relations between supposed invariant categories may be a mere *a priori* anthropology.

4. This is an absolutely minimal set of the most institutionalized person categories which will suffice here for giving our outline framework. Naturally, when analysing a particular body of ethnographic data we should set out the person field using the native categories themselves, and this would involve considering the less formal 'dramaturgical' roles as well.

one on a board which contains other persons with differently specified characteristics. Moreover, this one system intersects with others – with concepts of human actions, evaluatory ideas, and other systems of beliefs. We could say that to tackle 'witchcraft' as if it were an isolable problem would be like someone unfamiliar with the game of chess observing a series of movements and then writing a book on 'bishops'. The point is that the 'bishop' cannot be understood apart from – indeed exists only by virtue of – the whole system of definitions and rules which constitutes chess. In Saussurian terms (1949, p. 153 ff.), the value of the bishop (or witch) derives from all the other pieces which the bishop (or witch) is not. Neither has any significance in isolation – a striking demonstration of the way in which anthropology is a species of inquiry into the nature of semantic identities and not a matter of that Radcliffe-Brownian butterfly collector identifying natural species.

No doubt such a scheme will seem needlessly intricate to some, but the deficiencies in the functional approach make it necessary to work out a new framework in such an explicit manner. And the scheme is designed to encourage a greater empiricism in this area than has been shown in the past. The structure of the person system is itself an empirical matter. Certainly one will expect there to be recurring patterns cross-culturally – among other reasons because of the appearance of formal categories like marginality in all classifying structures – but it is an ethnographic matter how many pieces each puts on the moral board and what type of discriminations it makes between them.

Undoubtedly one source of past empirical shortcomings has been the enormous influence of Evans-Pritchard's monograph on subsequent studies. This analysis was only an interpretation of a belief structure in one society, and there was no reason to presume that detailed features of Zande thought would be found elsewhere. Unfortunately, however, it has become almost a model for witchcraft studies in general. In many cases it is patently clear that ethnographers have had the Zande scheme in mind when organizing their own data. Gluckman even boldly claimed that Evans-Pritchard's argument applied to 'all African tribes who believe in witchcraft' (1944, p. 61), despite the fact that one of his earliest articles on Zande thought specifically warned against the projecting of any one cultural scheme into a general model (1929, pp. 1–2).

It is unfortunately the case that a few excellent monographs have tended to become frameworks into which ethnographers could fit their own field material instead of paying more attention to the particularity of the culture they happen to have studied. Thus it is probably no exaggeration, in view of the enormous influence of Evans-Pritchard's study of the political system of the Nuer – although here too the most 'paradigmatic' insights were missed by his imitators – to suggest that a whole phase in British social anthropology of concern with lineage typologies would have been substantially different had he done his field-work elsewhere. In the case of witchcraft, the Zande distinction between the witch as the possessor of innate psychic power and the sorcerer who consciously manipulates objects, has clearly become the basis for ill-conceived taxonomic generalizations. Evans-Pritchard was not trying to impose on future studies a conceptual strait-jacket, yet this is what the distinction has become, despite protests from other anthropologists about the misguided nature of the enterprise (Turner, 1964). Middleton and Winter, for instance, argue that the witch/sorcerer opposition is vital for comparative work, although some of the cultures discussed in the volume where they make this claim obviously do not possess it (1963, p. 2). Mair is even prepared to defend the distinction on the basis that the anthropologist is able to find physical evidence in the one case but not in the other (1969, p. 23). It is not merely that the opposition is sometimes just imposed, or that it is normally presented along with suspiciously Western terms like 'spirit' and 'matter'; for even where a Zande-like scheme does appear, the difference between the witch and sorcerer only gets its meaning from the whole system of differences which makes up the set of person categories. Far from accepting this, some have even suggested that it is permissible to overlook the one opposition if it does appear in the effort to arrive at sociological generalizations (Marwick, 1965, p. 171). Yet others, given a host of cultural identities, think it sufficient to regard several differently named persons as different kinds of witch.

Clearly it would be better to follow the advice given by Leach in his attempt to rethink anthropology out of the taxonomic phase (1961, p. 10) – to take each case as it comes along. We need semantic analyses of conceptual fields of the kind Lienhardt made in his study of the terms related to the Dinka notion of *apeth* (1951). One need only think of whether the powers are regarded as hereditary or not, whether they are exercised consciously or not, whether the category is associated with 'foreignness' (Buxton, 1963, p. 105) or exactly the reverse, to see what a mass of disparate phenomena have been subsumed under the one label of witchcraft. It is not even the case that 'witchcraft' is always disapproved of, nor is the 'witch' always defined by a process of total symbolic inversion. Despite these well-known ethnographic facts, some (Mair, 1969) still persist in speaking of the 'universal image' of the witch.

Of course, because of their interest in the locus of accusations, the old-style writings on witchcraft have certainly established some patterns which definitely do recur in many societies. But the advantage of employing our framework of person identities and concepts of action is that we can go far beyond the functionalist statements about misfortune and social competition to make a more discriminating study of particular social ideologies. For instance, we can associate particular person categories with certain types of action and motivation. Among the Bakweri, for instance, there is a strong conceptual tie between *liemba* (witch) and *inona* (envy), and, not surprisingly for a people with an egalitarian ethic, a strong link between these and the possession of wealth (Ardener, 1973, p. 5). Witchcraft can only be understood when the complex which makes up the whole conceptual field in which a *liemba* acts is set out. For the Gonja we have evidence that the act of bewitching can be associated with two very different evaluations of action according to the sexual identity of the witch (Goody, 1970). Thus, female witches engage in an activity which is disapproved of, while using these powers is actually an accepted convention in the competition between males for authority. Further significant variations are found in terms of the victims of evil-doing. For instance, some categories of person with powers to harm are thought to use their evil indiscriminately, while others aim it at well-circumscribed sectors of the moral space of their culture, for instance those persons labelled 'affines'. Clearly it is by following up details like this that we shall be able to distribute those facts clustered into 'the witchcraft problem' into larger cultural schemes of action concepts, ethical theory, and person categories in ways which respect the particularities of each case.

One of the gains of the idea of a moral space is that it is a framework which can encourage an empirical approach to the cultural composition and full scope of the person system. For there is the danger that the alien nature of such categories as 'witch', 'diviner', and so on, because they are not part of the internal structuring of this classificatory plane in our culture, will lead anthropologists to close off this area as concerned with 'mystical belief' or suchlike. But this may badly disfigure the semantic structure of other cultures. Among the Lugbara, for instance, the symbolism which defines witchcraft and sorcery is only a part of a larger schema applied to differences in social distance and social time in general (Middleton, 1963, p. 271). Among the Safwa, witchcraft and sorcery operate in affinal and descent relationships respectively, which suggests that they are both partial refractions of a larger classificatory system (Harwood, 1970, p. 137–8).

There is certainly much evidence that 'political identities' should be included in the same person field as the witch, and political action in the general system of action/evaluation concepts. Religion and political structure are often quite explicitly aspects of a single coherent ideology, so that 'government' is not a separate sphere but merely a dimension of a total symbolic classification (Hocart, 1970; Coomaraswamy, 1942; Dumont, 1972). The outlook of the old-style British anthropologists – that political behaviour was 'real', and rituals and beliefs largely embellishments – obscured this vital semantic point. Hence the numerous instances where the two have been artificially ripped apart and then joined again by some functional hypothesis about the link between mystical beliefs and political structure, such as that ritual sacralizes political statuses and so supports the social order, and so on.

Nor is there any reason to presume that such explicit ideologies are confined to those cultures with an elaborate 'Great Tradition'. For instance, the Swat Pathans (who have been the central ethnographic case in the recent development of the transactional approach to politics (Barth, 1965)) clearly display a cultural schema containing the oppositions of power/passivity, violence/mediation, wealth/humility, which subsumes both religious statuses and political action. In Africa too where the institutional-functional tradition has been so strong in anthropology, symbolic analyses have also proved fruitful. Needham has shown 'complementary governance' systems to exist among the Nyoro and Meru (1967, 1960). And among the Nuer, an analysis of the identities 'priest', 'prophet', and 'bull' exposes a larger scheme based on the opposition of violence and peace (Beidelman, 1971a).

Using this kind of framework for these examples clearly shows that it is considerably more instructive to analyse the collective representations of a culture than make easy resort to the familiar political rhetoric of our own society, or to be concerned with whether it is appropriate to speak of 'chiefs' or not (Needham, 1960, pp. 124–5). But to do this we also need analytic terms with which to construct our analyses which will not distort the nature of cultural categories while framing them. We have suggested that the notion of a 'person' system may be of general value here; but there are other general notions which provide conceptual strands of the total moral space. For instance, with the examples used above the male/female opposition seems a likely basic syntactical component. It is an opposition which in many cultures is concordant with the witch/sorcerer distinction; in the Hindu scheme it emerges in the idea of the 'marriage' between the king and the *brahmin* priest; in the secular-mystical dyarchy of the Nyoro it is present in inverted form as the maleness of the princess and the femininity of the diviner. Clearly, also, such a discrimination forms a basic part of the field of kinship classification.

It may well be, then, that the general framework outlined for reshaping witchcraft has a value far beyond this problem. It may provide a scheme in which a good many other traditional areas of the subject can be recast. After all, it is a fairly obvious fact that other cultures are not organized along the lines by which the social sciences are taught in our universities, even if our introductory textbooks frequently give the opposite impression. Having sketched this analytical scheme, our semantic investigation can turn to some ideas from linguistic philosophy to aid our comprehension of the facts now that they have been rearranged.

Types of Discourse: The Point of the Rules: Speech Acts

A natural language is not a homogeneous structure. In English there are moral terms like 'good', for instance, which do not behave like ordinary descriptive words; and some would argue that there is a 'naturalistic fallacy' which acts as a general boundary marking off the ethical domain, so prohibiting the transmutation of moral concepts into naturalistic discourse about 'effectiveness', 'utility', and the like. There is no reason for thinking that a similar heterogeneity does not exist in other languages. The idea of different 'domains of discourse' may therefore be of wide value, especially in reminding us of features to remember when looking for the appropriate concepts in our own culture to translate those of other societies. If it is accepted here that ethical utterances may not be recast as scientific propositions, or judged by the same types of criteria, it is obviously vital to respond to the existence of corresponding prohibitions in other languages. Naturally, these domains and prohibitions will have to be established empirically; but if there are invariants to be discovered in comparative work on the moral field, we may presume that some of the deepest distinctions on which the configuration of our own domains are based may find parallels elsewhere.

These considerations are even more important when dealing with such problems as witchcraft, because ethical discourse is so closely bound up with human action and evaluation. This is why Wittgenstein's notion 'form of life', which emphasizes the relation of speaking to non-linguistic action by locating language in its broader cultural context, is so useful. Concepts, says Wittgenstein, express our interests (1953, para. 570). Thus, in order to understand a mode of discourse we must not only grasp the rules but also the 'point' of those rules. Meaning is part of a game whose conventions have some purpose (ibid., paras 564–5; Winch, 1964, pp. 26–7). Consequently it is vital to study the part which concepts play in the life of the community. In other words, if we wish to explain types of discourse we must do it by reference to the institutions and forms of social life with which they are associated (Hampshire, 1970, p. 14). By stressing rules and the relation of concepts to action we are able to make our explorations semantic rather than functional.

Zande moral concepts are social in a rather different way from that in which the theoretical terms of science are, for instance, because the links between concepts and action are different in the two fields. Perhaps certain of the 'unscientific' aspects of Zande thought become more intelligible, therefore, when we look at the relation between 'social knowledge' and 'social interests'. We know that Zande witchcraft beliefs have a practical point, also that the system is not logically complete, in the sense that there are problems an anthropologist could raise which have no interest for the Azande themselves (Evans-Pritchard, 1937, pp. 24–6). The anthropologist can expose 'conceptual synapses' – beliefs which are not brought together, ideas which are not pushed to a conclusion, questions that are not asked. They are not contradictions, for they lie precisely in areas which are not structured because the Azande see no point in thinking them out. It is too extreme to speak of Zande witchcraft as a system of action rather than a theory (Barden, 1972, p. 113); but we should certainly not forget the reason for these rules, which may rest in the close link of the concepts to social action. There is, for example, a great emphasis on particularity. The Azande are not so much interested in who is a witch as in who is causing one to be ill at a particular time (Evans-Pritchard, 1937, pp. 24–5). Hence, while they claim witchcraft to be hereditary, they punish only individuals.

Similar features appear in conceptual systems in other cultures which share a like location with respect to social interests and practical action. For instance, we ourselves speak about being moulded by external circumstances and influences stemming from early childhood, yet our law punishes a culpable individual. To a degree, therefore, our own legal notions operate by not following up certain lines of investigation. As the judge said in Samuel Butler's *Erewhon*, the fault was in the accused individual and he was not there 'to enter upon curious metaphysical questions as to the origin of this or that ... questions to which there would be no end were their introduction once tolerated, and which would result in throwing the only guilt on the tissues of the primordial cell'.

Some jurists have even emphasized that their task is a practical rather than a scientific one. A distinction like that between 'cause' and 'conditions' in jurisprudence is clearly related to this practical role. Evans-Pritchard discussing witchcraft beliefs and the practice of divination spoke of a 'socially relevant cause' (1937, p. 73), but essentially the same notion is expressed in Bacon's famous dictum '*in jure, non remota causa*;

sed proxima spectatur' (quoted in Cohen, 1950, p. 259, n 27). Since law is closely tied to conceptual structures and moral evaluations, the complexity of notions of causation in this sphere – for instance, attributing an event to 'negligence', 'accident', 'act of God', and so on – is well worth semantic investigation by anthropologists (see Hart and Honoré, 1956). *Mens rea*, for example, links culpability to certain conditions of knowledge and intention; in many branches of law a man is punishable only when a 'free' agent. Once the idea of agency in this sense is established, various lines of questioning need not be raised, for the agent is a responsible individual and is punishable as such. Facts which link him causally by chains which are relevant considerations in other contexts, no longer have any interest. To all intents and purposes, each man then becomes an island complete in himself.

Since law is evidently a field for detailed conceptual inquiry, it is unfortunate that the outlook which cast witchcraft studies into a micro-political form should also have led to an overwhelming stress on social control in the field of law. Of course we have come a good deal further than the taxonomies of social sanctions proposed by Radcliffe-Brown, and we possess some good monographs in the anthropology of law. On the other hand, the general approach has remained that of 'jural sociology', and references to the work of jurists and philosophers of law remain few. Even today some anthropologists (Mair, 1972a, p. 210) still almost instinctively separate law from those topics like religion which involve systems of belief as well as systems of action. But to suggest that law does not entail a study of conceptual relations is preposterous. The links between law, morality, and custom may be complex, and what should be included under law is therefore something of a problem. But whatever is included will be intricately related to the cultural systems of notions about statuses, human actions and ethical evaluation. Even if legal terms do not have quite the same sense as the concepts in ordinary language, they nonetheless relate to them. There are consequently areas of law where the rich conceptual structures of ordinary language relating to action – notions of culpability, chance, responsibility, excuses, free will, agency, cause, motive, intention, etc. – make their presence felt. In actual legal proceedings an outcome sometimes depends upon the minutest of distinctions contained in this field of concepts.

Some might argue that this conceptual complexity stems from literacy, or is the result of the existence of a legal profession, but it would be a gross prejudice simply to assume that similar systems could not be detected in primitive societies. Hence, the anthropology of law also needs to be a semantic investigation, and indeed in some cases might quite literally

357

be a linguistic one. The Yakan, for instance, lack our institutions of law; but litigation, as opposed to argument or just ordinary talking, is registered as a distinct style of speech (Frake, 1969). Clearly, it will not be possible for the more sociologically inclined to turn to jural and political relations as easy alternatives to tackling the more obviously semantic realms of religion or myth, or to profess an interest in law while declaring that language concerns another type of anthropologist. As all human action is of a conceptual order, there can be no adequate approach to any of the topics anthropology tackles which is not a study of meaning.

Legal actions are highly structured rituals involving the definition and redefinition of persons, and it may well be that Austin's idea of 'performative utterances' will be of great value here.[5] When a jury delivers a verdict it does not *state* that a man is guilty, it *makes* him so. 'Guilt' is a public legal status, and consequently a man is guilty when declared so independently of whether he actually committed the offence of which he has been accused. And when found guilty, a man can only escape this category by being part of a second legal performance which annuls the first – the mere discovery of new evidence is not enough. After all, it is not without significance that a jury is asked whether the accused is guilty or not guilty, and not whether he is guilty or innocent. We can therefore construe verdicts as 'performative definitions', so legal proceedings – and we could add the larger field of criminology (Maguire, 1974) – are largely concerned with systems of classification.

This kind of idea applies to witchcraft also. Accusations, denials, the findings of divination, change the public definitions of persons. In all these areas where belief and action are closely related, where utterances define situations and reclassify them, the notion of 'doing things with words' may provide fresh insights. Thus, to take a 'phenomenological' religion where ritual is a means of controlling experience (Lienhardt, 1961, pp. 234, 289 ff.), among the Dinka a sacrifice may be regarded as creating the situation which it describes (id., 1956, p. 327). Just as 'I name this ship the X' actually does confer the name on the ship, so the ritual sacrifice does not state a fact but actually brings a state into being. Hence we may see the ritual of cutting through the genitals of the slain beast as a clarification and redefinition of the articulation of moral space (id., 1961, pp. 284–5). Kinship ties are severed by the ritual itself, and the new distance created means that action which would have been labelled incest can, in the new space, not be so categorized. The performance (in Austin's

5. Finnegan has suggested that the notion may illuminate the fields of religion and ritual in general (1969, p. 550); Tambiah has applied the concept to magic (1973).

terms) is neither true nor false, but either happy or not depending on a highly complex set of conventions.

Because primitive cultures do not have the means of making a public record of events in the way our literate culture does, anthropologists will possibly find the idea of 'speech acts' of wide use. It will require detailed research to establish how fruitful a notion the 'performative' is. However, Austin's work has not gone uncriticized, and he himself thought that the distinction constative/performative would be absorbed into 'more general families of related and overlapping speech acts' (1962, p. 149). Certainly then, even if performative utterances throw valuable light on some problems, they cannot really be expected to solve more than a narrow range of semantic issues. It is clear that our attention is more profitably directed towards the more minute discriminations which compose the more general framework.

Just what contribution 'speech acts' can make to the development of a philosophical semantics is not clear: but anthropologists could at least aid its growth by providing the comparative perspective to what might otherwise easily be a severely culture-bound enterprise by virtue of the small number of societies with which philosophers are normally familiar. Given the total historical experience of humanity, literate industrial cultures are very unrepresentative. It has been an important development in philosophy that the stress should turn to the great diversity of ways in which ordinary language is used. It is a pity that anthropologists were not more interested in language than they have been, for then we might have been able substantially to aid the researches of another discipline. It seems likely that the ceremonial and instrumental uses of speech would be more evident in non-literate societies, so our researches could have put a general theory of speech acts on a firmer empirical basis.

Semantic Changes: Scope and Empiricism

The analysis in this paper has gathered together some ideas from linguistics and linguistic philosophy in order to demonstrate relatively concretely the difference of outlook and style which exists between semantic anthropology and the older sociological tradition in the discipline. Clearly, the discussion does not provide a new theory of witchcraft. It merely gives an outline of a theoretical framework in which a standard topic in structural-functional anthropology could be reformulated. Other topics, like law and politics, were included in the same general schema used to dissolve witchcraft in order to show that the framework possesses sufficient analytical power to help in a more widespread recasting of anthropology. This move was not one from a conceptual problem on to institutional relations, for our notion of human action renders this division nonsensical. By now we are more than prepared to see categories like 'totemism' or 'religion' dispensed with, but it is important to stress that labels like 'politics' may equally seriously impede our comprehension of other cultures.

It was necessary therefore to develop our argument concerning witchcraft by absorbing other topics, for our experience of the last ten years or so in British anthropology might badly mislead us as to the potential scope of the recent semantic trends. Because analytical advances have been so striking in the fields of kinship and symbolic classification, one might be tempted to infer that the discipline is amenable to this type of recasting only in certain limited areas, and that other topics like law and politics must forever remain fixed in the basic form they assumed under the old sociological identity of the subject. Our integrating several traditionally separate topics in the terms of one analysis was meant to demonstrate the fact that the divisions do not fall between different kinds of problems that anthropology studies, but rather that there are deep differences of outlook between different anthropologists over the general nature of the discipline itself. Thus it should not be thought that in our stressing language and meaning we are drawing attention to past deficiencies just in connection with subjects like religion or myth. The whole of anthropology covers a semantic subject matter, and so the kind of analytical interest which lay behind our recasting of witchcraft could radically change other areas, even those seemingly most remote from semantic concerns like ecology and economics. In other words, semantic anthropology is not a sub-department of anthropology; the semantic style covers all the territory which was included in the older functional social anthropology. The new anthropology cannot be an agglutinative discipline – a patchwork of sociological and semantic parts. Gradually, it is hoped, those same sorts of interests which have transformed major topics will infect the rest. Obviously we shall have to wait to see how semantic anthropology recasts these areas which have so far been virtually untouched by the developments of the last decade. But it is necessary to conclude by pointing out that, because of the broad nature of the aim of the analysis in this chapter, our argument has done little more than provide a suggestive outline framework for application in specific cases. It is vital to stress that semantic anthropology itself is far more detailed analysis than it is the formulating of general schemas. Indeed, we shall only know the value of our proposed recasting of witchcraft when the ideas we employed are applied to detailed bodies of ethnographic data.

Because the discipline is in a profound transition, much of the literature that has pointed the way has tended to be polemical and this has somewhat obscured the nature of the work that belongs to the new identity. We should never forget that Evans-Pritchard, who so significantly led the shift from function to meaning, was not a polemicist, and that by far his best work consists of monographs which resulted from his own fieldwork.

It is important to make this point because many of those who have expressed antipathy towards the recent trends in the discipline have alleged that anthropology is turning from an empirical science into abstract metaphysics. But this is to misperceive the nature of these developments entirely. Any unprejudiced reading of the typical articles which have established the break with the older functional style will see how much they are a matter of close attention to ethnographic facts. Indeed, many spectacular articles have been reworkings of classical functionalist monographs; and the experience has often been that the monographs themselves are shown to be severely deficient in crucial ethnographic information when exposed to modern analytical interests. Semantic anthropology certainly is far more dependent upon detailed ethnography than functionalism ever was.

Of course we can be proud of the fieldwork record of British anthropology during the past half-century. But when, nowadays, we draw attention to the theoretical shortcomings of structural-functionalism yet then praise its representatives for the thoroughness of their field research, we must not forget that the known influence of theoretical interests on research procedure lessens the weight of this compliment considerably. Obviously all theories are selective, and it would be unfair to expect functionalists to have gathered the facts which are relevant to our inquiries when they were not interested in our sorts of questions. This is why a fieldwork tradition must be a part of the newer anthropology: we must clearly gather new data by a process of investigation which is specifically directed by our own concerns.

But this is an issue which has more general implications, for the deficiency in functionalist fieldwork was of a far more fundamental kind than we have so far suggested (Ardener, 1971a, p. 450 ff.). It is clear from the speciousness which pervades so much functional writing that in a great many cases the functionalists did not even ask those questions which were vital to collecting the information necessary to supporting *their own* contentions. For a discipline which prided itself on its scientific nature and was proud of its fieldwork basis, it is striking how frequently there appeared general statements about the functional relationships between institutions entirely unsupported by any empirical evidence. The failing here was not that of selectivity, but a basic error concerning what scientific investigation of social life involved, and so a mistaken view of what constituted empiricism there. It is therefore doubly important that we emphasize here that our explorations in language have not been part of an effort to convert anthropology into philosophy, but merely an attempt, after a consideration of the character of the subject matter our science deals with, to do anthropology better. We must give attention to the sort of theoretical issues discussed above in order for our empiricism to be more effective. Indeed, unless one acknowledges the conceptual nature of human beings one cannot be scientific in describing their activities at all. It is for that very reason that, as semantic anthropology attempts to rectify some of the theoretical defects of the old style of investigation, it at the same time rectifies its empirical shortcomings too.

References

ARDENER, E. W. (1970), 'Witchcraft, economics, and the continuity of belief', in M. Douglas (ed.) (1970b), pp. 141–60.

ARDENER, E. W. (1971a), 'The new anthropology and its critics', *Man* (n.s.), vol. 6, pp. 449–67.

ARDENER, E. W. (1971b), Introductory Essay, in 1971 (ed.), pp. ix-cii.

ARDENER, E. W. (ed.) (1971), *Social Anthropology and Language*, Tavistock.

ARDENER, E. W. (1973), Some Outstanding Problems in the Analysis of Events. A.S.A. Conference Paper.

AUSTIN, J. L. (1962), *How To Do Things With Words*, Clarendon Press.

BARDEN, G. (1972), 'Method and meaning', in Singer and Street (eds) (1972), pp. 104–29.

BARTH, F. (1965), *Political Leadership among Swat Pathans*, Athlone Press.

BEIDELMAN, T. O. (1970), 'Towards more open theoretical interpretations', in M. Douglas (ed.) (1970b), pp. 351–6.

BEIDELMAN, T. O. (1971a), 'Nuer priests and prophets, charisma, authority, and power among the Nuer', in (1971b) (ed.), pp. 375–415.

BEIDELMAN, T. O. (ed.) (1971b), *The Translation of Culture*, Tavistock.

BUXTON, J. (1963), 'Mandari witchcraft', in Middleton and Winter (1963).

CHAPPELL, V. C. (ed.) (1962), *The Philosophy of Mind*, Prentice-Hall.

COHEN, F. S. (1950), 'Field theory and judicial logic', *Yale Law Journal*, vol. 59, pp. 238–72.

COLLINGWOOD, R. G. (1944), *An Autobiography*, Penguin.

COOMARASWAMY, A. K. (1942), *Spiritual Authority and Temporal Power in the Indian Theory of Government*, American Oriental Society.

DOUGLAS, M. (1967), 'Witch beliefs in Central Africa', *Africa*, vol. 37, pp. 72–80.

DOUGLAS, M. (1970a), *Natural Symbols, Explorations in Cosmology*, Cresset.

DOUGLAS, M. (ed.) (1970b), *Witchcraft Confessions and Accusations*, Tavistock.

DUMONT, L. (1961), 'Caste, racism and "stratification": reflections of a social anthropologist, *Contributions to Indian Sociology*', vol. 5, pp. 20–43.

DUMONT, L. (1972), *Homo Hierarchicus. The Caste System and its Implications*, Paladin.

DURKHEIM, E. (1906), 'The determination of moral facts', in (1953), pp. 1–34.

DURKHEIM, E. (1953), *Sociology and Philosophy*, Cohen & West Ltd.

EVANS-PRITCHARD, E. E. (1929), 'The morphology and function of magic: a comparative study of Trobriand and Zande ritual and spells', in Middleton (ed.) (1967a), pp. 1–22.

EVANS-PRITCHARD, E. E. (1937), *Witchcraft, Oracles and Magic among the Azande*, Clarendon Press.

FINNEGAN, R. (1969), 'How to do things with words: performative utterances among the Limba of Sierra Leone', *Man* (n.s.), vol. 4, pp. 537–52.

FORTES, M. and DIETERLEN, G. (eds) (1965), *African Systems of Thought*, Oxford U.P. for International African Institute.

FRAKE, C. O. (1969), 'Struck by speech: the Yakan concept of litigation', in Gumperz and Hymes (eds) (1972), pp. 106–29.

GEERTZ, C. (1966), *Person, Time, and Conduct in Bali. An Essay in Cultural Analysis*. Yale South East Asia Studies Cultural Report Series No. 14.

GLUCKMAN, M. (1944), Review of Evans-Pritchard (1937). *Human Problems in British Central Africa*, vol. 1, pp. 61–71.

GLUCKMAN, M. (ed.) (1972), *The Allocation of Responsibility*, Manchester U.P.

GOODY, E. (1970), 'Legitimate and illegitimate aggression in a West African State', in M. Douglas (ed.) (1970), pp. 207–44.

GUMPERZ, J., and HYMES, D. H. (eds) (1972), *Directions in Sociolinguistics. The Ethnography of Communication*, Holt, Rinehart & Winston.

HAMPSHIRE, S. (1970), *Thought and Action*, Chatto & Windus.

HART, H. L. A., and HONORÉ, A. M. (1956), 'Causation in the law', *Law Quarterly Review*, vol. 72, pp. 58–90, 260–81, 398–417.

HARWOOD, A. (1970), *Witchcraft, Sorcery and Social Categories among the Safwa*, Oxford U.P. for International African Institute.

HICK, J. (ed.) (1966), *Faith and the Philosophers*, Macmillan.

HOCART, A. M. (1970), *Kings and Councillors. An Essay in the Comparative Anatomy of Human Society* (ed. Needham), first published by University of Chicago Press (1936).

HORTON, R., and FINNEGAN, R. (eds) (1973), *Modes of Thought. Essays on Thinking in Western and Non-Western Societies*, Faber and Faber.

KEYNES, R. H. (1972), 'Witchcraft in sixteenth- and seventeenth-century England', *Journal of the Anthropological Society of Oxford*, vol. 3, pp. 149–57.

LEACH, E. R. (1961), 'Rethinking anthropology', in (1968), pp. 1–27.

LEACH, E. R. (1968), *Rethinking Anthropology*, Athlone Press.

LEWIS, I. M. (1970), 'A structural approach to witchcraft and spirit possession', in M. Douglas (ed.) (1970), pp. 293–309.

LIENHARDT, R. G. (1951), 'Some notions of witchcraft among the Dinka', *Africa*, vol. 21, 308–18.

LIENHARDT, R. G. (1956), 'Religion', in Shapiro (ed.) (1956), pp. 310–29.

LIENHARDT, R. G. (1961), *Divinity and Experience. The Religion of the Dinka*, Clarendon Press.

MACFARLANE, A. (1970), *Witchcraft in Tudor and Stuart England. A Regional and Comparative Study*, Routledge & Kegan Paul.

MACINTYRE, A. C. (1964), 'Is understanding compatible with believing?', in Hick (ed.) (1966), pp. 115–33.

MACINTYRE, A. C. (1971), *Against the Self-Images of the Age. Essays on Ideology and Philosophy*, Duckworth.

MAGUIRE, M. (1974), 'Criminology and social anthropology', *Journal of the Anthropological Society of Oxford*, vol. 5, pp. 109–17.

MAIR, L. P. (1969), *Witchcraft*, Weidenfeld & Nicolson.

MAIR, L. P. (1972a), *Introduction to Social Anthropology*, Clarendon Press.

MAIR, L. P. (1972b), 'Some recent writings on witchcraft', *Journal of the Anthropological Society of Oxford*, vol. 3, pp. 33–41.

MARWICK, M. G. (1965) 'Some promblems in the sociology of sorcery and witchcraft', in Fortes and Dieterlen (eds) (1965), pp. 171–91.

MARWICK, M. G. (ed.) (1970), *Witchcraft and Sorcery*. Penguin.

MARWICK, M. G. (1972), 'Anthropologists' declining productivity in the sociology of witchcraft', *American Anthropologist*, vol. 74, pp. 378–85.

MAUSS, M. (1938), 'Une categorie de l'esprit humain. La notion de personne, celle de "moi"', *Journal of the Royal Anthropological Institute*, vol. 68, pp. 263–81.

MIDDLETON, J. (1963), 'Witchcraft and sorcery in Lugbara', in Middleton and Winter (eds) (1963), pp. 257–75.

MIDDLETON, J. (ed.) (1967a), *Magic, Witchcraft, and Curing*, Natural History Press.

MIDDLETON, J. (ed.) (1967b), *Myth and Cosmos. Readings in Mythology and Symbolism*, Natural History Press.

MIDDLETON, J., and WINTER, E. (eds) (1963), *Witchcraft and Sorcery in East Africa*, Routledge & Kegan Paul.

NEEDHAM, R. (1960), 'The left hand of the Mugwe: an analytical note on the structure of Meru symbolism', in (1973) (ed.), pp. 109–27.

NEEDHAM, R. (1967), 'Right and left in Nyoro symbolic classification', in (1973) (ed.), pp. 299–346.

NEEDHAM, R. (1972), *Belief, Language and Experience*, Blackwell.

NEEDHAM, R. (ed.) (1973), *Right and Left. Essays on Dual Symbolic Classification*, University of Chicago Press.

READ, K. E. (1955), 'Morality and the concept of the person among the Gahuku-Gama', in Middleton (ed.) (1967b), pp. 185–230.

SAUSSURE, F. de (1949), *Cours de Linguistique Générale* (C. Bally and A. Sechehaye, eds), Payot.

SHAPIRO, H. (ed.) (1956), *Man, Culture and Society*, Oxford U.P.

SINGER, A., and STREET, B. V. (eds) (1972), *Zande Themes. Essays Presented to Sir Edward Evans-Pritchard*, Blackwell.

STANDEFER, R. (1970), 'African witchcraft beliefs: the definitional problem', *Journal of the Anthropological Society of Oxford*, vol. 1, pp. 11–17.

STRAWSON, P. F. (1958), 'Persons', in Chappell (ed.) (1962), pp. 127–46.

STRAWSON, P. F. (1964), *Individuals: An Essay in Descriptive Metaphysics*, Methuen.

TAMBIAH, S. J. (1973), 'Form and meaning of magical acts: a point of view', in Horton and Finnegan (eds) (1973), pp. 199–229.

THOMAS, K. (1970), 'The relevance of social anthropology to the historical study of English witchcraft', in M. Douglas (ed.) (1970b), pp. 47–79.

THOMAS, K. (1971), *Religion and the Decline of Magic. Studies in Popular Beliefs in Sixteenth-and Seventeenth-Century England*, Weidenfeld & Nicolson.

TURNER, V. W. (1964), 'Witchcraft and sorcery. Taxonomy versus dynamics', *Africa*, vol. 34, pp. 314–24.

WILDEN, A. (1972), *System and Structure. Essays on Communication and Exchange*, Tavistock.

WINCH, P. (1960), 'Nature and convention', *Proceedings of the Aristotelian Society* (n.s.), vol. 60, pp. 231–52.

WINCH, P. (1964), 'Understanding a primitive society', in (1972), pp. 8–49.

WINCH, P. (1972), *Ethics and Action*, Routledge & Kegan Paul.

WITTGENSTEIN, L. (1953), *Philosophical Investigation*, Blackwell.

34. W. D. Hammond-Tooke*

The Witch Familiar as a Mediatory Construct

W. D. Hammond-Tooke, 'The Cape Nguni witch familiar as a mediatory construct', *Man*, vol. (n.s.) 9, 1974, pp. 128–36.

I

This article is an attempt at a fresh look at the system of witch beliefs of the Cape Nguni in an effort to answer the question: why do the beliefs take this precise form? Recent trends in the anthropological study of religious systems (and it is maintained here that witch beliefs are an integral part of Cape Nguni cosmology) stress the desirability of seeing such systems, not only as 'reflections' of the social structure, but as cognitive systems in their own right, as primitive attempts to explain reality. Both Geertz (1966) and Spiro (1966) have strongly urged a more cultural, 'Tylorean', approach, but perhaps the most explicit formulation has been that of Horton in a series of seminal articles (Horton, 1962, 1964, 1967, 1970). He sees traditional cosmological ideas as being similar, in certain respects, to scientific theory-building, in particular the elaboration of explanatory models that search for, and postulate, a unity underlying the apparent diversity of natural events – in fact a search for *order*. His Kalabari material shows clearly how the pantheon of gods and spirits is not only consonant with the social structure but also 'explains' such things as village prosperity, individual misfortune and even social change, and, because their social system is the most constant factor in their lives, it provides a personified model that postulates the forces underpinning and operating on Kalabari society. Horton describes the spirits as fashioned in the image of ordinary Kalabari people but, as he says, 'Beyond this point they are bizarre in many ways' (Horton, 1970, p. 149). The Cape Nguni familiars we shall consider are decidedly not like humans – and they are bizarre almost beyond belief. Is it possible to understand why this should be so?

The system of witch beliefs in Cape Nguni cosmology is clearly closely

*I am grateful to Dr A. A. Dubb and Dr A. G. Schutte, of the Department of Social Anthropology, University of the Witwatersrand, for discussion on points of detail.

interlocked with the more purely 'religious' system of the ancestor cult.[1] It provides an alternative theory of misfortune to that occasioned by ancestral wrath and there is evidence that it is pressed into use to explain more dire misfortunes. Whereas the ancestors are basically benevolent and chastise their descendants more in sorrow than in anger for neglect of custom, the witch is ruthless and motivated by envy and malice, or perhaps by blind, irrational generalized hate. The witch system provides an explanation for evil and reflects the fact that conflict is inherent in society, in much the same way that Satan and his angels have been imported into the idea system of Judaeo-Christian monotheism as a logical and, indeed, essential counterpart to an all-good God.

Much has been written on the sociology of witchcraft but this important aspect does not concern us here.[2] What does need explanation is the cultural forms that Cape Nguni witch beliefs take. As among other Nguni, witches are typically believed to be women[3] and there is a whole bestiary of familiars. The two most common are the *uthikoloshe* and the ambiguous *impundulu* or 'lightning bird' which, although thought of as the bird of heaven, the beating of whose wings is thunder and excrement lightning, is also conceptualized as a handsome youth with whom the witch has sexual relations. The other familiars fall into three groups. *Ichanti* and *umamlambo* are snakes which, like the *impundulu*, have the power to change shape, but in a much more pronounced and kaleidoscopic way, *imfene* (baboon) and *impaka* (wildcat) are zooform beings, and *umkhova*, or *isithunzela*, is a disinterred corpse held captive by witches. What can we say of these beliefs: why precisely these forms?

II

Let us look at them more closely. The following descriptions are based mainly on Professor Wilson's very detailed account of the Mpondo (Hunter, 1936), but I myself have recorded basically similar material from Bhaca (Hammond-Tooke, 1962), Dushane (1970) and Mpondomise (unpublished). The system among Mfengu and Xhosa in

1. A detailed description of these beliefs will be found in Hunter (1936) and Hammond-Tooke (1962).

2. Specific data on the targets of witchcraft accusations in certain Cape Nguni societies will be found in Hunter (1936), p. 318, Wilson et al. (1952), pp. 182–5, and Hammond-Tooke (1970).

3. This is recorded in all the sources. Of 121 cases of witchcraft/sorcery recorded in the Eastern Cape only sixteen of the accused were males (Hammond-Tooke (1970), p. 38): 'The vast majority of accusations of witchcraft or sorcery are against women' (Hunter (1936), p. 316).

the south is identical (Wilson et al., 1952). The main variation is that the Bhaca do not have the *inyoka yabafazi* ('snake of women'), a small snake sent by women to bite babies and small children.

uthikoloshe

'*Thikoloshe* is a small hairy being, having the form of a man, but so small that he only reaches to a man's knee. He has hair all over his face and coming out of his ears, and his face is squashed up like a baboon. The penis of the male is so long that he carries it over his shoulder, and he has only one buttock. All *Thikoloshe* speak with a lisp ... *Thikoloshe* is kept by its owner in a store hut ... A woman *igqwira* (witch) who has a *Thikoloshe* always has a male and she has sexual relations with him ... The accusations of possessing *Thikoloshe* are usually against women' (Hunter, 1936, pp. 275–8).

impundulu (intaka yezulu)

'The [*izulu* or] *impundulu* is the lightning bird . . . which is there when the thunder strikes. An *izulu* is always possessed by a female witch, and it appears to her in the form of a very beautiful young man, who becomes her lover ... The manner by which it kills is a mystery' (Hunter, 1936, pp. 282–4). *Impundulu* can cause miscarriages, blindness and death to man and stock. I myself found that, in the Eastern Cape, the *impundulu* was the most feared of all familiars. Dushane informants believed that the *impundulu* sucked blood from its victims and that its insatiable hunger drove its owner to kill for "meat". Long wasting illnesses, accompanied by coughing, stabbing pains and shortness of breath, are believed to be caused by these vampire-like activities: sudden death from being kicked by the "bird of heaven" ' (Hammond-Tooke, 1970, pp. 28–9).

umamlambo

Umamlambo is a familiar possessed by men. Hunter refers to it as a 'charm' acquired from Whites or Indians (1936, p. 287) but the Bhaca conceive of it as a snake (Hammond-Tooke, 1962, p. 285) as do the Mfengu and Xhosa of Keiskammahoek who call it 'the snake of the men' (*inyoka yamadoda*). '*uMamlambo* has the power to take on any guise at all, such as a baby, a beautiful woman, a variegated charm, a tin or a mirror' (Wilson et al., 1952, p. 190).

ichanti

'*Ichanti* is a snake which lives in rivers and which has powers of metamorphosis, appearing in any form. "A man goes to a river and sees a tin dish. As he is looking it turns into a hat, and then into a bullock chain." "It runs like a bicycle; when it is going to a person it turns into a ball and races towards them" ... "Any person who sees an *ichanti* falls ill, and will die unless treated ..." "The illness is always severe" ' (Hunter, 1936, p. 286). 'Some Keiskammahoek informants content that *ichanti* is one of the River People' (Wilson et al., 1952, p. 1) but this is clearly not so in other groups.

imfene

'The baboon is a familiar peculiar to men, and used frequently for harming cattle ... witch who has a baboon keeps it in the store-hut ... and rides about on it at

367

night, with one foot on the animal's back, the other on the earth, he facing the animal's tail' (Hunter, 1936, p. 287).

impaka

'Another familiar believed to be possessed by women is the *impaka*, a small rodent. It is said to be sent by its owner to bite people's throats' (Hunter, 1936, p. 286). This familiar appears to be confined to the Mpondo.

isithunzela

It is not certain whether the *isithunzela* is a familiar in the same sense as the others. 'Witches ... raise the dead and enslave them ... The witch beats the grave with a switch, and the grave opens, and the body comes out. He drives a wooden nail into the dead man's head so that he becomes foolish, and pierces his tongue with a long bone needle, so that he cannot speak' (Hunter, 1936, p. 289). Bhaca say that *izithunzela* are extremely tall and black and have the power of hypnotizing (*ukuthwobula*) a person so that he will be drawn towards them like a bird attracted by a snake (Hammond-Tooke, 1962, p. 287). Their appearance is so ghastly that those who see them go mad.

Two problems arise at this point, namely, why is the witch conceptualized so frequently as a woman, and why are the two familiars, especially associated with women, thought of in blatantly sexual terms? Both the icthyphallic *uthikoloshe* and the *impundulu* are believed to have sexual intercourse with their owners and, indeed, frigidity in women is thought to result from this illicit congress. Monica Wilson has discussed the marked sexuality of Mpondo witch beliefs (Wilson, 1951) and postulates, albeit tentatively, that it derives from the fact that, through the rules of clan exogamy, a large number of otherwise potential mates within the area of a marriage isolate are thereby excluded. She contrasts this with the position in Nyakyusa age-villages where kinship does not operate and where witches harm for lust for meat, not for sex. It is difficult to assess the validity of this hypothesis. Certainly today, and presumably for some time in the past, Mpondomise lineages and clans are not basically local groups (Hammond-Tooke, 1968) and one has a wide choice of marriage partner from one's local area. An analysis of Mpondomise marriages showed that 6 per cent. of marriages were contracted between people living in the same neighbourhood, 23 per cent. between those living in the same location, 51 per cent. within the same chiefdom, and only 13 per cent. beyond, and a similar pattern is probably general among all Cape Nguni. Wilson's hypothesis may, of course, be a historical one in the sense that descent groups may have been more localized in the past and that the witch myth 'grew up' at a time in which kinsmen were more concentrated, continuing to operate today under its own inertia.

III

An alternative explanation derives partly from a consideration of inter-sex relationships in the society and partly from the clue given by Geertz (1966) that 'religious' ideas arise to cope with man's perplexity at the limits of his powers of comprehension and control. Cape Nguni women are perpetual minors, first as daughters in their father's homestead and later as wives. In particular, they have certain disabilities. They cannot themselves appear in court, they cannot hold political office, they are victims of a double standard in which men, but not they, may be poly-gynous or take lovers, they may be chastised (within limits) by their husbands and they are harmful to the all-important cattle. This is expres-sed in a special vocabulary and in respectful behaviour (*hlonipha*) to-wards all senior males of the husband's lineage. It is true that there is a complementarity of roles in the sexual division of labour and that women enjoy certain very material satisfactions. A woman is enabled to fulfil her basic role as wife and mother, as a senior wife she has control over junior wives and, as a mother-in-law, she may lord it over her daughter-in-law. Women, as a group, may or may not be happy in their subordinate role, and there is no real reason to think that traditionally the average woman was not – although one suspects that diviners* frequently use their position to break away from an intolerable situation.

But the matter should be looked at from the men's point of view – for, although we have no actual proof of the matter, presumably cosmolo-gical ideas are 'man-made', rather than 'woman-made'. Among all Cape Nguni, women are under the control of men. They are important com-modities in the exchange relationships of the bridewealth system, they are vehicles for the perpetuation of the lineage and a vital factor in the labour force. It is essential for society, for good order, that women should be controlled. And yet they are difficult to control. Like women everywhere they tend to dominate the hearth; the society is not purely pastoral and the important (if de-emphasized) fieldwork is in the hands of women (and probably supplies the real basis of subsistence) and, to change the level of analysis, as Gluckman (1955, pp. 98–9) has pointed out, in a very real sense women do cause disruption of the lineage by creating rivals to a husband and generating the segmentation that presages the future break-up of the descent group. Here, then, is an ambiguous situation – inferiors who frequently do not act as such, the weaker vessel who is, in fact, the sturdy container of lineage interests.

At this point in the argument I have to make assumptions. It seems to me that men must have a sneaking suspicion that *in fact* women are

*Among the Cape Nguni, most diviners are women (see below, p. 426) – *Ed.*

perhaps more important than they are. No matter how self-evident the principle of agnation the fact remains that it is a principle and lacks the poignant immediacy of an umbilical cord that must be cut with a blade of river grass.[4] If fertility is a basic value in the society, it is in women that fertility is most unambiguously located. What I am suggesting is that man's attitude to women is basically ambivalent, if not frankly antagonistic, and that there is a significant contradiction between the *de jure* and *de facto* perception of the woman's role and meaning.[5]

I am suggesting further that their awareness of what appears to be feminine deprivation makes men uneasy. They ask themselves how *they* would feel if roles were reversed, and answer – with resentment. Given, then, a belief in the mystical causation of misfortune through the activities of ill-disposed and malevolent fellow humans, who more likely to cherish negative emotions than the disadvantaged and (wrongly) undervalued women? I am suggesting, then, that the conceptualization of the witch in the image of a woman is a means of objectivizing this perception of inter-sex conflict (real or imaginary). It is not certain whether men feel guilty as to the position of women in the social structure but, if they do, the witch myth could provide an *ex post facto* rationalization for discrimination: in fact, the Cape Nguni do not seem to utilize this, but the ambivalence is expressed quite clearly in the notion of the ritual impurity (*umlaza*) of women (Hunter 1936, pp. 46–7).

IV

To focus now on the familiars themselves. It has been suggested that men are aware of feminine deprivation. It is almost certain that, men being men, they perceive the crux of the deprivation as *sexual* deprivation, for it is here that the principle of manhood finds its most meaningful expression. If a man would feel resentment, presumably women would do the same – and what more natural than they should take daemon lovers, who not only fulfil their inadequately satisfied sexual needs but can be used to wreak vengeance on male society. Note that this theory does not rest on the (empirical) fact of whether or not women *do* feel deprived by their culture, nor even on whether they are

4. It is interesting, in this connection, to note that the origin of man is thought to be from a bed of reeds, the constant proliferation of suckers being likened to the splitting off of tribes. Is it chance that the differentiation from the mother (and the founding of a new agnatic line) should be effected by means of a river plant?

5. One may note here that in some societies, notably in Australia, this ambivalence appears in an even more extreme form, as envy of women's position (Bettelheim (1955)).

in fact deprived, although Hunter notes that, among the Mpondo, 'There is a double standard of sexual morality and most of the quarrels between husband and wife turn on this' (Hunter, 1936, p. 42).[6] It rests on the perception *by men* of this state of affairs. And, if there is guilt, it is transmuted into righteous indignation. The most obvious and appropriate symbol of women's resentment of sexual deprivation is the compensatory image of the enormous penis of *uthikoloshe*: it is significant that an essential preliminary to a cure of bewitchment by the other 'sexual' familiar (*impundulu*) is a confession of having had intercourse with it (Hunter, 1936, p. 285).

What I am suggesting is that here we have a split between the traditional construction of reality (Berger and Luckmann, 1966), which is presented to men as part of their culture, and a perceived contradiction with the realities of the situation. This gives rise on the psychological level to cognitive dissonance (Festinger, 1957) and a drive to handle the contradiction intellectually in terms of a reconceptualization that itself now becomes part of the constructed reality. There is obviously a similarity here with Lévi-Strauss's contention that myths mediate contradictions in the social structure (Lévi-Strauss, 1963) and Rosen's recent suggestion of a similar function in pollution beliefs (Rosen, 1973). It can also be looked at, à la Mary Douglas, as an attempt to cope with category confusion (Douglas, 1966).

But what of the other pair of familiars – the *ichanti* and *umamlambo*? The striking feature of both these beings is their ability to change shape, an ability, significantly, also possessed by witches themselves. Both *ichanti* and *umamlambo* seem to be snakes in their primary form, but resort to rapid changes of form and, in the case of *umamlambo*, colour. There is some evidence that *umamlambo* is more often possessed by male witches and may metamorphose into a beautiful girl, and here the sex-antagonism hypothesis would not be so persuasive. But if we focus on another aspect of witchcraft, the belief that witches attack their nearest-and-dearest and thus strike at the heart of the social structure itself (kinship loyalty), it would seem that here (given the belief in witchcraft) we have another confusion of categories. The kinsman is the stranger: the neighbour is the enemy within the gates (Mayer, 1954, p. 17). And this perception reflects the true position. In fact it is between people

6. It is significant that neuroses of a markedly sexual character are common among Zulu women, who live in a society of essentially similar type. Lee found that 'crying hysteria' and nightmares of a sexual nature tended to take place while husbands were at home (i.e. not away on migrant labour) and that there was evidence of strong dissatisfaction on the part of women with their sexual role in marriage (Lee (1969), pp. 149–50).

locked together in the bonds of mutual obligation that tensions and conflicts arise. A Mpondo proverb states that 'Strife flares up on the (family) ash heap' (Hunter, 1936, p. 308) and the Mpondomise have a simile, 'They fight like brothers'. Mayer quotes an informant as saying 'The spirits remain in strongest form at a man's home, *where there are many enemies of all kinds*' (Mayer, 1961, p. 161, my emphasis). The social construct of reality stresses agnatic and neighbourly harmony: the perception is one of frequent tension. This ambiguity about kinsmen, this cognitive dissonance, is portrayed, and thus objectivized in cultural terms, in the shape (if that is the word!) of beings with ambiguous boundaries. It is significant, too, that the other familiar, the baboon, is an ambiguous creature which mediates between animals and man in that he is an animal but with marked man-like features. Finally, ambiguity and confused categories are symbolized vividly in the zombi-like *isithunzela*, existing in the twilight of a living death.

Perhaps the argument can be made clearer by the following reformulation. It is being argued that the nature of the belief in the witch and her familiars can be explained as a construct deriving from an attempt to mediate between two contradictory constructs, resulting from a perceived discrepancy between the ideal state of affairs and the actual state of affairs. In the following schematic exposition:

C^1 = primary construct
P = perception of discrepancy
C^2 = secondary construct
D = experience of dissonance (i.e. between C^1 and C^2)
WB = the system of witch beliefs (taken as given)
mC = mediatory construct (the *content* of the concept).
We thus get the schema presented on p. 373.

One may note, in passing, another theme, that of symbolic reversal (noted also from other areas, e.g. the Lugbara (Middleton, 1960)). Mpondo and Bhaca witches ride *backwards* on their baboons, and witches always approach the homestead of their victim going backwards.

V

To sum up. These (admittedly speculative) suggestions as to the symbolic meaning of witch familiars all derive from a theory of dissonance between the constructs of reality (cognitive maps) that people have of the nature of things (e.g. correct relations between the sexes, agnatic loyalty, good neighbourliness) and the perceived discontinuities between these and

Q1 Why are witches women?

	C^1	(P)	C^2	(D)	$[WB] > mC$
construct level	women accept control by men		women resent control by men		witches are women
action level	women control aspects of social life				
perception level		women play a vital role in social life		experience of cognitive dissonance	

Q2 Why are uthikoloshe and impundulu conceptualized in sexual terms?

	C^1	(P)	C^2	(D)	$[WB] > mC$
construct level	women accept their sex role		women reject their sex role		witches take daemon lovers
action level	intersex tension within and outside marriage				
perception level		women are sexually deprived		experience of cognitive dissonance	

Q3 Why do ichanti and umamlambo change shape?

	C^1	(P)	C^2	(D)	$[WB] > mC$
construct level	kinsmen are loyal		kinsmen are potentially dangerous; their attitude ambiguous		ambiguous monsters
action level	competition and tension in local group				
perception level		kin loyalty is uncertain		experience of cognitive dissonance	

373

things as they are. The resulting cognitive dissonance leads to a drive towards reformulation – or at least additional *ad hoc* constructs – to deal with the discrepancies, and this takes the form of the belief in witches and their familiars. The ambiguity of the cognition is reflected in the ambiguity of the familiars themselves.

The problem tackled in this article is how to explain a particular cultural form within a symbolic system. The object is to understand what the Cape Nguni are 'saying' in conceptualizing a witch in the image of a woman and witch familiars in the image of sexuality and ambiguity, in other words, the meaning of the symbols. And here it must be stressed that the meanings are not overt. The Cape Nguni themselves do not seem to have raised their metaphysic above the subliminal level. This need not dismay us. Jung has suggested that the effectiveness of symbols lies precisely in their unconscious nature and that most of their potency is lost if the meaning is borne out of them, and Turner 'consider(s) it legitimate to include within the total meaning of a dominant ritual symbol, aspects of behaviour associated with it which the actors themselves are unable to interpret, and indeed of which they may be unaware ...' (Turner, 1967, p. 27).

What I have postulated here is that the meaning of the images of the witch and her familiars derives from an (unconscious) attempt to mediate between contradictory constructs and that the precise form of the resulting images derives from their aptness to symbolize the contradiction. The 'development' of the symbols has been visualized in terms of a dialectical model that oscillates between cultural constructs (C^1, C^2 and mC) and perceived discrepancies between these 'models of' (Geertz) and the realities of social life. This formulation gives the appearance of a causal, developmental process. In fact, of course, the mediation must be thought of as occurring synchronically with the postulations. Men are born into a society whose culture presents them *at the same time* with C^1, C^2, [WB] and mC as part of a structured cognitive system.

References

BERGER, P. L. and LUCKMANN, T. (1966), *The Social Construction of Reality*, Penguin.

BETTELHEIM, B. (1955), *Symbolic Wounds: Puberty Rites and the Envious Male*, Thames & Hudson.

DOUGLAS, M. (1966), *Purity and Danger*, Routledge & Kegan Paul.

FESTINGER, L. (1957), *A Theory of Cognitive Dissonance*, Stanford U.P.

GEERTZ, C. (1966), 'Religion as a cultural system', in *Anthropological Approaches to the Study of Religion*, M. Banton (ed.) (Ass. Social Anthrop. Monogr.), Tavistock.

GLUCKMAN, M. (1955), *Custom and Conflict in Africa*, Blackwell.

HAMMOND-TOOKE, W. D. (1962), *Bhaca Society*, Oxford U.P.

HAMMOND-TOOKE, W. D. (1968), 'Descent group scatter in an Mpondomise ward', *African Studies* vol. 27, pp. 83–94.

HAMMOND-TOOKE, W. D. (1970), 'Urbanization and the interpretation of misfortune: a quantitative analysis', *Africa*, vol. 40, pp. 25–39.

HORTON, R. (1962), 'The Kalabari world-view: an outline and interpretation', *Africa*, vol. 32, pp. 197–220.

HORTON, R. (1964), 'Ritual man in Africa', *Africa*, vol. 34, pp. 85–104.

HORTON, R. (1967), 'African traditional thought and Western science', *Africa*, vol. 37, pp. 50–71, 55–87.

HORTON, R. (1970), 'African traditional thought and Western Science', in *Rationality*, B. R. Wilson (ed.), Blackwell.

HUNTER, M. (1936), *Reaction to Conquest*, Oxford U.P.

LEE, S. G. (1969), 'Spirit possession among the Zulu', in *Spirit Mediumship and Society in Africa*, J. Beattie and J. Middleton (eds), Routledge & Kegan Paul.

LÉVI-STRAUSS, C. (1963), *Structural Anthropology*, Basic Books.

MAYER, P. (1954), *Witches*, Rhodes University.

MAYER, P. (1961), *Townsman or Tribesman*, Oxford U.P.

MIDDLETON, J. (1960), *Lugbara Religion*, Oxford U.P.

ROSEN, L. (1973), 'Contagion and cataclysm: a theoretical approach to ritual pollution beliefs', *African Studies*, vol. 32, pp. 229–46.

SPIRO, M. E. (1966), 'Religion: problems of definition and explanation', in *Anthropological Approaches to the Study of Religion*, M. Banton (ed.) (Ass. Social Anthrop. Monogr.), Tavistock.

TURNER, V. (1967), *The Forest of Symbols*, Cornell U.P.

WILSON, M. (1951), 'Witch-beliefs and social structure', *American Journal of Sociology*, vol. 56, pp. 307–13.

WILSON, M., KAPLAN, S. and MAKI, T. (1952), *Social Structure*, Shuter & Shooter.

Part Four

Urbanization and the Meaning in Misfortune

Anthropologists, historians and sociologists have concerned themselves with the relation between general social changes – whether gradual over an extended period or relatively sudden as the result of revolution or of contact – and corresponding changes in belief systems. In particular they have sought to determine the social conditions under which accusations of witchcraft (in the generic sense) rise and those under which they fall. Of special interest to students of European witchcraft are the questions why, from the fifteenth century onwards, prosecutions for witchcraft increased, and why, in the late seventeenth and early eighteenth centuries, they gradually disappeared. In the excerpt from his book included in Part Two of these Readings, Thomas, in discussing the decline in European concern with witchcraft, points out that, while 'the history of witchcraft *prosecutions* in England ... reflects the intellectual assumptions of the educated classes who controlled the machinery of the law courts' ..., 'the history of witchcraft *accusations* on the other hand can only be explained in terms of the immediate social environment of the witch and her accuser' (1973, p. 697, italics in original). He concludes that '... There seems no way of telling ... how far the drop in indictments before the courts in the early eighteenth century was caused by the known hostility of judges and juries to such accusations, how far it reflected a dwindling demand for prosecution on the part of the villagers themselves' (loc. cit). A similar problem faces students of recent, and more sudden, changes to traditional societies. For instance, when African villagers are uprooted to become either temporary migrant labourers or permanent settlers in urban areas, how do their beliefs change? The slenderness of the evidence for settling this question either way has led anthropologists to speculate on the basis of those of their experiences that have impressed them most; and, not surprisingly, they have come to conflicting conclusions. Thus Richards (1935, p. 458), in analysing her study of the Mucapi movement among the Bemba, wrote in 1935,

Missionaries all over Africa are teaching a religion which casts out fear, but economic and social changes have so shattered tribal institutions and moral codes that the result of white contact is in many cases an actual increase in the dread of witchcraft, and therefore in the whole incidence of magic in the group.

The Wilsons, writing ten years later on the basis of their research experience in central Africa, came to a very different conclusion:

Increase in control of the material environment has been dependent upon a relatively non-magical religion, but non-magicality, like the development of wealth, knowledge and skill [,] is patchy. The proportion of occasions on which Africans attribute misfortune to witchcraft and sorcery is diminishing ... (1945, p. 120)

And they add in a footnote:

Accusations of witchcraft and sorcery are an expression of opposition, and in so far as the oppositions of everyday life are exacerbated by disequilibrium ... the number of accusations may have increased – we do not know. Nevertheless, we suggest that the *relative* importance of magic is declining and that of science increasing. Here we differ from Dr Audrey Richards (loc. cit.).

Subsequent writers have offered their views, again based on impressions rather than hard evidence. For instance, taking into consideration that many Ceŵa accusations of sorcery are related to tensions inherent in modern social situations, I found myself in closer agreement with Richards than with the Wilsons (Marwick, 1965, pp. 251, 289). The debate has continued; and, in this part, there are papers which may bring resolution closer. The first two papers involve a discussion, based on a few cases but ones recorded in some detail, of the ways in which misfortunes are explained by urban Africans. In the first of these, Mitchell points out that in the towns 'there is a preponderance of strangers not intimately and emotionally linked to each other as kinsmen are in a tribal society' (1965, p. 201). Thus a townsman is free to express openly his hostility towards most of his associates and he may resolve tensions by social separation without recourse to a catalytic agent such as witchcraft (loc. cit.). 'When [however] townsfolk are linked in co-operative enterprises ... in which competition is nevertheless an essential element, such as in work groups in factories or as rival brewers in a neighbourhood, the hostility is likely to be expressed in terms of accusations of witchcraft' (1965, pp. 201–2). But, since urban judicial institutions do not countenance witchcraft, the accuser or would-be accuser is allowed no direct retributive action, and, in the cases on which this analysis is based, he tends to see misfortunes ultimately in terms of the angry spirits of deceased kinsmen (1965, p. 202). Swartz, while agreeing in general with Mitchell's conclusion, extends his analysis by pointing out that to attribute witchcraft to an urban competitor would be an inappropriate way of expressing tension because 'the relations with the competitor are not of the sort that produces witchcraft' (1969, p. 31). The views of Mitchell and Swartz relating to the probably lower incidence of witchcraft in African urban areas become even more cogent when one notes their congruence with Simmel's theoretical statement, as presented by Coser, of the contrast in tension management between intimate and more diffuse social groups.

... The closer the group, the more intense the conflict. Where members participate with their total personality, and conflicts are suppressed, the conflict, if it breaks out nevertheless, is likely to threaten the very root of the relationship.

In groups comprising individuals who participate only segmentally, conflict is less likely to be disruptive. Such groups are likely to experience a multiplicity of conflicts. This in itself tends to constitute a check against the breakdown of consensus: the energies of the group members are mobilized in many directions and hence will not concentrate on one conflict cutting through the group (Coser, 1956, p. 206).

The remaining papers in this part report on quantitative surveys that have a bearing on the extent to which the incidence of explanations of misfortune changes with urbanization and with related variables such as education and religious affiliation. The paper by Mitchell and Mitchell (pp. 401–21) includes witch-beliefs in a wider range of notions relating to the causation of disease. The one by Hammond-Tooke (pp. 422–40) is more specifically directed to testing hypotheses concerning the changes expected to accompany urbanization in regard to how people explain the misfortunes befalling them. At the risk of oversimplifying their cautious conclusions, one could say that both these papers demonstrate that modern social changes tend to be accompanied by a progressive secularization of explanatory beliefs.

References

COSER, L. A. (1956), *The Functions of Social Conflict*, Free Press, as reprinted in L. A. Coser and B. Rosenberg (eds), *Sociological Theory*, Collier-Macmillan, 1964, pp. 151–6.

MARWICK, M. G. (1965), *Sorcery in Its Social Setting*, Manchester U.P.

MITCHELL, H. F., and MITCHELL, J. C. (1980), 'Social factors in the perception of the causes of disease', in J. C. Mitchell (ed.), *Numerical Techniques in Social Anthropology*, Institute for the Study of Social Issues.

MITCHELL, J. C. (1965), 'The meaning in misfortune for urban Africans', in *African Systems of Thought*, M. Fortes and G. Dieterlen (eds), Oxford U.P. for International African Institute.

Urbanization and the Meaning in Misfortune

RICHARDS, A. I. (1935), 'A modern movement of witch-finders', *Africa*, vol. 8, no. 4, pp. 448–61.

SWARTZ, M. J. (1969), 'Interpersonal tensions, modern conditions, and changes in the frequency of witchcraft/sorcery accusations', *African Urban Notes*, vol. 4, pp. 25–33.

THOMAS, K. (1971, 1973 ed.), *Religion and the Decline of Magic*, Weidenfeld & Nicolson and Charles Scribner's Sons, 1971; Penguin Books, 1973.

WILSON, G., and WILSON, M. (1945), *The Analysis of Social Change*, Cambridge U.P.

35. J. Clyde Mitchell

The Meaning in Misfortune for Urban Africans

J. Clyde Mitchell, 'The meaning in misfortune for urban Africans', in *African Systems of Thought*, preface by M. Fortes and G. Dieterlen, London: Oxford University Press for International African Institute, 1965.

Evans-Pritchard's (1937) classical study of witchcraft among the Azande showed, among other things, how the Azande are able to relate their misfortunes to the hostilities and fears that arise in the communities in which they live. The Azande blame witches for unusual or capricious events and then seek the witches among those whom they suspect bear them malice. The crucial link between witchcraft as the abstract causative element behind misfortune a man experiences and the network of social relationships out of which the witchcraft arises, is the divining seance. Evans-Pritchard was able to show that the victim deliberately tests the names for witchcraft of those whom he knows bear him malice. The divining seance then merely uncovers the hostilities and fears of which the victim himself was already secretly aware.

Marwick (1952), utilizing the rationale of the divining situation, has been able to extend Evans-Pritchard's argument and to show that witchcraft accusations are particularly likely to fall between persons who are in competition with each other and who are unable in terms of the mores to express their hostility openly. The accusations of witchcraft bring tensions into the open which previously lay hidden and give kinsmen a justifiable cause to attack their rivals who, as kinsmen, in other circumstances should rather be protected. Accusations of witchcraft, therefore, act as a catalyst in the process of segmentation. For Marwick then, the meaning which tribesmen read into misfortunes derives from latent strains in the positions they occupy in the social structure. My own studies among the Yao of Nyasaland lend support to this view (Mitchell, 1952, 1956).

These observations refer to tribal systems where the social structure has been studied in detail and where the consequences and circumstances of accusations of witchcraft can be easily traced. We are able here to interpret the meaning people attribute to misfortunes in terms of the set of social relationships in which they are personally involved.

If this hypothesis is valid we would expect the meaning which people

381

read into their misfortunes to change when they become part of an industrial urban community. These urban communities in Southern Africa are phenomena which have appeared in the last seventy-five years. In the Rhodesias they are even more recent – the Copperbelt having come into being only in 1927. The African populations in these towns are characterized by a set of particular social and demographic features. The most striking difference between the rural and urban communities is the heterogeneity of the towns. The labour required for industrial enterprises is drawn from a wide hinterland so that the people of many different tribes and language groups are thrown higgledy-piggledy together in the African townships. Since the demand is predominantly for able-bodied manual workers young men tend to be attracted to the towns more than women or older men. These men seldom sever relationships completely with the rural communities out of which they come but continue to consider themselves part of them. There is thus a great deal of mobility between town and tribal area. This mobility of the African population underlies and is further encouraged by the form of administration which has developed in industrial towns. Since the African workers were considered to be temporary residents only, the control of law and order and of housing and amenities have rested in the hands of various municipal and central Government officials. In a population so heterogeneous and so unstable residentially few institutions of social control have arisen spontaneously. Instead differences which arise must be ironed out informally by friends or kinsmen or formally by the agents of municipal or central Government.

Migrants who move into a town such as Salisbury, therefore, move into a community which is composed overwhelmingly of strangers. The migrant almost certainly knows a few kinsmen in the town and possibly a few other tribesmen. Among the others he gradually builds up a network of connection – among those employed at the same place, in the various Burial Societies which have developed to meet the needs such as his own, among members of the congregation of the church at which he worships, and among his neighbours. This then is the social context in which the African townsman has to interpret his misfortunes.

The first point to note is that, as in rural areas, Africans in towns interpret misfortunes in direct and personal terms. They are likely to see in a motor accident not 'bad luck' or an unfortunate misadventure but rather the machinations of some witch who owes the victim a personal grudge, or the action of some aggrieved ancestor spirit who has chosen this way to express his displeasure to his descendants. This explanation is specific to the individual concerned: it explains why the accident should befall that particular person and not his workmate who was perhaps travelling next to him. It explains, as Gluckman puts it, the *why* of the event, rather than the *how* (1955, p. 84).

This 'egocentric' interpretation of misfortune leads us to seek its meaning in the network of relationships in which the victim or his representative is involved. Consider, for example, this case history:[1]

Two African families in Salisbury were neighbours. The husbands in both families and the wife in Family B were from the Cewa tribe in Northern Rhodesia. The wife in Family A was an Ngoni also from Northern Rhodesia. Both wives were accustomed to brew and sell beer illicitly to supplement their family incomes. Illicit liquor brewing is very common in Southern African townships where the combined effects of poverty, the restrictions on the sale of liquor to Africans, and the unbalanced sex ratio leading to a keen demand from bored and unattached young men, drive many women into this lucrative trade. Each of these 'shebeen queens' in time builds up a 'name' and a regular clientele. Competition for trade between them for customers is thus likely to be sharp. The two wives in these families were able to compete amicably until a lodger came to live with Family B. This lodger soon started to have an affair with wife B. Since the two women were well known to each other, the lodger began to take an interest in wife A also. The latent hostility between the two women arising out of their economic competition had thus far been held in check by the bonds of a common tribal and territorial unity since the number of peoples from Northern tribes in Salisbury is very small. But when the additional competition over a lover arose the hostility became overt. The two women quarrelled openly in a beerhall one night and the friendship between the two husbands also began to cool now.

Soon after this quarrel wife A decided to brew beer and to obscure her activities from the authorities she took out a permit to buy beer from the Municipal Beerhall. Wife B, however, familiar with the tricks of the trade, recognized the import of the purchase of beer from the Beerhall and reported to the police that wife A was brewing beer illegally. The police duly raided the home of wife A and found her in possession of liquor. Unfortunately for wife B, however, the policeman who conducted the raid was one of wife A's previous lovers. He not only released her before a charge was laid but also told her how the police had become informed. The relationships between the women were now so tense that wife B openly threatened to knife wife A when she had the opportunity.

Very shortly afterwards a teacher brought a pubescent daughter from family A home from school. He reported that the girl had fainted there. A week later the girl was well enough to go back to school but she collapsed once again as soon as she got to the classroom. The teacher now confessed his fear that there was some 'foul play' afoot. The father of the girl consulted a fellow-tribesman who was a diviner and was told that an enemy of the family in the neighbourhood was 'throwing witchcraft' at the family but that since there was no blood relationship between the

1. I am indebted to Mr B. Lukhero for this case history.

383

parties the witchcraft was not very powerful. The 'doctor' then buried an egg wrapped in black cloth with a piece of root attached to it at each of the three entrances to the house. He explained that when the witch came to the house to do harm he would find the house like the eggs – without doors and in darkness. Both families withdrew from the shebeen trade and the lodger sought another landlady. The friendship of the two men has completely ended!

This is a straightforward account of the deterioration of relationships arising out of competition in both the sexual and economic fields, and the interpretation of misfortune in terms of these relationships. In contrast to what might have been the course of events in a rural area there are two specific points of interest. The first is that the witch was sought not in the family, as would almost certainly have happened among rural Ceŵa (Marwick, 1952, pp. 216–17). The fact that the girl had survived, however, was still explained in terms of belief that normally only kinsmen bewitch one another. The significant point is that while the family is the locus of much competition and hostility in Ceŵa rural life, in a town like Salisbury, where not only kinsmen but even tribesmen hold together and support one another in the face of a large majority of foreigners, the family is essentially a tightly integrated co-operative group. Tensions intrude, rather, from the larger society. Hostility and jealousy are likely to arise in those situations where individuals are linked in close personal relationships but who nevertheless compete with each other for advancement and success. This is likely to occur, particularly in the economic field.

Employment looms large in the life of Africans in towns. Most of them are in the town in the first instance as wage-earners. While they are able to find succour with some kinsmen for a spell if they lose their employment, in the end if they do not find work they must return to their rural homes. The control of employment, however, is largely in the hands of the Europeans who appear to behave capriciously and unpredictably. Whether a workman is engaged or discharged it seems, and indeed often is, so much a matter of luck that becoming and remaining a wage-earner is fraught with as much uncertainty as hunting dangerous animals, embarking on a long journey, or similar activities in which magic and ritual figure prominently. It is difficult to secure accurate information on the degree to which African work-seekers make use of charms in their search for employment. Of thirty-five men who visited a 'doctor' in Harare, fifteen of them sought treatment primarily for a straightforward medical complaint such as a headache, constipation, or something similar. Of the remaining twenty no less than ten sought charms to help them to secure employment or to stay in it. The remaining ten were seeking advice about sexual virility, love potions, gambling charms, or straightforward anti-witchcraft medicine.

The uncertainty of employment falls unequally on different occupational strata. A shrewd research assistant remarked that the clerks in a large tobacco firm feared witchcraft, while the unskilled workers did not. The clerks compete for a few highly paid permanent posts in which there are opportunities for personal advancement. There are not many of them and they work constantly together and know each other relatively well. The unskilled workers on the other hand work for a fixed wage which is the same for them all, there are several hundreds of them and they are seasonal workers. Their security lies in their tribal areas rather than in employment. Of thirteen unskilled workers who consulted the 'doctor' in Harare only two sought charms to get work or to keep them in it. Of the fifteen skilled and white-collar workers no less than eight sought work charms.

Among women the emphasis is likely to be on economic competition only if they happen to be traders or beer-brewers operating in the same neighbourhood and are thus known to each other. I have recorded several cases of accusations of witchcraft between 'shebeen queens' who were close neighbours. A more likely foundation to personal animosity is sexual jealousy where women compete for the attentions of the same man.

In the case history we have quoted we have seen that Family A interpreted the misfortune they suffered immediately in terms of the tensions which arose in the network of personal relationships in which they were involved and that they protected themselves with magic and avoided contact with Family B.

We have seen that in tribal areas lineage oppositions are likely to find vent in accusations of witchcraft. On these grounds kinsmen are able to appeal to the tribal authorities and demand punishment. In the towns, however, Europeans exercise authority and to them witchcraft beliefs are unreal. African women dare not make an accusation of witchcraft arising indirectly out of illicit liquor brewing to the authorities. Not only is liquor brewing illegal but to accuse another of witchcraft by Southern Rhodesian law is a criminal offence. The interpretation of misfortune in terms of witchcraft, therefore, does not lead naturally to a solution of personal difficulties as it may in rural areas. Casting the interpretation of misfortune in terms of witchcraft, although likely to be initially the most natural to townsmen, is unsatisfactory because they are unable to take action which they believe will be effective in removing the basic cause of the witchcraft. They must therefore seek an alternative explanation which will allow them an effective course of action. This is shown in the following case history.[2]

A Shona man who worked as a wine-steward in a Salisbury hotel for nine years earning a salary of £8 a month and a considerable income from tips, was relieved by another African to enable him to go home on leave. When he returned he found that his employers had decided to retain the substitute in his place. The displaced man consulted a diviner and he was told that his rival had obtained a charm to make the employers prefer him to the original wine-steward. The diviner warned the displaced man not to resort to vengeance magic for this would be likely to bring death or disaster upon himself.

Dissatisfied, the man consulted another diviner. Now he was told that his misfortunes could be traced to the action of the angered spirit (*ngozi*) of his father's brother's wife. It appeared that before he was born his mother had taken his elder sister then aged three to her home. There the child had died. The man's father had then forced his brother's wife, unwilling as she was, to return to the father's village with the body of the child on her back. When the man's father's brother's wife died misfortunes started to attend the family, and it was her spirit which had caused the man (and also his younger brother) to lose his employment. To overcome these misfortunes the diviner advised the man to give a heifer or £10 to the brothers of the man's father's brother's wife, so they could lay the angered spirit.

There are some similarities between this case and that of the two 'shebeen queens'. Once again the misfortune is interpreted initially in the light of economic competition, but once again the victim is helpless to take any direct action against the suspected witch. But there is a further development: the misfortune is later traced through the action of the ancestor spirits to the man's relationships with his rural kinsmen. This re-interpretation of the misfortune is particularly significant in the light of the administrative system in the towns. The victim is unable to take positive measures against his rival; measures which would enable him to redefine his relationships with his rival. The victim therefore seeks a new meaning in the misfortune and finds one which accords with tribal belief and one for which there is a recognized and customary remedial action. This double interpretation of misfortune may be seen as successive attempts to handle personal conflicts within a social framework which contains no institutionalized mechanism to achieve this.

Exactly the same sequence of events arises in a more complicated case history.[3]

The case concerns the misfortunes that befell a family raised in Salisbury by a Nyasaland man who had married a Shona wife. This man, a staunch Christian, died towards the end of 1959. His widow and her six children visited a diviner to

2. I am indebted to Mr M. Bganya for this case history.
3. I am indebted to Mr G. Chavunduka for this case history.

find out the cause of death. All these children it should be noted were relatively well educated, two of the sons having achieved University entrance standard, one of the others being a teacher and both daughters being trained nurses. The diviner indicated that three people were responsible for the death of the man. Two were church leaders who were rivals with the dead man for a position in the church organization. The other was a co-worker. The widow confessed later that she had always suspected the church leaders but being a staunch Christian she could herself take no action against them.

But the diviner noticed also that when the man's father had died in Nyasaland some time previously no one from the family had gone to take part in the mortuary rites. Again when the man's mother and other relatives in Nyasaland had died no one from this family had visited them: the widow, a Shona woman, in fact had never been to Nyasaland at all. The diviner suggested that the members of this family ought to buy a goat and sacrifice it at an expiatory feast to which all their kinsmen should come.

The feast was not held immediately, and before it was, the eldest son of the family took ill. In April he and his younger brother went to consult a 'doctor' about this illness some eleven miles outside Salisbury. Here, at a cost of £1 10s. 0d. the 'doctor' sucked some worms out of the sick man's body. Who was responsible for planting these worms in the man's body was obscure. The sick man returned to Salisbury and continued to be treated at the Harare* General Hospital.

In May the man had not improved much and sought aid from another 'doctor' who lived, once again, some miles outside Salisbury. This 'doctor' runs his practice along the lines of a modern clinic. He wears a white dust coat, keeps a register of his patients and keeps his herbs in stoppered bottles. The sick man and his wife went in to see the herbalist. The herbalist used a mirror to look into the sick man's body. After some time he removed a piece of rotten meat from the man's body, and a large dead worm which he said was a human kidney. After some additional treatment the sick man was allowed to return to Salisbury. The fee was £2 5s. 0d. Before the man left, however, he asked the 'doctor' who was bewitching him. The 'doctor' refused to tell him, saying that he was too weak to stand the shock of the revelation. He said that the sick man should return at a specified date later on when he would reveal the names of the man's enemies.

In the meantime the man's condition had not improved. He therefore sought out a third 'doctor', one who lived this time in Harare. The 'doctor' proceeded in much the same way as the others, finally removing several objects which looked like childrens' teeth and several worms. When the sick man asked the 'doctor' who had caused all this trouble the 'doctor' said that there were some rivals at his place of employment who were jealous of his social standing, and of the trust which the employer had placed in the sick man. When the sick man pressed the doctor to mention the names of the miscreants the doctor refused saying that he had been warned by a judge of the High Court not to mention the names of people in his treatments. He did, however, offer some vengeance magic for £5, but the sick man refused this. The doctor went on to assure the sick man that if he listened carefully

* A Salisbury African township – *Ed.*

to what people said to him he would not find it difficult to identify the guilty people. Later on the sick man noticed that two of his co-workers had greeted him by saying 'Hallo, Big Boss' when he first came to work, and he thought that this was strange. He would, however, not commit himself to saying that these were indeed the witches who were troubling him.

The man's health improved for a while and he was then convinced that the first two 'doctors' he had consulted were incompetent and that the third had in fact removed the objects which were causing his illness. Three days before he was due to return to the second 'doctor' to learn the names of the witches, the man fell seriously ill again and was admitted to hospital. As his condition seemed to be worsening his family hastily procured two black goats from a European farmer some 39 miles away at a cost of £2 each. Beer worth fifteen shillings was purchased from the beerhall, though not much of this was actually drunk by the family since they are staunch Methodists. However, all other members of the family including the sick man's brothers-in-law attended the rite. The sick man's father's sister from Nyasaland made the invocation to the ancestor spirits. The feast was held in Old Highfields Township and people who were there said that it was not held under ideal conditions. The sick man was obviously getting worse and this cloud hung over the gathering. Also curious visitors from the neighbourhood kept interrupting the proceedings.

Immediately after the feast a diviner was consulted to find out whether the spirits had accepted the sacrifice. This diviner said that the feast had been conducted satisfactorily but that he could not guarantee that the sick man would recover. He pointed out that while everything possible had been done to appease the spirits on the father's side, nothing had been done for the spirits on the mother's side. Those at the feast had all been Nyasas; the man's mother was the only Shona person there. Sources of dissatisfaction on the mother's side were said to be:

(a) The man's Nyasa father who had recently died had not paid the 'mother's cow' which is part of the traditional Shona marriage payment.

(b) The man's mother's mother had brought up two of the children of this family but had never been thanked by having some clothing brought for her. The sick man was in fact one of these children.

Two days after the feast, after several blood transfusions, the sick man died in hospital. The death certificate showed that the man had died from leukemia. The family are now faced with the duty of appeasing the ancestor spirits on the mother's side.

This case history shows the dual interpretation of misfortune very clearly. The sick man's father was thought to have been bewitched by his rivals for a church position or by a jealous fellow workman. But ostensibly because this was a Christian family his widow could take no action against them. Instead she found the ultimate explanation in the relationship between this urban family and their patrilateral kinsmen in Nyasaland whom they had never seen. Their immediate and feasible action therefore was to appease these spirits. The tragic history of the dead man's son follows exactly the same pattern. He has foreign objects removed by a number of 'doctors'. These 'doctors' were all extremely reluctant to indicate names of his tormentors, possibly because of the law which makes it an offence to do so. Eventually when the sick man does persuade a 'doctor' to reveal who the witches are he points to the jealousy of the sick man's co-workers. Yet the victim is unable to take action against them and once again his kinsmen interpret the misfortune in terms of the ancestor cult for which there are specific and definite procedures.

I argue then that town Africans in the main continue to interpret their misfortunes in 'personal' terms but the final meaning they attach to the misfortune must be of a type which will allow them to take effective action. There are institutionalized means of dealing directly with believed witches in rural societies, devices which assist the normal social processes of division and reintegration to take place. In the towns, however, there is a preponderance of strangers who are not intimately and emotionally linked to each other as kinsmen are in a tribal society. Hostility and opposition may be openly expressed towards strangers so that there is no need for accusations of witchcraft. Social separation is a feature of urban societies so that the tensions that arise in the towns do not call for a catalytic agent such as witchcraft accusations to provide a justification for segmentations. Where townsfolk are linked in co-operative enterprises, however, in which competition is nevertheless an essential element, such as in work groups in factories or as rival brewers in a neighbourhood, the hostility is likely to be expressed in terms of accusations of witchcraft. If hostilities are phrased in terms of witchcraft accusations, however, this is the end of the matter, for the accuser cannot use these beliefs to bring the opposition into the open as he would do for example among the Yao. The judicial processes in the town are part of an administrative system which does not countenance witchcraft beliefs. To see the hand of witchcraft in misfortunes may be the first reaction of a townsman, but it is an interpretation which in terms of the social and administrative structure of the urban community allows him no direct retributive action. He tends to see misfortunes ultimately then in terms of the action of the angered spirits of a deceased kinsman. There are, after all, time-honoured methods of adjusting the relationships of a man to his ancestor spirits, but none of dealing with a witch in the alien circumstances of the town. A man takes his ancestor spirits to town with him and if he sees their hand in the misfortunes that befall him he has the satisfaction of knowing that at least there is something he can do about it.

References

EVANS-PRITCHARD, E. E. (1937), *Witchcraft, Oracles and Magic among the Azande*, Clarendon Press.

GLUCKMAN, M. (1955), *Custom and Conflict in Africa*, Blackwell.

MARWICK, M. (1952), 'The Social context of Cewa witch-beliefs', *Africa*, vol. 22, pp. 120–35, 215–33.

MITCHELL, J. C. (1952), 'A note on the African conception of causality', *The Nyasaland Journal*, vol. 5, pp. 51–8.

MITCHELL, J. C. (1956), *The Yao Village*, Manchester U.P. for Rhodes-Livingstone Institute.

36. Marc J. Swartz

Modern Conditions and Witchcraft/Sorcery Accusations

Marc J. Swartz, 'Interpersonal tensions, modern conditions, and changes in the frequency of witchcraft/sorcery accusations', *African Urban Notes*, vol. 4, pp. 25–33.

Students of witchcraft and sorcery[1] in Africa are quite uniform in believing that witchcraft accusations are a reflection of interpersonal tensions. Marwick's formulation of this generally held view is perhaps the most widely accepted one. It maintains that witchcraft accusations will occur when three conditions are simultaneously present: first, that there is tension between individuals due to their competing for some highly valued end; second, that these same individuals are united in co-operation in other contexts; and, third, that their roles in the competition are not clearly defined and delimited.

If we accept Marwick's view (1952, 1965) of the genesis of witchcraft accusations, it will not come as much of a surprise that the social, economic and communications developments which are often spoken of as 'modernization' should have brought with them an increase in witchcraft accusation. This is so, of course, because the new economic opportunities arising out of developments in the last few score years have provided new highly valued ends to serve as the objects of competitions; the improved communications have ended or drastically lessened the isolation of ethnic groups and brought people into contact with new ways of behaving and new opportunities for social and spatial movement; many of these developments have lessened the strength and applicability of norms and values which may once have defined many interpersonal relationships more sharply than they do now and thereby increased the potential for conflict and tension over what it had been.

The sources of interpersonal conflict of the sort that Marwick and others identify as leading to witchcraft accusation have most certainly become more numerous than they were in most African (and I address

1. Instead of continuing to use both terms and distinguishing between them as Evans-Pritchard did for the Azande (1937) I will follow the usage of English-speaking East Africans and use the single term 'witchcraft' to refer to the attempt of an individual to harm other individuals by supernatural means whatever those means may be and whatever his alleged abilities and procedures may be.

myself primarily to East Africa) societies previous to the beginning of the changes which have been grouped together under the banner 'modernization'. At the same time and for even more complex reasons which cannot be explored in the confines of this paper, witchcraft's crucial function as an explanation for misfortune has become more crucial as the alternatives to witchcraft become less widely and less fully acceptable to many people. Witchcraft, as Evans-Pritchard pointed out thirty years ago, serves to 'explain the inexplicable' and provides a means for 'controlling the uncontrollable'. The major proselytizing religions have had substantial success in many areas of Africa in eradicating or seriously weakening belief in the supernatural power of ancestors and of other indigenous supernatural agencies and these shades and gods once provided an alternative – in some areas, at least, a more frequently used alternative – explanation for misfortunes of the 'inexplicable' sort, but these religions have had much less success in eradicating or weakening belief in witchcraft.[2] To some extent, perhaps, the newly introduced religions themselves present satisfying explanations for disasters and means for reacting to them, but there is little evidence that this is widely so and no one who has worked closely with large numbers of African Christians and Moslems can have failed to note that at least some, and probably most of them, at least sometimes consider the misfortunes they have experienced as due to agencies additional to those occupying the central place in the orthodox versions of their formally organized religions.

All this is to say that witchcraft belief and witchcraft accusation can be expected to increase under modern African conditions both because of the increase in the sorts of situations and relationships which give rise to them and because of the lessening importance of alternative means of satisfying a function well served by witchcraft belief and accusation. Although it is difficult to measure a change in rate over the relatively long period during which 'modernization' has been going on when there are no records at all from the early stages and when anti-witchcraft laws and attitudes make the records for even the most recent periods very incomplete and unsatisfactory, it can be said that older informants report that there *is* more witchcraft now in their groups than there was in their youth. My own experience with the Bena of southern Tanzania is that every informant over the age of fifty or so holds this opinion and many

2. The implication is not that the relative prevalence and strength of either witchcraft or ancestor/gods belief is to be understood solely, or even primarily, as a consequence of missionary effort. Why there has been a rather general difference in the response to missionary efforts in regard to the two kinds of beliefs is a vast question far beyond the scope of this paper.

other anthropologists report similar findings (e.g. Gluckman, 1963). This mass of evidence, despite its non-quantitative character, must convince most of those exposed to it that what we expect on theoretical grounds has, *mirabile dictu*, in fact occurred as concerns the change in frequency of witchcraft accusation, and the use of witchcraft as an explanation of personal disaster.

However, the smooth interdigitation of theoretically derived expectation and empirical fact encounters what is, at least, an apparent difficulty. This is that although witchcraft accusation and belief have increased in rural areas there is some fairly persuasive evidence to indicate that in urban areas there is less witchcraft accusation and, perhaps, less witchcraft-based explanation of misfortune than there is in the rural areas. Alas, for the sake of a neat fit between rather simple theory and empirical reality this should not be so. If the changes that affect the rural areas work to increase witchery, why should they not do so to at least the same extent in the cities? Why, in fact, do not the increases in opportunities, the lessening of rigid role definitions, and the enlarged sources of competition which developments are surely more advanced in cities than in rural areas lead to more rather than less witchcraft accusation? And why are there not more explanations of the almost surely greater number of 'inexplicable' events which assail the townsman, especially (and this is the group with which this paper is concerned) if that townsman is a transplanted villager who probably plans to stay in the town only temporarily?

Mitchell has recently written a paper (1965) which seeks to explain this issue and his stimulating argument merits close attention. Before turning to that argument a word about the data used in assessing urban witchcraft belief and accusation is essential, because we do not know at all clearly whether or not witchcraft is actually less active in the cities than it is in the rural areas. In fact, it may well be at least no less prevalent there than in the rural areas but the nature of the data and, especially, the conceptual schemes used by those who collect these data make it impossible for us to know how important witchcraft actually is to townsmen and how this importance is revealed.

The main source of data concerning urban witchcraft is court records (Crawford, 1967; Gelfand, 1967). This is largely negative evidence since there are very few court cases involving witchcraft in the cities. The presence there of laws and/or judges most emphatically opposed to witchcraft accusation is obviously a factor, and a key one, in the absence of such cases since the person who accuses a witch is more likely in most urban jurisdictions to be punished than is the accused witch. This is so because in these courts witchcraft is granted no standing and is viewed as harmful and malicious superstition. This does not apply equally in the rural areas where there are more sympathetic judges and a greater scope for 'traditional' law is more frequently allowed. Thus, although even in the villages many witchcraft cases are not brought before tribunals which keep records – my own field experience leaves me in no doubt on this score – in cities there are even more formidable reasons to avoid any sort of official airing of witchcraft accusations, so that there is reason to believe that the urban records may show even fewer of the actual cases of witchcraft accusation than do the rural ones.

If the court records were the only source of information, it would be bootless to pursue the issue of differences between rural and urban witchcraft frequencies since there would be no supportable reason to believe that there is any difference between the two. However, we do have another source and although this source has provided little published data as yet, what has appeared is sufficiently persuasive to continue this enquiry. This other source is the direct experience of anthropologists and others who are acquainted with rural African groups and who have also lived closely with an urban population so that they can compare what they have observed in the two sorts of areas. Only by intimate acquaintance with communities is it possible to get really worthwhile data on clandestine activities, and witchcraft accusation is certainly such an activity given the enforcement of laws against it in most – probably all – African cities. Thus on this issue a close observer's views are worth a great deal more than all the court records available.

Mitchell has done long and brilliant work in rural Malawi and, while connected with the University College in Salisbury, enquired into witchcraft beliefs and the use to which they were put in that city. Gelfand has also had experience in both rural and urban areas and he joins Mitchell in the view that there is relatively little witchcraft accusation in cities as compared to rural areas. Other researchers no doubt have information on this question but published accounts of their work are unaccessible and while awaiting further data, I can only throw into the balance the less reliable information derived from Bena informants who have lived in cities but who were back in their home villages when contacted. They too reported very little witchcraft accusation between townsmen, and although their views cannot be given the weight those of qualified and conscientious researchers are accorded, one cannot ignore them.

Taking all this admittedly slender information together, it is tentatively concluded that there is, in fact, less witchcraft accusation among townsmen than among villagers. At the same time another tentative conclusion is that there is no significant difference between the sort of townsmen with whom I am concerned and rural people so far as belief in witchcraft is concerned. It is much less difficult to find out about beliefs concerning witchcraft in general than it is about actual accusations of witchcraft. I have talked with many townsmen who freely discussed their general views on the subject and who clearly believed in witches and the power of witchcraft quite as much as did the Bena villagers. Both Mitchell and Gelfand make it clear that they too were convinced that townsmen believed in witchcraft as strongly as villagers did, the townsmen's lack of obvious accusations against witches notwithstanding.

How does one explain the apparently lower rate of witchcraft accusation in cities as compared to rural areas when the conditions which were said earlier to have brought about an increase in witchcraft accusation in the latter area appear to be even more powerful in the towns? Mitchell's argument is examined in this context.

His position has two basic explanatory approaches. One indicates a source for the lesser *applicability* of witchcraft beliefs to urban social situations and the other indicates a lesser *appeal* of witchcraft explanations of misfortune for urbanites.

The lesser applicability of witchcraft beliefs to city situations comes from the fact that competition, which Mitchell holds to be primarily economic in towns for the sort of townsmen considered here, usually takes place between individuals who are not united in cooperation in other respects and toward whom hostility can be directly expressed. In the countryside competition for some particular end occurs between kinsmen and others who are united in a broad scope of other shared ends and activities so that hostility arising from the tension of competition cannot be expressed in any direct or open way without harming one's own interests and commitments in other respects and contexts. Moreover, the avoidance of open hostility between such competitors is usually strongly enjoined by norms and values held not only by the observers of the competition but by the competitors themselves. In the cities this is much less commonly the case and competitors do not often find themselves bound together by ties which cut across the current competition. Moreover, social separation of competitors in the city is not impeded by common interests and if the tensions between individuals become intolerable it is often quite easy, given the structure of cities, for antagonists simply to part and have nothing more to do with one another. In the countryside accusations of witchcraft may be necessary before lineage-mates or brothers can bring themselves to sever the broad and important ties which bind them together however much the tension between them leads them to want to part; and only such grave accusations can justify the parting to those with whom the competitor-brothers must retain ties regardless of what they do regarding one another. Thus, a personal misfortune such as a child's death can be explained as the work of a witch and if a competing kinsman with whom ties are no longer tolerable can be identified as that witch, the accusation serves not only to put the misfortune in a cognitive and moral framework which is acceptable (as, say, a framework based on the operation of random chance is not) but also to provide a basis for breaking off relations which is acceptable to the kin who sever relations and to those with whom they retain relations and who judge the morality of what they do. It is not necessary, of course, that the victim and the accused be aware of all of this – or any of it – but all these functions can be served by witchcraft-based explanations of disaster and the accusations which result from them.

In the city competitors are most often not tied together by bonds other than mutual, opposed interest in the object of competition. They need no moral explanation for severing their relations if the tension between them becomes intolerable. Social separation is a constant, expected and accepted feature of city life.

So far, then, Mitchell's argument explains the lower rate of witchcraft accusation in cities by the different nature of the relations between competitors in city and country. He does not maintain that there are no competitors in the city between whom there are bonds which make separation difficult when tension becomes unbearable. He argues, rather, that such situations are uncommon in the city and very common in the country. Thus, his position is that despite the great amount of competition in the city and despite the looser rules governing this competition less witchcraft accusation occurs in the cities because the relations between the competitors are so often without the crucial ties between them which cross-cut their competition and complicate their separation.

Clearly, his argument is a convincing one and a contribution to our understanding of the problem to which this paper is addressed. There is, however, one aspect of this part of Mitchell's argument which could profitably be explored further. This useful further exploration stems from the fact that townsmen no less than villagers believe in witchcraft and its power and that they have a moral and cognitive scheme which depends heavily on this belief. If this is so, where do lost competitions fit into their understanding of the world? That is, it is doubtless true that townsmen can compete, generate intolerable tension in doing so, and separate easily without the competitors accusing one another of witchcraft, but how does the loser explain his loss? The point here is that although the number of competitions which are likely to engender witchcraft is reduced by the type of relations often or usually found between city competitors, the results of the competitions may require explanation for the loser. Given the very strong possibility that there are more competitions in the city than in the country it is doubtful that lacking more data it can be agreed that reducing the number of competitions involving people related to each other in a way likely to produce witchcraft really reduces the need for witchcraft explanation and, consequently, witchcraft accusation. One's competitors in the city assume the status of natural forces and are not proper objects for witchcraft accusation but they are sources for such accusations against someone insofar as the loser in the competition really views his misfortunes in a framework of witchcraft belief.

Mitchell addresses himself to this problem in the second part of his argument. He presents a case of a wine steward who, after eight years of service in this remunerative job, is permanently replaced by the man who took over his position when the steward went on leave to his home village. The steward's reaction was to go to a diviner who told him that the usurper of his position had won the job by means of a charm but that the steward should not make retributive magic against his usurper because it would only lead to the steward's own death or some other disaster. The steward was not satisfied and went to another diviner who told him he lost his job because of the anger of his father's brother's wife at mistreatment she had received from the steward's father during her lifetime. The diviner told the steward that he could only escape further difficulty if he gave money or a heifer to the brothers of the outraged spirit so that they could appease her. He accepted this explanation and did as the diviner suggested.

Mitchell cites a second case which followed the same basic lines as the wine steward's and formulates from these cases a generalization concerning what he calls 'dual interpretation'. This is stated clearly in his own words: 'Casting the interpretation of misfortune in terms of witchcraft although initially the most natural to (townsmen) ... is unsatisfactory because they are unable to take action which they believe will be effective in removing the basic cause of the witchcraft. They must therefore seek an alternative explanation which will allow them an effective course of action' (Mitchell, 1965, p. 197).

Dual interpretation involves first interpreting city misfortune within the context where the misfortune arose (i.e. blaming the competitor) but since that allows no effective action, the explanation is shifted to social tension in the victim's own rural, home area. In the two cases Mitchell presents the causes of the misfortunes arrived at in the second interpretation is the wrath of shades. This is probably generally true in the Central African area where Mitchell worked, but in southern Tanzania such an explanation probably would not appeal to temporary city dwellers since ancestors' wrath is a rare explanation for any misfortune. For the moment, however, that is a minor point which must not be allowed to obscure the main point.

This point revolves around the only substantial disagreement I have with Mitchell's views on the place of witchcraft in explaining city misfortunes. He says that the witchcraft of one's competitors is an unsatisfactory explanation because it allows no effective actions since the competitor cannot be accused of witchcraft. I agree that such an explanation is unlikely to be satisfactory very often but I do not agree that it is unsatisfactory because there is nothing the victim can do about having been attacked. My view is that the witchcraft of the competitor is an unsatisfactory explanation because the relations with the competitor are not of the sort that produces witchcraft and that, in fact, the competitor has the status of a part of a natural disaster not that of a malign, personal antagonist. The wine steward's usurper occupies the same position in the view of the steward as, say, malignant malaria would in the death of the steward's wife or child if that had been his misfortune. The emotional bonds and broad social ties involved in most witchcraft accusations are absent and the economic competitor needs to be explained in the same way any other disaster does, i.e. whose malignant ill-will caused *him* (my competitor) to happen to me? That is the crucial question.

The difference between my understanding of urban, dual interpretation and Mitchell's is rather penetrating in its implications. His view implies two different structures in that the steward (let him stand for the general case of the urban-dweller who has lost a competition or suffered some other misfortune) is seen as belonging in two different slots in separate, though overlapping, organizations. He seeks to act effectively in one structure and being barred from doing so by the laws of that structure (i.e. the anti-witch laws), he moves to the other structure where he can act effectively.

My view implies a social field in which the steward participates without moving from one compartment to another. He rejects the explanation of his loss due to his competitor's magic not because it is ineffective but because it is inappropriate to the organization of the total field within which he is operating. That field is composed of the people back in the home village with whom he has broad ties and deep attachments and of fleeting social objects and occurrences in the town which are intelligible in reference only to those ties and attachments. Whether he can act effectively or not, given the organization of his field, the only explanation he can accept is one which refers to that field and not only to the currently active fragment of it within which his misfortune happened to occur.

Given the field view of social structuring, the relative infrequency of witchcraft explanation and accusation is a function of the way the temporary townsmen we are here considering structure their fields while they are living in the city. Their city misfortunes *do* lead to witchcraft explanations and accusations (or to similar explanations concerning the shades when and where these beliefs are still potent) but these explanations and accusations do not occur in the city part of the arena but rather in the rural part of the arena where the sources of misfortune (i.e. conflict within relations also characterized by deep mutual commitments) reside. We do not have records of these distant accusations – that is, accusations in the rural area precipitated by urban misfortunes – at least because as far as I know they have not been sought. They may, of course, not occur, but so long as the city is seen as one structure and the rural area as another, investigators are far less likely to look for these sorts of phenomena than they are if they conceive of the events of interest as occurring in a single social field composed of all urbanites' effective associates and their total relation to the process in question (i.e. misfortune and accusation rather than their relation to one another within some assumed separate structure which is better conceived as a part of the total, fluid field).

From the perspective of this paper it would be too bold to say that witchcraft accusation (and explanation) are as prevalent in towns as they are in the country in that they are precipitated in the towns and actually occur in the country. Data may well prove that this is not the case and that there is really less witchcraft accusation not only in the towns but also stemming from processes in them. However, it does seem warranted to suggest that, so long as the town and the rural areas are considered separate structures and relationships are traced only within each, we are not likely to raise questions which concern the organization and development of the total social field surrounding processes such as changing rates of witchcraft accusation and differences in rates, which may or may not be real, depending on the structural limits we place upon our investigation of them.

References

CRAWFORD, J. R. (1967), *Witchcraft and Sorcery in Rhodesia*, Oxford U.P.

EVANS-PRITCHARD, E. E. (1937), *Witchcraft, Oracles and Magic among the Azande*, Clarendon Press.

GELFAND, M. (1964), *Witch Doctor: Traditional Medicine Man of Rhodesia*, Harvill Press.

GLUCKMAN, M. (1963), 'The logic in witchcraft', in M. Gluckman, *Custom and Conflict in Africa*, Blackwell.

MARWICK, M. G. (1952), 'The social context of Cewa witch-beliefs', *Africa*, vol. 22, pp. 120–35, 215–33.

MARWICK, M. G. (1965), *Sorcery in its Social Setting: A Study of the Northern Rhodesian Cewa*, Manchester U.P.

MITCHELL, J. C. (1965), 'The meaning in misfortune for urban Africans', in M. Fortes and G. Dierterlen (eds), *African Systems of Thought*, Oxford U.P. for International African Institute.

37. Hilary Flegg Mitchell and J. Clyde Mitchell

Social Factors in the Perception of the Causes of Disease

Hilary Flegg Mitchell and J. Clyde Mitchell, 'Social factors in the perception of the causes of disease', in *Numerical Techniques in Social Anthropology*, Philadelphia: Institute for the Study of Social Issues, 1980, pp. 49–68.

Orientations toward Illness and Disease

Illness and disease are personal misfortunes which people may explain in various ways. Among the African peoples of Central Africa, in particular the Shona-speaking and the Ndebele-speaking peoples of Rhodesia, disease and illness were explained traditionally in terms of several different causal categories, including the following:

1. Some illnesses and diseases were considered to be 'natural' or the result of processes that were not thought of as problematical. The diseases of very young children or the infirmities of the aged, for example, might be seen as requiring no further explanation than the natural condition of the sufferer.

2. Some illnesses and diseases were seen to be the natural consequences of the actions of those who suffered from them. For example, some of the diseases of young children who were considered to be 'ritually cold' were seen to be the consequence of their having been exposed to 'ritually hot' circumstances. In adults some chest conditions were thought to be the consequence of adultery.

3. Some illnesses were considered to be the consequences of the actions of wraiths or spirits and frequently followed some violation on the part of the patient, or one of his close kinsmen, of custom or kinship obligations.

4. Some illnesses and diseases were considered to result from the actions of sorcerers or witches.

5. Some illnesses, particularly fits, were considered to be due to the action of spirits, usually of kinsmen but not necessarily so, who had selected the patient as a medium through which they could speak.

These causal categories are essentially collective representations to which people may appeal in order to provide rationales for the misfortunes that assail them. As such, the categories influence the action people feel would be appropriate. Like all causal explanations, they are essentially constructions of reality which are open to reconstructions in

401

the light of the different interests of the actors in any social drama (Mitchell, 1965).

Modern scientific causal categories provide yet another way of explaining the same objective phenomena, and we would expect them to be used in the same way as traditional categories to provide a rationale for appropriate action.

Most observers have devoted more attention to the traditional categories of thinking than to the ways in which categories derived from Western thought have been used in the variety of social situations in which non-Western people find themselves.

It is common knowledge, and has been documented extensively, that so-called 'traditional' or 'folk' explanations of disease and those explanations that are called 'Western' or 'scientific' (or 'modern') are not mutually exclusive bases for action. In Rhodesia several observers have noted how patients made simultaneous use of 'traditional' and of 'Western' healing agencies.[1] There are thus many individual case histories reflecting the behaviour of individuals and even of groups who oscillate between medical practitioners and traditional healers, but we do not yet have data to show how most people are likely to behave or whether there is a trend one way or the other. We know that traditional healers flourish while at the same time hospitals are overcrowded, but we do not know how the patients themselves interpret the condition they suffer from when they seek treatment. This study does not purport to throw light directly on these questions, but it may suggest factors likely to influence change in the present situation.

The data in fact refer to the responses of a relatively large number of young Africans in Rhodesia to a set of items in a standard type of attitude questionnaire designed for a somewhat different purpose. Clearly data of this sort are heavily influenced by the situation in which they are generated. In this respect they are no different from data assembled by other procedures such as observation or interviewing. What is essential is that the constraints of the particular way in which the data were created in the first instance should explicitly condition the way in which the data are subsequently interpreted. Frequently attitude studies are pilloried by critics who unjustifiably attribute qualities to the data which they cannot possess simply because of the way in which they were generated. One of the simplest and crudest confusions of this sort arises when it is expected that people in day-to-day situations will in fact behave in accordance with

1. See, for example, Gelfand (1964, pp. 134–43; 1973), in particular the histories he took of his own patients, the case history described by J. C. Mitchell (1965), the comments by H. F. Mitchell (1967), and the detailed analysis made by Chavunduka (1973).

their responses to items in an attitude questionnaire. The way in which a respondent 'constructs the reality' of his attitude in a test situation is, of course, likely to be entirely different from the way in which he 'constructs the reality' of an everyday situation. To equate the two is to commit an elementary blunder.

In this study our aim is not to examine the disparity between these different 'constructions of reality'. Our more limited aim is to argue that we are able to arrange respondents along a continuum according to the way in which they answered certain selected questions. At one extreme would be the respondents who reacted to the questions in such a way as to lead us to suppose that they were operating predominantly within a 'traditional' orientation; at the other extreme would be those who were operating within a 'non-traditional' framework. Note that from the material available to us we cannot argue that the orientations we adduce have validity outside the specific test situation in which the questions were posed. This is something that other investigators, possibly using other research procedures, could settle. In this sense our analysis raises rather than answers questions. What we can do with this material, however, is to pose the following question: given that the respondents were operating within a predominantly 'traditional' or predominantly 'non-traditional' framework in answering the questions, do those with a particular set of personal characteristics tend to respond one way or the other, and if so can we postulate any relationship between these characteristics and the way in which the respondents answered the questions?

The Data

The data were collected in a study with a different purpose from the analysis presented here. One of us (H. F. M.) was engaged in a study of the incidence of cancer among Africans in Rhodesia, and in the course of this study had become aware of the extent to which cancer rates computed from the evidence collected for migrant populations in a large urban area may be seriously distorted because of the extent to which some patients important in cancer rates (as, for example, the old) might escape the diagnostic net of the survey (cf. Mitchell, 1967). It seemed essential, consequently, to understand something about the use of medical services by the African population, and a part of this study was to assess the attitudes toward these services of the 'rising' generation of educated young people.

For this purpose a survey was conducted among secondary school students and teachers in training in the larger African educational institutions in the southwestern part of Rhodesia. A population of this sort was able to participate in a study requiring a fair degree of literacy in English and could be conveniently organized at centers and in suitable groups to facilitate testing. It could in no way be thought of as representative of the whole African population of Rhodesia or even of the population of the southwest of Rhodesia since it was naturally both younger and better educated than the total population.

Elementary social characteristics of 2,663 respondents whose returns were usable are given in Table 6 (pp. 413–15). The loss rate by refusals and unusable returns was negligible: one respondent refused to co-operate on religious grounds and six returns were rejected because they were not completed satisfactorily. In all, fourteen schools and institutions of further education were included in the study. Two were situated in town and the rest in the rural areas, but the latter were boarding schools with students and trainees drawn from town and country. Some of the institutions were secular but the majority were mission controlled and run. The data were collected in February and March 1964.[2]

By arrangements with the principals of the institutions,[3] the scholars and students were assembled and seated at desks in a central hall. One of us (H. F. M.) then explained the purpose of the study and elicited the co-operation of those involved. She was accompanied and assisted by two African social workers throughout the field-work. The schedules, mimeographed on two sheets of paper of double foolscap size, were then distributed to the group and completed by them in silence and without reference to one another. At the conclusion of this session, usually after about half an hour, the research worker collected the schedules and then engaged in a general discussion with the group about medical topics.

The schedules, printed in English, covered two sets of data. The first related to a number of 'background variables' or social characteristics of the respondents which we thought might have some bearing on their attitudes toward the use of medical services. The names of respondents were specifically excluded. The second set consisted of a number of statements about medical services and the treatment of disease to which the respondents were asked to react in terms of five categories of intensity of agreement or disagreement.

2. The data were collected as part of the Geographic Pathology study of cancer in Rhodesia supported by the International Union Against Cancer and the British Empire Cancer Campaign. Preliminary results of the sociological findings of this study have been published in H. F. Mitchell (1967), which should be consulted for details concerning the original study.

3. We are grateful to the principals of the institutions concerned and to the students whose co-operation made the study possible.

Among the items in the second part of the schedule were ten that could be construed as reflecting the attitudes respondents might have toward the basic causes of illness. These items and the distribution of responses to them in terms of agreement and disagreement are presented in Table 1.

The crude distributions for these items are interesting in themselves. A common criticism of responses to formal questions of this sort is that they tend to reflect what the respondents think the investigators want them to say. In this case the study was conducted under the auspices of the African Studies Department of the University College of Rhodesia and Nyasaland, and those who supervised the completion of the schedules

Table 1

Responses to Items Relating to the Causation of Disease (Distribution in Percentage of Responses Excluding 'Don't Know' Responses)

Item[a]	SA^b	A^b	U^b	D^b	SD^b	D/K^c
23. *Abatakati*[d] or *varoyi*[d] can make people sick	61·8	20·8	8·6	2·8	6·0	13
24. *Amadhlozi*[e] or *midzimu*[e] can make people sick	41·5	23·6	18·2	5·5	11·2	43
27. For certain kinds of sickness it is better to ask the help of the *nyanga*[f] rather than the medical doctor	38·2	24·2	11·0	10·0	16·6	20
44. If a man is sick he should go first to the *nyanga* to see what is wrong with him *before* he goes to a medical doctor	16·5	12·5	15·3	24·0	31·8	15
49. *Abatakati* or *amadhlozi* can make people cough blood	21·2	18·3	28·0	12·6	19·9	45
50. *Abatakati* or *amadhlozi* can make people have sores on their bodies that do not heal	21·3	23·0	27·5	13·2	15·0	61
51. *Abatakati* or *amadhlozi* can make people have difficulty in swallowing food	17·4	23·3	28·2	15·2	16·0	65
52. *Abatakati* or *amadhlozi* can make people have a lump that grows in the body	25·2	25·7	24·4	11·5	13·3	56

405

Table 1 (*continued*)

Item[a]	SA[b]	A[b]	U[b]	D[b]	SD[b]	D/K[c]
53. *Abatakati* or *amadhlozi* can make people pass blood in the water	11·5	11·5	29·1	22·1	25·7	55
54. *Abatakati* or *amadhlozi* can make people fall down in fits (*situtwani* or *zvipusha*)[g]	30·3	24·2	22·6	10·4	12·6	52

[a]The item numbers shown are the actual item numbers in the questionnaire.

[b]SA = strongly agree, A = agree, U = uncertain (cannot decide), D = disagree, SD = strongly disagree.

[c]D/K = number of 'don't know' responses.

[d]These are the actual words used in the items. The vernacular terms *abatakati* (Ndebele) and *varoyi* (Shona) for sorcerers were used to make the meaning clear to the respondents, all of whom could understand at least one of these languages and many of them, both.

[e]The vernacular terms *amadhlozi* (Ndebele) and *midzimu* (Shona) were used for ancestor spirits.

[f]The vernacular word *nyanga* (Ndebele and Shona) was used for diviner.

[g]The vernacular words *situtwani* (Ndebele) and *zvipusha* (Shona) were added to explicate the word 'fits', which respondents may have had difficulty in understanding.

were associated with the largest African hospital in the region. Whether or not the respondents wanted to please the Department of African Studies at the university or the representatives of the medical services would be difficult to say, but it certainly did not prevent some 82·6 per cent of the respondents from agreeing with the statement that sorcerers could make people ill or 65·1 per cent from agreeing that ancestor spirits could make people ill. Substantially fewer, however, agreed that a sick person should consult a diviner before consulting a medical practitioner or that sorcerers or ancestor spirits could cause specific symptoms of disease.[4] Irrespective of whether or not these responses reflect accurately what people really think about these conditions, the point of immediate interest is that there is a certain amount of variability in the responses. The problem may be rephrased in terms of the differences in response of subjects with varying social backgrounds and how far these differences were in accordance with what we might expect from our understanding of the positions these respondents occupy in the social system as a whole.

4. It is interesting that a larger proportion agreed with the statement that sorcerers or ancestor spirits could cause 'fits' or 'lumps that grow in the body'. This is almost certainly related to common beliefs about these conditions as against hematuria which, because of the widespread infestation of bilharzia, is quite common in Rhodesia.

Table 2

Correlations among Items Relating to the Causation of Disease

Item	1	2	3	4	5	6	7	8	9	10
1. *Abatakati* or *varoyi* can make people sick	1·0000	0·4409	0·2205	0·2081	0·3117	0·3250	0·2874	0·3114	0·1718	0·3219
2. *Amadhlozi* or *midzimu* can make people sick	0·4409	1·0000	0·1954	0·2365	0·2984	0·2899	0·2797	0·2915	0·2006	0·2957
3. For certain kinds of sickness it is better to ask the help of the *nyanga* rather than the medical doctor	0·2205	0·1954	1·0000	0·3370	0·1439	0·1484	0·1198	0·1654	0·0739	0·1586
4. If a man is sick he should go first to the *nyanga* to see what is wrong with him *before* he goes to a medical doctor	0·2081	0·2365	0·3370	1·0000	0·2403	0·2039	0·2279	0·2118	0·1908	0·2192
5. *Abatakati* or *amadhlozi* can make people cough blood	0·3117	0·2984	0·1439	0·2403	1·0000	0·5011	0·5171	0·4519	0·4133	0·3738
6. *Abatakati* or *amadhlozi* can make people have sores on their bodies that do not heal	0·3250	0·2899	0·1484	0·2039	0·5011	1·0000	0·5770	0·5158	0·3547	0·4040
7. *Abatakati* or *amadhlozi* can make people have difficulty in swallowing food	0·2874	0·2797	0·1198	0·2279	0·5171	0·5770	1·0000	0·5490	0·4502	0·4306
8. *Abatakati* or *amadhlozi* can make people have a lump that grows in the body	0·3114	0·2915	0·1654	0·2118	0·4519	0·5158	0·5490	1·0000	0·3896	0·4778
9. *Abatakati* or *amadhlozi* can make people pass blood in the water	0·1718	0·2006	0·0739	0·1908	0·4133	0·3547	0·4502	0·3896	1·0000	0·4217
10. *Abatakati* or *amadhlozi* can make people fall down in fits (*siturwani* or *zvipusha*)	0·3219	0·2957	0·1586	0·2192	0·3738	0·4040	0·4306	0·4778	0·4217	1·0000

Based on 2,663 cases. 'Don't know' or missing responses for items are replaced by mean values of known responses for those items.

Traditional and Non-traditional Orientations toward the Causation of Disease

Regardless of the way in which respondents reacted independently to each of the ten items we have selected for analysis, it seems reasonable to argue that if a respondent consistently agreed, over all ten items, that diseases or specified symptoms of diseases (included in the survey) could be caused by ancestor spirits or sorcerers, then he was oriented, at least in the test situation, toward a traditional view of the etiology of disease. The extent to which respondents reacted to the items in a consistent way, of course, could be measured by product moment correlation coefficients.

Table 2 gives the correlations among these ten items. In order to compute the correlations, we assigned arbitrary values of 1 to 5 to the five categories of agreement/disagreement in accordance with the content of the item in such a way as to accord a 'traditional' orientation toward the causation of disease a low score and a 'non-traditional' orientation a high score. Where respondents had returned a 'don't know' response, a value equal to the mean of the known responses to that item was inserted. It is immediately apparent that the correlations were all positive and that they ranged from 0·5770 to 0·0739.

It is possible mathematically to decompose each correlation in a set of correlations of this sort into a number of constituent parts, each of which is accounted for by a separate underlying general 'factor'. Furthermore, because of the mathematical procedures used to estimate these 'factors', they are constrained to be independent numerically from one another; that is, the correlations among the 'factors' themselves must all be zero. Applying an analysis of this sort to the correlations in Table 2 resulted in two 'factors' of appreciable size.[5] The correlations of each of the separate items with the underlying factors, that is, the factor loadings, are given in Table 3.

From this table it is clear that all the items we have used in our analysis correlate positively with the first factor. Since these items refer to the belief that witches or spirits can cause symptoms of disease or to the role of the traditional healer (albeit to a lesser degree), we felt justified in treating this factor as one that would discriminate between those who thought of the causation of disease in traditional terms as opposed to those who saw it in non-traditional terms.[6]

5. 'Appreciable size' here refers to factors with an eigenvalue of 1·0 or more. This is a standard commonly accepted for deciding whether it is worthwhile to take a factor into account or not.

6. These items were all worded deliberately to encourage respondents to react in terms of a traditional orientation toward the causation of disease. The object was to try to counter-

Table 3

Factor Loadings on Items Relating to the Causation of Disease

Item	Factor 1	Factor 2
1. *Abatakati* or *varoyi* can make people sick	0·5026	0·3171
2. *Amadhlozi* or *midzimu* can make people sick	0·4855	0·3137
3. For certain kinds of sickness it is better to ask the help of the *nyanga* rather than the medical doctor	0·2791	0·3881
4. If a man is sick he should first go to the *nyanga* to see what is wrong with him *before* he goes to a medical doctor	0·3744	0·2966
5. *Abatakati* or *amadhlozi* can make people cough blood	0·6664	−0·0904
6. *Abatakati* or *amadhlozi* can make people have sores on their bodies that do not heal	0·6956	−0·1308
7. *Abatakati* or *amadhlozi* can make people have difficulty in swallowing food	0·7411	−0·2358
8. *Abatakati* or *amadhlozi* can make people have a lump that grows in the body	0·7002	−0·1186
9. *Abatakati* or *amadhlozi* can make people pass blood in the water	0·5514	−0·1928
10. *Abatakati* or *amadhlozi* can make people fall down in fits (*situtwani* or *zvipusha*)	0·6207	−0·0255
Percentage of variance explained	39·23	12·54

balance the reluctance of relatively well-educated respondents to admit to beliefs in traditional causal mechanisms. It is possible that, had we included items phrased positively from the perspective of adherence to modern rather than traditional notions of causation, then separate factors relating to intensity or belief in traditional and non-traditional types of causation may have emerged. This possibility is hinted at by the slightly lower loadings on factor 1 of the items that bear a reference to the 'medical doctor'. Our purpose, however, was not to examine the structure of beliefs *per se* but rather to try to point up factors that might influence the possible use of medical services. We felt justified in using the respondents' reactions to the totality of these items, suitably weighted as described in the text, to estimate the position of each respondent's orientation toward the causation of disease along a hypothesized 'traditionalism' dimension. We have deliberately avoided referring to the 'non-traditional' end of the dimension as 'modern' precisely because we do not have the data to justify that usage.

The correlations of the items with the second factor were somewhat smaller than with the first. This factor separated the items relating to the symptoms of disease from more general considerations of causation, a fact which is interesting in itself but which we do not pursue here.

Having established the extent to which each item relates to a hypothesized underlying dimension concerning traditional or non-traditional notions about the causation of disease, we may now use the correlations of each item with this underlying dimension, together with the responses of each respondent on each of the ten items, to produce a score reflecting the extent to which the respondent fell toward the traditional or the non-traditional end of a continuum. The weights so derived, adjusted by the standard deviation of each item, are presented in Table 4. These weights have been so adjusted that if a respondent were to disagree strongly with each item he would achieve a score of 100, whereas if he were to agree

Table 4
Weights Applied to Items to Determine Respondents' Positions along a Hypothetical Causation Orientation Continuum

Item	Weight
1. *Abatakati* or *varoyi* can make people sick	2·4512
2. *Amadhlozi* or *midzimu* can make people sick	1·9838
3. For certain kinds of sickness it is better to ask the help of the *nyanga* rather than the medical doctor	0·9907
4. If a man is sick he should go first to the *nyanga* to see what is wrong with him before he goes to a medical doctor	1·2308
5. *Abatakati* or *amadhlozi* can make people cough blood	2·8039
6. *Abatakati* or *amadhlozi* can make people have sores on their bodies that do not heal	3·1906
7. *Abatakati* or *amadhlozi* can make people have difficulty in swallowing food	4·4178
8. *Abatakati* or *amadhlozi* can make people have a lump that grows in the body	3·3572
9. *Abatakati* or *amadhlozi* can make people pass blood in the water	2·0369
10. *Abatakati* or *amadhlozi* can make people fall down in fits (*situtwani* or *zvipusha*)	2·5371

strongly with each item he would achieve a score of 0.[7] In other words, a score of 100 would represent the most extreme non-traditional position that a respondent could take, and a score of 0 would represent the most extreme traditional position. The actual scores of our respondents are shown in Table 5. These scores are, of course, entirely arbitrary: it would have been just as easy to arrange for the extremes to be reversed.

Table 5
Distribution of Scores on Continuum for 'Traditional'/'Non-traditional' Orientation toward the Causation of Disease

Orientation	Score	Number of respondents
Extreme traditional	0–9	172
Traditional	10–19	224
	20–29	375
Mixed traditional and	30–39	484
non-traditional	40–49	482
	50–59	349
Non-traditional	60–69	203
	70–79	133
Extreme non-traditional	80–89	89
	90–100	72
		2,583[a]

[a] The scores are for 2,583 respondents because information on background characteristics was missing for 80 respondents and these have been excluded from the rest of the analysis.

The distribution of scores is thus fairly even, with a mean of 42·15 and a standard deviation of 21·65. The majority of the respondents seem to occupy an intermediate position with respect to orientation toward the causation of disease, but nevertheless about one-tenth scored in the lowest range (say under 12) and one-tenth in the highest range (say over 75).

7. The score for individual i was derived from

$$S_i = 100 \left(\frac{\sum_{j=1}^{10} w_j (X_{ij} - X_{\min j})}{X_{\max j} - X_{\min j}} \right)$$

where $X_{\max j}$ is the maximum value item j could attain (i.e. 5), $X_{\min j}$ the minimum value item j could attain (i.e. 1). X_{ij} the score individual i had on item j, and w_j the weight, i.e. the factor coefficient derived from the first axis of a principal components analysis divided by the standard deviation for item j. If an individual returned a 5 response to all items his score would be 100, indicating a maximum orientation toward non-traditional views concerning the causation of disease. If he returned a 1 response to all items, his score would be 0, indicating a maximum orientation toward traditional views concerning the causation of disease.

411

Effect of Background Characteristics

Our immediate concern, however, was not with the interpretation of the scores *per se* but rather with the way in which the scores varied with combinations of different social backgrounds of the respondents. The material that can be collected on the social background of respondents in a test situation of this sort is, of course, limited to a number of fairly straightforward characteristics. Those that were included are listed in Table 6.

We are dealing here, as in all social analyses, with the operation of a large number of factors which we expect *ex hypothesi* to have some effect on the position of a respondent on the hypothetical attitudinal continuum relating to the causation of disease. All these variables operate simultaneously in the case of a single respondent. Analytically, however, we wish to separate the effects of one background factor from another so as to assess which of the factors is most likely to influence the position of the respondent along the continuum. There are several ways in which we could go about this, providing the approach handles the effect of all the measured factors simultaneously and not separately. We have elected to use regression analysis, mainly because the number of respondents is large enough to enable us to do so and because the techniques are well developed and reasonably robust. From a substantive point of view the procedure is constrained by the sort of variables we have been able to use in the analysis. Perhaps there were factors that would have had a much sharper effect on the respondent's orientation toward the causation of disease than those we have been able to include. This does not mean that they were not easily available to us, given the techniques of data collection we were using.

Considering that we are able to explore here only those variables included in our analysis, we are confronted with another difficulty. Normally regression analysis makes the assumption that the variables included in the analysis are continuous and measured on an interval scale. Quite clearly the material that we have to deal with cannot meet this assumption. Church affiliation, for example, or father's occupation could only be considered a nominal variable or at best an ordinal variable if, for instance, the religious groups or occupations could be arranged in some order in relation to the orientation toward the causation of disease. Recent developments in regression analysis in econometrics, however, have substantially overcome this difficulty even though they have not yet been used much in anthropological analyses. We refer here to what have come to be known as 'dummy' variable procedures. In these procedures a

Table 6
Effects of Variables on 'Traditional'/'Non-traditional' Orientation
toward the Causation of Disease

Variable	Proportion of respondents in category	Effect of variable on score
Type of school		
1. Urban secular schools	0·037	+9·41
*2 Large mission schools with teacher training facilities	0·623	45·49
3. Small mission schools without teacher training facilities	0·231	−4·34
4. Rural secular boarding schools (technical and agricultural)	0·109	−2·40
Respondent's educational level		
1. Nine or less years of schooling	0·377	−1·24
*2. Ten to twelve years of schooling	0·552	45·49
3. Thirteen or more years of schooling	0·071	−6·88
Type of course		
*1. Academic	0·424	45·49
2. Technical	0·537	−2·66
3. Agricultural	0·039	−1·22
Sex		
*1. Male	0·727	45·49
2. Female	0·273	+0·53
Age of respondent		
1. Sixteen years old and younger	0·502	+1·13
*2. Seventeen to twenty-one years old	0·348	45·49
3. Twenty-two years old and older	0·150	+1·20
Father's occupation		
*1. Rural agricultural (including subsistence)	0·438	45·49
2. Unskilled	0·041	−2·02
3. Skilled	0·166	−0·49
4. Supervisory	0·043	−3·18
5. Business and trading	0·039	+1·33
6. White-collar and professional	0·189	+3·17
7. Not recorded	0·084	−2·15

413

Table 6 (*continued*)

Variable	Proportion of respondents in category	Effect of variable on score
Mother's occupation		
1. Rural agricultural (including subsistence)	0·061	+1·05
*2. Unskilled (including housework)	0·775	45·49
3. Skilled	0·016	−1·02
4. Supervisory	0·001	+13·86
5. Business and trading	0·002	+5·62
6. White collar and professional	0·120	+0·34
7. Unrecorded	0·025	+4·69
Ethnic group		
1. Ndebele	0·358	−2·05
*2. Shona and Kalanga	0·522	45·49
3. Zulu and Shangaan	0·019	−0·03
4. Sotho and Tswana	0·041	−1·72
5. Others	0·060	+1·05
Birthplace		
*1. Urban	0·186	45·49
2. Rural	0·814	−0·78
Residence while attending school		
*1. At school	0·865	45·49
2. With own parents	0·097	−2·10
3. With relatives and non-relatives	0·038	−1·20
Years attending particular school		
1. Less than one year	0·363	+2·61
*2. One to two years	0·505	45·49
3. Five years or more	0·132	+1·24
Residence during school holidays		
*1. With parents and relatives	0·925	45·49
2. With non-relatives	0·007	+2·10
3. Elsewhere	0·068	+2·67
Father's educational level		
1. Nil	0·111	−0·05
*2. Primary only	0·637	45·49
3. Secondary	0·189	−1·54
4. Not known	0·063	−0·76

Table 6 (*continued*)

Variable	Proportion of respondents in category	Effect of variable on score
Mother's educational level		
1. Nil	0·142	+0·75
*2. Primary only	0·661	45·49
3. Secondary	0·101	−2·92
4. Not known	0·096	−2·49
Religious affiliation		
1. Roman Catholic	0·050	+1·17
2. Anglican	0·074	−2·77
3. Dutch Reformed, Presbyterian, C.C.A.P., Free Presbyterian Church of Scotland, Paris Evangelical, Lutheran	0·202	−0·88
*4. Methodist, Congregationalist (L.M.S.), Free Methodist, S.A.G.M.: Society of Friends, American Board Mission	0·295	45·49
5. Brethren in Christ, Salvation Army, Church of Christ, Baptist, Team, E.L.M.	0·249	−0·46
6. Seventh Day Adventist	0·090	+5·26
7. Jehovah's Witnesses and Full Gospel	0·003	0·00
8. Zionist, Simbabwe, Apostolic Church, Mai Chaza, American Methodist Episcopal, Assembly of God	0·012	+1·71
9. Independent African Church, United African Faith Church, African Lutheran Church	0·002	−3·01
10. No Christian affiliation	0·023	−7·75

Asterisks indicate variables excluded from the analysis.

variable that is not continuous and measured on an interval scale may be presented in a regression analysis as several distinct variables of a zero-one kind. If the respondent is a member of a particular Christian sect, for example, we could give him a score of unity on a dummy variable created to represent his religious affiliation. This implies that the respondent must of necessity be given a score of zero on other categories created to represent other religious affiliations, since we assume that the respondent can be a member of only one religious denomination. Using this procedure, we are able to represent variables of any complexity in a regression analysis. How we create the dummy variables, of course, will depend on what we are trying to achieve in the analysis. We would create the variables, for example, because we believe that a particular category is likely to be related to the dependent variable in a specific way.

In our analysis we did not use all the variables available to us partly because creating additional dummy variables would increase the number of variables we would have to handle and partly because we judged that they would not have any appreciable effect on the variable we wished to examine. The actual dummy variables we created and their effects on the score for orientation toward the causation of disease are given in Table 6.

Because of a technical problem concerned with solving for the effects of variables, one of the categories relating to each of the dummy variables must be excluded from the analysis.[8] We have marked with asterisks those which we have excluded. The choice of the category to exclude is purely arbitrary and makes no difference to the analysis except that if a category including only a very small number of cases is excluded, the determination of the effect of the remaining variables is likely to be unstable. The effect of the variables created as dummies is that the category excluded takes on a computed base value,[9] in this case a score of 45·49. The effects of the other categories in that variable (and in other variables as well) will be represented by departures from this value. For example, if we consider the variable relating to type of school, the excluded variable was large mission schools with teacher training facilities, which were attended by 62·3 per cent of the respondents. Respondents at this type of educational establishment would have an expected score of 45·49. We see from Table 6, however, that respondents at secular schools – the government schools in the town – would have an expected score some 9·41 points higher than this, that is, a score of 54·90, whereas respondents at small mission schools without teacher training classes would have an expected score 4·34 points less than 45·49, that is, a score of 41·15. Under the usual conventions of multiple regression, of course, it is assumed that the effects of all other variables included in the analysis have been allowed for in these scores. We may thus conclude that insofar as the attitude of respondents toward the causation of disease is concerned, the effect of different types of educational establishment may be interpreted as follows: respondents at small mission schools without teacher training facilities have the most traditional orientation

8. This is based on the consideration that if all categories were included, then one of the categories, given the others, would be fully determined. In these circumstances there could be no unique solution of the regression equations.

9. In fact the intercept value.

416

(score = 41·15); respondents at rural secular boarding schools have a slightly more non-traditional orientation (score = 43·09); students at large rural mission schools have a slightly more non-traditional orientation (45·49); but those at urban secular day-schools have the most non-traditional orientation of all. What in fact the use of dummy variables makes possible is an empirical determination of the effect of different categories of variables without assuming a direct linear relationship as do normal regression analyses using continuous variables. In particular, we are able to include, as a distinct category, respondents with 'don't know' responses, which were appreciable in the items relating to mother's and father's occupations. This would have been impossible with normal regression procedures.

When the operation of all these variables is taken into account, only a small proportion of the variance in the scores relating to the orientation toward the causes of disease is accounted for.[10] The implication of this is that if there are major causal factors that influence the orientation toward the causation of disease, these factors have not been included in the variables we have been able to use. Even if the explanatory power of the variables used is low, however, we are nevertheless able to examine the *relative* effect of the variables we have used. To do this we need to examine the extent to which each of the variables succeeds in explaining the variance in the disease causation orientation score. We can do this most simply by computing the diminution in the proportion of variance explained when specified variables are excluded from the analysis. These effects are given in Table 7.

It is clear from this table that the type of educational institution (and to some extent therefore the type of course being followed) is associated most directly with changes in the score in the disease causation orientation score. Religious affiliation has the next most important effect and then father's occupation. At the other end of the scale we see that birthplace and sex have virtually no effect on the scores.

Since our set of respondents was not drawn from a universe in a way that would enable us to use sampling theory, we could not estimate the probability that the relationship between the dependent variable and the independent variables we found in our analysis was likely to exist in the general population. However, it is apparent from Table 7 that there is a sharp decrement in the proportion of variance explained when we exclude the first three variables, from 'type of school' down to 'father's

10. The multiple correlation coefficient is 0·235, which implies that only 0·055 per cent of the variance in the scores is explained by the variables that have been used in this study.

Table 7

Percentage of Loss in Variance Explained When Specific Variables Are Excluded from the Analysis

Variable excluded	Percentage loss
Type of school	0·880
Religious affiliation	0·864
Father's occupation	0·544
Respondent's educational level	0·251
Type of course	0·225
Mother's educational level	0·213
Years attending particular school	0·202
Ethnic group	0·195
Mother's occupation	0·175
Residence while attending school	0·098
Age of respondent	0·057
Father's educational level	0·052
Residence during school holidays	0·047
Birthplace	0·017
Sex	0·009

occupation'. It would seem reasonable therefore to confine our comments to the effects of these three variables.

The specific effects of the variables that are most closely associated with variations in the disease causation orientation score may be assessed by examination of the increment values in Table 6. But the effect of religious conviction on the scores was not so simple. From Table 6 we see that being a Seventh Day Adventist led to the most 'non-traditional' expected score (50·75) of all the broad categories of religious persuasion. This group was followed by a category of fundamentalist sects with a score of 47·20, including several, such as the Apostolic Faith Church, which believed in divine healing. At the other extreme of the range of scores were the adherents to a number of African Independent sects with a score of 42·48 and those who did not profess to be Christians with a score of 37·74. We had anticipated that membership in mission churches, that is, in overseas-based churches that maintained expatriate mission staffs in Rhodesia, would have the most 'non-traditional' score, and we had expected that those who were members of local separatist sects and those who were not Christians would have scores indicating the most traditional orientation. While our expectations with respect to the non-

Christians and to independent churches of what Sundkler (1948) would have classified as Ethiopian churches were borne out, our expectations with regard to the mission churches were not. On reflection, the non-traditional orientation of the Seventh Day Adventists seems reasonable since in general they are noted for their hard-headed, practical approach to Christianity, but we have no adequate explanation of why the members of the Anglican Church should have returned such a relatively high 'traditional' expected score of 42·72, which is only slightly more 'non-traditional' than the expected score of members of the Ethiopian-type Independent Churches.

Following the effect of school type and religious affiliation on the orientation toward disease causation score, the occupation of the respondent's father seems to have had most influence on the level of that score. In relation to respondents whose fathers were in rural agricultural occupations (including subsistence cultivation), those whose fathers were in white-collar or professional occupations tended to reflect a more non-traditional orientation toward the causation of disease (expected score of 48·67 versus 45·49), while those whose fathers were in supervisory occupations, with an expected score of 42·31, and those whose fathers were in unskilled occupations, with an expected score of 43·47, reflected a more traditional orientation toward the causation of disease. In general, the trend in the expected scores of respondents whose fathers were in different occupational categories followed the general level of education associated with those occupations in that there is a clear trend of increasing score, indicating a more non-traditional orientation, as one moves from the unskilled to white-collar and professional categories. The one exception to this is the supervisory category. The probable explanation for this is that because of their role in the government administrative system, the occupations of 'headman' and 'chief', both of which required no educational background and both of which were essentially related to rural contexts, were coded as 'supervisory', a decision which in retrospect was unfortunate and could only be remedied by recoding the entire set of records.

Conclusions

In general, these findings are consistent with our expectations about the way in which people undergoing academic education and coming from homes in which parents are in white-collar or professional occupations would react to questions of this kind about the basic causes of disease. They are also consistent with our appreciation of how effective the teaching of fundamentalist sects can be in influencing the way in which their adherents react to questions of this type. The categories of respondents to which these expectations apply, however, are very different from one another. Although it is always easy to be wise after the event, we had not in fact anticipated the result we obtained from the Seventh Day Adventists.

But the exercise has been instructive in another way. We had included the original set of variables because we had anticipated on common-sense grounds that they would be related to the way in which young educated people appreciated medical services and to the factors underlying their beliefs about what made people ill. We had not anticipated that age or sex, for example, would make no difference at all to the way in which respondents reacted to the items. It is true that the age range of the respondents is small – the population was heavily selected from the younger ages of the population – but we had anticipated that respondents in the upper age range would have had more education and so would have reacted in a more non-traditional way than they did.

Our expectations with respect to respondents' living in boarding schools as opposed to home, their living in town as opposed to the country, the number of years of schooling they had had, and the level of education their parents had had were in general not confirmed.

We would not argue that the sort of analysis we have conducted here is a substitute for traditional anthropological field-work. Our view, rather, is that, providing appropriate analytic techniques are used,[11] surveys of this kind can be used to refine hypotheses and therefore to respecify questions that in the end may possibly only be answered using different methods of enquiry. There is clearly a dialectic between different methods of enquiry. Questions resolved by one method are likely to throw up questions of a different kind which can only be resolved by some other method.

References

CHAVUNDUKA, G. L. (1973), 'Paths to medical care in Highfield Rhodesia', *The Society of Malawi Journal*, vol. 26, part 2, pp. 25–45.

11. By 'appropriate' we mean techniques that violate as little as possible the assumptions upon which the data were generated in the first instance. We look upon multiple regression using dummy variables as a technique of this sort, as is the related technique called multiple classification analysis. There has recently been a rapid extension of procedures for analyzing data which do not assume interval-type measures, and anthropologists do not seem to have availed themselves of the facilities that these techniques offer. One reason may be that a procedure like multiple regression using dummy variables rapidly expands the number of variables which must be used, and this can be a disadvantage if sample sizes tend to be small.

GELFAND, M. (1964), *Witch Doctor*, Harvill Press.

GELFAND, M. (1973), 'The Shona Ng'anga as I know him', *The Society of Malawi Journal*, vol. 26, part 2, pp. 16–24.

MITCHELL, H. F. (1967), 'Sociological aspects of cancer rate surveys in Africa', *National Cancer Institute Monograph No. 25*, pp. 151–70.

MITCHELL, J. C. (1965), 'The meaning in misfortune for urban Africans', in G. Dieterlen and M. Fortes (eds), *African Systems of Thought*, pp. 192–203, Oxford U.P. for International African Institute.

SUNDKLER, B. G. M. (1948), *Bantu Prophets in South Africa*, Butterworth.

38. W. D. Hammond-Tooke

Urbanization and the Interpretation of Misfortune

W. D. Hammond-Tooke, 'Urbanization and the interpretation of misfortune: a quantitative analysis', *Africa*, vol. 40, 1970, pp. 25–39.[1]

The general aim of this paper is to test by quantitative methods Mitchell's statement (Mitchell, 1965, p. 193) that 'we expect the meaning which people read into misfortunes to change when they become part of an industrial urban community'. Mitchell was commenting (and elaborating) on the demonstration by Marwick (1952) that witchcraft accusations are particularly likely to occur between people who are in competition with one another, but who are prevented by the norms of the society from expressing their hostility openly. He suggests that Africans in towns continue to interpret their misfortunes in 'personal' terms but that 'the meaning that they attach to the misfortune must be of a type which will allow them to take effective action'. In the towns of the Copperbelt hostility and opposition may be openly expressed towards strangers, so there is no need for accusations of witchcraft (signalling interpersonal tensions), except where townsfolk are linked in co-operative enterprises in which, nevertheless, there is an element of competition, e.g. as between rival beerbrewers or fellow workers. In such cases open accusation tends to be inhibited and the interpretation recouched in terms of ancestral wrath. Mitchell sees, therefore, an increase in ancestor-centred explanation of misfortune in urban areas and implies a decrease in witch accusations.[2] Marwick has suggested, on the other hand, that 'the immediate effect of contact with Western influence is not a decrease but an increase in the African's preoccupation with magic, witchcraft and sorcery', due to new social alignments and social, economic and political changes, which create insecurity, anxiety, and impart a 'dangerous flexibility' to human relationships (Marwick, 1958, p. 106).

The specific aims of the investigation are twofold: to determine

1. Research was financed by a grant from the Institute for Social and Economic Research, Rhodes University, to which the author expresses his thanks. He is also grateful to Mr P. Qayiso, B. A., for much assistance in the field-work.

2. 'There are, after all, time-honoured methods of adjusting the relationships of a man to his ancestor spirits, but none of dealing with a witch in the alien circumstances of the town' (op. cit., p. 202).

whether the interpretation of misfortune (in terms of witchcraft/sorcery, ancestral wrath, or by non-mystical causation) differs significantly as between rural and urban communities, and whether, in the witchcraft/sorcery category, there is significant variation in the targets of witchcraft accusations. *Prima facie* one would expect conflict-reflecting accusations to occur mainly between kinsfolk and near neighbours in the rural area and between strangers competing for economic and prestige awards in the urban. Field-work was undertaken in two Xhosa-speaking communities in the Eastern Cape, Republic of South Africa, and we know, from the work of Professor Monica Wilson and her associates in the rural district of Keiskammahoek (Wilson *et al.*, 1952, p. 172), that among these mixed Mfengu-Xhosa, those accused of witchcraft and sorcery were related to their victims by consanguinity or affinity in 82 per cent of the cases recorded. This rural material provides comparative data for my rural figures; there is no comparable quantitative survey for the incidence of witchcraft in towns.

Method

Two areas were selected for detailed investigation – a conservative, predominantly 'Red'*, administrative area ('location'), Khalana in the Dushane chiefdom of the Ciskeian district of King William's Town,[3] and the African townships of Grahamstown, a small Eastern Cape educational and commercial centre situated about fifty miles away. Khalana has an estimated population of 900 persons: Grahamstown's African population is approximately 25,000. Grahamstown is one of the oldest established towns in South Africa, having been founded in 1812 as a military post on the frontier between White and Xhosa. Its African population is drawn almost exclusively from the Xhosa-speaking chiefdoms to the east, of which the Dushane is one. I have no figures for the number of Dushane in Grahamstown but the tribe, a part of the Xhosa tribal cluster,[4] is representative of the Cape Nguni culture complex, of remarkable uniformity.[5] Although a small town almost devoid of industries, the long-established nature of the community has resulted in a

---

* The Xhosa distinction between conservative 'Red' [-ochre-smeared] people and more westernized 'School people' is explained by Mayer (1961, pp. 3 f., 20–30, 40 f.) – *Ed.*

3. Mayer (1961, p. 298), in his Appendix II, gives the percentage of Red homesteads in Khalana as 96·5 per cent.

4. See W. D. Hammond-Tooke, 'Segmentation and fission in Cape Nguni political units', *Africa*, vol. 35, part 2 (1965), pp. 143–66.

5. See P. Mayer (1961, p. 3) for a discussion of the background of tribesmen in East London. The position is similar for Grahamstown.

comparatively westernized and sophisticated African population. Work done by Rhodes University's Institute of Social and Economic Research in 1966–7 revealed a large and active 'middle class' and intelligent informants comment on the urban, or big town, 'feel' of the townships. Obviously an investigation of this nature would have been better done in a large urban centre but, it is argued, if trends there be, these should be found even more developed in an urban conurbation. What is of interest are *patterns*, rather than absolute quantities: our results should apply *a fortiori* to highly industrialized urban communities.

Cases were collected for all misfortunes and deaths occurring in these two areas. A period of two months was spent in each community but the cases do not refer specifically to this period. The greater number were retrieved from the memories of informants and refer to the past, particularly to the last six years. No attempt was made to ask specifically for 'witchcraft' or 'ancestor' explanations. Rather was the question formulated: 'Have you ever suffered a misfortune?', and the case, with its 'explanation', recorded in detail.

Two points must be made in this connection. Marwick (1967, p. 243) has stressed the importance of expressing the incidence of witchcraft accusations as rates of occurrence rather than raw frequencies of incidence. 'Accusations of sorcery in each relationship category must somehow be expressed as proportions of the total amount of interaction characteristic of that category before comparisons can safely be made.' This obviously entails full genealogical and demographic data about the social universe and demands detailed face-to-face field-work within carefully delimitated small communities. Exigencies of time and finance made this a counsel of perfection. This type of participant observation is particularly difficult to achieve in the urban situation. An attempt was made, as indicated above, to randomize the sample, but there are undoubtedly built-in biases. Approximately 100 cases were collected from each of the two areas (Khalana 107; Grahamstown 99).

Secondly, Marwick has also laid great stress on the importance of recording, not only the relationship between accused and victim, but also that between accuser and accused. This has the advantage of 'providing a direct index of the tense relations rather than an indirect one through informants' own estimates of who might have attacked the victim' (Marwick, 1967, p. 240). This proved impossible in the South African situation. Accusations of witchcraft are a criminal offence since the passing of the Witchcraft Act (20 of 1895). In most cases, even in rural areas, there was no public, formalized accusation and the only realistic interview question was: 'What did the people say had caused the misfortune?' Even diviners refuse to specify witches by name. Rather do they indicate the sex, status, and perhaps relationship of the witch and leave their clients to form their own conclusions. In a few cases there was dual explanation: the people said the victim died of an accident (or drink) but his relative suspected witchcraft.

The theoretical presupposition is, of course, that Khalana represents an earlier 'stage' in the urbanization process – a stage through which the urbanites of Grahamstown have moved in the process of becoming town-rooted, in Mayer's phrase (Mayer, 1961). This attempt to inject time depth into what is essentially a synchronic study of differentially acculturated communities, has a respectable history in anthropology (e.g. Redfield's studies of Yucatan and Hunter's work on the Mpondo).[6] While the method does not tell us anything about the process whereby idea systems change, Khalana and Grahamstown can be regarded as providing points along a continuum towards increasing urbanization. In a study of changing social structures and relationships such an approach would be less than adequate; it is maintained here that, in a study limited to the structure of idea systems, the approach still has some value.

A serious omission was the failure to record the length of time urban victims had been resident in Grahamstown, so that relative 'urbanization' could be used as a variable. On the other hand, it can be argued that the stricter application of the influx control regulations since 1945 has reduced newcomers to Grahamstown to a trickle. The almost complete lack of industry means that the migrant category, documented by Mayer (1961), and also represented on the Copperbelt, is poorly represented in Grahamstown. This would appear to be one of the reasons for the lack of importance of the ancestor cult in town (see below) – although, as we shall see, it does not appear to be an important category of explanation in the rural areas either.

The cultural content of Cape Nguni ancestor and witch beliefs is well documented[7] and need not be recapitulated in detail here. All illness and misfortune, and all deaths, except from extreme old age, are explained as due to the activity of a witch or sorcerer or as being sent by the ancestors in punishment for some neglect of ritual. The concept of chance, essential to scientific causal explanation, is thus unknown as an indigenous category of explanation. Evans-Pritchard's terminology is analytically appropriate for the Cape Nguni although one word, *igqwira*, is used for both witch and sorcerer (Evans-Pritchard, 1937). The people can distin-

6. R. Redfield (1941), M. Hunter (1936).

7. e.g. M. Hunter (1936), W. D. Hammond-Tooke (1962), J. H. Soga (1931), W. D. Hammond-Tooke (1968).

guish, however, between *ukuthakatha* (the general term for witchcraft or sorcery) 'by means of familiars' (*izilwana*) and 'by means of medicines', and the classification here follows this usage. Allocation of blame to either witch/sorcerer or ancestor is determined through a diviner (*igqira* – the similarity of terms is suggestive) who is 'called' to the office and who divines through possession by her ancestral spirits (most diviners are women). This is the only instance of ancestral shades influencing others than their own descendants and is anomalous in the otherwise structurally determined ancestor cult. In the past reaction to what Mayer (1954, p. 17) calls 'the hidden enemy within the gate' was swift and violent. Alberti (1810), our earliest authority on the Xhosa, and a close and accurate observer, states that a discovered witch was either tortured by being pegged down and covered with 'a large black type of ant' or by being burnt with heated stones (both often resulting in death), clubbed to death on the order of the chief, or expelled from the tribe. 'In every case, the hut of such an unfortunate is burnt down and his cattle and other property become the property of the tribe ...' (p. 51). Diagnosis of ancestral displeasure puts the blame for misfortune squarely on the victim or his guardian, unlike witchcraft which can be looked on, in terms of one type of psychological theory, as a projection of guilt feelings.[8]

By far the greater number of alleged witches and sorcerers are women. Of the 121 cases of witchcraft/sorcery in both the rural and urban samples, only sixteen of the accused were males. In two of these cases they were believed to have used familiars; in all others, sorcery was the mode of attack (rural, 6; urban, 8).

However, something should be said of the 'folk model' as conceived by the people of Khalana today. Informants stressed that witches (*amagqwira*, sing. *igqwira*) were extremely active in the community and that of latter years they had developed more sophisticated techniques. There was much talk of 'flying machines' used to spirit away victims, usually to the Gwadana forest in the Willowvale district of the Transkei, renowned as the headquarters of witches from as far afield as the Transvaal and Natal. Gwadana is said to have a dark, silent lake surrounded by marshes which no human being can traverse and over which not even an aeroplane can fly. It is here that the witches hold their meetings. The flying machines are faster than an aeroplane, so that witches can fly to Johannesburg and back in the same night.

A witch is superficially a normal person 'yet deep down in her heart she has a great hatred for people'. Witches are touchy and malicious and will kill for minor, inadvertent slights. 'A witch may have borrowed salt and

8. C. Kluckhohn (1944).

tobacco from you for years, yet if you refuse once she might kill you.' Witches kill out of sheer sadism, to test their medicines, or to please a familiar, in particular the much-feared *impundulu* or lightning bird. Unlike the sorcerer, who uses medicines for the specific purpose of harming his victim, witch activity may be unconscious on the part of the witch, or forced upon her by her familiar. There are a number of such familiars, perhaps the most dreaded being the *impundulu*. *Iimpundulu* (pl.) suck blood from their victims and their insatiable hunger forces their owners to send them to obtain 'meat'. Long wasting illnesses, accompanied by coughing and stabbing pains and terminating in *iphika* (shortness of breath) and death, are believed to be caused by the vampire-like activities of an *impundulu*: sudden death is due to the victim's having been kicked on chest or head by this familiar. *Iimpundulu* are usually owned by women and inherited from the mother: 'This is one of the reasons why the daughter of a known witch often fails to get married.' If the *impundulu* is not passed on at the death of the witch it becomes an *ishologu*, an ownerless familiar that acts autonomously. The *impundulu* is by far the commonest form of familiar in both town and country: in the sample 70 per cent of rural witchcraft cases involved *iimpundulu* and 50 per cent of urban cases. 'It is the most feared because it has no mercy. As long as it has been directed to kill it will not rest until it has fulfilled its purpose. It will kill a whole family and keep on asking for victims. The owner is forced to direct it to other victims to prevent it turning on her.' The cases in the sample of mother/daughter and mother/son witchcraft are usually due to an *impundulu* demanding their sacrifice. Informants state (as a modern development) that *iimpundulu* today even make the *isithunzela*, the resurrected corpse, formally the work of witches (Hunter, 1936; Hammond-Tooke, 1962).

In contrast, the little, man-like, *uthikoloshe* or *uhili* is 'more merciful' and will sometimes spare a victim out of pity. *Ichanti* is a snake that usually accompanies the *uthikoloshe* and has the power of transforming itself into any type of object. It is particularly dangerous to cross the spoor of an *ichanti* as it causes enteritis and death. Other familiars are a mystical baboon *imfene*, usually kept by male witches, and *mamlambo*, a snake-like creature that demands the sacrifice of a close kinsman.

Relations with the ancestral shades are established and maintained by blood sacrifices performed by the lineage head on behalf of lineage members. Specific calling on the ancestors by name (*nqula*) is confined to piacular killings to propitiate the shades in times of misfortune diagnosed by a diviner as being caused by neglect of custom. In practice this custom concerns the ritual killings appropriate at life-cycle rituals, especially at birth (*bingelela*), initiation, and death. Neglect of the *guqula* killing, to end the mourning period and incorporate the deceased into the world of the shades, is a particularly common cause of ancestral wrath. Neglect of death ritual killings account for 50 per cent of all cases of ancestor wrath (66 per cent of rural cases).

Analysis of Survey Data

The allocation of explanations of misfortune between the various categories was found to be as follows:

Table 1
Explanations of Misfortune: Rural and Urban

Category	Rural		Urban	
	n	%	*n*	%
Witchcraft	39	36·4	20	21·0
Sorcery	38	36·4	24	24·0
Total W/S	77	72·8	44	45·0
Ancestors	9	8·2	7	7·0
River people	2	1·7		
Non-mystical causes	19	17·3	48	48·0
Grand total	107	100·0	99	100·0

It appears from the above that neither Mitchell's nor Marwick's predictions are fulfilled in this Eastern Cape situation. In the urban area there is a marked drop in witchcraft/sorcery cases from 72·8 per cent to 45 per cent (there is little change in the *ratio* of witchcraft to sorcery cases in this category) but there is no corresponding rise in ancestor cases. Rather is there a marked increase in the proportion of cases explained by non-mystical causation (from 17·3 to 48 per cent). This is what one would expect in an increasingly secularized, westernized community. The most unexpected result, however, is the small number of cases of misfortune explained in terms of ancestral wrath in the rural area, and the almost identical incidence of this category in both areas.

The general pattern is clear: the cases must now be analysed in greater detail.

428

Witchcraft and Sorcery

This is the area in which interpersonal tensions become significant and a few words must be said as to the social situations in which these conflicts occur.

All Cape Nguni are patrilineal pastoral-hoe-culturalists with by far the greater emphasis on cattle-keeping, which is highly ritualized. They are divided into chiefdoms that enjoyed complete independence in the past (Hammond-Tooke, 1965) and social life is regulated by a combination of descent-group membership and residence in local administrative areas under headmen. The ritual and economic unit is the patrilineage (or, more usually today, the lineage segment) which defines inheritance of property and the objects of worship (Hammond-Tooke, 1968a). Marriage is patrilocal, in most chiefdoms exogamy rules exclude marriage within the clans of all four grandparents and children come under the control of their agnatic ancestors. Women, on marriage, are incorporated into their husband's patrilineage by a ritual killing. The incidence of polygyny has dropped considerably. There are no figures as to its traditional incidence, but in the Keiskammahoek survey of 1952 only one case of polygyny was recorded. Comparative data for the conservative Mpondomise show not more than 5 per cent of male household heads had more than one wife (Hammond-Tooke, 1968b, p. 85). Lineages are still important kinship structures, especially in ritual matters, but no longer form exclusive local groups, if they ever did. Considerable inter-ward movement has meant the dispersal of agnatic kin, except for pockets composed mainly of lineage segments (Wilson *et al.*, 1952, p. 47; Hammond-Tooke, 1968b). Informants stated that witchcraft accusations were formerly more frequent between agnatic kin, due to quarrels over inheritance, but that today most accusations were between neighbours. This present day 'folk model' was not entirely borne out by the survey, in which 21 per cent of accusations in the rural area were between agnates as opposed to 23 per cent among neighbours, but these figures might indicate a significant shift from the position in the past.

In actual fact, as appears from Table 2, the great majority of accusations between kin occur, not between agnates, but between affines. Of these, 38 per cent occurred between a woman and her husband's brother's son, three with the husband's brother himself, and two with HBSS. This is in strong contrast to Keiskammahoek, where Wilson reports that 'The person most often accused of witchcraft or sorcery is a wife, and second to her a mother-in-law' (p. 173). The reason for the prevalence of the FBW as a target for witch accusations is probably due to the fact that she is the nearest lineage affine (and, therefore, stranger) not the actual wife or mother of the victim. There was only one case of a man's mother-in-law being accused (rural) and four cases each of a wife bewitching her husband in Khalana and Grahamstown. The *proportion* of husband–wife accusations differs, however. Whereas in the country they form only 9 per cent of inter-kin cases; in town they form 25 per cent. It is clear that inter-kin conflict is much less common in town and is

Table 2

Relationship between Victim and Accused in Witchcraft/Sorcery Cases

	Rural					Urban				
	Category V/ad	n	%	W	S	Category V/ad	n	%	W	S
KIN										
Affines	HBS/FBW	10		5	5					
	HB/BW	3		3						
	BW/HZ	2		1	1					
	HFBS/FBSW	1		1						
	HBSS/FFBW	2		2						
	HF/SW	1		1						
	HBW/HBW	1			1					
	Sil/Mil	1			1					
	BW/HB	1			1					
	HBSW/HFBW	1			1					
	HZS/MBW	1			1					
	Hclansm/W			1						
	Lineage Ws	1		1						
		26	26	33·7						
Patrikin	S/M*	3		2	1	S/M*	1		1	
	D/M*	3		3		Z/Z	1		1	
	FZ/BS	1		1		B/Z	1			1
	H/W	4		1	3					
	S/StepM	3		2	1	H/W	4		1	3
	BS/FB	2		2						
		16	16	21·0						
Matrikin	MB/ZD	1	1	1·1	1					
	Total kin		43	55·8	27	16	Total kin	7	16·0	3	4

Table 2 (*continued*)

Rural					Urban				
Category V/ad	n	%	W	S	Category V/ad	n	%	W	S
OTHER Neighbours	17	23·2	5	12	Neighbours	9	20·5	6	3
Employer/ Employee	2	2·6	2			1	2·5		1
Lovers	4	5·2	1	3		4	9·1	1	3
Cred/Debt	2	2·6		2		1	2·3	1	
Chrmn/mem	1	1·5		1		1	2·3		1
Co-drinkers	2	2·6		2		2	4·5	1	1
Brewer/client						2	4·5	1	1
Co-workers	1	1·5		1		5	11·5		5
Business rivals						3	6·8	1	2
Church member						2	4·5		2
D's lover						1	2·3		1
Rival gangs	1	1·5		1					
Unrelated						1	2·3	1	
Familiar wanted meat	4	3·5	4			5	11·1	5	
			12	22				17	20
Total other	34	44·2			Total other	37	84·0		
Grand total	77	100·0			Grand total	44	100·0		

*D/M and S/M cases usually involve a familiar's demand for the death of the victim due to jealousy.

confined to members of the nuclear family. That is what one would expect and reflects the isolation of the family from its matrix of kin in the urban situation.[9]

The large number of accusations between a wife and her husband's agnates needs explaining. Here the lack of detailed demographic data becomes apparent. It would appear that there is a greater tendency for uterine brothers to settle close to one another than in Keiskammahoek or

9. Mitchell (1965, pp. 195–6), on the other hand, has stated that witchcraft accusations are not frequent in the urban family. 'The significant point is that while the family is the locus of much competition and hostility in Cewa rural life, in a town like Salisbury ... the family is essentially a tightly integrated co-operative group. Tensions intrude, rather, from the larger society.'

among the Mpondomise. The great majority (seven) of reasons given for conflict in the ten cases between a woman and her husband's brother related either to jealousy because of greater material prosperity or jealousy of hardworking children (in one case the accused was childless). In three cases it was said that the woman was trying to kill off the family of her husband's elder brother so that her sons could claim the inheritance. In two other cases the cause was a grudge because of refusal to render economic assistance and one involved the discovery by the HBS of his aunt in actions indicating witch activity (she was mixing the cowdung and mud for floor-smearing with her own urine, and retaliated by attempting to poison him).

As we should expect, accusations between non-kin are much more frequent in Grahamstown than in Khalana (84 per cent : 44·2 per cent of the total). Here again the different categories must be expressed in percentages to give the true picture. Accusations against *neighbours* constitute 50 per cent of non-kin accusations in Khalana and 24 per cent in Grahamstown, although they both constitute approximately 20 per cent of the total incidence of witchcraft/sorcery in both areas. The category 'neighbours' refers to cases in which there was apparently no other significant relationship between victim and accused except their neighbourliness; the protagonists in other non-kin categories, e.g. co-drinkers, creditor/debtor, etc., may, of course, also happen to be neighbours, but the particular relationship seemed to be more significant in terms of conflict, and they have been so classified. Conflicts between neighbours in the rural area are predominantly due to envy of another's wealth and good fortune. Of the seventeen cases in this category eleven were because of economic jealousy, two because the reputed witch was childless and envied a neighbour's child, two because of quarrels (in one case a strayed horse: in the other refusal to lend food), and two cases unascertained.

Conflict between neighbours in the town is not so clearly related to economic envy. There was only one example of this in the nine cases, the other sources of conflict being jealousy of a neighbour's clever child (four cases) and quarrels over refusal to lend food or afford other help (four cases). Whereas in Khalana 79 per cent of witchcraft and sorcery cases involved kin and/or neighbours, reflecting a settled rural community, this category forms only 36 per cent of the urban cases. In Grahamstown 63·5 per cent of cases involved conflict between people due to causes other than kinship or propinquity and 36·5 per cent between kin and neighbours reflecting, in its turn, a greater heterogeneity and competitiveness on other grounds.

The actual *number* of non-kin witchcraft cases (as opposed to percentages) differs surprisingly little as between town and country. The great difference, as we have seen, is between the proportion of cases explained by the witchcraft/sorcery syndrome and what I have called 'non-mystical causation' (see below). It seems that the inter-kin witchcraft and sorcery category is supplanted, in town, by a tendency to explain misfortune in non-personal terms. This must be analysed in greater detail – but first something must be said of misfortunes caused by ancestral wrath.

The Wrath of the Ancestors

The most unexpected result of the investigation was the small number of misfortunes, in both rural and urban communities, diagnosed as having been caused by the ancestral shades (rural 8·2 per cent; urban 7·0 per cent). While perhaps not unexpected for the urban community (*pace* Mitchell) it is certainly so for the rural, which, as we have seen, is a predominantly Red area. Details are given in Tables 3 and 4.

Causes of ancestral wrath here involve the neglect of three types of ritual killing, viz. *bingelela*, a birth ritual; *izila*, a killing to 'accompany' the deceased; and *guqula*, a ritual to incorporate the shade of a dead father into the community of the ancestors. In only one case did death supervene and in some the symptoms were comparatively minor. It is interesting that, although all except two cases involved Red persons, a diviner was consulted in only four of the cases. The question arises: why

Table 3

Cases Explained by Reference to Ancestors: Rural

Symptoms	Neglected custom	R/S	D	WD
1. Diarrhoea in infant	*bingelela*	S	+	+
2. Pains, died, cattle died	*guqula* for FF	S	–	+
3. Fever, diarrhoea, pains in child	*bingelela*	R	–	–
4. Wasting, T.B.	*guqula*/F	R	–	+
5. Killed by car Jbg (son of No. 4)	*guqula*/F	R	–	–
6. Cattle lost	*izila*/F (anger of FF)	R	+	–
7. Mauled by dog: D sick	*izila*/F	R	–	–
8. Persistent headache	*guqula*/F	R	+	–
9. Swollen leg	*bingelela*	R	+	+

R = Red; D = Diviner consulted; WD = White doctor consulted; S = School.

Table 4

Cases Explained by Reference to Ancestors: Urban

Symptoms	Neglected custom	R/S	D	WD
1. Body pains	Dead F's request for meat (in dream) ignored	S	+	−
2. Pains, breathlessness, died	izila/F	S	+	+
3. S insane; victim died	imbeleko	S	−	−
4. Circ. wound not healing	intambo	S	+	−
5. Choked to death	izila/F	R	+	−
6. Wounded by police	imbeleko	S	+	−
7. Became deaf and dumb	izila/F	R	+	−

R = Red; D = Diviner consulted; WD = White doctor consulted; S = School.

were these cases thought to be ancestrally caused, particularly in the absence of divination? The answer would appear to lie in the comparatively minor nature of most of the misfortunes and in a conscious feeling of guilt for a known neglect of custom.

Two cases (not classified here) involving coughing, body pains, and madness, were diagnosed as being caused by the River People (*abantu bamlambo*): the victims had bathed in the Keiskamma River.[10]

The pattern appears to differ slightly for urban cases (Table 4) but the numbers involved are too small for definite conclusions to be drawn. Here the misfortunes seem more severe (three deaths, madness, dumbness). In almost all cases, diagnosis was performed by a diviner – a marked contrast to the position in the country. This may be due to a less active 'conscience' on the part of townsfolk, who do not automatically relate misfortune to neglect of custom and who thus need to have it specifically pointed out and confirmed. It would appear that there is little difference in the incidence of the category between town and country, a fact difficult to explain except on the grounds that, in any event, this type of explanation probably always formed a small proportion and that the ancestor cult is accepted uncritically in both areas. The figures do not indicate any change due to urbanization.

10. It is difficult to place the 'river people' in Cape Nguni religious systems. According to Wilson (1952, pp. 192 fn.) 'In Pondoland "the people of the river" are clan ancestors, but this connection was not made plain by informants in Keiskammahoek District.' From my investigations among the Xhosa it would appear that they are not ancestral spirits, although a relationship exists between them and certain clans, who sacrifice maize, millet, and tobacco to them at sacred pools.

Non-Mystical Causation

The allocation of recorded explanations to the category 'non-mystical causes' presented some difficulties. It is not a category represented in the traditional world-view, at least not in its modern form of cause and effect chains, subordinate to laws. Yet there was always (as far as we know) a residual category, 'old age', which fell outside the witchcraft/sorcery syndrome. All writers state that death from senility was regarded as part of the nature of things – and in both Khalana and Grahamstown a high proportion of cases in the category refer to this (rural 57·8 per cent; urban 19 per cent). It appears, though, that only extreme old age removed explanation from the supernatural sphere; the average age of rural and urban cases was eighty-six years!

The concept of non-mystical causation, as used here, does not necessarily mean the use of explicitly scientific theory to explain misfortune. There may or may not be an understanding of, say, germ theory in the minds of the explainers. More often than not it would appear to involve a failure to define explicitly the causative element – to let the search for explanation just rest at the noting of an event, or by expressing it as due to chance.

Cases of misfortune explained as due to non-mystical causes in Khalana (17·3 per cent of the total number from this area) are presented in Table 5.

The eight cases not involving old age need closer examination as they are *prima facie* anomalous in a traditional setting, particularly as all except one are the responses of Red people who, one would expect, still operate with traditional categories. One of the three cases which I have

Table 5

Cases Explained by Non-Mystical Causes: Rural

Category	n	%	nWD	nD
Old age	11	57·9	1	..
Sickness	3	15·8	2	..
Murder	2	10·5	..	1
Accident	2	10·5	..	..
Over-exertion	1	5·3	..	..
Total	19	100·0	3	1

WD=White doctor consulted; D=Diviner consulted.

recorded as 'sickness' involved a ten-year-old boy who fainted at school and began vomiting bile. He was cured by a White doctor and people said that he had too much bile, due to drinking excessive quantities of tea. His mother, though, was not satisfied and hinted darkly at witchcraft. A fifty-one-year-old male suffered an attack of fever, which was cured by herbs: 'The fact that he got better showed it was only fever, but it attacked him so severely that we began to wonder if there was nothing more' (i.e. witchcraft). Finally, a forty-seven-year-old female was suddenly attacked by body pains which resulted in an operation in hospital to remove what the White doctor called a 'worm'. The people accepted this, probably because the explanation was couched in familiar terms. It is perhaps significant that in all these cases the sickness was minor, or at least readily curable: and that in two cases there was the beginning of a suspicion of witchcraft.

The category 'murder' refers to a strangulation case in Khalana and a fatal assault case in Johannesburg on a thirty-eight-year-old Khalana migrant. In neither case was witchcraft thought to be involved. The two 'accidents' involved a man who died from taking too strong a dose of emetic so that he inhaled his vomit, and a woman who fell off a moving lorry and who suffered acute pains for some time.

The proportion of 17·3 per cent of non-mystical explanation is unexpectedly high. If, however, those classified as 'old age' are ignored, the number drops to eight, or 7·3 per cent, which is more in line with expectations.

Turning to the Grahamstown community the figures are as quoted in Table 6.

We have here a striking contrast between town and country. Excluding death from old age, we have an increase from 7·3 to 37·6 per cent in the proportion of non-traditional modes of explanation. As we have seen, this is not a category formally represented in the traditional world-view and its greater use in Grahamstown would seem to indicate a shift towards a more secular world-view. In twenty-two of the forty-eight cases (47 per cent) diagnosis had been made by a White doctor whose explanation presumably had been accepted by the community. As at Khalana, in only one case had a diviner been consulted. Explanations of 'sickness' included the following comments: 'He died from T.B. because he failed to carry out the doctor's orders'; 'The White doctor said it was a case of high blood-pressure'; 'He died from a T.B. infection which was made worse because he was a heavy drinker'; 'The people agreed with the (White) doctor's diagnosis of blood-pressure because she was very fat.' The large number of stabbing cases are shrugged off as an urban phenomenon, part

Table 6
Cases Explained by Non-Mystical Cases: Urban

Category	n	%	nWD	nD
Old age	9	19·0	4	..
Sickness	9	19·0	6	1
Drink	14	29·9	10	..
Stabbing	11	21·2	2	..
Car accident	1	2·2	..	..
Over-exertion	1	2·2	..	..
Dagga (Indian hemp)	1	2·2	..	..
Premature birth	1	2·2	..	..
Act of God	1	2·2	..	..
Total	48	100·0	22	1

WD = White doctor consulted; D = Diviner consulted.

and parcel of town life. It is significant that over half of the cases deal with such occurrences as excessive drinking and stabbings. While not unknown in the rural area, they can be looked on as 'new' misfortunes which possibly require a 'new' explanation. Drunkenness is, of course, not unknown in the reserves but in the towns the consumption of hard liquor and fortified concoctions is creating a social problem. Only two of the stabbings in the sample were due to a faction fight (the traditional expression of inter-neighbourhood conflict in the country): six of the ten stabbings resulted from drunken quarrels in shebeens.

The case classified as an 'Act of God' should properly not appear in the category of non-mystical causation. The victim was a well-known poultry thief. He had stolen a fowl and was lying by the fire waiting for water to boil, when some children upset the water over his face. The neighbours interpreted his death as a judgement of God, who had 'answered him for them' – an interpretation in terms of Christian theology.

Of all the victims recorded here, all except eight classified themselves or were classified as School, with varying degrees of education ranging from Standard I to Native Primary Higher (a teaching qualification). This contrasts with the position in Khalana where all but one of the misfortunes classified as caused by non-mystical means involved Reds: it seems that the Red/School dichotomy is not significant in affecting the incidence of non-mystical explanations. It is striking, though perhaps not unexpected, that both in town and country the classification of misfortune as due to non-mystical causes is correlated with the non-consultation of a diviner.

There is no doubt that the move from the country to the town involves a significant shift in the proportion of explanation in traditional terms towards secular, scientific categories. The reason for this is probably due to a higher proportion of School people in town and to education. The fact that in 47 per cent of urban cases a White doctor was consulted as opposed to 15 per cent of rural cases also points to an increased scientific approach.[11] On the other hand, there is some evidence that the type of misfortune so explained tends to be precisely that produced by specific urban conditions, especially alcoholism and the violence which so frequently accompanies it. One can argue that it is urban-generated misfortunes that tend to be explained in non-mystical terms rather than a progressive substitution of scientific for mystical theories of causation 'all along the line'.

Conclusions

The aims of this paper are limited, in the main, to providing quantitative data to test the frequently-made statement that witchcraft accusations increase in the town environment (due to increased insecurity, individualism, and competition) and to assess the importance of the ancestor belief system as an explanatory hypothesis in cases of misfortune. It is obvious that the type of data and the intensity of field-work on which this survey is based are not of such a nature as to answer many 'depth' questions of interest to anthropologists. No insights are given as to the process by which individuals change their categories of explanation on moving to town, nor are there data on possibly important variables, e.g. length of residence in town, adjustment to urban conditions, nature of employment, church membership, and education. What information I have on the latter score would seem to indicate that education is an important variable. In sixty of the ninety-nine urban cases the educational standard of both victim and accused was recorded. Taking only the victim (it is presumably *his* family that is most vitally interested in 'explanation') it was found that (although a third of the victims to whose misfortune a non-mystical cause was ascribed had no education) approximately 60 per cent of those with Standard V or less explained in terms of witchcraft or ancestors, whereas only 23 per cent of those with Standard VI or higher qualifications did so. Apart from this, not enough is known of the

11. In by no means every case was the diagnosis of the White doctors taken as final and frequently one or more diviners were consulted in addition. This refers particularly to cases eventually classified as 'witchcraft' or 'sorcery' and therefore not appearing on Tables 3–6.

social universe within which these 'explanatory decisions' take place. It is obvious, for instance, that the stress on kinsmen in rural areas is due to the fact that these are the people with whom rural tribesmen would be most likely to interact.

The data do show, however, that for this Eastern Cape area at least, urbanization has not meant an increase in explanations based on mystical causation. One of the main reasons for this difference in research findings is probably the non-migrant nature of the Grahamstown population and the long-established (157 years) nature of its African townships. There is a hospital and a number of clinics in the area and in 47 per cent of cases recourse was had to a White doctor. It is clear that people in both rural and urban areas operate with a threefold category system with which to explain misfortune: it is the proportions in which they select from one of these which differs significantly between the two areas.

An important aspect, which is also demonstrated by Mitchell, is what may be called serial situational explanation. Explanation of misfortune among the Xhosa of the Eastern Cape (as all explanation) is a relative matter. The satisfactoriness of an explanation is relative to the effective and cognitive interests of the person (or persons) for whom the explanation is important. Just as the explanation: 'The car does not go because there is something wrong with the engine' might satisfy a woman driver, but not a mechanic, explanation in terms of non-mystical causation may be satisfactory for one person, in a particular situation, but not for another. Cases of this appear in the sample – the child who had a liver attack from drinking too much tea, but whose mother suspected witchcraft; the man with so bad a case of fever that his family began to wonder 'if there was perhaps nothing more', and so on. A succession of misfortunes, or increasing deterioration in the victim's condition, may give rise to a *redefinition* of the cause.

Mitchell has suggested that explanation is only acceptable if people can thereby do something about the matter. This does not appear to be so important – in Grahamstown, at least. Explanation need not always lead to action. In an anomic society (and the Rhodes University's Institute of Social and Economic Research investigation referred to above has shown that to a large extent there is a marked lack of community spirit and intense rivalry in Grahamstown, especially among the élite – often expressed in the segmentation of voluntary associations such as football clubs) one can merely accept the explanation fatalistically. This is particularly true in cases of death from alcoholism and urban violence. The secularization of urban life finds its counterpart in the secularization of world-view.

References

ALBERTI, L. (1810), *De Kaffers Aan de Zuidkust van Afrika*, trans. by W. Fehr as *Alberti's Account of the Xhosa in 1807* (1968), Cape Town. Reference is made to this edition.

EVANS-PRITCHARD, E. E. (1937), *Witchcraft, Oracles and Magic among the Azande*, Clarendon Press.

HAMMOND-TOOKE, W. D. (1962), *Bhaca Society*, Oxford U.P.

HAMMOND-TOOKE, W. D. (1965), 'Segmentation and fission in Cape Nguni political units', *Africa*, vol. 35, part 2, pp. 143–66.

HAMMOND-TOOKE, W. D. (1968a), 'The morphology of Mpondomise descent groups', *Africa*, vol. 38, part 1, pp. 26–45.

HAMMOND-TOOKE, W. D. (1968b), 'Descent group scatter in a Mpondomise ward', *African Studies*, vol 27, part 2, pp. 83–94.

HUNTER, M. (1936), *Reaction to Conquest*, Oxford U.P.

KLUCKHOHN, C. (1944), *Navaho Witchcraft*, Beacon Press.

MARWICK, M. (1952), 'The social context of Cewa witch-beliefs', *Africa*, vol. 22, pp. 120–34, 215–33.

MARWICK, M. (1958), 'The continuance of witch beliefs', in P. Smith (ed.), *Africa in Transition*, Reinhardt.

MARWICK, M. (1967), 'The study of witchcraft', in A. L. Epstein (ed.), *The Craft of Social Anthropology*, pp. 231–44, Tavistock.

MAYER, P. (1954), *Witches*, Rhodes University.

MAYER, P. (1961), *Townsmen or Tribesmen*, Oxford U.P.

MITCHELL, J. C. (1965), 'The meaning in misfortune for urban Africans', in M. Fortes and G. Dieterlen (eds), *African Systems of Thought*, pp. 192–202, Oxford U.P. for International African Institute.

REDFIELD, R. (1941), *The Folk-cultures of Yucatan*, University of Chicago Press.

SOGA, J. H. (1931), *The Ama-Xhosa: Life and Customs*, Lovedale.

WILSON, M. *et al.* (1952), *Social Structure*, vol. 3, Keiskammahoek Rural Survey, Shuter and Shooter.

Part Five
Witch-Beliefs Throw Light on Other Problems

Anthropologists have long been preoccupied with the problem why beliefs in magic, witchcraft and sorcery, though palpably false, nevertheless continue to have influence. One of the most systematic resolutions of this problem is to be found in Evans-Pritchard's description of the protective devices, or secondary elaborations, by means of which oracle-based predictions that fail can be explained away; and those that succeed, emphatically recalled (Evans-Pritchard, 1937, p. 330). The steps non-literate peoples take to protect their beliefs from falsification give rise to closed, circular systems of thought which, though starting from different premises, are no less logical than ours. Such systems are of considerable relevance to the discussion of scientific methodology (see the Readings from Gluckman (p. 443), Polanyi (p. 452) and Marwick (p. 460)). Marwick's paper is an attempt to show how this relevance has been sharpened by the debate springing from the publication of Kuhn's *The Structure of Scientific Revolutions* (1962). On a more empirical plane, Cárdozo's paper (p. 469) on McCarthyism shows the gains that accrue from applying to the analysis of a modern political movement the generalizations emerging from the study of witch-crazes. In more recent papers not included here, Bergesen has made similar use of the witch-hunt model in analysing the Chinese Cultural Revolution (1978) and in making an international comparison of the implications of the dictum that 'ultimate national purposes require not only their worshippers, but also their enemies' (1977, p. 220). In another direction, the European witch-scare has provided material for the analysis of historical expressions of sexism (Anderson and Gordon, 1978).

References

ANDERSON, A., and GORDON, R. (1978), 'Witchcraft and the status of women – the case of England', *British Journal of Sociology*, vol. 19.

BERGESEN, A. J. (1977), 'Political witch hunts: the sacred and the subversive in cross-national perspective', *American Sociological Review*, vol. 42.

441

Witch-Beliefs Throw Light on Other Problems

BERGESEN, A. J. (1978), 'A Durkheimian theory of "witch-hunts" with the Chinese Cultural Revolution of 1966–9 as an example', *Journal for the Scientific Study of Religion*, vol. 17.

EVANS-PRITCHARD, E. E. (1937), *Witchcraft, Oracles and Magic among the Azande*, Clarendon Press.

KUHN, T. S. (1962), *The Structure of Scientific Revolutions*, University of Chicago Press.

The Logic of African Science and Witchcraft

Excerpts from Max Gluckman, 'The logic of African science and witchcraft: an appreciation of Evans-Pritchard's *Witchcraft, Oracles and Magic among the Azande* of the Sudan', *Human Problems in British Central Africa*, vol. 1, 1944, pp. 61–71.

I have selected this book for the first appreciation in our journal, because it is one of the most notable contributions to the scientific understanding of African problems. Though the researches on which it is based were made in the Sudan, the general argument applies to all African tribes who believe in witchcraft, oracles or divination, and magic. The author describes clearly the functioning of witchcraft and magic in a book that is fascinating to the specialist, and is also written so simply and vividly that every layman who begins it will not be able to leave it till he has followed the argument to its close. For an understanding of the behaviour of Africans, and, as will be seen, of ourselves where we do not act on scientifically valid grounds, it is a work which everyone should read. Since the book explains to us not only customs of the Sudan Azande, but also the basis of such wide fields of human behaviour, I shall here set out the general lessons which it teaches, and then touch on the differences between the Azande and our own peoples. However, as Evans-Pritchard does not consider in detail aspects of Zande behaviour other than what he calls the mystical, I begin by referring to these.

The title of this review poses the question: is there a fundamental difference between African and European logic, and if so, is it due to physical differences, or to psychological ones related to the different social conditions in which Africans and Europeans live? Without entering into the arguments for and against, I may say that the consensus of scientific opinion is that there is no proof of any great difference between the brains of various races. If there are any differences, they are altogether insufficient to account for the great differences between cultures and modes of thought, and above all, they cannot account for the rapid spurts in cultural development which some countries achieved in a very short time. That is, if we have to explain London and an African village, we cannot do so by bodily differences between Londoners and Africans: we must investigate their history and struggles, especially their contacts with other peoples, and other social factors. For if an African were brought up from birth by a Londoner, he would be a Londoner. We know that shipwrecked European children were distinguishable from their African foster-people only by their colour.

Therefore, if the mind of the African differs from the European's it is because he has grown up in a different society, where from birth his behaviour and ideas are moulded by those of his parents and fellows. If he inherits a 'mind', he inherits it socially, and not physically. [...]

In technological and administrative matters [...] [the African] reasons much as we do, though within much narrower ranges of facts, and of course without testing his theories by scientific experiment. This ability to reason clearly also appears where he works with beliefs and ideas that are different from ours, notably those about witchcraft and magic, a system of ideas which our civilization abandoned some 150 years ago. Many Europeans, particularly peasants, still hold them. That these beliefs subsisted till so recently in educated Europe and America shows that they are not innate in Africans, but are part of their culture, as they were of ours. Anyone who follows Evans-Pritchard's exposition of the intellectual aspect of Zande magic and witchcraft will be fascinated by their logical skills. [...]

The fundamental point is that the African is born into a society which believes in witchcraft and therefore the very texture of his thinking, from childhood on, is woven of magical and mystical ideas. More important still, since magic and witchcraft are lived, far more than they are reasoned about, his daily actions are conditioned by these beliefs, till at every turn he is confronted by the threat of witchcraft and meets it with divination and magic. The weight of tradition, the actions and behaviour of his elders, the support which chiefs give to the system, all impress on the African the truth of the system, and since he cannot measure it against any other system, he is continually caught in the web of its making. Evans-Pritchard stresses too, that the African does not go about his business in constant terror of witchcraft nor does he approach it with an awesome fear of the supernatural; when he finds it is working against him he is angry against the witch for playing a dirty trick on him.

These points emerge from a brief analysis of the essential characteristics of the system of witchcraft-divination-magic beliefs and behaviour. The Azande, like many other Central African tribes, believe witchcraft to be a physical condition of the intestines (as found in a corpse, it is probably a passing state of digestion), which enables the soul of the witch to go out at night and harm his fellows. There is also sorcery (which is more commonly believed in in South Africa) which is the use of magical substances for anti-social purposes. A man may have witchcraft in his body, and yet not use it: his witchcraft may be 'cool'. Africans are not interested in witchcraft as such, but in the particular witch who is bewitching them at a certain moment. They do not get the idea that they are being bewitched and are therefore going to suffer some misfortune, such as to fall ill and die. What happens is that they suffer misfortune and after it has occurred blame it on a witch: and if it is not a misfortune past and done with, they find out who the witch is and get him to withdraw his evil influence or tackle it with magic. Therefore Evans-Pritchard says he knows of no Zande who would die in terror of witchcraft, and this is confirmed by other trained observers.

The problem which the African answers with his belief in witchcraft is this: why misfortune to me? He knows that there are diseases which make people ill; he knows that hippos upset dugouts and drown people. But he asks himself: 'why should I be ill and not other people?' The man whose son has drowned when a hippo upset his dugout, in effect says, 'My son frequently travelled by dugout on the river where there are always hippo, why on this one occasion should the hippo have attacked and drowned him?' This he answers: 'because we were bewitched'. He knows full well that his son was crossing the river to visit his mother's family, and that the hippo, irritable because it had a calf, was migrating upstream when it met the dugout. We say that it was providence or ill-luck which brought the hippo and the son together so that the son died, as we do when a man crossing the road from one shop to another is run over by a car; when the African says it is witchcraft that caused these deaths, he is explaining a coincidence which science leaves unexplained, except as the intersection of two series of events. The African is fully aware that his son drowned because his lungs filled with water: but he argues that it was a witch, or a sorcerer by his medicines, who brought together the paths of dugout and an angry mother hippo to kill the son. The Azande explain it by a hunting simile. The first man who hits a buck shares the meat with the man who puts the second spear in it. 'Hence if a man is killed by an elephant Azande say that the elephant is the first spear (existing in its own right) and witchcraft is the second spear and that together they killed the man. If a man spears another in war the slayer is the first spear and witchcraft is the second spear and together they killed him.' [...]

Immediately they suffer misfortune Africans think that a witch has been working against them. Every kind of accident or of ill may be ascribed to witchcraft. But this does not mean that the African does not recognize lack of skill and moral lapses. For an unskilled potter to say that his pots broke in firing because he was bewitched, would not convince his fellows if he had left pebbles in the clay; but the skilled potter who had followed all the rules of his craft would be supported in saying this. It would not be a sound defence for a criminal to plead that he did wrong because he was bewitched to do so, for it is not believed that witchcraft makes a man lie, steal, betray his chief, or commit adultery.

This is how witchcraft works as a theory of causes. The African goes further. Witchcraft does not harm people haphazardly, for the witch wants to hurt people he hates, has quarrelled with, of whom he is envious. So that when a man falls ill, or his crops fail (for on good soil crops should not fail), he says that someone who envied him his many children, the favour of his chief, or his good employment by Europeans and his fine clothes, therefore hated him and has used medicines or evil power to do him ill. Witchcraft is thus a moral theory for witches are bad people, hating, grudging, envious, spiteful. A witch does not just attack his fellows, he attacks those whom he has reason to hate. There is a clear distinction between the man who has witchcraft in him but is a good man and does not use it against his fellows, and the man who wants to do others harm but has not the power of witchcraft or cannot get the evil medicines of sorcery, and the witch himself, the man who has the power to bewitch and uses that power. Since people are only interested in whether their fellows are witches when they suffer misfortunes, they seek among their enemies for those who may have this power. They think of someone with whom they have quarrelled, and suspect him of the evil deed. We find thus that witchcraft as a theory of causes of misfortunes is related to personal relations between the sufferer and his fellows, and to a theory of moral judgments as to what is good and bad.

When a man suffers a misfortune which he cannot remedy, such as the breaking of his pots in firing, he may just accept it, as witchcraft, just as we would say, 'Bad luck'. But when witchcraft is making him ill and may cause him to die, when it is blighting his crop, or when by divination he finds that it is threatening him in the future, he does not sit down hopelessly under it. He has to scotch its evil working. This he does by using medicines against it, which will stop the witchcraft and possibly kill the witch, or by calling in a diviner to find out who is the witch so that he can be put out of business, or persuaded to remove his witchcraft. The diviner does not seek for the witch haphazardly. Most methods of divination allow one of two possible answers, yes or no, to a stated question. For example, the Azande give a 'poison' (of course they do not know it is a poison) with strychnine properties to fowls which die or do not die to say 'yes' or 'no' to a question of the form: is A the witch who is harming me? Thus a man, seeking for the witch among the people he thinks wish him ill, must eventually get the answer 'yes' to one of them. This particular oracle is out of human control; others, including witchdoctors, are less trusted by the Azande as being subject to human manipulation. But even the Zande witchdoctor, though he works on his knowledge of local gossip, does not often deliberately cheat. He may seek, or be asked by his client to seek, for the witch among say four names: these are the names of enemies of the client, and though the witchdoctor may choose from these, or others whom he knows wish his client ill, by unconscious selection, there is a moment when by bodily sensation he knows that the medicines, which give him his divining power, say: it is A who is the witch, and not B. Or the diviner will indicate someone generally without specifying a name – e.g. 'one of your wives', 'an old woman' – and the client will fix on some definite person, among his neighbours, who is thus described and who therefore he thinks has reason to wish him ill. Charges of witchcraft thus reflect personal relations and quarrels. Often a man accuses not someone who hates him, or who is envious of him, but someone whom he hates or envies. The African knows this, and may stress it when he is not involved in the case or when he is the accused, but he forgets it when he is making the accusation. In Zululand a man accused his brother of having bewitched him because he was jealous of him. An old diviner, aware of psychological projection, told me: 'Of course, it is obvious that it is the complainant who hates his brother, though he thinks it is his brother who hates him'. But that diviner believed firmly in his own power to detect witchcraft.

Evans-Pritchard stresses that the Azande cannot thus set out the intellectual basis of their theory; this is what he has worked out from an observation of hundreds of situations involving charges of witchcraft, discussions about it, and so on. [. . .]

Since personal relations and spites determine who shall be accused of bewitching a man, we find that in different societies different types of people accuse each other of witchcraft. As witchcraft is hereditary, Zande princes who are all related, do not accuse each other of witchcraft, nor do other kinsmen, though an accuser of his brother could escape the imputed taint on himself by saying that his brother is a bastard. In all African societies courtiers suspect each other, and the jealousy of polygynous households breaks out thus. While the Azande do not accuse kinsmen, the Lozi almost always do, for reasons I have given in my *Economy of the Central Barotse Plain*. Among the south-eastern Bantu, for determinable reasons, it is the daughter-in-law who is often accused. If a sociologist can find where charges of witchcraft in a particular society fall, he can almost reconstruct the social relationships of the society.

The theory of witchcraft is thus seen to be reasonable and logical, even if it is not true. Since it explains the intersection of two chains of events by the enmity of people with evil power, it works in fields our modern science leaves unexplained. Thus the African cannot see that the system is untrue and moreover he has to reason with the system as we do with our scientific beliefs. Wherever the system might conflict with reality its beliefs are vague, and deal with transcendent non-observable facts: the witch works at night with his soul, the soul of the poison oracle (which is not personified, but has consciousness) finds out the witchcraft. The theory is a complete whole, in which every part buttresses every other part. Illness proves that a witch is at work, he is discovered by divination, he is persuaded to withdraw his witchcraft. Even though he may feel himself that he is not the real witch, he will at least show that he intends no harm to the sick man. Or he is attacked with magic. It is difficult for the African to find a flaw in the system. Scepticism exists, and is not socially repressed, and Evans-Pritchard writes that the

absence of formal and coercive doctrine permits Azande to state that many, even most, witch-doctors, are frauds. No opposition being offered to such statements, they leave the main belief in the prophetic and therapeutic powers of witch-doctors unimpaired. Indeed, scepticism is included in the pattern of belief in witch-doctors. Faith and scepticism are alike traditional. Scepticism explains failures of witch-doctors, and being directed towards particular witch-doctors even tends to support faith in others.

Even the witch-doctor who works by sleight of hand believes that there are doctors who have the magic to make this unnecessary.

In this web of belief every strand depends upon every other strand, and a Zande cannot get out of its meshes because this is the only world he knows. The web is not an external structure in which he is enclosed. It is the texture of his thought and he cannot think that his thought is wrong. Nevertheless, his beliefs are not absolutely set but are variable and fluctuating to allow for different situations and to permit empirical observation and even doubts.

Within this web, the African may reason as logically as we do within the web of scientific thought. If your house, which you have protected with lightning-conductors, is nevertheless struck by lightning you say that the workman was bad, the wires poor, or there was a break in the wiring. If the African has had his village protected with medicines against storms and it is struck by lightning, he says the magician was bad, his medicines poor, or a taboo was broken. [...]

Evans-Pritchard's analysis of witchcraft illuminates the working of human thought in other spheres. For instance, he makes this comparison. The Azande as we have seen exclude witchcraft as a cause of moral lapses.

448

As in our own society a scientific theory of causation, if not excluded, is deemed irrelevant in questions of moral and legal responsibility, so in Zande society the doctrine of witchcraft, if not excluded, is deemed irrelevant in the same situations. We accept scientific explanations of the causes of diseases, and even of the causes of insanity, but we deny them in crime and sin because here they militate against law and morals which are axiomatic. The Zande accepts a mystical explanation of the causes of misfortune, sickness, and death, but he does not allow this explanation if it conflicts with social exigencies expressed in law and morals.

I make one final point here, in answer to the oft-made statement that witchcraft charges are based on cheating. Evans-Pritchard emphasizes that the patient, who wishes to abolish the witchcraft harming him, above all people does not wish to cheat: for what good is it to him if he detects the wrong person as witch? But he does accuse his personal enemies.

When the African, with these beliefs, comes to deal with Europeans, there are many ways in which they affect his behaviour so that it seems incomprehensible to us. For example, he queries: it is true that the White doctors are very good in treating disease, but while they cure the disease they don't treat the witchcraft which caused the disease, and that will continue to do harm. Evans-Pritchard shows that the Zande's oracles are 'his guide and councillor', whom he consults about every enterprise. Evans-Pritchard himself lived thus, and found it as good a way as any other of ordering his affairs. But because of it, Europeans often cannot understand Zande behaviour: why a Zande will suddenly move from his home to shelter in the bush (because of witchcraft), why a homestead will suddenly be moved (because of witchcraft attacking them in that spot), and so on. Frequently his guests suddenly departed without bidding him farewell, and he was angry till he realized that the oracles had told them that witchcraft was threatening them.

I found that when a Zande acted towards me in a manner that we would call rude and untrustworthy his actions were often to be accounted for by obedience to his oracles. Usually I have found Azande courteous and reliable according to English standards, but sometimes their behaviour is unintelligible till their mystical notions are taken into account. Often Azande are tortuous in their dealings with one another, but they do not consider a man blameworthy for being secretive or acting contrary to his declared intentions. On the contrary they praise his prudence for taking account of witchcraft at every step. . . . With the European it is different. We only know that a Zande has said he will do something and has done nothing, or has done something different, and we naturally blame the man for lying and being untrustworthy, for the European does not appreciate that Azande have to take into account mystical forces of which he knows nothing.

Evans-Pritchard gave a feast to which a prince promised to come; he sent to tell that he would not come. Suddenly he arrived. He arranged to stay the night; in the night he disappeared. He had been told that witch-craft threatened him, and it was a great compliment to the sociologist that he attended the feast; his wayward actions were to deceive the witches. I myself had a favoured informant in my employ who kept replying to my summonses, that he would come; but stayed away until I moved my home. He had been threatened with witchcraft at the one spot, not the other. For notions of place and time in witchcraft thought vary from ours; witchcraft may threaten a man now from the future, so the future is in the present, and has to be avoided by not adopting a line of action which was contemplated, as going on a journey; or a man will decide to build his homestead on a certain spot, by eliminating other spots where witchcraft will threaten him, though he has not yet built on them.

There is a second way in which witchcraft behaviour may affect Africans when we deal with them. Under these beliefs, people who pro-duced good crops while their neighbours' harvests were meagre; who had large healthy families while all around was illness; whose herds and fishing prospered exceedingly; these fortunate people were sometimes believed to make good by magic and witchcraft at the expense of their fellows. We have seen in a quotation above that they believed themselves open to attack from witches. The Zande

knows that if he becomes rich the poor will hate him, that if he rises in social position his inferiors will be jealous of his authority, that if he is handsome the less favoured will envy his looks, that if he is talented as a hunter, a singer, a fighter, or a rhetorician, he will earn the malice of those less gifted, and that if he enjoys the regard of his prince and of his neighbours he will be detested for his prestige and popularity.

These are the motives that lead to witchcraft. Such beliefs were only possible in a society with nowhere to sell surplus goods, no profit motives, without storable goods, with no luxuries so that there was no heavy pressure on any member to produce more than he required for his own needs. Africans have come from a society with these beliefs into our economic system where they are expected to work long and hard, trying to outdo their fellows, and perhaps the beliefs deter them in this struggle and affect their efficiency. I know Africans who blame their misfortunes on witches envious of their higher wages, or their fine would-be European-style houses. It is possible that fear of witchcraft prevents Africans developing what skill and capacity they have, in their work for Europeans, though this fear would be unimportant in comparison with other factors preventing their development, such as disease and social barriers.

I have given part of the argument of Evans-Pritchard's book to set out the main framework of magic-witchcraft thought. I hope I have shown how skilfully the argument is set out. In my short review I am unable to do more than indicate its unlimited riches of delight, which make reading and re-reading it an unfailing fascination. Everyone who is interested in human problems in this region should own the book. But I must warn the layman that in applying its conclusions to our own tribes, he must do so with care. The central argument applies absolutely, but there are certain important differences. Among the Azande, witchcraft was not a crime but a delict, for which compensation was paid only on a death. In many Southern African tribes witchcraft is a crime, and the state punished witches by killing them. Also in Southern Africa sorcery (the deliberate use of evil magic) was believed to be at work, rather than witchcraft (causing ill by inherent evil power plus malice). This produces important changes in the whole system, which can be traced, e.g. in Hunter's *Reaction to Conquest* on the Mpondo.

In quoting Evans-Pritchard to show how beliefs in witchcraft affect Africans' behaviour and thought, I have emphasized that often their minds work in the same logical patterns as ours do, though the material with which they think is different, so that it is clear that if they were given the same education and cultural background as we have, they would think with the same materials and in the same way as we do.

40. Michael Polanyi

The Stability of Scientific Theories against Experience

Excerpts from Michael Polanyi, *Personal Knowledge*, University of Chicago Press, 1958, pp. 286–94.

Implicit Beliefs

The limitations of doubting as a principle can be elaborated [...] by extending our inquiry to the beliefs held in the form of our conceptual framework, as expressed in our language. Our most deeply ingrained convictions are determined by the idiom in which we interpret our experience and in terms of which we erect our articulate systems (Polyani, 1958, p. 80). Our formally declared beliefs can be held to be true in the last resort only because of our logically anterior acceptance of a particular set of terms, from which all our references to reality are constructed.

The fact that primitive people hold distinctive systems of beliefs inherent in their conceptual framework and reflected in their language was first stated with emphasis by Lévy-Brühl earlier in this century. The more recent work of Evans-Pritchard on the beliefs of Azande has borne out and has given further precision to this view (Evans-Pritchard, 1937). The author is struck by the intellectual force shown by the primitive African in upholding his beliefs against evidence which to the European seems flagrantly to refute them. An instance in point is the Zande belief in the powers of the poison-oracle. The oracle answers questions through the effects on a fowl of a poisonous substance called *benge*. The oracle-poison is extracted from a creeper gathered in a traditional manner, which is supposed to become effective only after it has been addressed in the words of an appropriate ritual. Azande – we are told – have no formal and coercive doctrine to enforce belief in witch-doctors and their practice of the poison-oracle, but their belief in these is the more firmly held for being embedded in an idiom which interprets all relevant facts in terms of witchcraft and oracular powers. Evans-Pritchard gives various examples of this peculiar tenacity of their implicit belief.

Suppose that the oracle in answer to a particular question says 'Yes', and immediately afterwards says 'No' to the same question. In our eyes this would tend to discredit the oracle altogether, but Zande culture provides a number of ready explanations for such self-contradictions.

Evans-Pritchard lists no less than eight secondary elaborations of their beliefs by which Azande will account for the oracle's failure. They may assume that the wrong variety of poison had been gathered, or a breach of taboo committed, or that the owners of the forest where the poisonous creeper grows had been angered and avenged themselves by spoiling the poison; and so on.

Our author describes further the manner in which Azande resist any suggestion that *benge* may be a natural poison. He often asked Azande, he tells us, what would happen if they were to administer oracle-poison to a fowl without delivering an address, or if they were to administer an extra portion of poison to a fowl which has recovered from the usual doses.

The Zande [he continues] does not know what would happen and is not interested in what would happen; no one has been fool enough to waste good oracle-poison in making such pointless experiments which only a European could imagine. ... Were a European to make a test which in his view proved Zande opinion wrong they would stand amazed at the credulity of the European. If the fowl died they would simply say that it was not good *benge*. The very fact of the fowl dying proves to them its badness (Evans-Pritchard, 1937, pp. 314–15).

This blindness of Azande to the facts which to us seem decisive is sustained by remarkable ingenuity. 'They reason excellently in the idiom of their beliefs, but they cannot reason outside, or against, their beliefs because they have no other idiom in which to express their thoughts' (Evans-Pritchard, 1937, p. 338).

Our objectivism, which tolerates no open declaration of faith, has forced modern beliefs to take on implicit forms, like those of Azande. And no one will deny that those who have mastered the idioms in which these beliefs are entailed do also reason most ingeniously within these idioms, even while – again like Azande – they unhesitatingly ignore all that the idiom does not cover. I shall quote two passages to illustrate the high stability of two modern interpretative frameworks, based on these principles:

My party education had equipped my mind with such elaborate shock-absorbing buffers and elastic defences that everything seen and heard became automatically transformed to fit a preconceived pattern (Koestler, 1950, p. 68).

The system of theories which Freud has generally developed is so consistent that when one is once entrenched in them it is difficult to make observations unbiased by his way of thinking (Horney, 1939, p. 7).

The first of these statements is by a former Marxist, the second by a former Freudian writer. At the time when they still accepted as valid the conceptual work of Marx or of Freud – as the case may be – these writers would have regarded the all-embracing interpretative powers of this framework as evidence of its truth; only when losing faith in it did they feel that its powers were excessive and specious. We shall see the same difference reappear in our appraisals of the interpretative power of different conceptual systems, as part of our acceptance or rejection of these systems.

Three Aspects of Stability

The resistance of an idiom of belief against the impact of adverse evidence may be regarded under three headings, each of which is illustrated by the manner in which Azande retain their beliefs in the face of situations which in our view should invalidate them. Analogous cases can be adduced from other systems of beliefs.

The stability of Zande beliefs is due, in the first place, to the fact that objections to them can be met one by one. This power of a system of implicit beliefs to defeat valid objections one by one is due to the circularity of such systems. By this I mean that the convincing power possessed by the interpretation of any particular new topic in terms of such a conceptual framework is based on past applications of the same framework to a great number of other topics not now under consideration, while if any of these other topics were questioned now, their interpretation in its turn would similarly rely for support on the interpretation of all the others. Evans-Pritchard observes this for Zande beliefs in mystical notions. 'The contradiction between experience and one mystical notion is explained by reference to other mystical notions' (Evans-Pritchard, 1937, p. 339).

So long as each doubt is defeated in its turn, its effect is to strengthen the fundamental convictions against which it was raised. 'Let the reader consider (writes Evans-Pritchard) any argument that would utterly demolish all Zande claims for the power of the oracle. If it were translated into Zande modes of thought it would serve to support their entire structure of belief' (Evans-Pritchard, 1937, p. 319). Thus the circularity of a conceptual system tends to reinforce itself by every contact with a fresh topic.

The circularity of the theory of the universe embodied in any particular language is manifested in an elementary fashion by the existence of a dictionary of the language. If you doubt, for example, that a particular English noun, verb, adjective or adverb has any meaning in English, an English dictionary dispels this doubt by a definition using other nouns, verbs, adjectives and adverbs, the meaningfulness of which is not doubted for the moment. Inquiries of this kind will increasingly confirm us in the use of a language.

Remember also what we have found about the axiomatization of mathematics; namely that it merely declares the beliefs implied in the practice of mathematical reasoning. The axiomatized system is therefore circular: our anterior acceptance of mathematics lends authority to its axioms, from which we then deduce in turn all mathematical demonstrations. The division of mathematical formulae, or of the asserted sentences of any deductive system, into axioms and theorems is indeed largely conventional, for we can usually replace some or all of the axioms by theorems and derive from these the previous axioms as theorems. Every assertion of a deductive system can be demonstrated by, or else shown to be implied as axioms of, the others. Therefore, if we doubt each assertion in its turn each is found confirmed by circularity, and the refutation of each consecutive doubt results in strengthening our belief in the system as a whole. [...]

A second aspect of stability arises from an automatic expansion of the circle in which an interpretative system operates. It readily supplies elaborations of the system which will cover almost any conceivable eventuality, however embarrassing this may appear at first sight. Scientific theories which possess this self-expanding capacity are sometimes described as epicyclical, in allusion to the epicycles that were used in the Ptolemaic and Copernican theory to represent planetary motions in terms of uniform circular motions. All major interpretative frameworks have an epicyclical structure which supplies a reserve of subsidiary explanations for difficult situations. The epicyclical character of Zande beliefs was shown above by the ready availability of eight different subsidiary assumptions for explaining a point-blank self-contradiction in two consecutive answers of an oracle.

The stability of Zande beliefs is manifested, thirdly, in the way it denies to any rival conception the ground in which it might take root. Experiences which support it could be adduced only one by one. But a new conception, e.g. that of natural causation, which would take the place of Zande superstition could be established only by a whole series of relevant instances, and such evidence cannot accumulate in the minds of people if each of them is disregarded in its turn for lack of the concept which would lend significance to it. The behaviour of Azande whom Evans-Pritchard tried to convince that *benge* was a natural poison which owed none of its effectiveness to the incantations customarily accompanying its administration, illustrates the kind of contemptuous indifference with which we normally regard things of which we have no conception. 'We feel neither curiosity nor wonder', writes William James, 'concerning things so far beyond us that we have no concepts to refer them to or standards by which to measure them.' The Fuegians in Darwin's voyage, he recalls, wondered at the small boats, but paid no attention to the big ship lying at anchor in front of them (James, 1890, p. 110). A more recent instance of this occurred when Igor Gouzenko, cypher clerk of the Soviet Embassy in Canada, tried in vain for two days in succession (5 and 6 September 1945) to attract attention to the documents concerning Soviet atomic espionage which he was showing round in Ottawa at the risk of his life.

This third defence mechanism of implicit beliefs may be called the principle of suppressed nucleation. It is complementary to the operations of circularity and self-expansion. While these protect an existing system of beliefs against doubts arising from any adverse piece of evidence, suppressed nucleation prevents the germination of any alternative concepts on the basis of any such evidence.

Circularity, combined with a readily available reserve of epicyclical elaborations and the consequent suppression in the germ of any rival conceptual development, lends a degree of stability to a conceptual framework which we may describe as the measure of its completeness. We may acknowledge the completeness or comprehensiveness of a language and the system of conceptions conveyed by it – as we do in respect to Azande beliefs in witchcraft – without in any way implying that the system is correct.

The Stability of Scientific Beliefs

We do not share the beliefs of Azande in the power of poison-oracles, and we reject a great many of their other beliefs, discarding mystical conceptions and replacing them by naturalistic explanations. But we may yet deny that our rejection of Zande superstitions is the outcome of any general principle of doubt.

For the stability of the naturalistic system which we currently accept instead rests on the same logical structure. Any contradiction between a particular scientific notion and the facts of experience will be explained by other scientific notions; there is a ready reserve of possible scientific hypotheses available to explain any conceivable event. Secured by its circularity and defended further by its epicyclical reserves, science may deny, or at least cast aside as of no scientific interest, whole ranges of experience which to the unscientific mind appear both massive and vital.[1]

The restrictions of the scientific outlook which I summed up as objectivism have been recurrent themes throughout this book. My attempt to break out of this highly stabilized framework and to enter avenues of legitimate access to reality from which objectivism debars us will be presently pursued further. At the moment I only wish to give some illustrations to show how, *within science itself*, the stability of theories against experience is maintained by epicyclical reserves which suppress alternative conceptions in the germ; a procedure which in retrospect will appear right in some instances and wrong in others.

The theory of electrolytic dissociation proposed in 1887 by Arrhenius assumed a chemical equilibrium between the dissociated and the undissociated forms of an electrolyte in solution. From the very start, the measurements showed that this was true only for weak electrolytes like acetic acid, but not for the very prominent group of strong electrolytes, like common salt or sulphuric acid. For more than thirty years the discrepancies were carefully measured and tabulated in textbooks, yet no one thought of calling in question the theory which they so flagrantly contradicted. Scientists were satisfied with speaking of the 'anomalies of strong electrolytes', without doubting for a moment that their behaviour was in fact governed by the law that they failed to obey. I can still remember my own amazement when, about 1919, I first heard the idea mooted that the anomalies were to be regarded as a refutation of the equilibrium postulated by Arrhenius and to be explained by a different theory. Not until this alternative conception (based on the mutual electrostatic interaction of the ions) was successfully elaborated in detail, was the previous theory generally abandoned.

Contradictions to current scientific conceptions are often disposed of by calling them 'anomalies'; this is the handiest assumption in the epicyclical reserve of any theory. We have seen how Azande make use of similar excuses to meet the inconsistencies of poison-oracles. In science this process has often proved brilliantly justified, when subsequent revisions of the adverse evidence or a deepening of the original theory explained the anomalies. The modification of Arrhenius's theory for strong electrolytes is a case in point.

Another example may illustrate how a series of observations which at one time were held to be important scientific facts, were a few years later completely discredited and committed to oblivion, without ever having

---

1. I have described similar stabilities before, when showing that two alternative systems of scientific explanation are separated by a logical gap and thus give rise to passionate controversy in science (Polanyi, 1958, pp. 150–59, 112–13).

been disproved or indeed newly tested, simply because the conceptual framework of science had meanwhile so altered that the facts no longer appeared credible. Towards the end of the last century numerous observations were reported by H. B. Baker on the power of intensive drying to stop some normally extremely rapid chemical reactions and to reduce the rate of evaporation of a number of commonly used chemicals (Baker, 1894, p. 611). Baker went on publishing further instances of this drying effect for more than thirty years (Baker, 1922, p. 568; 1928, p. 1051). A large number of allegedly allied phenomena were reported from Holland by Smits (1922)[2] and some very striking demonstrations of it came from Germany (Coehn and Jung, 1923, p. 695; Cohen and Tramm, 1923a, p. 456, 1923b, p. 356 and 1924, p. 110)[3]. H. B. Baker could render his samples unreactive sometimes only by drying them for periods up to three years; so when some authors failed to reproduce his results it was reasonable to assume that they had not achieved the same degree of desiccation. Consequently, there was little doubt at the time that the observed effects of intensive drying were true and that they reflected a fundamental feature of all chemical change.

Today these experiments, which aroused so much interest from 1900 to 1930, are almost forgotten. Textbooks of chemistry which thoughtlessly go on compiling published data still record Baker's observations in detail, merely adding that their validity 'is not yet certainly established' (Philbrick, 1949, p. 215), or that 'some (of his) findings are disputed by later workers, but the technique is difficult' (Partington, 1946, p. 483; Thorpe, 1947).[4] But active scientists no longer take any interest in these phenomena, for in view of their present understanding of chemical processes they are convinced that most of them must have been spurious, and that, if some were real, they were likely to have been due to trivial causes.[5] This being so, our attitude towards these experiments is now similar to that of Azande towards Evans-Pritchard's suggestion of trying out the effects of oracle-poison without an accompanying incantation. We shrug our shoulders and refuse to waste our time on such obviously fruitless enquiries. The process of selecting facts for our attention is indeed the same in science as among Azande; but I believe that science is often right in its

2. Baker's experiments are referred to (p. vii) as 'the most beautiful means of establishing the complexity of unary phases' postulated by the author.

3. These authors reported the stopping of the photochemical combination of hydrogen and chlorine by intense drying.

4. Thorpe reports Baker's 'interesting discovery' without any qualification.

5. Other examples of this procedure in which its results subsequently proved erroneous were given before in section 4 of this chapter to illustrate the equivalence of belief and doubt (Polanyi, 1958).

application of it, while Azande are quite wrong when using it for protecting their superstitions.[6]

I conclude that what earlier philosophers have alluded to by speaking of coherence as the criterion of truth is only a criterion of *stability*. It may equally stabilize an erroneous or a true view of the universe. The attribution of truth to any particular stable alternative is a fiduciary act which cannot be analysed in non-committal terms. [...] There exists no principle of doubt the operation of which will discover for us which of two systems of implicit beliefs is true – except in the sense that we will admit decisive evidence against the one we do not believe to be true, and not against the other. Once more, the admission of doubt proves here to be as clearly an act of belief as does the non-admission of doubt.

References

BAKER, H. B. (1894), *Journal of the Chemical Society of London*, vol. 65.
BAKER, H. B. (1922), *Journal of the Chemical Society of London*, vol. 121.
BAKER, H. B. (1928), *Journal of the Chemical Society of London*, part I.
COEHN, and JUNG, C. (1923), *Ber. deutsch. Chem. Ges.*, vol. 56.
COEHN, and TRAMM (1923a), *Ber. deutsch. Chem. Ges.*, vol. 56.
COEHN, and TRAMM (1923b), *Zeitschr. f. Phys. Chem.*, vol. 105.
COEHN, and TRAMM (1924), *Zeitschr. f. Phys. Chem.*, vol. 110.
EVANS-PRITCHARD, E. E. (1937), *Witchcraft, Oracles and Magic among the Azande*, Clarendon Press.
HORNEY, K. (1939), *New Ways of Psychoanalysis*, Routledge.
JAMES, W. (1890), *Principles of Psychology*, vol. 2, New York.
KOESTLER, A. (ed.) (1950), *The God that Failed*, Hamilton.
PARTINGTON, J. R. (1946), *General and Inorganic Chemistry*, n.p.
PHILBRICK, F. A. (1949), *Textbook of Theoretical and Inorganic Chemistry*, rev. edn, London.
POLANYI, M. (1958), *Personal Knowledge*, University of Chicago Press.
SMITS (1922), *The Theory of Allotropy*.
THORPE, E. (1947), 'Benzene and its homologues', *Dictionary of Applied Chemistry*, n.p.
VAN DER WAERDEN, B. L. (1954), *Science Awakening*, Gröningen.

6. The wise neglect of awkward facts may be of value even for the development of the deductive sciences. Greek mathematicians allowed themselves to be discouraged from developing algebra by the impossibility of representing the ratio of two incommensurable line segments in terms of whole numbers. B. L. Van der Waerden (1954, p. 266) says that 'it does honour to Greek mathematics that it adhered inexorably to such logical consistency'. But had their successors been as exacting in their logical scruples, mathematics would have died of its own rigor.

41. Max Marwick

Witchcraft and the Epistemology of Science

Max Marwick, 'Is science a form of witchcraft?', *New Scientist*, vol. 63, 1974, pp. 578–81 (Presidential Address, Section N, British Association for the Advancement of Science, Stirling Meeting, 1974).

By seeing the world through the eyes of members of societies other than our own, and from the viewpoint of our predecessors in earlier phases of our history, we can gain a clearer, more self-conscious awareness of our own cosmology. Seen in this comparative perspective our world-view is revealed as a socially constructed set of assumptions and axioms that underly our reasoning and place limits on our inquiries.

By exploring world-views, it may be possible to reveal some of the general principles, especially the social influences, according to which, in any society, presuppositions are made and sustained, ideas are formulated and transmitted, and changes of mind and position are initiated and brought about. Among many societies, the course of events is explained mainly in terms of a cardinal belief in witchcraft or sorcery, and this fact sets off their world-views sharply from ours – as sharply, perhaps, as ours is differentiated now from the one that prevailed in our society three and more centuries ago, when not only the masses but also the most intelligent and cultivated men and women of the time had no difficulties in assuming the existence of witches.

The analysis of witch-beliefs in their social setting throws light on two sub-disciplines – the sociology of conflict and tension management, and the sociology of knowledge. The latter application should help us to understand the principles according to which the social reality that confronts the members of any society including our community of scientists is constructed. My immediate task here is to explore some alien societies with world-views radically different from those of our own. And those in which beliefs in witchcraft, sorcery and magic occur provide the sharpest and most useful contrasts. What I hope to demonstrate is that, despite distinctly different kinds of assumptions about how the events of everyday life are to be explained, Africans are nevertheless involved, as we are, in the building of theories from traditional axioms and the testing of instantial hypotheses derived from these theories. It would appear that, according to one of the two opposed schools of thought, scientific tests, during the phase that Thomas Kuhn calls 'normal science', as in Africa do not upset fundamental presuppositions, whereas, according to the other school, they are at all times deliberately and conscientiously aimed at the falsification of conjectures and may at any time have fundamental repercussions on theory.

In many small-scale communities, a combination of normal stresses in the social structure with close personal interrelationships sustains a traditional belief that there are one or both of two types of persons who illegitimately harm their fellow men – witches, who are addicted to the habitual use against others of a mysterious supernatural baleful power, and sorcerers, who, driven by more understandable motives of jealousy and hatred, from time to time resort to destructive magic for attacking the objects of their resentment.

You can perhaps best appreciate the distinctive character that the cardinal belief in witchcraft brings to a society's cosmology if I ask you to share my experiences in a series of cases I recorded among the Ceŵa, a Bantu-speaking matrilineal people of eastern Zambia. I shall start with one that involved me personally and which is therefore not obscured by some of the complexities of the Ceŵa matrilineal kinship system. I call it the case of The Dancing Owls.

When we were among the Ceŵa, our house became infested with owls whose hooting and scrabbling on the ceiling – 'dancing' as a Ceŵa friend called it – kept us awake at night. This gave me an excellent opportunity of tackling a problem as one of my Ceŵa friends would have done; and thus, instead of seeking the advice of the Department of Game and Tsetse Control, I consulted a diviner. In Ceŵa terms, this was a rational thing to do; for in the Ceŵa language the owl's weird cry is heard, not as a meaningless inanity such as 'to wit to woo', nor is it a merry note, but a sinister warning. It comes over loud and clear as '*Muphe! Muphe! Nimkukute!* (Kill him! Kill him! That I may munch him!)' and thus confirms the traditional belief that owls are sorcerers' familiars, the reference to munching being a link with the sorcerers' believed practice of exhuming and eating human corpses.

The diviner, by skilfully involving me in an argument between himself and the speaking gourd he used, discovered that I had two surviving paternal uncles (as I, indeed, had at the time) and he found that one of these had sent the owls to plague me. His advice was that I should ask this uncle (identified as the one who didn't write often) to desist; and the diviner would have rubbed some of his medicines into incisions in my skin if I had been a more conscientious, stoical field-worker who takes participant observation to the ultimate limit. The important point about this incident is that I was subjected to a subtle examination of the state of my social relationships, to disturbances in which the Ceŵa, with an almost neo-Freudian emphasis, attribute most discomforts and misfortunes. Such social relationships play a central role in African systems of causality – and perhaps they should be taken into even greater account in the analysis of the epistemology of modern science.

My next case concerns the death of a Ceŵa village headman, and it illustrates the principle that, in Ceŵa terms, there are no accidents in the sense that we regard them as chance intersections of chains of events. The headman, whom I knew well, was killed in the provincial capital when a car driven by a drunken friend swerved so much that he jumped out and was crushed by it against the bank at the side of the road. This was the coroner's verdict, and his friend was subsequently imprisoned for manslaughter. Back in the headman's village, the official explanation of his death was regarded, not so much as wrong, as incomplete; for it told us *how* he met his death, which seemed beyond dispute, but did not even raise the important question of *why* he and not some other person had been the victim. Thus the villagers attributed the accident and its tragic consequence to sorcery. A minority blamed the headman's sister who, they said, had been angry with him because he stinted her and treated his favourite, their younger sister, more generously. The majority attributed the accident to the infidelity of the headman's second wife (he was a polygynist), saying that she was having affairs with several men, including the driver of the car, who because of this had used sorcery to cause the headman's death. A few supporters of this version said the driver had not used sorcery but had physically pushed the headman out of the car. (Note once more the importance of social relationships in the explanations of why the headman had been killed.)

Our Own Unanswered Questions

This tendency for believers in witchcraft to be unsatisfied by an explanation that goes no further than telling them *how* a certain event occurred and does not tell them also *why* it occurred was noted by Sir Edward Evans-Pritchard as long ago as 1937, when he pointed out that, even when a misfortune is clearly the result of an observable event, such as someone's being trampled by an elephant or his being injured because a granary, weakened by the ravages of termites, has fallen on him, the Azande nevertheless invoke witchcraft to account for the fact that the elephant killed this person and not some other, or to explain why the granary fell at the particular moment that the particular victim was

462

resting in its shade. In this way the Azande, as do the Ceŵa in the case I have just recounted, invoke witchcraft to answer a kind of question which we in our society leave unanswered. We, too, can observe, say, how a motor accident occurred, and we have elaborate machinery for apportioning blame, but we have no universally acceptable explanation of why it affected a certain person rather than someone else.

My next case is again one that provides enough information for us to construct a Western-type explanation of the events that took place – that is, to answer the question 'How?'. The Ceŵa, however, go further in their explanation than we do and answer both questions, 'How?' and 'Why?'.

A young man had a puppy that went mad and bit him. He failed to seek proper treatment, and in time became ill with symptoms similar, as my informant put it, to those of a dog suffering from the disease of the dogs. The young man attributed his illness to the sorcery of his father's matrilineal relatives, not naming any of them at this stage. In the past, these relatives had been critical of his father for favouring him in preference to them (illustrating a common form of role-conflict in a matrilineal society). The young man then went mad, accused two of his father's matrikin of using sorcery against him, burned down their huts and died. After his death his mother consulted a diviner who confirmed her deceased son's allegations; and, as a result, she left her husband. One of the two accused stayed away from the funeral and this was taken as confirmation of her sorcery.

This case raises the question of African theories of disease causation and again involves the subject of divination, to which I shall give more attention in a moment.

The persistence with which Africans retained beliefs in ancestor spirits and witches used to exasperate missionaries and colonial administrators, who were usually committed to imposing a Western system of causality on them. The preference for the native system is, however, not surprising when we consider theories accounting for illness and disease. The African theory, with its ancestor spirits and witches and breaches of taboo, provides more intelligible, dramatic and emotionally satisfying explanations than our rather colourless germ theory which attributes our ailments to organisms so minute that most of us have never seen them and have to accept their existence on the authority of the experts. Nor is it surprising that the African system can assimilate the Western one without itself changing much.

There is a hint of this assimilation in the case involving the disease of the dogs, where some notion of the way in which one can contract rabies seems to be entertained by the informant. Yet an explanation of why the rabies germ attacked a particular victim is called for, and sorcery, a reflection of tense social relationships, provides what for the Ceŵa is a necessary extension of our 'scientific', but in their view, incomplete, explanation.

Back in 1967, Professor Robin Horton made the important point that the validity of either the Western or the African theory of illness is always relative to the conditions in which it is applied. In Africa where, traditionally at least, potent antibiotics and artificial immunization techniques were not available, natural immunity left populations in a delicate state of balance between survival and death. Under these circumstances the ancestor-spirit/witchcraft theory of causation, which basically expresses the quality of the patient's social relations, is not as far-fetched as at first sight appears; for good or bad social relations could well tip the scales one way or the other.

Like Western scientific diagnosticians, Africans (and other peoples elsewhere) sometimes put instantial hypotheses derived from their theories of disease causation to what they recognize as reliable tests – that is, they resort to divination. I have described an instance of Ceŵa divination in the case of The Dancing Owls and you will remember a reference to it in the case of Death from the Disease of the Dogs. From Evans-Pritchard's account, the testing of hypotheses deriving from the general witchcraft theory, and the checking of conjectures made for other purposes, seem to be of very frequent occurrence among the Azande.

The Azande generally attribute accidents and illness to witchcraft. Their suspicions about *whose* witchcraft could have caused the misfortune they reduce to a short list with the aid of the rubbing board oracle (the slide rule, as it were, of Zande divining) and the names on this list they then check by means of the poison oracle (the computer of Zande divining, which is programmed by feeding a poisonous substance called *benge*, probably containing strychnine, to a chicken, after which the data, the short list of subjects, are fed in). In the first run of the oracle, if the chicken dies to a suspect's name, the suspicion is confirmed; if it doesn't, they try another name on another chicken, and go on in this way until the oracle identifies the witch responsible by causing the chicken to die to his name. At that point they do a re-run, employing a sub-routine which double-checks by reversing the instruction to the poison so that this time it will *spare* the chicken to the name of the identified witch. (To get the feel of it all, Evans-Pritchard tried using the poison oracle for coming to everyday decisions affecting his household in the field. He reported, in 1937, that he found it as satisfactory a method of domestic decision-making as any other he might have used.)

The Azande, having identified the witch, may use vengeance magic against him if they believe that what he has done is irreversible – for instance, if the victim is dead. But, if the victim is still alive and ailing, they take further steps. First, they make a public announcement in the village without naming anyone but asking whoever is responsible for the illness to withdraw his witchcraft. If this is to no avail, they send their oracular finding to the chief's deputy, asking him to confirm it by means of the chief's oracle. If it is thus confirmed, the wing of the chicken that died to the name of the alleged witch is spread out like a fan and sent to him with the request that he withdraw his witchcraft. Although the person thus accused may believe that he has had nothing whatever to do with the misfortune, he will generally agree to withdraw his witchcraft – if any, he is careful to add – because his refusal would be a sure sign of the very hostility of which he is being accused, in much the same way as failure to attend a victim's funeral among the Ceŵa would confirm people's suspicions. Unless, therefore, he is very tactless or very careless of his reputation, he ritually removes his witchcraft – 'if any' – by filling his mouth with water and spraying it out on to the chicken's wing.

But what's all this to do with the epistemology of science? Following the lead set by Professor Michael Polanyi in 1958, we can use this Zande material for the beginnings of an answer to this question. The aspect of Zande witch-belief that is relevant to the present discussion is the fact that witchcraft can provide an explanation for a wide range of misfortunes; and such an explanation is likely to be subject, not to sceptical testing, but rather to regular reinforcement by the alleged witch's carrying out of a ritual – such as the spraying of water from his mouth which, to the accuser, and possibly even to the alleged witch himself, confirms the existence of witchcraft.

It is true, so Evans-Pritchard reports, that the Azande are sceptical about both oracles and witch-doctors, but, as their scepticism is always directed towards particular oracles and particular witch-doctors, their faith in oracles and witch-doctors in general remains unscathed. In other words, they meet objections one by one and such objections cannot affect their attitude towards their total theory of causation. It is true, too, that they check and recheck the more important diagnoses of their oracles by putting their questions to a series of tests by the same oracle, but reversing the order of the instruction to the poison, and by submitting their findings for confirmation by the chief's oracle; but if a poison oracle contradicts itself or is contradicted by a superior oracle, this does not disconcert them, because they always have an explanation to account for the contradiction or for any predictive failure of the oracle.

Confusion by Elaboration

By means of what Evans-Pritchard calls 'secondary elaborations of belief' they may explain the failure of the oracle in no less than eight different ways – such as that the wrong kind of poison has been gathered, or someone has broken a taboo, or that someone else is using witchcraft to upset the oracle, or that the poison is stale, and so on. In this respect, Evans-Pritchard's findings confirm the suggestion made by Tylor in the nineteenth century that faith in the efficacy of magic (and divination usually involves magic) is perpetuated because, among other reasons, the magician always has so elaborate a procedure that it leaves him with the possibility of explaining away failures by pointing to some minor part of it that he has inadvertently omitted. Computer programs, I sometimes suspect, have a similar complexity performing a similar function.

Polanyi, a chemist turned philosopher, in his book *Personal Knowledge* (1958) analyses the typical Zande sequence of events I have described, and concludes that Zande institutions promote a pattern of thought with three outstanding characteristics. First, it is circular: someone falls ill, the oracles point to the witch responsible, he is induced to remove his witchcraft and the patient gets better – as most patients do anyway. Each element in this sequence supports every other. Secondly, this system of thought is epicyclical in the sense that it readily yields secondary elaborations of belief which will cover almost any conceivable eventuality and every anomaly. Thirdly, the system of thought has what Polanyi terms the principle of suppressed nucleation. Because it meets objections to its validity one by one, point by point, it prevents the accumulation of these objections into a rival system or, in Thomas Kuhn's phrase, a paradigm, which might threaten the established system (Jones, 1974). Rival conceptions are laughed out of court one by one and are never permitted to be perceived as a whole theory that might compete with and displace the prevailing theory.

Polanyi, having thus shown the foundations of the stability of Zande magical thinking, goes on, in a chapter significantly entitled 'The stability of scientific theories against experience,' to illustrate that scientific thinking, certainly in the short-term, has precisely the same kind of stability supported by the same three principles of circularity, epicyclical elaboration and suppressed nucleation. He does this mainly in reference to the history of his own subject, chemistry.

Since the 1950s, there has been an increasing recognition of this presuppositionalist character of scientific research, an important landmark being the publication in 1962 of Kuhn's *The Structure of Scientific*

Revolutions (1970). The many debates that have taken place since its appearance do not seem to have resolved the issues between Kuhn and his supporters on the one hand, and more orthodox philosophers of science, centring on Sir Karl Popper, on the other. Interestingly enough, each side tends to explain its failure to be reconciled in terms of its own theory.

I doubt whether the dust has yet settled and I would hazard the guess that most readers might well form two separate columns behind the respective banners of Kuhn and Popper. I would not dare to adjudicate. To me, the basic question seems to be whether Kuhn's originally sharp but now modified distinction between 'normal science' and revolutionary 'paradigm-switches' is a reality rather than an attention-getting heuristic device. I find his claims plausible, but, probably for the wrong reasons, they appeal to my somewhat disenchanted liberal political inclinations rather than to conclusions based on a sound knowledge of the history of science, which I do not possess. On the other hand, I find Stephen Toulmin's critical assessment (1972) of the development of Kuhn's ideas very cogent. For this reason I shall put my conclusion in a conditional form.

Let us address ourselves bluntly to the question: 'Do modern scientists think like African tribesmen?' Without necessarily accepting Kuhn's position, we can note that both hold theories of causation, both derive specific explanatory hypotheses from these theories, and both carefully apply recognized tests to these hypotheses; but the tests may be qualitatively different – confirmatory for Africans, but genuinely refutational (or potentially so) for modern scientists. However, if there is any validity in Kuhn's conception of 'normal science', with most scientists most of the time operating from a largely presuppositional base which their day-to-day activities do not lead them to question, then the parallel between science and witchcraft (in the general sense in which we are using the term) may be closer than we have hitherto assumed – with both scientists and tribesmen advancing hypotheses derived from *theories resting on authority* (for the time being in the case of scientists, for longer in the case of tribesmen); both using tests for solving day-to-day puzzles rather than disturbing fundamental propositions; and, last but perhaps most important, both either disregarding anomalies between tests and theories, or explaining them away.

I have illustrated the importance of social relationships in the explanatory schemes of the two African societies I have discussed. Perhaps this should prompt us to look even more exhaustively at the social relationships within the community of scientists in an attempt to improve our understanding of their influence upon the way in which scientists proceed.

In particular, perhaps we should study more fully the process of Maussian gift-exchange and its implied social controls that Hagstrom (1972) sees in the submission of 'acceptable' contributions in return for social recognition by the establishment in the community of scientists, a process which Mulkay (1972) has neatly reconciled with some of Kuhn's ideas.

References

BARNES, [S.] B. (ed.) (1972), *Sociology of Science: Selected Readings*, Penguin.

EVANS-PRITCHARD, E. E. (1937), *Witchcraft, Oracles and Magic among the Azande*, Clarendon Press.

HAGSTROM, W. O. (1965), 'Gift-giving as an organizing principle in science', in Barnes (1972) *q.v.*

HORTON, R. (1967), 'African traditional thought and Western science', *Africa*, vol. 37, pp. 50–71, 155–87.

JONES, B. (1974), 'Plate tectonics: a Kuhnian case?', *New Scientist*, vol. 63, pp. 536–38.

KUHN, T. S. (1970), *The Structure of Scientific Revolutions*, University of Chicago Press, 2nd ed. (first published 1962).

MULKAY, M. J. (1972), *The Social Process of Innovation*, Macmillan, for British Sociological Association.

POLANYI, M. (1958), *Personal Knowledge*, University of Chicago Press.

TOULMIN, S. (1972), *Human Understanding*, vol. 1, Clarendon Press.

42. A. Rebecca Cardozo

A Modern American Witch-Craze

Abridged version of A. Rebecca Cardozo, *Witches: Old and New*, 1968, original MS.

Common Features of Crazes

Social, political, economic and religious upheaval makes a society especially vulnerable to a craze. In an atmosphere of confusion and uncertainty, people become intolerant towards change; and it is primarily social, political and religious intolerance that provides the initial impetus for a craze. Influential members of society single out and identify an 'enemy of the people', e.g. the witch, the heretic, the Communist, the Jew. This infamous 'enemy' is then blamed for all evil and uncertainty. Malinowski describes this tendency as universally human and persistent. It permits the concentration of blame and hatred to fall 'on certain clearly defined groups suspected of causing evils for which one otherwise would have to blame all the members of the community, its government, the decrees of destiny, or other elements against which immediate reaction is not possible' (Malinowski, 1945, p. 97).

A myth is created about this diabolical threat to society. And the 'truth' of the myth is soon substantiated by evidence obtained in confessions of the accused. It is important to note, particularly in relation to the crazes to be discussed in this paper, that the persecutors obtain official authority or an influential position that enables them to proceed with the persecutions. Society, in effect, implicitly sanctions their efforts to eradicate the 'enemy'.

As a craze develops, a climate of fear and suspicion permeates throughout the society; and the consequence of the widespread fear and intolerance is the madness of 'the hunt'. Accompanying 'the hunt' are false accusations, torture, forced confessions, ruined reputations and death.

Crazes do not die out overnight. Rather, they can last and have lasted for centuries. The perpetuation of the hysteria associated with a craze can be accounted for in a number of ways. The mythological 'truths' stating the nature of the threatening enemy are disseminated throughout society and passed to succeeding generations in the language of local folklore. In modern times, the Press serves a similar purpose. However, it is fear itself that is primarily responsible for perpetuating a craze. Fear suppresses open dissent and resistance in the midst of widespread hysteria. Skeptics, in speaking out against the persecutors, risk their own persecution. In resisting persecutors' efforts to exterminate the 'enemy', skeptics are often accused of consorting with that enemy. Resistance easily leads to guilt-by-association. Thus, the persecutions continue, shielded from the skeptics' attacks.

At some point, however, the craze is brought to an end. Somehow the spell is broken. The ideology of the craze no longer suffices to justify the hunt. The breakdown may occur as a result of an Enlightenment such as Europe saw in the eighteenth century, or the spell may be broken by newly found courage of a country's leaders.

It is the purpose of this paper to examine the causes, development, consequences and decline of two crazes – the European witch-craze of the sixteenth and seventeenth centuries and McCarthyism from 1950 to 1954. Although these crazes are widely divergent with respect to the time, place, duration and circumstances of their occurrence, they are nevertheless strikingly similar.

The European Witch-Craze

It was religious intolerance that provided the initial impetus for the European witch-craze. Although, in the Middle Ages, beliefs in witch-craft seemed to be declining and were discouraged by both legal and ecclesiastical enactments, they were, from the twelfth century onwards, revived in the struggles between Western Catholicism and heretics in mountain areas such as the Alps and the Pyrenees (Trevor-Roper, 1967a, p. 9). The Dominicans soon began pressing for a revision of official Church policy towards witchcraft which they saw as inseparable from the heresies for the combatting of which their order had been founded. Their earlier attempts were resisted by the Church, but, by the late fifteenth century, the Inquisitors of the day were influential enough to induce Pope Innocent VIII to issue his famous bull, *Summis Desiderantes Affectibus* (1484), authorizing two of them, Heinrich Institor (Krämer) and Jacob Sprenger, to extirpate witchcraft in Germany. Two years later these two Dominicans issued the first great printed encyclopedia of demonology, the *Malleus Maleficarum* (the 'Hammer of Witches'), which consolidated the mythology of, and gave impetus to, a campaign that was to continue for two centuries (1967a, pp. 4, 8). Thus, as Trevor-Roper puts it, 'By 1490, after two centuries of research, the new, positive doctrine of witch-craft would be established in its final form. From then on it would be simply a question of applying this doctrine: of seeking, finding, and destroying the witches whose organization had been defined' (1967a, p. 4).

The fear of witches spread. The 'hunt' now had the official blessing of the Church; and people began to associate all deviant behavior with witchcraft. 'Those who believed that there were devil-worshipping societies in the mountains soon discovered that there were devil-worshipping individuals in the plains' (1967a, p. 20). In the course of time Dominicans and other Catholics were followed by Protestants and lay politicians in the war against witchcraft.

The consequences of these hunts were appalling. The fear was so great that judicial torture was allowed in the Courts of the Inquisition in order to force confessions from the accused. Of course people confessed even though they had been falsely accused; and, in the course of their confessions, set about 'creating witches where none were and multiplying both victims and evidence' (1967a, p. 17). If convicted, the victims were usually sentenced to burn. Thousands did burn.

It should be noted that the widespread confusion and fear prevailing during a craze is easily exploited, not only by the persecutors. Other members of society take advantage of 'the hunt' for purposes of personal and political revenge. To note one example, to accuse Joan of Arc of witchcraft was indeed a convenient way to get rid of her.

The European witch-hunt lasted for centuries. People continued to believe the 'truths' expounded in the *Malleus Maleficarum*. The ideology reached and influenced all of society, since it was disseminated in the language of local folklore and passed to succeeding generations.

It was not everyone, however, who believed that the persecutions could be justified. There were political and religious leaders as well as artists who opposed the massive witch-hunt (Trevor-Roper, 1967a, p. 21; 1967b, pp. 15 ff.). These skeptics were appalled at the false accusations and sentencing of innocent people to death. John Weyer, for example, attributed the actions of many of the accused to 'melancholia' rather than to witchcraft (Trevor-Roper, 1967b, pp. 15–16). But open dissent and resistance in the midst of the craze was a dangerous endeavor. 'Until the middle of the seventeenth century the orthodox always prevailed. The voice of dissent was powerless to stay the persecution. It could hardly be uttered in safety' (1967a, p. 23). Skeptics in their efforts to stop the 'hunt' were often accused of consorting with the Devil. Thus fear of accusation did a great deal to suppress resistance movements.

There was some skepticism which did reach and influence large numbers of people. It was apparently not this, however, that brought about the end of the craze. Trevor-Roper offers the following explanation of how the spell was broken: 'What ultimately destroyed the witch-craze, on an intellectual level, was not the arguments of the sceptics ... [but] the new philosophy, a philosophical revolution which changed the whole concept of Nature and its operations. [It was the Enlightenment] in which the duel in Nature between a Hebrew God and a medieval Devil was replaced by the benevolent despotism of a modern, scientific "Deity"' (1967b, pp. 29–30). It is difficult to tell what exactly he means by 'a modern scientific "Deity"', but his point is that the widespread belief expressed in witch-mythology, that there were witches consorting with the Devil, lent mass support to the persecutions, making 'the hunt' possible; but, as soon as certain fundamental beliefs changed in the eighteenth century, the fear of witches subsided – and with it the craze.

McCarthyism: 1950–1954

The United States in 1950 was hardly Europe in the late Middle Ages. But the causes, development, consequences and decline of McCarthyism closely resemble those of the European witch-craze. Political intolerance provided the initial impetus for the movement. To America and her allies in the 1950s, the threat of Communist infiltration was a mysterious but very real threat. At the time, very little was understood about the Communist movement, its tactics and its direction, and fear of it was considerable.

McCarthyism was possible because of this fear and ignorance of Communism. However, Joe McCarthy's initial reason for seeking out the 'Communists in government' was hardly as patriotic as it sounded. Actually, his own political ambitions prompted his first accusations. 'Communists in government' would make a good campaign issue for the 1952 election (Rovere, 1959, p. 119). His first attack on these 'enemies of the people' came on 9 February 1950, when, in a speech in Wheeling, West Virginia, he told the people: 'I have here in my hand a list of 205 names that were made known to the Secretary of State [Dean Acheson] as being members of the Communist Party and who nevertheless are still working and shaping policy in the State Department' (Anderson and May, 1952, p. 174). He made similar accusations on the floor of the Senate a few days later (*Congression Record*, 20 February 1950).

That McCarthy was a Senator made a difference. As a Senator, he had access to information he might not have otherwise had. The American people therefore took heed of his accusations. Most important in relation to his advantage as a Senator is the fact that Senators speaking in Congress are immune from libel suits. Undoubtedly this immunity gave McCarthy a certain amount of courage in making such serious accusations (Anderson and May, 1952, p. 205).

The myth of Communists in government created fear and suspicion throughout the country. The hunt for Reds was on. 'In [McCarthy's] demonology the Democratic leaders, the liberal intelligentsia, and a supposedly decadent Eastern aristocracy played the accomplice role that Hitler assigned to the Jews' (Rovere, 1959, p. 19). The accusations continued, becoming more personal and ugly. McCarthy said once, for example, 'The Democratic label is more the property of men and women who have ... bent to the whispered pleas from the lips of traitors ... men and women who wear the political label stitched with the idiocy of a Truman, rotted by the deceit of an Acheson, corrupted by the red slime of a [Harry Dexter] White' (Rovere, 1959, p. 11).

A Senate committee was appointed in February of 1950 to investigate the charges being made by McCarthy (Anderson and May, 1952, p. 174). 'Doggedly, Joe pursued the elusive "proof" he needed to back up his charges. He chased pink shadows through the maze of government bureaus and agencies; he set up his own private spy system; and he pestered newspapermen and petty officials for leads. He also telephoned Congressman Richard Nixon ... then a big gun on the House Unamerican Activities Committee ... and pleaded ... over the phone for a peek at the Unamerican Activities Committee's secret files ...' (p. 191).

The 'Tydings Committee' called in the State Department to testify to the validity of the charges against its employees (U.S. Senate, 1950, p. 151). Out of approximately eighty-one cases investigated, not one of the accused was proved to be a Communist. In effect, the members of the Committee were disgusted with McCarthy and his unfounded accusations. Senator Tydings in his report said the following: 'We have seen the technique of the "Big Lie", elsewhere employed by the totalitarian dictator with devastating success, utilized here for the first time on a sustained basis in our history. We have seen how, through repetition and shifting untruths, it is possible to delude great numbers of people' (pp. 151–2).

But McCarthy continued his search for Communists in government. And he was given the chance again to have the charges investigated by another Senate Committee. This time the chairman of the Sub-Committee on Internal Security was Pat McCarran, friend and supporter of McCarthy (Anderson and May, 1952, p. 340). An all-out effort was made to gather 'proof' by legal and illegal means. The story of how

McCarthy and his aides obtained files belonging to his victims is much too complicated to relate here (Anderson and May, 1952, p. 208).

The McCarran hearings also failed to prove the existence of card-carrying Communists in the government. Yet, in spite of the findings of the Committee, McCarthyism endured. How was it that McCarthy was allowed to continue making outlandish accusations with little forceful resistance outside the hearing room? The Senators were 'scared stiff'. They believed McCarthy could in some way determine their political futures, particularly if they openly criticized his tactics (Rovere, 1959, p. 35). Tydings had spoken out against McCarthy; and, in the 1952 election campaign, McCarthy set out to discredit Tydings and ensure his defeat. Tydings , who had been in the Senate for many terms, was defeated; and many other Senators attributed his defeat to McCarthy (Anderson and May, 1952, p. 295). Even by 1954, McCarthy was still considered powerful. As Rovere, a newspaperman, puts it, 'Evidence was not conclusive ... but politicians cannot afford to deal in finalities and ultimate truths; they abide, by and large, by probabilities and reasonable assumptions and the law of averages, and there was nothing unreasonable, in 1954, in assuming that McCarthy held enormous power in his hands, when it came to the question of deciding who should and should not sit in the United States Senate' (1959, p. 35).

Numerous other examples seemed to back up this assumption. It is now thought that McCarthy's influence on the electorate was considerably less than believed at the time; and that the defeat of several of McCarthy's enemies can be attributed as easily to the Eisenhower landslide as to McCarthy (Polsby, 1963, p. 820). But the Senators' fears nevertheless greatly suppressed open opposition to McCarthy, and their timid behavior, as well as that of influential members of society, directly aided in perpetuating McCarthyism.

The Press was also a vital force in helping McCarthyism to endure (Anderson and May, 1952, p. 266). Newspapers played up McCarthy's accusations in big headlines. McCarthy craved publicity, and he got it. More importantly, newsmen and editors also feared the Senator. A news article critical of McCarthy's efforts could leave the author wide open to accusation. Editorial opposition was suppressed because of these fears. Thus, what could have been a vital force against McCarthyism turned out as a force in his favor. It is said that 'if Joe McCarthy [was] a political monster, then the Press [had] been his Dr Frankenstein' (Anderson and May, 1952, pp. 266–7). Of course many people did believe that the Senator was doing the ultimate good for America; and, following news reports of his campaign against traitors, money poured into his office (p.

180). Indirectly, the Press was indeed an agent in McCarthy's favor, that is, until some newspapers regained their courage and openly condemned 'the hunt'.

Finally, in 1952, some Senators took a forceful stand against McCarthy. Senator Hubert Humphrey was one of these. After declaring that accusing people and demanding that they prove their innocence was 'Anglo-Saxon jurisprudence upside down', he added: 'I think it is time we stated that we are not going to let people be ruined, their reputations destroyed, and their names defiled because we happen to be in the great game of American politics' (Anderson and May, 1952, p. 330).

The United States Senate had regained its courage. For many, their renewed courage was too late in coming. 'The real victims of McCarthyism [had] been the men and women who had their careers damaged by being unjustly labeled "security" risks, or who were punished for "crimes" which were defined by no law and without being given an opportunity to fight back against their accusers' (Lubell, 1956, p. 242).

But the final assault against McCarthy was testimony to Americans' faith in the due process of law. In July 1954, Senator Flanders introduced a resolution to censure Senator Joseph McCarthy (U.S. Senate, 1954a, p. 8). Hearings followed to investigate the charges against him; and, on 22 December 1954, following recommendations by the Investigating Committee, McCarthy was censured by the Senate on two of the original five charges, one, for 'contempt of the Senate or Senatorial Committee, and two, for ridiculing a witness in a hearing and for violating certain rules of that committee' (U.S. Senate, 1954b, p. 67).

Censure destroyed McCarthy, and with him the era of McCarthyism. He became a thoroughly dejected man and died three years later. America began her recovery from a craze not unlike the European witch-craze at the close of the Middle Ages.

References

ANDERSON, J., and MAY, R. (1952), *McCarthy: The Man, The Senator, The 'Ism'*, Beacon Press.

Congressional Record, 20 February 1950.

LUBELL, S. (1956), *Revolt of the Moderates*, Harper.

MALINOWSKI, B. (1945), *The Dynamics of Culture Change*, Yale U.P.

POLSBY, N. (1963), 'Toward an explanation of McCarthyism', in N. Polsby *et al.*, *Politics and Social Life: An Introduction to Political Behavior*, Houghton Mifflin.

ROVERE, R. (1959), *Senator Joe McCarthy*, Harcourt, Brace.

TREVOR-ROPER, H. R. (1967a), 'Witches and witchcraft: an historical essay', *Encounter*, vol. 28, no. 5, pp. 3–25.

Witch-Beliefs Throw Light on Other Problems

TREVOR-ROPER, H. R. (1967b), 'Witches and witchcraft: an historical essay', *Encounter*, vol. 28, no. 6, pp. 13–34.

U.S. SENATE (1950), *Report of the Committee on Foreign Relations, Pursuant to Senate Resolution 231, State Department Loyalty Investigation.*

U.S. SENATE (1954a), *Hearings on Senate Resolution 301, Hearings Before a Select Committee to Study Censure Charges*, parts 1 and 2.

U.S. SENATE (1954b), *Senate Report no. 2508 on Censure Hearings.*

Further Reading

Several of the Readings in this volume are abridgements of, or excerpts from, longer books or articles which should be consulted in the original. Details of the longer versions will be found at the beginnings of the relevant Readings, i.e. nos. 4 and 17 (Thomas, 1971), 5 (Macfarlane, 1970), 8 and 11 (Caro Baroja, 1964), 14 (Harwood, 1970), 16 (Cohn, 1975), 18 (Midelfort, 1972), 21 (Marwick, 1950), 22 (Willis, 1968), 24 (Parsons, 1927), 25 (Malinowski, 1925), 26 (Kluckhohn, 1944), 31 (Crawford, 1967), 33 (Crick, 1976), and 40 (Polanyi, 1958).

Of the items listed below, about half have to do with European (including New England) witchcraft; and all the remaining ones, except two or three in general works, with witchcraft and/or sorcery in non-literate societies. They have not been classified, since in most instances their titles are reasonably good guides to their contents. Where necessary, chapter or page references have been given.

P. Boyer and S. Nissenbaum (eds), *Salem Village Witchcraft*, Wadsworth, 1972.

P. Boyer and S. Nissenbaum, *Salem Possessed*, Harvard U.P., 1974.

G. L. Burr, *Narratives of the Witchcraft Cases 1648–1706*, Scribners, 1914.

L. R. Caporael, 'Ergotism: the Satan loosed in Salem?' *Science*, vol. 192, 1976, pp. 21–26.

R. Cavendish, 'Magic: a revolt of the soul', *Observer Magazine*, 1 December 1968, pp. 20–23.

R. Cavendish (ed.), *Man, Myth and Magic*, Purnell, 1970–72.

C. Cross, 'The witches ride again', *Observer Magazine*, 1 December 1968, pp. 12–18.

M. Douglas (ed.), *Witchcraft Confessions and Accusations*, Tavistock, 1970.

K. T. Erikson, *Wayward Puritans*, Wiley, 1966.

E. E. Evans-Pritchard, *Witchcraft, Oracles and Magic among the Azande*, Clarendon Press, 1937.

C. L. Ewen, *Witch-Hunting and Witch Trials*, Kegan Paul, Trench, Trubner, 1929.

C. L. Ewen, *Witchcraft and Demonianism*, Heath Cranton, 1933.

A. H. Gayton, 'Yokuts-Mono chiefs and shamans', *University of California Publications in American Archaeology and Ethnology*, vol. 24, 1930, pp. 361–421, especially pp. 408 ff.

M. Gluckman, 'Social beliefs and individual thinking in primitive society', *Memoirs of the Proceedings of the Manchester Literary and Philosophical Society*, Session 1949/50, pp. 1–26.

M. Gluckman, *Custom and Conflict in Africa*, Blackwell, 1956, ch. 4.

M. Gluckman and E. Devons, 'Conclusions', especially pp. 240 ff., in M. Gluckman (ed.), *Closed Systems and Open Minds*, Oliver & Boyd, 1964.

C. Hansen, *Witchcraft at Salem*, Braziller, 1969.

Further Reading

M. Harner, 'The role of hallucinogenic plants in European witchcraft', in M. Harner (ed.), *Hallucinogens and Shamanism*, Oxford U.P., 1972.

M. Harris, *Cows, Pigs, Wars, and Witches*, Random House, 1974, pp. 207–76.

H. I. Hogbin, 'Sorcery and administration', *Oceania*, vol. 6, 1935, pp. 1–32.

M. Hopkins, *The Discovery of Witches*, 1647, M. Summers (ed.), Cayme Press, 1928.

M. Hunter [now Wilson], *Reaction to Conquest*, Oxford U.P. for International Institute of African Languages and Cultures, 1936, ch. 6.

A. Huxley, *The Devils of Loudun*, Chatto & Windus, 1952, Penguin Books, 1971.

G. L. Kittredge, *Witchcraft in Old and New England*, Harvard U.P., 1929.

E. J. Krige and J. D. Krige, *The Realm of a Rain Queen*, Oxford U.P. for International Institute of African Languages and Cultures, 1943, ch. 14.

H. Kuper, *An African Aristocracy*, Oxford U.P. for International African Institute, 1947, pp. 172 ff.

C. J. Larner, C. H. Lee and H. V. McLachlan (eds), *A Source-Book of Scottish Witchcraft*, University of Glasgow, 1977.

P. Lawrence, 'Sorcery among the Garia', *South Pacific*, vol. 6, 1952, pp. 340–43.

G. Lienhardt, 'Some notions of witchcraft among the Dinka', *Africa*, vol. 21, 1951, pp. 303–18.

L. Mair, *Witchcraft*, Weidenfeld & Nicolson (World University Library), 1969.

M. G. Marwick, 'The social context of Cewa witch-beliefs', *Africa*, vol. 22, 1952, pp. 120–35, 215–33.

M. G. Marwick, *Sorcery in Its Social Setting*, Manchester U.P., 1965.

M. G. Marwick, 'The study of witchcraft', in A. L. Epstein (ed.), *The Craft of Social Anthropology*, Tavistock, 1967.

J. Middleton, *Lugbara Religion*, Oxford U.P. for International African Institute, 1960.

J. Middleton and E. H. Winter (eds), *Witchcraft and Sorcery in East Africa*, Routledge & Kegan Paul, 1963.

J. Middleton (ed.), *Magic, Witchcraft and Curing*, Natural History Press (American Museum Sourcebooks in Anthropology), 1967.

A. Miller, *The Crucible*, Viking Press, 1952.

J. C. Mitchell, *The Yao Village*, Manchester U.P., 1956, ch. 6.

W. E. Mitchell, 'Sorcellerie chamanique: "sanguma" chez les Lujere du cours supérieur de Sépik', *Journal de la Société des Océanistes*, vol. 33, 1977, pp. 179–89.

E. W. Monter, *Witchcraft in France and Switzerland*, Cornell U.P., 1976.

E. W. Monter (ed.), *European Witchcraft*, Wiley, 1969.

W. Notestein, *A History of Witchcraft in England from 1558 to 1718*, American Historical Association, 1911.

G. K. Park, 'Divination in its social contexts', *Journal of the Royal Anthropological Institute*, vol. 93, 1963, pp. 195–209.

G. Parrinder, *Witchcraft*, Penguin Books, 1958.

B. Reynolds, *Magic, Divination and Witchcraft among the Barotse of Northern Rhodesia*, Chatto & Windus, 1963.

R. H. Robbins, *Encyclopedia of Witchcraft and Demonology*, Crown, 1959.

E. E. Rose, *A Razor for a Goat*, University of Toronto Press, 1962.

J. B. Russell, *Witchcraft in the Middle Ages*, Cornell U.P., 1972.

I. Schapera, *The Crime of Sorcery*, Royal Anthropological Institute (The Huxley Memorial Lecture), 1969.

R. Scot, *The Discoverie of Witchcraft*, 1584; reprinted with a Preface by H. R. Williamson, Centaur Press, 1964.

B. Simon and D. Cripps, 'Double, double, toil and trouble ...', *Observer Magazine*, 1 December 1968, pp. 24–5.

N. P. Spanos and J. Gottlieb, 'Ergotism in the Salem Village witch trials', *Science*, vol. 194, 1976, pp. 1390–94.

M. L. Starkey, *The Devil in Massachusetts*, Knopf, 1950, Dolphin, 1961.

D. Tait, 'A sorcery hunt in Dagomba', *Africa*, vol. 33, 1963, pp. 136–47.

H. R. Trevor-Roper, *Religion, Reformation and Social Change*, Macmillan, 1967, chapter 3.

V. W. Turner, *Schism and Continuity in an African Society*, Manchester U.P., 1957, chs. 4, 5, *et passim*.

V. W. Turner, *Ndembu Divination: Its Symbolism and Techniques*, Manchester U.P. (Rhodes-Livingstone Paper no. 31), 1961.

V. W. Turner, 'Witchcraft and sorcery: taxonomy versus dynamics', *Africa*, vol. 34, 1964, pp. 319–24.

V. W. Turner, 'Sorcery in its social setting', *African Social Research*, no. 2, December 1966.

B. B. Whiting, *Paiute Sorcery*, Viking Fund, 1950.

M. Wilson *et al.*, *Keiskammahoek Rural Survey*, vol. 3., *Social Structure*, Shuter & Shooter, 1952.

Acknowledgements

Permission to reprint the Readings in this volume is acknowledged from the following sources:

Reading 1   International African Institute
Reading 2   *Sudan Notes and Records*
Reading 3   Thomas Nelson & Sons Ltd
Reading 4   Weidenfeld & Nicolson and Charles Scribner's Sons
Reading 5   Routledge & Kegan Paul Ltd
Reading 6   *New Society*
Reading 7   Philip Mayer
Reading 8   Weidenfeld & Nicolson Ltd and University of Chicago Press
Reading 9   A. P. Watt & Son and Collins-Knowlton-Wing Inc.
Reading 10   A. P. Watt & Son and Collins-Knowlton-Wing Inc.
Reading 11   Weidenfeld & Nicolson Ltd and University of Chicago Press
Reading 12   Routledge & Kegan Paul Ltd and E. P. Dutton & Co. Inc.
Reading 13   The Royal African Society
Reading 14   International African Institute
Reading 15   Royal Anthropological Institute of Great Britain and Ireland
Reading 16   Sussex University Press
Reading 17   Weidenfeld & Nicolson and Charles Scribner's Sons
Reading 18   Stanford University Press
Reading 19   Joyce Bednarski
Reading 20   International African Institute
Reading 21   International African Institute
Reading 22   International African Institute
Reading 23   A. D. J. Macfarlane
Reading 24   Royal Anthropological Institute of Great Britain and Ireland
Reading 25   Society for Promoting Christian Knowledge
Reading 26   Peabody Museum of Archaeology and Ethnology
Reading 27   *Theoria*, University of Natal
Reading 28   University of Chicago Press
Reading 29   American Anthropological Association
Reading 30   *Australian Journal of Science*
Reading 31   Oxford University Press
Reading 32   M. J. Kephart
Reading 33   Malaby Press
Reading 34   Royal Anthropological Institute of Great Britain and Ireland
Reading 35   International African Institute
Reading 36   *African Urban Notes*

Acknowledgements

Reading 37   Institute for Study of Social Issues
Reading 38   International African Institute
Reading 39   Institute for Social Research, University of Zambia
Reading 40   Routledge & Kegan Paul and University of Chicago Press
Reading 41   *New Scientist*
Reading 42   A. Rebecca Cardozo

The Editor wishes to add his personal thanks to those authors who generously allowed him to use their unpublished material, Miss Joyce Bednarski, Miss A. Rebecca Cardozo, Dr A. D. J. Macfarlane and Ms M. J. Kephart, and to those who kindly consented to his abridging their articles, Professor E. E. Evans-Pritchard, Professor Max Gluckman, Dr Alan Harwood, Professor Norman Cohn, Dr Erik Midelfort, Dr R. G. Willis and Dr Florence R. Kluckhohn (Executrix to the Clyde Kluckhohn Estate). Despite many attempts, he was unable to contact the literary executor of the late Dr Elsie Clews Parsons and will be glad to receive any information that will enable him to regularize his having abridged her important paper and to make due acknowledgement in a subsequent edition.

He would also like to record his gratitude for invaluable help received, in assembling the materials from which the Readings in this volume have been selected, from Miss Anne Edmonds, Librarian of Mount Holyoke College, and her staff; and from Mr John Stirling, Librarian of the University of Stirling, and his staff, especially Miss Carolyn Jamie, who obligingly and expeditiously borrowed books and journals on Library Interloan and produced photocopies. He owes his then secretary, Mrs D. J. Kent, special thanks for the extra work she was involved in as a result of his preoccupation with assembling and editing the materials.

He would like to thank the Trustees of Mount Holyoke College in Massachusetts for having honoured him with the award of the Florence Purington Lectureship during the second semester of 1967–8, and the Council of Monash University in Australia, whose generous leave provisions made it possible for him to accept it. The lectureship, with its light teaching load and its complete freedom from administrative chores, gave him the time for assembling materials and the opportunity of exploring them in the company of a senior undergraduate seminar, whose gifted, enthusiastic and charming members became known as 'Mr Marwick's witches'. A fitting secondary dedication of this volume would be 'to the Enchantresses of Mount Holyoke'.

The Editor is indebted to the Council of Griffith University, Brisbane, Australia, for the generous grant of study-leave in 1978–9, part of which was devoted to the preparation of the Second Edition; and he is grateful for the hospitality of colleagues at the University of East Anglia, Norwich, and at Nuffield College, Oxford, to which institutions he was successively attached while on leave.

Index

This index aims at bringing out similarities and contrasts in the material presented in the forty-two Readings. Its scheme of classification reflects the principles that have been set out in the general introduction and in the introductions to the five parts. It was compiled by collecting references under headings of society, region and historical period or episode and then distributing them to categories that may be regarded as aspects of, or approaches to, witchcraft and sorcery and the events of everyday life that are related to them.

The geographical or historical identities of the items thus collected and distributed have, however, been preserved and are shown by labels that appear within the conceptual categories or their subdivisions wherever this is appropriate. Page numbers not preceded by labels are general references. In addition, the index has independent main entries for the various societies, peoples or periods, and these will enable the reader to find the more connected accounts of them quickly. In some of the main entries, e.g. the one for 'theories of witchcraft and sorcery', the names of authors associated with particular viewpoints have been placed in positions similar to those of the ethnographic or historical labels.

To keep the Index to a reasonable size it has been necessary to select from the very large number of proper names occurring in the Readings. Generally those names that appear only once or twice, and which are confined to the text, footnotes or reference list of the same Reading, have not been included unless there is some special reason for them to be indexed.

An *n.* suffixed to or following a page number indicates that the item referred to will be found in a footnote, an *r.* that it will be in a list of references.

absence of witch-beliefs among certain peoples, 55

Andaman Islanders, 60

accusations and suspicions of witchcraft and sorcery (*see also* social relations)

  arise from personal antipathy, 62

  as both symptoms and intensifiers of conflict, Shona, 314, 323–4

  as means of manipulating public opinion, 316–17

    Navaho, 257

    Shona, 324–6

  as projection of hatred or guilt, England, 171

    Gusii, 66

    Mesakin, 296

    Salem, 192

    Zulu, 447

  believed to recoil, Gusii, 66

  functions of, 63, 132, 330–35

  general reputation as a factor in, 64, 184ff.

  illegal in modern jurisdictions, 64, 693–4

    Gusii, 66

    Rhodesia, 385

    South Africa, 424

    Tswana, 115

  melancholy and isolation as factors in, 140, 181–2

  normative implications of (*see also* witches, negative role-models), 66

    Nyakyusa, 277

    Salem, 192

    Shona, 315–16

  precluded from certain relationships, Lobedu, 272–3

action against witches and sorcerers – *see* measures

Ady, T., 46, 47r., 158, 159n., 161n., 165n.

Akan of west Africa, 135

Alberti, L., 426, 440r.

alternatives to explanations in terms of witchcraft and/or sorcery, 59, 114

Ambo of east Africa, 320–21

Andaman Islanders, 60

Anderson, A., 441 and r.

Anderson, J., 472–5, 476r.

Anon., *Fuero juzgo*, 96 and n.

anthropology's failure to develop Evans-Pritchard's insights, Crick, 343–5

anti-sorcery cults as successors to the poison ordeal, 318–19

approaches to witchcraft and sorcery – *see* theories of witchcraft

Apuleius, 71, 81–6, 87–90

Ardener, E. W., 344, 345, 353, 361, 362r.

Arrhenius, 457

Ashanti of west Africa, 137

Austin, J. L., 358, 359, 362r.

Azande (sing. and adj., Zande) of north-central Africa, 12n., 18, 21, 23–7, 29–37, 41 and n., 57, 58, 119n., 125ff., 130, 206, 225, 280, 302, 310, 334, 338, 343, 344, 346, 351, 352, 356, 381, 391n., 443–51 *passim*, 452–9 *passim*, 462–6 *passim*

  'conceptual synapses' in thought of, 356

  formality brings order in stressful situations, 36–7

  mangu (witchcraft substance) morally neutral, Harwood, 125–6

  moral grading of magic among, 25

  normal growth of *mangu*, 31–2

  oracles form hierarchy, 34–6

  unilateral inheritance of witchcraft consistent with beliefs about procreation among, 30 and n., witchcraft may remain 'cool', 444–5

  witches' congress summoned by drum, 31 (*see also under* witches)

Baëta, C. G., 133, 138r.

Baker, H. B., 458 and n., 459r.

Bakweri of west Africa, 345, 353

Bali, 251

Banyang of west Africa, 133, 135, 137

Barden, G., 356, 362r.

Barth, F., 120, 130r., 354, 362r.

Baxter, R., 166

Beattie, J., 314

Bednarski, J., 190–200

Beidelman, T. O., 345, 354, 362r.

Index

5660